ENCYCLOPEDIA
of the
HOLOCAUST

ENCYCLOPEDIA
of the
HOLOCAUST

Israel Gutman, Editor in Chief

Volume 1

Yad Vashem
The Holocaust Martyrs' and Heroes'
  Remembrance Authority
Jerusalem

Sifriat Poalim Publishing House
Tel Aviv

MACMILLAN PUBLISHING COMPANY
NEW YORK

Collier Macmillan Publishers
LONDON

Macmillan Publishing Company
866 Third Avenue
New York, New York 10022
Collier Macmillan Canada, Inc.
Library of Congress Catalog Card Number: 89-13466
Printed in the United States of America

printing number
2   3   4   5   6   7   8   9   10

Library of Congress Cataloging-in-Publication Data

Encyclopedia of the Holocaust / Israel Gutman, editor in chief.
p.   cm.
Includes bibliographical references.
ISBN 0–02–896090–4 (set)
Trade edition ISBN 0–02–546705–0 (set)
1. Holocaust, Jewish (1939–1945)—Dictionaries.   I. Gutman,
Israel.

D804.3.E53   1990   89-13466
940.53'18'-03—dc20   CIP

Acknowledgments of sources
and permissions to use previously published materials
are made in Acknowledgments, page xix.

Contents

Editorial and Production Staff

Project Editor
Sylvia Juran

Editorial Consultants
Abraham J. Edelheit
Hershel Edelheit

Copy Editors
Eric L. Haralson   David Olivenbaum

Proofreaders
Jeffrey P. Edelstein   Emily Garlin   Candice L. Gianetti   Gloria Klatt

Production Director
Matthew M. Kardovich

Indexer
Cynthia Crippen

JERUSALEM STAFF

Translator into English
Mordechai Shalev

Illustrations Researcher
Moshe Shalvi

Illustrations Assistant
Yehudit Levin

Staff

Marianne Asaf   Eitan Ben-Noah   Shelly Berliner   Daphna Blumert
Tamar Blumert   Heftsibah Cohen   Eva Condor   Joan Hooper   Tirza Lavi-Muttath
Stephanie Nakache   Zvi Reiter   Jacqueline Rokhsar   Yaakov Stein   Tsiporet Yagil

PUBLISHER
Philip Friedman

MANAGING EDITOR, ENCYCLOPEDIAS
Elly Dickason

Foreword

Auschwitz will remain as the darkest, the cruelest, the most incomprehensible—and yet also the most documented—event in history. Thanks to the testimonies of the victims, the confessions of the killers and their accomplices, and the research of historians, we are able to know its essential features. The meticulous preparations for the "Final Solution" of the Jewish question at the highest level of the Third Reich, the active collaboration of all its ministers, the pernicious role played by Nazi propaganda, by the army, and by Nazi science, the economy, industry, and medicine—anyone who wants to learn the facts needs only to look into the archives. They exist. The effort of the SS to destroy them failed. The enemy did not succeed in erasing the traces of his crimes. Thus he has been defeated in at least one domain, that of remembrance.

That his total war against the Jewish people was also a war to the death against Jewish memory is no longer doubted by anyone. His aim was not only to exterminate all the Jews on the planet but also to torment them, to torture them, to humiliate them, to drive them to despair and shame—in short, to dehumanize them before casting them into the shadows of history, from which they would never again emerge.

Why this cold and calculated hatred—both rational and irrational, and elevated to the status of a national, even a universal ideology—for an ethnic, social, and religious minority which, over the centuries, has contributed so much to civilization and its progress?

Why did this hatred find such resonance in Germany itself and in most of the occupied countries? Why the Allies' conspiracy of silence and their indifference toward this war that the common enemy was fighting within the greater war?

A tragedy unlike any other, senseless, it defies answers. It could have been avoided; at least, its extent could have been diminished. We will never understand why the extermination of six million human beings was made possible. But we do know how. It is only necessary to read certain works of history, to study the documents, to investigate the accounts of witnesses. And to consult this monumental encyclopedia, on which the most knowledgeable specialists in the subject, under the editorship of Dr. Israel Gutman, the most eminent among them, have collaborated for many years.

Everything is here, in condensed form, of course. Cities and towns and villages, ghettos and prisons, important dates, reference books and statistics, massacres and revolts, names and pseudonyms, fighters and chroniclers, heroes and martyrs: do you want to know about their fate? You must. To turn one's back on this chapter of history means wanting to forget it. And he who forgets becomes an accomplice of the enemy. To forget the victims is to kill them a second time.

Certainly, we shall never understand either the dehumanized cruelty of the executioner or the human gentleness of his victims. Yet here it is not a question of understanding, but of knowing. To confess our incomprehension is a sign of humility; to refuse to learn the facts is a proof of arrogance. And of indifference.

That is the importance of this encyclopedia: the amount of knowledge accumulated in it is so extensive that it must be regarded as an indispensable source.

Elie Wiesel
New York, September 1989
Translated from the French
by Sylvia Juran

Preface

The decades since the end of World War II have witnessed a growing awareness throughout the world of the significance of the Holocaust as a central event in the history of the Jewish people and of Western civilization. The purpose of this encyclopedia is to put at the disposal of teachers, students, and all those interested in the subject a comprehensive and up-to-date work on the Holocaust: its background, its history, and its impact, written by the leading scholars and experts in Holocaust studies from many countries. The encyclopedia deals in depth with the sources and motivations for all manifestations relating to or forming part of the Holocaust. They include:

1. The rise and growth of racist ideology and Nazi-style hatred of the Jews, promoted by Hitler and the Nazi party, which Germany adopted as official policy when it came under Nazi rule.

2. The discriminatory racist legislation under which the Jews were excluded from human society in Germany, and the relentless policy of stripping the Jews of all their economic assets and sources of livelihood and of gradually excluding them from the Nazi-created Third Reich.

3. The process, instituted against the Jews in Poland during the war, of oppression, terrorization, starvation, imprisonment in ghettos, and deportation. In the critical phase of the war—the attack on the Soviet Union—this process turned into mass murder and, subsequently, into a campaign that aimed at the total destruction of the Jews of Europe. The decision on this course of action was taken at the top level of the German state and the Nazi party, by the leaders who bore responsibility to the highest degree; the planning was put into the hands of a state apparatus, and the process was implemented by special murder squads and in killing installations.

The encyclopedia devotes a substantial amount of space to the Jews in Nazi-dominated Europe: their leadership and organizations, their misery, the extent of their knowledge about what lay in store for them, their activities as they confronted a hopeless situation, their stubborn struggle for life and survival, and the desperate means of resistance to which they resorted in the face of the inescapable death closing in on them. Much attention is devoted to the countries under German occupation or control and the degrees and stages of oppression they underwent, to the fate of other civilian population groups, and, in particular, to Soviet prisoners of war, who were tortured in the camps and murdered en masse. According to Nazi racist principles, the people in these groups were inferior beings, lacking full human worth and the right to exist. Another issue dealt with is the attitude toward Jews manifested by various occupied peoples, their resistance attempts, and the actions they took, if any, to save Jews who were being driven to their death. Other subjects examined include the position taken by the free democracies and the Jews living in them, as well as by the Jewish community in Palestine (then administered by the British Mandatory government), with regard to the anti-Jewish persecutions and, later, the "Final Solution." Also explored are the postwar influences of the Holocaust on ideological and political concepts, and on the positions and policies of the various religions and their institutions; the way in which the world regards the Jews and the Jews regard themselves in the postwar period; the treatment of the Holocaust in historiography; and the repeated attempts to deny the Holocaust or to distort its meaning and the responsibility of its perpetrators.

The basic approach taken by the editors of the encyclopedia is that the Holocaust was a historical and ideological event that must be examined in the historical context and with the historian's tools and methods. At the same time, the editors realized that any attempt to understand the factors leading to the Holocaust, the persons involved in it, and the lessons to be derived from it requires the contribution of scholars from other disciplines—political science, sociology, religion, psychology, law, medicine, literature, and the arts.

While the need for a basic work on the Holocaust in encyclopedia format was not in doubt, the decision to carry out this project was taken after much considered thought. The first question confronting the initial team of editors was whether the research on the Holocaust to date had covered the many aspects of the subject sufficiently to justify undertaking such a comprehensive project. Preliminary investigations showed a firm base for such an effort, and now that the work has been completed we believe that this original assumption is borne out by the results. Another question arose concerning the form that the work should take—its style and its terminology. The Holocaust is a subject laden with powerful emotions. It is not only Holocaust survivors and persons who suffered directly who are so emotionally involved that they are not always capable of approaching the subject objectively and analytically. Even intellectuals, such as George Steiner, have stated that the bestiality of the Holocaust does not lend itself to the normal linguistic and associative means of expression that belong to our ethical and cultural tradition; in the face of the Holocaust and its horror, we are therefore silent and paralyzed, and the only possible reaction is one of mute, frozen communion. In a letter, Nelly Sachs

suggested that "an altar of silence be erected, made up of rocks—of unhewn words." Others have asserted that authors of fiction cannot cope with the challenge posed by the Holocaust. In many instances the diaries of victims and the memoirs of survivors create a more authentic picture of the Holocaust and make a stronger impact with the facts they describe and their distinctive power of expression than do the intuition and the imagery of the writer of fiction. It is not by chance that it was writers such as Tadeusz Borowski, Primo Levi, and Elie Wiesel who were able to give authentic articulation to the essence of the horror of the concentration camp universe, having themselves been prisoners in the camps; their personal experience of the war and the Holocaust constituted the motivating force and internal compulsion behind their literary work. The Israeli poet Abba Kovner, in a short essay, "Epilogue for Historians," warned of the natural inclination of historians to seek satisfactory answers to questions for which no answers exist: this may lead to a situation in which "the fog appears to lift and everything falls in place in accepted terms . . . and even the horror can be weighed and measured." Our work in the encyclopedia is based on criteria derived from conscientious and sound investigation. However, we had to retain at least a trace of the terrible shock that a person experiences when he or she touches on the Holocaust. We have also tried to avoid, as best we could, providing simple and clear-cut answers to complex and troubling issues, preferring to leave the questions partially unanswered, as food for thought and doubt, rather than trying to resolve them by smooth formulas that disregard facts.

The use of Nazi terminology was one of the problems we faced. Each case was decided individually, the criterion being how widely the name or term was used. We therefore chose to use the German terms *Kristallnacht, Judenrat, Selektion, Aktion, Arisierung, Anschluss,* and so on. These terms are unique in their Nazi context and lose much of their meaning in translation.

The very definition of the word "Holocaust" (in Hebrew, *sho'ah*) is not always uniform or generally accepted. Even scholars interpret it with different nuances. These differences apply not only to the term's origin and meaning; they also involve the categories of victims to which it relates. Throughout the course of human history, mass killings and bloodshed of other kinds have taken place during revolutions, social upheavals, civil wars, and retaliatory acts, especially in the twentieth century, and are subsumed under the term "genocide." Frequently, no distinction is made between these acts and the Holocaust carried out by the Nazi regime. As a result, such events as the Biafra tragedy or the mass killings in Cambodia are sometimes referred to as "holocausts"—a practice that blurs the uniqueness of the Holocaust. In our conception, the Holocaust in the Nazi period and during World War II was, above all, the process of the oppression and murder of some six million European Jews—the only one among Hitler's goals and war aims that he succeeded in accomplishing.

Several components of the persecution and murder campaign set the Holocaust apart from mass-murder phenomena of the past and of the twentieth century (even during World War II itself). The Holocaust did not originate in a real conflict between the German people and the Jews of Germany or the Jews of the world. In fact, the Jews of Germany were a loyal and devoted element of German society who made a great contribution to the development and flourishing of the country's economy, science, and culture. In many nations, especially in eastern Europe, Germany was highly esteemed among the Jews, who regarded it as an enlightened country that was tolerant toward its Jews. Quite often, the Jews of these countries were suspected of being loyal to Germany, and their Yiddish language (which is mainly based on a dialect of German origin) was sometimes thought to be an element used by the Jews to "Germanize" the non-Jewish population. Moreover, owing to such demographic processes as a low birthrate and rapid assimilation, the Jewish population of Germany was fast diminishing, and some were predicting its almost complete decline and its disappearance within a foreseeable period.

It follows that the discrimination against the Jews introduced by the Nazis in Ger-

many, their efforts to drive the Jews out of the country, and their decision for the total physical destruction of the Jews did not result from any confrontation between Germany and the Jews or from any threat posed by the Jews to Germany. This was an annihilation operation that had its source in Nazi racist ideology and was decided upon on that basis. In the Nazi concept, not only were the Jews different because of their origin and certain alleged peculiar physical attributes, but the Jewish race as such, in its biological substance and its blood, was believed to embody noxious traits and hereditary characteristics that could not be changed by evolution, education, or integration. If Jews mixed with other races, it was held, these negative traits and characteristics would predominate and determine the image and nature of society.

Such claims contradict scientific fact as well as the basic and hallowed tenets of Christianity. But Nazi racist ideology did not confine itself to defining the Jew as having acquired inferior racial biological traits in a perversion of the process of natural selection, adaptation, and survival according to the Darwinist theory. The guidelines laid down by Hitler stated that the Jews were neither a religious nor a national group but an ambitious and well-organized subversive race. The Jewish race had set itself the aim of disrupting the natural dynamics among the human races, and through conspiracy and manipulation it exerted influence in the world and prevented the "master race" (Herrenvolk—that is, the Nordic Aryans) from taking its rightful place as the ruler and inaugurator of a new social order and new principles of existence. In short, the Jews were deemed an "anti-race," the complete opposite of the Germans. For this reason, a campaign—no less significant than any military confrontation—was being waged whose purpose was to change the course of history. The Aryan race, and in particular its purer and more determined German component, was engaged in a struggle with the Jewish threat. Such were the groundless claims on which was based the "war" against the Jews, a war that increased in ferocity until it reached the stage of relentless physical annihilation.

Some researchers have tended to disregard the racial elements in Hitler's and the Nazis' ideology or to discount its role, and to concentrate on what they regard as the political pragmatism of the Third Reich's course. This approach ignores the historical reality. The regime's policy toward the Jews, the measures taken against them, and the fate that they suffered in all the areas under Nazi rule, occupation, and influence were determined, in principle and practice, by the dictates of fanatic and unrestrained racism. This fact represents the very essence of the Holocaust.

The Holocaust, as it was carried out, strove to physically destroy a blameless people—an ethnic entity that was not a participant in the war. This drive had as its purpose the persecution of every person of Jewish descent (according to the Nazi racial definitions) and the tracking down of every Jew who tried to elude the fate planned for him by going into hiding or converting to Christianity. When such a Jew was caught, he was dealt with in the most inhumane and merciless fashion. The objective was to trap and kill every Jew, irrespective of age, gender, political view, occupation, or social status. To this end a state apparatus of civilians, diplomats, and security and military forces, as well as personnel specifically assigned to the job of killing, was spread all over Europe and charged with the planning, organization, and execution of the campaign. That apparatus knew that its task constituted the Führer's highest priority, and it was tireless in its efforts to ensure that no Jewish community and no individual Jews escaped the bitter end planned for them. Even when the Third Reich's unconditional surrender had become inevitable and the only surviving Jews in most of the German-occupied areas were slave-labor forces working for the Nazi war machine, the Nazis did not put a halt to the murder of those human beings, whose only crime was that that they were Jews.

The most radical consequence of Nazi racism, the Nazi murder machine with its use of lethal gas, was, for the most part, applied solely to the Jews. Other categories and ethnic groups, however, were persecuted and murdered as well, including Gypsies, members of the Polish intelligentsia, and Soviet prisoners of war. Millions from these groups were killed, because the Nazis regarded them as enemies, as socially disruptive, or as racially inferior. These victims too are often seen as victims of the Holocaust. To judge by

the nature of the regime that the Nazis imposed on the occupied countries (especially the Slavic lands), and by General Plan East (*Generalplan Ost*), in which they outlined their future policy concerning these people, it can well be imagined how the Nazis would have treated the people that were "inferior" in their eyes, their opponents in other countries, and, indeed, all of mankind, had they succeeded in establishing their "New Order."

Nevertheless, a distinction must also be made between the Holocaust (which rested on the principles of racism and was expressed in the attempted total and immediate destruction of a people) and attacks on population groups that the Nazis considered harmful from the social, political, or military point of view and, consequently, expendable. No discriminatory legislation was enacted in the German Reich before the war against the Poles and the Russians, whom the Nazis considered to be racially inferior. Even during the war, Poles and Russians living in occupied countries such as France or Hungary were not persecuted or killed on account of their racial origin. There is, of course, no difference in the gravity of the crimes committed by the Nazis against the members of any people, as far as the individual victim is concerned, or the injury and sorrow inflicted on his family. It is when we define the Holocaust as a social, political, and historical phenomenon that a clear and fundamental difference emerges between it and all the other forms of persecution and mass murder committed by the Nazis.

The kind of antisemitism that spawned a negative image of the Jew on religious or other grounds did not arise during the Nazi period but preceded it. It is inconceivable that the Nazis could have succeeded in creating a hostile atmosphere against the Jews and in carrying out their design on the scale that they did—deporting and murdering Jews by the millions—had it not been for the distrust and hatred of Jews that antisemitism had legitimized and fostered over many generations. The Nazi experience proved in full, and in the most cruel manner, the rule that hatred based on religious and political grounds does not stop at the victim's doorstep but serves as a boomerang. Nazism was determined to wipe the Jewish people off the face of the earth, but it also attacked Western civilization, its norms of morality, and the political and social systems created and developed on the basis of those ethical concepts. In universal terms, Nazism was an attack that aimed at a total revolution: the uprooting of the standards of Western civilization, based on the Judeo-Christian tradition, and their replacement with a world in which racial criteria and a cult of raw, brutal power would hold sway.

The editorial board of the encyclopedia turned to experts in different parts of the world to contribute to the *Encyclopedia of the Holocaust*. On occasion, some contributors expressed views at variance with those of the board, but these were as a rule approved, out of the obligation to respect the contributors' right to express their ideas freely and to reflect as wide a range of theoretical approaches as possible. A determined effort was made to present major events and issues from a variety of different angles, and, above all, to base the material in the encyclopedia on the multifaceted sources at our disposal —German and Jewish, and from the occupied and Allied countries.

The encyclopedia's structure was based on a list of entries that included individual names, major events, the countries involved, the concentration camps, the ghettos, the extermination camps and murder sites, political movements and trends, and resistance movements. This list was made up of approximately one thousand entries that were classified in accordance with their relative importance and estimated length.

As in other encyclopedia projects, changes were made in the original structure of the work during the course of its preparation. Contributors were sometimes unable to keep to the allocated space and wrote at much greater length, involving the editors in a thankless job of cutting. At times it was felt that such reduction might impair the entry, and consequently the entire article was kept, in view of the importance and originality of the subject matter—even if this might lead to certain disproportions.

Collecting the vast reservoir of material and dealing with the complex problems presented in an encyclopedia of this size and standard was made possible by the systematic and ongoing research undertaken in many countries and in different languages. It included wide-ranging German studies of the historical background, the stages of Hitler's rise to power, and the structure of the Nazi regime and its components; examination by Polish scholars of the character of the occupation regime; research into the Holocaust conducted in Israel, which has provided monographs on ghettos, camps, and the resistance movement; analysis of the nature of totalitarian movements and of psychological and other effects of the Holocaust, centered in the United States; and the local research work that has been taking place in other countries. The works of such authors as Gerald Reitlinger, Léon Poliakov, Raul Hilberg, Nora Levin, Lucy Dawidowicz, Nathan Eck, and, most recently, Leni Yahil have been valuable contributions to the historical portrayal of the Holocaust in its various aspects. The major innovation and significance of the encyclopedia lies in the fact that it encompasses within a single work the Holocaust research of a great many authors, each writing in his or her area of expertise.

Almost every entry in the encyclopedia has a select bibliography attached to it, with preference given to books in English, but also listing basic books written in other languages. The encyclopedia also contains a great many photographs, maps, and diagrams. Among the appendixes are a glossary, a chronology, and a listing, by country, of the number of Jewish victims of the Holocaust. This enumeration is the first of its kind in that it represents not the calculations and assumptions of a single author, but the summing-up of data gathered by a group of experts.

The executive editorial board operated as a team, supervising the work in all its stages; the international board, serving as an advisory body, was of great help to the project in its execution. The initiative of the project was undertaken by the publisher, Sifriat Poalim, headed by Tsvi Raanan, who enlisted a team of technical and administrative personnel to help carry out the work of the encyclopedia. The work was done at the publisher's Jerusalem office and at Yad Vashem, without whose library, archive, collection of photographs, and staff the project could not have been accomplished.

ISRAEL GUTMAN
Editor in Chief
Jerusalem, June 1989

Introduction

This encyclopedia seeks to provide, insofar as its format allows, the widest possible scope of information on what has justly been called the worst event in human history. Its nearly one thousand entries cover manifold aspects of the Holocaust—here defined as the Third Reich's attempt, during the period of Nazi power (1933–1945), to physically destroy the Jews of Europe—from its antecedents to its postwar consequences. A primary aim has been to make knowledge that was previously available mainly to scholars accessible to the educated public at large.

Entries are of many kinds and fall into many categories. Examples of the latter, to cite only a few, are *geographical:* regions; countries (many in the form of paired articles, detailing the history of the Holocaust period from both the non-Jewish and the Jewish point of view); cities and smaller places; Nazi camps; sites of massacres; *biographical:* Nazis and collaborators; partisans; Jewish and non-Jewish leaders and resisters; rescuers of Jews; persons who relayed to the free world the facts of the Holocaust; entries concerning the *postwar impact:* survivors; trials of war criminals; reflections in literature, films, art, and music; education on the Holocaust; documentation centers. A dozen or so entries are in multiple form (several related articles grouped together) in order to cover different aspects of a major topic; examples are Museums and Memorial Institutes and Youth Movements.

The blind entries, located alphabetically throughout the encyclopedia (such as Nazi Doctors. *See* Physicians, Nazi), direct the reader to topics sought, or to closely related topics. Entry titles are almost invariably in the foreign language of origin, but English translations of these names and terms appear as blind entries (for example, "Stab-in-the-Back" Myth. *See* Dolchstosslegende). Acronyms are avoided as entry titles, but they too are found as blind entries (UNRRA, OSI, and so on). Some lengthy blind entries, such as that for Camps, appear as small essays guiding the reader to many relevant entries.

The encyclopedia's articles are further linked by a comprehensive system of cross-references. When the reader of an entry encounters a name or term in small caps, he or she is being advised that the name or term is the title of another entry, as in this example:

> In BIAŁYSTOK, the first announcement made by the JUDENRAT (Jewish Council), on German orders, stated: "As of the morning of July 10, 1941, all Jewish men, women, and children aged fourteen and over must wear a white armband on their left sleeve, with a blue Star of David on it" (*see* BADGE, JEWISH).

Cross-references are also found at the end of many entries, such as [*See also* Propaganda, Nazi] at the end of the entry Goebbels, Joseph. The cross-references and blind entries are adjuncts to the detailed index in the fourth volume of the encyclopedia.

In the interest of accuracy and authenticity, original foreign-language names and terms are used almost exclusively, with English translations provided in parentheses; for well-known organizations, the foreign acronyms are also included, as Reichssicherheitshauptamt (Reich Security Main Office;

RSHA). Toward this same end, diacritics are provided for all Latin-alphabet languages. Thus, Bełżec and not Belzec, Ustaša and not Ustasha. For non-Latin-alphabet languages such as Hebrew and Russian, nonscholarly transliteration systems are used. With few exceptions, italics are limited to foreign words and terms as such: *Ostarbeiter* (eastern [slave] laborer), *rampa* (railway platform). The basic source for place-names was *Webster's New Geographical Dictionary* (Springfield, Mass., 1984); preference was given to the name most commonly used during the Holocaust period. Variant names appear as blind entries.

What made the events described here possible? The response "racist fanaticism, combined with unlimited opportunity" fails to satisfy. As Elie Wiesel has observed, the "why" cannot be answered; we can only learn the "how." How the worst—men without substance, but with limitless malevolent energy—gained power, how they infected some and aroused fear and hesitation in others. How they quickly and easily, well before initiating World War II, became professional thieves and killers. How they ranged as predators, hunting down guiltless men, women, and children in order to destroy them. How, free of restraints, they covered occupied Europe with a grotesque network of "camps," into which they drove and lured the immense numbers of people whom they had forced from their homes. How, in the most obscene manner, they robbed these human beings—already robbed of home, family, possessions, and strength—of all there was left to take, their lives. Such was the outcome of the racist lunacy that constituted the very center and foundation of Nazi ideology.

Can it be that these crimes took place not so many years ago, within the lifetime of many of us? But for an accident of geography or birth this could have been our parents, our brothers and sisters, ourselves. These were people like ourselves, with the same thoughts and feelings as our own. Yet each was an individual, unique, who suffered as an individual.

The facts are here, but they are only a beginning. It is for each reader to bring them to life in his or her own heart. Having thought, and reflected, and wept, we ask: In the face of this terrible lesson, what must we learn, and what can we do? What is our responsibility?

To ensure that this will never happen again.

Most importantly, to remember the victims. Each day, each hour, as best we can, in our own lives, let us speak up for those who were made silent.

Thanks are due to the many people in Israel and the United States who cooperated in the work of the encyclopedia. For all concerned, this was a deeply emotional involvement. Brigitte Goldstein was an infallible source of help in German-language matters, and Sylvia Kanwischer made thoughtful and valuable suggestions during the encyclopedia's early stages. Karin Vanderveer was a capable, efficient administrative assistant. The expertise and judgment of Abraham Edelheit and Hershel Edelheit were relied on throughout. Above all, thanks and gratitude are due to Israel Gutman, the encyclopedia's editor in chief, to Robert Rozett, the associate editor, and to Moshe Shalvi, the project coordinator. Their commitment, their knowledge, and their warm-hearted support were unfailing and indispensable.

SYLVIA JURAN
Project Editor
New York, October 1989

Acknowledgments

We would like to thank Martin Gilbert for his permission to use some of the maps from *The Macmillan Atlas of the Holocaust* (New York, 1982).

We also wish to express our thanks and appreciation to the various institutions and libraries that have kindly granted us permission to reproduce photographs in their possession. Appropriate credit lines appear with each such photograph. All photographs without attribution were provided by the Yad Vashem archives in Jerusalem.

Alphabetical List of Entries

Directory of Contributors

A

MICHEL ABITBOL
Hebrew University of Jerusalem
Algeria
Libya
Morocco
Tunisia

SAMUEL ABRAHAMSEN
Brooklyn College
Norway

IRIT ABRAMSKI-BLIGH
Yad Vashem, Jerusalem
Husseini, Hajj Amin al-
Iraq
Libya: Forced-Labor and
  Internment Camps
Syria and Lebanon

UWE ADAM
Frankfurt am Main (deceased)
Anti-Jewish Legislation
Daluege, Kurt
Darré, Richard Walther
Frick, Wilhelm
Gas Chambers
Lammers, Hans Heinrich
Ley, Robert

JACQUES ADLER
University of Melbourne
Amelot
Conseil Représentatif des Juifs
  de France
Paris

Rayski, Abraham
Union des Juifs pour la Résistance
  et l'Entr'aide

MIKHAIL AGURSKY
Hebrew University of Jerusalem
Litvinov, Maksim Maksimovich
Molotov, Viacheslav Mikhailovich
Stalin, Joseph Vissarionovich

GABRIEL E. ALEXANDER
Jerusalem
Berlin

YITZCHAK ALPEROWITZ
Yad Vashem, Jerusalem (emeritus)
Bielski, Tuvia

DAVID ALTSHULER
*Museum of Jewish Heritage,
  New York*
Museums and Memorial Institutes:
  A Living Memorial to the
  Holocaust—Museum of Jewish
  Heritage

MORDECHAI ALTSHULER
Hebrew University of Jerusalem
Soviet Union

ZIVA AMISHAI-MAISELS
Hebrew University of Jerusalem
Art of the Holocaust

JEAN ANCEL
Yad Vashem, Jerusalem
Antonescu, Ion
Antonescu, Mihai
Bessarabia
Bogdanovka
Bucharest
Bukovina
Centrala Evreilor
Chernovtsy
Comisia Autonoma de Ajutorare
Cuza, Alexandru
Domanevka
Dorohoi
Edineti
Filderman, Wilhelm
Goga, Octavian
Iaşi
Iron Guard
Kishinev
Lecca, Radu
Marculeşti
Mogilev-Podolski
Odessa
Richter, Gustav
Romania: Jews during the
  Holocaust
Safran, Alexander
Secureni
Sima, Horia
Transnistria
Transylvania, Southern
Trials of War Criminals: Romania
Uniunea Evreilor Români
Vapniarka
Vertujeni

YITZHAK ARAD
Yad Vashem, Jerusalem
Aktion Reinhard
Bełżec
"Erntefest"
Extermination Camps
Family Camps in the Forests
Fareynegte Partizaner
    Organizatsye
Franz, Kurt
Gens, Jacob
Glazman, Josef
Jeckeln, Friedrich
Klooga
Kommissarbefehl
Kruk, Herman
Pechersky, Aleksandr
Ponary
Reichskommissariat Ostland
Sobibór
Treblinka
Vilna

SHLOMO ARONSON
Hebrew University of Jerusalem
Gestapo
Heydrich, Reinhard
Reichssicherheitshauptamt
SA
SS

HAIM AVNI
Hebrew University of Jerusalem
Spain: General Survey

GABRIEL BACH
Supreme Court of Israel
Eichmann Trial

ZVI BACHARACH
Bar-Ilan University
Funk, Walther
Galen, Clemens August Graf von
Grawitz, Ernst Robert
Hitlerjugend
Lichtenberg, Bernhard
Propaganda, Nazi
Wurm, Theophil

DAVID BANKIER
Hebrew University of Jerusalem
Baum Gruppe
Chamberlain, Houston Stewart
Deutscher Vortrupp, Gefolgschaft
    Deutscher Juden
Documentation Centers:
    Wiener Library
Four-Year Plan
Freemasons
Führerprinzip
Horst Wessel Song
Lebensraum
Mischlinge
Nazi Party
Nuremberg Laws
Reichsbund Jüdischer
    Frontsoldaten
Weltsch, Robert

AVRAHAM BARKAI
Tel-Aviv University; Leo Baeck
    Institute, Jerusalem
Arisierung
Boycott, Anti-Jewish
Schacht, Hjalmar
Warburg, Max

YEHUDA BAUER
Hebrew University of Jerusalem
Beriha
Gypsies
Joint Distribution Committee
Kasztner, Rezső
Mayer, Saly
Riegner Cable
Schwartz, Joseph J.
Totenkopfverbände
World War II

ARIE LEON BAUMINGER
Jerusalem
Bauminger, Heshek

MOSHE BEJSKI
Supreme Court of Israel
"Righteous among the Nations"

GRACIELA BEN-DROR
Moreshet Institute, Givat Haviva
Argentina

HEDVA BEN-ISRAEL
Hebrew University of Jerusalem
Great Britain: Appeasement of
    Nazi Germany
Munich Conference

ARIEH BEN-MENAHEM
Ramat Hasharon, Israel
Front of the Wilderness Generation
Grossman, Mendel

AVRAHAM BEN-YAKOV
Jerusalem
Bulgaria

SARAH BENDER
Tel-Aviv University
Białystok

MICHAEL BERENBAUM
United States Holocaust Memorial
    Museum
Museums and Memorial Institutes:
    United States Holocaust
    Memorial Museum

STEFAN BIERNACKI
Main Commission for Investigation
    of Nazi Crimes in Poland, Warsaw
AB-Aktion
Documentation Centers: Main
    Commission for Investigation of
    Nazi Crimes in Poland
Forster, Albert
Goeth, Amon Leopold

YSRAEL CH. BILETZKY
Bar-Ilan University
Literature on the Holocaust:
    Yiddish Literature

DANIEL BLATMAN
Yad Vashem, Jerusalem
Bund

SARA BLOOMFIELD
U.S. Holocaust Memorial Council,
    Washington, D.C.
U.S. Holocaust Memorial Council

NAHUM BOGNER
Yad Tabenkin Institute,
Ramat Efal, Israel
Cyprus Detention Camps

JACOB BORUT
Yad Vashem, Jerusalem
Frankfurt am Main

STEVEN B. BOWMAN
University of Cincinnati
Athens
Corfu
Greece
Koretz, Zvi
Rhodes
Salonika
Thrace

RANDOLPH L. BRAHAM
City University of New York
Baky, László
Becher, Kurt
Brand, Joel
Cluj
Dej
Endre, László
Freudiger, Fülöp
Gendarmerie, Hungarian
Hungary: Jews during the
  Holocaust
Kállay, Miklós
Kamenets-Podolski
Kaposvár
Krumey, Hermann Alois
Munkács
Munkaszolgálat
Relief and Rescue Committee
  of Budapest
Satu-Mare
Sighet Marmaţiei
Stern, Samu
Strasshof
Szálasi, Ferenc
Sztójay, Döme
Tîrgu- Mureş
Transylvania, Northern

MARTIN BROSZAT
University of Munich (deceased)
National Socialism

CHRISTOPHER R. BROWNING
Pacific Lutheran University
Auerswald, Heinz
Deportations
"Final Solution"
Frank, Hans
Ganzenmüller, Albert
Killinger, Manfred von
Lösener, Bernard
Ludin, Hans Elard
Luther, Martin
Madagascar Plan
Neurath, Konstantin Freiherr von
Nisko and Lublin Plan
Rademacher, Franz
Rauff, Walther
Reichskommissariat für die
  Festigung des Deutschen
  Volkstums
Ribbentrop, Joachim von
Sajmište
Thadden, Eberhard von
Wagner, Horst
Wannsee Conference
Weizsäcker, Ernst von

YEHOSHUA R. BÜCHLER
Moreshet Institute, Givat Haviva
Buchenwald
Dora-Mittelbau

JOZEF BUSZKO
Jagiellonian University, Kraków
Auschwitz
Höss, Rudolf
Płaszów

DANIEL CARPI
Tel-Aviv University
Italy: Aid to Jews by Italians
Italy: Concentration Camps

SHALOM CHOLAWSKI
Kibbutz Ein Hashofet
Atlas, Yeheskel
Baranovichi
Belorussia

Derechin
Diatlovo
Gomel
Grodno
Kaplinski, Hirsch
Koldichevo
Lachva
Lida
Maly Trostinets
Minsk
Mir
Mushkin, Eliyahu
Nesvizh
Novogrudok
Partisans
Rufajzen, Oswald
Slonim
Volozhin
Zorin, Shalom

YEHOYAKIM COCHAVI
Bet Loḥamei ha-Getta'ot; Haifa
  University
Centralverein Deutscher Staats-
  bürger Jüdischen Glaubens
Goebbels, Joseph
Göring, Hermann
Hilfsverein der Deutschen Juden
Hirsch, Otto
Kulturbund Deutscher Juden
Mittelstelle für Jüdische
  Erwachsenenbildung
Museums and Memorial Institutes:
  Bet Loḥamei ha-Getta'ot
SD
Speer, Albert
Zentralausschuss der Deutschen
  Juden für Hilfe und Aufbau
Zentralstelle für Jüdische
  Auswanderung

ASHER COHEN
Haifa University
Arrow Cross Party
Budapest
Horthy, Miklós
Youth Movements: Hungary

NAVA COHEN
Hebrew University of Jerusalem
Medical Experiments

RICHARD COHEN
Hebrew University of Jerusalem
Arendt Controversy
Baur, André
Blum, Léon
Consistoire Central des
    Israélites de France
France: General Survey
France: Jewish Responses to
    Persecution
France: The Jews and the
    Holocaust
Helbronner, Jacques
Hirschler, René
Jarblum, Marc
Jefroykin, Jules
Lambert, Raymond-Raoul
Meiss, Léon
Saliège, Jules-Gérard
Union Générale des
    Israélites de France

JOHN S. CONWAY
*University of British Columbia,
    Vancouver*
Barth, Karl
Bonhoeffer, Dietrich
Christian Churches:
    General Survey

ABRAHAM COOPER
*Simon Wiesenthal Center,
    Los Angeles*
Museums and Memorial Institutes:
    Simon Wiesenthal Center

LEONARD DINNERSTEIN
University of Arizona
Displaced Persons, Jewish

BARBARA DISTEL
Dachau Museum, West Germany
Dachau
Kaufering

ELLY DLIN
Yad Vashem, Jerusalem
Education on the Holocaust:
    United States and Israel

ELIEZER DOMKE
Haifa
Hamburg

JUDITH E. DONESON
Clayton, Missouri
Films, Nazi Antisemitic
Films on the Holocaust

TADEUSZ DREWNOWSKI
University of Warsaw
Literature on the Holocaust:
    Poland

KRZYSZTOF DUNIN-WASOWICZ
*Polish Academy of Sciences,
    Warsaw*
Pawiak Prison
Stutthof
Warsaw: General Survey
Warsaw Polish Uprising

EUGENIUSZ DURACZYNSKI
*Polish Academy of Sciences,
    Warsaw*
Armia Krajowa
Delegatura
Gwardia Ludowa
Polish Government-in-Exile
Sikorski, Władysław Eugeniusz

BENYAMIN ECKSTEIN
*Hebrew University of Jerusalem
    (deceased)*
Ebensee
Gunskirchen
Gusen
Mauthausen
Melk

ABRAHAM J. EDELHEIT
Touro College, New York
Biltmore Resolution
Historiography of the Holocaust
Silver, Abba Hillel
White Paper of 1939

LEO SHUA EITINGER
Oslo University (emeritus)
Survivors, Psychology of:
    Survivors of Ghettos and Camps

ISRAEL ELDAR
Hebrew University of Jerusalem
Blum, Léon

ELIZABETH E. EPPLER
Jerusalem
Einstein, Albert
Goldmann, Nahum

SHAUL ESH
*Hebrew University of Jerusalem;
    Yad Vashem (deceased)*
Entjudung

ROBERT A. EVERETT
Fairleigh Dickinson University
Parkes, James William

ANDREW EZERGAILIS
Ithaca College
Latvia: General Survey
Latvia: The Fate of Latvian Jewry

SIDRA DEKOVEN EZRAHI
Hebrew University of Jerusalem
Literature on the Holocaust:
    United States

JEAN-CLAUDE FAVEZ
University of Geneva
Red Cross, International

HENRY L. FEINGOLD
City University of New York
American Jewry and the Holocaust
Bermuda Conference
McDonald, James Grover
Morgenthau, Henry, Jr.
Roosevelt, Franklin Delano
United States of America
Wise, Stephen Samuel

GILA FLAM
*United States Holocaust Memorial
    Museum, Washington, D.C.*
Music, The Holocaust in

EVA FOGELMAN
*Jewish Foundation for Christian
    Rescuers/ADL, New York*
Survivors, Second Generation of

JOHN P. FOX
  Leicester University
  Education on the Holocaust:
    Great Britain

JÖRG FRIEDRICH
  West Berlin
  Trials of War Criminals:
    Dispensation of Justice
    in Germany
  Trials of War Criminals:
    Subsequent Nuremberg
    Proceedings

MARIAN FUCHS
  Żydowski Instytut Historyczny,
    Warsaw
  Music, The Holocaust in

YOAV GELBER
  Haifa University; Yad Vashem,
    Jerusalem
  Haavara Agreement
  Jewish Brigade Group
  Parachutists, Jewish
  Prisoners of War:
    Jewish Prisoners of War

HAIM GENIZI
  Bar-Ilan University
  American Committee for Christian
    German Refugees
  American Friends Service
    Committee
  Bergson Group
  Nonsectarian Refugee Organi-
    zations in the United States
  United States Army and Survivors
    in Germany and Austria

SHARON GILLERMAN
  Los Angeles
  Education on the Holocaust:
    United States and Israel

SEEV GOSHEN
  Haifa University
  Kahn, Franz
  Lidice
  Rathenau, Walther

HELGE GRABITZ
  Hamburg, West Germany
  Law and Judiciary in
    Nazi Germany

GIDEON GREIF
  Yad Vashem, Jerusalem
  Fleischmann, Gisi
  Reik, Haviva

WILLY GROAG
  Kibbutz Givat Hayyim
  Youth Movements:
    Bohemia and Moravia

LEO GROSS
  Tufts University (emeritus)
  Superior Orders

ISRAEL GUTMAN
  Hebrew University of Jerusalem;
    Yad Vashem, Jerusalem
  Anielewicz, Mordecai
  Anschluss
  Antisemitism
  Arierparagraph
  Axis
  Badge, Jewish
  Barasz, Efraim
  Berman, Adolf Abraham
  Blum, Abraham
  Christian Churches:
    After the Holocaust
  Czerniaków, Adam
  Diaries, Holocaust
  Dolchstosslegende
  Dubnow, Simon
  Edelman, Marek
  Feiner, Leon
  Gepner, Abraham
  Ghetto
  Gitterman, Yitzhak
  Glazer, Gesja
  Greiser, Arthur
  Grosman, Haika
  Hausner, Gideon
  Holocaust, Denial of the
  Kaplan, Chaim Aaron
  Kaplan, Josef
  Kapo
  Kolbe, Maximilian

Korczak, Janusz
Kovner, Abba
Levi, Primo
Lubetkin, Zivia
Muselmann
Nossig, Alfred
Oneg Shabbat
Partisans
Poland: The Jews in Poland
Rasse- und Siedlungshauptamt
Ringelblum, Emanuel
Robota, Roza
Schiper, Ignacy
Stroop, Jürgen
Szlengel, Władysław
Third Reich
Umschlagplatz
Warsaw: Jews during the
  Holocaust
Warsaw Ghetto Uprising
Wdowinski, David
Wilner, Arie
Wittenberg, Yitzhak
Youth Movements: General Survey
Zagan, Shakhne
Zimetbaum, Mala
Zuckerman, Yitzhak
Żydowska Organizacja Bojowa
Żydowski Związek Wojskowy
Zygelbojm, Samuel Artur
Zyklon B

AMY HACKETT
  New York
  Physicians, Nazi

DAVID HADAR
  Hebrew University of Jerusalem
    (emeritus)
  Bernheim Petition
  Glücks, Richard
  Gustloff, Wilhelm
  Hess, Rudolf
  Hindenburg, Paul von
    Beneckendorff und von

LEAH HADOMI
  Haifa University
  Literature on the Holocaust:
    Germany

ESTHER HAGAR
Yad Vashem, Jerusalem
Dvinsk
Kaiserwald
Liepāja
Riga

EDDIE HALPERN
Israel Broadcasting Authority,
Jerusalem
Music, The Holocaust in

JOSEPH HELLER
Hebrew University of Jerusalem
Jabotinsky, Vladimir
Lohamei Herut Israel

ESRIEL HILDESHEIMER
Jerusalem
Eppstein, Paul
Germany
Reichsvertretung der
Deutschen Juden

MOSHE HOCH
Institute for Conservation and
Research of Jewish Music of the
Holocaust, Givatayim, Israel
Music, The Holocaust in

COLIN HOLMES
University of Sheffield
Great Britain: Fascism in
Great Britain
Mosley, Sir Oswald

ARIEL HURWITZ
Kibbutz Galon
Fort Ontario
Intergovernmental Committee
on Refugees
Jewish Labor Committee
United States Department of State
World Jewish Congress

EBERHARD JÄCKEL
Stuttgart University
Hitler, Adolf
Mein Kampf

YESHAYAHU JELINEK
Ben-Gurion University of the Negev
Bratislava
Europa Plan
Hlinka, Andrej

Hlinka Guard
Slovakia
Slovak National Uprising
Tiso, Jozef
Transcarpathian Ukraine
Ústredňa Židov

KAROL JOŃCA
University of Wrocław
Nacht und Nebel

PRISCILLA DALE JONES
Wolfson College, Cambridge
University
Trials of War Criminals:
General Survey
Trials of War Criminals:
Subsequent British Trials

FELICJA KARAY
Tel-Aviv University
HASAG
Skarżysko-Kamienna

STEVEN T. KATZ
Cornell University
Jewish Philosophical and
Theological Responses
to the Holocaust

MENAHEM KAUFMAN
Hebrew University of Jerusalem
American Zionist
Emergency Council
B'nai B'rith
Proskauer, Joseph Meyer

YITZCHAK KEREM
Yad Vashem, Jerusalem
Athens
Greece

NILI KEREN
Seminar ha-Kibbutzim, Tel Aviv
Korczak-Marla, Rozka

HILLEL KLEIN
Hebrew University of Jerusalem
(deceased)
Survivors, Psychology of:
General Survey

SHLOMO KLESS
Hebrew University of Jerusalem
Weissmandel, Michael Dov

BRONIA KLIBANSKI
Yad Vashem, Jerusalem
Plotnicka, Frumka
Relief Committee for the War-
stricken Jewish Population
Tenenbaum, Mordechai

JOKE KNIESMEYER
Anne Frank Foundation,
Amsterdam
Frank, Anne

LIONEL KOCHAN
University of Warwick (emeritus)
Abetz, Otto
Best, Werner
Blomberg, Werner von
Brack, Viktor
Canaris, Wilhelm
Clauberg, Carl
Dannecker, Theodor
Dibelius, Otto
Frank, Karl Hermann
Frank, Walter
Gerstein, Kurt
Globke, Hans
Globocnik, Odilo
Hassell, Ulrich von
Himmler, Heinrich
Krupp von Bohlen
und Halbach, Gustav
Lenard, Philipp
Lohse, Hinrich
Ludendorff, Erich
Niemöller, Martin
Pohl, Oswald
Rauschning, Hermann
Röhm, Ernst
Rosenberg, Alfred
Rudel, Hans-Ulrich
Sauckel, Fritz
Schellenberg, Walter
Stahl, Heinrich
Stuckart, Wilhelm
Stülpnagel, Karl Heinrich von
Thierack, Otto
Veesenmayer, Edmund
Wirth, Christian

ARIEH JOSEPH KOCHAVI
  Haifa University
  United Nations Relief and
    Rehabilitation Administration

ALFRED KONIECZNY
  University of Wrocław
  Gross-Rosen
  Organisation Schmelt

RYSZARD KOTARBA
  Main Commission for Investigation
    of Nazi Crimes in Poland, Kraków
  Płaszów

SHMUEL KRAKOWSKI
  Yad Vashem, Jerusalem
  Althammer
  Auschwitz
  Bełchatów
  Bergen-Belsen
  Biebow, Hans
  Blechhammer
  Bor-Komorowski, Tadeusz
  Bothmann, Hans
  Chełmno
  Death Marches
  Deutsche Ausrüstungswerke
  Dora-Mittelbau
  Eicke, Theodor
  Fischer, Ludwig
  Katyn
  Koppe, Wilhelm
  Kraków
  Kramer, Josef
  Krüger, Friedrich Wilhelm
  Łódź
  Lublin
  Lublin-Lipowa
  Mengele, Josef
  Mikołajczyk, Stanisław
  Narodowe Siły Zbrojne
  Polnische Polizei
  Poniatowa
  Prisoners of War:
    Jewish Prisoners of War
  Radom
  Resistance, Jewish
  Rowecki, Stefan
  Rumkowski, Mordechai Chaim
  Rzeszów
  Stalingrad
  Volksdeutsche
  Werwolf

DAVID KRANZLER
  Queensborough Community College,
    New York
  Japan
  Schonfeld, Solomon
  Shanghai

BOGDAN KROLL
  Archive for Recent Documents,
    Warsaw
  Rada Główna Opiekuńcza

LESZEK KUBICKI
  Institute of State and Law, Warsaw
  Trials of War Criminals: Poland

OTTO DOV KULKA
  Hebrew University of Jerusalem
  Germany
  Reichsvertretung der
    Deutschen Juden
  Theresienstadt

ZBIGNIEW LANDAU
  Warsaw
  Forced Labor: Jews in
    Occupied Poland
  Ghettos, Nutrition in

HAGIT LAVSKY
  Hebrew University of Jerusalem
  Displaced Persons, Jewish

LUCIEN LAZARE
  Yad Vashem, Jerusalem
  Alsace-Lorraine
  Armée Juive
  Cohn, Marianne
  Darlan, François
  Fédération des Sociétés Juives
    de France
  French Police
  Gamzon, Robert
  Gaulle, Charles de
  Glasberg, Alexandre
  Lévitte, Simon
  Lublin, Lucien
  Oradour-sur-Glane
  Polonski, Abraham
  Rayman, Marcel
  Veil, Simone
  Weill, Joseph
  Youth Movements: France

SINAI LEICHTER
  Hebrew University of Jerusalem
  Częstochowa
  Kielce
  Piotrków Trybunalski

DOV LEVIN
  Hebrew University of Jerusalem
  Adamowicz, Irena
  Brizgys, Vincentas
  Elkes, Elchanan
  Estonia
  Irgun Berit Zion
  Kėdainiai
  Kovno
  Lietuviu Aktyvistu Frontas
  Lithuania
  Memel
  Ninth Fort
  Partisans
  Policiniai Batalionai
  Robinson, Jacob
  Rumbula
  Tallinn
  Vaivara
  Voldemaras, Augustinas
  Yelin, Haim
  Ziman, Henrik

YOSSEF LEWINGER
  Tel-Aviv University (emeritus)
  Bačka

HAYA LIFSHITZ
  Yad Vashem, Jerusalem
  Black Book of Soviet Jewry, The
  Kutorgiene-Buivydaité, Elena
  Šiauliai

ROBERT JAY LIFTON
  City University of New York
  Physicians, Nazi

GEORG LILIENTHAL
  University of Mainz
  Anthropology and
    National Socialism

DEBORAH E. LIPSTADT
  Los Angeles
  American Press and the Holocaust

FRANKLIN H. LITTELL
Temple University
Christian Churches:
　After the Holocaust
Niebuhr, Reinhold

YAACOV LOZOWICK
Yad Vashem, Jerusalem
Jäger, Karl

CZESŁAW LUCZAK
University of Poznań
Forced Labor: Fremdarbeiter
Haupttreuhandstelle
Umwandererzentralstelle
Warthegau

CZESŁAW MADAJCZYK
Polish Academy of Sciences,
　Warsaw
Generalgouvernement
Generalplan Ost
Museums and Memorial Institutes:
　Poland
Poland: General Survey

YITZCHAK MAIS
Yad Vashem, Jerusalem
HICEM

ZYGMUNT MANKOWSKI
University of Lublin
Majdanek
Sporrenberg, Jacob
Zamość

MICHAEL R. MARRUS
University of Toronto
Commissariat Général aux
　Questions Juives
Darquier de Pellepoix, Louis
France: The Jews and
　the Holocaust
Grynszpan, Herschel
Laval, Pierre
Pétain, Philippe
Refugees, 1933–1945
Statut des Juifs
Vallat, Xavier

FREDKA MAZYA
Kibbutz Haogen
Silesia, Eastern Upper

JACOB METZER
Hebrew University of Jerusalem
Menczer, Aron

MEIR MICHAELIS
Hebrew University of Jerusalem
Badoglio, Pietro
Ferramonti di Tarsia
Italy
Mussolini, Benito
Rome

ALAIN MICHEL
Centre Yair, Jerusalem
Eclaireurs Israélites de France
Les Milles
Oeuvre de Secours aux Enfants

DAN MICHMAN
Bar-Ilan University
Antwerp
Association des Juifs en Belgique
Belgium
Breendonck
Brussels
Mechelen

JOZEPH MICHMAN
Hebrew University of Jerusalem
　(*emeritus*)
Asscher, Abraham
Cohen, David
Hague, The
Joodse Raad
Mussert, Anton Adriaan
Nationaal Socialistische Beweging
Netherlands, The
Rotterdam
Seyss-Inquart, Arthur
Trials of War Criminals:
　The Netherlands
Visser, Lodewijk Ernst
Vught
Westerbork
Westerweel, Joop

SERGIO I. MINERBI
Hebrew University of Jerusalem
Kappler, Herbert
Pius XII

GEORGE L. MOSSE
University of Wisconsin, Madison
Racism

MARIAN MUSHKAT
Tel-Aviv University
Crimes against Humanity
Documentation Centers:
　Berlin Documents Center
Extradition of War Criminals
Genocide
Law Punishing Nazis and
　Nazi Collaborators
Lemkin, Raphael
Trials of War Criminals:
　Bergen-Belsen Trial
Trials of War Criminals: Norway
Trials of War Criminals:
　Nuremberg Trial
Trials of War Criminals:
　Zyklon B Trial
United Nations War Crimes
　Commission

TIKVA S. NATHAN
Haifa University
Survivors, Psychology of:
　Children of Survivors

SHLOMO NETZER
Tel-Aviv University
Będzin
Sosnowiec

FRANCIS R. NICOSIA
Saint Michael's College, Winooski,
　Vermont
Zionist Movement in Germany,
　1933–1939

AKIVA NIR
Kibbutz Shomrat
Banská Bystrica
Nováky
Sered
Sixth Slovak Brigade
Slovak National Uprising
Youth Movements: Slovakia

DALIA OFER
Hebrew University of Jerusalem
Aliya Bet
Rescue Committee of the
　Jewish Agency in Turkey
Struma

EFRAIM OFIR
Kibbutz Shuval
Youth Movements: Romania

WILA ORBACH
Yad Vashem, Jerusalem
Mińsk Mazowiecki

HARRY PAAPE
Netherlands State Institute for War
Documentation, Amsterdam
Documentation Centers:
Rijksinstituut voor
Oorlogsdocumentatie

MORDECAI PALDIEL
Yad Vashem, Jerusalem
Abegg, Elisabeth
André, Joseph
Baublys, Petras
Beccari, Arrigo
Benoît, Marie
Binkiene, Sofija
Bogaard, Johannes
Borkowska, Anna
Choms, Władysława
Deffaugt, Jean
Douwes, Arnold
Evert, Anghelos
Getter, Matylda
Grüninger, Paul
Hautval, Adelaide
Helmrich, Eberhard
Kowalski, Władysław
Le Chambon-sur-Lignon
Lipke, Janis
Lutz, Carl
N.V. Group
Nèvejean, Yvonne
Nicolini, Giuseppe
Overduijn, Leendert
Schindler, Oskar
Schmid, Anton
Sendler, Irena
Šimaite, Ona
Skobtsova, Elizaveta
Sousa Mendes, Aristides de
Sugihara, Sempo
Sztehlo, Gábor
Van der Voort, Hanna
Zabinski, Jan

STANLEY G. PAYNE
University of Wisconsin, Madison
Spain: Spanish Fascism
and the Jews

YAEL PELED (MARGOLIN)
Jerusalem
Draenger, Shimshon
Draenger, Tova
He-Haluts ha-Lohem
Liebeskind, Aharon
Montelupich Prison

ELI PFEFFERKORN
Silver Spring, Maryland
Wiesel, Elie

FALK PINGEL
Georg-Eckert-Institut Braunschweig;
University of Bielefeld
Columbia Haus
Concentration Camps
I.G. Farben
Jehovah's Witnesses
Kogon, Eugen
Natzweiler-Struthof
Neuengamme
Oranienburg
Ostindustrie GmbH
Sachsenhausen
Wirtschafts-Verwaltungshauptamt

CRISTIAN POPISTEANU
Bucharest
Romania: General Survey

DINA PORAT
Tel-Aviv University
Ben-Gurion, David
Gruenbaum, Itzhak
Joint Rescue Committee
Sereni, Enzo
Szenes, Hannah
"Tehran Children"
Yishuv

TERESA PREKEROWA
Warsaw
Aid to Jews by Poles
Białystok

Grobelny, Julian
Hotel Polski
Kossak-Szczucka, Zofia
Wolinski, Henryk
Zegota

TSVI RAANAN
Kibbutz ha-Zorea
Bormann, Martin

JOSEPH RAB
Moreshet Institute, Givat Haviva
Łódź Ghetto, Chronicles of the

GYÖRGY RANKI
Hungarian Academy of Sciences,
Budapest (deceased)
Hungary: General Survey

HANNU RAUTKALLIO
Tampere University
Finland

SHIMON REDLICH
Ben-Gurion University of the Negev
Ehrenburg, Ilya Grigoryevich
Eynikeyt
Jewish Antifascist Committee

JEHUDA REINHARZ
Brandeis University
Weizmann, Chaim

SHALOM ROBINSON
Talbiyeh Psychiatric Mental Health
Center, Hadassah Medical School,
Hebrew University of Jerusalem
Survivors, Psychology of:
Survivors in Israel

JACQUELINE ROKHSAR
Yad Vashem, Jerusalem
Barbie Trial
Joyce, William
Norway: General Survey
Quisling, Vidkun
Stürmer, Der

AVIHU RONEN
Tel-Aviv University
Merin, Moshe
Silesia, Eastern Upper

HERBERT ROSENKRANZ
Yad Vashem, Jerusalem
Austria
Löwenherz, Josef
Vienna

LIVIA ROTHKIRCHEN
Yad Vashem, Jerusalem
Beneš, Edvard
Bohemia and Moravia,
    Protectorate of
Czechoslovak Government-in-Exile
Prague
Tuka, Vojtech
Wisliceny, Dieter

ROBERT ROZETT
Yad Vashem, Jerusalem
Auschwitz Protocols
Budapest
Debrecen
Horthy Offer
Kistarcsa
Komoly, Ottó
Košice
Lutz, Carl
Mach, Alexander
Miskolc
Oradea
Pracovná Skupina
Protocols of the Elders of Zion
Przemyśl
Railways, German
Resistance, Jewish
Slovakia
Slovak National Uprising
Szeged
Timişoara
Trials of War Criminals: Hungary
Uzhgorod
Vyhne

ADALBERT RÜCKERL
Ludwigsburg, West Germany
    (deceased)
Denazification
Kriminalpolizei

Ludwigsburger Zentralstelle
Ordnungspolizei
Trials of War Criminals:
    West Germany

ADAM RUTKOWSKI
Centre de Documentation Juive
    Contemporaine, Paris (deceased)
Documentation Centers:
    Centre de Documentation Juive
    Contemporaine
Drancy
Gurs
Institut d'Etude des
    Questions Juives
Vittel

SUZANNE D. RUTLAND
Sydney College of Advanced
    Education, Australia
Australia, Jewish Refugees in

NANA SAGI
Hebrew University of Jerusalem
Board of Deputies of British Jews
Brodetsky, Selig
Great Britain: Jewish Refugees
Reparations and Restitution

MICHELE SARFATTI
Centro di Documentazione Ebraica
    Contemporanea, Milan
Documentation Centers: Centro di
    Documentazione Ebraica
    Contemporanea

CHAIM SCHATZKER
Haifa University
Education on the Holocaust:
    West Germany
Youth Aliya
Youth Movements:
    Germany and Austria

PESACH SCHINDLER
Hebrew University of Jerusalem
Kiddush ha-Hayyim
Kiddush ha-Shem

KARL A. SCHLEUNES
University of North Carolina
Hitler, Adolf

GITTA SERENY
London
Stangl, Franz

MILTON SHAIN
University of Cape Town
Greyshirts
South Africa

ELISHEVA SHAUL
Yad Vashem, Jerusalem
Bartoszewski, Władysław
Bernadotte, Folke
Dvoretski, Alter
Grojanowski Report
Homosexuality in the Third Reich
Karski, Jan
Schwarzbart, Ignacy Isaac

MENACHEM SHELAH
Haifa University; Yad Vashem,
    Jerusalem
Belgrade
Chetniks
Croatia
Jasenovac
Macedonia
Pavelić, Ante
Rab
Sarajevo
Serbia
Tito
Ustaša
Yugoslavia

DAVID H. SHPIRO
Tel-Aviv University
Eisenhower, Dwight David
Joint Boycott Council

DAVID SILBERKLANG
Yad Vashem, Jerusalem
American Jewish Committee
American Jewish Conference
Boycotts, Anti-Nazi
Council for German Jewry
Hirschmann, Ira A.
Hull, Cordell
St. Louis

SHMUEL SPECTOR
Yad Vashem, Jerusalem
Abugov, Aleksandr
Aktion 1005
Babi Yar
Bach-Zelewski, Erich von dem
Bandera, Stefan
Berdichev
Blobel, Paul
Brest-Litovsk
Brunner, Alois
Budzyń
Demjanjuk Trial
Dirlewanger, Oskar
Dnepropetrovsk
Einsatzgruppen
Fegelein, Hermann
Fomenko, Witold
Frankfurter, David
Gas Vans
Gildenman, Moshe
Gräbe, Hermann Friedrich
Hahn, Ludwig
Hilfswillige
Karaites
Kharkov
Kherson
Knochen, Helmut
Koch, Erich
Koch, Karl Otto
Kovel
Kovpak, Sidor Artemevich
Krasnodar
Kremenchug
Krimchaks
Kube, Wilhelm
Liebehenschel, Arthur
Lutsk
Melnyk, Andrei
Mogilev
Nazi-Soviet Pact
Novak, Franz
Oberg, Carl Albrecht
Ohlendorf, Otto
Opole Lubelskie
Orhanizatsyia Ukrainskykh
    Natsionalistiv
Ostbataillone
Partisans
Pinsk
Poltava

Prützmann, Hans-Adolf
Pruzhany
Rasch, Emil Otto
Ravensbrück
Red Orchestra
Reichskommissariat Ukraine
Rostov-on-Don
Rovno
Russkaya Osvoboditelnaya Armiya
Simferopol
Smolensk
Sonderkommando
Stahlecker, Franz Walter
Starachowice
Trawniki
Trials of War Criminals:
    Krasnodar Trial
Tuchin
Ukraine
Ukrainische Hilfspolizei
Ukrainska Povstanska Armyia
Vinnitsa
Vitebsk
Vlasov, Andrei
Wolff, Karl
Yad Vashem
Zhitomir

ELIYAHU STERN
Bet Loḥamei ha-Getta'ot
Danzig

ZEEV STERNHELL
Hebrew University of Jerusalem
Action Française
Fascism

CHRISTIAN STREIT
Mannheim, West Germany
Prisoners of War:
    Soviet Prisoners of War

YEHIEL SZEINTUCH
Hebrew University of Jerusalem
Gebirtig, Mordecai
Glik, Hirsh
Kaczerginski, Shmaryahu
Katzenelson, Itzhak
Literature on the Holocaust:
    Yiddish Literature
Spiegel, Isaiah
Sutzkever, Abraham
Zeitlin, Hillel

URIEL TAL
Hebrew University of Jerusalem
    (deceased)
Holocaust

JERZY TOMASZEWSKI
University of Warsaw
Zbąszyń

HAROLD TROPER
University of Toronto
Canada

YEHUDA TUBIN
Moreshet Institute, Givat Haviva
Museums and Memorial Institutes:
    Moreshet

JUDITH TYDOR-BAUMEL
Bar-Ilan University
Great Britain: Jewish Refugees
Rescue of Children, United States

MICHAL UNGER
Hebrew University of Jerusalem
Edelstein, Jacob

JOSEPH WALK
Yad Vashem; Leo Baeck Institute,
    Jerusalem
Baeck, Leo
Breslau
Documentation Centers:
    Leo Baeck Institute
Warhaftig, Zorah

JEHUDA L. WALLACH
Tel-Aviv University
Blitzkrieg
Jodl, Alfred
Keitel, Wilhelm
Manstein, Erich von
Reichenau, Walter von
Waldheim, Kurt

CHARLOTTE WARDI
Haifa University
Literature on the Holocaust:
    France

HENRY WASSERMAN
Yad Vashem, Jerusalem
Munich
Nuremberg

ABRAHAM WEIN,
Yad Vashem, Jerusalem
Documentation Centers:
    Żydowski Instytut Historyczny
Yizkor Book

DAVID WEINBERG
Bowling Green State University,
    Ohio
France: After the Holocaust

AHARON WEISS
Yad Vashem, Jerusalem;
    Haifa University
Berezhany
Biberstein, Marek
Brody
Chortkov
Drogobych
Gorodenka
Janówska
Judenrat
Jüdischer Ordnungsdienst
Katzmann, Fritz
Kolomyia
Lublin
Lvov
Nachtigall Battalion
Petliura Days
Rogatin
Sheptytsky, Andrei
Stanisławów
Stry
Tarnów
Ternopol
Zolochev

HANS-HEINRICH WILHELM
West Berlin
Abwehr
Ahnenerbe
Auslandsorganisation der NSDAP
Euthanasia Program
Kaltenbrunner, Ernst
Korherr, Richard
Müller, Heinrich
Nebe, Arthur
Oberg, Carl Albrecht
Organisation Todt
Papen, Franz von
Parteitage
Streicher, Julius
Wehrmacht

DAVID S. WYMAN
University of Massachusetts,
    Amherst
Auschwitz, Bombing of
Evian Conference
President's Advisory Committee
    on Political Refugees
War Refugee Board

LENI YAHIL
Haifa University (emeritus)
Denmark
Duckwitz, Georg Ferdinand
Eichmann, Adolf
Einsatzstab Rosenberg
Kristallnacht
Mauritius
Sprachregelung
Sweden
Switzerland
Wallenberg, Raoul

HANNAH YAOZ
Tel Aviv
Literature on the Holocaust:
    Hebrew Literature

JAMES E. YOUNG
University of Massachusetts,
    Amherst
Museums and Memorial Institutes:
    General Survey

RUTH ZARIZ
Bet Loḥamei ha-Getta'ot
Exchange: Jews and Germans
Luxembourg

IDITH ZERTAL
Tel-Aviv University
Exodus 1947

EFRAIM ZUROFF
Simon Wiesenthal Center for
    Holocaust Studies, Jerusalem
Kalmanowitz, Abraham
Office of Special Investigations
Rescue of Polish Jews via
    East Asia
Sternbuch, Recha
Va'ad ha-Hatsala
Wiesenthal, Simon

RONALD W. ZWEIG
Tel-Aviv University
Churchill, Winston
    Leonard Spencer
Eden, Sir Anthony
Great Britain: General Survey
Great Britain: Jewish Refugees

A

AB-AKTION (Ausserordentliche Befriedungs-aktion; Extraordinary Pacification Operation), extermination campaign directed against Poles. The immediate objective of the AB-Aktion was to suppress Polish resistance and put fear into the hearts of the Polish population by liquidating persons who were capable of inciting or organizing Polish resistance to the Germans. In that respect, the AB-Aktion was a continuation of previous terror operations, such as the political purge carried out in 1939.

The Reich security organizations did not possess precise information on the growing resistance movement, but the possibility of an uprising was taken into account, and the Wehrmacht had in fact warned of it. The GENERALGOUVERNEMENT chief, Hans FRANK, was in favor of forestalling the threat by destroying the Polish leaders.

In February and March 1940, the Reichsverteidigungsrat (Reich Defense Council; the military planning committee) discussed the subject and drew up plans, based on past experience gained by the Reich. A decision was made to exterminate, at one blow, potential leaders of a resistance movement —identified as the activists among the Polish intelligentsia—and thereby also to intimidate the population. On May 16, 1940, a few days after the Germans had launched their offensive in western Europe, Frank gave the order for the AB-Aktion to begin. Approximately thirty-five hundred persons whom the Germans regarded as belonging to the leadership class, as well as three thousand suspected of criminal activities, were arrested in the Generalgouvernement and massacred (one of the sites of the massacres was the Palmiry Forest). The plan had been to bring the operation to an end by the middle of 1940, but it continued until the fall, most probably because of the success of the German offensive in the west.

The operation failed to achieve its objective of destroying the resistance movement. For a while, the resistance organizations (for example, the Związek Walki Zbrojnej, or Union for Armed Struggle) had their membership reduced by a third, but the movement recovered and accelerated its operations. The danger that the Polish population would become disillusioned with resistance following the defeat of France, which had been a real threat, did not materialize.

The AB-Aktion, and the crimes committed in the course of that operation, were among the charges raised at the NUREMBERG TRIAL and at the series of war crimes trials held by the Supreme People's Court in Poland.

BIBLIOGRAPHY

Broszat, M. *Nationalsozialistischer Polenpolitik, 1939–1945.* Stuttgart, 1964.

STEFAN BIERNACKI

ABEGG, ELISABETH (1882–d. after 1957), German Quaker who saved Jews in Berlin during World War II. Raised in Strasbourg (Alsace) when it was part of Imperial Germany, Abegg became involved in activities

Elisabeth Abegg.

for the Quakers when she moved to Berlin. A history teacher at the Luisen girls' school, she was dismissed in 1933 by the Nazi school director for her pronounced anti-Nazi views.

In 1942, at the age of sixty and while looking after her bedridden mother and sick elder sister, Abegg began using her home in the Tempelhof district as a temporary shelter and assembly point for many Jews. She created a rescue network made up of friends from the Quaker movement, pastors, and former students, and over a period of almost three years helped dozens of Jews escape deprivation and deportation. Her activities included sheltering Jews either in her own home (in a building that also housed several Nazi party members) or in temporarily empty adjoining apartments in her care. Abegg found safe and permanent refuges both in Berlin and in more distant locations such as Alsace and East Prussia; she sent provisions to enable those who escaped to survive and provided them with false identities. She helped still others to escape across the Swiss border, selling her jewelry and other valuables in order to finance this work. She also

tutored Jewish children at her home to compensate for their not being able to attend school. Bringing false identification papers, money, and provisions, she visited her charges in various locations.

In a booklet dedicated to her on her seventy-fifth birthday in 1957, entitled "And a Light Shone in the Darkness," her former charges offered profuse praise of Elisabeth Abegg's dedication, care, and humanity.

BIBLIOGRAPHY

Leuner, H. D. *When Compassion Was a Crime.* London, 1966.

MORDECAI PALDIEL

ABETZ, OTTO (1903–1958), German ambassador to Vichy France during World War II. Abetz studied art and later taught drawing at a girls' school. His support for the Nazi party dates from 1931. In 1934, in addition to his teaching duties, he began to organize meetings of French and German ex-servicemen. In 1935, as a French expert, he entered the For-

Otto Abetz, Hitler's ambassador to Vichy France. [National Archives]

eign Office under Joachim von RIBBENTROP. He spent much time in France, but was expelled in 1939 in connection with the measures being taken against the Cagoulards, a secret fascist organization.

Abetz returned to France in 1940 and in August of that year was appointed ambassador to the Vichy government. He held this post for the next four years, advising the German military and police administration in Paris and dealing with all political questions in occupied and unoccupied France. In his efforts to secure complete French cooperation with Nazi objectives, Abetz enjoyed the support of Pierre LAVAL. As a party activist (he was appointed an SS-*Brigadeführer* in 1941), Abetz took a leading role in supporting the deportation of foreign Jews and then of French-born Jews, especially after the German occupation of southern France in November 1942. He was arrested after the liberation and in 1949 was sentenced by a military tribunal in Paris to twenty years' hard labor for war crimes, including the deportation of Jews and of French workers. He was found not guilty of complicity in the murder of Georges Mandel, the Jewish former minister of the interior.

Abetz served five years of his sentence. Released in 1954, he died four years later in a motor accident in the Rhineland.

BIBLIOGRAPHY

Browning, C. R. *The Final Solution and the German Foreign Office: A Study of Referat D3 of Abteilung Deutschland, 1940–1943.* New York, 1978.
Marrus, M. R., and R. O. Paxton. *Vichy France and the Jews.* New York, 1981.
Paxton, R. O. *Vichy France: Old Guard and New Order, 1940–1944.* New York, 1972.

LIONEL KOCHAN

ABUGOV, ALEKSANDR (b. 1913), Russian Jewish partisan commander. A native of Odessa, Abugov grew up in Kirovograd and became a locksmith. After his army service he studied at the Kharkov sports academy and worked as a fencing instructor.

When the Germans invaded the Soviet Union, on June 22, 1941, Abugov was called up and posted to the Ukrainian front, where he served as a second lieutenant in an armored-train unit. The unit was besieged and Abugov was taken prisoner of war. Seeing that the Germans were murdering the Jews among the prisoners, Abugov posed as an ethnic Russian. He passed through several prisoner-of-war camps—Uman, Vinnitsa, Shepetovka, Brest-Litovsk, and Kobrin—and finally reached the camp in KOVEL, from which he made his escape. He joined a partisan unit in the village of Dolsk, in Polesye. By September 1942, the group had grown in size and Abugov commanded its reconnaissance squad.

At the end of 1942 the unit moved east, where Abugov encountered Jews fleeing from the Serniki and Dubrovitsa ghettos. He was deeply moved by the difficult situation of the Jews and decided, with several friends, to leave his unit and together with Jewish youths to set up his own partisan unit. At the request of Gen. Vasily Begma, commanding officer of the two Rovno divisions, Abugov joined the Rovno division and was appointed commander of the reconnaissance battalion, a 400-man cavalry unit, with which he took part in the liberation of ROVNO in February 1944. On his discharge he became the district sports officer. He married one of the young women who had served with him and, together with other members of his family, moved to Poland. In 1949 he emigrated to Israel.

BIBLIOGRAPHY

Spector, S. *The Holocaust of Volhynian Jews, 1941–1944.* Jerusalem, 1986. (In Hebrew.)

SHMUEL SPECTOR

ABWEHR (full name, Amt Ausland/Abwehr im Oberkommando der WEHRMACHT; Foreign Bureau/Defense of the Armed Forces High Command), the German Reich's most important intelligence service in World War II. Established in 1938, the Abwehr was preceded by two intelligence branches, the Reichswehr Abwehr Abteilung (Army Intelligence Section) and the Abwehr Abteilung of the War Ministry. Until 1944 the Abwehr was headed by Adm. Wilhelm CANARIS. The navy and the air force each had an intelligence service as well. The civilian sector was the concern of the Foreign Ministry intelligence service; two intelligence services maintained by the SD (Sicherheitsdienst; Security Service), one headed by Walter SCHELLENBERG, dealing with foreign affairs, and the other, headed by Otto OHLENDORF, for internal affairs; and an intelligence service for economic affairs. The war zones had their own intelligence services: Fremde Heere–Ost (Foreign Armies–East; as of April 1, 1942, run by Reinhard Gehlen) and Fremde Heere–West, both of which were part of the Oberkommando des Heeres (Army High Command). On the lower command levels, the intelligence branches were frequently served by one and the same intelligence officer.

The effectiveness of the German military intelligence services in World War II is a highly controversial subject that has been embellished by many legends. The most successful spy operating on his own (his code name was "Max") has been identified by historian Herbert Rittlinger as "the Jew Klatt," a financier by profession, whom the Abwehr had inherited from the Austrian intelligence. "Max" is alleged to have had first-class connections in Moscow and the Balkan countries and to have been one of the most mysterious figures in modern espionage. Canaris's achievements as a military attaché in Madrid, Bucharest, Sofia, Ankara, Budapest, and other places cannot as yet be properly evaluated, since the relevant documents (assuming that they still exist) have not become accessible. It is known that until June 22, 1941, the day of the German attack on the Soviet Union, the German military intelligence's opinion of the Soviet military potential was so low that it bordered on the grotesque—an opinion, incidentally, that they shared with British and American intelligence. German radio intelligence was quite reliable, and its achievements were comparable to corresponding intelligence branches in other countries. During the course of the war, signals intelligence became the most important element of intelligence gathering.

The Abwehr made headlines mostly by virtue of the scandals and affairs in which it was involved, among them foreign-currency violations, corruption, diversion of funds to obscure purposes, passport violations, smuggling, and misuse of foreign army uniforms. There were instances when it failed to grasp enemy intentions in time; when its agents defected to the enemy at an opportune time; when it failed to detect double agents; and when treacherous disinformation agents talked too much and divulged true instead of misleading information. All these mishaps took place in the Abwehr and were regarded in professional German intelligence circles as hazards that were always present in intelligence work; the latter claimed that only to outsiders did they appear as unpardonable bungling.

More difficult to judge are the politically motivated "mistakes," "offenses," and failures to act. For example, did Canaris deliberately act against the interests of his employers when he recruited and surrounded himself with potential adversaries of the regime? These included members of the Freikorps, SA (Sturmabteilung; Storm Troopers) mercenaries, and National Bolsheviks serving in the special "Brandenburg" Regiment; Oberstleutnant Hans Groscurth, the pastor's son whom Canaris made head of the sabotage and subversion section; Generalmajor Hans Oster, an anti-Nazi whom Canaris appointed head of the central division and chief of staff of the foreign section; members of the anti-regime Bekennende Kirche (Confessing Church) whom Canaris used as couriers; Catholic priests, whom he trusted with secrets; and Ukrainian nationalists and Russian monarchists, whom he recruited to serve as a fifth column during the German attack on the Soviet Union. Was Oster betraying his country when he used various channels to transmit to the West in 1940 the presumed date of that attack, in such a way that nobody in the capitals concerned paid any heed to his warnings? Is it true that Canaris and Generalmajor Erwin Lahousen (Groscurth's successor) vigorously protested the slaughter of the Jews when, in the fall of 1941, they received the first detailed eyewitness account of the slaughter? By then, the fact that Jews were being murdered was undoubtedly known to both of them.

There is documentary evidence that the Geheime Feldpolizei (Secret Field Police), which was under the Abwehr's control, took active part in the murder of Jews in the Soviet Union. It has also been conclusively proved that Canaris forwarded to Joseph GOEBBELS a proposal made by the chief of the Abwehr's counterintelligence section, Generalmajor Franz Eccard von Bentivegni, to force all the Jews in Berlin to wear a sign identifying them as security risks, and to concentrate them in the eastern section of the capital.

The core of the resistance center that did exist in the Abwehr was smashed long before the July 20, 1944, abortive coup against Hitler. Hans von Dohnányi, Dietrich BONHOEF-FER, Josef Müller (an eminent Munich lawyer and devout Catholic, who had been attached by Oster to the Abwehr and who had good connections with the Vatican), and Oster were under arrest on twenty-four-hour surveillance from April 1943; and Canaris was under house arrest from February 1944. The Abwehr was disbanded and incorporated into the REICHSSICHERHEITSHAUPTAMT (Reich Security Main Office; RSHA) as the Military Bureau, and Groscurth was taken prisoner by the Soviets on the Stalingrad front. Nevertheless, in April 1945, Canaris, Oster, Bonhoeffer, and Dohnányi, who at the time were imprisoned in the FLOSSENBÜRG concentration camp, were summarily tried, sentenced to death, and hanged by the Germans.

BIBLIOGRAPHY

Brissard, A. *The Nazi Secret Service.* New York, 1974.
Buchheit, G. *Der deutsche Geheimdienst: Geschichte der Militärischen Abwehr.* Munich, 1966.
Hoetl, W. *The Secret Front: The Story of Nazi Political Espionage.* New York, 1971.
Hohne, H. *Canaris, a Biography.* Garden City, N.Y., 1979.
Hohne, H. *The Order of the Death's Head: The Story of Hitler's SS.* New York, 1969.

HANS-HEINRICH WILHELM

ACTION FRANÇAISE, French radical right-wing antisemitic movement. Action Française was founded in 1899, when the Dreyfus affair was at its height, to counter liberal intellectuals who were rallying to the defense of the Jewish army captain charged with treason.

The point of departure of the new movement was that the question of Dreyfus's guilt or innocence was irrelevant; at stake was the good of the nation and of the state, for which it was imperative that the army be free of all stain. The public interest was held always to take precedence over the interest of the individual—all the more so when that individual was a Jew, a foreign body in the French people.

Thereafter, until its formal dissolution at the end of World War II, Action Française was the spearhead of "integral nationalism," the nationalism of blood and soil. French "integral nationalism" regarded the nation as an organic entity, engaged in an unending struggle with four enemies that threatened to destroy it: Jews, foreigners, Protestants, and Freemasons. To defend itself and safeguard its survival, the nation had to fight all these elements and seek to banish them from its midst.

The central thesis of "integral nationalism" was that in order to put a stop to France's disintegration, the heritage of the French Revolution had to be discarded and monarchic rule restored. Nationalism—according to Charles Maurras (1863–1952), the founder and undisputed leader of Action Française—was not only a political value; it was also, perhaps above all, an aesthetic value. "Goddess France" was a creation unlike any other in the world, and the preservation of this unique entity required absolute national egotism; any element that weakened the body of the nation had to be destroyed. Heading the list of such elements was democracy, which was based on the principles of equality, individualism, and human rights, and which served as the arena for struggle among diverse interest groups and political parties.

Antagonism toward the Jews guided Maurras's actions throughout his life, and for nearly fifty years his movement was in the vanguard of French antisemitism. The history of the movement, in many ways, parallels Maurras's own life. Action Française derived its influence from his writings; Maurras was one of France's leading intellectuals and authors, a member (from 1939) of the Académie Française and a figure highly esteemed by many in the country's intelligentsia.

In World War II, Maurras led a virulent

campaign of anti-Jewish incitement and tried to gain recognition as the ideologue of the Vichy regime's "national revolution." He enthusiastically welcomed the racist laws introduced in October 1940. These laws were to serve the new regime's aim of removing the Jews from the life of the French people and thereby to erase 150 years of the country's history as a republic; this corresponded to the objectives of Action Française. Indeed, the movement had been founded for the purpose of liquidating the heritage and ideals of the French Revolution, which constituted the principles on which the Third Republic (1871–1940) was based.

When the war ended, Maurras was sentenced to life imprisonment for collaborating with the enemy. Action Française was always a small movement in size, but its intellectual influence was disproportionately large, not only in France, but also in Italy, Spain, Belgium, and countries of eastern Europe.

BIBLIOGRAPHY

Curtis, M. *Three against the Third Republic: Barrès, Maurras, Sorel.* Princeton, 1959.
Nölte, E. *Three Faces of Fascism: Action Française, Italian Fascism, National Socialism.* New York, 1966.
Sutton, M. *Nationalism, Positivism, and Catholicism: The Politics of Charles Maurras and French Catholics, 1890–1914.* Cambridge, 1982.
Weber, E. *Action Française: Royalism and Reaction in Twentieth-Century France.* Stanford, 1962.

ZEEV STERNHELL

ADAMOWICZ, IRENA (1910–1963), Polish liaison officer among various ghetto underground movements. Born in Warsaw, Adamowicz was a pious Catholic and a member of the leadership of the Polish scout movement. She graduated with a degree in social work at Warsaw University. In the 1930s she was greatly attracted by the Ha-Shomer ha-Tsa'ir movement and even participated in its social and educational work. In the summer of 1942, Adamowicz carried out many dangerous missions for the Jewish underground organizations in the ghettos of WARSAW, BIAŁYSTOK, VILNA, KOVNO, and ŠIAULIAI. In addition to the important information she conveyed, her vis-

its to the isolated ghettos brought moral encouragement to those imprisoned there. With her help, contact was established between the Jewish underground organizations and the members of the ARMIA KRAJOWA (Home Army).

After the war, Adamowicz maintained close relations with the survivors of the pioneer Zionist movements in Poland and with her friends from those movements in Israel. For her unique activity in the war years she was awarded the "RIGHTEOUS AMONG THE NATIONS" medal by YAD VASHEM in Jerusalem.

BIBLIOGRAPHY

The Jewish Partisans. Merhavia, Israel, 1958. (In Hebrew.)

DOV LEVIN

AFRICA, NORTH. *See* Algeria; Libya; Morocco; Tunisia.

AFSC. *See* American Friends Service Committee.

AHNENERBE (lit., "ancestral heritage"), the Society for Research into the Spiritual Roots of Germany's Ancestral Heritage (Studiengesellschaft für Geistesurgeschichte Deutsches Ahnenerbe), founded in Berlin on July 1, 1935, by Heinrich HIMMLER, Richard Walther DARRÉ, and the German-Dutch lecturer Herman Wirth. The society published a magazine, *Germanien*, whose object was to broaden support for Wirth's cult of "Germandom." Shortly after Ahnenerbe was founded, however, the leading "scientific" role in the society was put in the hands of Walther Wüst, the Nazi-appointed dean of the faculty of philosophy at Munich University, since Wirth was found to have no standing among the academic community.

From its very inception, Ahnenerbe concerned itself with esoteric, mostly pseudo-scientific, subjects. These included, in addition to ancient Germanic history, Hanns Hörbiger's universal ice theory (*Welteislehre*); the Atlantis myth; interpretation of the *Ex-*

ternsteine ("external stones," a peculiar outcrop of rock near Detmold, reputed to be the site of ancient pagan worship); revival of ancient Germanic customs; research into the runes (ancient Germanic letters of the alphabet); interpretation of symbols (such as the origin and meaning of the swastika); and promotion of the cult of the medieval German king Heinrich I (r. 919–936), "Conqueror of the Slavs," a fad of Himmler's that involved archaeological digs and memorial services at Quedlinburg (now in East Germany), where Heinrich I had resided.

Before long, Ahnenerbe branched out into various other fields, a process that was speeded up when Himmler took direct charge of the society in 1937 and eventually became its president. Ample funds now poured into Ahnenerbe's treasury. New projects undertaken by the society included a research expedition to Tibet; research into ancient forms of naturopathy; genealogical research; publications such as the *Atlas of German Folklore* and a book series, Forest and Trees in Aryan-German Thought and Culture; archaeological excavations at ancient settlements or at sites related to German legends, such as Altchristburg in East Prussia, Hohmichele near Sigmaringen, Haithabu in Schleswig, and Krimhildestuhl near Bad Dürkheim; speleological expeditions to the Altmühltal caves and Franconian Switzerland; research on the history of the Lombards; research on the art and culture of the Irish-Scottish Mission (sixth to ninth centuries); meteorological research; divination (by use of rods); reexamination of the occult sciences; research on astronomy; research on ownership marks and clan symbols; research on military geology (prospecting for war-essential metals); the study of paleontology; research on animal geography and history; and study of the development of a "national telescope." In the planning stage were expeditions to Hawaii, southern Nigeria, Manchuria, South America, Iceland, and Iran.

In 1939 Ahnenerbe launched its annual "Science Weeks," a lecture series at Salzburg. It also compiled and published lists of "Jewish scientists or scientists related to Jews by marriage" and confiscated libraries, such as the Jewish author Lion Feuchtwanger's Oriental-Semitic library and the library, consisting of 80,000 to 100,000 volumes, of the Salzburger Universitätsverein (Salzburg University Society), which had been disbanded by the Gestapo shortly after the ANSCHLUSS. Ahnenerbe representatives were sent to scientific congresses as observers; rival research organizations, such as the German Society of Celtic Studies and the Westphalian Native Lodge, were undermined to facilitate their takeover by Ahnenerbe, which also schemed against Alfred ROSENBERG, particularly Rosenberg's ambitious plan for establishing a *Hohe Schule* (academy of sciences) on the shore of Lake Chiem in Bavaria.

Many of these projects became outmoded as soon as the war broke out, and others were continued to enable the researchers to dodge military service. Soon, Germany's territorial expansion created new challenges, which Ahnenerbe was eager to tackle. Among these were the "recovery" of German church registers and archives in the Baltic states; the seizure of art treasures in Poland; the sifting of art collections in the museums of Kiev, Odessa, Rostov, and Novocherkassk; "archaeological excavations, on a larger scale" in the Dnepropetrovsk district; an investigation of Gothic memorial tablets in the Crimea; a study of the dialects of the Cimbri (an ancient Germanic tribe) in the South Tirol; folklore research in "Gottschee" (Kočevje, in Slovenia), Norway, and Flanders; historical research on the *limes* (ancient Roman imperial fortifications) and on Cossack life, designed to shore up Himmler's plans for the establishment of settlements populated by soldier-farmers; a plan for policy on science in the Greater German Reich; research into the history of the Mongols; a comprehensive exploration of Caucasia; and the breeding of a "superior steppe horse for use in war and agricultural colonization," by crossing the Przewalski and Gmelin wild-horse lines.

It was almost impossible to establish which projects were plain charlatanry, which were politically motivated research, and which were conventional scientific projects. Many projects never went beyond the preliminary stage, which was not surprising in view of the short time available, the lack of means, and the low regard of the scientific community for Ahnenerbe (the organization did not attract the better-qualified and established scientists).

In 1942 this obscure society was swallowed up by the *Reichsführer*'s personal staff. The fact that its very existence is still known is not because of any scientific achievement by its researchers but because of the evil experiments conducted under its auspices by the German air force medical officer Dr. Sigmund Rascher in DACHAU, and the skull collection created by Dr. August Hirt, professor of anatomy at the Reich University of Strasbourg, as of 1941. A favorite of Himmler's, Rascher most likely did not need his post at Ahnenerbe's Institute of Military-Scientific Applied Research (*Wehrwissenschaftliche Zweckforschung*) to conduct his carcinoma-test series and his experiments in high-altitude flights under conditions of low pressure and freezing temperatures. As an air force senior medical officer, he was acting on orders of Professor Erich Hippke, air force sanitation inspector; Professor Georg August Weltz of the Munich Institute for Air Force Medicine; and Dr. Siegfried Ruff of the Berlin Institute of Flight Medicine of the German Flight Research Institute; and with the knowledge of Erhard Milch, the inspector general of the air force.

In his freezing experiments, Rascher was assisted by Professor Ernst Holzlöhner, a Kiel physiologist acting on a research assignment from Hippke, and by Dr. E. Finke, another air force medical officer. All the machinery and installations required by Rascher for his experiments were provided by the air force. The Dachau concentration camp did not come under Ahnenerbe, and in his capacity as Ahnenerbe president, Himmler was not authorized to give instructions to the concentration-camp commandant. It was only as *Reichsführer*-SS and chief of the German police that Himmler was in a position to approve of Rascher's human experiments on prisoners in Dachau. Rascher's association with Ahnenerbe was therefore no more than a scientific cover for a favor that Himmler was doing for Hermann GÖRING's Luftwaffe. As far as Rascher's cancer research was concerned, Himmler had given his approval to Rascher himself, in a private capacity, as early as 1939.

Rascher's high-altitude experiments are reported to have been conducted on 180 to 200 prisoners, "mostly Jews, Germans, Russians, and Poles—including also some Christian clergymen," of whom about 80 perished as a result. In the freezing experiments, of which 400 were carried out, from 280 to 300 prisoners took part and between 80 and 90 of them died.

In 1945 Rascher was executed in Dachau by a shot in the neck, on Himmler's orders, as an accessory to at least eight cases of kidnapping children perpetrated by his wife; she was a close acquaintance of Himmler's and had falsely claimed to have given birth to children after the age of forty-eight. She was hanged in the RAVENSBRÜCK camp shortly before it was liberated, after attacking a female guard in the camp.

Hirt's skull collection, according to a memorandum he submitted to Ahnenerbe on December 10, 1941, was intended to close an existing gap:

> We have large collections of skulls of almost all races and peoples at our disposal. Of the Jewish race, however, only very few specimens of skulls are available and their processing cannot assure us of obtaining reliable results. The war in the east now presents us with the opportunity to overcome this deficiency. By procuring the skulls of the Jewish-Bolshevik commissars, who represent the prototype of the repulsive but characteristic subhuman, we have the chance now to obtain authentic scientific material.

In the future, all "Jewish-Bolshevik commissars" were to be handed over to the field gendarmerie, so as to enable medical students serving in the army to take the required anthropological measurements; then, after carefully severing the heads from the bodies, they were to dispatch the remains to Strasbourg in special lead containers filled with preservative fluid. Henceforth, Hirt's interests broadened: in November 1942 he was to receive "150 skeletons of prisoners, that is, Jews" from the AUSCHWITZ extermination camp for "certain anthropological examinations." Delivery of the order was delayed, however, and it was only in June of 1943 that Hirt was informed by one of his assistants of the receipt of "79 Jews, 2 Poles, 4 Central Asians, and 30 Jewesses, processed." In late

July and early August, 122 corpses (including the corpses of 29 females) were delivered, of persons whom the camp commandant had had killed in a special gas chamber, using for this purpose a chemical Hirt had selected.

A part of Hirt's skull collection is said to have been moved to the Mittersill castle in the fall of 1944. Hirt died in Schönenbach, in the Neustadt district (Black Forest), on June 2, 1945. He is presumed to have taken his own life.

[*See also* Medical Experiments.]

BIBLIOGRAPHY

Kater, M. H. *Das "Ahnenerbe" der SS, 1935–1945: Ein Beitrag zur Kulturpolitik des Dritten Reiches.* Stuttgart, 1974.

Mitscherlich, A., and F. Mielke. *Doctors of Infamy: The Story of the Nazi Medical Crimes.* New York, 1949.

HANS-HEINRICH WILHELM

AID TO JEWS BY POLES. A number of factors made it extremely difficult for Poles to come to the aid of the Jews in POLAND during World War II: the lack of contact between the Jews and the Polish environment; the antisemitism that spread in certain circles of Polish society; the regime of terror in Nazi-occupied Poland, which was aimed at the entire population, on a scale unparalleled in western Europe; and the death penalty the Nazis applied in Poland for giving aid to Jews.

Forms of Help. The most dangerous, and yet the most frequent, form of help given to the Jews was the offering of refuge in private dwellings. Most of the people who gave refuge to Jews also provided them with financial assistance. In the main the motivation for help was that of human compassion; devout Catholics felt obligated to abide by the commandment to "love thy neighbor." Others—chiefly among leftist and liberal circles—acted out of ideological and political considerations. Some of the Poles who gave help to Jews did so in return for financial reward, which was very high in certain cases. Those who gave help came from all walks of life. There were even a few cases in which

antisemites helped Jews. Aid to Jews was extended mainly in two centers—WARSAW (where twenty thousand to thirty thousand Jews were in hiding) and KRAKÓW.

At a later stage, aid in organized form was given by underground organizations, trade unions, and political parties—Democrats, Socialists, and Communists. In most of these cases, the recipients of the aid were Jews who were members, or relatives of members, of the respective organization. Beginning in early 1943, these organizations (except for the Communists) were assisted by ŻEGOTA (the Polish Council for Aid to Jews).

Some monasteries (primarily Franciscan) took in Jewish children; the Benedictine monastery near Vilna even extended aid to Jewish fighters. Several of the boy scouts from the underground Gray Ranks organization (Szare Szeregi, which was affiliated with the Home Army, or ARMIA KRAJOWA) cooperated with Ha-Shomer ha-Tsa'ir, acting as its intermediary between one city and another, and smuggling arms. It is difficult to estimate the extent of this kind of aid in figures.

According to postwar estimates by historians, several tens of thousands of Jews were saved by the local population. The number of "Aryans" who gave help to Jews (Poles and, in eastern Poland, also Belorussians and Ukrainians—the latter much more rarely) is variously estimated as ranging from 160,000 to 360,000, that is, 1 percent to 2.5 percent of the population. A list drawn up by the MAIN COMMISSION FOR INVESTIGATION OF NAZI CRIMES IN POLAND puts the number of non-Jews executed individually by the Germans for aiding Jews at 872, with several hundreds more murdered in mass executions (as when the Nazis burned down entire villages).

Military aid given to Jews was minimal. The information available concerning the earliest contacts with various groups is under dispute. These contacts were established by the ŻYDOWSKI ZWIĄZEK WOJSKOWY (Jewish Military Union), the second Jewish fighting organization in the Warsaw ghetto, whose nucleus consisted of members of the Revisionist Betar youth movement. It made contact with the Korpus Bezpieczeństwa (Security Corps; KB), an underground organization affiliated with the Armia Krajowa, which acted as a gendarmerie when the WARSAW POLISH UPRIS-

ING took place. It was only in the fall of 1942 that the ŻYDOWSKA ORGANIZACJA BOJOWA (Jewish Fighting Organization; ŻOB), after several abortive attempts, established links with Armia Krajowa headquarters, with the help of Henryk WOLINSKI. The Armia Krajowa planned an uprising against the Nazis that would take place only when the front line of battle was drawing near, since it did not believe that an earlier attempt stood any chance of success. The ŻOB, on the other hand, felt that the Jews had no time to lose and that a revolt had to be attempted even if it was hopeless. The Armia Krajowa, moreover, was not convinced that the ŻOB really meant to execute its schemes when it spoke of fighting the Nazis. For these two reasons, the quantity of weapons supplied to the ŻOB by the Armia Krajowa was very small.

During the WARSAW GHETTO UPRISING, the Armia Krajowa, the Gwardia Ludowa (later the ARMIA LUDOWA, or Polish People's Army), the KB, and the Socjalistyczna Organizacja Bojowa (Socialist Fighting Organization) carried out several actions to indicate their solidarity with the Jews and attacked German positions, losing men in these attacks. They also helped several groups of ghetto fighters to make their way through the Warsaw sewers to the city's "Aryan" side. At a later stage, when the question of establishing Jewish partisan units came up, the Armia Krajowa refused to cooperate, believing that such units would have a pro-Soviet orientation. The Gwardia Ludowa/Armia Ludowa gave the Jews some help, but the possibilities open to it were limited. In the Warsaw Polish uprising, in the summer of 1944, Jews fought in Armia Ludowa units.

A constant source of danger to the Jews who had gone into hiding was the so-called *szmalcowniki* (blackmailers)—gangs of robbers who roamed the countryside, blackmailed the Jews in hiding, and extorted ransoms from them, frequently also informing on them to the Germans. There were also instances when Poles who looked like Jews or gave help to Jews were blackmailed by the *szmalcowniki*.

These *szmalcowniki*, for the most part, came from the lower strata of the population. It was difficult to fight them, since only in rare instances was it possible for their vic-

tims to identify them. The *szmalcowniki* were also wanted by the Polish underground because they worked for the German police, and they were often sentenced to death by the underground tribunals. Several dozen such death sentences were carried out in 1943 and 1944, and as a result, the activity of the blackmailers diminished considerably.

Contacts Abroad. The Jewish underground's efforts to establish its own contacts with the outside world did not materialize. Beginning in 1942, however, the BUND and the Żydowski Komitet Narodowy (Jewish National Committee; the ŻOB's political arm) had the help of the DELEGATURA (the representative, in Poland, of the Polish government-in-exile), whose couriers carried letters back and forth between Poland and England and which also transmitted the two Jewish organizations' messages on current affairs by radio. The addressees in London were the Jewish representatives on the Polish National Council—Samuel ZYGELBOJM, and subsequently Emanuel Scherer and Isaac SCHWARZBART. Funds contributed in London by international Jewish organizations were transmitted to Poland (by parachute drops) together with funds for the Armia Krajowa and the Delegatura.

In 1940 the Polish underground also began transmitting to London reports on the situation of the Jews. Some historians believe that these reports were deliberately delayed, especially those concerning the deportation of the Jews from the Warsaw ghetto to the extermination camps. Other historians claim that the reports were transmitted promptly, and that it was the Allied governments who held them back. Ultimately, public statements made by the Polish government-in-exile and the testimony of emissaries from Poland—primarily that of Jan KARSKI—played an important role in dispelling the doubts of the free world about reports on the annihilation of European Jewry by the Germans.

BIBLIOGRAPHY

Bartoszewski, W., and Z. Lewin. *Righteous among Nations: How Poles Helped the Jews, 1939–1945.* London, 1969.

Datner, S. *Las sprawiedliwych: Karta z dziejów ratownictwa Żydow w okupowanej Polsce.* Warsaw, 1968.

Friedman, P. *Their Brothers' Keepers: The Christian Heroes and Heroines Who Helped the Oppressed Escape the Nazi Terror.* New York, 1957.

Gutman, Y. *The Jews of Warsaw, 1939–1943.* Bloomington, 1980.

Laqueur, W. *The Terrible Secret.* London, 1980.

Ringelblum, E. *Polish-Jewish Relations during the Second World War.* Jerusalem, 1974.

Tec, N. *When Light Pierced the Darkness: Christian Rescue of Jews in Nazi-occupied Poland.* New York, 1986.

TERESA PREKEROWA

AJ. *See* Armée Juive.

AJB. *See* Association des Juifs en Belgique.

AKIVA. *See* Youth Movements.

AKTION "ERNTEFEST." *See* "Erntefest."

AKTION 1005, code name for a large-scale activity that aimed to obliterate the traces of the murder of millions of human beings by the Nazis in occupied Europe. A decision to undertake this action was made in Berlin after news of the mass murders began to emerge in the Allied countries, and when the hastily buried corpses began to pose a serious health hazard in the early summer of 1942.

The operation's code name originated in an important letter from the Gestapo commander Heinrich MÜLLER to Martin LUTHER in the Foreign Office, who had forwarded an anonymous letter complaining about the corpses flooding the WARTHEGAU area. At the head of the letter, under the name of the ministry, appeared the number 1005 in brackets, and this became the code by which the operation was known. The units that put it into effect were called Sonderkommandos 1005.

The operation commenced in June 1942 with attempts to burn the corpses in the CHEŁMNO extermination camp. At the same time, SS-Standartenführer Paul BLOBEL was appointed head of Aktion 1005. He created a small staff in Łódź, and in an initial stage, between the summer of 1942 and that of 1943, supervised the burning of bodies in the AKTION REINHARD extermination camps (BEŁŻEC, TREBLINKA, SOBIBÓR), in the Chełmno camp, and at AUSCHWITZ (until the crematoria were installed there). An architect by profession, and a member of the engineering corps in World War I, Blobel developed systems for burning on pyres, installations for crushing bones, and methods of scattering ashes.

In a second stage, beginning in early June 1943, liquidation of the mass graves in areas of the occupied USSR and Poland began. The first site seems to have been the JANÓWSKA camp in Lvov, where the Sonderkommandos 1005 later employed in the other areas studied the methods used.

Each Sonderkommando 1005 consisted of several SD (Sicherheitsdienst; Security Service) and Sicherheitspolizei (Security Police; Sipo) officers, who supervised the work, and several dozen German policemen from the ORDNUNGSPOLIZEI (German regular police), who were charged with guarding the workers and the area. The labor was carried out by scores or hundreds of prisoners, mainly Jews. Pyres were built with long, thick wooden beams 23 to 26 feet (7–8 m) long, soaked with a flammable liquid, and the corpses were placed in layers between them. In the extermination camps, railway tracks were used for the foundation of the fire. The prisoners were divided into three groups: one opened the graves and exhumed the bodies, the second brought the corpses on stretchers and arranged them on the pyre, and the third was employed in sifting the ashes, crushing the bones, collecting any valuables overlooked earlier, and scattering the ashes. One or two prisoners were responsible for kindling the pyre and counting the corpses burned. The capacity of one pyre at Janówska was about two thousand bodies a day. Upon termination of work at the site, reconstruction was carried out, such as leveling the terrain, harrowing, and replanting. Since Aktion 1005 was defined as a "Reich secret" (*geheime Reichssache*), the Germans in the unit had to sign declarations promising secrecy, and the prisoners were killed on completion of their work.

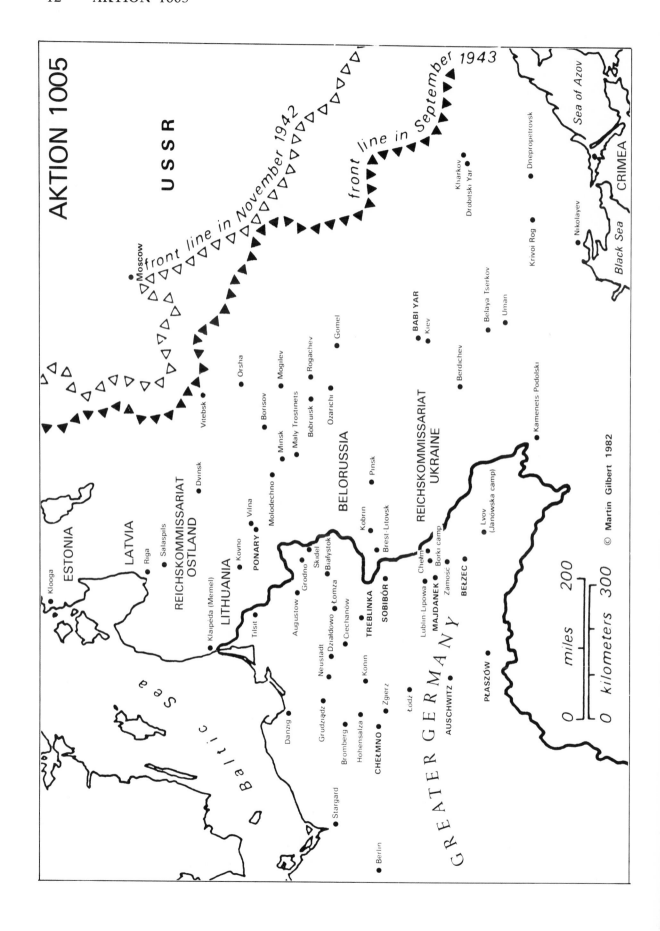

AKTION 1005

USSR

front line in November 1942

front line in September 1943

Moscow

Sea of Azov

CRIMEA

Black Sea

Dnepropetrovsk

Kharkov
Drobitski Yar

Nikolayev

Krivoi Rog

Belaya Tserkov

Uman

BABI YAR
Kiev

Berdichev

Kamenets Podolski

Orsha

Mogilev

Borisov

Rogachev

Bobrusk

Ozarichi

Gomel

Maly Trostinets

Vitebsk

REICHSKOMMISSARIAT
OSTLAND

Dvinsk

Minsk

BELORUSSIA

Pinsk

Kobrin

REICHSKOMMISSARIAT
UKRAINE

Brest-Litovsk

Lvov
(Janowska camp)

ESTONIA

Klooga

LATVIA

Riga

Salaspils

Klaipėda (Memel)

LITHUANIA

Kovno

Vilna

PONARY

Grodno

Skidel

Białystok

© Martin Gilbert 1982

Chełm

Borki camp

Lublin Lipowa

MAJDANEK

Zamosc

BEŁZEC

Baltic Sea

Tilsit

Augustow

Neustadt

Działdowo

Łomza

Ciechanów

TREBLINKA

SOBIBÓR

Konin

Zgierz

Łódź

GREATER GERMANY

PŁASZÓW

AUSCHWITZ

Danzig

Bromberg

Grudziądz

Hohensalza

CHEŁMNO

Stargard

Berlin

0   miles   200

0   kilometers   300

In early November 1943, the prisoners of the Sonderkommando 1005 in Janówska saw that their work was drawing to a close, and planned to attack the police at night and escape. On November 19, their plan was partially carried out. Of the scores of Jews who fled, a few individuals survived, including Leon Weliczker, who had recorded his impressions when he was in the unit, and later published them.

After the German defeat at Stalingrad and the retreat from the Ukraine in the first half of 1943, Blobel sped to Kiev in order to organize the erasing of the mass graves there. It was Blobel who supervised the slaughter at BABI YAR near Kiev, at Drobitski Yar in KHARKOV, and in many other places. In the first half of August 1943, two units were formed in Kiev: Sonderkommando 1005-A and Sonderkommando 1005-B. SS-Sturmbannführer Hans Zohns was appointed to head the entire operation. On August 18, Sonderkommando 1005-A began to remove the bodies at Babi Yar; it received 327 prisoners for this task, including about 100 Jews. On September 29 the prisoners learned that they were to be put to death the next day. A group that sought to escape had prepared saws for their chains and a key to open the grille at the entrance to the dugout in which they were locked, and it was decided to break out that night. At midnight, under cover of darkness, a group of 25 shouting prisoners stormed the guards and took advantage of the confusion reigning among them; about 15 men reached freedom.

After Kiev, Sonderkommando 1005-A continued to burn bodies in Berdichev, in Belaya Tserkov, and in Uman. After a short holiday the unit worked at KAMENETS-PODOLSKI, until it was disturbed by the approach of the Red Army. It transferred to ZAMOŚĆ in the Lublin area, and finished in ŁÓDŹ, then accompanying the last of the Jews from the Łódź ghetto to Auschwitz.

Sonderkommando 1005-B supervised the burning of bodies in Dnepropetrovsk, in Krivoi Rog, and in Nikolayev and the surrounding area. On April 9, 1944, after a holiday, the unit was sent to RIGA. It established its base near the Salaspils camp, burned about twenty thousand bodies, and also operated in DVINSK and other places.

Aktion 1005 in Belorussia was divided into two units. In eastern Belorussia, which was under military rule, the *Aktion* was carried out by Sonderkommandos 7a and 7b and by Einsatzkommandos 8 and 9 under the command of a Dr. Siekel, an Einsatzkommando 8 officer. From the fragmentary information available, it is known that the activity was carried out in the districts of GOMEL (7.5 miles [12 km] northwest of the city, and near Ozarichi and Rogachev), Mogilev (near the villages of Pashkovichi and Pulkovichi), Bobruisk, and VITEBSK (near Orsha and Borisov). In October 1943 in western Belorussia, which was under civilian rule, Blobel's deputy, Arthur Alexander Harder, created Sonderkommando 1005 Mitte (Central), the base of which was in the SS camp MALY TROSTINETS, and which came under the command of Max Krahner.

Sonderkommando 1005 Mitte began its activity by burning the bodies of the forty thousand to fifty thousand Jews of MINSK and the Reich who had been killed and buried in the vicinity of Minsk. The unit continued its work in different towns in the area of Minsk and Molodechno, and from there it went on to the districts of Brest-Litovsk, PINSK, Kobrin, and Lomza. On August 16, 1944, this unit was transferred to Łódź to escort the transports of the Jews from the ghetto to Auschwitz.

In the Baltic countries, 1005 is known to have been active in Lithuania—in PONARY, near Vilna; and in the NINTH FORT in Kovno. The activity in these two vicinities began in September 1943, and in both, the Jewish prisoners organized an escape. In Kovno all seventy of the prisoners employed fled on December 24, 1943; only thirty-four of them survived, however. In Ponary the escape took place on the night of April 15, 1944, and of the forty prisoners who escaped, fifteen survived. The Sonderkommando 1005 organized in Tilsit (Sovetsk) burned thousands of corpses of Soviet prisoners of war near Pegegen in the Klaipėda (Memel) region. The operation in Latvia has been mentioned above. In Estonia the bodies were burned when the KLOOGA camp and its subcamps were liquidated at the approach of the Red Army. The Germans did not have time to set fire to all the pyres, and Red Army photographers filmed a pyre prepared for burning.

In the Białystok district, which was a separate administrative unit, a Sonderkommando 1005 was established and functioned from mid-May until mid-July 1944 in the towns of Augustów, Grodno, and Skidel, and the village of Grabowka. On July 13 the prisoners were brought to a pit where they were to be killed, but the forty-three Jewish prisoners took flight and eleven of them managed to escape.

In the GENERALGOUVERNEMENT, Sonderkommando 1005 was active in LVOV and the Lvov region, as noted above, and in Zamość in the Lublin district. In the same district a unit operated in the Borki camp near Chełm, using Jewish prisoners of war (formerly in the Polish army) from the LUBLIN-LIPOWA camp. The corpses burned were mainly those of Soviet and Italian prisoners of war. The Jewish prisoners planned an escape and hewed out a tunnel, and on the evening of December 24, 1943, ten of them fled. Four reached partisan units, and after the war they gave evidence on what they had seen at Borki.

As the Soviet army approached in mid-1944, the principal 1005 activity in the Generalgouvernement began. A meeting was convened by Wilhelm KUBE, the *Höherer SS- und Polizeiführer* (Higher SS and Police Leader) in Kraków, with the participation of all the SD and Sipo commanders and the police of the districts. Each commander undertook to establish a Sonderkommando 1005 in his area. A similar instruction came from Berlin to the SS and police leaders in the areas of Poland annexed to the Reich, where tens of thousands of Poles had been killed in the early days of the occupation in 1939. Sonderkommando 1005 units were active in Soldau (now Dzialdowo) in the Ciechanów region; in the Gau Danzig (Gdańsk) region in West Prussia in the towns of Graudenz (now Grudziądz), Bromberg (now Bydgoszcz), Stargard, Neustadt (now Nowe Miasto), Cronau (now Kronowo), and Kulm (now Chełmno); and in the Warthegau district in the vicinities of Konin, Zgierz (Gornau), and Hohensalza (Inowrocław).

Outside eastern Europe, Aktion 1005 activity was carried out in Yugoslavia near the village of Jajinci in the area of the SAJMIŠTE camp, where there were about eighty thousand corpses, including those of about eleven thousand Jews. The operation began on November 6, 1943, and up until the flight of one of the prisoners engaged in the activity, about sixty-eight thousand bodies were burned.

Most of the Germans employed in Aktion 1005 were not returned to their units but were assembled in early October 1944 in Salzburg, Austria. There they were formed into Einsatzgruppe "Iltis," for special tasks under the command of Paul Blobel, particularly to fight against the Yugoslav partisans in the region of Carinthia.

Although burning the bodies from the mass graves did not efface the Nazi crimes, it did cause difficulties in determining the facts of the crimes and in drawing up statistics on the number of victims. In many cases, the commissions investigating Nazi crimes in the USSR and in Poland found no trace of the mass graves, and they encountered difficulty in reaching estimates.

BIBLIOGRAPHY

Spector, S. "Aktion 1005 to Obscure the Murder of Millions during World War II." *Yahadut Zemanenu* 4 (1986): 207–225. (In Hebrew.)
Weliczker-Wells, L. *Brygada śmierci (Sonderkommando 1005: Pamiętnik)*. Łódź, 1946.

SHMUEL SPECTOR

AKTION REINHARD, code name for the operation that had as its objective the physical destruction of the Jews in the GENERALGOUVERNEMENT, the territory in the interior of occupied Poland, within the framework of the "FINAL SOLUTION." The name was coined by the SS men in charge of the operation, several months after it had been launched, in memory of Reinhard HEYDRICH, the chief planner of the "Final Solution" in Europe, whom members of the Czech underground had assassinated on May 27, 1942. The aim of Aktion Reinhard was to kill the 2,284,000 Jews then living in the five districts of the Generalgouvernement— Warsaw, Lublin, Radom, Kraków, and Lvov (Eastern Galicia)—according to the German data as stated in the minutes of the WANNSEE

CONFERENCE of January 20, 1942.

Preparations for Aktion Reinhard began in October and November of 1941. Himmler appointed Odilo GLOBOCNIK, *SS- und Polizeiführer* (SS and Police Leader) in the Lublin district, to head the program, with Hauptsturmführer Hans Höfle as chief of operations, in charge of organization and manpower. The operational headquarters was in Lublin, and its tasks were as follows:

1. Overall planning of the deportations
2. Construction and operation of extermination camps
3. Coordination of the deportations from each of the five districts
4. The extermination process in the camps
5. Confiscation of the victims' possessions and valuables and their dispatch to the appropriate authority in the Reich.

For security reasons, Globocnik's orders on the extermination process were given to him orally. Deporting the Jews from the ghettos

AKTION REINHARD

© Martin Gilbert 1982

and escorting them to the extermination camps—an integral part of Aktion Reinhard—were the responsibility of the SS and police in the various districts, and were not under the direct authority of Globocnik and his staff.

The personnel who were put at Globocnik's disposal for the operation included a team of 450 Germans. At its core was a group of 92 men, headed by Kriminalkommissar Christian WIRTH, who had been assigned to Globocnik for the EUTHANASIA PROGRAM. That operation had been broken off in mid-1941, and for security reasons the men who had taken part were not posted to the front. Their assignment to Aktion Reinhard provided Globocnik with personnel who had gained experience in the use of gas as a means of killing people, as practiced in the Euthanasia Program. It was this group from which the key German staff was chosen for Reinhard, including the commanders of the extermination camps; each camp was allotted 20 to 30 German staff.

The Aktion Reinhard headquarters recruited a special auxiliary unit for its purposes, consisting of Ukrainian volunteers, most of them Soviet prisoners of war. They were billeted in the SS training camp at TRAWNIKI, where they were provided with black uniforms, given arms, organized into platoons and companies, and put through a brief training program. The platoon and company commanders were Germans, some of them VOLKSDEUTSCHE (ethnic Germans); the local population referred to them as "Trawniki men" or "Askaris." Each extermination camp was assigned from 90 to 120 Ukrainians; "Trawniki men" were also employed in deporting Jews from the ghettos and in escorting the transports on their way to the camps.

Three extermination camps were established under Aktion Reinhard: BEŁŻEC, SOBIBÓR, and TREBLINKA. A number of considerations determined the location of the camps. They had to be close to a railway, so that transportation would not pose a problem; for security reasons, they had to be in an isolated area, as remote as possible from population centers; and in order to lend a semblance of credence to the cover being used for the operation—that the Jews were being transferred to work "somewhere in the east," in occupied Soviet territory—the camps had to be near the eastern border of the Generalgouvernement.

The first camp to be set up, between November 1941 and March 1942, was the one in Bełżec, on the Lublin-Lvov railway line. The killings there began on March 17, 1942. The camp at Sobibór, east of Lublin, was constructed in March and April of 1942, and it began operations in early May 1942. The Treblinka camp, 50 miles (80 km) northeast of Warsaw, was established in June and July 1942, and the murder operations there were launched on July 23, 1942, coinciding with the start of the mass deportation from the Warsaw ghetto. The gas used in all three camps was carbon monoxide, generated by gasoline or diesel engines placed outside hermetically sealed gas chambers and pumped into them through a system of pipes. The Aktion Reinhard camps were not equipped for the cremation of bodies; the victims were buried in huge pits, and it was not until the end of 1942 and the beginning of 1943 that bodies were burned in huge pyres, the purpose being to erase evidence of the crimes that had been perpetrated there. The camps were constructed by Polish workers living in the area, augmented by Jews on forced labor, and the latter became the first victims.

For manual labor the camps used, by the hundreds, Jewish prisoners who were retained for this purpose from the transports that were put through the extermination process. As a rule, these prisoners were killed after working in the camps for several weeks or months, to be replaced by new arrivals from the transports. Only a few remained alive for any length of time.

The program of deportations to the extermination camps was based on the existing division of the Generalgouvernement into five districts, and the determining factor was proximity to a given camp and to the railway line that led there. Thus, Jews from the Kraków and Lvov (Eastern Galicia) districts were sent to Bełżec, from the Warsaw and Radom districts to Treblinka, and from the Lublin district to Sobibór. This pattern, however, was subject to change, and some of the Jews from the Lublin district were sent to Bełżec and Treblinka.

The method of deportation from the ghettos was uniform for most places in eastern Europe. Its principal elements were surprise, speed, terrorization, and keeping the victims unaware of their real destination. The authorities in charge of the deportation announced it the day before it was to take place, and at times without a single day's notice; the announcement was made to the local JUDENRAT (Jewish Council), which in turn had to pass it on to the ghetto population (the Judenrat was told that the Jews were being transferred to work camps in the east). At the same time the ghetto was encircled with a heavy guard of German security units, to prevent anyone from escaping. In the large ghettos, which contained tens of thousands or even hundreds of thousands of Jews, the deportation could not be completed in one day; therefore, in each separate *Aktion* the Judenrat was told to gather several thousand people for deportation. If the Judenrat was unable to supply the required quota, even with the help of the Jewish police at its disposal, German and Ukrainian reinforcements were sent in, to break into the houses and courtyards where the Jews were hiding and drag them out.

In the large ghettos, there were many *Aktionen* over a period of weeks and months, for as long as was necessary to clear the ghetto of all its inhabitants. In the small ghettos the *Aktionen* were a one-time operation, taking a day or two. Many persons were shot inside houses, in the street, or in the hiding places where they had taken refuge; among those shot were the elderly and the sick who were too feeble to walk on their own, as well as anyone who offered resistance.

Once they were removed from the ghetto, the Jews were taken to the railway station, usually by foot, where they were loaded into freight cars. The cars were crowded to suffocation, sometimes containing as many as one hundred and fifty persons each. The trip from the loading point to the extermination camp, which under normal circumstances lasted a few hours, sometimes took days, the trains being stopped for many hours en route, either in stations or on the railway line. Owing to the unbearable conditions in the cars—overcrowding, lack of water and sanitation, intense heat in the summer and cold in the winter—many died on the way; when the trains arrived at the death camp, there were often dozens or even hundreds of corpses aboard.

In order to ensure the exclusive and total control by the SS over the Jews in the "Final Solution" stage, and to raise the efficiency of the deportation process, the entire Jewish population of the Generalgouvernement was removed from the control of the German civil administration and placed under the authority of the SS, on June 3, 1942. When the Treblinka camp was put into operation in July of that year, deportations proceeded at a record pace, so much so that there were not enough trains available for the transports. At this time the German attack on Stalingrad and Caucasia was at its height, and the German army on the front was in urgent need of all the rolling stock that the railway administration had at its disposal. It required Heinrich HIMMLER's personal intervention with Theodor GANZENMÜLLER, the Transport Ministry's state secretary in charge of the German railways (Reichsbahn), for the required amount of rolling stock to be allocated to the deportation of the Jews.

In mid-July 1942, Himmler paid a visit to the Aktion Reinhard headquarters and to the camps under its control. Following his visit, on July 19, he issued an order according to which the deportation of the Jews in the Generalgouvernement to the extermination camps was to be completed by December 31, 1942. Beyond that date, only a few Jews were to be left whose retention was essential for the war effort, and these would be held in special work camps that were to be established in Warsaw, Kraków, Częstochowa, Radom, and Lublin.

The order, which called for deporting nearly the entire Jewish population from the ghettos, caused manpower problems for factories and workshops engaged in the war effort, and the military officials in charge of war production protested against this blow to the output of essential supplies needed by the armed forces. According to data submitted by the army, out of the 1 million workers employed in its plants in the Generalgouvernement, 300,000 were Jews, and of these one-third were skilled craftsmen. As a result of the army's appeal against Himmler's order, it was decided to keep some Jewish workers in several of the large ghettos until further notice.

The deportations continued, and, according to German data, by about the end of December 1942, 136,000 Jews in all remained in four of the Generalgouvernement districts; in the fifth, Lvov, 161,000 remained. The ghettos in these districts were liquidated in the period between January and June 1943 and the Jews in them removed; most were deported to extermination camps, while several tens of thousands, mostly young and skilled workers, were put in concentration camps and work camps.

In the last few months of 1942, when the deportations from the Generalgouvernement under Aktion Reinhard were coming to an end, the operation's scope was extended to include Jews from the Białystok district, numbering some 210,000. Most of the Białystok Jews were deported to Treblinka, and several transports went to Auschwitz; by August 1943 all the Jews of the Białystok district had been sent to extermination camps. From the Kraków district, the Jews were deported to Bełżec up to October 1942, and afterward to Płaszów and Auschwitz. Not all of the Jews in the Generalgouvernement found their end in the concentration and extermination camps; thousands were shot on the spot, where they lived. In the Lvov district alone, over 160,000 Jews were murdered in local *Aktionen*.

In the course of Aktion Reinhard, the Germans seized a huge amount of property, which the Jews of Poland had accumulated by hard work and manifold economic activities over the hundreds of years that they had been living in the country. This included real estate—houses, buildings, industrial plants, and land—the value of which cannot even be estimated in financial terms. In addition, an enormous quantity of movable property was left behind in homes and factories and was confiscated by the German authorities, although some of it fell into the hands of the non-Jewish local population. The Jews who were being deported took along those articles that they were allowed, including cash and valuables; all this accumulated in the camps where they were killed, and passed into German hands.

There was stiff competition over the control of Jewish property among the various official German bodies, especially between the civil administration of the Generalgouvernement, which regarded itself as the local government, and the SS with its several branches, which considered itself in charge of all aspects of the "Final Solution," including the property of the Jews. On September 26, 1942, the WIRTSCHAFTS-VERWALTUNGSHAUPTAMT (Economic-Administrative Main Office; WVHA) issued guidelines for the use of Aktion Reinhard headquarters and the commandant of the Auschwitz camp on the procedure to be followed in dealing with the money and valuables brought by Jewish victims to the extermination camps. According to these guidelines, all the cash and valuables accumulated in the camps were to be forwarded to the WVHA; other items, such as watches, clothing, eating utensils, and bedding, were to be distributed among the Economy Ministry, the army (for handing out to the troops), the SS workshops, and the *Volksdeutsche* in the occupied countries.

The Aktion Reinhard headquarters set up a special camp in Lublin, attached to the Majdanek camp, as a collecting center for the possessions left behind by the victims at Treblinka, Sobibór, and Bełżec. The site was an old airfield, and its hangars were used as warehouses for the loot. Jewish prisoners, mainly women, were employed in the warehouses. On December 15, 1943, the Aktion Reinhard headquarters submitted an account of the moneys, gold, and valuables taken from the Jews in the extermination camps for which the Reinhard headquarters was responsible. The figures were quoted in German marks (the rate of exchange of the reichsmark against the United States dollar at the time was 2.5 to 1). The report contains the particulars of the various categories: United States currency, about $1,100,000 in cash and $250,000 in gold coins; other foreign currency, from forty-eight countries; other gold coins, from thirty-four countries; 2,910 kilograms (6,415 lb) of gold bars; 18,734 kilograms (41,301 lb) of silver bars; diamonds totaling 16,000 carats. The report ends with the sum totals of the value of all the Jewish possessions collected.

Cash in Polish zlotys and German marks	RM73,852,080.74
Precious metals	8,273,651.60
Foreign currency, in cash	4,521,224.13
Foreign gold coins	1,736,554.12
Precious stones and other valuables	43,662,450.00
Textiles	46,000,000.00
Total	RM178,045,960.59

In addition, vast quantities of possessions were appropriated by German officials, SS men, Ukrainian camp guards, police, and local residents.

Aktion Reinhard, which began in mid-March 1942, continued until early November 1943, when the last Jews in the Majdanek, Poniatowa, and Trawniki camps were murdered; this operation was given the name "ERNTEFEST" ("Harvest Festival") by the Germans. In all, more than two million Jews of the Generalgouvernement were killed in Aktion Reinhard.

BIBLIOGRAPHY

Arad, Y. *Belzec, Sobibor, Treblinka: Operation Reinhard Death Camps.* Bloomington, 1987.
Gutman, Y., and L. Rothkirchen, eds. *The Catastrophe of European Jewry.* Jerusalem, 1976.
Hilberg, R. *The Destruction of the European Jews.* 3 vols. New York, 1985.
Reitlinger, G. *The Final Solution.* London, 1968.

YITZHAK ARAD

AKTION T4. *See* Euthanasia Program.

ALGERIA, republic in central North Africa; the largest of the Atlas Mountains states. Algeria was conquered by the French in the period from 1830 to 1847, and the Europeans who settled there—French, Italians, and Spaniards—were given the rights of citizens of FRANCE. In 1870 the Jews of Algeria also became French citizens, under a decree signed by the French minister of justice, Isaac-Adolphe Crémieux. On the eve of World War II the *colons* (French citizens in Algeria) accounted for nearly one-eighth of the total population.

Jews had been living in Algeria since the time of the Roman empire. In the fifteenth and sixteenth centuries they were joined by Jewish refugees from Spain. On the eve of World War II the Jewish population of Algeria was 120,000 (1.5 percent of the total, and

ALGERIA

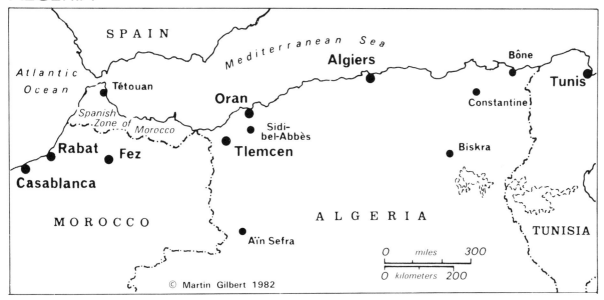

© Martin Gilbert 1982

one-eighth of the number of French citizens). More than half of the Jewish population was concentrated in three large cities—Algiers, Oran, and Constantine.

Under Muslim rule the Jews had the status of *dhimmi* (protected people); that is, they were officially protected and tolerated, but also humiliated, discriminated against, and occasionally persecuted. Under French rule their economic and political situation improved greatly, especially when they acquired French citizenship, in 1870. Unlike the situation in TUNISIA and MOROCCO, which were French protectorates, in Algeria—which was originally a French colony and then officially became a part of France—French policy was designed to assimilate the Jews. This policy led first to the abolition of the traditional community organization and its replacement by a Consistoire (1845), in accordance with the French model, and then to the granting of citizenship to the Jews under the Crémieux Decree.

The improvement in the situation of the Jews was accompanied by a deterioration of their relations with the non-Jewish population. A wave of antisemitic violence and pogroms struck Algeria immediately after the Crémieux Decree and reached its climax in the 1880s, when antisemitic circles and political parties gained control of all the local European government institutions. A second wave came in the mid-1920s and lasted until the end of World War II. This wave also spread to Morocco and Tunisia, carrying along the Arab population, who were incited by propaganda beamed from Berlin and Rome and were also the objects of an anti-Zionist campaign promoted by the local Arab nationalists active on the eve of World War II.

Under the provisions of the French-German armistice of June 1940, North Africa was considered part of unoccupied France. The Germans had no foothold there until the Allied invasion of Algeria and Morocco in November 1942, to which the Axis powers reacted by occupying Tunisia. As in France itself, Marshal Philippe PÉTAIN and his Vichy regime enjoyed tremendous support among the European population of the Maghrib (Morocco, Algeria, and Tunisia), which welcomed the armistice and accepted the claim that France's defeat had been caused by the degeneration of France's republican regime. For this reason the Europeans in Algeria were not inclined to defend democratic institutions, and these were indeed abolished when the Vichy regime was installed. There was no need for Vichy to purge the French administration in North Africa, since most of the senior officials rallied to Pétain's side—either out of opportunism or out of conviction—

and diligently applied all the orders they received from Vichy, including those relating to the Jews.

In the sphere of anti-Jewish legislation, Algeria was singled out for special attention by the Vichy regime. Since Algeria was considered an integral part of France, all French laws and regulations applied to it; for the Jews of Algeria this meant that their legal status was similar to that of the Jews in unoccupied France. This fact alone, however, does not explain the special measures taken against the Algerian Jews, since the Vichy regime also persecuted, with no less determination, the Jews of Morocco and Tunisia, who were not French citizens but had the status of a subject people. Actually, the Vichy regime saw in the three countries a single geopolitical entity containing a large Jewish population, sandwiched in between a Muslim majority, whose loyalty to France was doubtful, and a European minority, which had adopted antisemitism as its political credo.

The anti-Jewish legislation was therefore applied to Algeria not only because it fitted in with the Vichy regime's ideological orientation. The Vichy authorities believed that it could also serve the double purpose of catering to the wishes of the Europeans and gaining for France the sympathy and support of Algeria's Muslim population. Under the "New Order" introduced by Vichy, a series of laws were enacted that discriminated against the Jews and set them apart both from the rest of the French population and from the general population of Algeria. The first step in this direction was the repeal of the Crémieux Decree, by an ordinance issued on October 7, 1940, that deprived the Jews of Algeria of their French nationality, except in a few cases, such as that of Jews who had been awarded military distinctions. In this way the regime complied with a demand that antisemitic circles had been making for seventy years. The ordinance was followed within a few days by another anti-Jewish decree, of even broader implications—the STATUT DES JUIFS (Jewish Law).

The Algerian version of the Statut des Juifs was identical with the French: it defined as a Jew any person who had three Jewish grandparents, or who had a Jewish spouse and two Jewish grandparents. It imposed various restrictions and prohibitions on the Jews—excluding them from the public service, the teaching profession, the courts, the local councils, the army, the media, the film industry, and the theater. In the following two years the COMMISSARIAT GÉNÉRAL AUX QUESTIONS JUIVES (General Office for Jewish Affairs) issued several more sets of anti-Jewish decrees, all of which were applied to Algeria as well as to Vichy France. Thus, an "Aryanization" office (see ARISIERUNG) was established in Algeria that was authorized to confiscate Jewish-owned property and was in charge of dismissing Jews from banks, insurance companies, and the stock exchange. A 2 percent *numerus clausus* (quota) was imposed on Jews in the professions—doctors, lawyers, druggists, registered nurses, and so on; the number of Jewish students at the University of Algiers was drastically reduced to 3 percent; and Jewish children were excluded from secondary and elementary schools (a measure that was not put into effect even in metropolitan France). In 1941 a general census of the Jews of Algeria was undertaken, and by 1942 preparations were under way to set up a JUDENRAT (Jewish Council) on the model of the UNION GÉNÉRALE DES ISRAÉLITES DE FRANCE (General Council of French Jews), but these were brought to a halt by the Allied invasion on November 8, 1942.

The extent of German involvement in Algerian affairs is unclear. While the WANNSEE CONFERENCE included North African Jews under the heading "France," these Jews did not attract the Germans' attention before the latter's occupation of Tunisia, in November 1942. But account must be taken of the atmosphere created by the antisemitic organizations in Algeria and the existence of dozens of labor camps on the southern border of Morocco, where thousands of Jews—mostly foreigners but including a number of native Jews—were held, having been charged with subversive activities or black-market operations. The Bedeau camp, near the town of Sidi-bel-Abbès, served as a concentration camp for Algerian Jewish soldiers, who had been formed into a special unit, the Groupement de Travailleurs Israélites (Jewish Workers' Group), and subjected to exceptionally hard forced labor under the command of Foreign Legion officers.

In general, it may be assumed that the Jews of Algeria, like their French counterparts, thought that German pressure was to blame for the racist laws that were introduced against them. As a result, despite their loss of status, property, and livelihood, they never abandoned their loyalty to France and would not believe that the "Jewish laws" were a French creation. This state of mind also explains the fact that hundreds of Algerian Jews flocked to the underground when it came into being in late 1940. Indeed, the preponderance of Jews in the underground was such that it could well have been regarded as a Jewish organization, although the motivation of those who joined it was in no way "Jewish."

The Algerian resistance movement had its start when a few young Jews, some of them former French army officers, organized into a self-defense unit, under the cover of a sports club. At the same time, unconnected with the "sports club," other Jewish resistance groups sprang up in Algiers and Oran, whose membership included scions of the Jewish social elite, headed by members of the Aboulker family in Algiers. In the course of 1942 the various Jewish organizations formed a link and established contact with some French politicians and senior officers of the French secret service, who had come to Algeria on their own initiative in order to prepare the ground for resuming the fight against the Germans. Though this group apparently shared Pétain's ideology and political views, the Jewish underground accepted their authority since it was only through them that it could establish contact with the United States.

At the end of October 1942 the Americans informed the Algerian resistance of their planned landings on the shores of Algeria and Morocco, requesting them to take an active part in the operation by seizing the strategic points in Algiers, Oran, and Casablanca in order to neutralize them for several hours until the Allied forces could make their entry into these cities. In Oran and Casablanca the resistance organizations failed completely in this mission, but in Algiers the underground

accomplished its task in full, attaining all of its objectives efficiently and with perfect discipline. Of the 377 resistance members who seized control of Algiers during the night of November 7–8, 315 were Jews. The plan had been for the United States advance team to enter Algiers within two hours of the landings, but fierce opposition by the French coast guard delayed its arrival until the evening of November 8, leaving the resistance to fend for itself. However, the fighters held out, at great risk to their lives, maintaining control of most of the points they had seized for the whole day that elapsed before the Americans appeared on the scene.

In the meantime, the Americans entered into negotiations concerning a cease-fire with Adm. François DARLAN, the designated successor to Pétain, who had arrived in Algiers two days earlier under mysterious circumstances. Darlan agreed to the cease-fire, but only after he had been given assurances by the Americans that the Allies would permit the Vichy regime to stay and would not interfere with internal affairs in North Africa, such as the "Jewish question." Darlan was then appointed High Commissioner of North Africa. For the short while that he held that post—until he was murdered, on December 24, 1942—Darlan remained loyal to Pétain, adamantly refusing to abolish any of the racist laws. The Americans kept the agreement they had signed with Darlan and lent their protection to a regime that, in its ideology and practice, violated the principles of democracy. The Jews—especially those who had been members of the resistance—were sorely disappointed, having expected that the American conquest of Algeria would have an immediate beneficial effect on their condition. Not only did the Vichy regime stay in office, but in many places attacks on Jews became even more frequent, since they were now also accused of collaborating with the Americans.

Anti-Jewish incitement reached new heights in the wake of Darlan's assassination. All the former leaders of the Jewish underground were arrested on the charge of collaborating with the assassins. To their great surprise, the Jewish prisoners now found out that the order for their arrest had been given by none other than their former leaders in the resistance—the senior French officers who, on the day after the American invasion, had taken their places in Darlan's Vichy-style administration.

News of the Jewish leaders' arrest was brought to the knowledge of Robert Murphy, President Franklin D. ROOSEVELT's personal representative in North Africa. The American diplomat was preoccupied with his search for a replacement for Darlan and did not want the affair reported in the United States press. Newspapers were already expressing misgivings about the American moves in the area and publishing eyewitness accounts and background articles on the condition of the Jews in Algeria and the sufferings of concentration camp prisoners. Though Jews in the United States were far from indifferent to this state of affairs, they were cautious in expressing their dissatisfaction with the continued presence of the Vichy regime in North Africa, lest their attitude be misused by American isolationist elements. Their apprehension increased when Gen. Henri Giraud, Darlan's successor, appointed as governor-general of Algeria Marcel Peyrouton, who as minister of the interior in Pétain's first cabinet had signed the racist laws issued by Vichy in October 1940.

Pressure by the American media forced the United States government to ask Giraud to abolish the racist laws. Giraud agreed, but only when it was made clear to him that refusal to do so might mean that the military aid he had requested would be denied. Giraud annulled the racist laws on March 14, 1943, but on the same day he reinstated the law that had abolished the Crémieux Decree, on the pretext that the decree discriminated against Algeria's Muslims.

Thus, within a period of less than three years, Algerian Jews were twice deprived of their citizenship—once by Pétain and once by Giraud. The "repeal of the repeal" of the Crémieux Decree aroused much resentment among the Jewish organizations in the United States, leading them to renew their fight against the Giraud regime with increased vigor. While the United States government went out of its way to protect Giraud, Gen. Charles de GAULLE lent a receptive ear to the Jewish organizations, since his ri-

valry with Giraud over who was to be the leader of the struggle for the liberation of France was then at its peak. It was obvious that the outcome of the struggle between the two generals would have an impact on the fate of the Crémieux Decree. The Gaullist movement's growing strength inside France, however, dampened its enthusiasm to restore political rights to the Jews of Algeria. When de Gaulle took over in Algeria, on May 3, he refrained from officially canceling his predecessor's decision. Not until three months had passed from the date of that decision without any regulations being issued for its implementation, as required by law, did de Gaulle take advantage of this legal loophole to inform the leaders of Algerian Jewry that the Crémieux Decree was again in force. It took many more months, however, for the last vestiges of the Vichy period to disappear. Late in 1944 dozens of Jewish refugees were still imprisoned in concentration camps, and it took even longer to purge the Algerian administration fully of all the pro-Vichy elements, who, as long as they were in office, persisted in treating the Jews as though nothing had changed since November 1942.

BIBLIOGRAPHY

Abitbol, M. *North African Jewry during World War II*. Detroit, 1989.

Amipaz-Zilber, G. *The Jewish Underground in Algeria, 1940–1942*. Tel Aviv, 1983. (In Hebrew.)

Ansky, M. *Les Juifs d'Algérie du Décret Crémieux à la Libération*. Paris, 1963.

Danan, Y. M. *La vie politique à Alger de 1940 à 1944*. Paris, 1963.

Murphy, R. *Diplomat among Warriors*. London, 1964.

Szajkowski, Z. *The Jews and the French Foreign Legion*. New York, 1975.

MICHEL ABITBOL

ALIYA BET ("illegal" immigration), entry into Palestine during the period of the British Mandate by other than the official way—a permit issued by legal representatives of the authorities. The phenomenon was given different designations, each expressing a value judgment: (1) Aliya Bet (*aliya* in Hebrew means "immigration," and *bet* refers to "B," illegal, in contrast to "A," or legal, immigration); (2) *ha'apala* (lit., "climb," "struggle upward"); (3) independent immigration; and (4) illegal immigration. The first three were designations used by Zionist elements; two of them, Aliya Bet and Ha'apala, were current within the Labor movement and became the idiom in spoken and written Hebrew, while the third designation, "independent immigration," was used by the Revisionists and their activists. The fourth, "illegal immigration," was the term used by the British Mandatory authorities. The immigrants who entered Palestine by this method were called Ma'apilim (from Ha'apala) by the Jews in Palestine and "illegal immigrants" by the British.

There were several patterns of Aliya Bet: immigration undertaken by individuals on their own initiative, and immigration initiated by Zionist organizations that encouraged and assisted their members. The majority of these immigrants traveled by boat and tried to land in Palestine without being detected. The boats used for this purpose were antiquated freighters that were no longer in regular use; living conditions on these boats were difficult and at times quite unbearable. Some immigrants journeyed by an overland route, from eastern Europe to countries bordering on Palestine, and then tried to cross the border. Other "illegals" were persons who had entered Palestine legally, as tourists, and stayed on, without obtaining a residence permit from the authorities. Still another method was to use legal entry permits without being entitled to them, for example, through fictitious marriages contracted for this purpose, or by using forged entry visas.

All Aliya Bet movements had a common origin—a situation in which large numbers of Jews felt a growing urgency to depart from their countries of residence, at a time when the rate of authorized immigration did not keep up with the demand. The pressure for such departure, for political or economic reasons, became so strong that people were willing to take enormous risks, including the risk of running afoul of the law. Preceded by spontaneous attempts by individuals, organized Aliya Bet provided ideological motivation for people to leave their homes and make their way to Palestine by this method,

and gave it the dimensions of a mass movement. Of the 530,000 immigrants who entered Palestine up to the establishment of the state of Israel, 25 percent—some 130,000 persons—came by way of Aliya Bet. Of these, 104,000 arrived by sea, in 136 boats; 52,000 of these were caught by the British and deported to internment camps in Cyprus (*see* CYPRUS DETENTION CAMPS).

Before World War II. Aliya Bet began before World War I with the modern settlement of Palestine by Jews, when the Ottoman rulers were obstructing the entry of Jews into the country. When World War I ended, the British military authorities who were then in control did not permit entry to anyone who had not lived in the country before the war, and this compelled a large number of young Jews to organize and enter Palestine in defiance of existing regulations. It is estimated that under the postwar military administration (1917 to 1920), two thousand immigrants entered Palestine either by posing as prewar residents or by jumping the border.

The first immigration law, enacted in the summer of 1920, established the criteria for the admission of immigrants to Palestine. In the summer of 1922, definitive laws and regulations on immigration were issued, and these remained in force until the publication of the British WHITE PAPER of May 1939, which severely restricted Jewish immigration. From 1922 on, the number of immigrants to be admitted into the country was an issue that put a constant strain on the relations between the British Mandatory government and the Zionist political leaders. In the 1930s, the authorities approved about one-third of the requests for immigration certificates submitted by the Jewish institutions. It was this gap between the number of requests submitted and the number approved by the British, reinforced by the rising pressure by Jews in Europe after the advent of Adolf Hitler to be permitted to emigrate to Palestine, that created the Aliya Bet movement under the British Mandate.

In the 1930s, Aliya Bet was a significant element in the growth of the Jewish population in Palestine. When the first international Jewish sports gathering, the Maccabiah, was held in Palestine in 1932, it attracted more than twenty thousand tourists to the country,

On facing page and above: arrival of the illegal ship *Haumot Hameukhadot* (The United Nations) at Naharia, Palestine, on January 1, 1948. Civilians waited on shore to mingle with the new arrivals in order to prevent them from being easily identified by British soldiers. Those who were caught were loaded onto British military trucks and transported to detention camps. One of the boats used to convey illegal immigrants from ship to shore bore the name of a member of the Ha-Irgun (Revisionist underground), Alexander Rot. [A Living Memorial to the Holocaust—Museum of Jewish Heritage, New York]

and about ten thousand of these visitors remained there after their visas had expired. There was also a rise in the number of fictitious marriages for purposes of immigration, and this ruse made it possible for two people to use one certificate.

In the latter half of the 1930s, most of the immigrants to Palestine arrived by ship. This method, for Aliya Bet purposes, was first employed in 1934 by Polish He-Haluts members in two voyages on a ship named *Vellos*, and by Betar members on a ship named *Union*. In both cases the immigrants were motivated by ideological and social considerations and felt that they could not wait until their turn came to be granted an official certificate.

The plight of Jews in Europe—especially the Nazi persecutions in Germany and Austria and the antisemitism in Poland—drove a growing number among the general Jewish public, as well as members of the Zionist movement and the youth movements, to participate in Aliya Bet in 1937 and 1938. In the summer of 1938, Vienna and Prague, after Warsaw and Berlin, were its centers. During the initial phase, the Aliya Bet ships left from Greek ports, with the immigrants arriving by train; later, the main route was by boat down the Danube, via the Black Sea to the Mediterranean. Aliya Bet was an ideological and social protest movement against the established Zionist leadership (which initially disapproved of this form of immigration) and against the British policy on Jewish immigration to Palestine. It was also a means of escape from Nazi-ruled and other endangered countries, and thus became part of the general movement of Jewish refugees fleeing from central and eastern Europe (*see* REFUGEES, 1933–1945).

By 1939 the Zionist movements had set up their own organizations for Aliya Bet, and the private operators also greatly extended the range of their enterprises. In that year, more than seventeen thousand Jews came to Palestine via Aliya Bet, while only eleven thousand arrived on official immigration permits. The New Zionist Organization (NZO), which had been established by the Revisionists, opened its own Immigration Center, with offices in Paris and London, and in Palestine the Mosad le-Aliya Bet (Organization for Aliya Bet, or Mosad for short) was created jointly by the Jewish Trade Union Federation, the Histadrut, and the underground Jewish defense organization, the Hagana. The two bodies assumed the overall task of organizing and planning Aliya Bet and making the decisions for implementation in various centers of Jewish population. Their emissaries in those centers had the job of selecting and organizing the immigrants, raising the required funds, and obtaining the agreement of the respective local authorities for the Jews to leave or to pass through the country; for this last purpose the emissaries had to cultivate local political elements.

The Immigration Center concentrated its efforts on unifying and organizing the Aliya Bet operations ("independent immigration," in Revisionist terminology) that members of the NZO had established in places with a significant Jewish population. The top leaders of the NZO—including its president, Vladimir JABOTINSKY—participated in establishing the center. In Jabotinsky's view, "independent immigration" represented the Jews' own way of battling Great Britain, and a means of recruiting masses of Jews to the movement that could arouse and activate the Zionist youth's potential. In fact, he had been propagating these ideas since 1932. The NZO leaders thought that the Immigration Center, by means of an agreed-upon policy, would be able to set up a system that would take into account the conflicting interests of Betar, the underground movement Irgun Tseva'i Le'ummi associated with them, and the Revisionist party, and would fix the order of precedence for their respective candidates for immigration, as well as mediate between the movement's activists in the various centers and coordinate their work. The actual result was that several Revisionist activists who had been organizing immigration—such as Paul Haler, Herman Flesch, and Avraham Stavsky—preferred to continue their work in a private capacity. Some of the activists felt that privately organized immigration was more efficient, and others regarded it as a potential source of considerable financial profit. These different attitudes caused friction between the Immigration Center of the NZO and the "independent immigration" offices of the private activists in the various countries.

Other private persons organized immigration on their own as well. One well-known figure among them was Dr. Baruch Confino, a member of the Zionist movement in Bulgaria, who is credited with having arranged the immigration of 3,000 persons. The Mosad le-Aliya, which took over the work of Aliya Bet from He-Haluts in Poland, operated as a centralized body. It was headed by a Hagana man, Shaul Meirov (later Avigur), who had a number of prominent He-Haluts activists working with him in the Mosad center in Paris. Some of the He-Haluts emissaries from Palestine in Europe became Aliya Bet orga-

The "illegal immigration" ship *Atrato VII*, which sailed from the Romanian port of Constanţa on the Black Sea with 390 Jewish refugees on May 20, 1939. Mosad le-Aliya Bet, the Jewish immigration authority in Palestine, organized the voyage. The ship arrived in Palestinian territorial waters on May 28 and was intercepted by the British navy. [Hagana Archives, Tel Aviv; Beth Hatefutsoth]

nizers in various Jewish communities (Moshe Averbuch-Agami in Vienna, Pino Ginzburg in Berlin, and Joseph Barpal and Ruth Klüger-Aliav in Romania). The candidates for immigration were selected from members of the youth movements and the veteran Zionists in the Jewish communities. The ships were chartered by persons who had this specific assignment, and places were allocated to the various communities on the basis of overall planning, coordinated with the emissaries in the communities. The raising and distribution of funds were also centralized. Most of the immigrants did not pay the full costs of the fare, but well-to-do immigrants from Germany and Austria were asked to pay more than their share, in order to help finance the passage of young people who had no means of their own. This system also came to be adopted by the Revisionist immigration organizers.

The Mosad did not have the full support of the Zionist organization's political leadership (contrary to the all-out support received by the Revisionist Immigration Center from its movement's political leaders). Members of the kibbutz movement, Ha-Kibbutz ha-Meuhad, gave Aliya Bet enthusiastic support, and most of the field operators were recruited from among its members. The labor leaders in the Jewish Agency Executive, such as David BEN-GURION and Eliezer Kaplan, at first were not in favor of Aliya Bet, and even when they changed their stand they differed with the Aliya Bet activists on the aims of the operation and the methods it was to employ. These differences were the result of their political approach, which saw mass immigration as the primary condition for the realization of the Zionist goals—a condition that could be achieved only in cooperation with Great Britain. As long as they believed such cooperation was possible, they were not prepared to give their support to operations that could create friction and sow the seeds of hostility between Palestinian Jewry and the British authorities.

It was only in late 1938 that Ben-Gurion became a supporter of Aliya Bet, after realizing that British policy was undergoing a radical change, switching from support of the Zionist enterprise to accommodation with the Arabs. At that point Ben-Gurion came to regard Aliya Bet as the major instrument that the Jews had at their disposal in the struggle for their future. The shift in the attitude of leading political figures strengthened the hand of those who supported Aliya Bet for moral reasons—saving Jewish lives and Jews' mutual responsibility for one another. This camp was led by the Labor leader, Berl Katznelson, who at the Zionist Congress in August 1939 depicted the refugee wandering from one end of the earth to the other as not only the symbol of Jewish distress, but also the banner and guide of Zionism in action.

Still, considerable opposition to Aliya Bet persisted in the Zionist organization, one of the opponents being Chaim WEIZMANN. Abba Hillel SILVER, the American Zionist leader, also expressed strong opposition to Aliya Bet at the congress. One reason for the continued opposition was the complaints circulating in the Zionist organization about the Revisionist and private Aliya Bet organizers, who were charged with exploiting the refugees' plight for the sake of easy profits.

In World War II. When the war broke out, Aliya Bet had to contend with new problems and uncertainties. Shipowners were expecting that the war would provide easier and more lucrative business opportunities, and they doubled and trebled the price for charters and also failed to keep their commitments. Governments, for their part, restricted the free use of vessels over which they had control. These difficulties, plus a lack of funds and a political reassessment of Aliya Bet, caused Zionist-organized Aliya Bet to slow down, and, in 1941 and 1942, to come to a complete halt.

There were second thoughts about continuing Aliya Bet in a war in which the Jewish people and Britain had an identical interest —to defeat the Nazis. The dilemma facing the Zionist leaders was how both to struggle against Britain and at the same time to cooperate with it. The Nazis were still permitting Jews to emigrate, whereas the British adhered to their tough policy on immigration, prohibited the entry of "enemy aliens," reduced legal immigration to a minimum, and found a new way of punishing the "illegal" immigrants when caught, by deporting them (to MAURITIUS). The quandary meant that no clear policy could be adopted on Aliya Bet, and in the absence of substantive support it became very difficult to cope with the problems involved in the operations. The Mosad made efforts to complete the processing of groups ready to leave, but did not always succeed in doing so. There was the case of the so-called Kladovo Group (Kladovo is a town in Yugoslavia on the Danube River, about 90 miles [145 km] southeast of Belgrade), which had left Reich territory and was stranded in Yugoslavia. The Nazis caught up with them in the fall of 1941 and murdered them on the spot. An example of the conflict, in moral and Zionist terms, between Aliya Bet operations and cooperation with the British was the case of the *Darien*, a ship that Mosad operators had purchased for the Kladovo refugees. In July 1940, when it seemed that the Kladovo Group could not be brought to the ship, the *Darien* was sold to the British, for joint British-Jewish sabotage operations. These operations, however, were delayed. In September 1940 the Mosad operators thought that they should use the ship for Aliya Bet, and they defied orders received from the Hagana chief, Eliyahu Golomb, to hand over the ship to Hagana men who were engaged in joint intelligence and aid operations with the British in Greece. Instead, they put 789 immigrants on board the ship, which reached the shores of Palestine in March 1941. These immigrants, however, were not the ill-fated Kladovo Group for whom the ship had originally been designated.

The leaders of the NZO also looked for ways to cooperate with the British in the war against the Nazis, and they had to face similar moral questions. NZO-organized immigration came to a halt about six months after the outbreak of the war, with the departure of the *Sakarya*, most of whose passengers had been ready to leave since the summer of 1939. The NZO thereafter never resumed "illegal" immigration on an appreciable scale.

"Private enterprise" Aliya Bet also came almost to a complete halt during the war, with the exception of Baruch Confino, who kept on sending boatloads of Jewish refugees from Bulgarian ports. Of the three boats at his disposal, one, the *Rudnichar*, made three successful trips to the shores of Palestine (September, November, and December 1939); another, the *Libertad*, made one such trip (July 1940); the third boat, the *Salvador*, sank in a storm in the Sea of Marmara and most of its 220 passengers drowned. Confino at this point suspended his operations, but he resumed them after the war. The largest group of immigrants to reach Palestine by private enterprise was that organized by Berthold Storfer, acting in behalf of the Vienna Jewish community, with the consent of the Nazi authorities; he dispatched three ships. Between November 1 and November 24, 1940, the three ships, *Pacific*, *Milos*, and *Atlantic*, arrived at the Haifa port, where they were impounded by the British and their passengers transferred to the *Patria* for deportation to Mauritius. The Hagana, with the help of the immigrants, sabotaged the ship to prevent its departure, but a miscalculation caused the *Patria* to sink, with a loss of 267 lives. The survivors were interned at the Atlit camp near Haifa, and 1,600 of the *Atlantic* passengers were deported to Mauritius on December 9, 1940, where they remained until the end of the war.

During 1942, following the sinking of the STRUMA, the Mosad reorganized its immigration operations. These were resumed in the spring of 1944. The new port of departure was Constanţa on the Black Sea, where the immigrants were put on small freighters, converted for passenger use, that sailed to Turkey. There they were issued immigration permits and resumed their trip, this time by train. The ships that were used did not meet the usual safety standards and could not be insured. They did not sail under the protection of the International RED CROSS or of a neutral country, and had not been assured of safe conduct by the Germans; this meant that they were in danger of warlike action from either side.

The resumption of immigration in this form was the result of a combination of several factors: a clear-cut decision by the Jews of Palestine, once they became aware of the meaning of the "Final Solution," to take up rescue operations; cooperation between Mosad le-Aliya, the representatives of the political department of the Jewish Agency in Turkey, and British intelligence agents; and the joint teams set up by the Jewish communities in Romania, with the help of the Palestinian Jewish representatives in Istanbul (*see* RESCUE COMMITTEE OF THE JEWISH AGENCY IN TURKEY). In addition, the operation benefited from the facts that the downfall of Nazi Germany was clearly drawing near and the United States was now taking political action in behalf of the rescue of Jews. From the British point of view this immigration was legal, in line with a British government decision, in July 1943, to issue an immigration permit to Palestine to any Jewish refugee reaching Turkey.

Up to the end of the war, ten groups took this route, totaling over three thousand persons; most of them were refugees from Poland, Hungary, and Transnistria. Much haggling and struggling went on before the final choice was made of the persons who were to join the trip, since many of those who wanted to felt that this was the only way to save themselves. The guidelines suggested by the Palestine Jewish organization on how the immigrants were to be chosen were not relevant to the actual conditions, and there were cases of persons of means being preferred. One of the ships, the *Mefkura*, sailing in August 1944, was sunk by a Soviet submarine by mistake, and only five of the passengers on board were saved.

In the immediate postwar years, Aliya Bet reached new records, as a result both of the pressure exerted by the She'erit ha-Peletah (Holocaust survivors) and of the excellent organization of the operation, which now enjoyed political support and priority. The Mosad le-Aliya, still headed by Shaul Avigur, became a highly efficient body with agents who were highly expert in their work. The ships acquired were manned by volunteers —officers and crews who were members of Palyam (the naval arm of the Hagana's striking force, the Palmaḥ) or Jewish sailors from the Western world (including 200 volunteers from the United States). Well-trained signal personnel on shore and on board the ships monitored the movement of the ships at sea in order to coordinate their time of arrival and ensure the safe landing of the passengers. On shore, experienced people awaited the new arrivals, to help them disembark and to distribute them as quickly as possible among the Jewish settlements, so as to prevent their detection by the British. On a budget of 7 million pounds, the Mosad moved 70,691 of these immigrants to Palestine on sixty-four ships. The British, however, caught most of the boats and deported their passengers to Cyprus.

Aliya Bet became the very heart of Zionist activity. It focused attention on the issue of rehabilitating the survivors of the Holocaust and assuring their future—an issue that had become a moral, political, and economic challenge for the nations of Europe—and presented the Zionist solution as the only possibility, in view of the complex relations between the Jews and European nations in the wake of the Holocaust. Support for Jewish immigration to Palestine became a political issue that enjoyed wide public sympathy and persuaded governments to favor the establishment of a Jewish state, despite Arab opposition. Aliya Bet also became a unifying factor in the Jewish world; it had the support of all the Jewish organizations once it became clear that masses of Jews, survivors of the Holocaust, were longing to get to Palestine. Aliya Bet was capable of fulfilling their desire, in numbers far exceeding the official rate of immigration permitted by the British—a meager 1,500 per month.

Immigration centers were set up all over Europe: in France, Italy, Yugoslavia, Greece, and other Balkan countries, staffed by fifty Mosad emissaries. It was only in 1946, however, that the Aliya Bet operation really resumed on a large scale; up to the end of 1945, only eight boats, with 1,022 passengers, were brought to Palestine in this way. In each Aliya Bet center the *modus operandi* was adapted to local conditions. In Italy, which was the point of departure for about half of all the sailings, the center was headed by Yehudah Arazi and Ada Sereni, who developed their own methods, concentrating on cultivating ties with political leaders, public figures, and intellectuals. In particular, Arazi attached great importance to the political

goals of Aliya Bet, and he believed that these would be achieved only if there was an ongoing flow of ships en route to Palestine and if the number of passengers was large enough to impress public opinion.

The principal center of the Mosad's operations was in France. It was to France that Jewish children were brought from the Netherlands and Belgium (where they had been saved, many in convents), and France was the gathering point for Jews from the DISPLACED PERSONS' camps. In order to arrange for them to be able to depart for Palestine, political contacts had to be cultivated, a process in which the Mosad operators made use of the French officials' hostility to the British. Conditions in France for the Mosad's work were more difficult than in Italy, because of the greater efficiency of French central control. The EXODUS 1947 affair was linked to these operations in France, and the positive attitude of the French in that affair was an example of the effectiveness of the Mosad work there. The fate of this ship and its passengers, who were returned to Germany, galvanized world public opinion and dramatized the tragic plight of the Holocaust survivors and their desperate determination to get to Palestine.

Regarding Aliya Bet from eastern and southern Europe, there was concern that countries in these regions would close their borders and prohibit the exit of Jews (as was the case in the Soviet Union); the immigrants had to be ransomed to enable them to leave. Emigration operations from Romania and Bulgaria were complicated and extensive, with twenty-one thousand emigrants leaving these countries in five sailings. Of these, fifteen thousand were passengers on the *Pan Crescent* and *Pan York*, two ships that sailed straight to Cyprus, by prior agreement with the British. In Yugoslavia the Mosad operators had the benefit of sympathy for persecuted Jews among persons who were close to the ruling circles, and this enabled them to channel over eight thousand immigrants through that country, in four sailings.

In August 1946 the British had come to the conclusion that in order to hold down the flow of "illegal immigration" they had to revert to the deportation procedure, and they selected Cyprus as the place to which the "illegals" would be deported. This policy led to fifty-two thousand of the would-be immigrants being deported to Cyprus, from thirty-two ships that had tried to bring them to Palestine. In Cyprus the deportees were held in camps, most of them staying there until after the state of Israel was established.

BIBLIOGRAPHY

Avneri, A. *From Velos to Tauras: The First Decade of Jewish Illegal Immigration to Mandatory Palestine (Eretz Yisrael), 1934–1944.* Tel Aviv, 1985. (In Hebrew.)

Habas, B. *The Gate Breakers.* New York, 1963.

Hadari, Z. V. *Refugees Defeat an Empire: Chapters of Illegal Immigration, 1945–1948.* Tel Aviv, 1986. (In Hebrew.)

Kimche, J., and D. Kimche. *The Secret Roads.* London, 1954.

Ofer, D. *Illegal Immigration during the Holocaust.* Jerusalem, 1988. (In Hebrew.)

Zweig, R. W. *Britain and Palestine during the Second World War.* London, 1986.

DALIA OFER

ALSACE-LORRAINE, two provinces in northeastern FRANCE, bordering on Germany; a historical bone of contention between the two countries. France controlled Alsace-Lorraine during the seventeenth and eighteenth centuries. From 1871 to 1918 the area was held by Germany; in 1919 it reverted to France. It was again in German hands from 1940 until the fall of 1944, when it was returned to France following the Allied conquest.

Jews lived in Alsace-Lorraine from the ninth century. In 1939 the Jewish population was twenty thousand, the largest community being that of Strasbourg (Ger., Strassburg), followed by that of Metz. In the wake of the MUNICH CONFERENCE of September 1938, violent demonstrations took place in Alsace-Lorraine, in the course of which Jewish shops in Strasbourg and other places were attacked. Jewish youth movements in Strasbourg set up a coordinating committee for their struggle against the antisemitic elements. German agents and members of the Nazi party smuggled antisemitic propaganda into Strasbourg, which became a distribution center of such material for all of France. Jewish relief organizations were established in Strasbourg and Metz to facilitate the absorption of Jewish refugees from central and eastern Europe.

When World War II broke out in September 1939 the French authorities evacuated the inhabitants of the border areas, among whom were fourteen thousand Jews. They were moved to the central area of western France, in and around the cities of Poitiers, Limoges, and Périgueux. With the fall of France in June 1940, some five thousand Jews from Alsace-Lorraine fled to southern France, which was not under German occupation. The following month the Germans expelled the remaining Jews of Alsace-Lorraine, and the area was now *judenrein* ("cleansed of Jews").

It was in Strasbourg that Professor August Hirt, director of the Anatomical Institute at the local Reich University, set up a collection of Jewish skulls and skeletons for the study of the theory of race, as authorized by Heinrich HIMMLER. On June 21, 1943, seventy-three Jewish men and thirty Jewish women were moved from AUSCHWITZ to the NATZWEILER-STRUTHOF camp, where they were gassed to death; their corpses were handed over to Hirt's laboratory.

A large percentage of the Jews from Alsace-Lorraine, dispersed over various parts of France, were active in the Jewish resistance organizations. Some two thousand Alsace-Lorraine Jews perished in the Holocaust. When the war ended most of the remaining Jews of Alsace-Lorraine returned to their homes and reestablished Jewish communities and communal institutions.

BIBLIOGRAPHY

Marrus, M. R., and R. O. Paxton. *Vichy France and the Jews.* New York, 1981.

LUCIEN LAZARE

ALTHAMMER, concentration camp in Poland established in mid-September 1944 near Ruda Śląska, a town 10.5 miles (17 km) west of Katowice, as a satellite camp of AUSCHWITZ. There were about five hundred Jewish prisoners in the camp. Most were from the Łódź ghetto, and the rest were from Hungary and France, in addition to a few Greek Jews. The camp also had a small number of "privileged" German prisoners, all of whom were functionaries. The Althammer inmates were employed in the construction of a nearby power station. As a result of the harsh working conditions and starvation, a third of the camp population was sick. The camp commandant, SS-Oberscharführer Josef Mirbeth, acted with great cruelty, torturing the prisoners with his own hands and shooting some to death. On January 19, 1945, four hundred prisoners were put on a death march, in the direction of Gliwice; most of them were killed en route. Of the remainder—those who were sick and had stayed in the camp—the majority were murdered by the Germans before the retreat; the survivors reached the Nordhausen camp in Saxony. A few dozen prisoners succeeded in escaping and were liberated by the Red Army on January 27, 1945.

BIBLIOGRAPHY

Piper, F. "Podoboz Althammer." *Zeszyty Oświęcimskie* 13 (1971): 137–153.

SHMUEL KRAKOWSKI

AMELOT, Jewish organization established in June 1940 to coordinate assistance to the French Jewish community; it was situated in Paris on Rue Amelot, from which it took its name. On June 15, 1940, as the German troops entered Paris, some immigrant Jewish activists—members of the FÉDÉRATION DES SOCIÉTÉS JUIVES DE FRANCE (FSJF), Po'alei Zion, the BUND, and other groups—met and decided to pool their resources and reactivate communal institutions. With the return to Paris of David Rapoport, a central figure in the FSJF before the war, the amalgam was solidified. The FSJF's welfare organization, the Colonie Scolaire, became its center.

Amelot was reluctant to adhere to the Comité de Coordination des Oeuvres Israélites de Bienfaisance (Coordinating Committee of Jewish Welfare Societies), formed under Nazi pressure in January 1941, but it nevertheless joined the committee out of recognition of communal needs. However, increasing Nazi control over the committee led Amelot to resign from it in May 1941. From then on it followed its own line, although it was dependent on the committee.

In May and August 1941, when eight thousand Jewish men were interned, Amelot further extended its relief activities. When the UNION GÉNÉRALE DES ISRAÉLITES DE FRANCE (UGIF) was formed in January 1942, Amelot maintained its independence, with UGIF agreement. Since Amelot was an immigrant-based committee, the July 1942 mass deportations temporarily interrupted its activities, but by August, with the necessary UGIF protection, they were resumed.

Amelot also assisted Jews who had escaped deportation and could not be helped by the UGIF. Disregarding precautions, Amelot, under Rapoport's leadership, hid children and distributed forged papers. In June 1943, Rapoport was arrested and deported. Under Abraham Alpérine, a new leadership was established. Early in 1944, Amelot was a constituent member of the Comité Général de Défense in Paris, which united all Jewish resistance forces and campaigned for the UGIF's closure. Under the FSJF, Amelot maintained itself throughout the war and saved over one thousand children, helped thousands of adults, and through its four canteens distributed thousands of meals. From its inception it followed a policy of self-help, working with Communists and the UGIF when required. It made an important contribution to the survival of the Jews of Paris.

BIBLIOGRAPHY

Adler, J. *The Jews of Paris and the Final Solution.* New York, 1987.

JACQUES ADLER

AMERICAN COMMITTEE FOR CHRISTIAN GERMAN REFUGEES (ACCR), American Protestant relief agency that provided help to Christian refugees from Nazism in the United States. Many Protestants shared the generally apathetic attitude of the American people toward refugees from Nazism, in spite of the fact that one-third of those reaching American shores were Christian refugees who had fled Nazi-dominated countries on account of political, religious, and ethnic persecution. In order to alleviate the distress of German co-religionists by providing immediate relief and resettlement services, the American Committee for Christian German Refugees was established in February 1934. The committee had to struggle for years to maintain its existence, meeting with many disappointments. Because of Christian apathy, even toward the plight of Christian refugees, Jewish organizations came to the rescue of the ACCR in certain crises.

Although given only very limited support by the churches, the committee acted as an arm of the churches, mainly those affiliated with the Federal Council of Churches, for the purpose of refugee relief administration. Possibly owing to its close relationship with the liberal-minded Federal Council, the ACCR failed to gain the support of the conservative theological communities. Even liberal circles did not support the committee, because Protestants thought of themselves in denominational terms (such as Baptists, Methodists, or Lutherans), rather than in general terms, as Protestants or Christians. Therefore, the ACCR, as an interdenominational agency, was unable to attract widespread moral or financial support. Its poor resettlement record—three hundred persons between 1935 and 1945—is a proof of that failure.

Chronic shortage of funds and high overhead resulted in a weak organization with a limited program. However, the report of 1940, the busiest year of the committee, showed certain progress. With an annual income of $226,214 and a staff of thirty-three, the ACCR that year took care of 4,413 migration cases (not all of whom reached the United States), gave vocational advice to 678, granted scholarships to 38 students, located jobs for 256, and retrained 127 refugees.

With the establishment of the Committee on Foreign Relief Appeals in the Churches (1939), and mainly with the foundation of the Federal National War Fund (August 1943), the ACCR's financial problems were largely solved, and it gradually emerged as the nation's first and greatest Christian refugee agency. In the decade from September 1935 to December 1945, it expended $1,481,436 for services to approximately 15,000 refugees from forty-two countries. It gave advice, granted affidavits, secured jobs, settled newcomers, offered vocational training, and sent funds abroad to help European co-religionists. The moral support was sometimes as important as the practical aid. Bearing in mind the strong anti-alien atmosphere, Thomas Mann, a refugee himself, in 1945 summed up the ACCR's achievements, saying that the committee functioned as "the conscience of America."

With the termination of the National War Fund's support and the establishment, in 1946, of the Church World Service, which became the agent of the churches for relief work, there was no justification for the ACCR's continuing existence. Its diminished importance was also attested by the fact that from 1945 it brought into the United States only eight hundred displaced persons. In July 1947 the ACCR was liquidated, its sixty-one staff members were dismissed, and its cases were transferred to the Church World Service.

[*See also* Refugees, 1933–1945.]

BIBLIOGRAPHY

American Committee for Christian German Refugees. *Toward a New Life: Ten Years of Stewardship.* New York, 1945.

Davie, M. R. *Refugees in America.* New York, 1947.

Genizi, H. *American Apathy: The Plight of Christian Refugees from Nazism, 1933–1945.* Ramat Gan, Israel, 1983. See pages 96–136.

Nawyn, W. E. *American Protestantism's Response to Germany's Jews and Refugees, 1939–1941.* Ann Arbor, Mich., 1981. See pages 159–181.

Ross, R. W. *So It Was True: The American Protestant Press and the Nazi Persecution of the Jews.* Minneapolis, 1981.

HAIM GENIZI

AMERICAN FRIENDS SERVICE COMMITTEE (AFSC). The Society of Friends, or Quakers, constitutes one of the smaller religious groups in the United States. In 1933 they numbered 112,000 members. The Quaker belief that God is within every man leads to a respect for all men as individuals, thus pre-cluding a resort to violence and war. Quakers believe that religious experience and social concern are inextricably related.

The American Friends Service Committee was established in 1917 with the dual purpose of giving Quakers an opportunity for constructive service to humanity and a means by which they could find their moral equivalent for military service during World War I. Through Quaker centers in different parts of the world they engaged in relief work, community development, educational programs, and social-action projects.

As its first project, the AFSC conducted a feeding program for 1.2 million German children suffering from World War I. Owing to this relief work, the Friends gained German appreciation, which, along with their non-partisanship and dedication to human need, elevated them into a position to intervene more efficiently on behalf of victims of persecution than almost any other agency. Even the Nazis treated them with respect.

During the first years of Adolf Hitler's regime, the scope of the AFSC's activities on behalf of refugees was surprisingly small, unlike that of the European Quakers. This was probably the outcome of a dilemma faced by the Quakers as a result of the anti-Jewish measures in Germany. Some feared that supporting the Jewish cause would seriously compromise the Quakers' reputation in Germany. Their close relationship with Friends in Germany, whom they did not wish to offend or harm, also led to inaction. Therefore, American Quakers were almost completely silent publicly with regard to the Nazi anti-Jewish policy.

The institutionalized help of the AFSC appeared only after the KRISTALLNACHT pogrom of November 1938. A Refugee Division was established, with headquarters in New York City, that provided services only in certain fields not provided through other agencies. The Quakers were eager to go "beyond relief into the more far-reaching openings for reconstruction and rehabilitation." Through hostels, American seminars, college workshops, and other educational projects, the AFSC concentrated on orientation and Americanization. These were only small pilot projects that demonstrated to the large relief

agencies "the Quaker way" in which refugees should be treated. Although members of the AFSC, under the leadership of Rufus M. Jones as chairman and Clarence E. Pickett as executive secretary, enthusiastically labored on behalf of refugees, the rank and file of Quaker communities in the United States failed to contribute to the cause either financially or by absorbing refugee families.

For the AFSC operations abroad, the picture was quite different. As a "foreign-minded" organization, the Foreign Service Section was much more effective than the Refugee Division. In response to a request from the American Jewish JOINT DISTRIBUTION COMMITTEE (JDC), the Quakers sent a commission to Germany in 1939 to ascertain the exact situation of Jews and Christians and to provide help if necessary. Indeed, from 1933 through the war, the warm relationship between the AFSC and Jewish agencies such as the JDC, HICEM, and OEUVRE DE SECOURS AUX ENFANTS was an example of interfaith cooperation on refugee matters. As a result of the division of work among the relief agencies, the AFSC devoted its major efforts to helping Christian refugees, but Quaker assistance to Jewish refugees in Paris, Marseilles, Lisbon, and Madrid was sometimes crucial. Feeding and rescuing children in France, helping refugees in neutral Portugal, and coordinating the activities of relief agencies in Spain were among the achievements of the AFSC. Over the course of a decade the scope of its services for victims of Nazi persecution was meaningfully expanded, from an expenditure of $17,000 in 1934 to $1,911,300 in 1944, with more than two hundred paid workers and many volunteers.

While during the Hitler era Jews and "non-Aryan" Christians were the main beneficiaries of AFSC help, after 1945 the Quakers focused their attention on helping Germans, Japanese, Indians, and Chinese, among others. Since 1948 the AFSC has been providing relief in Palestinian Arab refugee camps in the Middle East. In appreciation of its relief work for refugees during and after World War II, the AFSC, along with the British Service Council, received the Nobel Peace Prize in 1947.

BIBLIOGRAPHY

Byrd, R. O. *Quaker Ways in Foreign Policy*. Toronto, 1960.

Genizi, H. *American Apathy: The Plight of Christian Refugees from Nazism, 1933–1945*. Ramat Gan, Israel, 1983. See pages 172–214.

Pickett, C. E. *For More than Bread*. Boston, 1953.

Vining, E. G. *Friend of Life: The Biography of Rufus M. Jones*. Philadelphia, 1958.

HAIM GENIZI

AMERICAN JEWISH COMMITTEE (AJC), United States Jewish defense organization founded in 1906 with the aim of protecting the civil and religious rights of Jews anywhere in the world. The committee was oligarchic and until 1931 was limited to sixty members, all of German-Jewish origin and all from the upper socioeconomic stratum of American Jewry. Membership was expanded to 350 in 1931 and to thousands via chapter membership, introduced in 1944.

Cyrus Adler was the committee's president until his death in 1940. He was succeeded by Solomon Marcuse Stroock for one year, and then by Maurice Wertheim, who served until 1943. Wertheim was replaced by Judge Joseph M. Proskauer. Throughout this period, the committee followed a generally non-Zionist line in defining both its internal and American Jewish policies, in opposition to "Diaspora nationalism" and its stance vis-à-vis the Nazi regime. Whereas this policy-making became somewhat more pro-Zionist under Wertheim, it moved in an anti-Zionist direction during the first years of Proskauer's tenure.

The committee's approach to dealing with the Nazis was one of quiet diplomacy, in contrast to the protests and mass demonstrations undertaken by the American Jewish Congress and other organizations in the United States. In 1933 the committee, together with other organizations, approached President Franklin D. ROOSEVELT and Secretary of State Cordell HULL to request a State Department protest (*see* UNITED STATES DEPARTMENT OF STATE) to the German government regarding the treatment of the Jews in Germany. While the two leaders expressed their sympathy, they declined the request.

The committee sought to publicize information on Germany, but attempted to have this information and any protest action dealt with by non-Jews. Therefore, the AJC opposed the anti-Nazi rally sponsored by the American Jewish Congress in March 1933, and refrained from joining similar rallies afterward. Similarly, the committee opposed the anti-Nazi boycott movement (*see* BOYCOTTS, ANTI-NAZI) that developed during the early part of the Nazi regime.

During World War II, the committee maintained its prewar diplomatic policy, but its willingness to participate in joint protests with other groups increased after the United States entered the war in December 1941 and as information regarding the murder of the European Jews reached the United States. For nearly a year, from the late fall of 1942 to the early fall of 1943, the committee cooperated with the American Jewish Congress and other organizations to present current rescue projects and postwar proposals to the government. The AJC was one of eight organizations forming the Joint Emergency Committee on European Jewish Affairs, established in March 1943. This committee submitted a twelve-point rescue proposal to the BERMUDA CONFERENCE and organized mass meetings to inform the public of the Nazis' murder of the Jews.

In April 1943, the AJC agreed to join the AMERICAN JEWISH CONFERENCE to further American-Jewish unity in defining policy in face of the disaster in Europe. However, the conference's September 1, 1943, resolution calling for the establishment of a Jewish commonwealth in Palestine led the committee to withdraw from the conference in October 1943. In protest against this controversial move, 10 percent of its membership resigned from the committee.

The AJC continued its activities relating to postwar Jewish issues, and in 1944 established the Research Institute on Peace and Post-War Problems, directed by Dr. Max Gottschalk, to plan proposals for securing Jewish rights in the postwar world. The committee remained influential in government circles, and was one of the two American Jewish organizations (together with the

American Jewish Conference) designated by the State Department as consultants to the United States delegation at the San Francisco Conference, which founded the United Nations in April 1945. The AJC was also represented at the Paris Peace Conference in 1946.

BIBLIOGRAPHY

Cohen, N. W. *Not Free to Desist: The American Jewish Committee, 1906–1966.* Philadelphia, 1972.

Lazin, F. A. "The Response of the American Jewish Committee to the Crisis of German Jewry, 1933–1939." *American Jewish History* 68/3 (March 1979): 283–304.

DAVID SILBERKLANG

AMERICAN JEWISH CONFERENCE, American Jewish umbrella organization established in August 1943 in an attempt to unite American Jewry for planning Jewish postwar policy. At the initiative of Henry Monsky, the president of B'NAI B'RITH, representatives of thirty-two national Jewish organizations met in Pittsburgh on January 23, 1943, two months after the State Department (*see* UNITED STATES DEPARTMENT OF STATE) had confirmed to Stephen WISE reports of the Nazi plan to kill the European Jews (*see* RIEGNER CABLE). At the Pittsburgh meeting a resolution was made to convene a conference, to be named the American Jewish Assembly, with 500 delegates—375 elected and 12 appointed by cooperating organizations. A three-part agenda was to be addressed: (1) Jewish rights and status in the postwar world; (2) the implementation of Jewish rights regarding Palestine; and (3) the election of a delegation to carry out the assembly's program in cooperation with Jewish representatives around the world. The rescue of European Jewry was added to the agenda in late July of 1943, one month before the American Jewish Conference convened.

The AMERICAN JEWISH COMMITTEE (AJC) and the JEWISH LABOR COMMITTEE, which had declined Monsky's invitation to the Pittsburgh meeting for fear of Zionist domination,

joined the conference in April and May, respectively. The effect of the negotiations leading to the AJC's joining was both to expand the conference and to weaken its authority, since complete freedom of action was guaranteed to each participating organization. As a result of these negotiations, the assembly was renamed a conference, in order to avoid Jewish nationalist overtones.

Rescue was the first of the three main topics (rescue, Palestine, and postwar issues) discussed at the five-day conference, but the resulting conclusion was in effect merely a reiteration of several earlier proposals by various American Jewish groups. Whereas the conference's discussion of rescue was lackluster, its treatment of the Palestine issue was electrified by Abba Hillel SILVER's impassioned speech of August 30, which called for the creation of a Jewish state to end "the immemorial problem of our national homelessness, which is the principal source of our millennial tragedy." Silver's passion swept the conference, and on September 1 a resolution calling for a Jewish commonwealth in Palestine was passed by a vote of 477 in favor, 4 against, and 20 abstaining.

The American Jewish Committee withdrew from the conference on October 24, 1943, citing the Palestine resolution as its reason, while other organizations gave only limited cooperation to the conference. The American Jewish Conference never succeeded in unifying American Jewry or in gaining acceptance by the United States government as the representative of American Jewry on rescue, postwar, and Palestine issues. In 1944 the conference was reconvened, and it was subsequently able to exercise limited influence on the United States government and the United Nations on postwar questions. But having failed in its attempt at unity, it gradually diminished its activities and declined in importance until it disbanded in 1949.

BIBLIOGRAPHY

Kohanski, A. S., ed. *The American Jewish Conference: Its Organization and Proceedings of the First Session, August 29 to September 2, 1943.* New York, 1944.

DAVID SILBERKLANG

AMERICAN JEWISH CONGRESS. *See* World Jewish Congress.

AMERICAN JEWISH JOINT DISTRIBUTION COMMITTEE. *See* Joint Distribution Committee.

AMERICAN JEWRY AND THE HOLOCAUST. During the 1930s, when American Jewry was compelled to confront the crisis befalling the Jews of Europe, it lacked organizational cohesiveness and could not speak to power holders with one voice. That internal division partly accounted for its ineffectiveness during the years of the Holocaust. But even had it been unified, it is unlikely that by itself it could have altered wartime priorities, in which the rescue of European Jewry had no place. No American ethnic group possessed the power to alter single-handedly the major priorities of public policy, especially during wartime. Jews, despite antisemitic depictions of them as wielding great behind-the-scenes power, were no exception to this rule.

The disunity within American Jewry was reflected first in its inability to reach a common ground for appraising the threat posed by the advent of the National Socialist regime in Germany in 1933. Organizations like the JEWISH LABOR COMMITTEE, representing the still-powerful elements of the democratic Left anchored in the Jewish labor movement, would have no dealings with the National Socialists. But elements farther to the left slavishly followed the Comintern line, which moved from a united-front strategy to its opposite, a nonaggression pact with Germany, signed in August 1939. The AMERICAN JEWISH

Anti-Nazi demonstration organized by the American Jewish Congress in New York City on May 10, 1933, to protest the Nazi burning of books written by Jewish and non-Jewish authors.

COMMITTEE—which represented the more Americanized, affluent, Germanic elements of the community—shared the erroneous but popular conventional wisdom which held that the responsibilities of power would tame Hitler and that the Germany of Goethe and Heine was only temporarily eclipsed. The committee preferred quiet behind-the-scenes diplomacy to ameliorate the deteriorating condition of German Jewry. In contrast, the American Jewish Congress, which represented the more liberal and relatively less Americanized eastern European Jewish immigrants and their offspring, was convinced that an aroused public opinion could improve the situation, and called for a continuing round of protest rallies. Neither agency's strategy proved effective. The National Socialist regime was as immune to moral suasion as it was to diplomatic.

These defense and community-relations agencies represented different constituencies in the Jewish community. What appeared ultimately as differing political ideologies was really the outer manifestation of different degrees of acculturation. Not only were the political assumptions of the committee and the congress different, but so were their approaches to the tenets of the Jewish faith. The committee was composed of wealthy, assimilated German Jews, who saw Judaism as a religion only. The congress was composed of poor and middle-class, partly acculturated eastern European Jews who, though no longer Orthodox, still saw Judaism as a cultural and "national" community, that is, as an ethos. Such disparities characterized the entire world of American Jewish organizations, so that it is difficult to speak of an American Jewish community in the 1930s and 1940s. The common base in culture, language, and experience that might have engendered such a sense of communalism was not yet in place. Instead, there were small communities loosely grouped together as Jewish. Only in the eyes of the American antisemites and in their rhetoric, which was strident during this period, were the Jews of America a single unified entity.

These constituencies, represented by their organizations, differed on all major issues: the nature of the Nazi threat, the efficacy of a boycott, the centrality of the YISHUV (the Jewish community in Palestine), the apportionment of philanthropic funds, the proper strategy against the 1939 British WHITE PAPER restricting immigration to Palestine, the desirability of a Jewish army, and even the advisability of Jews, as a group, advocating the removal of restrictive barriers to immigration into the United States. There were also considerable differences on domestic political issues generated by the welfare-state program and the foreign policy of the New Deal.

Voluntary Organizations. At the same time, changes developed in the 1920s in the way the community was led and how it influenced public policy. In the free voluntaristic environment of America, it was always difficult to say who was being represented by the various Jewish organizations. They had no legal basis for their actions, and their leaders operated in the capacity of interested individuals. Earlier, in the first part of the century, men like Louis Marshall, Jacob Schiff, and Justice Louis Brandeis had assumed leadership positions by means of these organizations and were so recognized by officials of the American government, who spoke to the Jewish community through them. During the 1930s this pattern changed, as many nominal Jews gained high places in the Roosevelt administration because of their prominence in one of the elite groupings of American society: the law establishment, organized labor, the business community, the news media, the universities, and the political parties themselves. Men like Sidney Hillman, a labor leader; Samuel Rosenman, a lawyer involved in Democratic politics; Justice Felix Frankfurter; Henry MORGENTHAU, Jr., who began his career with Franklin D. ROOSEVELT in New York state politics; and Herbert Lehman, an investment banker and governor of New York, were often marginally Jewish and sometimes unhappily so. Earlier leaders, raised in a more intact Jewish environment, had had no doubt about the responsibilities to the Jewish interest that wealth and position assigned to them. The newer people who had reached the top during the Roosevelt period considered themselves Americans who happened to be Jewish. They would not risk their careers for a Jewish need. Yet it was through these people, who were only tenuously connected to the Jewish community, that the needs of American Jewry were ad-

American Zionist leaders at the British embassy in Washington to protest against the White Paper (1940). (1) Solomon Matz; (2) Nellie Ziv; (3) Leon Gellman; (4) Isadore Breslau; (5) Solomon Goldman; (6) Hayim Greenberg; (7) Stephen S. Wise; (8) Louis Segal; (9) Herman Hollander; (10) Israel Goldstein. [Keren Hayesod–United Israel Appeal, Jerusalem]

dressed by the government. The amount of cooperation they gave varied with time and circumstance, but, except in the case of Morgenthau, it was rarely sufficient to fill the need. In a real sense the American Jewish community was leaderless, since people like Rabbi Stephen S. WISE could speak to the administration only through these nominal spokespersons. How different the case might have been is illustrated by the actions of Morgenthau in using his influence to establish the WAR REFUGEE BOARD, which marked the zenith of the American rescue effort in 1944.

Yet the picture was not totally gloomy. Despite its low level of leadership, the community was able to unify for limited objectives. The Jewish agenda was eventually made known to Roosevelt, and in the area of philanthropy a tenuous unity was achieved when the United Jewish Appeal was estab-

lished in 1939. Most importantly, the American Jewish JOINT DISTRIBUTION COMMITTEE, known in the Jewish world as "the Joint," which was established in 1914 to extend relief to Jewish communities abroad, maintained the apolitical character mandated in its charter and was thereby able to avoid the contention dividing the remainder of the highly politicized community. It did loyal service for the beleaguered Jewish community, even providing supplemental allotments of kosher food for Palestinian Jews serving in the British army. At the same time the Joint, working through proxy agencies in Europe, financed the rescue and sheltering of thousands of Jews in the neutral countries. It was in philanthropy and rehabilitation rather than politics and power that the strength of American Jewry lay.

Economic Depression. The Great Depression and the domestic political and social condition it brought in its wake, rather than the disunity within American Jewry, were the principal factors in the Roosevelt administration's response to the Holocaust. The depression was the major preoccupation of government during the 1930s.

During the critical years between 1937 and 1941, just before America entered the war, the economy was still in decline. That condition not only caused policymakers to enforce the restrictive immigration laws, which were administered to curtail the flow of refugees, but it also created intergroup tensions within American society that made the role of rescue advocates more difficult.

The strident antisemitism of the 1930s traumatized the Jews of America. It had a paralytic effect that even the new visibility of Jews in high places in the Roosevelt administration did not allay. Many believed that the antisemitic rantings of demagogues like Gerald L. K. Smith and Father Charles Coughlin, who spoke to millions over the airwaves, were a portent that "it could happen here." As a group the Jews were emerging from the depression faster than any other ethnic group in the nation. This rapid recovery generated envy and resentment, especially among the Irish, who controlled the hierarchy of the Catholic church. The Jews had been welcomed into the ethnic urban coalition on which the strength of the Roosevelt administration was based, but within that coalition all was not in harmony. Without the support of key elements of that coalition, which might amplify Jewish political influence, the sheltering and rescue of European Jewry, a major item on the Jewish agenda, could not be achieved. Moreover, the antisemitism of the 1930s awakened the defense instinct of Jewish organizations like the American Jewish Committee, which channeled a great deal of energy and funds into fighting the domestic enemy and proportionately less into alleviating the danger faced by European Jewry. It was, of course, far more possible to influence opinion and policies at home than it was abroad.

Intracommunity disunity and strife were partly alleviated when news of the "FINAL SOLUTION" was received in the fall of 1942. But the AMERICAN JEWISH CONFERENCE, which was organized in 1943 by the major Jewish organizations to impose a policy of unified action, at least for limited objectives, foundered on the rift of community strife. The role of the BERGSON GROUP became a focal point of subsequent Holocaust dialogue.

The Bergson Group. It is too early to give a fair verdict on whether the activities of the Bergson group helped or hindered the rescue effort. The "Bergson boys," so called after their leader, Peter Bergson (a pseudonym of Hillel Kook), differed from other sources of disunity in that they were a group of Zionist Revisionists who came to the United States from Palestine, rather than an indigenous product of the American Jewish community. Under several different names, the group variously advocated the creation of a Jewish army of stateless and Palestinian Jews and a militant rescue program based on the strategy of separating the rescue issue from the issue of establishing a Jewish homeland in Palestine. The second issue was the centerpiece of the Zionists' BILTMORE RESOLUTION (May 1942), adopted by the American Jewish Conference in 1943.

The Bergson group never became a mass organization, but it skillfully utilized the media and cultivated political leaders to make its program known. It demonstrated a flair for publicity that became an annoyance to the mainline organizations. They tried to silence the new organization, and in one instance, Dr. Nahum GOLDMANN, acting for the mainline Zionist organizations, proposed to government officials that the group be deported to Palestine. So bitter did the strife become that it was carried to the secular press by means of expensive full-page advertisements in which each party accused the other of everything from draft dodging to misuse of funds.

Some historians believe that in their misunderstanding of how American Jewry operated and was managed, especially the notion of having a democratic mandate, the Bergson group aggravated disunity. Its rescue program was in any case mostly beyond the realm of political possibility. But there are others who think that it was precisely organizations like the Bergson group and the ultra-Orthodox Agudat Israel that had a more realistic understanding of the disaster. They saw the threat better because they were not locked into the secular assumptions of indigenous agencies. They understood that a "business-as-usual" attitude was not appropriate, given the scale of the catastrophe. Such researchers point out that virtually every step for rescue, including finally the creation of a special government agency with the specific objective of rescuing Jews (the War Refugee Board), was suggested and then initiated by the Bergson group. Whatever the case, the bitter conflict stands today as a monument to the tragedy of the American Jewish posture during the Holocaust.

Any fair examination of the role of American Jewry during that time must take great care not to read the contemporary condition of relative coherence and effectiveness back into the past. This is a comparatively new development, which, ironically, was accelerated by the bitter lesson that American Jews learned about the high price of disunity.

The basic truths of American politics have not been altered. One of the most basic is that a minority ethnic group or special-interest group may have "a voice but not a veto" in the shaping of public policy. During the years between 1933 and 1945, American Jewry had such a voice. Its message to decisionmakers was sometimes muddled, but the fact that it desperately wanted its European brethren to be saved was understood. The steps it proposed were interpreted as an interference with the major American aim, which was to win the war, and were rejected.

BIBLIOGRAPHY

Bauer, Y. *American Jewry and the Holocaust: The American Jewish Joint Distribution Committee, 1939–1945.* Detroit, 1981.

Bauer, Y. *Out of the Ashes: The Impact of American Jewry on Post-Holocaust Jewish Europe.* Oxford, 1989.

Feingold, H. L. "Courage First and Intelligence Second: The American Jewish Secular Elite, Roosevelt, and the Failure to Rescue." *American Jewish History* 72/4 (June 1983): 424–460.

Feingold, H. L. *The Politics of Rescue: The Roosevelt Administration and the Holocaust, 1938–1945.* New York, 1982.

Wyman, D. S. *The Abandonment of the Jews: America and the Holocaust, 1941–1945.* New York, 1984.

HENRY L. FEINGOLD

AMERICAN LITERATURE ON THE HOLOCAUST. *See* Literature on the Holocaust: United States.

AMERICAN PRESS AND THE HOLOCAUST. The treatment accorded by the American press to the destruction of the Jews during World War II can best be described as a "sidebar," the name given by journalists to a story that is ancillary to the main story. The press coverage of the Nazi persecution of the Jews paralleled United States policy regarding refugee rescue. It was not an issue of primary importance. The press's behavior reflected the United States' attitude of "rescue through victory." It was relatively rare for more than the isolated paper to call for action to assist Jews.

A great deal of information, including that about the "FINAL SOLUTION" and the systematic destruction of the Jews, was available long before the end of the war. Practically no aspect of the Holocaust remained unknown by 1945. However, significant information was often buried on the inside pages of newspapers. For instance, the June 1942 announcement that two million Jews had been killed as a result of planned annihilation was placed at the bottom of page 6 of the *Chicago Tribune* and given thirteen lines. The story was treated similarly by other major papers. Many readers probably missed this story and similar ones published well inside the paper. Those readers who did see it had cause to assume that the editors did not really believe it; had they believed it, a reader might have reasoned, they would have accorded it more prominent placement.

From the beginning of the Nazi regime, the press in the United States generally failed to take Hitler's prewar and, in certain cases, wartime threats against Jews seriously. It generally did not grasp that ANTISEMITISM was a, if not the, keystone of Nazism. Consequently, what was done to the Jews was often attributed to opportunistic and political motives or to war-related privations.

American reporters who were in Germany could transmit reports until December 1941 (some reporters were repatriated only in May 1942). Though their movements in Germany were stringently circumscribed, they were still able to send out significant information. Some reporters went to the railway stations in order to listen to the conversations of soldiers on their way home from the front. These reporters always faced the threat of expulsion.

After the United States entered the war, news of the fate of European Jewry was released primarily by governments-in-exile or Jewish sources. The press was inclined to discount this news because it came from "interested parties," that is, the victims. Ironically, news released by the perpetrators was treated with far greater credulity than that released by the victims, as was the case with the LIDICE story.

During World War I, reporters had been told atrocity stories about the Germans. These stories, which were the products of propagandists' imagination, had left their legacy. In World War II, reporters doubted the reports of German atrocities because they seemed too similar to exaggerated World War I reports. Sometimes reporters in Europe believed the news, while editors and publishers in the United States did not. Moreover, the number of victims made it more plausible for the press to dismiss the news as "beyond belief." Stories detailing the deaths of several hundred were sometimes given more credence than reports of the deaths of millions.

The press's behavior can be explained partly by the magnitude of the numbers, the absence of "independent" eyewitnesses, the inability to obtain confirmation from "impartial" sources, and the experience with World War I atrocity stories. Even when the news was confirmed by the Allies, reports were still buried in small articles on inside pages. The government's desire to ignore the story also kept the press from focusing on it.

While the unprecedented nature of the events made it easier, particularly at the outset, to discount this kind of news, by 1943 and certainly by the time of the destruction of Hungarian Jewry in 1944, a great deal of evidence had become available. Most reporters seemed to know about the Holocaust, and some papers published editorials lamenting what was happening. But they generally maintained their practice of placing the stories in inconspicuous places and reacting dis-

passionately. It is impossible, of course, to determine whether increased press attention would have prompted the government to follow a different policy.

Many Americans, including much of the press, felt that the Jews were continuously "wailing" about their fate and demanding special attention. Ironically, early reports sometimes received more attention than did later, more horrifying news of death and atrocities. By mid-1943 the news of the persecution of the Jews was regarded as an "old story," and therefore most newspapers carried it on inside pages.

There were, however, newspapers and magazines that pursued the story of the fate of the Jews with persistence and energy. Among them were a disproportionate number of liberal publications, including *P.M., The New Republic, The Nation, Commonweal,* and the *New York Post,* as well as the liberal journalists Dorothy Thompson, William Shirer, Arthur Koestler, Sigrid Schultz, Freda Kirchwey, I. F. Stone, Max Lerner, and Alexander Uhl. The Hearst papers also focused on the story when they became strong supporters of the BERGSON GROUP, and repeatedly demanded action on behalf of the Jews. In marked contrast to the behavior and reaction of the general press, the Jewish press in the United States believed the stories that were coming from Europe and treated the news with urgency and concern.

BIBLIOGRAPHY

Laqueur, W. *The Terrible Secret: An Investigation into the Suppression of Information about Hitler's "Final Solution."* London, 1980.
Lipstadt, D. E. *Beyond Belief: The American Press and the Coming of the Holocaust, 1933–1945.* New York, 1986.
Wyman, D. *The Abandonment of the Jews: America and the Holocaust, 1941–1945.* New York, 1984.

DEBORAH E. LIPSTADT

AMERICAN ZIONIST EMERGENCY COUNCIL, coordinating body of United States Zionist organizations, originally (1939) called the Emergency Committee for Zionist Affairs. From January 1942 its name was the American Emergency Committee for Zionist Affairs, and from the fall of 1942, the American Zionist Emergency Council. The council was created by the Zionist Executive on the outbreak of World War II to represent the latter in the United States, given the possibility that restrictions might be placed on the activity of the Zionist leadership in London and Jerusalem as a result of the war.

One of the council's main tasks was to convince the American public of the centrality of Palestine in the future of the Jewish people. Its founding members were the senior Zionist leaders of America and representatives of the four major American Zionist bodies: the Zionist Organization of America, the Hadassah Women's Zionist Organization, the Labor Zionists, and Mizrachi, the religious Zionist movement. From 1939 to 1941, the council had no strong leadership and encountered severe organizational difficulties. It was most hesitant in its political activity against the British 1939 WHITE PAPER, which had restricted Jewish immigration to Palestine and land purchase there; and during the deportation of "illegal" Jewish immigrants to MAURITIUS. At this time the United States was still neutral, and the council shied away from publicly supporting the Zionist demand for the establishment of a Jewish army to combat the Nazis.

The Emergency Council did not focus its efforts on activity for the Jews persecuted under Nazi rule. By agreement among the American Zionists, this task was assumed in the main by the American Jewish Congress, most of whose members were Zionists and whose leaders, especially Stephen S. WISE, were heads of the Emergency Council. The council dealt only with problems related to Palestine and the Zionist movement, such as rescue immigration. Extended arguments with the American Jewish JOINT DISTRIBUTION COMMITTEE on financing such immigration led at times to delays and failures. In the winter of 1940 the Zionists of America were asked to raise the sum of $20,000 for purchasing a ship to transport to Palestine 1,150 young Jews stranded at Kladovo, Yugoslavia, on the frozen Danube River. The Emergency Council failed in this task, and the refugees were eventually massacred by the Germans.

In the area of rescuing Zionist activists from occupied Europe by obtaining immigration visas to the United States, the Emergency Council was forestalled by the JEWISH LABOR COMMITTEE and the VA'AD HA-HATSALA (Rescue Committee) of the Union of Orthodox Rabbis of the United States and Canada. Several Zionist activists were saved as a result of a change in the UNITED STATES DEPARTMENT OF STATE's visa policy. On the other hand, the Emergency Council financed the expenses of about one thousand agricultural pioneers from VILNA who immigrated to Palestine by way of the Soviet Union.

After the sinking of the STRUMA in February 1942, the Emergency Council sent protest cables to President Franklin D. ROOSEVELT and Prime Minister Winston CHURCHILL, but it did not organize demonstrations, since the British embassy had warned that it would see this as a "declaration of war against Great Britain."

In 1942 and 1943, the council participated in protest meetings organized by American Jewry against the "FINAL SOLUTION," but these activities had little influence on the events in Europe. Before the AMERICAN JEWISH CONFERENCE convened in August and September 1943, extensive discussions were held in the council. It had failed as an effective leadership for American Zionists, and even Chaim WEIZMANN, president of the World Zionist Organization, concluded that with its existing composition and structure, the council was not suited to political activity on the required scale. A reorganization was undertaken, and the American Zionist leader Rabbi Abba Hillel SILVER was appointed head of the board of directors of the council. The Holocaust of European Jewry was discussed at the American Jewish Conference, but no steps were resolved to further rescue work, and the debates focused on the postwar program for a Jewish commonwealth in Palestine.

Immediately after the war, under Silver's leadership, the Emergency Council became a pressure group. In the wake of the Holocaust, it waged a political struggle between 1945 and 1948, emphasizing the obligation of the United States to guarantee a home for the Holocaust survivors in a sovereign Jewish state. Despite the State Department's refusal to comply with the Zionist demands, the council convinced a large sector of American public opinion of the justification of these demands. The council continued assisting the "illegal" immigration of survivors to Palestine as well as the struggle for a Jewish state until the latter was established on May 15, 1948. In 1949, the Emergency Council was reorganized as the American Zionist Council.

BIBLIOGRAPHY

Halperin, S. *The Political World of American Zionism.* Detroit, 1961.
Silverberg, R. *If I Forget Thee O Jerusalem.* New York, 1970.
Urofsky, M. I. *American Zionism from Herzl to the Holocaust.* Garden City, N.Y., 1975.

MENAHEM KAUFMAN

ANCESTRAL HERITAGE. *See* Ahnenerbe.

ANDRÉ, JOSEPH (1908–1973), Belgian abbot who helped to rescue hundreds of Jewish children. In liaison with the Comité de Défense des Juifs, an underground Jewish organization searching for secure hiding places for Jews in distress, Abbé André coordinated his rescue activities out of his parish office, which was located next to the German military headquarters in Namur.

Abbé André found hiding places for many Jews. He kept an eye on all Jews whom he had directed to secure shelters. If convinced that a certain place had become unsuitable or that the treatment given was inadequate, he immediately took steps to have the Jew transferred to a new location. His role was especially significant in the rescue of children.

Traveling from place to place, he implored at monasteries, convents, and private homes that they take Jewish children under their protective wings. It did not take long for the Gestapo to realize that Abbé André was frustrating its designs for the deportation of all Belgian Jews, and they trailed his movements. He eventually became a marked man and had to go into hiding until the liberation of Namur by the United States Army in September 1944.

Abbé Joseph André, standing in the front row, fourth from the right. He is shown here with the people he saved during the Holocaust, at a tree-planting ceremony on October 30, 1968, at Yad Vashem, when he received his medal and scroll as a "Righteous among the Nations."

He then undertook the arduous task of gathering the children and returning them to their parents or to Jewish organizations. André never thought of trying to convert the children. On the contrary, he always emphasized the duty of maintaining every person's own faith, to the extent that many children under his care knew the "Hatikvah" (the Jewish national anthem).

Abbé Joseph André was recognized as one of the "RIGHTEOUS AMONG THE NATIONS" by YAD VASHEM in 1968.

BIBLIOGRAPHY

Friedman, P. *Their Brothers' Keepers.* New York, 1957.

MORDECAI PALDIEL

ANIELEWICZ, MORDECAI (1919 or 1920–1943), commander of the WARSAW GHETTO UPRISING. Anielewicz was born into a poor family living in a Warsaw slum quarter; he graduated from the Laor Jewish secondary school and joined the Zionist Ha-Shomer ha-Tsa'ir movement, where he distinguished himself as an organizer and a youth leader.

On September 7, 1939, a week after the outbreak of the war, Anielewicz fled from Warsaw and, together with the senior members of his movement, made his way to eastern Poland, assuming that the Polish forces would establish their defense line there. On September 17, however, eastern Poland was occupied by the Soviet army. Anielewicz reached the southern part of the Soviet-occupied area and tried to cross into Romania and establish a route for Jewish youth trying to get to Palestine. He was caught by the Soviets and put in jail; when he was released, he decided to return to Warsaw—by then under German occupation—and on the way he stopped at many towns and cities, visiting the Jewish communities. He stayed in Warsaw for a short while only and left for Vilna, which by then had been incorporated into Lithuania. It contained a large concentration of refugees from Warsaw, among them members of the youth movements and political parties. Anielewicz called on his fellow Ha-Shomer ha-Tsa'ir members to send a team of instructors back to German-occupied Poland, where they would resume the movement's educational and political activities in the underground. He and his friend Mira Fuchrer set an example by being the first to volunteer for this assignment.

By January 1940, Anielewicz had become a full-time underground activist. As the leader of the Ha-Shomer ha-Tsa'ir underground movement, he set up cells and youth groups, organized their activities, helped publish an underground newspaper, arranged meetings and seminars, and made frequent illegal trips outside Warsaw, visiting communities and his movement's chapters in the provincial ghettos. He also found time to study for himself, especially Hebrew, and read much history, sociology, and economics. It was in this period that, in his attempts to comprehend the situation, he crystallized his views, giving them expression in lectures and in articles that he published in the underground press.

Under the impact of the first reports of the mass murder of Jews in the east, following the German invasion of the Soviet Union in

Mordecai Anielewicz.

June 1941, Anielewicz revised his policy and concentrated on the creation of a self-defense organization in the ghetto. His first efforts to establish contacts with the Polish underground forces who were loyal to the POLISH GOVERNMENT-IN-EXILE in London were unsuccessful. In March and April 1942 he joined others in the formation of the Antifascist Bloc; the bloc, however, did not fulfill the expectations of its Zionist components, and after a wave of arrests, including those of Communist activists in the bloc, it ceased to exist.

At the time of the mass deportation from Warsaw in the summer of 1942, Anielewicz was staying in Zagłębie (the southwestern part of Poland, which had been incorporated into Germany). There he worked at transforming the underground youth movements into an armed resistance movement. On his return to Warsaw after the mass deportation, he found that only 60,000 of Warsaw's 350,000 Jews were left in the ghetto, and that the small ŻYDOWSKA ORGANIZACJA BOJOWA (Jewish Fighting Organization; ŻOB) in the ghetto lacked arms and was in a dire situation, having suffered failures and lost members. Anielewicz embarked upon a determined drive to reorganize and reinvigorate the ŻOB and achieved rapid results; following the mass deportation, there was far more support in the ghetto than previously for the idea of armed resistance and its practical organization. Most of the existing Jewish underground groups now joined the ŻOB, and a public council, consisting of authorized representatives, was established in support of the ŻOB (the Żydowski Komitet Narodowy, or Jewish National Committee, and the Coordinating Committee, the latter also including the BUND). In November 1942 Anielewicz was appointed commander of the ŻOB. By January 1943 several groups of fighters, consisting of members of the pioneering Zionist youth movements, had been consolidated, contact had been established with the ARMIA KRAJOWA (Home Army) command, and a small quantity of arms had been obtained from the Polish side of the city.

On January 18, 1943, the Germans launched the second mass deportation from the Warsaw ghetto. Caught unawares, the ŻOB staff was unable to meet in order to decide on what action to take in response, but in one part of the ghetto the armed groups of ŻOB fighters decided to act on their own. There were two foci of ŻOB resistance, with Anielewicz commanding the major street battle. The fighters deliberately joined the columns of deportees and, at an agreed signal, attacked the German escorts at the corner of Zamenhofa and Niska streets, while the rest of the Jews fled from the scene. Most of the fighters belonging to the Ha-Shomer ha-Tsa'ir group fell in that battle. Anielewicz was saved by his men, who came to his aid in the close-quarters fighting. The resistance action taken on January 18 was of great importance, because four days later the Germans halted the deportation, a step that the ghetto population interpreted as meaning that the Germans were drawing back in the face of armed resistance by the Jews. The following three months, from January to April 1943, were used by the ŻOB for intensive preparations for the decisive test ahead, under the supervision of the organization's headquarters, led by Anielewicz.

On April 19, the eve of Passover, the final deportation of Warsaw Jews was launched, an event that served as the signal for the Warsaw ghetto uprising. In the first few clashes, the Jewish resistance fighters held the upper hand and the Germans suffered losses. The clashes and street fighting in the ghetto lasted for three days. The Germans introduced a large military force, against which the few hundred Jewish fighters, armed only with pistols, had no chance whatsoever; but the fighters did not surrender. Neither, for the most part, did the Jews who were in the bunkers; the appeals and promises they heard from the Germans did not lure them out of their hiding places, and the Germans had to burn down the ghetto, house by house, in order to destroy the bunkers. The fighting in the ghetto went on for four weeks, in the course of which the Germans and their helpers suffered constant losses. It was only on May 16 that SS-Brigadeführer Jürgen STROOP, the commander of the German force, was able to report that the *Grossaktion* ("major operation") had been concluded and the ghetto conquered.

In the first days of the fighting, Anielewicz was in command, in the midst of the main fighting forces of the ghetto. When the street fighting was over, Anielewicz, together with his staff and a large force of fighters, retreated into the bunker at 18 Mila Street. This bunker fell on May 8, and the main body of the ŻOB, including Anielewicz, was killed. In his last letter, of April 23, 1943, to Yitzhak ZUCKERMAN (a member of the ŻOB staff who was then on assignment on the Polish side), Anielewicz wrote:

What has happened is beyond our wildest dreams. Twice the Germans fled from the ghetto. One of our companies held out for forty minutes and the other, for over six hours. . . . I have no words to describe to you the conditions in which the Jews are living. Only a few chosen ones will hold out; all the rest will perish sooner or later. The die is cast. In the bunkers in which our comrades are hiding, no candle can be lit, for lack of air. . . . The main thing is: My life's dream has come true; I have lived to see Jewish resistance in the ghetto in all its greatness and glory.

Kibbutz Yad Mordecai in Israel has been

named after Mordecai Anielewicz, and is the site of a memorial in his honor.

BIBLIOGRAPHY

Gutman, Y. *The Jews of Warsaw, 1939–1943.* Bloomington, 1980.

Gutman, Y. *Revolt of the Besieged: Mordehai Anielewicz and the Uprising of the Warsaw Ghetto.* Merhavia, Israel, 1963. (In Hebrew.)

Ringelblum, E. " 'Comrade Mordechai': Mordechai Anielewicz—Commander of the Warsaw Ghetto Uprising." In *They Fought Back*, edited by Y. Suhl, pp. 108–114. London, 1968.

ISRAEL GUTMAN

ANNE FRANK HOUSE. *See* Frank, Anne.

ANSCHLUSS, the takeover of AUSTRIA by Germany in March 1938 (the term is usually translated as "connection," "union," or "annexation"). The concept, denoting the inclusion of Austria in a united Greater Germany, entered German political terminology in 1918. Under the Treaty of St. Germain, the 1919 peace accord between Austria and the victorious allies, Austria was forbidden to join Germany and was made an independent republic. In the 1930s Engelbert Dollfuss, leader of the Christian Socialist party in Austria, set up a Fascist-style dictatorship, based on an alliance with Italy and opposed both to Austria's Social Democrats and to its Nazis. In July 1934 the Nazis made an attempt to seize power; they failed, owing to Italian intervention, but they did succeed in murdering Dollfuss in his chancellery office. Dollfuss's successor, Kurt von Schuschnigg, tried to reach an understanding with Nazi Germany, but Hitler would not settle for less than Austria's annexation to the Reich. As a result of the rapid rise of the Nazi movement in Austria, and the withdrawal of Italy's protection following the creation of the Rome-Berlin Axis, the Austrian regime lacked the strength to resist Hitler's pressure. The Anschluss, which took place on March 13, 1938,

In the days following the Anschluss (March 13, 1938), Jewish citizens of Vienna were forced to scrub away the election slogans of the Vaterländische Front (Fatherland Front, a party founded by Engelbert Dollfuss in 1933) from buildings and streets.

was in effect a dictate by Hitler, with massive support from the Austrian Nazis and with the agreement of Italy (which for Hitler was proof of Mussolini's loyalty and friendship). Britain and France went along with the Anschluss, despite the fact that it clearly violated a treaty that also bore Germany's signature.

BIBLIOGRAPHY

Kindermann, G.-K. *Hitler's Defeat in Austria, 1933–1934.* Boulder, 1988.

Luža, R. *Austro-German Relations in the Anschluss Era.* Princeton, 1975.

Schuschnigg, K. von. *The Brutal Takeover: The Austrian Ex-Chancellor's Account of the Anschluss of Austria by Hitler.* London, 1971.

Suval, S. *The Anschluss Question in the Weimar Era: A Study of Nationalism in Germany and Austria, 1918–1932.* Baltimore, 1974.

ISRAEL GUTMAN

ANTHROPOLOGY AND NATIONAL SO-CIALISM. The strong desire of anthropologists and "racial hygienists" to put their concepts of population policy to practical use came to the fore in the 1920s. German anthropologists considered the Weimar Republic unwilling and ill suited to transform their concepts into official policies, and they expected Adolf Hitler to pave the way for their plans.

The anthropologists' urge for action was not exclusively motivated by "racial hygiene" (Ger., *Rassenhygiene;* the Nazi term for eugenics) but also had its sources in the demands of everyday life. Law courts, for example, were eager to base determinations of illegitimate paternity on reliable evidence. On the other hand, eugenicists found it unbearable that a relatively large group of persons was excluded from a selective population policy because their genetic value could not be determined, owing to their unknown paternity.

In 1926 Otto Reche, head of the Institute of Anthropology in Vienna, drew up the first genetic reports on disputed paternity. Independently of Reche, Otmar von Verschuer delivered his first reports in Berlin, in 1928, at the Kaiser Wilhelm Institute for Anthropology, Genetics, and Eugenics.

The reports were based on analyzing similarities of the phenotype (the visible characteristics). Between 120 and 130 features (for example, the ear, nose, eyes, hair, head, and fingerprints) of the mother, child, and assumed father were examined. After they had determined all the similarities between mother and child, anthropologists tried to identify as many characteristic features of the child as possible with those of the disputed father. Each statement was summed up in a final result, and was graded according to its probability.

This procedure was soon accepted in Austrian courts. In 1931 the Supreme Court of Vienna declared that a genetic examination in proceedings tracing paternity should be obligatory. In Germany, however, law courts took a skeptical view of this new evidence. There, the gradual public acceptance was closely connected with the antisemitic politics of the National Socialists. As part of the Law for the Restoration of the Professional Civil Service (*Gesetz zur Wiederherstellung des Berufsbeamtentums*) of April 7, 1933, all Jewish civil servants were removed from their places of work. This law served as a background for the legal definition of a Jew. Such a definition was given its final form in the first implementing order of November 14, 1935, which said that a Jew was a person descended from at least three fully Jewish grandparents. A "partial Jew" (*see* MISCH-LINGE) was a person who had one or two Jewish grandparents. During the following years, special laws were enacted that systematically restricted the professional and social life of the Jews, and almost everywhere proof of one's "Aryan" identity, the *Ariernachweis,* was demanded.

The anti-Jewish legislation raised the problem of establishing racial descent. As a rule, such descent was proved by family documents. Sometimes, however, the necessary papers were not available. Proving descent was especially important to the Nazi authorities when Jewish descent was suspected, and it had to be determined whether the person in question was a "quarter Jew" (a *Mischling* of the second degree), a "half Jew" (a *Mischling* of the first degree), or a "full Jew" (*Volljude*). Therefore, the *Mischlinge,* whose officially estimated number varied between 115,000 and 750,000, became a focal point for the work of the Reichssippenamt (Reich Genealogical Office), which had been set up to clarify disputed cases of "Aryan" descent following the issuing of the Civil Service Law in 1933.

Only the Reichssippenamt was authorized to decide on "Aryan" descent, which was certified with a document, the *Abstammungsbescheid* (certificate of Aryan descent). First, the Reichssippenamt tried to establish a complete genealogy, with documentary evidence, of the person under investigation. This procedure, however, was prone to failure if birth or marriage certificates or entries were missing (usually in cases of illegitimate birth). In such cases the Reichssippenamt was entitled to draw upon "genetic and racial reports," if these concerned the "racial classification of individual persons." Such examinations functioned as a last resort and served as a basis for the *Abstammungsbescheid*, together with the previously obtained genealogical evidence.

Owing to its new function, the ordinary genetic report on disputed paternity developed into a "genetic and racial report." Its methodical basis remained principally unchanged: the genuine father was sought by means of genetic features. However, there were innovations. First, the purpose had changed. The object was not to unite an illegitimate child with its true father, in order to help it develop an emotional bond and to guarantee its rights, but to find out whether the offspring belonged by race to the German people, in order to determine whether or not the child should be granted its personal rights and liberty. The child's individual needs were of no importance. Second, the method suffered from its changed goal. Whereas the father was the center of attention in the former procedure, the emphasis now lay on the child. It was not as important to know the identity of the father of a child as it was to ascertain whether an offspring was of Jewish or German descent. Third, a racial classification was eventually made on the basis of alleged racial characteristics, and a largely intuitive racial analysis was carried out in search of Jewish features.

At first, only the Reichssippenamt had the right to conduct investigation about Jewish or non-Jewish descent, but beginning in 1938 law courts were also entitled to do so in certain cases. The public prosecutor was authorized to challenge the legitimacy of a child in the interest of the public, if its "racial classification" was disputed. In 1939, petitioning to determine one's blood relationship was allowed. Proceedings could be instituted if there was reasonable suspicion that legal and biological paternity were not identical. "Genetic and racial reports" became highly esteemed evidence, leading to a constantly increasing demand for them.

The genetic and racial tests were not conducted in the Reichssippenamt but exclusively in qualified institutions—mainly university institutes—whose directors were appointed by the Reich Ministry of the Interior as official experts. In a law of March 27, 1936, the Reich Ministry of Justice named nine such institutes, the majority of them institutes of anthropology and the rest institutes of genetics and racial hygiene. In 1943 the list of authorities that were entitled to issue such "genetic and racial reports" comprised twenty-two institutes and twelve individual experts. (The institutes were not obliged by the government to accept reports from the individual experts.) The institutes were as follows:

1. Berlin, Kaiser-Wilhelm-Institut für Anthropologie (Kaiser Wilhelm Institute for Anthropology; Prof. Dr. med. Freiherr Otmar von Verschuer [before 1942, Prof. Dr. med. Eugen Fischer])
2. Berlin, Institut für Rassenbiologie (Institute for Race Biology; Prof. Dr. phil. Wolfgang Abel)
3. Berlin, Institut für Rassenhygiene der Universität (University Institute for Racial Hygiene; Prof. Dr. med. Fritz Lenz)
4. Berlin, Erbpathologische Abteilung d. I. Medizinischen Klinik d. Charité (Heredity-Pathology Department of the First Medical Clinic of Charité; Prof. Dr. med. Friedrich Curtius)
5. Breslau, Anthropologisches Institut der Universität (University Anthropological Institute; Prof. Dr. phil.nat. Egon Freiherr von Eickstedt)
6. Cologne, Universitätsinstitut für Erbbiologie und Rassenhygiene (University Institute for Heredity Biology and Racial Hygiene; Prof. Dr. med. Ferdinand Claussen)
7. Frankfurt, Universitätsinstitut für Erb-

biologie und Rassenhygiene (University Institute for Heredity Biology and Racial Hygiene; Prof. Dr. med. Heinrich Wilhelm Kranz)

8. Giessen, Institut für Erb- und Rassenpflege (Institute for Heredity and Racial Cultivation; Prof. Dr. med. Hermann Boehm)

9. Greifswald, Institut für Menschliche Erblehre und Eugenik (Institute for Human Heredity Studies and Eugenics; Doz. Dr. phil. Fritz Steiniger)

10. Innsbruck, Erb- und Rassenbiologisches Institut der Universität (University Heredity and Racial Biological Institute; Prof. Dr. med. Friedrich Stumpfl)

11. Kiel, Anthropologisches Institut der Universität (University Anthropological Institute; Prof. Dr. rer.nat. Hans Weinert)

12. Königsberg, Rassenbiologisches Institut der Universität (University Racial Biological Institute; Dr. med. Bernhard T. Duis)

13. Leipzig, Institut für Rassen- und Völkerkunde an der Universität (University Institute for Race and Ethnology; Prof. Dr. phil. Otto Reche)

14. Munich, Anthropologisches Institut der Universität (University Anthropological Institute; Prof. Dr. med. Theodor Mollison)

15. Prague, Institut für Erb- und Rassenhygiene der Deutschen Karls-Universität (Institute for Heredity and Racial Hygiene of the German Charles University; Prof. Dr. med. Karl Thums)

16. Prague, Lehrstuhl und Institut für Rassenkunde der Deutschen Karls-Universität (Professorial Chair and Institute for Racial Studies of the German Charles University; Prof. Dr. phil. Bruno K. Schultz)

17. Strasbourg, Institut für Rassenbiologie der Reichs-Universität (Institute for Racial Biology of the Reich University; Prof. Dr. med. Wolfgang Lehmann)

18. Tübingen, Rassenbiologisches Institut der Universität (University Racial Biological Institute; Prof. Dr. phil. Dr. med. Wilhelm Gieseler)

19. Vienna, Anthropologisches Institut der Universität (University Anthropological Institute; Doz. Dr. phil. Karl Tuppa)

20. Vienna, Rassenbiologisches Institut der Universität (University Racial Biological Institute; Prof. Dr. med. Lothar Loeffler)

21. Weimar, Thüringisches Landesamt für Rassewesen (Thuringian State Department for Racial Knowledge; Prof. Dr. med. Karl Astel)

22. Würzburg, Rassenbiologisches Institut der Universität (University Racial Biological Institute; Prof. Dr. phil. Günther Just)

Among the individual experts allowed to issue such reports were:

1. Dr. Richard Günther, Vienna

2. Dozent Dr. phil.habil. Michael Hesch, Curator and Head of the Anthropological Department of the State Museum for Zoology and Ethnology, Dresden

3. Prof. Dr. phil. Dr. med.habil. Friedrich Keiter, University Racial Biological Institute, Würzburg

4. Dr. Werner Pendl, Vienna

5. Dr. Hella Pöch, Salzburg

6. Prof. Dr. med. Rudolf Polland, Director of the University Institute for Heredity Studies and Racial Hygiene, Graz

7. Prof. Dr. med. Dr. phil.nat. Andreas Pratje, University Anatomical Institute, Erlangen

8. Prof. Dr. med. Ernst Rodenwaldt, Director of the Hygienic Institute, Heidelberg

9. Dozent Dr. med. Dr. phil. Johannes Schaeuble, Head of the Department for Heredity and Race Lore of the Anatomical Institute, Freiburg im Breisgau

10. Dr. Josef Wastl, Custodian and Director of the Anthropological Department of the Natural History Museum, Vienna

After five years of their activities, and in view of the new legal regulations of 1938 and 1939, anthropologists and racial hygienists decided to meet at the Anthropological Institute of the University of Munich under the chairmanship of Otto Reche, on March 23, 1939. Most of the senior experts and their assistants attended the meeting, which served as an exchange of experience as well as of views.

Reche, in his dual function as rapporteur for the Munich conference and spokesman of the Rassenpolitisches Amt der NSDAP (Racial Policies Office of the Nazi Party), pointed out the aim of "genetic and racial reports" very clearly: "Only with this method is it possible to separate kinship and genetic lines and prevent foreign blood [*Rassenblut*] and hereditary diseases from being passed into the family. . . . Especially with illegitimate persons, the danger of hereditary taint and the infiltration of foreign blood is very great. It is well known, for example, that the Jews have given birth to many illegitimate half-castes."

The events of the KRISTALLNACHT pogrom in November 1938 did not prevent anthropologists and racial hygienists from using their science to determine the selection of Jews. The number of reports increased constantly during the Hitler period. For example, the Polyclinic of Genetics and Racial Hygiene in Berlin-Charlottenburg delivered 52 reports annually from 1935–1936 to 1937–1938, but its output of reports increased in 1938–1939 to 142, and in 1939–1940 to 314. The total number of all reports is unknown for the later years, but as of July 1942, ten out of twenty institutes delivered at least 3,700 reports.

At the end of 1942, the Reichssippenamt stated that applications for expert opinion had increased greatly, since applicants wanted to achieve a more favorable racial classification through genetic and racial examination. The increasing number of such applications was a decisive factor in the gradual fulfillment of the anthropologists' and racial hygienists' 1939 demand that new institutes be founded and that the group of experts be broadened.

The experts accepted the extension of ordinary genetic reports on disputed paternity to reports of racial descent, and they therefore also accepted the change in the aim, which was now that the true father of an illegitimate child should be determined in order to find out whether the candidate was a Jew or a *Mischling*. Anthropologists closed their eyes to the fact that Jewish descent could not be determined in the way that Negroid descent, for example, could be. Therefore, the Nazi laws now provided also for the determination of religious affiliation. A Jew continued to be a person who had at least three completely Jewish grandparents. His (or her) racial classification, however, derived from his affilia-tion to the Jewish religious community. Anthropologists did not make use of this fact to reject racial testimony because of its insufficient scientific basis. But even if Jewish descent could have been determined by genetic means, the aim would have remained immoral: first to deprive a human being of his rights, and, after 1941, to physically destroy him.

During World War II, the cooperation of anthropologists and racial hygienists with the Nazi party and government concerning their selection policies began to function less smoothly than previously. Appeals to courts in proceedings to determine Jewish descent had consequences that could not have been foreseen by their initiators. The appeals offered a final and very slim chance for Jews to escape persecution (and, eventually, death) with the help of the same bureaucracy that pursued their extermination. Thus, Jews increasingly contested the paternity of their legal and often legitimate fathers and claimed illegitimate descent from men of "German blood," in order to be classified as "Aryans" if they had been listed as *Mischlinge*, or to be accepted as *Mischlinge* if they had been listed as *Volljuden*.

In their desperation they sometimes tried to deceive the authorities. For example, the writer Rolf Italiaander, who was regarded as a *Mischling* by the Reichssippenamt, successfully concealed the Jewish descent of his grandparents on his father's side. First he declared his grandfather to be an illegitimate child of an Englishman. Then he found a photograph of an "Aryan"-looking man in a Berlin junk shop, soaked it in water, and rubbed it with cigarette ash to imbue the photograph with the patina of past decades. He then handed it in as a picture of his late grandfather. In addition, he destroyed the entry for the Jewish mother of his grandfather in the registration office of Düsseldorf, tearing it out of the entry list and swallowing it. Finally, his grandmother untruthfully affirmed that her husband had been the illegitimate son of an English sailor. In this way, Italiaander saved himself and forty members of his family from greater harm.

The authorities and party offices were not unaware of the attempts of Jews to disguise relationships with the help of these newly established legal possibilities in order to increase the chances of their survival. For this reason, from February 1943 on the Reich Ministry of Justice endeavored to limit the scope of courts regarding their decisions. Both the Reich Ministry of the Interior and the Reich Ministry of Justice tried to bind the authorities involved in the proceedings to the more rigorous antisemitic party line. Thus, the experts Rudolf Polland, Karl Tuppa, and Josef Wastl aroused the superior authorities' indignation because of reports they composed that were favorable to Jews.

Once the experts had accepted scientifically dubious evidence (such as yellowed photographs) to determine a candidate's descent, it was not far to actual manipulation, under the prevailing conditions. Thus, the anthropologists and racial hygienists had maneuvered themselves into a dilemma. Those who out of humanity manipulated the facts were, in official terms, deceivers—though morally they were justified. Those who worked objectively, at least from 1941 on, were accomplices to murder.

[See also Racism.]

BIBLIOGRAPHY

Grenville, J. A. S. "Die Endlösung und die 'Judenmischlinge' im Dritten Reich." In vol. 2 of *Das Unrechtsregime: Internationale Forschung über den Nationalsozialismus*, edited by U. Büttner, pp. 91–121. Hamburg, 1986.

Müller-Hill, B. *Murderous Science—Elimination by Scientific Selection of Jews, Gypsies, and Others: Germany, 1933–1945.* Oxford, 1988.

Noakes, J. "Wohin gehören die 'Judenmischlinge': Die Entstehung der ersten Durchführungsverordnungen zu den Nürnberger Gesetzen." In vol. 2 of *Das Unrechtsregime: Internationale Forschung über den Nationalsozialismus*, edited by U. Büttner, pp. 69–84. Hamburg, 1986.

Proctor, R. *Racial Hygiene: Medicine under the Nazis.* Cambridge, Mass., 1988.

Seidler, H., and A. Rett. *Das Reichssippenamt entscheidet: Rassenbiologie im Nationalsozialismus.* Vienna, 1982.

GEORG LILIENTHAL

ANTI-JEWISH LEGISLATION. More than two thousand anti-Jewish measures were enacted in Germany (in its January 1, 1937, borders) under Nazi rule. Owing to the federal structure of the Reich, it is difficult to ascertain their precise number. The figure cited here refers only to laws passed by the Reich and the larger *Länder* (states and provinces), and represents only a part of the total number of anti-Jewish regulations. If the smaller political units and the autonomous bodies are taken into account, the total exceeds three thousand.

The Nazi party program adopted in February 1920 contained four anti-Jewish objectives:

1. Jews should not be citizens, and should have the legal status of foreigners;
2. Jews should not be public officials;
3. Jews should be barred from immigrating into Germany;
4. Any Jew who is the owner or editor of a German newspaper should be removed from that position.

At the time these demands were not new, nor could they be regarded as particularly radical. They were no more than a repetition of the views advocated by all pre-1914 antisemitic parties and political groups, and corresponded to the ideas held by wide circles of the German population.

In retrospect, three distinct and separate waves of anti-Jewish legislation can be discerned. The first wave welled up in March 1933, and by April 7 had culminated in one of the major Nazi objectives—the enactment of the Law for the Restoration of the Professional Civil Service. This law authorized the dismissal of "non-Aryan" civil servants, except for those who had held that status since August 1, 1914, who had fought at the front for Germany in World War I, or whose father or son had been killed in action in that war. A "non-Aryan" was defined as a person "descended from non-Aryan, and especially from Jewish, parents or grandparents," even if only one parent or grandparent fitted that category.

This law became the model for measures excluding Jews from other occupations—for example, lawyers and tax consultants—and dismissing all "non-Aryan" employees; doctors and dentists were barred from the panels of social-medicine institutions. Under a law (the *Reichskulturkammergesetz*) that was passed on September 22, 1933, reestablishing a Reich Chamber of Culture, "non-Aryans" were removed from organizations and enterprises related to literature, the press, broadcasting, the theater, music, and art.

The legislation barring Jews from various professions and occupations was further augmented by measures designed to make these occupations inaccessible to them in the first place. The first such measure was the Law against the Overcrowding of German Schools and Institutions of Higher Learning (April 7, 1933), which restricted the admissible number of "non-Aryan" students to a certain percentage of the total. All regulations governing training and examinations for state-controlled occupations contained an ARIERPARAGRAPH ("Aryan clause"), which prohibited "non-Aryans" from sitting for final state examinations and thus closed all such occupations to them. The *Arierparagraph* was also introduced into the bylaws of professional organizations, societies, and clubs, and as a result it became increasingly difficult for Jews to protect their interests or take part in social activities.

Financial easements were denied to Jews: Jewish high school and university students were no longer eligible for reductions of school fees, scholarships, or any other kind of assistance; and newly married couples were not granted the usual matrimony loans if one of the partners was "non-Aryan."

Another category of laws and regulations was designed to discriminate against the Jewish religion and hamper observance of its practices and customs. Jewish ritual slaughter was outlawed as early as April 1933. Jewish judges could at any time be rejected, on grounds of bias. Local authorities, in ever-growing numbers, prohibited Jews from visiting public baths; Jewish students who did not attend classes on the Sabbath or Jewish holidays were penalized; and Jewish prisoners no longer had the right to receive kosher food. By mid-1935 these measures had severely restricted Jewish life in Germany. Jews, for the most part, maintained contact only with other Jews.

The second major wave of anti-Jewish legislation came on September 15, 1935, when the Reichstag, meeting in Nuremberg, passed two laws, drafted on short notice, that pro-vided for the final legal and social separation between German Jews and the German people. Under the *Reichsbürgergesetz* (Reich Citizenship Law), the Jews were deprived of all voting rights and became *Staatsbürger 2 Klasse* (second-class citizens). One immediate effect of this law was the dismissal, by December 31, 1935, of all the Jewish civil servants, employees, and workers who still held their jobs. The broader function of the citizenship law was to serve as the legal basis for no fewer than thirteen further decrees, each relating to a different set of circumstances.

The other law passed that day was the *Gesetz zum Schutze des deutschen Blutes und der deutschen Ehre* (Law for the Protection of German Blood and German Honor), which forbade marriage between Jews and nationals of German or kindred blood. In the wake of that law, a complicated classification system was enacted defining various degrees of Jewishness, ranging from *Volljude* (full Jew) to *Geltungsjude* (person regarded as a Jew, even though he or she had two "Aryan" grandparents) to *Mischling* (partial Jew, i.e., a person of mixed blood), divided in turn into first and second degrees, with each degree having its own specified privileges, rights, and disabilities (*see* MISCHLINGE).

The third wave of anti-Jewish legislation related to the remaining sphere of Jewish activity: the economy. Though this wave began during 1936 and 1937, its timing was most directly connected to measures taken after the rioting on KRISTALLNACHT (November 9–10, 1938). In 1938 the status of the Jewish community as a recognized public authority entitled to subsidies and tax exemption was rescinded. On November 12, Nazi anti-Jewish legislation entered its final phase. A collective fine of 1 billion reichsmarks was imposed on the Jews as a body, as a penalty for the murder of a German diplomat in Paris, the ostensible impetus for the riots; in addition, they had to repair out of their own resources all damage they suffered in the rioting. The *Verordnung zur Ausschaltung der Juden aus dem deutschen Wirtschaftsleben* (Measure for the Elimination of Jews from the German Economy) completed the list of occupations from which Jews were already barred; as of January 1, 1939, there was no occupation a Jew could join or practice unless he dealt only with Jews.

In the period following November 9, 1938, more legislation was passed, in three different areas:

1. The seizure and confiscation of Jewish-owned assets (ARISIERUNG, or "Aryanization"), which was a legalized form of plunder by the state.

2. The separation of the Jews from the Germans, in both location and time: Jews were forbidden to enter certain places or show themselves in public at certain times. As of February 1939, for example, they could no longer enter railway sleeping or dining cars; in April 1939, local authorities were permitted to restrict Jews to specific houses or residential districts.

3. The concentration of all significant political affairs relating to "Jewish questions" in the hands of the SS organs, and the liquidation of Jewish institutions.

On November 9, 1938, Hermann GÖRING had succeeded in obtaining from Hitler authorization to deal with all Jewish political affairs. This enabled him, on January 24, 1939, to appoint Reinhard HEYDRICH as chief of the ZENTRALSTELLE FÜR JÜDISCHE AUSWANDERUNG (Central Office for Jewish Emigration), which in practice gave the SS the power of decision on all matters affecting the Jews. In legislative terms, this situation was expressed in the *Zehnte Verordnung zum Reichsbürgergesetz* (Tenth Implementation Decree under the Reich Citizenship Law) of July 4, 1939, which provided for the establishment of the Reichsvereinigung der Juden in Deutschland (Reich Association of Jews in Germany). This organization, responsible for the organization and implementation of emigration and all related matters, as well as for separate Jewish education and social welfare, was under the supervision and control of Heydrich in his capacity as chief of the Sicherheitspolizei (Security Police) and SD (Sicherheitsdienst; Security Service).

Even prior to the outbreak of war, German Jews were trapped in a legislative net that, by the sheer number of its component parts as well as by its single-mindedness, had no precedent in the history of the treatment of minorities. When war broke out, the existing regulations were extended in every possible direction and tightened up. Jews were forbidden to leave their residences after 8:00 p.m. (September 1, 1939); their radio sets were confiscated (September 20, 1939); their food rations were reduced (December 7, 1939), as were their other rations (January 23, 1940); their purchases were restricted to limited hours and to certain stores; their telephones were taken away (July 19, 1940). From the beginning of the war, the Jews were put on forced labor, with none of the provisions of labor legislation applicable to them. As of September 19, 1941, they had to wear the Jewish BADGE in public and, with a few exceptions, were not permitted to use public transportation. On October 23 of that year, Jewish emigration was prohibited.

The "FINAL SOLUTION"—launched in Germany with two transports of Jews to the east in October 1941—was reflected inside the Reich by the enactment of regulations that had the sole purpose of depriving the Jews of the last of their possessions, of discriminating against them in every possible way, and of taking from them whatever rights they still had left. The Jews who were deported to the east automatically lost their German citizenship (November 25, 1941). At the end of June 1942, the remaining Jewish schools were closed down. Germans who maintained friendly contacts with Jews ran the risk of having to spend three months in a concentration camp (October 24, 1941); German hairdressers were no longer permitted to attend to Jews (May 12, 1942); and Jews were no longer allowed to keep "German" house pets. The final anti-Jewish law, dated July 1, 1943, provided that when a Jew died, his estate would be forfeited to the Reich.

In the countries allied with Germany, or conquered and occupied by it, the extent and severity of anti-Jewish legislation depended on the regime and on the political and military pressure exerted by Germany—or, conversely, on the degree to which the country could convince Germany to respect its status under international law. Thus, after the annexation of Austria on March 13, 1938, no time was lost in applying Nazi racial legislation to Austria. The same applied, even more keenly and ruthlessly, to the Protectorate of BOHEMIA AND MORAVIA and the GENERAL-GOUVERNEMENT, the residual Polish "state," whose territory, as soon as it was seized, was used for the harshest and most brutal anti-Jewish measures, which were passed months and even years before they were applied in the Reich itself.

In the countries that were militarily defeated—France, the Netherlands, Luxembourg, Norway, Yugoslavia (Serbia and Croatia), and Greece—the local German military commander or the puppet regime generally introduced legal measures defining who was to be regarded as a Jew and eliminating Jews from the country's economic life. This also occurred in states allied with Germany (Italy, Slovakia, Bulgaria, Romania, and Hungary), although in such cases the Reich had to exert varying degrees of pressure to overcome the resistance shown by most of these governments. The only country under German control that enacted no anti-Jewish legislation was Denmark, whose situation and status saved it from German pressure, and which also succeeded in saving most of its Jewish population when the Germans finally resolved to deport that country's Jews in July 1943.

[See also Bernheim Petition; Entjudung; Law and Judiciary in Nazi Germany; Nuremberg Laws; Statut des Juifs.]

BIBLIOGRAPHY

Adam, U. D. *Judenpolitik im Dritten Reich*. Düsseldorf, 1972.

Adam, U. D. "An Overall Plan for Anti-Jewish Legislation in the Third Reich." *Yad Vashem Studies* 11 (1976): 33–55.

Hilberg, R. *The Destruction of the European Jews*. 3 vols. New York, 1985.

Schleunes, K. A. *The Twisted Road to Auschwitz: Nazi Policy toward German Jews, 1933–1939*. Urbana, Ill., 1970.

Walk, D., ed. *Das Sonderrecht für die Juden im NS-Staat*. Heidelberg, 1981.

UWE ADAM

ANTISEMITIC FILMS. *See* Films, Nazi Antisemitic.

ANTISEMITISM (Ger., *Antisemitismus*). The term "antisemitism," denoting opposition to and hatred of Jews, became widely accepted from the end of the 1870s. Principally it referred to the views at the core of the anti-Jewish political trends that appeared throughout Europe in the period following the Emancipation of the Jews in the nineteenth century. These were sociopolitical movements with nationalist and racist concepts, which placed opposition to Jews and to the threat which the Jews allegedly posed at the center of their outlook and activities. With the passage of time, "antisemitism" came to denote hatred of Jews in all its forms, throughout history.

The causes of antisemitism, as well as its enduring nature and intensity, are based primarily on the religious and spiritual creed of Judaism and on the role played by Jews in the economy and other spheres of life in the Western world. Furthermore, through the centuries the term "Jew" has been associated with concepts, stereotypes, images, and calumnies that together formed a negative composite image on both the conscious and the emotional level, often almost without any relationship to Jewish society as it really was.

Many believe that the principal roots and causes of antisemitism lie in the confrontation and antagonism between Christianity and Judaism. According to this view, the antipathy to Jews that existed in the Greco-Roman world, based on Jewish monotheism and different life-style, was of marginal and temporary significance, and it is from Christianity that antisemitism derives its real force and its continuity. The essence of the conflict between the two religions, which have a common root, is mainly theological, grounded in the issue of Jesus as the Messiah, and in the place of Judaism and the Jews in the Old and New Testaments. The Christian church ascribes to the Jews as such the guilt of deicide, and the inferior status to which Christianity relegated the Jews was interpreted not only as an expression of Christianity's superiority, but also as proof of its veracity, of the "victory of the Church over the Synagogue." Within these components of Christian dogma are to be found some of the bases of what became the cornerstones of antisemitism. The guilt ascribed to the Jews was a collective guilt; not only the Jews who lived at the time of Jesus' crucifixion were

A Hungarian antisemitic poster. The text reads: "Brother! If you want to have a change, join and fight with us, the Arrow Cross Party. Our leader is Count Sándor Festetics. Our district leader is István Fehér. The center: Szeged."

deemed guilty, but all the seed of Israel, for ever and ever. The distinction made between Christians, seen as personifying God's truth and mercy and representing the true Israel, and the Jews, seen as heretics wallowing in sin, developed into simplistic folk motifs in which the Jew is the embodiment of evil, the schemer and bearer of harm and disaster —that is, he is linked to and endowed with demonic powers.

In time the anxieties and fears, as well as the stereotypical image of the Jews, entered the folklore of Christian peoples, their cultural legacy, their literature, and their education, and were no longer mere components of religious thought but part of the general cultural background of Western society. Some of these concepts became rooted in antisemitism and accompanied it in all its forms.

First, the wrongdoing of an individual Jew is not the manifestation of a personal flaw but an expression of the negative characteristics of all Jews, and the responsibility for such individual wrongdoing falls on all Jews. Second, the Jew is *eo ipso* to be suspected as having a hand in natural disasters, epidemics, and other crises, and there is no need to look for a rational explanation or pertinent evidence to prove his complicity in such events. Third, the Jews are a closed and unified community that formulates rules of morality and ethical standards for its own kind, different from those for outsiders. Out of the immense quantity and great variety of writings composed by the Jewish people in the course of its long history—sometimes in a spirit of openness and tolerance and sometimes reflecting the impact of outside pressure—the antisemites extracted those elements (especially from Talmudic literature) that could be misrepresented as proving Jewish hatred of and alienation from non-Jews, and identified as characterizing the Jews. Fourth, the Jews despise physical work, especially farming, and worship money and moneylending for interest; their role in human society is parasitic and unproductive. In some European languages the term "Jew" is synonymous with cheating and the extraction of usurious interest.

Modern antisemitism is a by-product of ideological and social developments during the period of the Enlightenment and the rise of the middle classes. In revolutionary FRANCE the "Jewish question" arose not as a separate issue but in connection with the now-accepted universalistic principle that equal civil rights should be granted to all men, regardless of religion or origin. In discussions in the National Assembly of France on the question of granting equal civil rights to Jews, the argument was raised that these rights should be denied to the Jews because they were not only a religious entity but a nation. Even the most ardent advocate of equal civil rights for Jews, Count Stanislas de Clermont-Tonnerre, declared, in December 1789, that "Jews should be given nothing as a nation, but everything as individuals." In the time of Napoleon, the questions put to the Sanhedrin (1807), a Jewish assembly convened in France by the emperor, were meant to inquire into Jewish observance and to ascertain whether the commandments of the Jewish religion stood in opposition to loyal citizenship and integration into the French nation. It is quite true that the granting of civil rights to Jews also posed difficult dilemmas and caused fierce arguments within the Jewish community, involving as it did the surrender by the Jews of the autonomous social frameworks that for many generations had been the foundation of the separate Jewish community, and the surrender of juridical and legal decisions according to Jewish law (halakha), the Sabbath as the day of rest, kosher food, and marriage within the Jewish community.

There were significant differences, however, between the granting of civil rights to Jews in France and the United States, and the process of the Jewish emancipation in GERMANY. In the United States, independence and the structure of national life were predicated on severance from the past, on founding the new nation on the basis of equality, and on the separation of church and state, which placed religion in a category that existed alongside the state structure. The different ethnic and national groups, living in a society that allowed much room for pluralism and recognized the right of entities to follow unique and diversified lines of development, were able to integrate into the national body and become partners in it.

This pluralism, to be sure, did not imply a partnership among equals, and from the first the white Anglo-Saxon Protestants dominated. The founders of the United States and their descendants determined the national challenges and norms of behavior and retained in their own hands the central positions of authority and the key economic positions. The problem of slavery confronted the American nation and society, and in its wake the problem of the blacks and the path toward its solution was strewn with internal strife and divisiveness. At times of turmoil, as during the Civil War or when the loss of hegemony by the ruling class and threats to its norms seemed to be in the offing, portents of antisemitism or restrictions on immigration (that is, quotas) appeared. Such a time of turmoil was the fateful period between the two world wars, when an anti-Jewish tendency appeared on the scene that had grave ramifications for the destiny of the Jews in Europe. Men of stature and influence in American culture, for example Henry Adams and Henry James, expressed antisemitic views in the face of the rapid urbanization and changes in American society that followed the Civil War. The noted anthropologist Madison Grant, in his book *The Passing of the Great Race* (1916), openly claimed that the flooding of the United States by great numbers of weak, broken, and mentally deficient people of all races, from the lowest strata of society in the Mediterranean countries and the Balkans to the wretched multitudes from the ghettos of Poland, endangered the American way of life and the "Nordic" racial structure of the people whose ancestors had founded America.

ŻYD
TO OSZUST
jedyny Twój wróg

SIEKANINA

CHLEB

MLEKO

Stań! Przeczytaj widzu miły,
Jak Cię żydy osaczyły.
Zamiast mięsa szczura sieka.
Brudnej wody da do mleka.
Roszczyn ciasta z robakami.
Ugniatany jest nogami.

Nazi antisemitic poster in Polish, "The JEW is a swindler. Your only enemy." The tags read (from top to bottom): Meat, Water, Milk, Bread. The text reads: "Stop, dear reader, and see how the Jews cheat you. Instead of meat he [the Jew] grinds a rat; adds filthy water to the milk; and kneads the worm-infested dough with his feet."

After World War I, Henry Ford contributed his money and influence to further the distribution of the PROTOCOLS OF THE ELDERS OF ZION in the United States, and the book *The International Jew*, which appeared under his name, helped spread the ideas contained in the *Protocols* throughout the world. American antisemitism often took the form of social separation and rejection—the refusal to accept Jews into exclusive clubs and certain hotels, and the blocking of their paths to senior posts and leading positions in certain companies. Antisemitism was keenly felt in the United States during the twentieth century and was influenced from outside by various forces, including the Nazis. It continued to be felt keenly until after the end of World War II, but it never took on a generally brutal and violent character, and never led to the passage of restrictive national laws specifically against Jews. Even at the height of the Great Depression in the United States,

whose source was the financial crisis that engendered massive unemployment, the Jews were never blamed for the situation, as had happened more than once in Europe during financial and economic collapses in such countries as France and Germany. Indeed, Jews took an active role in the economic recovery that President Franklin D. ROOSEVELT initiated, and his policies had the effect of broadening the spheres of American life in which Jews could participate. At no time did American antisemitism accrue political power as in Europe. The United States represents the kind of government and culture that, through a process of permutation, evolution, and material progress on a vast scale, has succeeded in integrating masses of people of different ethnic and religious backgrounds and cultures without destroying their identities, without oppression, and without abandoning the principles of democracy.

Germany passed through a process different from either the United States or France. A few of the Germans who tried to institute reforms in the social structure of the German states during the time of Napoleon's conquests supported improvement of the Jews' status. After Napoleon's defeat, however, such changes were regarded as part of the order imposed upon Germany by the enemy, and therefore were neither binding nor popular. The stages in the formation of the German nation were not motivated primarily by the adoption of revolutionary ideas advocating social change, but rather by the desire to unify the different parts of the German people into one strong national body. A prevailing goal was to derive inspiration and ideals from the German past and from spiritual and literary movements such as Romanticism, which embraced the traditions of medieval Germany. Whereas the character of the French and American revolutions allowed breadth of opportunity and belief in the perfectibility of man within the new laws and regimes, developments in Germany tended toward the suppression of outcasts and those who were different. The refusal to bestow equal rights in a single package and the fact that it took several generations before the process was fully accomplished also had a restraining influence, and heightened the unwillingness to accept the equality of the Jews, even when it had been legally granted.

Some well-known German philosophers expressed opposition to the integration of the Jews into the German nation. Among them was Johann Gottlieb Fichte, who enlisted his philosophy for the consolidation of the idea of modern German nationalism. In his view the Jews should be deprived of the right to belong to the German nation. He regarded Christianity as a basic component of German nationalism and asserted that the Jews are a nation within a nation, casting doubt on the possibility of changing the Jews and making them into an organic part of the German people. In Fichte's view, as human beings Jews must be given full rights, but not the privileges of citizenship. He saw only one way to make them worthy of such privileges: "to cut off their heads one night and replace them with new ones, free from all Jewish ideas."

Bruno Bauer, a philosopher and theologian of the Young Hegelian school of thought, published two essays in 1843 advocating that Jews should not be granted emancipation. According to Bauer, who identified with the trend calling for the end of the rule of religion over the thoughts of man, Christianity had arrived at the stage of development in which the state and the public had been freed from the chains of religion. In contrast, Judaism was a static and anachronistic religion, unable to adapt itself to changing times. Accordingly, Jews should not be granted emancipation, or, at least, emancipation should be withheld from them as long as they were not ready to abandon their religious beliefs. In his critique of Bauer, the young Karl Marx opposed the denial of emancipation for Jews. Marx differentiated between political and civil emancipation and human emancipation. The first was one of the distinguishing marks of the new state and freed the citizen from the yoke of state religion, a liberation that would also affect the Jews. The second was a higher state whose purpose it was to do away with the alienation and inequality that divide human groups from one another, especially because of the unequal distribution of wealth. With regard to progress toward full human emancipation, apart from equality as citizens, Marx viewed the Jews as an obstacle belonging entirely to the past; for him, Judaism and its commandments were egotistical. Through the Jew (and also by other means), money became material and gained control over the Christian people. Marx's conclusion was that "the social emancipation of the Jew is the emancipation of society from the Jew."

Frenchmen of the generation after the Revolution who had a radical socialist outlook, such as Charles Fourier, Alphonse Toussenel, and Pierre-Joseph Proudhon, were disappointed in the Revolution for not solving the troubling problems of society, and advocated diverse concepts. Some called for living in communes or cooperative communities (Fourier), while others had anarchic tendencies (Proudhon). Most, however, saw the main evil in the lack of equality in wealth and in the power of capital. Proudhon came out strongly against wealth that was not the product of a man's direct labor, but rather came from the exploitation of fellow men. He did not distinctly define the Jews, but the terms "nation" and "race" in references to Jews appear in his writings, and he saw in them the power behind the inequality and exploitation of society. In his view, "we are given into the hands of the Jews for good or for evil." The Jews, he said, are characterized by their unproductive parasitism, and a world plot connects them in the pursuit of their aims. Toussenel, who belonged to the school of Fourier and did not deal much with the subject of society, excelled in unbridled hatred of the Jews, writing a book titled *The Jews: Kings of the Period.*

From the time of the Congress of Vienna (1815) until the granting of full emancipation to the Jews (1871), expressions of antisemitism never disappeared in Germany. In 1819 the country was swept by the "Hep! Hep!" disturbances (the source of the cry is not fully clear), which caused material and physical damage, but not loss of life. Violently anti-Jewish writings continued to appear, such as those of Hartwig Hundt (known as Hundt-Radowsky), who called for the deportation or destruction of the Jews. Nor was there any lack of demagogues who advocated that the Jews return to their ghettos, wear a special badge, and pay special taxes. Even among the liberals who advocated the improvement of society, national unity, and changes in the government, there were severe critics of Jews

Nazi antisemitic poster in Polish, "Soviet Pyramid." The workers and peasants at the base of the pyramid are crushed by the Soviet army men above them, who, in turn, support the Jewish "bankers" conferring with Stalin.

and Judaism. Their accusations were based on analysis of the phenomena and characteristics ascribed to the Jews; the conclusions they arrived at sometimes generated wide repercussions, and in general constituted an attempt to halt the process of emancipation. The dominant personality and influence among them was the Heidelberg theologian Eberhard-Heinrich Paulus. Paulus engaged in a debate with Gabriel Riesser, a Jewish intellectual and ardent fighter for emancipation who played an important role in the Pan-German Parliament, held in Frankfurt during the revolutions of 1848–1849. According to Riesser, the Jews were a religious group similar to other religious groups. Paulus, how-

ever, saw Christianity as a religion that brings the believer to moral behavior, whereas Judaism is based on cult and on mechanical and abased ceremonies. He would grant equal rights only on condition that the Jewish commandments be abrogated. Paulus also maintained that Christian messianism had a universal appeal, whereas for the Jews messianism meant national salvation.

Notwithstanding these negative views, this period was marked by progressive and continuous evolution toward emancipation. The breaking up of the corporative frameworks, the desire to establish a unified German state, and developments in the economy and culture all contributed to this trend. Jews who left the ghettos achieved significant success in finance (the best-known example is the house of Rothschild) and in intellectual endeavors. Personalities like Heinrich Heine and the essayist and publicist Karl Ludwig Borne, although converts to Christianity, were influenced by Judaism in their creativity. An integral part of the progression toward equality was the abrogation of various prohibitions, such as those that forbade Jews to live in certain places or that limited them to certain professions. In 1830 the *Landtage* (state parliaments) enacted liberating laws, and a decisive stage was reached in the discussions and conclusions at the Pan-German Parliament. Jews and many gentiles believed that equality and the integration of the Jews into the German nation were inevitable and only a matter of time, and that the voices of the opponents and vilifiers, in the words of Borne, were no more than the last lingering shadows of the Middle Ages that were seeking to obscure—in vain—the dawn of a new age.

During the 1870s the granting of equal citizenship and legal rights to Jews was achieved throughout western and central Europe. With the completion of the cycle of emancipation, which appeared to signal general agreement for the integration of the Jews into the nation, antisemitism paradoxically appeared in a new form, which would bring disaster upon the Jews. It was not the antisemitism of the opponents of emancipation, even though that opposition, with its ancillary argumentation and demagoguery, was a factor in keeping antisemitism in the public eye. Neither was it a question of disappointment at the "reform" of the Jews (that is, at the attempt to end their isolation and wean them away from religious tradition, which many regarded as a precondition for emancipation), even though many who felt that improvements in the Jewish situation would lead to a general desertion from Judaism found their expectations unfulfilled.

The antisemitism in its new form, as it emerged from the 1870s, moved the allegations against the Jews and the concept of their innate disability into the national, and indeed the universal, social and political sphere. The Jews ceased being a separate category, judged through their behavior and deeds; the new antisemitism (the old antisemitism in its new guise) became a general ideology, a *Weltanschauung* with its own existence and at times without a real connection to Jews or Jewish society. It claimed to clarify the complex and troubling problems of modern man and to reveal the sources of economic crisis and poverty, of political conflicts, of societal ferment and war, and, in fact, of all the sicknesses that trouble mankind. The old antisemitism, in the view of the advocates of the new version, had been merely an impulsive emotion, whereas the new antisemitism was regulated and rational, based on objective scientific analysis that discovered the Jewish role in society. The very name of antisemitism, with which the advocates of the new version chose to define their ideology, was meant to emphasize the difference between it and earlier Jew-hatred. The name "antisemitism," which was taken from the Greek, was also intended to endow the ideology with a sort of scientific basis. In actuality, antisemitism was never directed against other "Semites," such as the Arabs, but only against the Jews. The new version of antisemitism was destined, in the twentieth century, to play a major and destructive role in the lives of Jews and all mankind. The German scholar Reinhard Rürup has stated that "Germany is the cradle of both the movement and the term antisemitism," from which they spread through countries in western, central, and eastern Europe. The question of whether one type of antisemitism spread generally, or whether indigenous varieties sprouted in each locality,

has yet to be answered conclusively. It is reasonable to assume, however, that both general external and particular internal factors led to its spread.

It may be asked whether there was any connection between the early antisemitism, which from the mid-nineteenth century until the 1870s was marked by a significant retreat, and the antisemitism that emerged in Europe and became one of the dominant elements in the political, economic, and social struggle from the 1870s onward. Some have addressed themselves to this issue, such as the philosopher Jean-Paul Sartre, who tried to understand the meaning of the new antisemitism of the years from 1870 to 1944. He set forth his ideas in *Réflexions sur la question juive* (1946; published in English as *Antisemite and Jew*, 1965). Sartre wrote that the essence of antisemitism is not grounded in historical fact relating to the Jews, but in the concept that the forces of history have created for themselves of the Jew. He emphasized that it is not the antisemite's personal experience with Jews that evokes his hatred toward them, but rather his tendency to see the source of his own personal failings in his abstract perception of Jews. Psychologists explain this type of antipathy in times of stress as a projection of the frustration of the modern anonymous masses and the consequences of this frustration on an object outside their circle. The Jew is the available scapegoat and meets these basically paranoid needs.

Hannah Arendt severed the new antisemitism from its past and claimed that in modern times, the Jews lost the support of rulers and protective regimes during and after the stage of the formation and acceptance of nationalism. As a result, the Jews were left with only the prop of money, which caused antipathy and left them vulnerable to attack. The importance Arendt ascribes to the Jewish role in the creation of the new antisemitism is schematic and simplistic and is not difficult to refute.

It is clear that even if the components of antisemitism in its new form are diverse and emanate from a new viewpoint, the old characterization of the Jew and the accompanying stereotypes have both played a part in the way that individuals and society as a whole conceive of the Jew. Moreover, even before the advent of political and racial antisemitism in Europe, the antisemitic factions, organizations, and claims, which at first had only a marginal influence, contained the potential to accrue power and momentum.

An important element in the new antisemitism is the identification of the Jew with modernism, capitalism, and urbanization. Social strata that were harmed by the swift changes in Germany during the last decades of the nineteenth century, as well as religious fundamentalists and conservatives, saw in modernization, capitalism, and urbanization a break away from tradition, the destruction of the traditional way of life, and the abolition of the framework that provided Germany with stability and its essential uniqueness. The Jews were regarded as the pioneers of change and the breakdown in tradition, and were seen as the principal beneficiaries of the new system. This found expression in the nationalist political *völkisch* movement, whose leading representatives opposed the industrialism and secularism that characterize modernity and that, in their view, undermine the foundations of the spiritual and cultural uniqueness of the German people. In the writings of advocates of the *völkisch* movement, much responsibility, or even the main responsibility, for undermining the German way of life can be ascribed to the Jews. The well-known biblical and Near Eastern scholar Paul Lagarde, who stood fast by his religious views and who hated liberalism, saw in the Jews a foreign and unifying force that bore within itself the germ of decay. In his view, "with germs one should not argue"; rather, they must be destroyed. Lagarde did not put forth a fully developed racist concept, but in his writings and in his refusal to consider conversion a solution to the "Jewish problem" can be seen the seeds of racism. One of his disciples, Ludwig Schemann, disseminated in Germany the ideas of the French racist Count Joseph-Arthur de Gobineau.

Another *völkisch* thinker was the cultural scholar Julius Langbehn, who was a generation younger than Lagarde and was active after the emancipation. Langbehn was an unstable megalomaniac who often changed his place of residence and area of study, yet he possessed great talent and intellectual curiosity. At one point he decided to devote himself to repairing the image of German culture, and his publications on the subject were widely read. Langbehn was willing to come to terms with traditional Jews, but he viciously lambasted the assimilated Jews. He opposed conversion, which he saw as merely a Jewish attempt at camouflage.

The challenge to emancipation focused on the negative characteristics and influence of Jews who became Germans by their own national self-identification. According to antisemitic arguments, these Jews were not satisfied with equality and did not integrate quietly into a working society. Instead, they aspired to take over wide areas of important but nonproductive branches of the economy, and to penetrate into science, art, literature, and the press, where they caused damage. According to their critics, the Jews destroyed good taste in Germany by engaging in imitation and dilettantism. Since their creativity was not deep-rooted and since they had no real contact with their new surroundings, they turned to radicalism and nihilism, which undermine patriotism and the national resilience. Even a composer of the stature of Richard Wagner, who during the revolutions of 1848–1849 was a radical liberal, changed his views; in his essay *Das Judentum in der Musik* (The Jews in Music), he accused the Jews of lacking original creativity and destroying artistic taste. Wagner's racism never reached full formulation. It was his son-in-law, Houston Stewart CHAMBERLAIN, who gave RACISM its character as a crystallized concept and lived to have contact with Hitler. Eventually, other intellectuals were harnessed to serve racism. Among them were scholars as eminent as the Nobel prize–winning physicist Philipp LENARD, who distinguished between "German physics" and "Jewish physics," the latter represented by Albert EINSTEIN and his theories.

The claim that the Jews were "a nation within a nation" was expanded. The more moderate of the new antisemites complained that the Jews had not fulfilled expectations and had not ended their national separatism. They did not identify unreservedly with the nation in the midst of which they lived, and they continued to maintain ties of communication and solidarity with Jews in other lands. According to the extreme antisemites, the Jews have an international leadership that functions in a secret fashion, similar to that of the FREEMASONS, intentionally entering the host nation and deliberately weaving a plot to take over other nations and eventually the entire world. The methods with which the Jews work, united in their secret international plot, are diverse and changing, but the Jews are not particular about the methods they use and keep their eyes on their final goal, of imposing their dominion over all mankind. In pursuit of this goal the Jews have concentrated capital in their hands and have turned it into a tool to promote their machinations. They have sought to inculcate political and social ideas in the guise of capitalism, liberalism, and socialism—ideologies that lead to national disintegration and direct men toward false universalistic concepts in the spirit of Judaism. Substantially there is no difference between these ideologies, because all of them are extensions of the one strategic plan of the Jews. Not only the traditional Jews but also the modern assimilated Jew is subject to the secret leadership, according to the antisemites, and supposed internal differences of opinion among the Jews are only a pretense to mislead non-Jewish society; the Talmudic dictum that the gentile world is to be hated must be followed by all Jews.

Blood libels (the accusation that Jews kill gentiles to obtain their blood for Jewish rituals) became numerous in the countries of western, central, and eastern Europe. Most infamous was the 1882 blood libel in the Hungarian village of Tisza Eszlar. During the trial the name of August Rohling, a professor of theology from Prague, also gained world attention. In 1871 Rohling published *Der Talmudjude* (The Talmud Jew) and offered to appear before a court to prove, using Talmudic sources, his claim that Jews use blood for ritual purposes. When it was demonstrated in Rohling's presence that he did not know how to read Talmudic sources and that his words were nothing but an evil libel, Rohling was forced to back down. As happens in such libels, however, sensational rumors proved to be hardier than the truth. The blood libel of which Mendel Beilis was accused in Russia and for which he was tried in 1913 also received worldwide publicity. Eventually the judges freed Beilis, but as in the Tisza Eszlar case, blood libel as such was not categorically denounced as a baseless invention.

According to extreme antisemites, a Jewish leadership working deep underground was orchestrating a long-range plan. At times certain institutions and organizations were said to be manifestations of this leadership. Among them were the Alliance Israélite Universelle, a Jewish philanthropic organization based in France that was devoted to spreading enlightened education to Jews in the Balkans, Asia, and North Africa. The Zionist Congresses were also tied to the leadership. In 1868 a novel, *Biarritz*, was published by Hermann Goedsche, under the pseudonym Sir John Redcliffe (Retcliffe). Its first chapter describes a secret meeting of the twelve Jewish tribes at night in the Prague Jewish cemetery. There, with the aura of an esoteric ceremony accompanied by prayer, oaths, and fire, those present survey the progress made by the Jews in their efforts to take over the Christian world, and formulate their future plans. This chapter went through different variations, all of which were presented as authentic. Redcliffe, who in reality was a post-office clerk, was described as a courageous man who had uncovered a Jewish plot that threatened the entire Christian world. In 1871 in Basel, Osman Bey's pamphlet *The Jewish Conquest of the World* was published, putting forth similar fabricated ideas.

Other variations on these themes appeared in different forms, but the version that became most important and influential, and that still continues to exert influence, is the *Protocols of the Elders of Zion*. The *Protocols*, which were disseminated in Russia from the beginning of the twentieth century, were a transparent plagiarism of a parody of Napoleon III by Maurice Joly, a long-forgotten French author. They were initially used by the Russian secret police to deflect political unrest toward the Jews. Remarkably, the *Protocols*, which were taken to the West by Russian emigrés at the time of the Bolshevik

An illustration from *Trau keinem Fuchs auf grüner Heid und keinem Jud bei seinem Eid* (Don't Trust a Fox in the Chicken Coop or a Jew at His Word), a children's book by Elvira Bauer published in Germany by Stürmer Verlag in 1936. [A Living Memorial to the Holocaust—Museum of Jewish Heritage, New York]

Revolution, reached Germany and other lands and were accepted by many as the truth. Even the London *Times* tended for a while to give credence to the *Protocols*, although later it exposed them as a forgery.

The success of the *Protocols* and similar works can be better understood against the background of the widely held accusation that Jews were among the leaders of the wave of revolutions that swept Europe during and after World War I; in particular, that they were among the leaders of the Bolshevik Revolution. The participation of Jews in these revolutions was prominent: personalities such as Leon Trotsky in Russia, Béla Kun in Hungary, and Rosa Luxemburg and Kurt Eisner in Germany were born Jews, although their politics and actions estranged them from Judaism. Nevertheless, their Jewish origins and those of other revolutionaries were emphasized everywhere, and aroused suspicions among many who had not previously been antisemitic.

Racial ideas also played a part in secular political antisemitism. The earlier vague antisemitism was superseded by claims supposedly based on objective scientific criteria. With the aid of caricatures projecting the ideas of ugliness, greed, and promiscuity, the image of the ugly Jew became established. The division of mankind by race, for which Gobineau had sought a basis, was originally conceived to give a foundation to the idea that the aristocracy, which had been displaced by the French Revolution, was really superior.

These ideas did not take root in France, but they did succeed in Germany. Those who hoped to divert dislike of Jews into a racial track found a sympathetic chord among many Germans. The Jews were virtually the only ethnic group dispersed throughout Europe on which an alien racial identity was pinned. The racial perspective allowed a mark to be placed on the Jew after all the other signs of stereotypical differences had virtually disappeared; the Jew now dressed like a German or Frenchman, behaved like a German or Frenchman, spoke impeccable German or French, and became a patron of music, art, and literature. The Jew-haters felt the need to transfer their hatred to an intangible and mysterious sphere, and racism fit the bill; if the Jew had characteristics that could not be changed, then it was justifiable to refuse to grant him equality. When the evil in the Jew, in all its aspects, was based on biology and blood, there was nothing different that was visible or could be erased; the cause was deeper. This held true for all Jews, whether traditional, assimilated, or converted to Christianity. In fact, the danger was seen as greater when Jews had acquired the language and outer appearance of Germans and had professedly left their own religion and race than when their Jewishness was transparent to all.

It is not incidental that an antisemite like Theodor Fritsch, who was known as a professional and eclectic antisemite (that is, one who was ready to adopt any and every reason or idea that would further his cause), in the end became a racist. Patriotism, which in the Second Reich (1871 to 1918) became strident nationalism, embodied by blood, war, and steel, reinforced by rapid industrialization, and translated into imperial designs, derided and detested tolerance and the values of equality. Heinrich von Treitschke, the ambitious historian and publicist of the Second Reich, who himself was a liberal in the days when liberalism flourished, claimed that the Jews were not completely loyal to Germany. He used the phrase "Die Juden sind unser Ungluck" ("The Jews are our misfortune"). His young pupil Heinrich von Class, who was active in reactionary right-wing circles during the Weimar Republic, went a step further, adopting racism and calling for the passage of discriminatory laws against the Jews.

Adolf Stoecker, a lay preacher who rose from humble beginnings to become the imperial court chaplain, was saturated with an anti-Judaism that was rooted in religion, and he imparted a public dimension to anti-Judaism. Stoecker tried to establish a Christian Socialist party to stop the growing Social Democrats, but when religious arguments did not work, he turned to antisemitism as a means of garnering mass support. Stoecker's antisemitism was still somewhat restrained, but that of Eugen Dühring, an eccentric philosopher with his own personal theory of socialism and a critic of the Christian church, was not restrained in the least. Dühring spoke clearly of a Jewish race that was totally evil. He advocated the abrogation of the Emancipation and the ousting of Jews from various spheres of life, and, finally, he viewed the deportation of the Jews as a desirable solution.

In periods of crisis, or in the face of failure or public outbursts of anger, an accusing finger was pointed at the Jews. Such was the case at the time of the *Gründerkrise* (the Founders' Crisis), which followed the prosperity after the victory over France in 1871 and the flow of reparations money; that prosperity led to the growth of speculative investments and profits, which in turn caused a crisis. Jews were at times represented as the cause of a calamity that at the same time struck other countries besides Germany. Men like Otto Glagua, who was among those badly hurt by the financial collapse, were not satisfied with accusing the Jews; they publicly aired the theory that Jews by nature turn to business, capital, and the stock market. In other words, said Glagua, the Jewish role in society is that of an unproductive parasite. Politicians and parties arose that exploited the circumstances and used antisemitism to pave their way to the Reichstag. In 1881, 300,000 people signed a petition calling for the expulsion of Jews from government jobs. During the 1880s in Germany antisemitic congresses were held that supposedly were international, but in reality the only non-Germans in attendance were from the Austro-Hungarian Empire, and their position was dictated by the Germans.

In the 1890s the antisemitic parties in Germany were in a state of decline. However, the right-wing conservative parties incorporated antisemitism as part of their platforms. With signs of defeat in World War I becoming apparent, strident antisemitism again became prominent. During the war, rumors were rife that Jews were not serving at the front but had infiltrated noncombat positions, and military leaders ordered that the matter be checked. Jews were also accused of fostering defeatism in the rear during the revolutionary period of 1918 and 1919. The frustration that came in the wake of the collapse of the war effort, the economic crisis during the Weimar Republic, and the revulsion felt by many toward the republic all engendered anti-Jewish ideas and feelings.

Political antisemitism was not only a German phenomenon but embraced all of Europe, and, as mentioned, it struck roots in France. There, during the last decades of the nineteenth century and the beginning of the twentieth, the Jewish issue was a component of the long debate between the republicans and royalists. The Dreyfus affair of the 1890s is seen as an anti-Jewish campaign that made a profound and stormy imprint on Europe. Eduard Drumont, the author of the book *La France juive* (Jewish France), whose anti-Jewish activities began before the Dreyfus affair and reached their apogee during it, has been appraised by the historian Jacob Katz as having expressed views as extreme and severe as those of the Nazis during the Weimar Republic.

Drumont raised the cry "France for the French." He wrote prolifically, published antisemitic books and newspapers, and was widely read. For a short time he also coordinated the antisemitic faction in the French parliament and led an antisemitic political party. French antisemitism sometimes dovetailed with the anti-Freemasonism that was fostered by the Catholic church. The connection between the Freemasons and the Jews did not exist to the same extent in Germany because there, Jews as a rule had not been admitted to Masonic lodges. Some believe that the reason why antisemitism in France did not reach the level of its German counterpart was that the Jews in France comprised a smaller percentage of the population than in Germany; and when the regions of Alsace

and Lorraine were transferred to Germany after the German victory over France in 1871, a focal point and main arena of French antisemitism disappeared. In France several financial scandals contributed to antisemitism, such as the collapse of the Union Générale bank, which was under the aegis of Catholics and was a competitor of Jewish banks; the collapse of the stock of the Panama Canal company; and several instances of corruption in which Jews as well as some well-known members of the social elite and the regime were involved. However, racial Darwinist ideas were never widely accepted in France. In general, the "Jewish question" was not at the core of any of the powerful political factions. The "Jewish question" in France was often an issue of the differences between Jews: the Jews who had been in France for a long time, were rooted in its culture, and had contributed to the French war effort, as contrasted to recently arrived foreign Jews. The latter were the main object of discrimination and antipathy, especially between the two world wars. Léon Blum, as the leader of the Socialist party, and at times the premier, was a target for incitement and outbursts owing to his Jewish background, yet it is doubtful whether in this period a Jew in Germany could have risen to a similar position. The closest, Walther RATHENAU, who filled various crucial posts in Germany during World War I and whose outlook tended toward the right, was assassinated in 1922, not long after he became Germany's foreign minister.

The situation of Jews in states with one dominant nationality, like Germany and France, must be distinguished from that in states where the Jews were one of many large minorities. In AUSTRIA, the Germans after World War I lost the dominance they had held in the former large Austro-Hungarian Empire, and moreover remained isolated from other Germans. Antisemitism was strong there, with foundations both in popular culture and in a nationalist ideology. In MEIN KAMPF, Adolf HITLER claimed that VIENNA was for him a school in antisemitism. The effective and popular mayor of Vienna, Karl Lueger, was (in the late nineteenth century) the first person of high rank in the Austro-Hungarian Empire who openly expressed antisemitic ideas and knew how to sell them to the Catholic majority. Another antisemitic leader who influenced Hitler, according to the latter's writings, was Georg von Schönerer, an advocate of Pan-Germanism who was close to the nationalist racist concept but whose influence in Austrian politics was limited. Although antisemitism increased and was directed primarily toward Jews who came to Vienna from eastern Europe, it never played an important role in internal Austrian politics or Austrian foreign relations between the two world wars. Antipathy toward the Jews attained a brutal, totally unrestrained expression with the ANSCHLUSS in 1938, and more than one of the Nazi leaders who were extreme in the persecution and murder of the Jews were of Austrian origin.

In HUNGARY, and to some extent in POLAND during the 1860s and 1870s, the trend was to bring the Jews closer to the nationalist movement within the multinational state structure, to make them a part of the population that identified with Hungarian or Polish nationalist aims. In the last decades of the nineteenth century, political antisemitism with an ideological tone increased in both countries. Both had long-standing, brutal, and vulgar antisemitic traditions, as in Germany. In both, Jews constituted a relatively high percentage of the urban population and controlled a significant proportion of trade, finance, and the professions. Since the Jews were considered outsiders, and since they themselves often maintained their uniqueness and separateness from the gentiles (in particular in Poland and ROMANIA), to a certain extent there was in these countries a real conflict or problem with regard to the Jews. The dominant antisemite in Hungary before World War I, Victor Istoczy, defined himself as an advocate of sociopolitical antisemitism, and spoke of "defense" against the Jews. He was in contact with prominent antisemites in Germany and took part in the first antisemitic congress, in Dresden. Istoczy spoke of "racism," but it seems that racism did not play a significant role in his anti-Jewishness.

In Poland during the 1890s a national democratic movement, that of the Endeks, arrived on the scene and adopted a platform emphasizing antisemitism. The party's authoritarian leader and ideologist, Roman Dmowski, was an aggressive antisemite, and at times wielded great influence in the party. As early as 1907 Dmowski called the Jews an ethnic entity that was foreign to the Polish mentality, was not able to assimilate, and was likely to spread foreign and repulsive ways among the Poles. Therefore, he maintained, the assimilation of the Jews, except in a few cases, was not desirable. Later, Dmowski and his circle asserted that the Jews had allied themselves with Poland's historical enemies (Russia, Prussia, and Austria-Hungary) and had derived benefit therefrom. Moreover, he declared, they bore much of the responsibility for Poland's sorry state. In 1912 Dmowski organized an anti-Jewish boycott, and from then on the economic component in political anti-Jewish propaganda—"Jewish Bolshevism"—became more prominent in the party's platform and policy. Between the world wars, antisemitism became a significant component of public and government opinion.

Except for Czechoslovakia, the situation of the Jews deteriorated in the countries of central and eastern Europe that had been created after the end of World War I. Although these states signed minority treaties, it was not within their power to uphold them, especially with regard to protecting the Jews' rights. Moreover, the desire of the largest ethnic group in each state to impose its own stamp on the country harmed all the minorities, and the Jews as a weak minority suffered more than others. The Romanians succeeded in abrogating the rights of Jews in the territories that Romania had annexed, and conducted a fierce anti-Jewish propaganda campaign. During the White Terror in Hungary (1919–1920) the Hungarians avenged themselves on the Jews for their alleged role in the revolution, which was led by Béla Kun. Hungary became the first country to invoke a *numerus clausus* (quota) in institutes of higher education, restricting the number of Jews who could study in them. In Poland, anti-Jewish policy was applied primarily in the economic sphere. The economic difficulties that struck the countries of central and eastern Europe strengthened anti-Jewish attitudes. For the most part, antisemitism in these countries was not racial or biological.

"Der ewige Jude" (The Eternal [or Wandering] Jew), a poster for the 1937 antisemitic exhibition arranged by the Nazis in Munich. The exhibition was also mounted in Vienna, on August 2, 1938. The text of the poster reads: "A large political exhibit in the library building of the Deutsche Museum in Munich from November 8, 1937. Open daily 10:00 to 21:00."

Among other reasons, the deep religiosity prevailing in them did not permit that kind of racist antisemitism to spread, and the relative isolation of the Jews prevented a search for ways of separating them out.

In the second half of the 1930s, after the 1933 Nazi rise to power, open and strident antisemitism received a great boost and legitimation as an acceptable policy. In Hungary and Romania fascist parties with a clear antisemitic tone were active. In Poland the right-wing parties and (after the death of the authoritative leader, Józef Piłsudski) the po-

litical camp in power supported a mass exodus of Jews. The extreme rightist movements wanted to speed up such an exodus by using violence and pogroms. The governing bloc, on the other hand, wanted to achieve this goal by political means. Hungary saw itself as an ally of Germany and a partner in territorial revisionism, and in 1938 and 1939 it passed antisemitic and racial laws. For a while in Romania pillaging, violence, and pogroms took place under government auspices.

The position of these peoples and nations during the period of Nazi rule and occupation is a separate and important chapter. The Poles did not take an active part in the annihilation of the Jews, but the dominant attitude of the population and the underground was one of indifference during the murder of the Jews, most of which, through no fault of the Poles, was carried out on their soil. The Romanians participated actively in the mass murder, but in the last stages of the war they recoiled from handing over Jews for total destruction. In Hungary the situation of the Jews during most of the war years was relatively tolerable, but with the German invasion of Hungary in March 1944 and the beginning of deportations to extermination camps, the Hungarian authorities helped in the work of annihilation, and much of the Hungarian population also played a shameful role.

Russian antisemitism has special characteristics. For centuries Russia was closed off to Jews. Jews were concentrated in the western district, which the tsarist empire had annexed from Poland and Romania. Stringent laws prevented Jews from leaving the area known as the Pale of Settlement to settle in the large cities of central Russia. The authorities attempted to break down Jewish separateness through administrative measures. For a long time antisemitism in Russia was government policy, and only small groups of Jews were permitted to play any part in the nation's economic development. Radical intellectuals viewed the antisemitism of the masses of peasants as a sign of their political awakening. The wave of pogroms that swept Russia during the 1880s, even when initiated not by the government but by extremist organizations close to it, was not opposed by the regime. These developments spurred the emigration of large numbers of Jews from Russia to countries overseas, especially to the United States. Only after the February 1917 revolution were Russian Jews granted equal rights. The wave of emigrés that left Russia after the 1917 revolution contributed to the spread of antisemitic ideas in the countries where they took refuge. Between the two world wars, antisemitism in the Soviet Union was illegal, and therefore hidden. The roles filled by individual Jews in the Soviet regime contributed to a new kind of antisemitism, one with new motives, which during World War II and the Holocaust had a deadly effect in the Nazi-occupied areas of the Soviet Union. In the opinion of some historians, Stalin's campaign against the old Bolsheviks was not free of an anti-Jewish motive.

In Germany, political antisemitism was first and foremost ideological in nature, claiming that the Jew played a key role in the confrontation between universalist philosophies and in current social and political conflicts. The brutality and violence of pogroms and persecutions that marked antisemitism in eastern Europe were not, at the beginning, part of German political antisemitism. However, the future would teach that a theory of racial antisemitism, which did not advocate force but rather spoke of "rational" solutions to the "Jewish question" as an answer to the problems of the nation and the entire world, contained within it sparks that would ignite a raging fire.

The division of people into races seemed to concur with the Darwinian interpretation of natural selection. It led to the conclusion that natural selection in nature (which balances or provides parameters for propagation, and improves through adaptation and survival those better suited to their surroundings) does not play a role in human society only because of artificial human intervention. Such intervention disrupts the process of evolution, which is based on competition and the elimination of the weak and unsuccessful. It is clear that this conclusion clashes with concepts that are rooted in religions ascribing to humans a special status as having been created in God's image.

A major place in the development of racism in Germany belongs to Houston Stewart Chamberlain, who added to it the dimension of historical evolution and the struggle within that evolution. Chamberlain was an Englishman who became Germanized and believed that he had a mission to the German people. According to Chamberlain, the Jews had declined over time. Neither King David nor Jesus was Jewish, and the great achievements ascribed to the Jews had actually been accomplished by gentiles. On the other hand, Chamberlain said, the Germans had developed into the elite Aryan race, and they enjoyed a spiritual singularity that enabled them to create great achievements. Chamberlain's book *Die Grundlagen des 19. Jahrhunderts* (The Foundations of the Nineteenth Century) was written to describe and explain this evolution and the racial struggle conducted throughout history. It was also written to make the Germans aware of the geographic expansion they deserved, and of the enemies surrounding them.

In Germany, racism, more than any other theory (aside from nationalism), was the substance of NATIONAL SOCIALISM. National Socialism did not adopt one anti-Jewish line, while abandoning the others. The authorities of the Third Reich were faced with the challenge of defining who was an Aryan and determining who was a Jew. They never attempted to define a person's race by means of elements in his blood, the shape of his skull or nose, his hair color or body type, and so on, realizing that such criteria would undoubtedly lead to many Nazis being defined as Jews and many Jews being considered pure Aryans. Therefore the Nazis turned to religion as the measurement of race, even though Hitler had claimed many times that the Jews did not constitute a religion but a race, and that it was race which determined their identity as Jews. The religious criteria that were instituted required that a check be made of the religious affiliation of persons who had abandoned Judaism or had intermarried. Some of the MISCHLINGE (people of mixed German and Jewish ancestry) were classified with the Jews, although they belonged to families that were German by any definition.

Long before the Nazi rise to power in Germany, it became clear that providing basic education to the masses and granting them political rights would not automatically strengthen liberalism, democracy, and mutual understanding among men and nations, as liberal and socialist circles had hoped and conservative nationalists had feared. It turned out that the superstitions and prejudices absorbed by popular culture over the course of generations had a firm hold on the people's soul and consciousness. Alongside innovative and progressive trends, another direction began to make headway, which opposed internationalism and socialism and claimed to have found the solution for the problem of the underprivileged in a national framework. This new direction, without being revolutionary in the accepted sense, manifested dynamism—albeit a nationalist dynamism—and the ability to capture and hold the imagination of the people. For the most part, antisemitism was an inseparable or dominant element in that trend and its motivation.

It has not been substantiated that antisemitism affected the entire German nation or even that the majority of Germans adopted an actively antisemitic outlook, and it would be wrong to make such a claim. From the mid-nineteenth century to the 1870s, emancipation and the ideas of liberalism had gained momentum in Germany and had made constant progress (which the antisemites and supporters of the old regime sought to stop). This situation changed, however, during the Second Reich. The liberal movement, which had come to be largely identified with Jews and which protected Jewish rights, weakened. Jews and non-Jews who opposed antisemitism had to organize in order to safeguard the rights already granted, and they were being put more and more on the defensive. The Social Democrats regarded Jew-hatred as an element undermining their ideological basis and found antisemitism to be the "socialism of fools," as the Social Democrat leader, August Bebel, put it. This recognition notwithstanding, the socialist camp tried not to be identified as defending the Jews, a position viewed as unpopular, and socialist propaganda was not above mentioning the connection that existed between Jews and capitalism.

Political antisemitism was a sign of the crisis that struck society and nationalism at the end of the nineteenth and in the first decades of the twentieth century. Countries in which democracy was rooted and flourishing—such as Great Britain, the Netherlands, and the Scandinavian nations—were not hurt much by the various radical movements and by antisemitism. The other countries, however, suffered great turmoil. The interwar period is regarded by many historians as an era in which fascism spread all over Europe. Yet these scholars tend to differentiate between National Socialism, which had antisemitism at the core of its ideology, and fascism in Italy and other countries of western Europe. The latter for a long time rejected antisemitism, and even when they accepted it, did not adopt racism as a main ideological component.

In Germany, the Jews had been asked to give up many elements of their tradition and organizational pattern in order to be worthy of equal rights and integration into German society. As a result, the greater part of German Jewry passed through a profound metamorphosis. The Jews, primarily urbanized and representing only about one percent of the population, adopted religious reforms that did away with many of their commandments and traditions, changed their marriage habits, and significantly reduced their birthrate. Many Jews turned to higher education and the professions to which it led, and tried to excel in them. Certain areas of advancement, however, remained closed to them, such as the officers' corps, and higher posts in the academic field and in the government administration. As a result, many Jews became concentrated in certain professions, including law and medicine, and also turned in significant numbers to the natural sciences, the press, and the arts. The number of German Jews who won Nobel prizes was many times greater than their proportion in the population. The Jews' drive to excel and their disproportionate numbers in some professions made them conspicuous and exposed them to suspicion and hatred. To escape from this hatred and to attain positions from which they were barred, many Jews converted; yet even then they did not cease to be Jews in the searching and watchful eyes of their professional rivals and the Jew-haters. In the opinion of sociologists and demogra-

Antisemitic graffito on a Jewish shopwindow in Germany (1938). The text is written in "pidgin German" to mock the "nonethnic" German Jew. It reads: "Am I not a good German?" [Bildarchiv Preussischer Kulturbesitz]

phers, the Jews of Germany would have disappeared within a few generations through assimilation and a declining birthrate, and it was only the influx of Jews from the east that slowed down this inevitable decline. Politically, most of the German Jews were liberals, and their first preference was for the further development of liberal policies. With the weakening of liberalism in Germany, the Social Democrats became a reliable barrier against antisemitism. Many Jews voted for the Social Democratic Party and supported it, even though they apparently did not fully identify with its ideology, and as a persecuted and besieged group were only looking for a helping hand. German Jews were great patriots, with a profound love for German culture and the German landscape. Even Orthodox Jews, who would never consider giving up their religious principles, were ardent

German patriots. For many Jews, their world was destroyed when Germany turned its back on them and they found out that their love for their country had been a one-sided, unrequited love.

During the Nazi period "anti-Jewishness" became part of an overall outlook, in several ways. First, it was integral to the Nazi ideology, not as just one among many different concepts, but as a central element. Second, it was considered a powerful and effective propaganda weapon, used to explain all the existing inadequacies and failures and to shore up the opposition to the liberal parliamentary regime. Third, with Hitler's rise to power, anti-Jewish racism became a political component of the means employed by the government to implement its policies—of excluding the Jews from social, cultural, and economic life; separating them, insofar as possible, from the rest of the population; and, in the end, getting rid of them altogether in all the lands under German control.

Anti-Jewishness in the Nazi period followed the directives laid down by Hitler in the 1920s. It was not based on an emotional approach and did not take the form of outbursts, but constituted a consistent "rational" policy, grounded in legislation. The Nazi anti-Jewishness did not confine itself to any particular set of charges against Jews but made use of all the many and varied antisemitic calumnies and libels that had been thought up over the generations.

At one stage the Nazi state tried to replace the term "antisemitism" with "anti-Jewishness." This was done both for political reasons ("antisemitism" could be considered to apply to Arabs as well as to Jews) and because Jew-hatred was no longer a separate subject, but a fundamental part of a political ideology. Although this effort did not succeed and the term "antisemitism" remained in use, certain new terms did enter circulation, such as "Jewish blood" and, conversely, "German and related blood." The Nazis took pains not to speak of the export of racism, since according to the principles of the Nazi version of that ideology, the different peoples of Europe would not be promised equality and partnership with the German master race. To the extent that the Nazis did try to disseminate and export antisemitism, they did so in the belief that it would help obscure their long-term goals and deflect public attention abroad from the emerging Nazi threat.

Political antisemitism did not lead directly and inevitably to Nazism, and the Nazi takeover of Germany was not mainly a result of antisemitism. Nazism came to power as a form of German nationalism, aided by the prevailing circumstances of defeat and crisis. Yet antisemitism helped Nazis to gain power and win the hearts of the German masses. Even though the Nazis did not particularly emphasize antisemitism on the eve of their rise to power, it was a well-known element in their creed and action, and was no obstacle to their takeover. Nor did it engender very much opposition from the army, the churches, or German society as a whole.

Between the two world wars antisemitism was on the increase all over Europe, as an ideology and, in some countries, also as a practical policy applied to the Jews. This development derived from the growing influence of the Third Reich and the various fascist movements, and it was particularly strong in the countries of eastern Europe. The democracies did not accept antisemitism—indeed, they opposed it—but they preferred to downplay their disapproval so that their policies and actions would not be interpreted as a defense of persecuted Jews, since in the Nazi period such a "reputation" was unpopular and considered politically detrimental. In general, the Nazi policies against the Jews caused the Nazis only minor damage in the democratic and liberal countries, and except in extreme instances, such as the KRISTALLNACHT pogrom in November 1938, they did not encounter any real opposition. With the outbreak of the war it became clear that the Nazis were not confining their anti-Jewish policies to the territory of Greater Germany. They applied these policies with increasing severity against the Jews in every place they occupied and in every country where they attained political power and ideological influence.

The "FINAL SOLUTION" may be said to have been the all-out implementation of two closely related tendencies in the Nazi party and the Third Reich's ideology and policy: the Nazis' racist anti-Jewish ideology, which regarded the confrontation with the Jews as a struggle in which there could be no compromise; and the conclusion reached by the Nazis that the threat inherent in "Jewish blood" could be removed only by spilling that blood. The dynamics of the anti-Jewish policies and the relentless escalation of the methods applied by the Nazis reached the point where the only means left to be used was indiscriminate mass murder. It was this combination of ideology and its practical outcome that led to the "Final Solution." Undoubtedly, the crystallization of the diabolic plan was facilitated by the climate of resignation to the Third Reich's anti-Jewish policies and, at times, by the approval and collaboration that the Nazis found nearly everywhere they went, even at the stage of the "Final Solution" itself.

After World War II antisemitism was

An antisemitic parade (late 1930s) in Vienna. Twenty thousand National Socialists demon-strated against the treaties of St. Germain and Versailles and the "Jewish" press.

greatly weakened in the West, and the Western churches on many occasions admitted the fatal mistake they had made in cultivating the Christian aspects of antisemitism. In the Soviet Union and its satellites, however, strong expressions of antisemitism recurred a few years after the end of the war, and in times of crisis and change antisemitism was once again employed as a tactical tool. Not only was this a denial of the ideas and principles that the Soviet Union and socialism in general had adopted, but it was also a strange paradox. The state and the system that radical antisemites had claimed were a Jewish creation were now turning to the cynical and brutal exploitation of antisemitism. Over the years antisemitism began to appear under the guise of "anti-Zionism." The United Nations gave this development its blessing in a resolution, passed in November 1975, that equated Zionism with racism. The denial of the Holocaust (*see* HOLOCAUST, DENIAL OF THE) is also essentially a form of antisemitism, seeking to eradicate the truth in order to permit the resurrection of Jew-hatred as it existed in the past. There have been expressions of antisemitism in countries that have no Jews living in them; one such example was the widespread dissemination of antisemitic literature in Japan in the 1980s.

It is difficult to know or to predict whether, despite these various manifestations, antisemitism is in a process of decline or is only hibernating, waiting for some trauma to strike the world that will revive it and once again make it a powerful factor. Above all, it is clear that the struggle against antisemitism requires eternal vigilance and counter-action, not only to ensure that the genie does not escape from the bottle, but also to excise this disease from the body of mankind.

BIBLIOGRAPHY

Almog, S., ed. *Antisemitism through the Ages.* Oxford, 1988.

Davies, A. T. *Antisemitism and the Christian Mind: The Crises of Conscience after Auschwitz.* New York, 1969.

Ganger, J. G. *The Origins of Anti-Semitism.* New York, 1985.

Katz, J. *From Prejudice to Destruction: Antisemitism, 1700–1933.* Cambridge, Mass., 1980.

Massing, P. W. *Rehearsal for Destruction: A Study of Political Anti-Semitism in Imperial Germany.* New York, 1949.

Parkes, J. *Antisemitism.* Chicago, 1964.

Pinson, K. S., ed. *Essays on Antisemitism.* New York, 1946.

Poliakov, L. *Suicidal Europe, 1870–1933.* Vol. 4 of *The History of Anti-Semitism.* New York, 1985.

Pulzer, P. G. *The Rise of Political Anti-Semitism in Germany and Austria.* London, 1988.

Rürup, R. *Emancipation und Antisemitismus.* Göttingen, 1975.

Zimmerman, M. *Wilhelm Marr, the Patriarch of Anti-Semitism.* Oxford, 1986.

ISRAEL GUTMAN

ANTONESCU, ION (1882–1946), Romanian general and statesman; ruler of ROMANIA from 1940 to 1944. In World War I, Antonescu distinguished himself as a member of the general staff, and in 1933 he was appointed its chief. In 1937 and 1938 he was minister of defense in the cabinet headed by Octavian GOGA and Alexandru CUZA, the first Romanian cabinet that was outspokenly antisemitic. Antonescu did not belong to the antisemitic fascist movement headed by Corneliu Codreanu, but he did act as liaison between that movement and the traditional political establishment.

The fall of France in the summer of 1940 shattered Romania's political status, and it was forced to cede large parts of its territory to the Soviet Union, Hungary, and Bulgaria. During this severe national crisis—which threatened Romania's continued existence as an independent state—Antonescu was ap-pointed prime minister by Prince Michael. Prior to this appointment, he had been confined on King Carol II's orders to a monastery after blaming the king and the military establishment for not preparing the Romanian army for war.

Upon being appointed prime minister, on September 5, 1940, Antonescu forced King Carol to abdicate in favor of his son Michael. Antonescu, however, was the real ruler. Together with Horia SIMA, chief of the IRON GUARD, Antonescu established the National Legionary Government, whose declared purpose was to draw close to Germany and Italy and to purge Romania of "foreign elements" and "foreign influence." Soon after assuming his post, he met with Hitler and gained his trust and esteem. Fearing that the Red Army was planning to seize the part of Moldavia still left in Romania's hands, Antonescu called on the German army to enter Romania, which it did in October of that year.

Soon after, Antonescu encountered problems with his Iron Guard partners, because of the violent and uncontrolled means they employed in seizing property—including the property of Jews—and in removing officials of the old regime from their posts, actions creating economic chaos and political unrest. In January 1941, the Iron Guard Legionnaires openly rebelled against Antonescu, who with Hitler's help was able to subdue them, henceforth ruling as dictator without setting up his own political party. Antonescu joined Germany in the invasion of the Soviet Union in June 1941 in order to recover BESSARABIA and northern BUKOVINA, which the Soviets had taken from Romania in June 1940. He also occupied TRANSNISTRIA, the considerable area of the Ukraine located between the Dniester and Bug rivers.

When he was in his thirties and serving as a military attaché in London, Antonescu had married a French Jewish woman, whom he later divorced; his stepmother too had been Jewish. Nevertheless, he was imbued with traditional antisemitic views and attitudes. These were based on economic and religious considerations according to which the Jews were exploiters who wanted to control Romania's economy, especially its commercial life, and therefore had to be removed from the villages and from economic positions. Antonescu, however, did not accept the racist Nazi-style doctrine, and throughout the war years he maintained public contact with representatives of Romania's Jewish community.

In his policy toward the Jews, Antonescu differentiated between Old Romania (the Regat, or pre–World War I Romania) and southern TRANSYLVANIA on the one hand, and Bessarabia and northern Bukovina on the other. In a secret draft order, he prepared for a purge of Bessarabia and Bukovina—extermination of the Jews in the rural areas, and imprisonment of the urban Jews in concentration camps and ghettos.

In Romania proper (Old Romania and southern Transylvania), Antonescu, on June 19, 1941, ordered the expulsion of 40,000 Jews from villages and towns to urban Jewish centers. He confiscated and nationalized Jewish property and imposed on the Jews a special levy of 4 billion lei (about $40 million). He did not, however, permit the 300,000 Jews of these areas to be handed over to the Germans or murdered.

Late in the summer of 1941, Antonescu ordered the expulsion of 150,000 Jews from Bessarabia, Bukovina, and the Dorohoi district, survivors of earlier massacres, to Transnistria. There, many of them were murdered, starved to death, or succumbed to disease and epidemics. For two years Antonescu stood firm in refusing to permit the return of the survivors from Transnistria, and it was only at the end of 1943 that certain categories of Jews, such as orphaned children, were permitted to go back to Romania. In the wake of an explosion on October 22, 1941, in the Romanian headquarters in ODESSA (which Romanian troops had occupied), Antonescu ordered punitive measures to be taken against Communists and Jews; for every Romanian or German officer killed, 200 persons were ordered to be killed, and 100 for every Romanian or German of other rank; 25,000 Odessa Jews were murdered in these retaliatory measures.

Although he had agreed to the German program for the "final solution of the Jewish question" in Romania, according to which all the Jews of his country were to be deported to the BEŁŻEC extermination camp in Poland, he hesitated in permitting its implementation and in the end withdrew his consent. For a

while (until the spring of 1942) Antonescu permitted the Zionist movement to operate, in order to solve the "Jewish question" by emigration of the Jews from Romania; this policy was defeated by German pressure, and by the British refusal to permit Jews from an enemy country to enter Palestine.

On August 23, 1944, as the Soviet army was advancing into Romania, Antonescu was arrested on the order of King Michael. He was taken to the Soviet Union, and subsequently sent back to Romania to be tried there. Sentenced to death, he was executed as a war criminal on June 1, 1946.

BIBLIOGRAPHY

Ancel, J., ed. *Documents concerning the Fate of Romanian Jewry during the Holocaust.* 12 vols. Jerusalem, 1986.

Simion, A. *Preliminarii politico-diplomatice de insurectiei române din August 1944.* Cluj, 1979.

Yust, W., ed. *Eventful Years.* Vol. 3. Chicago, 1947. See pages 828–834.

JEAN ANCEL

ANTONESCU, MIHAI (1907–1946), Romanian political figure. Antonescu was a lawyer and served as a professor of international law in Bucharest. He was not a member of any antisemitic or fascist party; as a young man he had expressed disapproval of anti-Jewish discrimination at the universities.

During the period of King Carol's dictatorship (1938–1940), Antonescu struck up a friendship with Ion ANTONESCU (they were not related), based on mutual opposition to the king's policy. Mihai Antonescu was never known as a supporter of the IRON GUARD, but he also refrained from denouncing its actions in public. In September 1940, when Ion Antonescu formed his first cabinet, the National Legionary Government (Governul National-Legioner), Mihai Antonescu was appointed minister of propaganda. In the period immediately preceding his appointment to the cabinet, Mihai Antonescu, who until then had voiced anti-Nazi attitudes, switched to support of Nazi Germany and its policies.

As Ion Antonescu's closest confidant, Mihai accompanied the premier on his January 1941 visit to Germany and took part in talks with Hitler and other leading figures in the Nazi regime. Acting in behalf of Ion Antonescu, Mihai coordinated the tactical moves against Iron Guard chief and deputy premier Horia SIMA, and, following the suppression of the Iron Guard elements, became deputy premier and foreign minister (February 1941) and the Romanian dictator's closest adviser. Mihai Antonescu incurred the hatred of the Legionnaires (the Iron Guardsmen), and on several occasions they threatened his life.

Mihai Antonescu was put in charge of censorship, and he instructed the media, especially the veteran Romanian newspapers, to adopt a rabidly antisemitic line, thereby preparing the ground for the exclusion of the Jews from Romanian society. As deputy prime minister he also concentrated on drafting the laws for the dispossession of Jewish property; in March 1941, Jewish-owned property in the cities—buildings, apartments, stores, and so forth—was confiscated. Antonescu initiated laws and administrative regulations that further restricted the opportunities available for Jews to earn a livelihood, caused their dismissal from posts they held, barred them from certain occupations, and "purged" the civil and public administrations of their Jewish employees.

On the eve of the war against the Soviet Union, Mihai and Ion Antonescu drew up the *Curatirea Terenului* (Cleansing of the Ground) edict, for "purifying" BESSARABIA and BUKOVINA of Jews. In a cabinet meeting held on July 3, 1941, Mihai Antonescu openly discussed the plan. He chaired a meeting of the officials designated to head the civil administrations of Bessarabia and Bukovina, at which, *inter alia*, he ordered them to get rid of the Jews there, who, he charged, were traitors to Romania and supporters of communism and the Russians.

In the initial phase of the war, until October 1941, Mihai Antonescu ran the country because Ion Antonescu was preoccupied at the front, directing the Romanian forces fighting the Russians. It was in that period that the Jews of Old Romania (the Regat) suffered the worst blows: they were expelled from the towns and villages, confined to detention and labor camps, and robbed of their belongings. Worst of all was the pogrom in

IAŞI, which began on June 29, 1941, and continued for several days. The degree to which Mihai Antonescu was directly involved in the pogrom cannot be determined. In meetings he had with Jewish community leaders in that period (until September 1942), Mihai Antonescu claimed that he took a "humane" approach, abhorred criminal action in all its forms, and was concerned solely with safeguarding the interests of the Romanian people. This, however, did not prevent him on occasion from issuing threats against the Jewish leaders, for example, Dr. Wilhelm FILDERMAN.

In talks with Hitler and other Nazi leaders, Mihai Antonescu praised the Nazis for the example they were giving the world on how to solve the "Jewish question." In November 1941 he consented to the request made by the German ambassador to Romania, Manfred von KILLINGER, to stop emigration of Jews from the country, and a few weeks later he agreed to withdraw the Romanian state's protection from Jews in the Nazi-occupied countries of Europe who had Romanian passports. As a result, most of these Jews were deported to extermination camps. Mihai Antonescu cooperated with Gustav RICHTER, the adviser on Jewish affairs in the German legation in Bucharest, and on Richter's demand he disbanded the Federatia Uniunilor de Comunitati Evreesti (Federation of Jewish Communities) and in its place established the CENTRALA EVREILOR (Jewish Center), a kind of JUDENRAT (Jewish Council). In the summer of 1942 Antonescu gave Richter written assurance on behalf of the government of Romania that the country's Jews would be deported to the extermination camps in Poland.

In the fall of 1942, under the impact of the sharp dispute with Hungary over northern Transylvania, the critical situation on the front, and the heavy economic and financial burden that Germany had imposed on ROMANIA, Mihai Antonescu began to look for ways to extricate Romania from the war and bring about a rapprochement with Britain and the United States. Ion Antonescu gave full support to these efforts, and resisted pressure by the Germans to dismiss the deputy premier from his post. The latter was convinced that the Jews would play an important role in

Mihai Antonescu during his trial in 1946.

influencing public opinion in the Allied countries.

Supported by orders from his chief, Mihai Antonescu embarked upon a new policy. He put a stop to the deportation of Jews from Romania and renewed contacts with the leaders of Romanian Jewry, especially with Filderman, Chief Rabbi Alexander SAFRAN, and the heads of the Zionist movement, Misu Benvenisti and Abraham Leib Zissu. Together with these leaders he explored possibilities for enabling as many Jews as possible to emigrate from Romania. With this end in mind, he agreed to the establishment of an emigration office and, in effect, to the resumption of the Zionist movement's activities. He put the diplomatic pouch at Filderman's disposal for communicating with the heads of the JOINT DISTRIBUTION COMMITTEE and other Jewish organizations in the free world, conducted the negotiations for the repatriation of orphans and other survivors of the deportations to TRANSNISTRIA, and alleviated some of the day-to-day burdens of the Jews. From mid-1943 his speeches had few antisemitic overtones and made no specific mention of the Jews.

In foreign policy, Mihai Antonescu attempted to persuade the Germans to bring the war in the West to an end and concentrate on the war against the Soviet Union and the Slav peoples. He failed in his attempt to extricate Romania from the war together with Italy, but protected the American ambassador's family after Romania severed relations with the United States at the end of 1941. He also protected the Italian ambassador himself when Italy surrendered to the Allies in September 1943. After the fall of Stalingrad, Mihai Antonescu tried to revise the documents that bore his signature and to destroy the written evidence of his criminal liability.

Mihai and Ion Antonescu were arrested on August 23, 1944; in 1946 they were sentenced to death and executed. Unlike Ion Antonescu, Mihai Antonescu behaved poorly during the trial. He tried to put the blame on others and to stress the modest steps he had taken to relieve the plight of the Jews.

BIBLIOGRAPHY

Ancel, J., ed. *Documents concerning the Fate of Romanian Jewry during the Holocaust.* Vols. 3, 5, 8, 9. Jerusalem, 1986.
Seton-Watson, H. *The East European Revolution.* London, 1961. See chapter 5.

JEAN ANCEL

ANTWERP, city in Flanders in northern BELGIUM, close to the Dutch border. Antwerp is Belgium's largest port and one of the major ports on the European continent. On the eve of the German invasion some fifty thousand Jews lived in Antwerp, of whom only 10 percent were Belgian nationals. Thousands of Jews fled Belgium at the time of the invasion; consequently, during the German occupation, the city had a Jewish population of about thirty thousand, representing 40.4 percent of the country's Jews, compared to the 51.4 percent of Belgian Jewry living in Brussels. Despite its smaller size, the Jewish community of Antwerp was the more prominent, by virtue of its distinct Jewish character and its range of activities. Antwerp had three separate Jewish communities: two Ashkenazic, named Maḥzikei Hadas and Shomrei Hadas, and one Sephardic. There were thirty-four synagogues and prayer houses; two comprehensive elementary schools (Yesodei ha-Torah and Taḥkemoni); four Hebrew schools; two rabbinical academies (yeshivas); twenty-two social organizations, including burial societies and foundations of various kinds (especially for mutual aid); and four aid organizations (Alliance Israélite Universelle, the Central Charity and Social Assistance Organization, the Committee for Jewish Refugees, and Tomkhei Aniyyim [Supporters of the Poor]). Six publications, in Yiddish, French, and Dutch (Flemish), appeared regularly. Several Zionist and non-Zionist political parties were active in the community, as were nineteen youth movements, six professional organizations, and three sports clubs.

The Antwerp Jewish community was of relatively recent vintage and for the most part consisted of immigrants from eastern Europe and, to a much lesser degree, from Germany. It was the eastern European style that determined the community's daily and organizational life. A substantial number of Jews were merchants and peddlers, but there was also a large Jewish proletariat. The diamond trade played a very important role in the life of the Jews and the general economic life of Antwerp. In the years just preceding the German occupation, there was an increase in the number of antisemitic incidents in Antwerp, which the Jews tried to cope with as best they could. The mayor of Antwerp, the Socialist Camille Huysmans, was friendly to the Jews and tried to be of help to them in various ways.

Under the German occupation, the fate of the Jews of Antwerp was essentially the same as that of the rest of Belgian Jewry, but a number of events and developments affected only Antwerp. During the fighting many Antwerp Jews tried to flee; some of them made their way to the south of France, but most had to turn back. Community life and the economic situation were partially restored, and for the first few months daily life was fairly undisturbed. Despite plans made before the German occupation to transfer the diamond industry to Britain, most of the diamond dealers and workers and the merchandise itself had remained in the city. The diamond industry was reactivated in the first

phase of the occupation and even flourished for a while, especially the trade in industrial diamonds.

Following a German decree under which foreign nationals could be removed from the coastal area of Flanders, the Antwerp military command, on its own initiative, decided to apply the decree to Jews who had immigrated to Belgium after 1938. On December 23, 1940, a first group, consisting of 222 men and women and 21 children, left for the Limbourg province; as time went on, the number of expellees rose to 3,334. They were distributed over forty-five villages and towns, the local authorities providing them with accommodation in various places, and Jewish and other institutions helping them to maintain themselves. In March 1941 the expellees were able to return to Antwerp, in several groups, although some of them were detained for a few months in the Overpelt camp. By January 1942 all had returned.

Antwerp was the scene of the only pogrom against Belgian Jews under the occupation. On April 10, 1941—the eve of Passover—small numbers of members of right-wing groups incited riots in the Jewish quarter. Four days later, on April 14, the film *Der ewige Jude* (The Eternal Jew) was screened at a meeting of the Volksverwering (People's Defense; a pro-Nazi organization headed by the attorney René Lambrichts). When the meeting ended, some of the participants proceeded to break into two synagogues and into the residence of Rabbi Marcus Rottenberg, setting fire to Torah scrolls, other religious objects, and furniture. Members of other right-wing movements joined the rioters in the pogrom, among them the Flemish SS. The fire department and the police were ordered not to interfere. The pogrom was apparently initiated by the local German authorities, and the German military commanders in Belgium disapproved of it.

The economic situation of the Jews took a turn for the worse in the summer of 1941, when "Aryanization" was introduced in Belgium. In several instances, the German police broke into diamond-polishing plants and confiscated the merchandise. When the ASSOCIATION DES JUIFS EN BELGIQUE (AJB) was formed, late in 1941, a branch was also set up in Antwerp, and Nico Workum was appointed its chairman (in addition to his appointment as deputy chairman of the AJB). One of the branch's tasks was to enroll into local Jewish schools the Jewish children who had been evicted from the general public-school system.

Under the occupation, the Jewish political parties reduced their activities to a minimum, and when the deportations were launched even that minimum was abandoned, for all practical purposes. In contrast, the youth movements, especially the Zionist movements, resumed their operations and, for many Jewish youngsters, became a home away from home. They ran very active programs and took part in efforts to obtain food from nearby farms and distribute it among Antwerp Jews. In 1942 and 1943, the youth movements made various attempts to smuggle members into Switzerland and Spain. Scores of young people reached Switzerland (the exact number is not known).

At the time when Belgian Jews were being deported to northern France for forced labor there, four such deportations took place in Antwerp in the course of 1942—on June 13, July 14, August 15, and September 12. Deportations to the east commenced in early August 1942. Even earlier, at the end of July 1942, the first orders were issued for Jews from Antwerp to report to the Dossin camp in MECHELEN (Malines). This step was followed by mass arrests: on August 13, 1942, Romanian nationals were arrested, and on Sabbath eve, August 14, another large group of Jews was seized. On September 10, the eve of the Jewish New Year, Jews were apprehended in the streets of Antwerp. Only those who could prove their Belgian nationality were released, while the rest were taken to Mechelen. In the following months, individual arrests were made from time to time. One such arrest was that of Rabbi Rottenberg, who was later released from Mechelen, and then sent to the VITTEL camp in France; he met his death in AUSCHWITZ, to which he was deported at the end of 1944. The last arrests of Jews took place on the night of September 3–4, 1943, and this time it was Belgian nationals who were taken. From the end of 1942, only a handful of Jews were left in Antwerp, since the majority of the Jewish population had not been Belgian nationals. The

school and welfare systems were sharply reduced and even so ran into great difficulties in trying to maintain their operations.

According to testimony given shortly after liberation, some three thousand Jewish men and women and three hundred children went into hiding in Antwerp and its vicinity; of these, some 30 percent were Dutch nationals. Later estimates came up with a lower figure, but precise data do not exist. Many Antwerp Jews were connected with the Comité de Défense des Juifs and took part in the committee's efforts to provide hiding places for Jewish children and adults; others belonged to various resistance movements, such as the Mouvement National Belge.

Following the liberation of Antwerp, on September 4, 1944, the surviving Jews orga-

Arnold and Lilian Buschel, who were deported from Antwerp to Auschwitz in September 1943.

nized an Aid Committee for Jewish War Victims (Hiso-Hulp aan Joodse Slachtoffers van de Oorlog), which assisted Jews who returned to Belgium, as well as others who were in need. Soldiers of the JEWISH BRIGADE GROUP also helped in the rehabilitation efforts. Some of the survivors of Antwerp emigrated and others helped restore prewar Jewish community life, albeit on a reduced scale. The number of Jews in Antwerp in 1969 was estimated at ten thousand five hundred.

BIBLIOGRAPHY

Brachfeld, S., ed. *Uit vervlogen tijden.* Herzlia, Israel, 1987.

Schmidt, E. *L'histoire des Juifs à Anvers (Antwerpen).* Antwerp, 1969.

Steinberg, M. *L'étoile et le fusil.* Vols. 1–3. Paris, 1983–1986.

Steinberg, M. "The Trap of Legality: The Association of the Jews of Belgium." In *Patterns of Jewish Leadership in Nazi Europe, 1933–1945.* Proceedings of the Third Yad Vashem International Historical Conference, edited by Y. Gutman and C. J. Haft. Jerusalem, 1979. See pages 353–376.

DAN MICHMAN

APPEASEMENT. *See* Great Britain: Appeasement of Nazi Germany.

ARCHIVES. *See* Documentation Centers.

ARENDT CONTROVERSY. Hannah Arendt (1906–1975) was a philosopher and political scientist whose study *The Origins of Totalitarianism* (1951) has become a classic. Her book *Eichmann in Jerusalem,* published in 1963, was the cause of a sharp public polemic. Arendt had been sent by *The New Yorker,* a weekly magazine, to cover the EICHMANN TRIAL in Jerusalem in 1961. Her report, first published serially in the magazine and then in book form, dealt with the process of destruction, Eichmann's role in it, and the trial's legal aspects. Among other subjects, she discussed the responses of the European Jewish communities to the Holocaust and the Nazi occupation, and the social and political implications of the trial in Israeli society.

The account was written in a pungent style, giving the historical evidence a distinct theoretical conceptualization.

The major theses that provoked the controversy centered on Arendt's analysis of Adolf EICHMANN and her portrayal of Jewish behavior, based to a great extent on Raul Hilberg's study *The Destruction of the European Jews* (1961). Viewing Eichmann within the framework of a totalitarian society and a social structure that had consecrated evil, Arendt refused to see his participation in the "FINAL SOLUTION" as being anything more than normal and his actions and thoughts as reflecting the antisemitic ideology of National Socialism. Reduced to a Nazi bureaucrat and unmotivated by antisemitic feelings, Eichmann was seen as a paradigm of "the banality of evil." In contradistinction to her portrayal of Eichmann, Arendt assessed the Jewish communities in Europe, and especially their leadership, with a sterner moral yardstick. In the behavior of Jews across Europe she found a common denominator: a lack of moral responsibility that expressed itself most blatantly in the predisposition to protect vested elements in the community, often at the price of sacrificing others. Arendt summarized her conclusions in this regard with the statement that had the Jewish community been left leaderless and in a state of anarchy, "there would have been chaos and plenty of misery but the total number of victims would hardly have been between four and a half and six million people."

Eichmann in Jerusalem sparked a public airing of historical issues relating to the Holocaust in which laymen, journalists, intellectuals, jurists, social scientists, and historians, both Jewish and non-Jewish, took part. Not all of Arendt's critics were negatively inclined; some praised her essay as a brilliant exposition on man's predicament in the face of totalitarianism. Others condemned the work for what they considered its disrespectful treatment of the Jewish victims. Her critics generally posited that an inquiry into the Holocaust necessitated a knowledge of the facts, an understanding of the catastrophe derived from experience, and the avoidance of overly rationalistic interpretations. Moreover, it was felt that the "true nature" of the persecutors and their victims must be preserved, as well as a clear-cut delineation between them. Moral judgment also had its limits and restrictions: the Jews, the tragic victims of the Holocaust, were above reproach, and historians who had not experienced their suffering were expected to refrain from judgment. The opposite was true regarding the Germans. Here there existed a moral imperative for contemporary society to uncover and condemn the moral collapse of Germany during the war. An important element in facing the Holocaust required a constant evocation of German cruelty in order to avoid a further catastrophe.

Eichmann in Jerusalem provoked responses from survivors and interested observers in America, Europe, and Israel, many of whom related publicly to the Holocaust for the first time. As such, the polemic provides a unique perspective for evaluating the public conception of the Holocaust in the early 1960s. Moreover, although it originally aroused anger and resentment, Arendt's book eventually stimulated serious thought and historical scholarship.

BIBLIOGRAPHY

Barnouw, D. "The Secularity of Evil: Hannah Arendt and the Eichmann Controversy." *Modern Judaism* 3 (1983): 75–94.

Hausner, G. *Justice in Jerusalem.* New York, 1968.

Krummacher, F., ed. *Die Kontroverse: Hannah Arendt, Eichmann und die Juden.* Munich, 1964.

Muller, S. "The Origins of *Eichmann in Jerusalem*: Hannah Arendt's Interpretation of Jewish History." *Jewish Social Studies* 43 (1981): 237–254.

Robinson, J. *And the Crooked Shall Be Made Straight.* New York, 1965.

RICHARD COHEN

ARGENTINA. The years from 1930 to 1943 in Argentina are known as the "shameful decade." In 1930 the Nationalists seized power in a corporative and military revolution, but in late 1931 the neo-Conservatives promised the presidency to Gen. Agustín Pedro Justo. Justo's presidency, which lasted until 1938, was paved with electoral corruptions designed to maintain the Conservatives in power. The army and the church cooperated with the regime, the heads of the economy supported it, and, despite the ideological disagreements prevailing in the country, the government met with very little opposition.

In 1938, Roberto M. Ortiz became president. From a radical party background, Ortiz tried to reorganize the regime along democratic lines. Following the example of the United States and of other Latin American countries, Ortiz adopted a position of neutrality when war broke out in Europe. In May 1940, however, he stated in the Argentine Congress that neutrality does not mean passivity and insensitivity, and expressed sympathy for the victims of the Nazi occupation. In this respect, Ortiz appeared as a liberal tending toward support for the Allies. However, in September 1940, with Ortiz incapacitated by illness, the conservative and nationalist vice president, Ramón S. Castillo, became acting president, and his brand of neutrality in World War II was an expression of sympathy toward the Axis countries.

In World War II. In 1943, a group of generals seized control and established a military dictatorship with a strong Catholic orientation. The parties were disbanded, and Catholic education was introduced in the state schools. It was from this group of generals that the populist rule of Gen. Juan Domingo Perón, the future president of Argentina, emerged in 1946. Unlike most of the Latin American countries, Argentina continued its policy of neutrality. Only in January 1944 did it yield to American pressure and sever its relations with Germany. It declared war on Germany as late as March 1945, whereas most of the Latin American countries had done so in 1941 and 1942, after the United States entered the war. The belligerent neutrality of Argentina was anti-American, anti-democratic, and anti-Communist, matching the position of the Spanish dictator, Francisco Franco, and was considered desirable from an economic viewpoint.

At the outbreak of World War II, nationalist groups in Argentina supported a neutrality with a pro-German bias. Despite the small size of the Movimiento Nacionalista (Nationalist Movement) and its internal divisions, its extensive propaganda penetrated influential sectors in the country, including the army, the Catholic church, and many groups within the nationalist intellectual elite. The movement opposed liberalism, communism, and the democratic camp, and at times professed antisemitism. It apparently succeeded in implementing its goals, in anticipation of the military putsch of June 1943. Catholic circles in Argentina were split between a nationalist, antiliberal majority and a pro-Western democratic minority. A number of the nationalist, military-minded groups adopted the Nazi ideology and were financed by the German embassy in Buenos Aires.

Following disquieting reports of the penetration of Nazi propaganda in Argentina, a parliamentary inquiry commission was set up, and, on the basis of its conclusions, a number of German Nazi institutions working under the cover of cultural or commercial activity were declared illegal. Most members of the German community in the country openly supported Nazi Germany, teaching its racist ideology in the German schools and cultural institutions, and enjoying the support of nationalist bodies.

On the other hand, antifascist and antiracist groups also existed in Argentina, and in mid-1937 they had created the Committee against Racism and Antisemitism. In the wake of the German invasion of the Netherlands and Belgium, Acción Argentina was created by democratic and anti-Nazi intellectuals, who cautioned against the presence of a potentially treacherous "fifth column" in the country and strove for the severing of relations with Germany.

The Immigration Laws. A law dating from 1876 allowed free immigration to Argentina. As a result of the Great Depression of 1929, Argentina, like most of the Latin American countries, took steps to restrict immigration. On November 26, 1932, a government decree was issued according to which potential immigrants had to prove that they had a profession or a place of work guaranteeing their livelihood, given the difficulties caused by the rising unemployment in the wake of the world crisis. This was a turning point, concluding the period of mass immigration and inaugurating a policy of selective immigration. Immigration was still possible by virtue of the articles of the law providing for reunification of families or concerning agricultural settlement. However, the gates of the country

were in the process of closing. A decree passed in October 1936 prohibited immigration stemming from ideological reasons, in order to curtail immigration of Communists and anarchists.

In July 1938, with increasing Nazi pressure for the emigration of refugees from the Reich following the German annexation of Austria (*see* ANSCHLUSS), the EVIAN CONFERENCE was convened on the initiative of the American president, Franklin D. ROOSEVELT. The Argentine representative at the conference promised to make every effort to help find a solution for the refugee problem. The Argentine government, however, after a reconsideration of its immigration policy, on July 28, 1938, passed a decree specifying new restrictions and placing stricter supervision along its borders to prevent illegal immigration, claiming that foreigners were infiltrating Argentina, particularly by way of Brazil and Uruguay. The reasons given in this decree point to its connection with the events in Europe and the fear of large-scale immigration. The stated focus of the problem was not the fear of unemployment but the "current international situation," as a result of which an immediate increase was expected in the number of people wishing to settle in Argentina. The toughening of the entry procedures was designed to give precedence to immigrants meeting the needs of Argentina's "society, culture, and economy." The word "Jews" was not explicitly mentioned in the decree, but is implied in the argumentation it contained, especially in face of the increasing applications by Jewish refugees and potential Jewish immigrants. Argentina's policy did not change even after the KRISTALLNACHT pogrom in Germany (November 9–10, 1938) and the widespread echoes of Nazi violence in the world press.

In early December 1938 the eighth Pan American Conference met in Lima, Peru, and approved a resolution against persecution carried out for reasons of race and religion. It also resolved that every country in the Western Hemisphere would try to absorb immigrants from any country of North and South America or of Europe in accordance with its internal needs and according to the characteristics and professions of the immigrants.

Argentina was very active at the conference, and frustrated American pressures for a binding resolution on immigration. Moreover, emphasis was placed on the continuation of selective immigration, which would prevent the entry of refugees forced to flee, in contrast to immigrants coming of their free choice. In addition, at a conference held by the finance ministers of Brazil, Argentina, Uruguay, and Paraguay, in February 1939, it was resolved to work to prevent the transit of people not possessing the required documents and visas, and the transit of people considered dangerous to public order, or undesirable by virtue of their past. These categories embraced refugees from the collapsing Spanish republic, as well as democrats, socialists, anarchists, and Jewish refugees who for various reasons had no documents. Argentine policy was influenced by this coordination among the four countries of the region, and Jewish refugees on thirty-five ships arriving in the Buenos Aires harbor in the years from 1938 to 1942 were refused entry. Most of them were sent back to Europe; a small minority found refuge in Chile and Curaçao.

Reactions of public figures and extensive press coverage alerted the public to the case of the Jewish refugees arriving in February 1939 on board the *Conte Grande,* and in October 1941 on board the *Cabo de Buena Esperanza.* But despite all the efforts on their behalf, they were not allowed to enter Argentina. Finally, passengers on board the *Conte Grande* were allowed to enter Chile, and those on board the *Cabo de Buena Esperanza* were allowed to enter Curaçao.

Throughout the war the closed-gates position continued. The local officials, the consuls in Europe, and the senior echelon of policymakers in Argentina all strictly enforced this position. Yet despite all the difficulties and restrictions, some 39,400 Jews arrived in Argentina during the Holocaust period, 26,500 legally and the rest illegally.

Thus, Argentina during the Holocaust period maintained a closed-gates policy vis-à-vis the Jewish refugees, notwithstanding its broad expanses of vacant territory and its need for development in a variety of fields. Support for the Jews by circles in the center and to the left of the political spectrum was of little avail, since they were unable to influence the government, which determined the immigration policy. In the decisive years, when chances of rescue still existed, there was an increasing disparity between the number of refugees applying for entry into Argentina and the limited number that Argentina was willing to absorb.

BIBLIOGRAPHY

Ebel, A. *Das Dritte Reich und Argentinien: Die diplomatische Beziehungen unter besonderer Berücksichtigung der Handelspolitik (1933–1939).* Cologne, 1971.
Frye, A. *Nazi Germany and the American Hemisphere, 1933–1941.* New Haven, 1967.
Nolberg, H. *Auslandsdeutschtum und Drittes Reich: Der Fall Argentinien.* Cologne, 1981.
Walter, R. J. *The Province of Buenos Aires and Argentine Politics, 1912–1943.* Cambridge, 1985.

GRACIELA BEN-DROR

ARIERPARAGRAPH ("Aryan clause"), regulation barring "non-Aryans" (that is, Jews) from membership in German political parties, economic establishments, various voluntary associations (especially student and sports groups), social clubs, and so forth. Clauses of this nature made their appearance in Germany during the nineteenth century in the bylaws of student societies and political and social organizations of a nationalist and racist character, and were applied by them to exclude Jews.

In the Third Reich the *Arierparagraph* represented a transitional stage. It was introduced in April 1933 in a number of laws enacted to provide for the "legal" purge of the Jews from various spheres of society, including the government and public sector, universities and other institutions of learning, and professional societies. The NUREMBERG LAWS, passed in September 1935, raised this anti-Jewish racist criterion to the status of a general, basic law.

[*See also* Anti-Jewish Legislation.]

BIBLIOGRAPHY

Schleunes, K. A. *The Twisted Road to Auschwitz: Nazi Policy toward German Jews, 1933–1939.* Urbana, Ill., 1970. See pages 92–120.

ISRAEL GUTMAN

ARISIERUNG ("Aryanization"), term used to denote the transfer of Jewish-owned independent economic enterprises to "Aryan" German ownership throughout the Third Reich and the countries it occupied. The process had two stages: "voluntary" sales of Jewish-owned businesses, in the period from 1933 to 1938, arising from the exclusion of Jews from the economic life of the country; and forced transfer, under law, in the final phase of the *Entjudung der deutschen Wirtschaft* ("de-Judaization" of the German economy), following KRISTALLNACHT, the November 1938 pogrom.

"Voluntary" Stage. At the beginning of 1933, there were some one hundred thousand Jewish-owned enterprises in Germany. About half of these were retail stores, dealing mostly in clothing, footwear, or furniture; the rest were factories and workshops of various kinds, publishing firms, newspapers, and independent practices of medicine, law, and other professions. In the early years of the Nazi regime, the economic boycott and exclusion process focused more on those fields of commerce that had a high proportion of Jewish-owned enterprises, and less on the Jewish firms that had international contacts and prestige. The "free professions" (those requiring higher education) were targeted as early as April 1933, when a special law was passed "for the restoration of the career public service" (*Gesetz zur Wiederherstellung des Berufsbeamtentums*); this was the first Nazi law to make Aryan descent a condition for public employment, and the condition also came to be applied to self-employed doctors and lawyers. The campaign against the Jewish-owned retail trade, on the other hand, was not at first based on formal legislation, and consisted mainly of boycotts and intimidation, inspired from above and often accompanied by violence (*see* BOYCOTT, ANTI-JEWISH). The government offices in Berlin, mainly the ministries of the economy and the interior, from time to time issued prohibitions of "partisan actions" (*Einzelaktionen*), and similar instructions were also put out by the central party institutions. These did not, however, stop the boycott propaganda and actions aimed at the exclusion of Jews from the country's economy. There were more and less harsh periods, but the process went on steadily, relentlessly, and most efficiently, so

much so that by the spring of 1938, 60 percent to 70 percent of the Jewish enterprises in Germany had been liquidated.

The methods used in the boycott campaign included the publication of conspicuous street posters and newspaper advertisements denouncing any German who bought from Jews as a "traitor to his people." From time to time uniformed patrols were posted in front of Jewish stores threatening potential customers and keeping them out. Non-Jewish customers who were seen entering Jewish stores were photographed and had their pictures and names published in the local press or on special billboards (the latter also displayed copies of the antisemitic paper *Der* STÜRMER). In addition to such sporadic actions, administrative measures were taken by the authorities without legal basis; Jewish enterprises did not receive any orders from public institutions, even when they had won public tenders; Nazi party members were prohibited from buying in Jewish-owned stores (a prohibition that was broadened to apply also to employees of local government authorities); and welfare recipients were not permitted to use their food stamps for buying in Jewish stores. Local newspapers were forbidden to publish advertisements of Jewish enterprises.

The "creeping" boycott actions affected mainly the Jewish retail trade. Of the more than fifty thousand Jewish retail stores that existed in 1933, only nine thousand were left in 1938. On the other hand, factories and workshops, especially those that were labor-intensive or export-oriented, were able to sustain themselves during the first few years of the Nazi regime and even to some extent to thrive on the general boom of the German economy. This was also true of the private Jewish banks, even though they had long been the butt of Nazi propaganda against "international Jewish financial capital." The continued existence of some Jewish enterprises had a variety of causes: the Nazi regime's concern about unemployment, which was still rife up to 1936; the staying power of large industrial plants and stores; and, in the case of the banks, their international connections, which affected German exports and the influx of foreign currency (of which there was a shortage).

The *Arisierung* measures were orchestrated

by the *Gauwirtschaftsberater* (economic counselors) of the Nazi *Gauleiter* (district leaders) in close cooperation with the local chambers of commerce and industry, economic organizations, and local and central economic and tax authorities. The declared purpose of the joint apparatus was to make sure that veteran party members would get the best businesses. For this purpose, detailed and up-to-date files were kept in the offices of the economic counselors to keep track of the Jewish enterprises in their respective *Gau* (district), and every *Arisierung* deal had to be approved by the competent economic counselor. All available "persuasion" and pressure tactics were employed in order to prevail upon the Jewish owners to sell their enterprises at a fraction of their value, ranging from economic boycott to physical attacks and even imprisonment in concentration camps and accusations by the Gestapo of having committed various crimes. As a rule, measures of this kind were used against small and medium-sized enterprises. More sophisticated means were used on the owners of large businesses, as long as a semblance of legal procedure was still maintained. Such enterprises were acquired by large and prestigious companies, and sometimes arrangements were made that enabled the Jewish owner to receive at least a part of his capital. But there were also cases of wealthy owners being jailed or put in concentration camps and held until they agreed to give up their enterprises. In some well-known instances, huge plants were confiscated in favor of the Reich without any compensation being paid, as in the case of the Simson armament factory in Suhl (Thuringia) in 1935, and the Petschek family firm in the Sudetenland in 1938.

Compulsory Stage and Final Liquidation. The second stage, that of compulsory *Arisierung*, began immediately after the November 1938 pogroms; in large measure, it was the result of political developments and the war preparations. Compulsory *Arisierung* was one of the points in the legislation announced by Hermann GÖRING on November 12, 1938, in his program to "exclude the Jews from the economic life of Germany" (*Ausschaltung der Juden aus dem deutschen Wirtschaftsleben*). The new regulations prohibited all independent economic activity by Jews, except for

certain services that they could continue to render to Jews only. Jewish enterprises that had not yet been sold were put under a government-appointed trustee (*Treuhänder*), whose task was to "Aryanize" the enterprise, for a fee that amounted to a substantial percentage of the price at which it was sold. A special regulation, which Göring enacted on December 10, 1938, provided for the first time that a part of the profits of *Arisierung* would go to the state. Compulsory *Arisierung* was applied to all Jewish businesses, factories, and workshops that were still in existence at the time; apartment houses, however, were explicitly postponed to a later date, apparently because of the impending plan to restrict Jews to living in Jewish-owned apartment houses (later known as *Judenhäuser*).

Compulsory *Arisierung* was the more conspicuous and drastic stage, but by that time the process of eliminating the independent economic activity of Germany's Jews was well advanced, and all that compulsory *Arisierung* accomplished was to liquidate the little that was left in a single stroke and within the space of a few weeks. The value of the property held by the Jews of Germany in 1933 had been estimated as in excess of 10 billion reichsmarks (RM). A census of Jewish property, in April 1938, within the borders of "Greater Germany," put its value at 8 billion RM; one-quarter of this property was in Austria. Only a little over 1 billion RM was classified in the census as working capital (*Betriebsvermögen*); 2.5 billion RM were said to be invested in real estate. A confidential Reich government document stated that 5 billion RM were liquid assets, available for immediate seizure. This last sum was made up for the most part of proceeds from the sale of enterprises in the earlier, "quiet" stage of *Arisierung*.

A census of Jewish holders of assets over 5,000 RM was one of several measures initiated at the end of 1937 that aimed to put an end to all remaining Jewish economic activity. Preparations had begun a year earlier by government departments in the wake of the FOUR-YEAR PLAN. This plan, which was derived from a secret memo of Hitler, was designed to prepare Germany's army and economy for war. From that point on, Göring, who headed the Four-Year Plan organization, was also in charge of the "purge of Jews from the German economy," the aim being to use the confiscated Jewish assets to finance the production of German armaments. Further measures included a census, taken in July 1938, of all Jewish enterprises still in existence; a law barring Jews from various branches of trade and brokerage; and the final annulment of all remaining licenses to practice held by Jewish doctors. Two months later, in September 1938, Jewish lawyers still in practice were also deprived of their licenses. Throughout 1938, pressure on Jewish enterprises, by boycott and harassment, increased and was extended to include industrial manufacturing enterprises. The process of "voluntary" *Arisierung* and liquidation of Jewish enterprises was correspondingly speeded up. No data are available as to which proportion of the Jewish enterprises were liquidated and which passed into "Aryan" German hands during the entire period of the two stages of the *Arisierung*. The more profitable and well-established of these enterprises were no doubt highly attractive prizes to large, well-known German firms, individual Nazis bent on getting rich, and ordinary Germans. Prominent among a variety of legal and administrative steps taken in preparation for the liquidation of the remnants of Jewish economic activity were the orders issued by Reinhard HEYDRICH to the banking system. In July 1938, in addition to his other posts, Heydrich was put in charge of the Devisenfahndungsamt (Foreign Currency Investigation Bureau). He gave the banks until the end of October to complete preparations for introducing special blocked accounts (*Sperrkonten*) for Jews, which would facilitate supervision of these accounts and restrictions on their use.

The final liquidation of economic activity by German Jews had been carefully prepared to go into effect immediately after the November 1938 pogroms. At a closed meeting held on October 14, 1938, Göring declared: "The time has come for the Jews to be driven out of the economic life, [and] their assets have to flow into the hands of the Reich . . . rather than serve as a source of riches for incompetent party members." The shots fired by Herschel GRYNSZPAN at the German diplomat Ernst vom Rath in Paris, and the pogroms that followed, were only welcome pretexts, used for propaganda purposes, to implement within a few weeks a program that had been planned and prepared for months.

The November 1938 pogroms marked the transition to open and undisguised robbery of Jewish property in Germany by official institutions of the Nazi regime. The first step was the imposition of a collective contribution, the so-called *Sühneleistung* ("atonement payment") in the amount of 1 billion RM. This penalty payment was promulgated in Göring's special decree of November 12, 1938, and took the form of a direct individual tax, in the amount of 20 percent of the declared capital, to be paid by every Jew who had assets of over 5,000 RM. In practice, the rate was raised to 25 percent, and 1.25 billion RM were collected. In addition, the Reich authorities confiscated 250 million RM in insurance money due to Jews as compensation for the material damage caused to them in the pogrom.

In the period from 1938 to 1941, 140,000 Jews were able to emigrate from Germany, leaving behind most of their property. Part of that property fell into the hands of the authorities on the spot, in the form of the *Reichsfluchtsteuer* ("escape tax") and other "legal" levies; the rest was kept in special blocked accounts in the name of the depositors. No precise figures are available, but there is no doubt that the Jews who emigrated were able to save only a small fraction of the 8 billion RM in assets that the Jews of Germany and Austria had declared in April 1938. As for the remaining Jews, their private assets, from early 1939, were kept in blocked accounts in special banks, from which the owners could draw only a fixed monthly sum, the minimum they needed for their living expenses.

From 1939 until the summer of 1943, when the deportations to the extermination camps were completed, some of the private Jewish property and the property of the Jewish communities and Jewish organizations in Germany was accumulating in the coffers of the Reichsvereinigung der Juden in Deutschland (Reich Association of Jews in Germany). On orders of the authorities, all the assets of Jewish communities that had been liquidated, or the proceeds from the sale of such assets, were turned over to the Reichsvereinigung, and the remaining communities functioned as branches of that (Nazi-controlled) body, which was also responsible for their financial administration. As long as emigration from Germany continued, the Jews who left the country were in effect forced to "donate" all their remaining property to the Reichsvereinigung. These funds were kept in a special "emigration account" that was under Gestapo control, and any withdrawal from it required Gestapo approval. Some of the money in that account was used to finance the operations of the Reichsvereinigung, as were the taxes and other compulsory payments that the Reichsvereinigung kept on collecting from Jews who still had some money left. The Reichsvereinigung used these funds to finance the community organizations, the schools, and the medical establishments—in effect, to maintain a growing proportion of the Jewish population, by welfare subsidies, old-age homes, and other social services. In addition to the expanding staff employed by community institutions, a self-contained Jewish economic sector existed, in which Jews supported themselves with their remaining assets and savings.

According to estimates made by the Reichsvereinigung, German Jews in October 1941—on the eve of the mass deportations—had in their possession private assets in the amount of 300 million RM; an additional amount of over 100 million RM was held by the Reichsvereinigung in its accounts. On orders of the Gestapo, the persons selected for deportation had to "donate" their remaining assets to the Reichsvereinigung, which in turn put the assets into a special account. The Jews who were earmarked for deportation to THERESIENSTADT had to sign a "home purchase agreement" (*Heimeinkaufsvertrag*) with the Reichsvereinigung. According to this agreement, the Reichsvereinigung undertook to take care of them for the rest of their lives, in exchange for their depositing a minimum of 1,000 RM, or, alternatively, their entire remaining assets, with the Reichsvereinigung.

During the deportations to the east, the entire property of the deportees, as well as the moneys held in the special blocked accounts of emigrants, was to be confiscated in favor of the state treasury, on the basis of Regulation 11 of the Reich Citizenship Law (*see* NUREMBERG LAWS) of November 23, 1941. In actuality, this was one of the Gestapo's manipulations designed to preempt the Finance Ministry's departments and acquire the remnants of Jewish property in the country. An explicit order by Heinrich HIMMLER declared that the proceeds of this property were to finance the costs of the "Final Solution," on which the Gestapo was the supreme authority. Although the Gestapo made use of the Reichsvereinigung accounts and staff to collect and temporarily hold Jewish property, it was clear that the Reichsvereinigung's ownership of these accounts was a fiction and that in practice it could not withdraw the smallest amount without the special permission of the Gestapo representative. No data are available on the amounts held in these accounts and their ultimate disposal following the dissolution of the Reichsvereinigung in July 1943. There are indications that certain sums were in fact transmitted to the Theresienstadt ghetto administration. It is not known how much of the money was finally passed on to the German state treasury and how much was kept by the Gestapo or by the SS and its commanders.

The deportees' apartments were handed over to the city governments, which arranged for transfer of the titles by the appropriate agency. The contents of the apartments and the valuables of the former owners were passed on to the Finance Ministry. Works of art, libraries, and especially Jewish traditional items were forwarded to the collection that Alfred ROSENBERG had set up, with the help of the EINSATZSTAB ROSENBERG staff.

BIBLIOGRAPHY

Barkai, A. *Vom Boykott zur "Entjudung": Der wirtschaftliche Existenzkampf der Juden im Dritten Reich, 1933–1943.* Frankfurt, 1988.
Genschel, H. *Die Verdrängung der Juden aus der Wirtschaft im Dritten Reich.* Göttingen, 1966.
Margaliot, A. "Trends and Courses in the Economic Struggle of German Jewry during the Period of Racial Discrimination." In vol. 2 of *Nation and History*, edited by S. Ettinger, pp. 339–355. Jerusalem, 1984. (In Hebrew.)
Schleunes, K. A. *The Twisted Road to Auschwitz: Nazi Policy toward German Jews, 1933–1939.* Urbana, Ill., 1970.

AVRAHAM BARKAI

ARMÉE JUIVE (Jewish Army; AJ), French Jewish resistance and fighting organization founded in Toulouse in January 1942. The initiative for creating the Armée Juive was taken by Abraham POLONSKI and Lucien LUBLIN, two militant Zionists who had made up their minds, at the beginning of the German occupation of FRANCE, to create a fighting force. Apart from the threat posed to the AJ by the Gestapo and the Vichy government, the organization also had to contend with distrust on the part of the Zionist leaders. The AJ recruited its members in secret, swore them in on the Bible and the blue-and-white Zionist flag, and began training them even before it obtained any weapons. There is no information available about the number of members recruited by the AJ.

In the fall of 1943 the AJ launched an operation in which it organized from among its members groups of trained men who crossed the Pyrenees into Spain—sometimes under unbelievably harsh conditions—in order to get from there to Palestine and join the Jewish forces attached to the British army. The total number of Jews that the AJ succeeded in transferring to Spain was 300; of these, 80 were He-Haluts members from the Netherlands who had fled to France. AJ squads of armed partisans took action against informers and Gestapo agents in Toulouse, Nice, Lyons, and Paris; in Nice, the partisans liquidated a particularly dangerous gang of "physiognomists" (informers capable of recognizing persons as Jews by their facial features and expression) who were working for the Gestapo.

The AJ group in Lyons distributed tens of millions of francs to rescue organizations and fighting units; the money had been allocated to the Jewish resistance movement by the Jewish Agency and the American Jewish JOINT DISTRIBUTION COMMITTEE and smuggled into France from Switzerland. In the Tarn department, the AJ formed a fighting unit, and AJ forces attached to the French Forces of the Interior (FFI) of the Montagne Noire (in the south of France, near Montpellier) raised the blue-and-white flag and took part in the heavy fighting that the FFI was conducting. Four AJ officers fell in Lyons and Toulouse.

The AJ suffered its heaviest losses in two Gestapo operations: in May 1944 the Gestapo traced five of the organization's members who were operating in Paris (belonging to the Dutch group), and in July 1944 it arrested twenty-five AJ fighters in Paris, thereby liquidating the AJ's French group in the capital. After being tortured, the AJ men were put on the last deportation train to leave the DRANCY camp (August 17, 1944). However, fourteen of the AJ prisoners jumped off the train and escaped. The AJ's French groups took part in the general uprising of August 1944 in Paris, Lyons, and Toulouse.

BIBLIOGRAPHY

Avni, H. "The Zionist Underground in Holland and France and the Escape to Spain." In *Rescue Attempts during the Holocaust*, edited by Y. Gutman and E. Zuroff, pp. 555–590. Jerusalem, 1977.

Latour, A. *Jewish Resistance in France (1940–1944)*. New York, 1981.

Lazare, L. *La résistance juive en France*. Paris, 1987.

Poliakov, L. "Jewish Resistance in France." *Yivo Annual* 8 (1953): 252–263.

Steinberg, L. *Jews against Hitler (Not as a Lamb)*. New York, 1974.

LUCIEN LAZARE

ARMIA KRAJOWA (Home Army; AK), the underground military organization in occupied POLAND, which functioned in all areas of the country from the fall of 1939 until its disbanding in January 1945.

The AK originated from the Służba Zwycięstwu Polski (Polish Victory Service), created in late September 1939 by Gen. Michael Torkarzewski-Karaszewicz. That December, Gen. Władysław SIKORSKI replaced this organization with the Związek Walki Zbrojnej (Union for Armed Struggle), which became the AK in February 1942. The AK's first commander was Stefan ROWECKI (known as Grot, or "arrowhead"), until his arrest; he was succeeded by Tadeusz BOR-KOMOROWSKI, from July 1943 until the latter's capture in September 1944. The last commander was Leopold Okulicki, known as Niedźwiadek ("bear cub").

The executive branch of the AK was the

operational command, which was composed of many units. Estimates of the AK membership in the first half of 1944 range from 250,000 to 350,000, with more than 10,000 officers. Most of the other Polish underground armies were incorporated into the AK, including the Bataliony Chłopskie (Peasants' Battalions), a large military organization of the Stronnictwo Ludowe (People's Party); the Socjalistyczna Organizacja Bojowa (Socialist Fighting Organization), established by the Polska Partia Socjalistyczna (Polish Socialist Party); the Narodowa Organizacja Wojskowa (National Army), established by the Stronnictwo Narodowe (National Party); and, from March 1944, part of the extreme right-wing organization, the NARODOWE SIŁY ZBROJNE (National Armed Forces).

The AK divided itself organizationally in Poland into sixteen regional branches, subdivided in turn into eighty-nine inspectorates, which were further divided into 278 districts. The supreme command defined the main tasks of the AK as preparation for action and, after the termination of the German occupation, general armed revolt until victory. Power was then to be seized in Poland by the DELEGATURA establishment, the representatives of the London-based POLISH GOVERNMENT-IN-EXILE; and by the government-in-exile, which would return to Poland.

While the AK did not engender a general revolt, its forces were responsible for intensive economic and armed sabotage. In 1944 it acted on a broad scale, one of its operations being the WARSAW POLISH UPRISING, which broke out on August 1, 1944, and was quelled by the Germans only on October 2. AK units carried out thousands of armed raids and daring intelligence operations, bombed hundreds of railway shipments, and participated in many partisan clashes and battles with the German police and Wehrmacht units.

In February 1942 the Operational Command of the AK Information and Propaganda Office created the Section for Jewish Affairs, directed by Henryk WOLINSKI. This section collected information about the situation of the Jewish population, on the basis of which reports were drafted and sent to London. It also centralized contacts between Polish and Jewish military organizations. Only a few Jews were accepted into the ranks of the AK, which generally turned down Jewish applicants. The AK provided the Warsaw ghetto with about sixty revolvers, several hundred hand grenades, and ammunition and explosives. During the WARSAW GHETTO UPRISING, AK units carried out holding actions outside the ghetto walls.

BIBLIOGRAPHY

Ciechanowski, J. M. *The Warsaw Rising of 1944.* Cambridge, 1974.

Gutman, I., and S. Krakowski. *Unequal Victims: Poles and Jews during World War II.* New York, 1986.

Korbonski, S. *The Polish Underground State.* New York, 1981.

Terej, J. J. *Na rozstajach dróg: Ze studiów nad obliczem i modelem Armii Krajowej.* Wrocław, 1978.

EUGENIUSZ DURACZYNSKI

ARMIA LUDOWA. *See* Gwardia Ludowa.

ARMY. *See* Armée Juive; Russkaya Osvoboditelnaya Armiya; Ukrainska Povstanska Armyia.

ARMY, JEWISH. *See* Armée Juive.

ARROW CROSS PARTY (Nyilaskeresztes Párt), Hungarian fascist party and movement created by Ferenc SZÁLASI in 1937. The name is also often used, inaccurately, to designate other parties (such as the party of the National Will and the Hungarian National Socialist party) that were also founded and led by Szálasi.

Szálasi labeled his theories *Hungarizmus.* They were a hardly intelligible mixture of romantic agrarian, anticapitalist, anti-Marxist, nationalist, and, above all, aggressively antisemitic ideologies. The movement's leadership, like Szálasi himself, came from the ranks of ex–army officers, journalists, and middle-ranking government and county officials. Popular support came mainly from officers, students, impoverished intellectuals, and the lowest classes of the urban and agrarian proletariat. In the 1939 national election, the only election in which the party took part, the Arrow Cross obtained over 25 percent of the vote (in Budapest it received 72,383 votes, compared with 95,468 for the government party) and became the most important opposition party.

Although the Arrow Cross advocated a consistent pro-German foreign policy, the party was not included in the pro-Nazi government, even after the German occupation of HUNGARY on March 19, 1944. Only after the deportation of Jews was stopped on July 7 and after Miklós HORTHY's attempt to make a separate armistice was aborted on October 15 was a coalition government led by the Arrow Cross formed, under German pressure. During the short Arrow Cross rule the deportation of Jews was resumed, and eighty thousand Jews were expelled from Hungary, most of them women, in a severe and murderous march to the Austrian border. Many of the deportees died en route. In Budapest during this time, several thousand Jews were murdered and their bodies thrown into the Danube. The government came to an end when the Red Army took Budapest in January 1945.

After the war, Szálasi and most of the prominent Arrow Cross leaders were tried as war criminals by the Hungarian courts. The majority of the party's rank and file were reintegrated into civilian life, many of them after joining the Communist party.

BIBLIOGRAPHY

Lacko, M. *Arrow Cross Men and National Socialists, 1935–1944.* Budapest, 1968.
Macartney, C. A. *October Fifteenth: A History of Hungary, 1929–1945.* New York, 1957.

ASHER COHEN

ART OF THE HOLOCAUST. Responses in painting and sculpture to the Nazi persecution of the Jews began in the early 1930s, when artists reacted to Adolf Hitler's rise to power and early discriminatory measures. They were continued during the period of the Holocaust, and they continue unabated to this day. The art involved can be divided into different categories, dependent on the status of the artist (inmate, survivor, liberator, refugee, nonparticipant, memorial builder), the goals set forth (witness report, depiction on the basis of photographs, personal expression, denunciation, affirmation of identity, symbolization, memorialization), and the style (realist, expressionist, surrealist, abstract).

One of the best known of these categories is the art produced by the inmates of the camps and ghettos under impossible conditions, often at the risk of their lives. Whereas some were involved in the production of "official art" for the Germans, most camp artists set themselves two major goals. First, their art was to serve as an eyewitness report of what went on in the camps, thus undermining the German wish for secrecy on the subject. They therefore depict every phase of camp life, from the cattle cars and *Selektionen*, through brutal labor, to the gas chambers and the stacks of dead left unburied toward the end of the war. These artists have stressed that their work, done for the most part in a realistic style, was to be judged not as art but as documentation. Second, but equally important, inmate art was a form of resistance to dehumanization in allowing the inmate both to retain a personality of his own and to be able to order his life, at least on paper. This affirmation of individual identity through the very act of creation gave the artist a reason to live. The combination of these two needs —to bear witness and to affirm life by resisting dehumanization—accounts for the many relatively idealized portraits that have survived, works that both bear witness to the individual subject's existence and show us the way he wished to be remembered, as healthy and full of life rather than starving to death.

A special place among inmate artists is held by the group of underground artists at THERESIENSTADT—Leo Haas, Bedrich Fritta, Karel Fleischmann, and Felix Bloch—who, aside from their realistic official art, secretly produced expressionistic works that stripped the veneer off the "model camp" and exposed the starvation and death that lay at its core. These drawings are radically different from those produced by other artists in the camps. However, the level of anger expressed in them and their expressionistic style can also be found in the works of artists such as Boris Taslitzky and Zoran Music, who were active during the last days of the camps, after discipline had broken down, and in the works of many artist-survivors after the liberation.

The final group of witnesses were the liberators who entered the camps and were confronted by conditions beyond their wildest nightmares, including gruesome piles of corpses and *Muselmänner* (*see* MUSELMANN) with no will to live. These liberators depicted the sights that met their eyes. They recorded the scenes objectively, as did Feliks Topolski, or obsessively, as did Corrado Cagli, and occasionally tried to reconstruct events in the camps by interviewing the inmates, as did Zinovii Tolkatchev.

It was the photographers among the liberators who had the most immediate impact on the public at large, flooding magazines and newsreels with their reports on the camps, and turning every bystander, no matter how far away, into an eyewitness. It is for this reason that among the most common images of the Holocaust in the public imagination are those of the mounds of corpses, the emaciated, bald survivors barely able to stand or move, and the inmates standing crowded together behind barbed wire, scenes that were recorded in countless photographs.

The corpses and the survivors were to enter art because of the powerful impression these photographs created on artists. In contrast, the depictions of people behind barbed wire represented the primal image of the camps that had emerged in art in the mid-1930s and that dominated it during the war years in all countries. This motif was based on the knowledge that the camps were surrounded by barbed-wire fences, and it remains a potent image to this day, reappearing in George Segal's *Holocaust* memorial as a clear symbol of the camps.

Other common motifs can also be discerned in non-inmate art, although none has remained as well known. Thus, for instance, images of refugees were extremely common in art from the late 1930s until 1948, as a reaction to the sights that artists in the Allied countries most frequently encountered. They expressed the problems of artists who were themselves refugees, and reflected the plight

"This Is Nazi Brutality," a 1942 poster by New York artist Ben Shahn (1898–1969). Shahn was born in Kovno, Lithuania, and from 1942 to 1944 he worked as an artist in the Office of War Information, where this poster was printed. It protested the killing of 199 Czech men and boys by the Nazis in the mining village of Lidice, in reprisal for the assassination of SS general Reinhard Heydrich by two Czech patriots. [A Living Memorial to the Holocaust—Museum of Jewish Heritage, New York]

Overleaf: Four drawings by Helga Weissová-Hosková, a Czech artist now living and painting in Prague. In 1941 she and her family were deported to Theresienstadt. As a teenager there, she illustrated daily life in the ghetto. In one of the drawings, internees are cutting bunks down from three tiers to two, in anticipation of the 1944 inspection visit by the International Red Cross, whose standards for "humanitarian conditions" stipulated beds with no more than two tiers. [A Living Memorial to the Holocaust—Museum of Jewish Heritage, New York]

"Throw away [down] your baggage and run to the trucks." Arrival at Auschwitz. A drawing by Alfred Kantor, who survived the Theresienstadt, Auschwitz, and Schwarzheide concentration camps. Other such sketches, with explanatory notes, give a graphic day-by-day picture of inmate life in the camps. They were later published in *The Book of Alfred Kantor* (1971). [A Living Memorial to the Holocaust—Museum of Jewish Heritage, New York]

of the survivors who became DISPLACED PERSONS after the war. The subject slowly disappeared from art after 1948, because the state of Israel was seen as a solution to this problem.

The same is true of themes of Jewish resistance, especially that of the WARSAW GHETTO UPRISING, which were immensely popular during and immediately after the war. Artists from William Gropper in New York to Lea Grundig in Palestine and Raphael Mandelzweig in eastern Europe characterized the

Jewish nature of this resistance by adding a bearded Jew to the group of young men and women fighting the Nazis.

The image that created the deepest and most lasting impression—the mounds of corpses—was one that also posed the greatest aesthetic and emotional problems, especially for those artists who encountered it only in photographs. Haunted by this image, they sought ways to translate it into art, usually following the lead of Pablo Picasso, whose *Charnel*

House dealt with the theme by means of semi-abstraction, or by concentrating on isolated groups of corpses, as did Rico Lebrun, Hans Grundig, and Gerhart Frankl. The aim was to establish a human context and an emotional relationship with the spectator that would allow him to overcome his repugnance to the forms before his eyes long enough to take in the artist's message. Jews and Christians often handled this subject differently. Whereas the latter felt free to use the photographs as a basis for their art, Jewish artists usually felt unable to do so, and the images of death that obsessed artists such as Hyman Bloom and Leonard Baskin are drawn from other visual sources, or, when based on Holocaust photographs, as in the works of Ben Shahn, are used to express deaths ostensibly entirely unrelated to the Holocaust.

Other symbols of the camps were formed from single objects that one could more easily adapt to different contexts. For example, from 1945 on, the crematorium chimney became synonymous with the camps, and the placement of such a chimney in the background of the works of Cagli and Hans Grundig anchors the scene within a camp context. The same is true of the works of Samuel Bak, for whom the chimney is a literal stand-in for the camps, whether set on an island dominated by the dice of chance, in the desert, or protruding from a humanoid pear and feeding on its lifeblood. In like manner, when Friedensreich Hundertwasser decided to express his own Holocaust past, he did so by juxtaposing three symbols: the crematorium chimney, a garden of blood, and his own personal symbol of hiding, the labyrinth. The symbol of the chimney is so well known that it is constantly used or alluded to in monuments, and even Buky Schwartz's *Pillar of Heroism* at YAD VASHEM, although composed of three concave surfaces, is immediately perceived from the distance as a chimney.

Even more far-reaching and adaptable as a Holocaust symbol is barbed wire, a strand of which immediately conjures up images of human beings behind a barbed-wire fence. Barbed wire can be used alone in an abstract composition, as Igael Tumarkin used it in the early 1960s to give a specific Holocaust meaning to his work, or it can be set before or around a hand or another object, as in works by Chaim Gross. Its meaning is so clear-cut that it can be used in other contexts to make Holocaust analogies. Thus, a Russian artist, Marc Klionsky, wraps a strand of barbed wire around a Russian Jew to symbolize his imprisonment in Russia, which is likened to a concentration camp. On the other hand, Tumarkin in the 1980s wrapped barbed wire around a prayer shawl that covers a mound of earth, in order to protest the establishment of Israeli religious settlements in the West Bank. The settlement is thus compared to a ghetto behind barbed wire, divided from the land around it, and the image suggests the possible destruction of the settlement in the future.

All the above symbols were taken from the camp experience itself. But artists who were interested in learning moral lessons from the Holocaust had from the early 1930s employed other images culled from religion and mythology to convey their ideas. These revolve around three main themes, each standing for a protagonist in the drama, and each conveying several alternate messages.

For instance, resistance to Nazism after 1933 was usually suggested through the image of David killing a Nazi Goliath, or in more general terms by Prometheus slaying the vulture. Jacques Lipchitz popularized both images in this context, using the first to stress the Jewish element in the conflict, and the second to bring home to non-Jews that Nazism was a threat to everyone and not only to the Jews. By emphasizing in some statues the physical resemblance between Prometheus and the vulture, Lipchitz also suggested that Nazism was an evil within man that he must defeat.

The victim, on the other hand, had several biblical symbols, each containing different nuances of meaning. Several artists attempted to use the traditional image of the sacrifice of Isaac in a Holocaust context, an image that is particularly potent in literature. However, since the usual artistic image of the sacrifice depicts the moment when the angel *stops* the slaughter, only a few artists succeeded in using this image. Mordechai Ardon portrays Sarah crying out at God in anguish on beholding her son dead on the altar, while Frederick Terna, a survivor, has done a

Pablo Picasso, *The Charnel House*, 1944–1945. Oil and charcoal on canvas, 6'6″ × 9'½″. [Museum of Modern Art, New York]

series of works in which he shows the angel pushing the knife in Abraham's hand into Isaac, thus blaming God for the Holocaust; or Abraham aiming the knife at God or at himself, unwilling to perform the sacrifice. Job, too, was used to protest the Holocaust to God, as he demands an explanation for the crime. Ivan Meštrović's emaciated Job accuses God, while Nathan Rapaport's Job, with a number on his arm, retains his faith despite everything.

By far the most frequently invoked symbol of the Holocaust victim was the crucified Jewish Jesus, who often wears a prayer shawl to make his identity clear. Here the artist, be he Christian like Otto Pankok or Jewish like Marc Chagall, turns to address not God but the Christian world, pointing out to the Christians that they are slaying Christ again when they kill his brothers, the Jews. This imagery, which became dominant in the 1930s, was reinforced when cruciform corpses were discovered in the camps, inspiring artists such as Graham Sutherland to make a direct use of Holocaust imagery in his 1946 portrayal of Christ. Many of the artists who used this imagery, such as Giacomo Manzù, Ernst Fuchs, and Mauricio Lasansky, used it also to denounce the church for not doing enough to save the Jews, linking the church clearly with Christ's killers rather than with Christ himself.

The third protagonist of the Holocaust, the Nazi aggressor, posed many problems for the

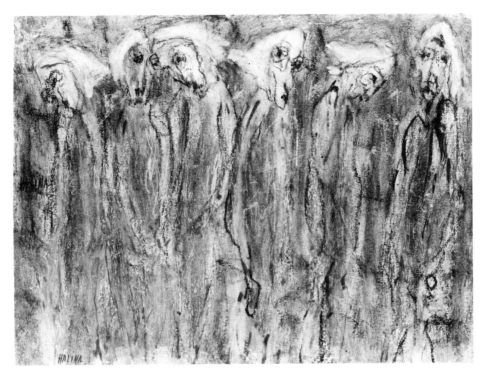

Halina Olomucki, *Before the Roll Call at Auschwitz*, 1950. Pastel, 12.6″ × 13.65″ (26.5 × 35 cm). [Yad Vashem Museum]

artist. A few tried portraying him realistically, but were overwhelmed by the limited expressiveness of such images of the "banality of evil." Most artists therefore portrayed the Nazis as monsters and images of death, using images that had been developed by artists like John Heartfield and George Grosz in Germany in the 1920s as part of their battle against the Nazi party. After the Holocaust, artists came to the conclusion that, as Lipchitz had put it, there is an evil beast in all of us. Matta, Francis Bacon, Leon Golub, and others present ambiguous figures that combine victim and oppressor in a highly problematic manner, implying both an inability to draw a clear line between good and evil, and a pessimistic view of all mankind as tending toward the monstrous. This attitude is seen most clearly in the works of Maryan (Pinhas Burstein), a survivor of AUSCHWITZ. Embittered by his experience, he turned all of humanity into a monstrous race, exuding excrement from every orifice.

Maryan's extreme reaction brings up the problem of the art of the survivors. All of the artist-survivors, after the liberation, described their experiences in their art, and many of them felt that this therapeutic activity freed them from the weight of the Holocaust. Whereas some went on documenting the Holocaust, believing, as Halina Olomucki did, that it was their sacred duty to the dead to record their agony, most artists—Maryan included—turned their backs on their past and tried to become entirely engrossed in modern art. Some of these, such as Avigdor Arikha, maintain this position; having moved from abstract expressionism to realism, Arikha focuses on the individual object, refusing to recognize any reality beyond it. Most of the other artists, like Hundertwasser, Maryan, Erich Brauer, Isaac Celnikier, Yehuda Bacon, and Osias Hofstatter, returned at some point in their maturity to the Holocaust, expressing it in terms of the style and iconography they had meanwhile developed. Often this return was motivated by world events, such as the EICHMANN TRIAL, the wars of Israel, or the continuing massacres in a world that had learned nothing

Mordechai Ardon, *Sarah*, 1947. Oil on board, 54½″ × 42¾″ (138.4 × 108.6 cm). [Zvi Reiter]

from the past. Many of these artists feel threatened, and they take a highly pessimistic stance. Thus, Bak sees Judaism as a destroyed and patched-up reality that will never be the same, and Zoran Music states his lament in the titles of his paintings of the 1970s, which he based on his 1945 drawings of camp corpses: *We Are Not the Last!*

Other Jewish artists, who did not experience the Holocaust themselves, felt a need in its wake to relinquish in part their socialist or assimilationist views and to return openly to Judaism. This is particularly notable among American artists, including Shahn, Gropper, Max Weber, Jack Levine, who began painting Jewish subjects in the 1940s. These works included biblical themes, praying men, shtetl scenes, and Hebrew inscriptions. On the other hand, younger artists, such as R. B. Kitaj, returned to an affirmation of their Judaism, not by dealing with traditional Jewish themes but by working on pictures related to the Holocaust. This interrelationship between Jewish identity and the Holocaust is a growing phenomenon, especially among secular Jewish artists, whose only knowledge of Judaism is compounded of pogroms, persecutions, and the Holocaust.

A more positive view of events was generated by the creation of the state of Israel, which artists such as Chagall and Lipchitz immediately saw as an answer to their questions regarding the Holocaust and as a solution to the plight of the survivors still in displaced persons' camps. However, Israel's continuing wars, and especially the threats to its existence in 1967 and 1973, forced some artists to a more pessimistic expression; they saw in every conflict an inherent renewal of

Buky Schwartz, *The Pillar of Heroism*, 1967, at Yad Vashem. Stainless steel, height 68.9 feet (21 m). [Zvi Reiter]

the Holocaust. On the other hand, the relations between Jews and Arabs since 1967 have caused both left-wing artists like Matta and Israeli artists like Igael Tumarkin to adapt Holocaust imagery to the new conflicts, with the Palestinians replacing the Jews as the victims. This generalization of Holocaust imagery is, in fact, part of a wider phenomenon, in which these images are applied, especially by artists associated with the Communists, to any current conflict, from Korea to Vietnam. In these works, the Americans and their allies are given the role of Nazi murderers. The artists thus attempt to activate an inbred, unquestioning hatred against those who have been clothed in the despised Nazi images.

The anxiety felt by many artists—not only survivors—in the postwar world is often linked by Jewish artists to the Holocaust. This is especially evident in the works of Jonathan Borofsky, all signed with numbers rather than with his name. Several of these works reflect his fear of being victimized by a Hitler-like person or by Gestapo dogs. These

Elsa Pollak, *Auschwitz*, 1985, at Yad Vashem. Bronze, height 9.8 feet (3 m). [Zvi Reiter]

fears have developed particularly in response to the millennial feeling that man is about to destroy himself. Artists like Robert Morris have joined survivors such as Music in depicting Holocaust corpses in an attempt to tell the world that catastrophe looms and that we can avert it if we act before it is too late.

A recent development has been the imagery created by the children of survivors, many of whom, like Yocheved Weinfeld, try to put themselves in their parents' place and imagine their own reactions had they been in the camps. On the other hand, young German artists, such as Anselm Kiefer, have begun to take tentative steps toward dealing with the past. Kiefer's art stresses the need to do so in order that healing may begin.

BIBLIOGRAPHY

Blatter, J., and S. Milton. *Art of the Holocaust.* New York, 1981.
Costanza, M. S. *The Living Witness: Art in the Concentration Camps and Ghettos.* New York, 1982.
Czarnecki, J. P. *Last Traces: The Lost Art of Auschwitz.* New York, 1989.
Frommhold, E. *Kunst im Widerstand.* Dresden, 1968.
Kampf, A. *The Jewish Experience in Twentieth Century Art.* South Hadley, Mass., 1984.
Museo Civico Bologna. *Arte e resistenza in Europa.* Bologna, 1965.
Novitch, M., L. Davidowicz, and T. L. Freudenheim. *Spiritual Resistance: Art from the Concentration Camps, 1940–1945.* New York, 1981.
Reith, A. *Monuments to Victims of Tyranny.* New York, 1969.
Roskies, D. G. *Against the Apocalypse.* Cambridge, Mass., 1984.
Thompson, V. *A Mission in Art: Recent Holocaust Works in America.* Macon, Ga., 1988.

ZIVA AMISHAI-MAISELS

ARYAN CLAUSE. *See* Arierparagraph.

"ARYANIZATION." *See* Arisierung.

ASIA. *See* Japan; Rescue of Polish Jews via East Asia; Shanghai.

ASSCHER, ABRAHAM (1880–1950), Dutch Jewish public figure. Asscher was proprietor and chief executive of the most important diamond firm in Amsterdam, a member of the Amsterdam chamber of commerce, and one of the leaders of the Liberal party, which he represented on the North Netherlands Regional Council from 1917 to 1940. He was active in many Jewish institutions and was a member of the Zionist movement. In 1932 he was elected chairman of the standing committee of the Union of Ashkenazic Communities and chairman of the Amsterdam Jewish Community Council. He thus became the outstanding personality of Dutch Jewry and its chief spokesman.

Together with his friend David COHEN, Asscher formed the Comité voor Bijzondere Joodse Belangen (Committee for Special Jewish Affairs) in reaction to developments in Germany, and was its head as long as it existed (it was dissolved in March 1941). Shortly after the occupation of the NETHERLANDS by the Germans in May 1940, Hermann GÖRING paid a visit to Asscher's diamond factory and purchased diamonds in the amount of 1.4 million guldens. On February 12, 1941, the German authorities asked Asscher to form a Jewish Council (JOODSE RAAD), which, together with Cohen, he did, and the two men served as the council's co-chairmen. Asscher took little part in the day-to-day operations of the Joodse Raad, but he chaired all its plenary sessions and did all he could to save Jews from deportation to Poland. The German Sicherheitspolizei (Security Police) granted Asscher certain favors, despite the fact that in his talks with the Germans he denounced the Nazi regime in no uncertain terms; many of his relatives and friends, for example, were spared and were not deported to Poland. By nature a tempestuous and courageous man, Asscher wanted to protest the German persecution of the Jews, but Cohen always managed to persuade him not to resign his position and to keep cooperating with the German authorities.

On September 23, 1943, Asscher, together with all the other members of the Joodse Raad, was arrested, sent to the WESTERBORK camp, and from there to BERGEN-BELSEN (the fate of the other Dutch diamond merchants as well). When the war was over and Asscher was free, he returned to the Netherlands. The Dutch government charged him with collaborating with the enemy, and Asscher was arrested; following an investigation, however, the file against him was closed. A Jewish tribunal acting on behalf of the Jewish communities found him guilty and barred him from participating in any form of Jewish communal activity. Asscher, however, did not acknowledge the tribunal's competence to judge him, and broke off all ties with the Jewish community. When he died, he was buried in a non-Jewish cemetery.

BIBLIOGRAPHY

Michman, J. "The Controversial Stand of the Joodse Raad in the Netherlands." *Yad Vashem Studies* 10 (1974): 9–68.
Michman, J. "The Controversy Surrounding the Jewish Council of Amsterdam." In *Patterns of Jewish Leadership in Nazi Europe, 1933–1945.* Proceedings of the Third Yad Vashem International Historical Conference, edited by Y. Gutman and C. J. Haft, pp. 235–258. Jerusalem, 1979.
Presser, J. *The Destruction of the Dutch Jews.* New York, 1969.

JOZEPH MICHMAN

ASSOCIATION DES JUIFS EN BELGIQUE

(AJB; Flem., Jodenvereeniging van Belgie), the organizational framework forced upon the Jews of BELGIUM in World War II. The military administration introduced by the Germans in Belgium differed from that of neighboring occupied countries and left to the local authorities a considerable measure of freedom of action. However, a consistently hostile policy was pursued toward the Jews from the very beginning of the occupation in May 1940, starting with the introduction of anti-Jewish legislation and the elimination of the Jews from the economic life of the country. One measure considered was making the Jews a separate sector of the population, supervised by a special administration, to be headed by an appointed body.

As early as the fall of 1940, a coordinating committee—the Comité de Coordination des Communautés Israélites—was set up by the Jews, which, however, had no legal standing. In 1941, when the Nazi anti-Jewish policy took a turn for the worse in all parts of occupied Europe, the concept of central Jewish leadership crystallized, the idea being to establish it in every country, in accordance with local circumstances. In Belgium, the German Sicherheitspolizei (Security Police; Sipo) decided in the late spring and summer of 1941 to establish a compulsory countrywide Jewish organization. The form proposed was similar to that of organizations set up in Germany, France, and the Netherlands, but it took into consideration the special situation in Belgium, where, for all practical purposes, the Jews were concentrated in only four cities—BRUSSELS, ANTWERP, Liège, and Charleroi. The plan for their organization was submitted to the various branches of the German military administration in Belgium, and, after discussion, the order for the creation of the Association des Juifs en Belgique was published, on November 25, 1941.

The order, consisting of eight paragraphs, made it compulsory for all Jews (who came under the definition of that term, as promulgated on October 28, 1940) to belong to the association; established the association as a body recognized by public law; and imposed on it certain functions, including the encouragement of emigration and responsibility for educational and welfare institutions. Formally, the association was put under the Belgian ministries of health and the interior, but all its substantial decisions were subject to the approval of the German military administration. The association was empowered to collect money, and the Belgian government was made responsible for any deficit that it might incur.

The November 25 order emphasized the association's Belgian character, but this was not borne out in practice; its main function, in 1942 and 1943, was the registration of Jews for forced labor and for deportation to the extermination camps in eastern Europe.

An executive board was appointed on December 22, 1941. Rabbi Salomon Ullmann, a Belgian citizen whose parents had immigrated from Hungary, was appointed chairman. Ullmann had been the chief Jewish chaplain and had become chief rabbi in November 1940, replacing Josef Wiener, who had fled the country; in April 1941 the Germans had also appointed Ullmann chairman of the coordinating committee of Jewish communities. Nico Workum, of Antwerp, was appointed deputy chairman. Other members of the executive body were Salomon Van den Berg, Noë Nozyce, and Juda Mehlwurm—representing the Jewish communities of Brussels, Liège, and Charleroi, respectively—and Joseph Teichmann and Maurice Benedictus, who were both from Antwerp and had not previously been involved in Jewish matters. Benedictus eventually became the association's leading figure, first as its secretary and later as its executive director. Teichmann resigned after serving on the board for a while. Only three members of the executive board were native Belgians; this was an indication not only of the composition of Belgian Jewry, but also of a clear-cut German policy to separate the Jews, as a body, from the Belgian people. The association's executive board had four local committees working under it—in Brussels, Antwerp, Charleroi, and Liège—and a number of administrative departments.

From the AJB's inception, it was not widely trusted or respected by the Jews. This attitude was expressed in written material, as well as in the fact that thousands of Jews failed to report for registration in the association offices when ordered to do so in March and April of 1942. This attitude changed somewhat in the summer of that year, when Belgian Jews were being sent for forced labor in northern France. Working for the association was then regarded as an essential occupation, and persons listed as association employees were exempt from this forced labor. For this reason, many Jews applied for work in the association, which responded so liberally that eventually many of those listed as its employees did little real work; the list of employees came to include even intellectuals and underground members who were opposed to the association in principle.

German pressure on the association increased as the time for deportations to the east drew near, and this also meant a growing involvement of the Sipo in the association's affairs. When the wearing of the Jewish BADGE was introduced, by an order published on May 27, 1942, the association, of its own accord, helped in distributing the badge in its offices, so that the Jews could meet the deadline for wearing it (June 3). On July 15, Benedictus was put in charge of the "mobilization for work" operation; thus he became in effect personally responsible for the association's role in the deportation of the Jews.

On Saturday, July 25, 1942, a group of Jewish Communists, members of the underground, occupied the AJB's offices and burned the lists they found there. They told the association employees who happened to be there that they were causing harm to the Jews. The loss of the lists had no effect on the Germans' plans for the deportations since they had their own copies. But German pressure on the association grew, and the Germans now insisted on more direct cooperation by the association in preparing for the deportations. Benedictus was removed from his job as head of the section for work mobilization (*Arbeitseinsatz*), and his successor, Robert Holcinger, was more amenable to German demands for cooperation. The first call-up notices for "work" were sent out to Belgian Jews at the beginning of August, together with a circular from the association urging the Jews to respond to the order and warning them, "in view of the grave actions committed in the last few days," that "failure to comply with the order will lead to serious consequences for your families and indeed for the entire Jewish population in the country." But despite this warning, and assurances that the call-up was indeed for purposes of work, resistance among the Jews became more determined, although some Jews did report. On the night of August 15–16 the Germans launched raids against the Jews. That month saw the first five transports of Jews leave the MECHELEN (Malines) camp for AUSCHWITZ. Following another raid on the Jews, on August 28 and 29, a group of Jewish members of the underground "armed partisans" organization attacked and killed Holcinger.

The standing of the association in the eyes of the authorities and of the Jewish community, and in its own eyes, suffered greatly as a result of the assassination. A further deterioration took place in the wake of continued arrests and raids (the worst of these occurring on September 11 and 12, 1942—the eve and first day of the Jewish New Year). Rabbi Ullmann resigned from his post on September 8, and at the end of the month the Charleroi local association committee decided to disband. (Even before taking this step, the committee had been involved in underground activities.)

In an effort to exert pressure on the AJB, the Sipo's section for Jewish affairs summoned dozens of leading Jews to a September 24 meeting with the section chief, Kurt Asche. Asche uttered threats against the Jews assembled in his office and arrested six of them, including Rabbi Ullmann, Salomon Van den Berg, Alfred Blum, and Maurice Benedictus. They were sent to the BREEN-DONCK camp, but released after fifteen days, on the intervention of Cardinal Joseph-Ernst van Roey and in response to pressure by the military administration. The association emerged from these events as a more submissive—and weaker—organization. Its role in the arrest and expulsion of Jews was now mainly confined to providing food and clothes to Jews on the eve of their deportation and to those interned in Mechelen; to looking after the families left behind by the deportees; and to overseeing education and health.

The new chairman of the association was Marcel Blum, a native of Belgium, who was the president of the Brussels Jewish community; he was nominated for the post by the association and approved by the authorities (the candidate proposed by Asche having been turned down by the military administration). Another reorganization of the association's structure and operations took place in the wake of Operation "Iltis," on September 3 and 4, 1943, in which Belgian Jews were arrested. The Antwerp local committee was abolished and the Brussels local committee merged with the association's central office, its activities now consisting of the maintenance of several orphanages, welfare centers, and hospitals. Most of the Jews still legally left in Belgium were either employed by the association or housed in one of its institutions. In this period the association also served as a cover for illegal operations, many of its employees being members of the underground.

In the middle of August 1944, the AJB was ordered to submit an updated list and photographs of all of its personnel. It delayed its response as long as possible. On August 24, Rabbi Ullmann was arrested and sent to Mechelen. Four days later, on August 28, the association board held its last meeting and decided to close its offices and cease operations. Six hundred orphan children who had been housed in the association's institutions were put into hiding, in a special operation to save them from arrest.

The association had been in existence from the end of 1941 until a few days before the entry of Allied forces into Brussels on September 3, 1944. It disbanded of its own accord, rather than on German orders. Generally, it had been submissive to the German authorities, but it played much less of a role as an instrument in the deportation of Jews than did similar organizations in other European countries. This was due both to the fact that the Jewish community of Belgium disregarded its orders, and to the success of efforts by Jewish underground groups to undermine its authority. On the other hand, the existence of the association as a legal organization enabled it to provide welfare and educational services to the Jews up to the very last days of the German occupation.

BIBLIOGRAPHY

Schirman, I. *La politique allemande à l'égard des Juifs en Belgique, 1940–1944: Mémoire de licence.* Brussels, 1971.

Schmidt, E. *L'histoire des Juifs à Anvers (Antwerpen).* Antwerp, 1969.

Steinberg, M. *L'étoile et le fusil.* Vols. 1–3. Brussels, 1983–1986.

Steinberg, M. "The Trap of Legality: The Association of the Jews of Belgium." In *Patterns of Jewish Leadership in Nazi Europe, 1933–1945.* Proceedings of the Third Yad Vashem International Historical Conference, edited by Y. Gutman and C. J. Haft, pp. 353–376. Jerusalem, 1979.

DAN MICHMAN

ATHENS. When the Greek capital fell under Italian occupation in April 1941, its Jewish community numbered approximately 3,500, out of a total population of 1.5 million (including the port city of Piraeus). Some of the Athens Jews were descendants of Sephardic immigrants who had come from SALONIKA, Izmir, and Larissa in the nineteenth century. Others came later from Kastoria and Ioannina. All the Jews in Athens, however, were united around the central synagogue. Already Greek-speaking, they were little affected by the Hellenizing and nationalizing policies of the interwar period.

During the spring and summer of 1941, the Germans stripped all of occupied GREECE of its agricultural produce and industrial resources, plunging the country into a serious famine. Jews suffered greatly along with the general population during the harsh winter of 1941–1942. Estimates record three hundred famine-related deaths a day among the Greek population.

The Italian occupation effected no anti-Jewish measures. Gen. Carlo Geloso, the Eleventh Army commander of Italian-occupied Greece, was respected by the community for his civility, his friendship toward leading Athenian Jews, and his efforts to protect Jews and foil Gestapo efforts to implement Nazi anti-Jewish measures. Geloso's successor (after May 3, 1943), General Vecchiarelli, similarly refused to carry out German demands. The Italians could not, however, prevent the Germans from establishing a Gestapo office, which arrested the leaders of the community council and other important Jews, and confiscated libraries and the communal archives.

In the summer of 1941, Greek fascists formed the Ethniko-Socialistike Patriotike Organosis (ESPO), under Dr. Speros Sterodemas, whose youth movement persecuted Jews and ransacked the synagogue on Melidoni Street. Rabbi Eliahu Barzilai, who had been chief rabbi since 1935 and was made community president by the Gestapo on July 20, 1941 (he was confirmed as such by the Italian and Greek authorities on September 1), managed to save the building with the aid of the Italian police. Immediately afterward the Jewish community officially dissolved itself, but it set up a secret committee that assisted the resistance. On September 22, 1942, Kostos Perrikos blew up the ESPO center, killing Sterodemas and a number of German soldiers. During the Day of Atonement services the Gestapo took ten important Jews as hostages in retaliation (they were later released owing to Italian intervention).

Throughout the Italian occupation Jews escaped from the German and Bulgarian occupation zones of Greece, many with their families, to Athens, whose Jewish population consequently rose to some eight thousand to ten thousand. This haven became a potential trap after the fall of Italy in September 1943. On September 8 the German army occupied Athens, accompanied by EINSATZSTAB ROSENBERG. Dieter WISLICENY, from Adolf EICHMANN's office, went to Athens on September 20 and set up a JUDENRAT (Jewish Council). It was headed by Moses Sciaki, who was murdered in January 1944; his aide, Isaac Kabelli, succeeded him. (Kabelli survived the war and wrote prolifically on the role and fate of Greek Jewry, but he was ostracized as a collaborator by the survivors.) On September 21, 1943, Rabbi Barzilai was ordered to hand over the communal lists of Jews. He replied that the ESPO had destroyed them during their raid on the synagogue, but he was then ordered to produce new lists within twelve hours. The rabbi destroyed the extant lists and warned the community to flee. He himself was escorted (or kidnapped, according to Baruch Shibi of the resistance) by the partisan network to the mountains of central Greece. There he issued calls to the Western powers to aid the main Greek resistance group, the National Liberation Front (Ethnikon Apeletherotikon Metopon, or EAM), in its efforts to save Jews and fight the Germans.

On October 7, 1943, an order by SS general and police chief Jürgen STROOP, who had been transferred to Athens after his Warsaw assignment, appeared in the local newspaper *Eleftheros Vima*, instructing the Jews to register with the community; only two hundred did. Eventually, two thousand registered, including three hundred of Italian and two hundred of Spanish nationality. The following month all Jewish property was confiscated for the Greek state in retaliation for the poor registration showing.

Following a rumor that the Gestapo was distributing unleavened bread, Jews assembled at the Melidoni Street synagogue on March 24, 1944. About 350 were seized, and their families as well were soon arrested, bringing the total to 800. They were all imprisoned in the notorious Haidar prison, and on April 2 formed part of a Jewish transport going from Greece to AUSCHWITZ. Arriving nine days later, on April 11, 433 of the Athenians were selected for labor details; only about 40 of them survived the war. A further transport, arriving on June 6, contained Jews from CORFU and Athens.

There were numerous protests by Greek leaders to the Greek government and the Italian and German occupiers. One hundred and fifty Salonika lawyers, after an approach to Simonides, the Greek governor of Macedonia, appealed to the government in Athens to at least shift the deportations from Poland to a Greek island. The response was that the Germans would not allow it. Jewish refugees from Salonika in Athens, aided by Athenian Jews, tried to pressure the government. They were joined by the intellectual and religious leadership, especially Archbishop Damaskinos and the heads of the institutions of higher learning, who argued eloquently on behalf of the Jews. Dr. Constantine Logothetopoulos, the head of the government in 1943, had the idea of settling the Orthodox refugees of Bulgarian-occupied Thrace in the vacant Jewish quarters of Salonika. His half-hearted attempt to stop the deportations through a letter to Guenther Altenberg, the German plenipotentiary in Athens, on March 23, 1943, arrived too late. On March 29 Athenian nongovernment leaders made an appeal, unprecedented in occupied Europe, to halt the deportations of loyal Greek citizens. This too failed because Salonika was in the German zone. The government of Ioannis Rallis protested to the Gestapo over the deportations and helped to foster an atmosphere in which Greek Jews were assisted by the population. In particular, Professor Nikolaos Louvaris (the minister of education, and later of communications) expended considerable effort to save the Jews.

Some of the Jews of Athens, including those who took refuge there, survived with the support of the resistance, the police, the church, the intelligentsia, ordinary people, and the government. The metropolitan of Athens, Archbishop Damaskinos, called upon his church and the nation to protect the Jews. Some one hundred and fifty baptismal certificates were issued; hundreds of Jewish children were placed under church protection; the police issued numerous false papers; and individual gentiles in the resistance hid Jews, assisted them to escape to the free mountains, and ferried approximately one thousand to Turkey. The Phoenix Chapter of the Athens Masonic Order also assisted Palestinian Jews who had served in the British Expeditionary Force to escape from their German captors.

STEVEN B. BOWMAN

After the War. The Jewish population of Athens increased owing to immigration, primarily from Salonika, but also from cities like Chalcis, Ioannina, and Volos, where the Holocaust had left only a handful of Jews. The Jewish community revived with the help of the American Jewish JOINT DISTRIBUTION COMMITTEE. The Organization for the Assistance and Rehabilitation of Greek Jews was formed under Greek government supervision to administer property reparations. In 1945 the Jewish Board of Communities was established in Athens; it played a key role in rehabilitating the Jewish community of Athens and other Jewish communities, particularly in Thessaly. In the 1950s, ORT (the international organization for developing skilled trades and agriculture among Jews through training) set up a technical school in Athens, and the city's Jewish community continued to maintain its own elementary school. The community numbered slightly under three thousand at the end of the 1980s.

YITZCHAK KEREM

BIBLIOGRAPHY

Avni, H. "Spanish Nationals in Greece and Their Fate during the Holocaust." *Yad Vashem Studies* 8 (1970): 31–68.

Carpi, D. "Notes on the History of the Jews in Greece during the Holocaust Period: The Attitude of the Italians (1941–1943)." In *Festschrift in Honor of Dr. George S. Wise*, edited by H. Ben-Shahar et al., pp. 25–62. Tel Aviv, 1981.

ATLAS, YEHESKEL (Yehiel; 1913–1942), physician and partisan commander. Born in Rawa Mazowiecka, in the Warsaw district, Atlas studied medicine in France and Italy. The outbreak of war in 1939 found him in Kozlovshchina, near Slonim, in the area occupied by the Soviet army. His parents and sister died in the ghetto there on November 24, 1941, five months after the Germans had conquered the area. Atlas stayed on, serving the farmers of the neighborhood as a physician and giving medical assistance to Soviet troops who had survived in the forest. When the DERECHIN ghetto was liquidated, on July 24, 1942, Atlas organized those who escaped into a Jewish partisan company under his command. Numbering 120, the company was subordinated to a Soviet partisan leader named Bulat, who headed a battalion that fought in the Lipiczany Forest.

On August 10, Atlas initiated an attack on

Derechin in which forty-four German policemen were captured and executed. Though the Soviet authorities wanted the "fighting doctor" to practice medicine for the partisans, after the Derechin attack the partisan leadership, recognizing his gifts as a tactician, did not want to lose him as a combat commander. Atlas and his men blew up a train on the Lida-Grodno line, burned down a bridge on the Neman River, and, on September 5, launched an attack on Kozlovshchina in which over thirty Germans were killed.

The company gained fame throughout the region for its daring exploits and was mentioned in dispatches for its role in the Ruda-Jaworska battle of October 10, during which 127 Germans were killed, 75 captured, and a considerable amount of much-needed war material seized. Atlas also assisted the family camp attached to his company that housed escapees from nearby ghettos. Following the second *Aktion* that took place at DIATLOVO, on August 6, its refugees too were helped by Atlas. His personality, military exploits, and acts of revenge made a profound impression on both the Jewish and non-Jewish partisans in the region.

On December 5, 1942, Atlas was wounded in a battle at Wielka Wola; after handing the command over to Eliyahu Lipshowitz, he died from his wounds.

BIBLIOGRAPHY

Eckman, L., and C. Lazar. "Dr. Yehezkiel Atlas." *Jewish Combatant* 1/2 (Fall 1980): 8–13.
Kahanovitch, M. "Organizers and Commanders." In *The Fighting Ghettos*, edited by M. Barkai, pp. 134–147. Philadelphia, 1962.

SHALOM CHOLAWSKI

Yeheskel Atlas.

AUERSWALD, HEINZ (b. 1908), Nazi official; German commissar of the WARSAW ghetto from May 1941 until November 1942. Auerswald was one of the "ghetto managers" in eastern Europe who worked to maintain the ghettos for the efficient and productive exploitation of Jewish labor in the period before the regime made its decision regarding the ultimate disposition of the Jews.

Auerswald was a lawyer by career. He

joined the SS in June 1933 but gained party membership only in the late 1930s. Performing his military service with the Schutzpolizei (the regular police), Auerswald was sent to Warsaw with a police battalion in the fall of 1939. He was soon transferred to the civil administration that was established to govern the occupied city. There he was in charge of VOLKSDEUTSCHE (ethnic Germans) affairs until his appointment as commissar of the Warsaw ghetto, with its population totaling at least 400,000 people.

In his new capacity, Auerswald sought to foster a growing ghetto economy on the one hand and to halt the spread of epidemics on the other. While the former involved a more rational use of Jewish labor and marginally better provisioning for the working segment only, the latter involved further constrictions of the ghetto boundaries—intensifying the existing overcrowding—and the imposition of the death penalty for Jews caught outside the walls. The diary of Adam CZERNIAKÓW, the head of the Warsaw JUDENRAT (Jewish Council), reveals that on at least one occasion Auerswald spoke with the Jewish leader as a fellow human being—treatment virtually without parallel in the history of the Holocaust. In the days immediately before the deportations began, however, Auerswald cynically denied to Czerniaków that any danger threatened the ghetto.

Following the mass deportations from Warsaw to TREBLINKA between July and September 1942, Auerswald became the district administrator (*Kreishauptmann*) in the Ostrów area in November 1942 and was drafted into the army the following January. He was investigated by German judicial authorities in the 1960s but was not indicted.

BIBLIOGRAPHY

Browning, C. R. "Nazi Ghettoization Policy in Poland, 1939–1941." *Central European History* 19/4 (December 1986): 343–368.

Gutman, Y. *The Jews of Warsaw, 1939–1943: Ghetto, Underground, Revolt.* Bloomington, 1982.

Hilberg, R., S. Staron, and J. Kermisz, eds. *The Warsaw Diary of Adam Czerniakow.* New York, 1979.

Trunk, I. *Judenrat: The Jewish Councils in Eastern Europe under Nazi Occupation.* New York, 1972.

CHRISTOPHER R. BROWNING

AUSCHWITZ (Pol., Oświęcim), largest Nazi concentration and extermination camp, located 37 miles (60 km) west of Kraków. Auschwitz was both the most extensive of some two thousand Nazi concentration and forced-labor camps, and the largest camp at which Jews were exterminated by means of poison gas.

On April 27, 1940, the head of the SS and German police, Heinrich HIMMLER, ordered the establishment of a large new concentration camp near the town of Oświęcim in Polish Eastern Upper SILESIA, which had been annexed to the Third Reich after the defeat of Poland in September 1939. The building of the camp in Zasole, the suburb of Oświęcim, was started a short while later. The first laborers forced to work on the construction of the camp were three hundred Jews from Oświęcim and its vicinity. Beginning in June 1940, the Nazis brought transports of prisoners into the camp. During the first period, most of them were Polish political prisoners. On March 1, 1941, the prison population was 10,900, most of it still Polish.

Very soon Auschwitz became known as the harshest of the Nazi concentration camps. The Nazi system of torturing prisoners was implemented here in its most cruel form. In one of the camp's buildings, the so-called Block 11, a special bunker for the severest punishments was erected. In front of that building stood the "Black Wall," where the regular execution of prisoners took place. Ironically, above the main gate of the camp was a large inscription that declared: "Arbeit macht frei" (Work leads to freedom).

In March 1941, Himmler ordered the erection of a second, much larger section of the camp, which was located at a distance of 1.9 miles (3 km) from the original camp. This was called Auschwitz II, or Birkenau. The original camp became known as the *Stammlager* (main camp)—Auschwitz I. In addition to the inhabitants of the Zasole suburb of Oświęcim, about two thousand Poles from the villages of Babice, Budy, Rajsko, Brzezinka (in German, Birkenau, which became the name for the entire camp of Auschwitz II), Broszkowice, Pławy, and Harmęże were expelled from their homes, which were destroyed in order to build these two parts of the Auschwitz camp. A large expanse of

AUSCHWITZ and Sub-Camps

Concentration and Extermination Camp

Sub-Camp

Death Marches

Administrative Divisions of Poland under German Occupation, 1939-1945

1 Pomerania
2 Brandenburg
3 Saxony
4 Lower Silesia
5 Upper Silesia
6 Warthegau
7 Danzig (West Prussia)
8 East Prussia
9 Generalgouvernement
10 Białystok Region

© Polish National Publishing House (Państwowe Wydawnictwo Naukowe) Warsaw, 1979

about 15.5 square miles (40 sq km) was declared a prohibited area.

In October 1941, intensive work on the construction of barracks and other camp installations started in Auschwitz II. In the final stage, Auschwitz II was composed of nine sub-units, which were isolated from one another by electrically charged barbed-wire fences. These components were designated as camps BIa, BIb, BIIa, BIIb, BIIc, BIId, BIIe, BIIf, and BIII.

In March 1942 a *Frauenabteilung* (women's section) was established in the main camp, Auschwitz I, but was moved on August 16,

1942, to a section of Birkenau. The first groups of women to be imprisoned in the section in Auschwitz I were 999 German women from the RAVENSBRÜCK camp, and an equal number of Jewish women from Poprad, Slovakia; by the end of March more than 6,000 women prisoners were being held in the new section. In nearby Monowitz (Pol., Monowice) a third camp was built, which was called Auschwitz III (Buna-Monowitz). The name Buna derived from the Buna synthetic-rubber works in Monowitz. Other subcamps affiliated with Monowitz were set up, and they too were included as part of

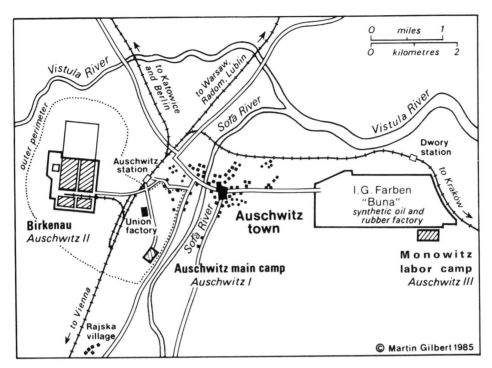

The three camps of Auschwitz.

Auschwitz III. In the course of time, another forty-five subcamps were built. Auschwitz II (Birkenau), which was the most populated camp of the Auschwitz complex, also had the most cruel and inhuman conditions. The prisoners of the Birkenau camps were mostly Jews, Poles, and Germans. For a time, the Gypsy family camp and the family camp of the Czech Jews were located there.

In Birkenau the gas chambers and the crematoria of the Auschwitz killing center operated. Auschwitz III (Buna-Monowitz and the other forty-five subcamps) were mainly forced-labor camps; the most important were Budy, Czechowitz (Czechowice), Gleiwitz (Gliwice), Rajsko, and Fürstengrube (Wesola). The inmates, chiefly Jews, were worked to the point of total exhaustion for German firms, among them I.G. FARBEN, Oberschlesische Hydriewerke, Deutsche Gasrusswerke, and Erdöl Raffinerie.

The Process. As the trains stopped at the *rampa* (railway platform) in Birkenau, the people inside were brutally forced to leave the cars in a great hurry. They had to leave behind all their personal belongings and were made to form two lines, men and women separately. These lines had to move

quickly to the place where SS officers were conducting the *Selektion*, directing the people either to one side (the majority), for the gas chambers, or to the other, which meant designation for forced labor. Those who were sent to the gas chambers were killed that same day and their corpses were burned in the crematoria, or, if there were too many for the crematoria to process, in an open space. The belongings left in the cars by the incoming victims were gathered by a forced-labor detachment ironically called "Kanada" (so termed because Canada was a symbol of wealth to the prisoners). Under the strict supervision of the SS, those prisoners had to store the property in specially built warehouses, to be shipped later to Germany for the benefit of the Third Reich's coffers.

Those victims not sent to the gas chambers were sent to that part of the camp called the "quarantine." But first they were taken to the camp's bath, the "sauna." There their clothes and every last personal belonging were taken from them, their hair was shorn—men and women alike—and they were given striped prisoners' garb. In the quarantine a prisoner, if not soon transferred to slave labor, could survive only for a few weeks; in the forced-

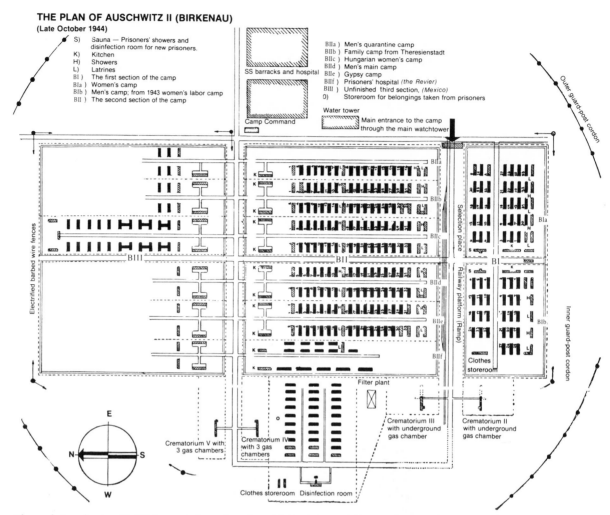

THE PLAN OF AUSCHWITZ II (BIRKENAU)
(Late October 1944)

S)   Sauna — Prisoners' showers and disinfection room for new prisoners.
K)   Kitchen
H)   Showers
L)   Latrines
BI)   The first section of the camp
BIa)   Women's camp
BIb)   Men's camp; from 1943 women's labor camp
BII)   The second section of the camp

BIIa)   Men's quarantine camp
BIIb)   Family camp from Theresienstadt
BIIc)   Hungarian women's camp
BIId)   Men's main camp
BIIe)   Gypsy camp
BIIf)   Prisoners' hospital (the Revier)
BIII)   Unfinished third section, (Mexico)
0)   Storeroom for belongings taken from prisoners

Plan of Auschwitz II (Birkenau), late October 1944. Adapted from *The Death Factory*, by Ota Kraus and Erich Kulka (1966).

labor camps the average life expectancy was extended to a few months. After that time, many of the prisoners became what was called in the camp jargon a MUSELMANN, a person so emaciated and weak that he could hardly move or react to his surroundings. It was no wonder that every prisoner tried to get out of quarantine as soon as possible.

Most of the prisoners were sent to Auschwitz subcamps or other concentration camps; some were directed to different work in Auschwitz I or III. One of the most dreaded institutions in Auschwitz was the roll call (*Appell*), which occurred early in the morning and in the late afternoon after the inmates had returned from their places of work, but sometimes also in the middle of the night. The inmates were made to stand to attention, motionless, usually sparsely clad, for many hours in the cold, in rain and snow, and whoever stumbled or fell was sent to be gassed. One of the most terrible tasks was that of the prisoners assigned to a special working group called the SONDERKOMMANDO. They were forced to work in the crematoria, burning the corpses of the victims who had been killed in the gas chambers on that day.

Prisoners were registered and received numbers tattooed on their left arm upon leaving the quarantine in Birkenau for forced labor in Auschwitz or in one of the subcamps. The same procedure applied to those prisoners who were directed straight to Auschwitz I; 405,000 prisoners of different nationalities were registered in this way. Not included in any form of registration were the vast majority of the Auschwitz victims, those men and women who, upon arrival in Auschwitz II, were led to the gas chambers and killed there immediately. Also not included in the registration were those prisoners who were sent to work in other concentration camps not belonging to the Auschwitz system, such as GROSS-ROSEN or STUTTHOF. Still another group of unregistered prisoners were those who were designated for execution after a short stay in the camp. That group consisted mainly of hostages, Soviet army officers, and partisans.

A day in the life of a prisoner, as many authors of concentration camp memoirs have so aptly described, is divided into a lengthy series of duties and commands. Some are dictated by camp routine, whereas others are unforeseen, a result of an order from above or an arbitrary outburst of violence on the part of the camp commandant. Some are directed against all the prisoners; others are aimed at an individual prisoner or a particular group of prisoners. All of the inmate's physical and mental capacities are unceasingly employed in an effort to get through the torturous stages that constitute an ordinary day—waking at dawn, straightening one's pallet, morning roll call, the journey to work, hours of hard labor, standing in line for a meal, the

Jewish brothers arriving at Auschwitz on a transport from Hungary in May 1944.

return to camp, block inspection, and evening roll call. "In camp, a small time unit," noted Victor Frankl, "a day, for example, filled with hourly tortures and fatigue, appeared endless." Any aberration or slip on the part of the prisoner—as a result of an incident in the work battalions or in the block, or a personal weakness or disease—very often meant death.

Besides those who were selected for forced labor upon arrival at the *rampa* in Birkenau, there was another, much smaller, group that was spared for the time being and not sent to the gas chambers. These were the people who were selected for pseudo-MEDICAL EXPERIMENTS. Many of these "experiments" were carried out on young Greek Jewish men and women. They underwent unbelievable suffering and torture. In July 1942, Himmler proposed instituting sterilization of Jewish women in Auschwitz. A German physician, Professor Carl CLAUBERG, who had the rank of SS-*Brigadeführer* and who had initiated such experiments with Himmler's permission at Ravensbrück, was given the task of establishing a similar experimental station for sterilizing women and for other criminal pseudomedical experiments in Block 10 of Auschwitz I. Among the victims selected for these experiments were groups of twins (including children) and dwarfs. Clauberg was assisted by a group of Nazi physicians who also usually conducted the *Selektionen* on the *rampa*

The "Kanada" slave-labor detachment.

This photograph, as well as the next nine, is from *The Auschwitz Album*. They were probably taken by Ernst Hoffman, a German photographer working in the Identification Service at Auschwitz. The series of photographs shows the arrival at Auschwitz-Birkenau of a transport of Hungarian Jews from the Transcarpathian Ukraine in June 1944. Here, the transport arrives at the *rampa*.

in Birkenau. The best known of this group was Josef MENGELE, who earned the notorious nickname "the Angel of Death" in the camp. His own barbarous experiments were mainly carried out on infant and young twins and on dwarfs.

On January 20, 1944, the total number of prisoners in Auschwitz was 80,839: 18,437 in Auschwitz I; 49,114 in Auschwitz II (22,061 in the men's section and 27,053 in the women's section); and 13,288 in Auschwitz III (of whom 6,571 were in Monowitz). By July 12, 1944, 92,208 prisoners were being held, and by August 22, that number had risen to 105,168. In addition, 50,000 other Jewish prisoners were held in the satellite camps. The total number of prisoners in that period was 155,000. The prison population was constantly growing, despite the periodic changes resulting from mass deaths, and despite the high mortality rate caused by starvation, hard labor, contagious diseases, and the total exhaustion of the prisoners.

In his memoirs, Rudolf HÖSS explained how Auschwitz was established as a killing center:

In the summer of 1941, I cannot remember the exact date, I was suddenly summoned to the *Reichsführer-SS*, directly by his adjutant's office. Contrary to his usual custom, Himmler received me without his adjutant being present and said, in effect:

"The Führer has ordered that the Jewish question be solved once and for all and that we, the SS, are to implement that order.

"The existing extermination centers in the east are not in a position to carry out the large actions that are anticipated. I have therefore designated Auschwitz for this purpose, both because of its good position as regards communications and because the area can easily be isolated and camouflaged."

We discussed the ways and means of effecting the extermination. This could only be done by gassing, since it would have been absolutely impossible to dispose by shooting of the large numbers of people that were expected, and it would have placed too heavy a burden on the

Two lines: men; women and children.

SS men who had to carry it out, especially because of the women and children among the victims.   (Höss, pp. 183–184)

The first, relatively small gas chamber was built in Auschwitz I. Here the experimental gassing using ZYKLON B gas first took place, on September 3, 1941. The victims were 600 Soviet prisoners of war and 250 other prisoners chosen from among the sick. After that experiment, the firm J. A. Topf and Sons received a contract to build much larger, permanent gas chambers connected with very large crematoria in Auschwitz-Birkenau, where the mass exterminations were mainly carried out. Altogether four such installations—II, III, IV, and V—were built in Birkenau. Each had the potential to kill 6,000 persons daily. The gas chambers were built to resemble shower rooms. The arriving victims were told that they would be sent to work, but that they first had to undergo disinfection and to shower.

Electrically charged barbed-wire fences 4 meters in height were erected around both Auschwitz I and Auschwitz II. They were guarded by SS men, who staffed the many watchtowers, and were equipped with machine guns and automatic rifles. In addition, Auschwitz II was surrounded by a network of canals 8 miles (13 km) in length. The whole complex of Auschwitz I and II was, moreover, enclosed by a chain of guard posts, two-thirds of a mile (1 km) out from the system of barbed-wire fences. The chain, called the *Postenkette* (outposts), was guarded by SS men with dogs; this unit was known as the *Hundestaffel* (dog battalion).

Auschwitz I, II, and III and the forty-five subcamps were overseen by one staff residing at the main camp, Auschwitz I. The commandants of the camp were, successively, Rudolf Höss, Arthur LIEBEHENSCHEL, Richard Baer, and again Rudolf Höss. They had the rank of SS-*Obersturmbannführer*. The most important division, noted for the cru-

The *Selektion*.

elty of its *Kommandatur* (command), was the Politische Abteilung (Political Division). The whole system was guarded by a specially organized regiment of the SS TOTENKOPF-VERBÄNDE (Death's-Head Units), an SS Totenkopfsturmbann (Totenkopf battalion) consisting of twelve guard companies, numbering at different times from twenty-five hundred to six thousand SS men.

The Nazi staff of the camp was aided by a number of privileged prisoners who were offered better food and conditions and more chances to survive, provided they helped to enforce the terror regime on their fellow prisoners. These prisoners were KAPOS (prisoner orderlies), *Blockälteste* (block elders, responsible for a certain block of prisoners' barracks), and *Vorarbeiter* (foremen, responsible for a group of prisoner workers).

As of March 1942, special trains organized by the REICHSSICHERHEITSHAUPTAMT (Reich Security Main Office; RSHA), containing Jews from the occupied countries in Europe, began arriving in Auschwitz-Birkenau almost

daily. Sometimes several, usually freight trains, arrived on the same day. In each of these trains, from one thousand to several thousand Jewish victims were forcibly brought in by the Nazis from the liquidated ghettos in Poland and other eastern European countries, as well as from countries in the west and south. The trains stopped at a special siding track that had been built within the Auschwitz-Birkenau camp. Its platform, called the *rampa*, became the busiest railway station in all of Nazi-occupied Europe, with one particular difference—namely, that people only arrived there, and never left again.

The first victims of the mass murder in Birkenau were Jews from Silesia. At the end of March 1942, transports of Jews started arriving from Slovakia and France; in July, from the Netherlands; and in August, from Belgium and Yugoslavia. In October, transports from the THERESIENSTADT ghetto began arriving; in November, transports from Greece and from the Ciechanów and

Białystok regions of Poland followed. The first transport from Berlin arrived in January 1943. Throughout 1943, transports continued to arrive from various countries under Nazi rule. One transport, of September 8, 1943, contained over five thousand inmates from the Theresienstadt ghetto who, surprisingly, arrived as entire families; they were not led to the gas chambers but were interned in a section of Birkenau that came to be known as the Theresienstadt family camp. After a stay of six months in this camp the inmates were suddenly driven out to the gas chambers and killed. On May 2, 1944, the first transport of Jews from Nazi-invaded Hungary arrived, presaging the large wave that would begin arriving on May 16 and would continue until the second week of July. The transports from Hungary were followed by transports from Łódź, the last ghetto to be liquidated in Poland, which came to Birkenau throughout August 1944.

Not only Jews but also about twenty thousand GYPSIES were deported to Auschwitz-Birkenau by the RSHA's order of January 29, 1943. The vast majority of them were killed in the gas chambers. A few hundred Polish political prisoners were also murdered in the gas chambers.

Resistance. Despite the severe conditions, the prisoners offered constant resistance to their oppressors. It took various forms, the most common being mutual help. However, there were also many instances of physical resistance and sabotage. One unidentified Jewish woman, on arriving on October 23, 1943, in a transport from BERGEN-BELSEN together with women who were led to the gas chambers, pulled a pistol out of the hands of an SS man and shot two others, Oberscharführer Schillinger and Unterscharführer Emmerich. The other women also resisted; all of them were killed by the SS reinforcement that arrived immediately. A very common form of resistance was escape; 667 prisoners, most of them Poles, Russians, and Jews, escaped under the most difficult conditions. However, 270 of the escapees were caught not far from the camp and afterward executed. The best-known and most dramatic escape was that of a Polish-Jewish couple, Mala ZIMETBAUM and Edward Galinski. They were caught and executed on September 15,

1944, in front of other prisoners who were forced to watch.

A well-known successful escape was that of two young Jews, Alfred Wetzler and Walter Rosenberg (Rudolf Vrba), on April 7, 1944. The two managed to reach Bratislava and contact some of the Jewish leaders still remaining there. They wrote a very detailed report on Auschwitz that was smuggled out to the free world (see AUSCHWITZ PROTOCOLS).

In 1943 a multinational resistance organization was formed on the initiative of Austrian prisoners; its name was Kampfgruppe Auschwitz (Auschwitz Fighting Group). This group operated in the main camp and in Birkenau; Monowitz had a group of its own, and the two were in contact with each other. The resistance movement in the camp was active in many spheres: helping the prisoners with medicines and food; documenting the Nazi crimes against the prisoners; organizing escapes, sabotage, and political action; seeking to place political prisoners in positions of responsibility; and preparing for an uprising in the camp.

Jewish leaders in the free world demanded that the Allied powers bomb Auschwitz (see AUSCHWITZ, BOMBING OF). This could well have stopped the continuation of the mass murders. As early as the fall of 1943, the Allied air forces could have destroyed the death installations in Auschwitz without much difficulty, from their newly conquered bases in Italy. In fact, they conducted bombardments of industrial targets in the vicinity of the camp. The destruction of Auschwitz by the Soviet forces would have been even easier. From July 1944, the Soviet front line was no more than 93 miles (150 km) from Auschwitz.

None of the Allied powers did anything to stop the mass murder in Auschwitz. No gas chamber was destroyed by the Allied air forces. The prisoners of the Sonderkommando, however, organized an uprising that took place on October 7, 1944, and did destroy at least one of the gas chambers. All the participants of that uprising fell in battle. After the uprising, the SS discovered that it was a group of young Jewish women from the Monowitz camp, led by Roza ROBOTA, who had smuggled out and supplied to the Sonderkommando the gunpowder that had been used in the uprising. Four of these

"Able-bodied" men after the *Selektion.*

Non-"able-bodied" men after the *Selektion.*

Striped prisoners' uniforms.

women, including Robota, were executed on January 6, 1945.

Prior to the uprising, the prisoners of the Sonderkommando accomplished another very important act of resistance: some of them managed to keep diaries, in which they described in detail the events at Auschwitz. These diaries were hidden in the ground. Discovered after the war, they provide the most significant, terrible, and authentic documents on Nazi barbarity in Auschwitz (*see* DIARIES, HOLOCAUST). The most important of these diaries are those of Zalman Gradowski and Zalman Levental.

Last Months. Immediately after the Sonderkommando uprising ended, the killing in the gas chambers came to a halt, and Himmler gave orders to demolish the crematoria. During November and December 1944, the technical installations of the gas chambers and crematoria I and II were dismantled, so that they could be transferred to the Gross-Rosen camp. Special Sonderkommandos of male and female prisoners were formed whose task was to clean up the crematoria pits, which were then to be filled with the human ashes from the crematoria, covered with earth, and planted with grass. Some of the warehouses containing the goods stolen from the Jews were hastily emptied of their contents; the valuable items were sent to Germany by train, and the rest of the booty was destroyed. Between December 1, 1944, and January 15, 1945, no fewer than 514,843 items of men's, women's, and children's clothing and underwear were shipped from the camp.

In the middle of January 1945, the Soviet army started an offensive in the direction of Kraków and Auschwitz. The Nazis began a hasty withdrawal. The fifty-eight thousand prisoners, most of them Jewish, were driven out of the Auschwitz camps and put on DEATH MARCHES. Most of them were killed during these marches; others were murdered even before the camps were evacuated.

On January 27, in the afternoon, soldiers of the Soviet army entered Auschwitz. In Birkenau they found the bodies of 600 prisoners who had been killed by the Nazis hours before the camp was liberated. However, 7,650 sick and exhausted prisoners were saved: 1,200 in Auschwitz I, 5,800 in Auschwitz II–Birkenau, and 650 in Auschwitz

III–Buna-Monowitz. The haste in which they had to withdraw made it impossible for the Germans to force these last prisoners on the death marches. Their hurried retreat also prevented them from emptying the rest of the warehouses of the victims' plundered property. In the warehouses, the Soviets found 350,000 men's suits, 837,000 outfits for women, and large amounts of children's and babies' clothing. In addition, they found tens of thousands of pairs of shoes and 7.7 tons (7,000 kg) of human hair in paper bags, packed for shipping.

Auschwitz was the largest graveyard in human history. The number of Jews murdered in the gas chambers of Birkenau must be estimated at up to one and a half million people: men, women, and children. Almost one-quarter of the Jews killed during World War II were murdered in Auschwitz. Of the 405,000 registered prisoners who received Auschwitz numbers, only about 65,000 survived. Of the 16,000 Soviet prisoners of war who were brought there, only 96 survived. According to various estimates, at least 1,600,000 people were murdered in the killing center at Birkenau.

After the war, several trials were held in Poland and West Germany of German Nazis who had committed crimes in Auschwitz. The former camp commandant, Rudolf Höss, was tried in March 1947 in Auschwitz before a Polish court and sentenced to death on April 2, 1947. While in the Polish prison he wrote his memoirs, which were published in Poland in 1956; they appeared in English in 1959. In November and December 1947, another trial took place in Kraków before a Polish court. Of the forty Nazis from Auschwitz indicted, twenty-three were sentenced to death and sixteen were sent to prison. Between 1963 and 1966 the so-called Auschwitz Trials I, II, and III took place in Frankfurt am Main before a court of the German Federal Republic. These ended with prison sentences for the twenty-two defendants accused of committing crimes in Auschwitz. Nine were sentenced to life imprisonment, and the others to terms ranging from three to nine years.

The horrors of Auschwitz have become legendary, and the name itself has passed into international usage as a byword for all that is bestial in humankind.

"Able-bodied" women after the *Selektion*.

Non-"able-bodied" women and children after the *Selektion*.

Women with shorn hair after "delousing."

On the way to the gas chambers. "For these crimes, there is no adequate punishment . . . this kind of guilt, in contrast to all criminal guilt, goes beyond and
destroys every system of law and justice. . . . And as non-human as this guilt is, so
is the innocence of the victims. As innocent as the victims were in front of the gas
chambers, no human being can ever be. . . . This kind of guilt . . . is beyond all
crime" (Hannah Arendt in a letter to Karl Jaspers, 1946).

BIBLIOGRAPHY

Gilbert, M. *Auschwitz and the Allies*. New York, 1981.

Gutman, Y., and A. Saf, eds. *The Nazi Concentration Camps: Structure and Aims; The Image of the Prisoner; The Jews in the Camps*. Proceedings of the Fourth Yad Vashem International Historical Conference. Jerusalem, 1984.

Höss, R. *Commandant of Auschwitz*. London, 1959.

Kielar, W. *Anus Mundi: Fifteen Hundred Days in Auschwitz-Birkenau*. New York, 1980.

Kraus, O., and E. Kulka. *The Death Factory: Documents on Auschwitz*. New York, 1966.

Langbein, H. *Auschwitz-Prozess: Eine Dokumentation*. 2 vols. Vienna, 1965.

Langbein, H. *Menschen in Auschwitz*. Vienna, 1972.

Levi, P. *Survival in Auschwitz: The Nazi Assault on Humanity*. New York, 1981.

Lukowski, J. *Bibliografia obozu koncentracyjnego Oświęcim-Brzezinka*. 5 vols. Warsaw, 1970.

Mark, B. *The Scrolls of Auschwitz*. Tel Aviv, 1985.

SHMUEL KRAKOWSKI and
JOZEF BUSZKO

AUSCHWITZ, BOMBING OF. By the spring of 1944, the massive killing operations under way at AUSCHWITZ were well known to the Allied governments (*see* AUSCHWITZ PROTOCOLS). By that time the Allied air forces controlled the skies of Europe and clearly had the range to strike Auschwitz as well as the railways leading to it. Yet no effort was made to bomb the gas chambers or the deportation railways, despite numerous requests for such action.

Great Britain's Prime Minister Winston CHURCHILL and Foreign Secretary Anthony EDEN supported a proposal made by the Jewish Agency for Palestine to bomb Auschwitz and the railways to it. But officials in the British Air Ministry and the Foreign Office managed, by stalling, to choke the plan to death, without ever looking carefully into its feasibility. The official British reply to the Jewish Agency dishonestly stated that "technical difficulties" made the proposed operations impossible (*see* GREAT BRITAIN).

The United States government also received requests, mostly from Jewish sources, to smash the Auschwitz killing installations and the railways to Auschwitz. These proposals became numerous in the spring of 1944, as the deportation of the large Hungarian Jewish community began. The first of the requests was turned down by the United States War Department in late June 1944 on the ground that "it could be executed only by diversion of considerable air support essential to the success of our forces now engaged in decisive operations."

In reality, the War Department's negative decision was not based on any analysis of air force operations. The department never looked into the feasibility of carrying out such bombing operations; it did not even consult the air force commanders based in Italy who were in the best position to strike Auschwitz.

What happened was that the War Department officials, when first confronted with the issue in June 1944, looked into their own files in Washington. There they found that several months earlier, the War Department had secretly established a policy of noninvolvement in rescue activities. This policy had come in response to President Franklin D. ROOSEVELT's formation of the WAR REFUGEE BOARD (WRB) in January of that year. The president's executive order establishing the WRB had specified that the State (*see* UNITED STATES DEPARTMENT OF STATE), Treasury, and War departments each had a special responsibility to help the WRB in its rescue endeavors. War Department officials, alarmed that this might mean that military forces would be diverted to rescue missions, unilaterally decided on a policy of noninvolvement in rescue. This was done despite awareness that it was in violation of the president's executive order. The policy was kept secret.

When the first bombing request came to the War Department, forwarded through the WRB, War Department officials checked their files and found the department's no-rescue policy. On that basis they decided against the proposal, without even looking into its feasibility. Obviously, they could not inform the WRB of the real reason for rejecting the bombing request. Instead, they used the best argument available: that it would divert military power from essential war operations.

Aerial bombing map of Auschwitz used to plan runs over Auschwitz by United States forces. The industrial areas were targeted, leaving the railway lines to the camp intact. [A Living Memorial to the Holocaust—Museum of Jewish Heritage, New York]

With this, the die was cast. Each of the several succeeding requests to bomb the gas chambers and the railways was rejected for the same reason as the first. The last such request was turned down in mid-November 1944. It is now known that these bombings were definitely within the capability of the United States Air Force based in Italy; in fact, they could have been accomplished in connection with essential war operations.

Because the Auschwitz complex included a major industrial area adjacent to the camp, Auschwitz itself was a military target. The primary objective there was a synthetic oil refinery. The Germans had seven other synthetic oil plants in the region, all based on the vast coal resources of Upper Silesia and all within 45 miles of Auschwitz. From July through November 1944, more than twenty-eight hundred American heavy bombers pounded the eight oil installations. En route to their targets, all these aircraft flew along or over key deportation railways. On two occasions (August 20 and September 13), large fleets of American bombers struck the industrial area at Auschwitz itself, less than 5 miles from the four huge gas chamber installations.

Yet on August 14, 1944, the War Department insisted, in a letter to Leon Kubowitzki (Aryeh Kubovy) of the World Jewish Congress, that bombing the Auschwitz killing installations and the deportation railways was not possible because such actions "could be executed only by the diversion of considerable air support essential to the success of our forces now engaged in decisive operations elsewhere." This was a word-for-word repetition of the June refusal. It was at variance with the facts and was no more than an excuse for inaction.

BIBLIOGRAPHY

Gilbert, M. *Auschwitz and the Allies.* London, 1981.
Wyman, D. S. *The Abandonment of the Jews: America and the Holocaust, 1941–1945.* New York, 1984.

DAVID S. WYMAN

AUSCHWITZ PROTOCOLS, two detailed reports about mass killings at AUSCHWITZ that were based on information provided by four escapees from the camp in the spring of 1944.

On April 7, 1944, with the help of the Auschwitz underground, two Slovak Jews, Rudolf Vrba (Walter Rosenberg) and Alfred Wetzler, began the steps that would lead to their escape from the camp. Members of the Auschwitz underground prepared a hideout for them in a gap in a woodpile that was located beyond the camp's inner perimeter. To confuse the dogs that would inevitably search for them, strong Russian tobacco that had been soaked in gasoline was spread around them. For three days and two nights Vrba and Wetzler waited for the search to end, and then fled toward Slovakia.

Two weeks later they arrived in Žilina, where they met Erwin Steiner, a representative of the Jewish Council. After hearing their story, Steiner contacted the Bratislava Jewish Council and spoke to Oscar Krasnansky on the phone. Krasnansky immediately arranged permission to travel by train to Žilina. At Steiner's house, he heard the two escapees' testimony and wrote a thirty-page report based upon it. Vrba and Wetzler described the workings of the camp, gave estimated statistics of Jews who had been killed (about 1.75 million), and warned that preparations were being made for the murder of the nearly 800,000 Jews of Hungary and the 3,000 Czech Jews who had been brought from THERESIENSTADT six months earlier.

In Bratislava, the report was passed on to Rabbi Michael Dov WEISSMANDEL of the PRACOVNÁ SKUPINA (Working Group) in Slovakia. A follow-up report was supplied by two more escapees, Czesław Mordowicz and Arnost Rosin, who reached the Slovak border on June 6, 1944, following their escape from Auschwitz on May 27. Meeting with Krasnansky, they added fresh information about Auschwitz. Among other things, they told of the arrival and murder of about three thousand Greek Jews, and the beginning of the murder of Hungarian Jews—90 percent of whom were killed immediately upon arrival. Their information was combined with the first report.

Attempts to smuggle the protocols abroad met with mixed results. First, the Pracovná Skupina tried to dispatch the Vrba-Wetzler report to Istanbul, giving it to a supposedly reliable courier. However, instead of passing it on to the representatives of the Rescue Committee of the Jewish Agency in Istanbul, the courier apparently handed over the report to the Budapest Gestapo. Rabbi Weissmandel then tried to use his contacts with Swiss Orthodox Jews to transmit it to the West. At first this channel failed him, but on May 16, 1944, the Pracovná Skupina sent a message that reached Isaac Sternbuch, the representative of the Orthodox Va'ad ha-Hatsala (Rescue Committee) in Switzerland. The message contained an abridged version of the Auschwitz protocols, and exhorted the Allies to bomb the extermination camp and the railway lines leading to it. In addition, the group suggested that Hungary be warned, the facts of the mass killings be publicized, the International RED CROSS be allowed into the camp, and money be provided to help rescue Hungarian Jews.

With the hope that it would later reach the free world, the report was also disseminated to key people in Bratislava. Krasnansky and Oskar Neumann (a member of the Pracovná Skupina) gave Rezső KASZTNER of the RELIEF AND RESCUE COMMITTEE OF BUDAPEST a copy of the Vrba-Wetzler report on April 28, 1944, when he visited the city. Apparently Kasztner brought it back to Budapest, but did not publicize it for fear the information would disrupt the rescue negotiations taking place between Hungarian Jewish leaders and the

Nazis. In mid-May, Rabbi Weissmandel also sent the report to Fülöp FREUDIGER (the leader of the Orthodox Relief and Rescue Committee in Budapest), specifically warning him that the Nazis were about to begin the liquidation of Hungarian Jewry. According to his testimony at the trial of Adolf EICHMANN, Freudiger forwarded the information to the Zsidó Tanács, the Jewish Council of Hungary; Angelo Rotta, the papal nuncio; and the Hungarian regent, Miklós HORTHY. The papal chargé d'affaires in Bratislava, Giuseppe Burzio, was also given the report and sent it to Rome on May 22, 1944. It is not known for certain when it reached the Vatican, but the notes on the Vatican's copy are dated October 22 and 25, 1944.

Following the arrival of the escapees Mordowicz and Rosin, the expanded report was sent to the West. Dr. Jaromir Kopecky, the Geneva representative of the CZECHOSLOVAK GOVERNMENT-IN-EXILE, received a copy from the Pracovná Skupina's courier on June 13, 1944. He informed Gerhart Riegner of the WORLD JEWISH CONGRESS, who in turn sent a telegraphic summary of the report (see RIEGNER CABLE) and a cover letter by Kopecky to Elizabeth Wiskemann of the British legation in Bern. She dispatched the information to Allen Dulles, the head of United States intelligence in Switzerland, who sent it to the American representative in Bern, Roswell McClelland, and he in turn forwarded it to the Department of State in Washington on June 16. Others received the report soon thereafter. The BBC broadcast some of the details on June 18, and the Swedes received a copy of the report on June 23, 1944. With the reception of the protocols in the West and the dissemination of the information contained in them, the true purpose of the Auschwitz extermination camp became clear to the free world.

BIBLIOGRAPHY

Gilbert, M. *Auschwitz and the Allies*. New York, 1981.
Mendelsohn, J., ed. *The Holocaust: Selected Documents in 18 volumes*. Vol. 11. New York, 1981.
Wyman, D. S. *The Abandonment of the Jews: America and the Holocaust, 1941–1945*. New York, 1984.

ROBERT ROZETT

AUSLANDSORGANISATION DER NSDAP (Foreign Organization of the NSDAP), organization founded in 1930 on the initiative of Bruno Fricke, from Paraguay, and Gregor Strasser, who at the time was in charge of the NAZI PARTY organization in Germany. Initially the organization had 300 members, residents of foreign countries. On August 7, 1931, the first Nazi party branch abroad, in Buenos Aires, was officially recognized. It was followed, on October 5, by a branch in Rio de Janeiro. On August 20 of that year the first nationwide organization was established, in Paraguay.

The Auslandsorganisation's first director was Hans Nieland, who was in charge of the Nazi organization in Hamburg and became a member of the Reichstag in 1930. Originally named Bund der Freunde der Hitlerbewegung (League of Friends of the Hitler Movement), for internal purposes its name was the Auslandsorganisation of the NSDAP. When the Nazis came to power in early 1933, over 160 local party branches were in existence in foreign countries, with 3,100 members. In the spring of 1933 Robert LEY appointed Ernst-Wilhelm Bohle to head the Auslandsorganisation. In his first report, submitted to the Nuremberg party rally at the end of August 1933, Bohle stated that since 1929, 230 local and countrywide branches had been set up in foreign countries. During the years that followed, Bohle's organization sought to enroll in the Nazi party the VOLKSDEUTSCHE (ethnic Germans) all over the globe; their number, in 1937, was estimated at 7 million. Nearly all of them, however, were assimilated into the society of the countries in which they lived, and the plan made little headway.

In 1937, Bohle was appointed head of the Auslandsorganisation section in the German Foreign Ministry, in order to improve coordination of the supervision of Nazi party members abroad. The staff of the Auslandsorganisation in Germany was estimated, in 1938, to number 800 (the figure apparently also included persons holding honorary posts); their assignment was to supervise 600 party cells and bases, local and countrywide branches abroad (consisting of 29,099 members), and 23,000 party members serving in the merchant marine. At that time the Foreign Ministry, headed by Joachim von RIBBENTROP, had a staff of 2,665 officers and employees serving abroad. Germans who were permanently resident abroad numbered over 500,000, of whom 6 percent were party members. The fourth convention of the Auslandsorganisation, held in Erlingen in September 1936, was attended by over 5,000 *Amtsleiter* (office managers) from all over the world. The fifth convention, held a year later in Stuttgart (which had been declared the "city of Germans residing outside Germany"), attracted over 10,000 Germans from abroad.

A highly significant event in the organization's history was the assassination of Wilhelm GUSTLOFF, the national director of the Auslandsorganisation in Switzerland, by a young Jew, David FRANKFURTER, on February 4, 1936. In his eulogy of Gustloff, Hitler compared Gustloff to the "martyrs" who had sacrificed themselves for the Nazi movement and called the deed "a declaration of war."

The foreign-trade section of the Auslandsorganisation and the "Germany" section of the Foreign Ministry opposed the HAAVARA AGREEMENT, the purpose of which was to facilitate the emigration of German Jews to Palestine. Until 1939, they had little success. They felt that the export of goods from Germany for which no payment was made in return and which would promote the establishment of a Jewish national state was against Germany's interests. In the period from 1933 to 1938, imports to Germany rose much faster than exports, and one of the Auslandsorganisation's goals was to promote exports. To this day there is no consensus on the importance of the role that the Auslandsorganisation played in the field of foreign affairs, but it seems to have been overrated. In November 1941 Bohle resigned from his post in the Foreign Ministry, an act that was regarded as an admission of the Auslandsorganisation's failure as far as Germany's foreign interests were concerned.

BIBLIOGRAPHY

De Jong, L. *The German Fifth Column in the Second World War.* London, 1956.

McKale, D. M. *The Swastika outside Germany.* Kent, Ohio, 1977.

HANS-HEINRICH WILHELM

AUSSERORDENTLICHE BEFRIEDUNGS-AKTION. *See* AB-Aktion.

AUSTRALIA, JEWISH REFUGEES IN. Adolf Hitler's assumption of power and the persecution of Jews in Germany after 1933 created a refugee problem for the British dominion of Australia that grew steadily worse throughout the 1930s. As each new crisis occurred, the Australian government was pressured to change its alien migration policies, and between 1936 and 1939 a more generous quota was gradually introduced.

In the 1930s, Australia was seen as a suitable place of refuge because of its small population, low birthrate, and democratic traditions. In both London and Australia, Jewish representatives requested the Australian government to permit more Jewish REFUGEES to settle in Australia, but until 1936 such requests met with a negative response. Only aliens possessing 500 pounds in landing money or dependent relatives of aliens already residing in Australia were allowed to enter. This policy of virtual exclusion meant that few Jewish refugees arrived before 1936.

Between 1936 and 1939, owing to the intensification of Nazi antisemitism and the slow improvement of economic conditions in Australia, there was a gradual relaxation of alien immigration policies. In 1936 the government reduced the landing-money requirement to 50 pounds and agreed that a responsible Jewish organization could act as guarantor. Aliens without a guarantor needed 200 pounds' landing money, and there was a quota system for the issue of landing permits. At the government's instigation, the Australian Jewish Welfare Society (AJWS) was formed in 1937, under the presidency of Sir Samuel Cohen, to coordinate efforts for Jewish refugees. This replaced the German Jewish Relief Fund, created in New South Wales in 1936 to raise funds to assist German Jews escaping from Nazism. In June 1938, at the EVIAN CONFERENCE, the Australian government announced that it would not increase its alien immigration quotas. After the devastation of the KRISTALLNACHT pogrom in Germany in November 1938, the government revised its policy. In a major ministerial statement on December 1, 1938, the minister for the interior, John McEwen, announced that Australia would admit 15,000 refugees over a period of three years, although this statement was not as liberal as it appeared on the surface since the Australian high commissioner in London, S. M. Bruce, had proposed a figure of 30,000. The outbreak of war in September 1939 ended the flow of refugees; by this time some 7,200 had arrived, 5,080 of them in 1939.

With the pressures of the arrival of the Jewish refugees, the AJWS grew rapidly by 1938 from a small organization run largely by volunteers to a large-scale association with fourteen full-time employees, located at the Maccabean Hall in Sydney. With financial assistance from the Refugee Economic Corporation, founded by American philanthropist Charles J. Liebman, the Mutual Enterprises organization was created to assist refugees to establish themselves in business, and Mutual Farms was founded to settle refugees on the land. A training farm was opened at Chelsea Park, Baulkham Hills, Sydney. These schemes operated in New South Wales, while in Victoria a Welfare Society also developed, under the leadership of Isaac Herbert Boas and in cooperation with the Melbourne Jewish Aid Society, which provided interest-free loans to newcomers.

The origins of Australian Jewry date back to Australia's foundation in 1788. Organized Jewish communities did not develop until the 1830s and 1840s, following the arrival of free English Jewish settlers. A number of German Jews settled in Victoria during the gold rushes of the 1850s, while a trickle of east European Jews arrived between 1880 and 1914; in the 1920s, about 2,000 Polish Jews settled in Australia, mainly in Melbourne. According to the census of June 30, 1933, the number of Jews in Australia was 23,553, or 0.36 percent of the population.

Most of the foreign Jews were absorbed into the Australian community and, until the 1930s, Australian Jewry remained Anglo-Jewish and very conservative in outlook. The community enjoyed a high economic and social status. The Jews were very Australianized, and responded to the refugees in a cold, unfeeling, and materialistic manner. Their social rejection of the newcomers, who were

seen as a threat to Australian Jewry's social and civic status, was a result of fear and distrust and also of a sense of conformity in this isolated and parochial community. In addition, there was a language barrier, especially in New South Wales, where, before 1939, very few in the established Jewish community spoke German, Polish, or Yiddish. The refugees were instructed not to speak German in the streets or streetcars, and not to walk in groups "loudly speaking in a foreign language," because "the welfare of the old established Jewish community in Australia as well as of every migrant depends on your personal behavior." The Jewish refugees were encouraged to make themselves as inconspicuous as possible and to assimilate quickly into Australian society.

Most Australians favored migration from the British Isles and opposed admission of large groups of aliens. The refugees represented the intrusion of an alien way of life, and Australians generally could not understand their different behavioral patterns and mode of dress. Many Australians believed that European Jews were different in ethics and morality from the Anglo-Jews whom they respected and admired. There was also fear of economic competition and the undermining of living standards, especially during the time of economic hardship in the 1930s. These factors created a sense of hostility toward the refugees and led to mounting accusations of various malpractices and unsavory behavior. The accusations were used to justify anti-refugee feelings—despite the fact that the refugees contributed to Australia's industrial development by bringing new skills, and to its cultural development, especially in music.

A small group of Australians were influenced by fascist ideas, and a few right-wing fringe organizations were formed during the 1930s. Most important of these were the New Guard in New South Wales, under the leadership of Eric Campbell, and the Australia First movement, which adopted Nazi racial policies and published large tracts of Hitler's speeches in its newspaper, the *Publicist*. A German Nazi party was also formed in Australia. Nazi influence was increased by the activities of the German consul general, Dr. Rudolph Asmis. In addition, the Social Credit movement of Canada, founded on the financial theories of Maj. C. H. Douglas (a former British army officer who believed that poverty existed amid plenty because of the banks' monopoly over credit), established roots in Australia with antisemitic overtones. This was evident in its Victoria publication, the *New Times,* and in the activities of its correspondent, Eric Butler.

With the outbreak of war, Australia joined the Allied war effort, and Australian forces were sent to fight in France and the Middle East. Later some of these forces participated in the fighting in Italy (1943), Normandy (1944), and various sections of the eastern front. Members of the Australia First movement were interned.

During the war, the Australian Jewish community became aware of the Nazi destruction program. Following the Allies' joint announcement on December 17, 1942, of their recognition of the massacre of the Jews in Poland, the United Jewish Emergency Committee was formed in Sydney by Dr. Jona M. Machover, a leading Zionist, originally an emigré from the Russian Revolution who settled in London and was stranded in Australia during the war. In Melbourne, the United Jewish Overseas Relief Fund (UJORF) was founded, under the presidency of Leo Fink, to raise funds and collect goods to assist the suffering brethren in Europe. At the same time, the Palestine Jewish community cabled the Australian government, informing it of the slaughter of Polish Jews and appealing to it "to open the gates of free countries to those who seek refuge from that inferno on earth." By 1943, communal documents recorded the destruction of 3 million to 4 million European Jews, and in November of that year a resolution, endorsed by the Jewish communities in all the Australian states and referring to the parlous state of European Jewry, was presented to Prime Minister John Curtin. It urged him to support Jewish immigration to both Australia and Palestine, and to participate in "any international scheme for the provision of relief to the survivors of Nazi atrocities." Despite these developments, most people were not aware of the full extent of the Holocaust or the exact details of the extermination program until after the war, and the Australian government made no positive response to the appeals during the war years.

Lack of understanding of the plight of European Jews was evidenced in the fact that refugees from Germany, Austria, and later Hungary were labeled as "enemy aliens" and were required to report regularly to the local police, to obtain a police pass if they wished to travel outside their police area, and to surrender their radios. Some of these refugees were also interned initially at Hay in New South Wales and later at Tatura, Victoria. There they joined some two thousand four hundred refugee internees who had been sent to Australia by Britain on the *Dunera* in September 1940 and internees from Singapore and other parts of East Asia.

The story of the *Dunera* became particularly notorious in the wake of British hysteria about Nazi agents among refugees. The *Dunera* was dispatched to Australia with 2,542 men on board. Included in the transport were 200 former Italian Fascists and 251 German prisoners of war, mostly seamen. The overwhelming majority of the passengers were "C" class aliens, that is, those who had been classified as potentially least dangerous to British security.

The *Dunera* had been built to accommodate sixteen hundred passengers, and the resultant overcrowding of the ship led to insufferable conditions during the voyage. The food was inedible, and the crew often behaved with barbaric cruelty. Many refugees were beaten, and all had their belongings ransacked. The refugees tried to make the best of their situation. Lectures were given, Torah study groups formed, and a constitution was written. These activities continued in the Hay and Tatura camps. The constitution was refined, and a makeshift college was set up where camp inmates could study subjects ranging from mathematics to metaphysics, besides a great variety of languages. A theater company, a rabbinical academy (yeshiva), and Zionist study groups were also established. Many of the *Dunera* internees returned to Britain toward the end of the war. Around one thousand remained; most of them volunteered for service in the Australian military forces employment companies, which engaged them in essential nonmilitary wartime work.

The total number of Jewish refugees reaching Australia between 1933 and 1945 was eight thousand two hundred, and their status was eventually redefined as that of "friendly aliens." Of the three thousand five hundred male refugees between the ages of eighteen and forty-five, nearly every one volunteered for military service as soon as refugees were permitted to do so, and one thousand two hundred were accepted. Of the rest, most were engaged in industries classified as essential to the Australian war effort; Jewish refugees also contributed their scientific knowledge to the war effort.

Because of their sense of isolation during the internment period and their disillusionment at the lack of support from the established Jewish leadership, the refugees instituted their own separate organizations. In Melbourne the Association of Jewish Refugees was formed under the leadership of the dynamic liberal rabbi Dr. Herman Sanger, who had arrived from Germany in 1936. In Sydney the Association of Refugees, led by Dr. Max Joseph, followed suit.

During the war years the "thirty-niners," as the refugees who arrived in the late 1930s were called, provided the impetus and manpower to introduce significant changes into Jewish communal management. These affected every aspect of Jewish life in Australia, including the growth of orthodox and liberal Judaism, the establishment of the first Jewish day school, the North Bondi Jewish Kindergarten and Primary School in Sydney, the creation of B'nai B'rith, and the evolution of a more democratic communal structure through the Board of Deputies and the formation of the Executive Council of Australian Jewry in 1944. Attitudes toward Zionism, previously a fringe movement in the community, also changed as a result of the impact of the newcomers. After the war, the Jewish immigration increased. By 1954 the total number of pre- and postwar Jewish refugees settled in Australia was approximately 25,500, while the total Jewish population had increased to 48,436.

BIBLIOGRAPHY

Blakeney, M. *Australia and the Jewish Refugees, 1933–1948.* Sydney, 1985.

Kwiet, K., and J. A. Moses, eds. "On Being a German-Jewish Refugee in Australia." *Australian Journal of Politics and History* 31/1 (1985): entire issue.

Pearl, C. *The Dunera Scandal: Deported by Mistake.* Sydney, 1983.

Rutland, S. D. "The Coming of the Refugees." In *Edge of the Diaspora: Two Centuries of Jewish Settlement in Australia.* Sydney, 1988.

SUZANNE D. RUTLAND

AUSTRIA. The German core of the Austro-Hungarian Empire, Austria became a separate republic in 1918 when the empire broke up into its national components and Habsburg rule came to an end. The country has an area of 32,432 square miles (84,000 sq km), and its population in 1937 was 6,725,000. Jews are believed to have lived in Austria from Roman times; in the Middle Ages, periods when the Jews enjoyed material and cultural prosperity alternated with periods of persecution and expulsions. In the modern era, Austria was one of the centers of the Jewish modernization process and the integration of Jews into the country's overall culture. In 1849 the Jews were given the right to organize as a community, and in 1867 they

AUSTRIA, November 1938

© Martin Gilbert 1982

Courtyard of the central synagogue in Vienna on March 18, 1938, when the Gestapo closed the Jewish community offices and institutions and arrested the officers and leaders. Among the SS men is Adolf Eichmann (left, facing the camera).

were granted equality of rights. During the second half of the nineteenth century and the first few decades of the twentieth, the Jewish population of Austria grew rapidly as a result of immigration from all parts of the empire, the greater part of the newcomers converging on the capital, VIENNA.

Jews played an important role in the economic and cultural life of Austria, which became a center of Jewish culture and the cradle of Zionism. At the same time the country was one of the first and most virulent centers of modern antisemitism. The Jewish population in Austria reached its height during World War I, approaching 250,000, as a result of the influx of war refugees from Galicia and Bukovina. After the war the Jewish population declined, to 191,000 in 1934 (176,000 in Vienna) and 185,000 in 1938 (170,000 in Vienna, 8,000 in Lower Austria, 1,000 in Upper Austria, 2,000 in Styria, 3,200 in Burgenland, and a few hundred in other parts of the country).

The Anschluss. On March 11, 1938, Adolf Hitler sent his army into Austria and on March 13 the annexation (ANSCHLUSS) of Austria to the Reich was proclaimed in Vienna. Most of the population welcomed the Anschluss enthusiastically, and this fervor also expressed itself in widespread antisemitic rioting and an almost total absence of resis-

tance to the Nazis. The Austrian Nazis lost no time in following the pattern, established by their fellow Nazis in Germany, of attacking Jews and expelling them from the country's economic, cultural, and social life—indeed, they outdid the German Nazis.

This greater scope of Nazi violence and brutality in Austria was also inspired from the top: on March 18, 1938, the German minister of the interior, Wilhelm FRICK, gave Heinrich HIMMLER extraordinary powers, enabling Himmler to operate in Austria beyond the limits set by law, in order to "preserve order and security." That same day Himmler set up a Gestapo headquarters in Vienna (in the Hotel Metropol, which had been confiscated from its Jewish owners), vesting in it political and police authority in Vienna and Lower Austria. The following day, Chief of Police Reinhard HEYDRICH empowered the chief of the Gestapo headquarters in Vienna, Franz Josef Huber, to establish Gestapo Lower Austria. The following day, Chief of Police Reinhard HEYDRICH empowered the chief of the Gestapo headquarters in Vienna, Franz Josef Huber, to establish Gestapo branch offices in Linz, Graz, Salzburg, Klagenfurt, Innsbruck, and Eisenstadt. By March 18, the offices of the Jewish community and the Zionist institutions in Vienna were closed down, and their officers were put in jail; 444

Jewish societies in Vienna and 181 in the provinces were forced to terminate their operations. A total of 110 public personalities, bankers, and businessmen were arrested and deported to DACHAU in the first two groups to be sent there from Vienna, on April 1 and May 15, respectively. In the first night following the Anschluss, March 13–14, the Gestapo launched an organized campaign of looting Jewish apartments, confiscating artworks, rugs, furniture, and other valuables, and shipping the loot to Berlin. The Gomperz and Rothschild art collections (their owners had been arrested) were transferred to the museum in Linz and to the private collections of Hitler and Hermann GÖRING. Göring was put in charge of Austria's economy on March 15, 1938.

In the very first week after the Anschluss, Jews were dismissed from their posts in theaters, community centers, and public libraries, and, on March 26, from employment in universities and colleges, and later in markets and slaughterhouses. Ritual slaughter was outlawed. On March 14, three Jews serving in the Austrian army refused to take an oath of loyalty to the Führer, and as a result all Jews were dismissed from the army. This step, however, did not absolve the Jews from having to go through the humiliating process of reporting for the draft when they reached conscription age, going through the medical examination, and then being rejected for service because they were Jewish.

In Graz the synagogues were desecrated and four Jews were killed, and in Vienna the main synagogue was used as a place where Jews were subjected to torture. All over Austria Jews were arrested and held in jail until they were ready to sign a statement that they were voluntarily giving up their property. In Graz, the Jews who were tortured and kept in jail for two months included Nobel prize winner Professor Otto Loewi and Chief Rabbi Professor David Herzog. The number of suicides monthly among Jews jumped from four in February 1938 to seventy-nine in March and sixty-two in April. The official reason given for the arrest of the Jewish community leaders and activists was that their names had been found on a list of contributors to the last election campaign of the Austrian chancellor. That same list also served as the pretext for the first "contribution" levied on the Jews of Austria, the sum of 500,000 marks.

Gauleiter Josef Burckel, whose job it was to implement Austria's unification with Germany, set up an office in Vienna for the seizure of Jewish property, with branches in the provincial capitals. Most of the 26,236 Jewish-owned businesses existing in March 1938 were modest enterprises, but they did not escape the furious "Aryanization" drive (see ARISIERUNG) that marked the first few weeks of the Anschluss, or the robberies that took place in full daylight, often with police protection. Among those affected were the large department stores, such as Shiffmann Brothers. When Walter Raffelsberger took over the Jewish-property office, the Vermögensverkehrstelle (Property Transfer Office), he introduced order into the ongoing removal of the Jews' belongings. According to figures he published on July 21, 1938, almost all the Jewish-owned property in the provinces and 30 percent of the property in Vienna had already been seized.

On June 29, all Jews and all partners in mixed marriages who were employed in the private sector—some forty thousand persons—were dismissed from their jobs. The number of German "supervisors" of Jewish property rose from 917 in July 1938 to 2,787 that November, and the number of businesses they were supervising rose from 1,624 in July to 5,210 in September. The drop in exports forced the Nazi authorities to keep Jews in key export branches temporarily in their posts, especially those branches that dealt with exports to southern and eastern Europe. By the summer of 1939, 18,800 Jewish enterprises had been closed down: 606 factories (out of 986), 8,145 commercial enterprises (out of 11,402), and 9,485 workshops (out of 13,046). According to Nazi estimates, the difference between the real value of the large Jewish-owned enterprises and the total sum that their Jewish owners were paid for them amounted to more than 35 billion reichsmarks. In one instance a business valued at half a million reichsmarks, with liabilities of 50,000 reichsmarks, was "bought" at a price of 20,000. The Jewish owner was arrested on a charge of negligence in running the business, since he was unable to come up with the 30,000 reichsmarks needed to cover the debt.

Emigration. The emigration of the Jews from Austria was handled by Adolf EICH-MANN. At the first meeting Eichmann held with leaders of the Jewish community and the Zionist movements, a meeting held in the Palestine Office (which dealt with Palestinian affairs, including immigration) two days after the Anschluss, he pretended to have been born in Palestine and to be familiar with the practices of Judaism. The executive director of the Vienna Jewish community, Dr. Josef LÖWENHERZ, reorganized the work of the Jewish Community Office in accordance with instructions dictated to him by Eichmann. The office was reopened on May 2, 1938, with Löwenherz as executive director, assisted by a council of eight section chiefs. That August, a special section was added to deal with provincial affairs, the Provinzreferat. Dr. Eduard Pachtmann, who had no previous experience in the field, was appointed head of the Zionist organization, in place of Dr. Oskar Grünbaum (who was in jail). He was joined by Zionist Youth Union leader Georg Überall (later, in Israel, he took the name Ehud Avriel) and by representatives of the Zionist National Funds and the Women's International Zionist Organization.

The Palestine Office was headed by Dr. Alois Rothenberg, who joined forces with the He-Haluts pioneering Zionist organization, headed by Ze'ev Willy Ritter; the nonpartisan organized Zionists of the eighteen-to-thirty-five age group; the YOUTH ALIYA (the fifteen-to-seventeen age group); and the young religious Zionist pioneers. A bitter controversy broke out between Rothenberg, who wanted to allocate the limited number of immigration permits for Palestine to the veteran Austrian Zionists, and Ritter, who demanded that they all be reserved for He-Haluts members and organized young skilled tradesmen and professionals. The Vienna Jewish Community Office, the Palestine Office, and the provincial communities all had to submit periodic reports to Eichmann —biweekly, monthly, and bimonthly—with the emphasis on the progress being made in the emigration of the Jews.

In addition to pressure from the top, there was terror in the streets. Emigration, in all its aspects, was concentrated in Vienna, so that community representatives and individuals trying to obtain the required documents had to stay in Vienna and stand in long lines, night and day, in front of the municipal and police offices. There they were exposed to humiliation and tortures by Nazi party thugs, the HITLERJUGEND (Hitler Youth), and brutal security men. The Jews of Austria were not allowed to share in the arrangements made with the Jews of Germany, whom the German Foreign Office permitted to emigrate in an orderly fashion to Palestine and other countries, together with a portion of their assets, under the HAAVARA AGREEMENT.

In August 1938 the ZENTRALSTELLE FÜR JÜDISCHE AUSWANDERUNG (Central Office for Jewish Emigration) opened offices in the Rothschild palace, which the Nazis had confiscated. Eichmann was in charge, assisted by Rolf Günther, who made wide use of extortion in his work. By systematic bureaucratic methods the Jews emigrating from the country were automatically divested of all their assets. Most of the financing of the emigration was funded by the levy that every emigrant had to pay, in proportion to the assets that he declared. The American Jewish JOINT DISTRIBUTION COMMITTEE and the British COUNCIL FOR GERMAN JEWRY agreed to provide the foreign currency needed for travel expenses and for the sum that the emigrant had to have in his possession on arrival at his destination. This was on condition that Eichmann release an equivalent amount from the blocked account of the community, to be used for welfare services and for assistance to emigrants who did not have enough means of their own to finance their departure. In the period from May to July 1938, 25 percent of the emigrants required full or partial assistance from the community, the number rising to 33 percent from August to October, 50 percent in November and December, and 75 percent between February and May 1939. In the first two months of the Anschluss, some seven thousand Jews crossed the border to Switzerland or Italy, and when these borders were closed to them the Jews tried to make their way to countries in western Europe. Sometimes the border police of the country they tried to enter forced the Jews back into Germany.

In the November 1938 KRISTALLNACHT pogroms, Eichmann imprisoned Jews in concentration camps as a means of extorting money from them and forcing them to speed up their emigration. When such a detainee was released, he was given a time limit in which to make his emigration arrangements; if he was still there after the limit had passed, he was again imprisoned. As a result there were a growing number of instances when adults or heads of families emigrated and left behind elderly parents and children. The number of old and infirm persons who had no relatives to care for them grew to 25,000, and there was a comparative rise in the number of abandoned children. Following the November pogroms, countries of western Europe agreed to accept 10,000 children, but only 2,844 children, in forty-three groups, were able to make use of this offer from December 1938 to August 1939. Some of the children were later seized by the Germans when they occupied these countries, and perished. Most of the children—2,262 of them—went to Britain.

Styria. Special treatment was granted by Eichmann to the Jews of Styria, whose capital, Graz, was declared the capital of the Nazi uprising in Austria and therefore aspired to be the first Austrian city to become *judenrein* ("cleansed of Jews"). In order to achieve this coveted goal by April 20, 1939 (Hitler's birthday), the chairman of the Zionist organization in Graz, Elias Grunschlag, was permitted to work closely with the Gestapo and the customs authorities to speed up the liquidation of debts owed by would-be emigrants and to deal collectively with the passports and other documents required for emigration. Eichmann also agreed to apply to the Jews of Styria the Haavara provisions and enable them to export to Palestine property and machinery in the amount of 5 million reichsmarks. This arrangement, however, was not put into effect before November 1938, and thereafter its scope was greatly reduced. The *Gauleiter* in Linz, August Eigruber, also granted special dispensation to his former friend and business partner, Max Hirschfeld, giving him a free hand in arranging for the emigration of Jews. Hirschfeld made full use of this opportunity. A similar relationship existed in Klagenfurt, the capital of Carinthia, between the Jewish community chairman, Nathan Kriegsfuss, and the local Nazi authorities.

Burgenland. The Jews of the "seven communities" of Burgenland, which were centers of Jewish learning and had been inhabited by Jews for hundreds of years, were driven out of their homes in the first few months after the annexation. On the Sabbath, March 26, 1938, the Jews of Frauenkirchen, under threat of deportation, were forced to come up with a "contribution" of 80,000 reichsmarks. This did not, however, prevent the Nazis from deporting ten of the wealthy families and forcing them across the border, after first compelling them to confirm, in writing, that they were voluntarily abandoning their property and leaving penniless. In the course of 1938 all the Burgenland Jews were driven out, on the pretext that they were too close to the borders of Hungary and Czechoslovakia and their presence there was jeopardizing the security of the Reich. About half were expelled to Vienna, and the rest had to wander from one border to the other. On April 26, 1938, the secretary of the religious Jewish organization Agudat Israel, Julius Steinfeld, gave a written promise to arrange for the emigration of all the Burgenland Jews. This was accomplished, with the cooperation of the Vienna Jewish community, the Jewish Agency, and the Rabbinical Aid and Rescue Committee in Britain, and with the granting of emigration priority to the Burgenland Jews.

Persecutions. In the city of Wiener Neustadt, all "Aryan" landlords were ordered to evict their Jewish tenants from their apartments. In Horn, the tombstones in the Jewish cemetery were desecrated in May 1938, and on September 18 the Jews had to leave the city without a day's notice. The Jewish communities were impoverished to the extent that they had to close their rented prayerhouses, and on August 7 they informed the Vienna community that they were no longer able to take care of their needs. Social life among the Jews in all the provincial communities came to a standstill, except for Graz, where there was still an active community.

In the November 1938 pogrom it was primarily the synagogues and the purification rooms (for washing the dead before burial) that were desecrated. In Klagenfurt the synagogue furnishings were destroyed by axes and Jewish apartments were vandalized. The impressive Graz synagogue with its cupola was blown up, as was the purification room, and 300 Jewish males were deported to Dachau. The worst pogroms took place in Innsbruck, where all the Jews were beaten up, an elderly Jewish couple were drowned, and the Zionist organization chairman and a wealthy merchant were murdered.

The November pogrom accelerated the liquidation of the Jewish communities. By May 1939, twenty-seven out of a total of thirty-three communities were closed down. Their property was confiscated by Eichmann and transferred to the Emigration Office in Vienna. On February 23, 1940, the authorities officially withdrew their recognition of the provincial communities.

Prior to the outbreak of the war, 126,445 Jews emigrated from Austria. Of the 58,000 who were left, 32,000 required welfare assistance. Another 2,000 managed to emigrate in wartime to other European countries up until November 10, 1941, when emigration of Jews was finally banned altogether. Of the 55,505 Jews who emigrated from Austria to European countries, 30,850 went to Britain; 15,000 were caught by the Nazis in their western European conquests and deported to extermination camps. The number of emigrants to North America was 28,700 (82 to Canada); to Central and South America, 11,580; to Asia, 28,700 (18,120 to China, mainly Shanghai); to Palestine, 9,190; to Australia and New Zealand, 1,880; and to Africa, 650. All in all, 128,500 Jews emigrated from Austria, to eighty-nine countries.

With the outbreak of the war, preparations for emigration continued, and technical training in anticipation of a new life was maintained. More than five thousand children studied in educational institutions under the auspices of the Jewish communities. Provision was made for some twenty-four thousand aged and ailing people for whom emigration would not be possible. At the beginning of October 1939, after the conquest of Poland, 1,048 young and elderly people, some stateless and some with Polish nationality, were deported to BUCHENWALD, where they were killed. Later in October two more transports, totaling 1,584 people, were dispatched to Nisko (see NISKO AND LUBLIN PLAN) from Moravian Austria (Moravská Ostrava),

in the vicinity of the Protectorate of BOHEMIA AND MORAVIA. Most of the deportees were expelled across the San River into the area conquered by the Soviet army; only 199 of the Austrian deportees employed in building the camp in Nisko later returned to Vienna.

During February and March 1941 about 5,000 Austrian Jews were deported to the KIELCE district in Poland, and were subsequently murdered in 1942 in the BEŁŻEC and CHEŁMNO camps. With the onset of the mass expulsions in mid-October 1941, 5,000 Jews were deported to Łódź, together with 5,000 GYPSIES from the Burgenland district of Austria. Later that year, more than 5,000 were sent to the Łódź ghetto and another 3,000 to ghettos in the Baltic area. Following the WANNSEE CONFERENCE in January 1942, the deportations were accelerated: 3,200 Jews were sent to Riga, 8,500 to Minsk, and 6,000 to the Lublin region. In the second part of 1942, almost 14,000—nearly all of them aged—were deported to the THERESIENSTADT concentration camp. When the Vienna community was dissolved in November 1942, only 7,000 Jews remained in Austria, most of them married to non-Jews. All those who were fit were put on forced labor. The community organization, the Kultusgemeinde, was replaced by the Ältestenrat (Council of Elders) in Vienna, which represented all of Austrian Jewry before the authorities and ran the Jewish hospital, the home for the aged, and a soup kitchen. Josef Löwenherz headed the council until the end of the war.

Deportations continued on a smaller scale and the community virtually disappeared. At the end of the war about 1,000 Jews survived in Vienna. Some were partners of mixed marriages, and the Gestapo employed a number of their offspring in sorting out the vast quantities of confiscated Jewish property. About one-third of the survivors remained alive by living under cover.

In the second half of 1944, tens of thousands of Hungarian Jews were deported to Vienna and Lower Austria for forced labor in building fortifications. About 8,000 Jews, scattered among small labor camps in Vienna, were assisted by the remaining staff of the Vienna Jewish Hospital, which even opened a maternity ward. It also maintained the last vestiges of organized Jewish religious ritual in Vienna. More than 65,000 Austrian Jews died in the ghettos and concentration camps of eastern Europe, from which only 1,747 returned to Austria at the end of the war. They were eventually joined by some of the Austrian Jews who had emigrated before the war, but the bulk of the postwar Austrian community consisted of Jews who arrived from other countries, mostly of eastern Europe, after the end of the war. This community became the center for the BERIḤA organization.

[See also Youth Movements: Germany and Austria.]

BIBLIOGRAPHY

Bauer, Y. My Brother's Keeper: A History of the American Jewish Joint Distribution Committee, 1929–1939. Philadelphia, 1974.
Fraenkel, J., ed. The Jews of Austria. London, 1967.
Gedye, J. E. R. Fallen Bastions: The Central European Tragedy. London, 1940.
Moser, J. "Die Verfolgung der Juden." In vol. 3 of Widerstand und Verfolgung in Wien 1934–1945, pp. 194–326. Vienna, 1975.
Oxaal, I., et al. Jews, Antisemitism, and Culture in Vienna. London, 1987.
Rosenkranz, H. Verfolgung und Selbstbehauptung: Die Juden in Österreich 1938–1945. Vienna, 1978.

HERBERT ROSENKRANZ

AXIS (Ger., Achse), the political, military, and ideological alliance of Nazi GERMANY and Fascist ITALY. In the first three years of Nazi rule (1933–1935), Italy's political interests and its concern over Nazi aspirations for territorial expansion prevented any alliance between the two regimes, despite their ideological affinity. Benito MUSSOLINI's policy of ensuring the independence of Austria so that it would serve as a buffer between Italy and Germany even led him, in April 1935, to reach an agreement with France and Britain that was clearly directed against the Third Reich. This agreement called for the maintenance of peace within the framework of the League of Nations, expressed the signatories' opposition to "any unilateral violation of treaties which would jeopardize European peace," and promised concerted action against such steps.

Mussolini's attitude changed in the wake of Italy's invasion of Ethiopia in October 1935. The League of Nations strongly opposed the invasion, and sanctions—albeit ineffective ones—were imposed on Italy, leading to a break between that country and Britain and France. The ensuing political crisis led to a rapprochement between Italy and Germany, a process that was accompanied by a virulent propaganda drive against the "degenerating democratic West." This rapprochement was accelerated and reinforced by the Spanish Civil War, which broke out in July 1936, with both Italy and Germany lending military support to the anti-republican side. After Mussolini first used the term "Rome-Berlin axis," in a speech at Milan in November 1936, it became widespread.

At first, the two countries stressed their joint political interest in opposing the democratic powers and their regimes; Mussolini and Italian Fascism still had reservations about racism in general and its antisemitic version in particular. It was only in 1938, when the relative international weight carried by the two dictators had shifted, the Third Reich had grown in power, and the international crisis had deepened, that Mussolini adopted racism and launched an anti-Jewish drive. In May 1939, following the dismemberment of Czechoslovakia and a few months before the outbreak of war, Germany and Italy concluded the so-called Pact of Steel. Earlier, in November 1937, Italy had joined the Anti-Comintern Pact. In September 1940, a tripartite alliance was forged between Germany, Italy, and Japan to which the three countries committed themselves for ten years; this was known as the Berlin-Rome-Tokyo Axis. During World War II the term "Axis countries" also came to be applied to other states allied with Germany that had joined the Anti-Comintern Pact: Hungary, Romania, Slovakia, and Bulgaria.

BIBLIOGRAPHY

Duroselle, M. Les relations internationals de l'Allemagne et de l'Italie de 1919 à 1939. Paris, 1967.
Petersen, J. Hitler-Mussolini: Die Entstehung der Achse Berlin-Rom, 1933–1936. Tübingen, 1973.
Wiskemann, E. The Rome-Berlin Axis: A History of the Relations between Hitler and Mussolini. London, 1949.

ISRAEL GUTMAN

B

BABI YAR, ravine, situated in the northwestern part of Kiev, where the Jews of the Ukrainian capital were systematically massacred. At the southern end of the ravine were two cemeteries, one of which was Jewish.

Kiev was captured by the Twenty-ninth Corps and the Sixth German Army on September 19, 1941. Of its Jewish population of 160,000, some 100,000 had managed to flee before the Germans took the city. Shortly after the German takeover, from September 24 to 28, a considerable number of buildings in the city center, which were being used by the German military administration and the army, were blown up; many Germans (as well as local inhabitants) were killed in the explosions. After the war, it was learned that the sabotage operation had been the work of an NKVD (Soviet security police) detachment that had been left behind in the city for that purpose.

On September 26, the Germans held a meeting at which it was decided that in retaliation for the attacks on the German-held installations, the Jews of Kiev would all be put to death. Participating in the meeting were the military governor, Maj. Gen. Friedrich Georg Eberhardt; the Higher SS and Police Leader at Rear Headquarters Army Group South, SS-Obergruppenführer Friedrich JECKELN; the officer commanding Einsatzgruppe C, SS-Brigadeführer Dr. Otto RASCH; and the officer commanding Sonderkommando 4a, SS-Standartenführer Paul BLOBEL. The implementation of the decision to kill the Jews of Kiev was entrusted to Sonderkommando 4a. This unit consisted of SD (Sicherheitsdienst; Security Service) and Sicherheitspolizei (Security Police; Sipo) men; the third company of the Special Duties Waffen-SS battalion; and a platoon of the No. 9 police battalion. The unit was reinforced by police battalions Nos. 45 and 305 and by units of the Ukrainian auxiliary police.

On September 28, notices were posted in the city ordering the Jews to appear the following morning, September 29, at 8:00 a.m. at the corner of Melnik and Dekhtyarev streets; they were being assembled there, so the notice said, for their resettlement in new locations. (The text had been prepared by Propaganda Company No. 637 and the notices had been printed by the Sixth Army printing press.)

The next morning, masses of Jews reported at the appointed spot. They were directed to proceed along Melnik Street toward the Jewish cemetery and into an area comprising the cemetery itself and a part of the Babi Yar ravine. The area was cordoned off by a barbed-wire fence and guarded by Sonderkommando police and Waffen-SS men, as well as by Ukrainian policemen. As the Jews approached the ravine, they were forced to hand over all the valuables in their possession, to take off all their clothes, and to advance toward the ravine edge, in groups of ten. When they reached the edge, they were gunned down by automatic fire. The shooting was done by several squads of SD and Sipo personnel, police, and Waffen-SS men of the Sonderkommando unit, the squads relieving one another every few hours. When the day

Babi Yar, where Sonderkommando 4a of Einsatzgruppe C carried out the mass slaughter of 33,771 Kiev Jews on September 29 and 30, 1941.

ended, the bodies were covered with a thin layer of soil. According to official reports of the Einsatzgruppe, in two days of shooting (September 29 and 30), 33,771 Jews were murdered.

In the months that followed, many more thousands of Jews were seized, taken to Babi Yar, and shot. Among the general population there were some who helped Jews go into hiding, but there were also a significant number who informed on them to the Germans and gave them up. After the war, the officer in charge of the Sipo and SD bureau testified that his Kiev office received so many letters from the Ukrainian population informing on Jews—"by the bushel"—that the office could not deal with them all, for lack of manpower. Evidence of betrayal of Jews by the Kiev population was also given by Jewish survivors and by the Soviet writer Anatoly Kuznetsov.

Babi Yar served as a slaughterhouse for non-Jews as well, such as GYPSIES and Soviet prisoners of war. According to the estimate given by the Soviet research commission on Nazi crimes, 100,000 persons were murdered at Babi Yar.

In July 1943, by which time the Red Army was on the advance, Paul Blobel came back to Kiev. He was now on a new assignment, in

coordination with SS-Gruppenführer Dr. Max Thomas, the officer commanding the SD and Sipo in the Ukraine: that of erasing all evidence of the mass carnage that the Nazis had perpetrated. For this purpose, Blobel formed two special groups, identified by the code number 1005. Unit 1005-A was made up of eight to ten SD men and thirty German policemen, and was under the command of an SS-Obersturmbannführer named Baumann. In mid-August the unit embarked on its task of exhuming the corpses in Babi Yar and cremating them. The ghastly job itself was carried out by inmates of a nearby concentration camp (Syretsk), from which the Germans brought in 327 men, of whom 100 were Jews. The prisoners were housed in a bunker carved out from the ravine wall; it had an iron gate that was locked during the night and was watched by a guard with a machine gun. They had chains bolted to their legs, and those who fell ill or lagged behind were shot on the spot. The mass graves were opened up by bulldozers, and it was the prisoners' job to drag the corpses to cremation pyres, which consisted of wooden logs doused in gasoline on a base of railroad ties. The bones that did not respond to incineration were crushed, for which purpose the Nazis brought in tombstones from the Jewish cem-

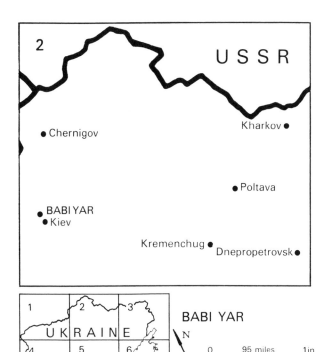

geni Yevtushenko published a poem, "Babi Yar," which begins with the lines:

> No gravestone stands on Babi Yar;
> Only coarse earth heaped roughly on the gash:
> Such dread comes over me.

A year later, Dmitri Shostakovich set the poem to music, incorporating it into his Thirteenth Symphony. (Under pressure from the authorities, changes were made in the original text, and it is the amended text that is used today when the symphony is performed in the Soviet Union.) Both the poem and the musical setting had a tremendous impact in the Soviet Union, as well as beyond its borders. Demands increased for a memorial to be built at Babi Yar, but it was not until 1966 that architects and artists were invited to submit proposals, and it took eight more years for the memorial to be built. Since 1974 a monument stands in Babi Yar, but the inscription does not mention that Jews were among the victims there.

etery. The ashes were sifted to retrieve any gold or silver they might have contained. Cremation of the corpses began on August 18 and went on for six weeks, ending on September 19, 1943. The Nazis did their job thoroughly, and when they were through no trace was left of the mass graves.

On the morning of September 29, the prisoners learned that they were about to be put to death. They already had a plan for escape, and resolved to put it into effect the same night. Shortly after midnight, under cover of darkness and the fog that enveloped the ravine, twenty-five prisoners broke out. Fifteen succeeded in making their escape; the others were shot during the attempt or on the following morning.

It took a long time after the war for a memorial to be erected at Babi Yar. The demand for a memorial was first voiced during the "thaw" that set in during the Khrushchev regime, by which time Babi Yar had become a place of pilgrimage. Among those who made this demand were the writers Ilya EHRENBURG and Viktor Nekrasov, but their call was not heeded. In 1961, the poet Yev-

Monument erected in 1966 at Babi Yar. The Ukrainian text reads: "On this site there will be a monument for the victims of fascism during the German occupation of Kiev, 1941–1943."

BIBLIOGRAPHY

Ehrenburg, I., and V. Grossman, eds. *The Black Book of Soviet Jewry.* New York, 1981. See pages 3–12.
Korey, W. "Babi Yar Remembered." *Midstream* 15/3 (1969): 24–39.

Kuznetsov, A. *Babi Yar.* New York, 1967.
St. George, J. *The Road to Babi Yar.* London, 1967.

SHMUEL SPECTOR

BACH-ZELEWSKI, ERICH VON DEM

(1899–1972), SS commander. Born in Lauenburg in Pomerania, Bach-Zelewski served as a private during World War I and then joined the police. He became a member of the Nazi party in 1930 and the following year enrolled in the SS.

After the Nazis' rise to power, Bach-Zelewski's career progressed rapidly, and in 1938 he was appointed SS commander in Silesia, with headquarters in Breslau (now Wrocław). After September 1939, the Polish part of Silesia was incorporated into his district of command and he was responsible for the expulsion of tens of thousands of Jews from the area. When the Germans invaded the Soviet Union on June 22, 1941, Bach-Zelewski became the Higher SS and Police Leader in central Russia, attached to the Central Army Group; in November of that year he was promoted to the rank of SS-*Obergruppenführer* and general of police. His duties also included command of Einsatzgruppe B, which mass-murdered Jews in Belorussia. In 1942, Bach-Zelewski was appointed Heinrich HIMMLER's representative in the fight against the partisans, and from January 1943 he was the commanding officer of all the forces fighting the partisans in eastern Europe. Between August and October 1944 he commanded the forces that suppressed the WARSAW POLISH UPRISING. Bach-Zelewski's units taking part in these operations became infamous for the mass murder of civilians and for the destruction of numerous villages and towns and of large parts of Warsaw. From the end of 1944 he was in command of various army corps.

After the war Bach-Zelewski appeared as a prosecution witness at the NUREMBERG TRIAL, before the American military tribunal there; at the Einsatzgruppen trial; at the trials of senior SS and army officers; and at the Warsaw trial of Ludwig FISCHER, who had been governor of the Warsaw district. Bach-Zelewski was held in prison; in 1951 he was given a ten-year sentence in a trial held in Munich, but was released after serving five years of his sentence. Re-arrested in 1958, he was sentenced at Nuremberg in 1961 to a further four and one-half years.

BIBLIOGRAPHY

Bartoszewski, W. *Prawda o von dem Bachu.* Warsaw, 1961.
Reitlinger, G. *The SS: Alibi of a Nation.* New York, 1956.
Zawodny, J. K. *Nothing but Honor: The Story of the Warsaw Uprising, 1944.* Stanford, 1978.

SHMUEL SPECTOR

BAČKA, district in YUGOSLAVIA that now forms the western part of the autonomous province of Vojvodina. Jews lived in Bačka in ancient times, but the first known organized Jewish communities were established there at the end of the eighteenth century.

Prior to the German invasion of Yugoslavia in April 1941, Bačka had a Jewish population of some sixteen thousand, representing 20 percent of Yugoslav Jewry and 2 percent of the district's population. There were seventeen Neolog communities, following a Conservative rite, and nine Orthodox communities. One-third of the Jews were engaged in trade and commerce, 20 percent were office workers, 10 percent were professionals (doctors, lawyers, and so on), and a similar number were skilled craftsmen and industrial workers. The Jewish community had a considerable impact on Bačka's cultural and educational life and on charitable activities. In the 1930s the Zionist movement gained the majority within most of the Jewish communities, and Zionist youth movements—Ha-Shomer ha-Tsa'ir (with twelve hundred members), Tekhelet Lavan (Blau-Weiss, with seven hundred), and Betar (with four hundred)—played an important role by running summer camps and *hakhsharot* (training schools for agriculture) and issuing their own regular publications. The clandestine Communist youth movement also had a substantial number of adherents among Bačka Jews. Some three hundred Bačka Jews had moved to Palestine, and Bačka communities helped tens of thousands of legal and "illegal" immigrants from

Germany and German-occupied countries to make their way to Palestine.

The anti-Jewish legislation introduced in Yugoslavia in 1940 generated resistance among Bačka Jews to the growing Nazi pressure. They supported the anti-Nazi coup of March 27, 1941, with most of the young Jewish men volunteering for the army in the April 1941 fighting. Several dozen were killed or wounded, or became prisoners of war.

When Yugoslavia was defeated and its territory carved up, Bačka was allotted to Hungary. Compared to the German occupation of neighboring SERBIA, the Hungarians were the lesser evil; but even in the early days of the occupation the Hungarians staged incidents to serve as an excuse for murdering thousands of Serbs and Jews. Many others were expelled and handed over to the Nazis; the leaders of the Jewish community and the Zionist movement were taken hostage; thousands of Jews were deprived of their citizenship and most of their possessions, by force or intimidation; and the communities had to pay a war levy. By May 1941, male Jews were being drafted for hard labor, in the course of which they were beaten up and tortured.

Terror against Jews and Serbs was stepped up in July 1941, when Hungary joined the war against the Soviet Union. Many Jews joined the TITO-led partisan movement, and the number of young Jews involved in the struggle against the Nazis was considerably larger than their proportion in the population. By the end of 1941 all male Jews, up to the age of sixty, were drafted into labor battalions (*see* MUNKASZOLGÁLAT) of the Hungarian army. For the most part they were posted to the Soviet front in the Ukraine, where they were worked to the bone, starved to death, left to freeze in the cold, or murdered by their guards. Some of the men managed to cross the lines, and it was these "deserters" who took the initiative to form the First Yugoslav Armored Brigade in the Soviet Union, which in the summer of 1944 was moved to the Serbian front.

In December 1941 and January 1942, incidents between a mobile partisan force and the Hungarian army served as a pretext for the slaughter of Serbs and Jews, under the cover of a *Razzia* (raid, roundup) that the Hungarian government had sanctioned on the recommendation of Hungarian and local Nazi ele-

ments. To carry it out, two special units were formed, under the command of Gen. Ferenc Feketehalmy-Czeydner, Col. László Deák, Maj. Gen. József Grassy, Capt. Márton Zöldi, and other Nazi agents. Over five thousand men were murdered in the course of January 1942, half of them Jews. Six Jewish communities were totally exterminated. Thousands were brought before "selection commissions" made up of Hungarians, which decided the way in which they were to be killed—by shooting, bayoneting, hanging, or other horrible methods. The city of Novi Sad was ransacked by units of the Second Combat Regiment, commanded by Grassy. On the very first day of the *Razzia*, dozens of Jews and Serbs were murdered; and on the third day, January 23, 1942, the gendarmes staged an incident that served as the excuse for mass slaughter; hundreds were murdered in the streets, the cemeteries, and the stadiums. The number of Jews murdered accounted for a third of the entire Jewish population in Bačka. The killing was stopped on the intervention of moderate elements, among them Endre Bajcsy-Zsilinsky, a member of parliament representing the Smallholders' party.

The massacre caused angry reactions among the Hungarian public and in neutral states, including Switzerland, Sweden, Spain, and Turkey. Miklós KALLAY, the Hungarian premier who had taken office in March 1942, had to admit that innocent people had been murdered. In the course of 1943 the men responsible for the carnage were put on trial but managed to flee to Germany, where they were given asylum. In March 1944, when the German army entered Hungary, the culprits in the Bačka crimes returned to the country and took part in the deportation of Hungarian Jews to extermination camps.

The situation of the surviving Jews of Bačka improved a little in 1943, but this did not prevent many young Jews from joining the mobile partisan units. Zionist functionaries took an active part in the rescue operations. Dr. Moshe Schweiger, a leader of the Ihud Olami (Zionist Labor) party in Bačka, took the initiative in setting up a committee in Budapest to care for the hundreds of refugees from Bačka in the Hungarian capital, to provide them with housing and employment, and to ensure that they would not be expelled. Dr.

BAČKA

Meir Weltmann-Tuval, an Ihud Olami member and leading Zionist, was very active in behalf of Bačka Jews at the Istanbul Jewish Agency office. He was joined by Dr. Francis Ofner, a Betar leader in Bačka, who had succeeded in escaping from the Hungarian murderers. Together, the two men arranged for dozens of Bačka Jews—children, youths, and adults—to make their way to Palestine.

After the Germans occupied Hungary, on March 19, 1944, German SS units, together with the Hungarian gendarmerie, came to Bačka and embarked on the deportation of the remaining Jews to extermination camps. Over a third of Bačka's Jews (which at the time numbered eight thousand) were deported to AUSCHWITZ and other extermination camps in May of that year. Of Bačka's prewar Jewish population of sixteen thousand, only twenty-five hundred survived to witness the liberation of the district. Many of these had volunteered for service in the Yugoslav army; some of Bačka's Jews fell in the final battles against the USTAŠA forces in Croatia, or even against SS units. The survivors reorganized themselves into ten communities, but eleven hundred went to Israel after the establishment of the state in 1948 and four hundred left for the West. Only a few hundred Jews were left in Bačka.

BIBLIOGRAPHY

Lewinger, Y. "Assassination of Jews in Bačka during the Police Raids, January 1942." *Studies* on the Holocaust Period 1 (1978): 189–212. (In Hebrew.)

Peric, M. *Demographic Study of the Jewish Community in Yugoslavia.* Belgrade, 1973.

YOSSEF LEWINGER

BADGE, JEWISH, distinguishing sign that Jews in Nazi Germany and in Nazi-occupied countries were compelled to wear to facilitate their identification as Jews. Such a distinctive sign had been imposed on Jews in ancient times, in the form of the color or shape of the clothes, shoes, hats, or scarves they were obliged to wear in order to differentiate between them and the rest of the population and humiliate them in other people's eyes. The first to introduce such a sign were the Muslims, who in the eighth century decreed that all the *dhimmi* (protected people)—Christians, Jews, and Samaritans—must wear clothes that set them apart from the Muslims. In Yemen such clothes were obligatory for Jews until the twentieth century. In Christian countries, distinctive signs for Jews were introduced on the basis of a canon issued by the Fourth Lateran Council in 1215, under Pope Innocent III (1198–1216), which laid down that Jews "of both sexes, in all Christian lands, shall be differentiated from the rest of the population by the quality of their garment." The form of this differentiation was not specified, but the decision makes it clear that its purpose was to prevent sexual intercourse between Jews and Christians.

The Lateran Council decision was not applied in all Christian countries at all times, or in a uniform manner, but the introduction of a "Jewish badge" did spread, and it became a means of shaming and humiliating Jews. The pointed hat, as a distinctive sign for Jews, is known to have been in use from the thirteenth century in various Germanic countries. Yellow as a distinguishing color for Jews had been decreed earlier, in Muslim countries, and the practice may have been taken over by Christian countries, though the reason for choosing this particular color is not clear.

A distinction must be made between the voluntary concentration of Jews in a certain part of a town and their forced confinement to a ghetto; between distinctive clothes and outward appearance that Jews adhered to of their own will, out of loyalty to their tradition, and the distinctive signs imposed on them by a hostile government for purposes of humiliation.

In modern times the Jewish badge was gradually abolished, disappearing altogether during the nineteenth-century Emancipation. Under the Nazis the term "yellow badge" first appeared in Robert WELTSCH's article "Tragt ihn mit Stolz, den gelben Fleck" ("Wear the Yellow Badge with Pride"), published in the *Jüdische Rundschau* on April 4, 1933, in reaction to the anti-Jewish boycott of April 1, 1933 (*see* BOYCOTT, ANTI-JEWISH). At that point no official Jewish sign was in existence and there were no plans to introduce such a sign. Weltsch was apparently referring to the slanderous and abusive inscriptions painted on the windows of Jewish-owned stores and businesses in "Operation Boycott" of April 1, and the relapse to medieval times that it signified. The proposal to impose a distinctive mark on the Jews was first made by Reinhard HEYDRICH at a meeting held in the wake of the KRISTALLNACHT pogrom, in November 1938.

At the height of the fighting in Poland, in September 1939, local German military and civilian authorities issued the first decrees ordering Jewish stores to be marked as such. Later decrees required Jews to wear a distinctive sign. In November 1939 the Jews of Lublin, for example, were ordered to wear a yellow badge on the left side of their breast, bearing the inscription *Jude*. On November 23, Hans FRANK, in one of the first regulations he issued as *Generalgouverneur*, stipulated that as of December 1, 1939, all "Jews and Jewesses" over the age of twelve living in the GENERALGOUVERNEMENT were to wear, on the right sleeve of their jacket or dress and on their overcoat, a white band at least 4 inches (10 cm) in width, with a blue Star of David inscribed on it. The Lublin order requiring a yellow badge was promptly withdrawn, and the Lublin Jews had to wear a white armband, like the Jews in the rest of the Generalgouvernement.

On November 14, SS-Brigadeführer Friedrich Übelhör, *Regierungspräsident* (administrative president) of the Kalisz district, issued an order for "all Jews, irrespective of sex or age, to wear a band 10 centimeters [4 inches] in width on the right arm, below the armpit, of Jewish-yellow color [*judengelber Farbe*]." On December 12, Übelhör issued a revised order: "Reichsstatthalter [Reich governor] Arthur GREISER has decreed that all Jews in the WARTHEGAU [must] wear a uniform distinctive sign. Accordingly, my order of November 14 under which Jews were obliged to wear a yellow band is amended, and I now order [that] Jews have to wear a yellow badge in the form of a Star of David, 10 centimeters in height, on the right side of their breast and on their back." In Zagłębie, a district that was also annexed to the Reich, like the Warthegau, the Jews were ordered to wear a band on the left sleeve, with a blue Star of David painted on it; this was later replaced by a badge.

When the Germans invaded the Soviet Union, in June 1941, they lost no time introducing into the newly occupied areas the various marks and methods used in Poland for differentiating between the Jews and the rest of the population. The guidelines on the treatment of Jews issued in 1941 by Hinrich LOHSE, the *Reichskommissar Ostland* (Reich Commissar of the Occupied Eastern Territories), contained the provision that "orders have to be issued that Jews be at all times identifiable as such by a yellow six-pointed star, clearly visible, at least 10 centimeters high, on the left side of their breast and on the back." In BIAŁYSTOK, which had its own civil administration, the first announcement made by the JUDENRAT (Jewish Council), on German orders, stated that "as of the morning of July 10, 1941, all men, women, and children aged fourteen and over must wear a white armband on their left sleeve, with a blue Star of David painted on it; the Star of David has to be 10 centimeters high and its outline at least 10 centimeters wide." The next order issued by the Białystok Judenrat, on July 11, 1941, however, spoke of "a yellow badge, as ordered"; the first order was presumably amended within a few days, and the armband was replaced by a yellow badge.

Forcing the Jews to wear a distinctive sign was one of the tactics of harassment that enabled the Germans to recognize Jews as such on sight, and was designed to create a gulf between the Jews and the rest of the population. The Jews were themselves responsible for acquiring the badges and distributing them. Even when the Jews were separated from the general population by being confined to ghettos, the orders requiring them to wear distinguishing signs remained valid and were strictly enforced. Jews who left the badge at home when they went out or whose badges did not meet the regulations were subject to fines and prison sentences. In WARSAW, warnings were posted in the hallways of apartment buildings, reminding Jews not to forget the badge when they went out. An announcement by the Białystok Judenrat of July 26, 1941, stated: "The authorities have warned that severe punishment—up to and including death by shooting—is in store for Jews who do not wear the yellow badge, on back and front."

In some ghettos various other distinctive badges were introduced—for identifying Jewish police, doctors, Judenrat employees, and people who held jobs in one of the many official factories. The purpose of these additional badges was to replace the Jewish badge and give the bearer a sense of being better protected and more favored than the anonymous masses in the ghetto. One of the Warsaw ghetto diarists drew up a list of nineteen different kinds of badges—in addition to the regular badge that all Jews had to wear—that were in use, at one time or another, during the existence of the ghetto. In May 1942 a decree was published in Warsaw forbidding the wearing of additional badges by the factory employees and confining the use of special badges to the Jewish police.

Frank's November 1939 decree on the wearing of distinctive signs in the General-gouvernement was followed by a regulation issued by the governor of the Warsaw district, Hauptamtsleiter SA-Brigadeführer Dr. Ludwig Fischer; the regulation stipulated that the decree applied to Jews by "race" and was therefore also binding on converts to Christianity and their progeny. The converts living in Warsaw appealed to the RADA GŁÓWNA OPIEKUŃCZA (Central Welfare Council; RGO), which was approved by the Germans, to intervene on their behalf so that they might be exempted from this shameful obligation. When the RGO applied to the Germans on the converts' behalf, the Germans requested a list of the persons to be ex-

empted, but on receiving it, they rejected the RGO's request. In October and November 1940, when the Warsaw ghetto was set up, the Germans used the list to round up the converts and force them to enter the ghetto with the Jews.

Inside the Third Reich, the regulation requiring a yellow badge to be worn by the Jews (a *Judenstern*, or "Jewish star," in the regulation's wording) was promulgated in September 1941, that is, nearly two years after it had been imposed on the Jews of Poland. The regulation also applied to the Protectorate of BOHEMIA AND MORAVIA and officially also to the Polish areas that had been incorporated into the Reich, even though in the latter areas the practice had been introduced shortly after the German occupation of Poland. The September 1941 regulation required all Jews over the age of six to wear a yellow six-pointed star, the size of a fist, on the left side of the breast, with *Jude* inscribed on it in black. As in the other places where it was applied, the yellow-badge decree in the Reich and the areas annexed to it was one of a series of anti-Jewish measures and signified a further intensification of the anti-Jewish line. The distinctive mark imposed on the Jews in Germany became an integral part of the preparations for the "FINAL SOLUTION." That same month, restrictions were imposed on freedom of movement by the Jews in Germany; in October, emigration of Jews from Germany was prohibited; and this was followed in November by an announcement that Jews "who are not employed by factories essential to the country's economy" would be dispatched to the east in the next few months.

The Jewish badge was also adopted by Germany's satellite states. On September 9, 1941, a "Jewish code" became law in Slovakia, stipulating in part that the Jews of that country were to wear a yellow badge, and that only the president of the country could exempt certain individuals from this obligation. German authorities ran into difficulties when they tried to introduce the wearing of the badge in the occupied countries of western Europe and Vichy France. The opposition seems to have come both from local quarters that still wielded a measure of power in the internal administration of these countries

Three examples of badges worn by Jews. In France the yellow Star of David had the word *Juif* in Hebraic-looking letters at the center; in the Netherlands the word *Jood* figured on the badge. In Bulgaria a yellow-and-black button was sewn on clothing to identify Jews. [A Living Memorial to the Holocaust—Museum of Jewish Heritage, New York]

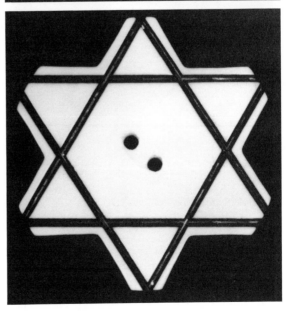

and, in rare instances, from German military authorities on the spot. In December 1942 the Germans began exerting pressure on the Vichy regime to impose the wearing of the yellow badge on the Jews of France—a preparatory step for the planned deportation and annihilation of the Jews of German-occupied western Europe. Adm. François DARLAN, Vichy premier at the time, rejected the German proposal, arguing that the anti-Jewish measures being applied in France were adequate and that a distinctive sign for Jews would come as a "great shock" to the French people. Adolf EICHMANN's office continued to press for the yellow badge to be applied in France, Belgium, and the Netherlands. In March 1942 the subject was discussed at meetings in Berlin and Paris, at one of which Helmut KNOCHEN, *Chef des SD und der Sicherheitspolizei* (Chief of the Security Service and the Security Police) for occupied France and Belgium, stated that in his opinion the yellow badge was "another step on the road to the final solution." The implementation of the yellow-badge decree was delayed, however, owing to the resistance shown by the French and the reservations raised by the German military administration, and also because the question of how to deal with Jews who were nationals of neutral countries or of Allied countries remained to be resolved.

In the Netherlands—where it was easier for the Germans to overcome resistance and obstacles—a decree was issued on April 29, 1942, according to which all Jews were obliged to wear a yellow star on the left side of their breast with the word *Jood* inscribed on it, in black ink. In Belgium the same decree was issued on May 27, 1942, to go into effect on June 3. In occupied France the decree was issued on June 7; it ordered all Jews aged six and over to wear a yellow star, the size of a clenched fist, on the left side of their breast, with the word *Juif* (Jew) or *Juive* (Jewess) inscribed on it. In the unoccupied zone of France the wearing of the yellow badge was not introduced, since the Vichy government persisted in its opposition to the measure. Some scholars of the Holocaust believe that the main reason for the Vichy regime's opposition—apart from concern over the reaction of the French public—was the fact that while the imposition of the yellow badge did not apply to Jews who were foreign nationals, Vichy authorities themselves would not be empowered to grant exemption from the badge to French Jews who had rendered distinguished service to France and French culture. In the end the Germans refrained from imposing the Jewish badge in Vichy France, even after November 1942, when they seized control of all of France, apparently because of the many manifestations of public opposition to the measure that they had encountered in occupied France.

In the satellite states and states that were otherwise dependent on Germany, the Nazis brought their power and influence to bear in order to have the Jewish badge adopted. In Hungary such pressure was applied in December 1942, but the government there was able to resist it. In March 1944, however, when the German army occupied Hungary, the first decision on Jewish affairs adopted by the new government under Döme SZTÓJAY, on March 31, was to impose the yellow badge on the country's Jews. Romania applied the yellow badge in the new territories that it occupied (BUKOVINA and BESSARABIA in July and September 1941, and TRANSNISTRIA in June 1942). The intention was to introduce the yellow star also in the Regat (the pre-1914 borders of the country), but Jewish intervention succeeded in foiling this design, except in Moldavia, in the final phase of the war (May 1944), when the yellow badge was applied "because the area is close to the battlefront." In BULGARIA, where there was strong opposition to anti-Jewish legislation and the persecution of the Jews, the government, in August 1942, decided to introduce a distinctive sign for Jews, in the form of a small yellow button. Even the wearing of that sign, however, was not strictly enforced, and most of the Jews in the country did not observe the order.

In DENMARK the German authorities considered introducing the yellow badge, but at no point did they dare risk making it mandatory. According to legend—which has also found its way into nonfictional writings—King Christian X threatened that if the Jewish badge were to be introduced in Denmark, he would be the first to wear one. While the king's opposition to anti-Jewish measures, like his personal courage, is unquestionable, he in fact never made such a declaration; the Germans, who were well aware of the Danes' unconditional resistance to anti-Jewish measures of any sort, never even attempted to force the yellow badge on Denmark.

The Jewish population's reaction to the yellow badge and the non-Jewish population's opposition to the measure in the German-occupied countries and in Germany itself were broadly as follows. In Poland, where a distinctive sign for Jews was first introduced, it initially had a considerable psychological impact, but further measures, much more severe in their effect on the Jews, overwhelmed this initial impact. Diaries from the period contain bitter and sarcastic references to the Jewish badge, such as one that compares the ghetto to Hollywood, because both are full of stars. The threat of severe penalties accounted for the almost uniform observance of the wearing of the Jewish badge; exceptions included members of the underground who served as illegal liaison officers among the ghettos, and Jews who had escaped from the ghetto to the "Aryan" side of the city.

In Germany the introduction of the Jewish badge was followed by a wave of suicides. Some Jewish sources report that there were a few instances of Germans' displaying solidarity with the Jews in the matter of the yellow badge. On the other hand, an internal SS report on the public mood, dated November 1941, includes an item to the effect that among the German population, surprise was voiced about the many Jews still to be found in Germany, as revealed by the yellow badges. The report mentions the special problem of persons classified as Jews under the Nazi racist legislation who were Christians by religion; congregants attending church services allegedly complained of having to sit next to persons wearing the yellow badge. Though Protestant clergymen were not prepared to exclude wearers of the yellow badge from services, they considered assigning them separate seating. Among the Catholic clergy, Cardinal Adolf Bertram in Germany and Cardinal Theodor Innitzer in Austria opposed such separation.

In western Europe many Jews defied orders and did not wear the yellow badge. In occupied France it had been estimated that more than one hundred thousand Jews would have to wear the badge, but in the weeks that followed the issuance of the order, only eighty-three thousand persons came to pick up the badges. Among the French population the yellow badge caused great dismay, and quite a few took effective steps against it. For example, yellow became a fashionable color, and some people wore stars or other items to express solidarity with the Jews. Even the French police, which had a poor record in its treatment of Jews, either found it difficult to overcome the defiance of the order to wear the yellow badge, or did not care to collaborate in this effort. Passersby who were asked to identify themselves because they looked Jewish sometimes turned out to be ''proper'' Frenchmen, and this experience too seems to have deterred policemen from trying to arrest violators of the yellow-badge decree. In the Netherlands there were many instances of demonstrative solidarity with the Jews. On May 1, 1942, a Dutch underground newspaper printed 300,000 stars bearing the inscription ''Jews and non-Jews are one and the same.''

In the Nazi concentration camps, prisoners were marked by triangular patches in various colors (in the case of Jews, by a Star of David consisting of two triangles in different colors) and by letters, the purpose being to indicate the ethnic and national identity of the prisoner and the prisoner's particular ''offense.'' Poles brought to Germany on forced labor were marked by the letter *P*, and severe restrictions were imposed on them in their day-to-day contacts with Germans; but special distinctive marks, in all occupied countries or countries under the influence of the Third Reich, were applied only to Jews.

BIBLIOGRAPHY

Blau, B. ''Der Judenstern der Nazis.'' *Judaica* 9 (1953): 34–47.

Friedman, P. ''The Jewish Badge and the Yellow Star in the Nazi Era.'' In *Roads to Extinction: Essays on the Holocaust,* edited by A. J. Friedman, pp. 11–33. New York, 1980.

Kisch, G. ''The Yellow Badge in History.'' *Historia Judaica* 4 (1942): 95–114.

Marrus, M. R., and R. O. Paxton. *Vichy France and the Jews.* New York, 1981.

Presser, J. *Ashes in the Wind: The Destruction of Dutch Jewry.* London, 1965.

ISRAEL GUTMAN

BADOGLIO, PIETRO (1871–1956), Italian soldier and statesman. Badoglio was made a marshal of Italy in 1926. He served as chief of staff of the Italian armed forces from 1925 to 1940; governor of Libya from 1928 to 1933; commander of the armed forces in East Africa from November 1935 to May 1936; and prime minister of Italy from July 25, 1943, to June 10, 1944, after Benito MUSSOLINI's downfall. Like most Italian officers, Badoglio accepted the Italian Jews as full members of the Italian nation; on the other hand, he was critical of the self-segregation of the Libyan Jews, who had not undergone a similar process of assimilation and ''Italianization.'' When Mussolini adopted antisemitic policies, Badoglio proclaimed his support of Fascist racial programs, if only to curry favor with his master. After Mussolini's

Marshal Pietro Badoglio (right) talking with Gen. Werner von Blomberg. [National Archives]

downfall on July 25, 1943, he headed the new government but refused to repeal the anti-Jewish laws, having made a public pretense of continuing the war at Germany's side. Badoglio arranged an armistice with the Allies on September 3, 1943, and finally abrogated the anti-Jewish laws on January 20, 1944; by that time, however, he controlled only the smaller part of Italy, the rest of which was under total German control. He wrote *L'Italia nella seconda guerra mondiale* (Milan, 1946; published in English as *Italy and the Second World War,* 1988).

BIBLIOGRAPHY

De Felice, R. *Storia degli Ebrei italiani sotto il fascismo.* Milan, 1977.

Michaelis, M. *Mussolini and the Jews: German-Italian Relations and the Jewish Question in Italy, 1922–1945.* Oxford, 1978.

Zuccotti, S. *The Italians and the Holocaust: Persecution, Rescue, and Survival.* New York, 1987.

MEIR MICHAELIS

BAECK, LEO (1873–1956), rabbi, philosopher, and community leader. Born in Lissa, in the Posen province of Germany, Leo Baeck studied at the Jewish Theological Seminary in Breslau and the Hochschule für die Wissenschaft des Judentums (College for Judaic Studies) in BERLIN, where he was ordained a rabbi in 1897.

From 1897 to 1907 Baeck was rabbi of Oppeln, in Upper Silesia, and from 1907 to 1912, in Düsseldorf; from then on, until 1942, he was rabbi in Berlin, and a lecturer at the Hochschule. In World War I, he served as an army chaplain.

As early as 1897, Baeck demonstrated his intellectual integrity, when he refused to join the declaration against Zionism issued by a group of German rabbis (who came to be known as the "Protest" Rabbis). He gained a name for himself as an original scholar in 1905, with the publication of *Das Wesen des Judentums* (The Essence of Judaism; 1936), which was a response to the 1900 book by the Protestant theologian Adolf von Harnack, *Das Wesen des Christentums* (The Essence of Christianity). In the following years, Baeck published many articles on Jewish religion,

Rabbi Leo Baeck at Theresienstadt (1944).

dealing especially with the Second Temple period.

In 1922 Baeck was elected chairman of the General Association of German Rabbis, and in 1924 and 1927 respectively, Grandmaster of the B'nai B'rith Lodge in Germany and member of the committee of the CENTRAL-VEREIN DEUTSCHER STAATSBURGER JÜDISCHEN GLAUBENS (Central Union of German Citizens of Jewish Faith). In 1920 he joined the executive board of the Palestine Foundation Fund (Keren Hayesod) as a non-Zionist; in 1926 he became a member of the Palestine Committee, and in 1929, of the committee of the newly founded Jewish Agency.

In 1933, when the REICHSVERTRETUNG DER DEUTSCHEN JUDEN (Reich Representation of German Jews) was established, Baeck became its president, by common agreement of the organization's founders. As such he had to preserve the internal unity of German Jewry and act as its accredited representative. He was twice arrested by the Gestapo, but each time he was released and reinstated in his position. Baeck refused to avail himself of opportunities to leave Germany, even when the situation of the Jews in Germany deteriorated and his own safety was threatened, and he remained at the head of the Reichsvertretung. In 1939 the Nazis changed its name to Reichsvereinigung der Juden in Deutschland (Reich Association of Jews in Germany), and it continued to function, under the supervision of the REICHSSICHER-HEITSHAUPTAMT (Reich Security Main Office; RSHA), until June 1943, when it was dissolved.

At the beginning of 1943, Baeck was deported to the THERESIENSTADT ghetto, where he became a member of the Ältestenrat der Juden (Jewish Council of Elders) and with his sermons and speeches made a significant contribution to the morale of the ghetto population. Opinions vary, however, as to whether Baeck was justified in keeping to himself the information that reached him in the ghetto concerning the fate that awaited those Jews who were being deported to AUSCHWITZ. After the liberation of the ghetto and its dissolution in 1945, Baeck settled in London. There he devoted himself to public affairs, as chairman of the Council for Jews from Germany, and to teaching and research in Jewish institutions of higher learning in Britain and the United States.

Among the institutions commemorating Leo Baeck are the Seminar for Progressive Rabbis in London, the LEO BAECK INSTITUTE in Jerusalem, London, and New York, and a secondary school in Haifa, Israel.

BIBLIOGRAPHY

Adler, H. G. *Theresienstadt 1941–1945—Das Antlitz einer Zwangsgemeinschaft: Geschichte, Soziologie, Psychologie.* Tübingen, 1960.
Baker, L. *Days of Sorrow and Pain: Leo Baeck and the Berlin Jews.* New York, 1978.
Friedländer, A. H. *Leo Baeck: Teacher of Theresienstadt.* New York, 1968.

JOSEPH WALK

BAKY, LÁSZLÓ (1889–1946), Hungarian antisemite who was among those chiefly responsible for the destruction of Hungarian Jewry in 1944. Baky played a leading role in the Hungarian counterrevolutionary movement of the early 1920s and in many ultrarightist organizations. One of the most outspokenly antisemitic members of the Hungarian officers' corps, he retired as a major general from the gendarmerie in 1938 in order to devote his time to the extreme right. In May 1939 he was elected to the nation's parliament as a leading figure of the Hungarian National Socialist party (Magyar Nemzeti Szocialista Párt). Shortly after Hungary's occupation by the Germans on March 19, 1944, he became an undersecretary of state in the puppet government of Döme SZTÓJAY, a position he held until September 1. Following the ARROW CROSS PARTY coup of October 15, 1944, he played an active role in the Ferenc SZÁLASI regime as well. As undersecretary of state in the Ministry of the Interior, Baky was one of the leading architects of the deportation of the Jews from Hungary. He fled Hungary with the retreating Nazi forces, but was captured by the Americans, who extradited him to Hungary in October 1945. He was tried as a war criminal and executed.

BIBLIOGRAPHY

Braham, R. L. *The Politics of Genocide.* New York, 1980.
Katzburg, N. *Hungary and the Jews, 1920–1943.* Ramat Gan, Israel, 1981.

RANDOLPH L. BRAHAM

BANDERA, STEFAN (1909–1959), Ukrainian leader. Bandera was born in Eastern Galicia into the family of a priest of the Uniate church. When he was in his twenties he joined the ORHANIZATSYIA UKRAINSKYKH NATSIONALISTIV (Organization of Ukrainian Nationalists; OUN), and soon became one of the leaders of the national organization in the western UKRAINE. In 1932 and 1933 Bandera, along with his comrades Yaroslav Stetsko and Roman Shukhevich, gained control of the organization's national executive, which functioned clandestinely, dictated an extremist fascist-oriented nationalist policy, and called for an armed struggle. After the assassination of the Polish minister of the interior, Bronisław Pieracki, Bandera was arrested on January 13, 1936, and given a life sentence. When Poland was occupied by the Germans in September 1939, Bandera was released by the Russians and moved to German-occupied Poland.

Bandera brought about a split in the OUN

at its national conference in Kraków on February 10, 1940. The majority, led by him, was called the Revolutionary OUN (OUN-R), or the Bandera OUN (OUN-B). Prior to the German invasion of the Soviet Union in June 1941, Bandera helped the Nazis to set up two Ukrainian battalions, the NACHTIGALL BATTALION and the Roland Battalion, with the purpose of carrying out intelligence activities. The OUN-B organized "mobile units," which moved into the Ukraine with the German forces and established the local government and the UKRAINISCHE HILFSPOLIZEI (Ukrainian Auxiliary Police).

On June 30, 1941, Bandera's representatives in Lvov announced the establishment of an independent Ukrainian government, but since the Germans objected to this, Bandera was arrested, on September 15, 1941, and sent to the SACHSENHAUSEN camp. He maintained contact with the members of his organization throughout the Ukraine, and on his instructions the UKRAINSKA POVSTANSKA ARMYIA (Ukrainian Insurgent Army) was organized at the end of 1942. Bandera was released on September 25, 1944, and conducted negotiations with the Germans. At the end of the war he settled in Munich. From there he continued to lead the movement until he was shot and killed in 1959 by a Soviet agent.

SHMUEL SPECTOR

BANSKÁ BYSTRICA, town on the Hron River in SLOVAKIA. It had a population of thirteen thousand on the eve of World War II, of whom one thousand were Jews.

During the SLOVAK NATIONAL UPRISING in 1944, Banská Bystrica was the capital of the area liberated. When German forces marched into Slovakia in order to destroy the partisans, Gen. František Catlos, minister of defense in President Jozef TISO's government, ordered the country's armed forces to offer no resistance to the invaders. The headquarters of the field forces in Banská Bystrica, however, disobeyed this order and instructed the troops under its command to fight the Germans.

Banská Bystrica became the military, political, and administrative center of the Czechoslovak republic in the heart of Tiso's fascist Slovakia. It was the seat of the Slovak National Council (Slovenská Narodna Rada)—the government of the liberated area —the plenum of which functioned as the parliament. It was also the headquarters of the First Czechoslovak Army, the British, American, and Soviet military missions, and the Palestinian parachutists (*see* PARACHUTISTS, JEWISH). In addition, the trade unions had their head office in Banská Bystrica, and six newspapers were published in the town.

Jews from the areas invaded by the Germans took refuge in Banská Bystrica, their number estimated at five thousand. The team of parachutists from Palestine—Haviva REIK, Chaim Hermesh, Rafael (Rafi) Reiss, and Zvi Ben-Yaakov—were active among the Jews, with Abba Berdiczew serving in the British military mission. The parachutists arrived at a time when the battles were at their height, and the original plan of forming a fighting Jewish unit under their command was not feasible, since the Jewish fighters were dispersed among the various units in the field. The parachutists organized a relief committee for Jewish refugees, provided them with lodging and employment, and generally looked after them. Before the town fell into German hands, the parachutists retreated with a group of Jewish community leaders and members of youth movements.

The Germans broke the rebels' resistance by a concentrated attack involving seven divisions, and captured the town on October 27, 1944. President Tiso—who was a Catholic priest—then went to the town to offer a thanksgiving service.

Zvi Ben-Yaakov and Abba Berdiczew were taken to MAUTHAUSEN and killed. The Banská Bystrica jail was filled with fighters and other opponents of the regime, including Haviva Reik and Rafael Reiss; from the jail the prisoners were taken to nearby Kremnica, where they were killed.

A handful of Jewish refugees managed to flee into the mountains before the town's fall. Most of the Jews in the area that had been liberated were caught; some of them were murdered in Kremnica and Nemecka. The rest were taken to the SERED camp, from which they were then deported, primarily to THERESIENSTADT, SACHSENHAUSEN, and AUSCHWITZ.

BIBLIOGRAPHY

Lipscher, L. *Die Juden im slowakischen Staat, 1939–1945.* Munich, 1980.

Nir, A. *Paths in a Ring of Fire.* Merhavia, Israel, 1967. (In Hebrew.)

Venohr, W. *Aufstand in der Tatra: Der Kampf um die Slowakei 1939–1944.* Königstein, West Germany, 1979.

AKIVA NIR

BARANOVICHI (Pol., Baranowicze), city in Brest Oblast (district), Belorussian SSR. In the interwar period it was part of independent Poland; it was occupied by the Red Army in September 1939 and annexed to the Soviet Union, together with the rest of eastern Poland.

On the eve of World War II, 12,000 Jews were living in Baranovichi, constituting over half the town's population. When the Germans entered Baranovichi, on June 27, 1941, the Jewish population stood at 10,000. A JUDENRAT (Jewish Council) was set up, with Yehoshua Isikson, a prominent figure in the city, as its chairman. A few days after they had occupied the city, the Germans murdered 73 Jews on charges of being Communists. At the end of June 1941, Einsatzkommando 8 and Wehrmacht troops murdered 350 Jews. Some time later, 750 Jews were sent to their death at the KOLDICHEVO concentration camp.

The Germans demanded that Isikson provide them with a large number of Jews for forced labor, even those who were physically unfit, but Isikson refused to comply. On March 3, 1942, 2,300 Jews were murdered. Isikson and his secretary were forced to witness the killing and then they too were murdered. He was replaced as chairman of the Judenrat by Shmuel Yankelevits. Following the March 3 *Aktion*, Jews from various other places—Liakhovichi, Kletsk, Meitshet, Stolbtsy, and Gorodishche—were brought to Baranovichi.

In the spring of 1942, three underground organizations were formed in the ghetto, one headed by Eliezer Lidovski, another by Momeh Kopelovits, and the third by Zaritskevits. Lidovski's group was also joined by the Jewish ghetto policemen. After a while the three groups united into a single organization, with some two hundred members, most of them in the sixteen-to-thirty age group. Its members engaged in sabotage, accumulated arms, and established contact with partisans.

A heated debate went on in the underground as to whether the forthcoming battle should be fought in the ghetto or in the forests. It was decided that the uprising would take place in the ghetto, and July 19, 1942, was fixed as the date. A plan was worked out, with the ghetto divided into several sectors and a commander appointed for each sector. A considerable quantity of weapons was smuggled into the ghetto by the underground members, mostly from the German warehouses where they worked; by the fall of 1942 the ghetto had 70 rifles, 2 machine guns, 40 pistols, 15,000 rounds of ammunition, 500 hand grenades, and several cases of gunpowder. At the beginning of July, the underground command decided to put off the date for the uprising, mainly out of consideration for the rest of the ghetto population. From then on, the underground's main effort was directed at escaping from the ghetto.

On August 19, 1942, 700 young Jews were seized and sent to Molodechno, in the northwest of the Belorussian SSR. A second *Aktion*, launched on September 22, lasted for ten days and resulted in the killing of 3,000 Jews. Throughout the days that the *Aktion* was raging, the underground was debating whether to start an uprising. Its armed members had gone into bunkers but did not open fire. The young people in the ghetto demanded that a decision be made to escape into the forests. When the *Aktion* came to an end, groups of Jews began to flee the ghetto; some of those who took part in the escape returned to the ghetto to help more groups get out. On December 17, 1942, the Germans launched a third *Aktion*, murdering 3,000 Jews and liquidating the ghetto. Only three remaining locations still had a concentration of Jews, totaling 700: the ORGANISATION TODT forced-labor camp, the Feldbauleitung (field construction office), and the Gestapo offices, where Jews were used for cleaning and other services. In the course of the *Aktionen* there were instances of individual Jews defying the murderers and jumping off the trucks.

At least 450 Jews fled to the forests from the ghetto and the labor camps in Baranovichi. The uprising had been scheduled to take place when the underground members were certain that the final liquidation of the ghetto was being launched; but they were never sure that this was indeed happening, either during the second *Aktion* or the third. The rest of the ghetto population also withheld their support for an uprising as long as they felt that there was still a chance to live and that not all of the ghetto inhabitants were doomed.

BIBLIOGRAPHY

Baranowicze Memorial Book. Tel Aviv, 1953. (In Hebrew.)

Foxman, J. *Baranowich in Martyrdom and Resistance*. New York, 1964. (In Yiddish.)

Lidovski, A. *In the Forests*. Tel Aviv, 1946. (In Hebrew.)

SHALOM CHOLAWSKI

BARASZ, EFRAIM (1892–1943), executive director of the Jewish community in BIAŁYSTOK and chairman of the Białystok ghetto JUDENRAT (Jewish Council). Born in Volkovysk, Białystok district, into an affluent and prominent Jewish family, Barasz had both a Jewish and a general education, studying in Germany and earning an engineering degree there. He joined the Zionist movement while still in his youth. During World War I, he lived in Russia with his family, returning to Volkovysk at the war's end. He became a businessman, was active in many Jewish institutions, and chaired the local Zionist organization. Moving to Białystok in 1934, Barasz kept up his activities in Zionist affairs, and was appointed executive director of the Białystok Jewish community, a post in which he excelled because of his initiative and his organizational talents. He visited Palestine in the early 1930s, in order to prepare for his family's immigration there. His son, whom he had enrolled in the Hebrew University, joined the British forces in World War II and became one of the first Jewish fighter pilots from Palestine.

At the end of June 1941, following the German occupation of Białystok, Rabbi Gedaliah

Efraim Barasz.

Rosenmann was appointed chairman of the Judenrat, but in actuality it was Barasz, the deputy chairman, who was in charge, both of the first Judenrat and its successor a month later. Many of the members of the Białystok Judenrat had previously held major posts in the organized Jewish community.

The ghetto in Białystok, established on July 31, 1941, held about thirty-five thousand Jews. Białystok came to be incorporated into a district that was joined to East Prussia. In the fall of 1942 the Białystok region was subjected to deportations and the liquidation of ghettos, although the Białystok ghetto itself was not affected. Barasz was aware of the mass murder of Jews by the EINSATZGRUPPEN, of the deportations, and of the destruction of Jewish communities, but he believed that work would "serve as a protective shield," as he put it: "Our main rescue effort has to be based on the establishment of a highly developed industry." Following this concept, Barasz did all he could to enlist the ghetto inhabitants in the work drive, issued stern warnings against sabotage acts, and even took part in the deportation of some of the ghetto population in February 1943 (in the course of which nine thousand to ten thousand Jews were driven out or murdered on the spot). At the same time, Barasz maintained close contact with the Białystok ghetto underground and, for a while, coordinated his activities with those of Mordecai TENENBAUM (Tamaroff), who later became the commander of the ŻYDOWSKA ORGANIZACJA BOJOWA (Jewish Fighting Organization; ŻOB) in Białystok and of the Białystok ghetto uprising. Barasz gained Tenenbaum's confidence, gave assistance to the commune of the He-Haluts Zionist youth movement that was set up in Białystok, provided the underground with laboratory facilities and experts for the manufacture of arms, and supplied it with funds for onward transmission to the ŻOB in Warsaw. Shortly before the ghetto uprising, however, Barasz's relations with the underground deteriorated and finally came to a complete break.

On the basis of his contacts with German officials, Barasz continued to believe that the German administration and police in Białystok wanted to keep the working ghetto in existence. He thought he could save the ghetto from total liquidation and the Jews from total annihilation.

The final phase of the liquidation of the ghetto came on August 16, 1943, and was followed by the uprising in the ghetto. Between August 21 and 27, twenty-five thousand Jews were deported to the TREBLINKA extermination camp, in five trains; several hundred Jews—Barasz, Rabbi Rosenmann, and other members of the Judenrat among them—were kept apart from the rest and put into a "small ghetto," the designation given to one of the streets of the former ghetto. In September the Jews from this "small ghetto," including Barasz, his wife, and the members of the Judenrat, were deported to the MAJDANEK concentration camp. From there the last of Białystok's Jews were apparently taken to the PONIATOWA camp, where all the Jewish prisoners were murdered, in November 1943. No precise details are available concerning the date and circumstances of Barasz's death.

BIBLIOGRAPHY

Blumenthal, N., ed. *Conduct and Actions of a Judenrat: Documents from the Białystok Ghetto.* Jerusalem, 1962.
Grosman, H. *People of the Underground.* Merhavia, Israel, 1965. (In Hebrew.)
Tenenbaum-Tamarof, M. *Pages from Fire.* Naharia, Israel, 1987. (In Hebrew.)
Trunk, I. *Judenrat: The Jewish Councils in Eastern Europe under Nazi Occupation.* New York, 1972.

ISRAEL GUTMAN

BARBIE TRIAL, criminal proceedings against former SS-Untersturmführer Klaus Barbie (b. 1913), held in Lyons, France, mainly between May 11 and July 4, 1987. Barbie joined the Nazi party in 1932 and the SS in 1935. He began working for the Gestapo in 1942, and in November of that year was posted to Lyons, where he served as the Gestapo chief for the next twenty-one months. During that period he directly committed or was responsible for numerous atrocities, earning him the nickname "the Butcher of Lyons." Among his most infamous acts was the torture of Jean Moulin, a hero of the French Résistance.

After the war Barbie became a counter-intelligence agent for the United States in Germany. In 1951 he emigrated to Bolivia, settling in La Paz. He acquired Bolivian citizenship in 1957, under the pseudonym Klaus Altmann. In 1952 and again in 1954 Barbie was tried *in absentia* in France. Both times he was convicted of specific war crimes and sentenced to death. He was discovered in La Paz by the Nazi hunter Beate Klarsfeld in 1971. In the following years the French government requested his extradition many times, but it was only in 1983 that the Bolivians finally expelled Barbie and he was brought to France to stand trial.

Barbie was charged with crimes against humanity, which were not subject to the French statute of limitations. The specific charges were: responsibility for a raid on the headquarters of the UNION GÉNÉRALE DES ISRAÉLITES DE FRANCE on Rue Ste. Catherine in Lyons on February 9, 1943, where some 85

Jews were arrested and later sent to AUSCH-WITZ; responsibility for the deportation of 44 Jewish children who were discovered by the Gestapo to be hiding in the village of Izieu, 43.4 miles (70 km) east of Lyons; and responsibility for ordering the last transport from Lyons to Auschwitz, on August 11, 1944. In all, Barbie was charged with responsibility for the deportation of 842 people from Lyons, about half of them Jews and half of them members of the French Résistance.

The Barbie trial was followed closely throughout the world. It aroused much controversy in France. Some Frenchmen feared it would raise questions on the French collaboration with the Nazis, especially regarding the arrest and killing of Jean Moulin. Others feared it might cause a new wave of antisemitism. Still others thought the trial might blur the distinctions between he Holocaust and other Nazi atrocities perpetrated during the war. In connection with the trial, neo-Nazis and some activists in Holocaust denial (see HOLOCAUST, DENIAL OF THE) tried to claim that Barbie's behavior was no different from that of many of the Allied forces during the war and of a number of nations after the war.

On July 4, 1987, Barbie was found guilty of crimes against humanity and was sentenced to life imprisonment, the maximum penalty under French law at the time.

[See also Trials of War Criminals.]

BIBLIOGRAPHY

Bower, T. Klaus Barbie: Butcher of Lyon. London, 1984.
Paris, E. Unhealed Wounds: France and the Klaus Barbie Affair. Toronto, 1985.
Ruzie, D. "The Klaus Barbie Case: War Crimes versus Crimes against Humanity." Patterns of Prejudice 20/3 (July 1968): 27–33.
Ryan, A. J., Jr., ed. Klaus Barbie and the United States Government. Frederick, Md., 1984.

JACQUELINE ROKHSAR

BARTH, KARL (1886–1968), Swiss Protestant theologian. Barth was the most prominent theologian in the Reformed (Calvinist) tradition in the first half of the twentieth century. He was educated in Germany, but in 1914 turned against his theological mentors because of their uncritical support of German nationalism and war aims. His commentary on the Epistle to the Romans (1919) was an outright attack on the "cultural Protestantism" of the nineteenth century and denied the identification of the Kingdom of God with human or national progress. Theology, for Barth, consisted not in man's attempt to find God, but solely in describing God's justification of man through faith. From 1921 to 1935, Barth was a professor of theology in Göttingen, Münster, and Bonn, establishing his school of "dialectical" theology, which looked to biblical revelation as the sole source of authority in the church and rejected any accommodation with nationalist or racial ideologies. From 1933 on, Barth was the theological leader of the German Confessing Church (Bekennende Kirche), in opposition to the pro-Nazi "German Christians"; he was the principal author of the 1934 Barmen Declaration, in which the supporters of the Confessing Church joined to defend their position against the totalitarian demands of the state. In 1935 he was expelled from Germany and returned to his native Basel, where he continued working on his unfinished major work, Church Dogmatics (13 vols.).

Barth's hostility to Nazi antisemitism was based on his biblical theology, though he did not at first recognize the need to make the "Jewish question" the central point of church resistance. Following his expulsion from Germany, he became more outspoken on behalf of the Jews, and from 1938 on his theology clearly affirmed the solidarity of Christians and Jews as the common heirs of biblical revelation. The second volume of Church Dogmatics (1942) contained a pointed chapter on the church's indissoluble dependence on and foundation in Israel. In later volumes of this work, he strongly criticized traditional Christian triumphalist attitudes, regarded Christian missionary activity to the Jewish people as theologically inadmissible, and repudiated the view that the Christian church had displaced Judaism as the sole channel of salvation. Despite his dogmatic views on modern Judaism and his exclusivist Christology, Barth's influence in the postwar period was significant, particularly in such bodies as the World Council of Churches, in rethinking the theological relationship between Christianity and Judaism.

Barth's writings that bear on such matters include *Church Dogmatics* (London, 1936–1969), *Der Römerbrief* (Oxford, 1933), and "The Jewish Problem and the Christian Answer," in *Against the Stream: Shorter Post-War Writings, 1946–1952* (London, 1954).

BIBLIOGRAPHY

Busch, E. *Karl Barth.* London, 1976.

JOHN S. CONWAY

BARTOSZEWSKI, WŁADYSŁAW (b. 1922), Polish anti-Nazi who aided Jews during the Holocaust. Bartoszewski was imprisoned in AUSCHWITZ from September 1940 to April 1941, and from 1942 to 1945 was a member of the ARMIA KRAJOWA (the Polish Home Army). He also belonged to the underground organization of young Catholics, the Front Odrodzenia Polski (Front for the Rebirth of Poland), and in September 1942 helped to set up a provisional committee that later became the ZEGOTA welfare organization. When the latter's permanent council was set up, on December 4, 1942, Bartoszewski became one of the two DELEGATURA representatives who regularly attended Zegota's board meetings. He was active in the underground and helped transmit to the POLISH GOVERNMENT-IN-EXILE reports on the Nazi terror against the Poles and on the situation of the Jews. In 1963 YAD VASHEM designated him a "RIGHTEOUS AMONG THE NATIONS."

A prolific writer and historian, Bartoszewski has published a number of books, dealing mostly with the history of Warsaw during the war, the Polish Jews, and the rescue of Jews by Polish gentiles. They include *Warsaw Death Ring, 1939–1944* (1968) and *Righteous among Nations: How Poles Helped the Jews, 1939–1945* (1969). Bartoszewski is the president of the PEN Club in Poland, serves as a professor on the faculty of the Catholic University of Lublin, and frequently lectures in many countries.

ELISHEVA SHAUL

Władysław Bartoszewski.

BAUBLYS, PETRAS (d. 1974), pediatrician and head of an orphanage in Kovno, Lithuania. Upon being contacted by an underground Jewish organization operating in the Kovno ghetto, Baublys agreed to use the orphanage facility (located in the Slobodka section of the city, where the ghetto was situated) as a temporary shelter and a conduit for transferring Jewish children to permanent, safe locations. Dozens of children and infants were accepted into the orphanage, some abandoned on the doorsteps by fleeing Jewish mothers. Children knowing a smattering of Lithuanian were kept within the orphanage compound for relatively longer periods; others, as well as children over the permissible age, were quickly spirited to hiding places with Lithuanian families, with Baublys providing free medical care for the sick children he visited. In order to minimize the danger of betrayal to the authorities, only a select group of the orphanage staff knew of this undertaking.

Baublys, his brother Sergejus, and his

sister-in-law Jadvyga (who hid a Jewish child in their home) were recognized by YAD VASHEM as "RIGHTEOUS AMONG THE NATIONS" in 1977.

MORDECAI PALDIEL

BAUM GRUPPE (Baum Group), clandestine anti-Nazi organization in Berlin, composed mainly of Jews who belonged to YOUTH MOVEMENTS and who during the Nazi rule joined the German Communist party or its youth organizations. Most of the group's members were Communists, but it also included Zionists, members of the left-wing Zionist youth movement Werkleute, and some who were recruited from Zionist youth movements such

Edith Fraenkel, a member of the Baum Gruppe, was sent to Theresienstadt and then to Auschwitz, where she died in 1944.

Monument to the Baum Gruppe in the Weissensee cemetery, East Berlin. The text reads (top): "To the members of the Herbert Baum group executed in 1942/43"; (bottom): "They fell in the battle for peace and freedom."

as Ha-Shomer ha-Tsa'ir and Ha-Bonim. Out of thirty-two militant members, only four were over the age of nineteen in 1933. The leaders of the group, Herbert Baum and his wife, Marianne, started their underground activity at the beginning of the Nazi regime.

In 1936 the Jewish members were instructed by the Communist underground to set up an independent group and found Communist cells in Jewish youth organizations. Between 1937 and 1942, the activities of the group, which maintained links with all major similar groups in Berlin, included the distribution of illegal brochures and the organization of educational evenings, political training courses, and cultural events. The group also sought to strengthen the morale of Jews due to be deported to the east. On May 18, 1942, several members of the group set fire to different areas of *Das Sowjetparadies* ("The Soviet Paradise"), an anti-Bolshevik exhibit set up in Berlin by the Nazi Ministry of Propaganda; the group's action was considered a major anti-Nazi manifestation. Most members of the group were caught, either denounced by an informer planted by the Ge-

Heinz Birnbaum, one of the leaders of the Baum Gruppe.

Lotte Rotholz, a member of the Baum Gruppe. She died in Auschwitz.

stapo or because of their lack of training in conspiratorial work. Five hundred Berlin Jews were also arrested in revenge. Half of them were shot and the others sent to the SACHSENHAUSEN concentration camp and killed in the fall of 1942. Baum was tortured to death, and the other members were arrested and prosecuted in separate trials between July 1942 and June 1943; most of them were executed. Nearly all the other members were later deported to the east and died in AUSCHWITZ.

Werner Steinbrink, a leading member of the Baum Gruppe, was apprehended and executed on August 18, 1942.

BIBLIOGRAPHY

Eschwege, H. "Resistance of German Jews against the Nazi Regime." *Leo Baeck Institute Year Book* 15 (1970): 143–180.

Kwiet, K., and H. Eschwege. *Selbstbehauptung und Widerstand.* Hamburg, 1984.

Mark, B. "The Herbert Baum Group: Jewish Resistance in Germany in the Years 1937–1942." In *They Fought Back*, edited by Y. Suhl, pp. 55–68. New York, 1962.

Pikarski, M. *Jugend im Berliner Widerstand: Herbert Baum und Kampfgefährten.* Berlin, 1978.

DAVID BANKIER

Zvi Bauminger.

BAUMINGER, HESHEK (Zvi or "Bazyli"; 1919–1943), one of the commanders of the Iskra (Spark) fighting organization in KRA-KÓW. Bauminger, who was born in Kraków, received a Zionist religious upbringing and attended the Hebrew high school in Kraków. At the age of sixteen he joined Ha-Shomer ha-Tsa'ir, and he eventually became the head of the movement's branch in Kraków.

When World War II broke out he was drafted into the Polish army, ending up in Lvov. After the Germans invaded the Soviet Union on June 22, 1941, Bauminger was drafted into the Red Army and fell into German captivity. He managed to escape and make his way to Lvov, where fellow Ha-Shomer ha-Tsa'ir members provided him with Aryan papers. He then made his way back to Kraków on foot, reaching the ghetto in early 1942. There he met with the surviving members of his movement and with leaders of Akiva, reporting to them on the horrendous mass murders that the Germans had perpetrated on the Jews of Eastern Galicia and the Ukraine, and advocating an armed struggle against the enemy.

In mid-1942 a unified Jewish command, the ŻYDOWSKA ORGANIZACJA BOJOWA (ŻOB), was established; headed by Bauminger, it included members of Akiva, Dror, Iskra, and other organizations. Using hit-and-run tactics, each movement engaged in its own sporadic actions, but major operations were carried out jointly and directed by the unified command. The most important of these, con-ducted on December 22, 1942, was called the "Cyganeria Night" (Cyganeria being the name of the café that was the target). Nine German officers were killed in the attack and thirteen wounded; this was the first time that Kraków residents saw Germans killed and wounded. The escape plan was for the He-Haluts ha-Lohem fighters to make their way back to their headquarters at 24 Skavinska Street, while the Iskra fighters were to go to their headquarters in Czerwony Pradnik, a Polish workers' section of the city, several kilometers from the ghetto. The Germans, however, found out about the meeting at the He-Haluts ha-Lohem headquarters. They broke in, killing some of the members and capturing the rest.

Bauminger and his men continued fighting the Germans, carrying out acts of sabotage on German installations in and outside the ghetto. In March 1943 the Germans broke into the place where he lived. Bauminger fired at them, saving the last bullet to shoot himself in the temple.

BIBLIOGRAPHY

Bauminger, A. *The Fighters of the Kraków Ghetto.* Jerusalem, 1987. (In Hebrew.)

Bauminger, A., M. Bosak, and N. M. Gelber. *The Kraków Book: A Jewish Mother-City.* Jerusalem, 1959. See pages 381–429. (In Hebrew.)

Krakowski, S. *The War of the Doomed.* New York, 1984.

ARIE LEON BAUMINGER

BAUR, ANDRÉ (1904–1943), Jewish leader in Paris. Born in Paris, Baur was reared in a distinguished Jewish family of rabbis and community figures, and he himself became the president of the Paris Reform synagogue (on Rue Copernic) in the late 1930s. A well-to-do banker, Baur could easily have left Paris during the great exodus of Jews in 1940 but opted to remain and serve the community.

In March 1941 the Comité de Coordination, the recently established umbrella organization of Jewish welfare societies in Paris, was at a crossroads, and new responsible Jewish personalities were needed to invigorate it. Called upon by his uncle Julien Weill, who was the Chief Rabbi of Paris, Baur entered the Comité and tried to turn it in constructive directions and increase relief to the Jews of the occupied zone. Although he succeeded in bringing together reputable individuals to head the Comité, he was unable to obtain the suppport of the community for his welfare schemes.

In the fall of 1941, Baur held talks with Xavier VALLAT, head of the COMMISSARIAT GÉNÉRAL AUX QUESTIONS JUIVES (established by the Vichy government), on the creation of the UNION GÉNÉRALE DES ISRAÉLITES DE FRANCE (UGIF), and he became its vice president. From the outset of the UGIF's existence, Baur directed it to abide by legal methods of operation, and even in moments of great crisis (such as the mass arrest of Jews in Paris in July 1942), he adhered strictly to this outlook, hoping thereby to alleviate the plight of the Jewish community. Constantly concerned with the needs of Jews, Baur went to great efforts to guarantee the UGIF's resources, even to the point of proposing a more "harmonized" and authoritarian organization that would have eliminated the autonomous existence of UGIF-South, the UGIF division in the unoccupied zone. Baur fought valiantly to save his immigrant employees from dismissal in early 1943, but gave in to the German pressure when it threatened the UGIF's continuation.

Baur was a man of principle, deeply devoted to succoring the needy. His policy came to an impasse in July 1943, when SS-Hauptsturmführer Alois BRUNNER devised a scheme in which the UGIF would encourage relatives of interned Jews to voluntarily unite with their family members in DRANCY. With the full support of his council, Baur rejected turning the UGIF into a police arm of the SS and sought the intervention of Prime Minister Pierre LAVAL. As a result of his objection to carrying out Brunner's plan, Baur, his wife, and their four children were arrested and sent to Drancy. From there they were deported in December 1943 to AUSCHWITZ, where Baur perished.

BIBLIOGRAPHY

Adler, J. *The Jews of Paris and the Final Solution: Communal Response and International Conflicts, 1940–1944.* New York, 1988.

Cohen, R. I. *The Burden of Conscience: French Jewish Leadership during the Holocaust.* Bloomington, 1987.

Cohen, R. I. "The Jewish Community of France in the Face of Vichy-German Persecution, 1940–1944." In *The Jews in Modern France,* edited by F. Malino and B. Wasserstein, pp. 181–204. London, 1985.

RICHARD COHEN

BECCARI, ARRIGO, priest in Nonantola, near Bologna in northern ITALY, who together with Giuseppe Moreali, a local physician, saved the lives of 120 Jews, mostly children. In July 1942, an initial group of fifty Jewish children arrived in Nonantola, after having resided for a while in the Italian zone of occupation in northern Yugoslavia. They had earlier been separated from their parents, whose whereabouts remained unknown. With the increase of partisan activity in the Italian zone, the friendly Italian authorities suggested to Josef

Itai, the group leader, that he move his children to the safety of Italy proper (then at war on the side of Nazi Germany). With the aid of Delasem (Delegazione Assistenza Emigranti Ebrei), the Jewish welfare agency officially recognized by the Fascist government, the children were housed in Villa Emma, in the village of Nonantola. There they were joined by an additional fifty children, recent refugees from Nazi terror. When the Germans overran northern Italy on September 8, 1943, the children were no longer safe, and preventive measures had to be taken immediately to avoid their falling into German hands. Without seeking the approval of his superiors in Modena, Arrigo Beccari, an instructor in a nearby Catholic seminary whom Itai had earlier befriended, opened the seminary's doors to the children. Others were housed with surrounding villagers, while the food for all was prepared within the seminary walls. When the seminary rector first saw the children, who included girls, he crossed himself and exclaimed: "For a thousand years, a woman's foot has not trodden on these grounds, but let God's will be done."

With the Nazis intensifying their search for Jews in hiding, a plan was prepared to move the children and their adult caretakers, a total of 120 persons, out of the occupied zone. At first, the thought was to smuggle them across Allied lines south of Rome. But as this proved impractical, it was decided to trans-

fer them to the Swiss border to the north. With the help of Giuseppe Moreali, the town doctor, false identities were provided and all 120 children and their caretakers were taken by train to the Swiss border, which they crossed on the eve of the Day of Atonement of 1943. The dangers attending the convoy of such a large group of children and their Italian guides on their trek to the Swiss border were great. The children, for instance, bore Italian names on their false credentials but were hardly proficient in that language.

The Gestapo, belatedly discovering the children's flight, seized Beccari and interrogated him to elicit the names of persons involved in the rescue operation and the location of other Jews in hiding. Beccari withstood the terrible ordeal of Nazi torture and was released after many months of incarceration in a notorious Bologna prison.

Arrigo Beccari and Giuseppe Moreali were recognized by YAD VASHEM as "RIGHTEOUS AMONG THE NATIONS" in 1964.

BIBLIOGRAPHY

Zuccotti, S. *The Italians and the Holocaust*. New York, 1987.

MORDECAI PALDIEL

Arrigo Beccari, left, and Dr. Giuseppe Moreali, right.

BECHER, KURT (b. 1909), Nazi official. Born in Hamburg, Becher arrived in Hungary with the rank of SS-*Obersturmbannführer* shortly after the German occupation on March 19, 1944, having served for several years on the Russian front. His alleged assignment from the SS headquarters was the procurement of horses and equipment for horse-drawn units of the Waffen-SS. Becher played a decisive role in the acquisition of German control over the giant Weiss-Manfred Works. He was also the chief SS negotiator with whom the RELIEF AND RESCUE COMMITTEE OF BUDAPEST, and especially Rezső (Rudolf) KASZTNER, had to deal. Becher was involved in the arrangement of the "Kasztner transport" and its eventual transfer from the BERGEN-BELSEN concentration camp to Switzerland. In this context he also met (having received Heinrich HIMMLER's consent) with Saly MAYER, the American Jewish JOINT DISTRIBUTION COMMIT-

TEE head in Switzerland, and with Roswell McClelland, the WAR REFUGEE BOARD representative, in Saint Gall on November 4, 1944. Considering the latter as "the personal representative of President Franklin Delano ROOSEVELT," Becher attached great importance to the meeting, transcending the rescuing of Jews.

A few months after Becher's promotion to SS-*Standartenführer* in January 1945, Himmler appointed Becher to serve as *Reichssonderkommissar für sämtliche Konzentrationslager* (Special Reich Commissioner for All Concentration Camps). Traveling in the company of Kasztner, Becher worked toward preventing the destruction of the camps in the last weeks of the war.

Becher was arrested by the Allies after Germany's surrender. He escaped prosecution as a war criminal, and was released from prison in Nuremberg on Kasztner's personal recommendation.

BIBLIOGRAPHY

Braham, R. L. *The Politics of Genocide: The Holocaust in Hungary.* New York, 1981.
Lévai, J. *A fekete SS fehér báránya.* Budapest, 1966.
Pintér, I. and L. Szabó, eds. *Criminals at Large.* Budapest, 1961. See pages 150–164.

RANDOLPH L. BRAHAM

BĘDZIN, town in the Katowice district in PO-LAND, founded in the Middle Ages. In the latter half of the nineteenth century, Będzin entered a stage of rapid development and attracted industry as a result of its location in an area rich in coal and iron ore. A Jewish community came into existence in Będzin in the late Middle Ages. In 1931 the Jewish population numbered 21,625 (45.4 percent of the total), and by the eve of World War II it had grown to approximately 27,000.

The German occupation of the city, on September 4, 1939, exposed the Jewish inhabitants of Będzin to maltreatment and harassment. On September 9 the Germans set fire to the main synagogue and fifty adjacent houses without giving the residents advance warning, and a number of Jews were burned to death. A series of anti-Jewish economic decrees was enacted, providing for the confiscation of Jewish property and the imposition of personal restrictions on the Jews.

The A. Rossner tailor shop in Będzin, which supplied uniforms for the Germans (March 4, 1941).

A JUDENRAT (Jewish Council) was established at an early stage of the occupation, headed by local Jewish public figures. After a while the local Judenrat was subordinated to the Judenräte center in SOSNOWIEC, and a new local Judenrat chairman, Chaim Molczadski, was appointed. The most difficult anti-Jewish decree ordered Jews to report for forced labor, which at times led to their being seized and deported to forced-labor camps in Germany. It soon became the Judenrat's task to organize these deportations. The Judenrat also helped establish workshops (known as "shops"), owned by Germans and using Jews as workers, on the assumption that by engaging in work benefiting the Germans, the city's Jews would be saved. The local Jewish YOUTH MOVEMENTS resumed their educational activities and also took on the teaching of children (who had been left without any schools) and vocational training, with an emphasis on agriculture. The Judenrat allocated a 100-acre (.404 sq km) plot of land at one end of the city to establish a *farma* (farm).

In May 1942, deportation of the Będzin Jews to the AUSCHWITZ extermination camp was launched, in the guise of "resettlement." The deportation reached its peak on August 12, when all the Jews of the city had to assemble on a central city plot, ostensibly in order to have their papers stamped. A *Selek-*

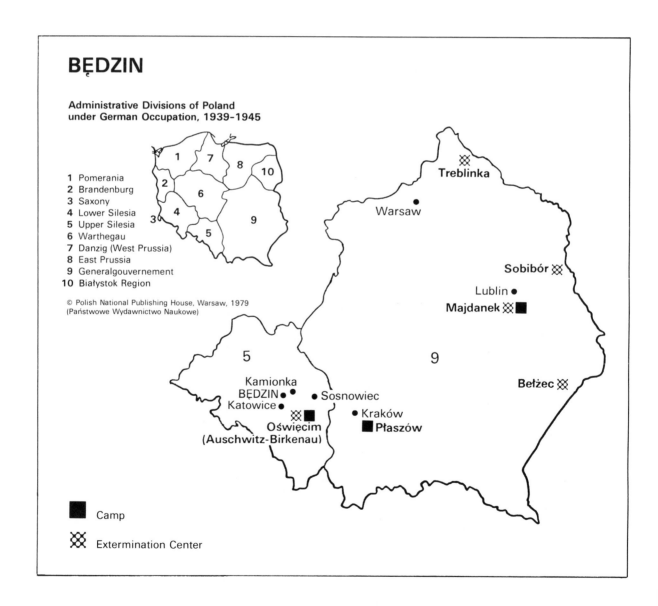

BĘDZIN

Administrative Divisions of Poland under German Occupation, 1939–1945

1 Pomerania
2 Brandenburg
3 Saxony
4 Lower Silesia
5 Upper Silesia
6 Warthegau
7 Danzig (West Prussia)
8 East Prussia
9 Generalgouvernement
10 Białystok Region

© Polish National Publishing House, Warsaw, 1979
(Państwowe Wydawnictwo Naukowe)

Treblinka

Warsaw

Sobibór

Lublin
Majdanek

Bełżec

Kamionka
BĘDZIN
Katowice
Sosnowiec

Oświęcim
(Auschwitz-Birkenau)

Kraków
Płaszów

■ Camp

✖ Extermination Center

tion was made, and 5,000 Jews were dispatched to their deaths.

The youth movements intensified their operations, embarked on an anti-Judenrat information campaign, and cautioned the Jews not to report for the deportations. The *farma* was used as the site of clandestine meetings with leaders of the ŻYDOWSKA ORGANIZACJA BOJOWA (Jewish Fighting Organization; ŻOB). One of them was Mordecai ANIELEWICZ, the future leader of the WARSAW GHETTO UPRISING, who told the local youth movement activists about the extermination of Jews in the GENERALGOUVERNEMENT and helped organize a local resistance organization. The *farma* became the center of the youth movements' underground operations and the site of a defense headquarters, in which representatives of all the youth movements took part. The leadership consisted of Frumka PLOTNICKA (who had come from Warsaw), Zvi Brandes, Herschel Springer, Shlomo Lerner, and Ezriel ("Yozek") Koszok.

The Będzin Jewish underground made attempts to establish contact with the Polish underground, but these failed, as did the attempts to stage an armed uprising outside the ghetto. During a sortie that a fighting unit made from the ghetto, it was ambushed and killed. The underground concentrated its efforts on acquiring weapons, preparing for defense, and constructing bunkers; these efforts were accompanied by a debate among the youth movements, between those who demanded that the emphasis be on the struggle inside the ghetto walls and those who stressed the search for escape routes, mainly by way of the border with Slovakia.

In the spring of 1943, the Będzin Jews were confined to a ghetto that was set up in Kamionka, a suburb close to Środula, where the Sosnowiec Jews were held. On August 1, 1943, the final liquidation of the ghetto was launched. Youth movement members offered armed resistance in several bunkers. The operation took more than two weeks, the Jews being deported to Auschwitz. Some of the survivors in the ghetto escaped to Slovakia and Hungary, where they resumed underground operations. A handful of Będzin Jews returned to the city after the war, but the Jewish community was not revived.

BIBLIOGRAPHY

Brandes, A., and H. Reshef, eds. *Zvi Brandes: A Leader of the Zaglembian Haluts Underground.* Tel Aviv, 1972. (In Hebrew.)

Gilbert, M. *The Holocaust.* New York, 1985.

Mazia, F. *Comrades in the Storm: The Struggle of Zionist Youth against the Nazis.* Jerusalem, 1964. (In Hebrew.)

Rappaport, J. *Pinkas Zaglembie: Memorial Book.* Tel Aviv, 1972. (In Hebrew, Yiddish, and English.)

Stein, A. S., ed. *Pinkas Bendin: A Memorial to the Jewish Community of Bendin (Poland).* Tel Aviv, 1959. (In Hebrew.)

SHLOMO NETZER

BEŁCHATÓW, town in the Łódź district, Poland. On the eve of World War II it had six thousand Jews, comprising 60 percent of the total population. About one-third of the Jews left in the first few months of the German occupation. On March 1, 1941, a ghetto was set up in Bełchatów; in the fall of that year it took in the Jews of nearby towns—Zelów, Widawa, and Szczerców—as well as those from several villages who had been driven out of their homes. As a result, the ghetto was crowded to suffocation and sanitary conditions deteriorated.

Between August 1941 and April 1942, 1,950 men from the Bełchatów ghetto were transferred to forced-labor camps in the Poznań area, where they all met their death. The ghetto was liquidated from August 11 to 13 of that year by SS units stationed in the area, with the participation of the civilian German population led by the mayor, Josef Tramler, and the chief of the Łódź ghetto administration, Hans BIEBOW (who made a special journey to Bełchatów for this purpose). In the course of the liquidation, 5,000 Jews were deported to the CHEŁMNO extermination camp and were murdered there, 850 were transferred to the Łódź ghetto, and 150 managed to flee, although most of them were later caught and killed.

BIBLIOGRAPHY

Belchatow (In Memoriam). Buenos Aires, 1951. (In Yiddish.)

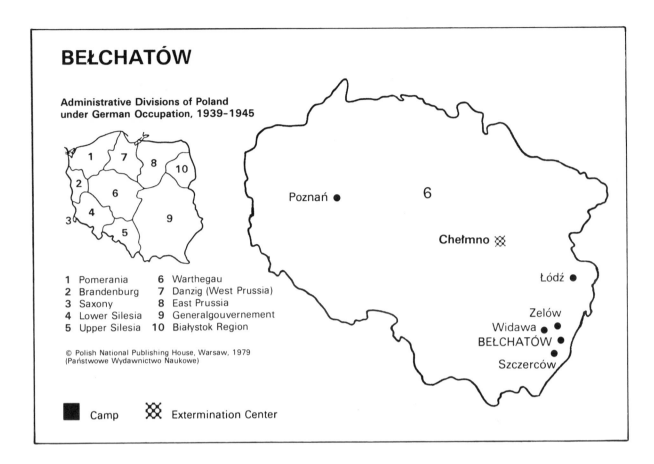

BEŁCHATÓW

Administrative Divisions of Poland
under German Occupation, 1939–1945

1 Pomerania   6 Warthegau
2 Brandenburg   7 Danzig (West Prussia)
3 Saxony   8 East Prussia
4 Lower Silesia   9 Generalgouvernement
5 Upper Silesia   10 Białystok Region

© Polish National Publishing House, Warsaw, 1979
(Państwowe Wydawnictwo Naukowe)

■ Camp   ⊗ Extermination Center

Poznań ●

6

Chełmno ⊗

Łódź ●

Zelów ●
Widawa ●
BEŁCHATÓW ●

Szczerców

Dobroszycki, L. *The Chronicle of the Lodz Ghetto.*
New Haven, 1984.

SHMUEL KRAKOWSKI

BELGIAN JEWS, ASSOCIATION OF. *See*
Association des Juifs en Belgique.

BELGIUM. In the Middle Ages the area that is
now Belgium had a small Jewish population,
but in the fourteenth century the existing
communities were liquidated. In the sixteenth century, Marranos (Jews concealing
their Judaism) from Portugal settled in the
Belgian cities, and by the seventeenth century a more or less overt Jewish community
had come into being in Antwerp. During the
eighteenth century Ashkenazi Jews also settled in Belgium, and by the century's end
they had achieved equal rights. In 1830,
when Belgium became an independent country, its Jewish population was a little over

1,000; by the end of the nineteenth century
that number had greatly increased. During
that period, however, Belgium was primarily
a transit station for Jewish refugees from
eastern Europe on their way to overseas destinations and, as a result, the Jewish community's size and institutions were not of a sta-
ble character. It was only from the early
1920s that Belgian Jewry steadily grew in
size, with Jews arriving from the multinational countries that had been broken up
(Russia and the Austro-Hungarian Empire)
and, in the 1930s, from Nazi Germany. On
the eve of the Nazi invasion Belgium had a
Jewish population of 66,000 (out of a total of
8.3 million), but only 10 percent of the Jews
were Belgian citizens.

The Jewish population was concentrated in
four cities, Brussels, Antwerp, Liège, and
Charleroi, but mostly in the first two. The
official Belgian Jewish community was organized into a central Consistoire, but many of
the immigrants formed their own communities, congregations, and associations, outside

BELGIUM

the Consistoire framework. The immigrants spoke Yiddish, but especially among the younger generation, French became the predominant language. All the shades of Jewish political opinion that had developed in Poland in the interwar period were present in Belgium, most prominently the socialist trends—Zionist and non-Zionist, including the BUND—and other, more radical leftist ideologies. This situation led to the development of very close ties between the Jews and the Belgian leftist movements, a factor that proved of great importance in the rescue efforts and the resistance during the Holocaust period.

German Occupation. German forces invaded Belgium on May 10, 1940, and on May 28, on the orders of King Leopold III, the Belgian army surrendered. The king stayed in Belgium, but the prime minister and some of the cabinet members fled the country, their first stop being France. After a great deal of internal discussion and controversy, a government-in-exile was established in London on October 31, 1940. As a result, two centers of official Belgian authority were now in existence, each with its own policy and objectives. The king, recognizing the new balance of power in the country, was inclined to cooperate with the Germans, and on one occasion even met with Adolf HITLER, but he refrained almost totally from overt activity. The government-in-exile supported the

Allies, and neither of the two sides recognized the authority of the other. Hitler had no definite plans for Belgium's ultimate political status in the "New Order" that was to be established in Europe after a German victory, and the absence of such plans had a marked effect on the administration that the Germans installed in the occupied country.

The first four years witnessed a military administration (*Militärverwaltung*), under Gen. Alexander von Falkenhausen. In July 1944 a civil administration (*Zivilverwaltung*) took its place, the Germans now planning to turn Belgium into two *Reichsgaue* (territorial units) annexed to Germany: *Reichsgau* Flanders and *Reichsgau* Walonia; Josef Grohé was appointed *Reichskommissar* for Belgium. Under the military administration, a complex set of relationships existed between the administration and the other branches of the German government and Nazi party that had a foothold in Belgium: the Foreign Ministry and the SS in general, especially the REICHSSICHERHEITSHAUPTAMT (Reich Security Main Office; RSHA). The latter two bodies, which were both under Heinrich HIMMLER's authority, made strenuous efforts to expand their influence, while the military administration tried to curb them. The Belgian administration continued to function on a regular basis under the *secrétaires généraux* (principal secretaries), who held regular meetings to coordinate their activities and constituted a kind of mini-government; from time to time, personnel changes took place among the *secrétaires généraux*.

In early September 1944, Brussels and Antwerp were liberated by Allied forces, and by early November all of Belgium was set free. However, in the winter offensive that the Germans launched in the Ardennes in December 1944, they reoccupied areas in the southeast, and it was only in January 1945 that the last German troops were driven out.

According to data published in 1980, the Jewish population of Belgium at the time of the German invasion was 65,696 (not 90,000, as claimed in earlier studies); 34,801 Jews were imprisoned or deported, and of these, 28,902 perished, representing 44 percent of the total Jewish population. This was a lower percentage of Jews murdered than in the

Netherlands, mainly for three reasons: (1) the different kind of administration established by the Germans; (2) the different mentality of the Belgian Jews; and (3) the attitude of the local population.

In Belgium, German rule had all the attributes of Nazi anti-Jewish policy: eliminating Jews from all positions of influence, depriving them of their possessions and livelihood, putting them on forced labor, isolating them from the rest of the population, and, finally, deporting them to their death. Here, however, the German administration served as a restraining factor on the volume, intensity, and tempo of the anti-Jewish measures.

In the first two years of the occupation, before the deportations began, eighteen anti-Jewish decrees and regulations were issued, at relatively long intervals, creating the impression that the measures were on the whole quite moderate. On October 23, 1940, ritual slaughter was prohibited. Two decrees announced October 28 defined who was to be regarded as a Jew under the law, ordered the Jews to conduct a census and draw up a list of all their enterprises and occupations, and eliminated Jews from the public administration, the legal and teaching professions, and the media. On May 31, 1941, two decrees were issued, ordering Jews to display signs identifying their enterprises as Jewish and to declare their capital and other assets (including real estate), and restricting withdrawals by Jews from their bank accounts to a fixed monthly amount. On August 29 of that year Jews had their freedom of movement restricted; they were permitted to reside only in the four major cities, and they were subject to a nightly curfew, from 8:00 p.m. to 7:00 a.m.

A decree issued on November 25, 1941, established the ASSOCIATION DES JUIFS EN BELGIQUE (Association of Jews in Belgium; AJB), to which every Jew had to belong. Within a week, another decree ordered the expulsion of all Jewish children from the public-school system, and the AJB was required to set up its own elementary and secondary schools (the order was implemented only four months later). On January 17, 1942, Jews were forbidden to leave the country. A general labor draft issued on March 3 of that year was amplified by a decree dated March 11 that imposed special forced labor on the Jews. At the bidding of the RSHA, a decree was issued on May 27 ordering the Jews to wear the yellow badge (see BADGE, JEWISH). These orders and regulations were implemented by the military administration, which tried to restrict the influence of the SS and the RSHA and to stay in control. It was only when the "Final Solution" was initiated, in the spring of 1942, that RSHA and its various divisions became the predominant force controlling Jewish affairs. The differences of approach to the Jewish question are reflected in the reports submitted by Eggert Reeder, head of the military administration staff in the early stage of the occupation. They state that "Jewish influence in the economy is generally quite small, except for the diamond industry" (April 1941) and "the Jewish question . . . does not play the same role as in most other European countries" (July 15, 1941).

Deportation. In the summer of 1942 the deportation of Jews from Belgium was launched, in coordination with the deportations from the Netherlands and France. The preparations had been made by Adolf EICHMANN's section in the RSHA. At a meeting held in Eichmann's office in Berlin on June 11, 1942, the SS officials in charge of Jewish affairs in the Netherlands, Belgium, and France were ordered to prepare for the deportation of the Jews, to begin within a few weeks. Differences of opinion among the various branches of the regime delayed the beginning of deportations in Belgium, and they were begun only on August 4. On July 15, the AJB was ordered to set up a special bureau for coordinating the "labor draft" (Arbeitseinsatz) of the Jews. The deportations continued for over a year, coming to an end in September 1943 with "Operation Iltis," in which Jews of Belgian nationality were dispatched to the east (until then their deportation had been deferred).

The deportations were handled by a small staff in the Bureau of Jewish Affairs on Avenue Louise in Brussels; the roundup of Jews and their actual deportation was carried out, for the most part, by the German Feldgendarmerie (field police). By far the greater number of the deportees perished in AUSCH-

WITZ; some small groups were also sent to BUCHENWALD, RAVENSBRÜCK, and BERGEN-BELSEN. By an agreement between Himmler and Albert SPEER, the minister of armaments, groups of men were taken off the transports in late August and early September of 1942, to be put to work in Koźle (Cosel), a subcamp of the Auschwitz complex. The Belgian Jews in these groups manifested a better ability to survive under the horrible conditions than did the Dutch Jews.

Economic Measures. Economic measures against the Jews were introduced toward the end of 1940. In the early months of the occupation, no such measures had been taken, and for a while it even seemed that the Jews would be able to carry on a reasonable level of economic activity. Some Jews who had fled to France (mainly to southern France) when Belgium was occupied even returned to Belgium and resumed their economic activities there, especially in the diamond industry in Antwerp. But in November 1940 Hermann GÖRING ordered the Belgian economy to be "Aryanized," and as a result various German enterprises showed interest in acquiring Jewish businesses. In practice, "Aryanization" was launched only in late 1941, its "legal" basis being decrees of October 28, 1940, and May 21, 1941. The rate at which Aryanization proceeded was accelerated in March and April 1942, when the systematic liquidation of Jewish businesses in the textile, leather, and diamond industries was set in motion. The process of Aryanization, however, was never completed; according to a comprehensive survey drawn up by the Germans, the large Jewish enterprises stayed in existence and kept their assets intact. A similar situation prevailed with Jewish-owned real estate.

In 1942, several decrees dealing with economic affairs were enacted, requiring the confiscation of property owned by German Jews (decrees of April 22 and August 1), placing severe restrictions on the practice of medicine (June 1), and forbidding the sale of real estate without special permission (September 29) during the period when Jews were being deported to the camps.

German plunder of Jewish property also took the form of confiscation—of the property of Jews who did not return to their homes or were deported, and of Jewish insti-

tutions and art collections. This form of plunder was in the hands of EINSATZSTAB ROSENBERG (Operational Staff Rosenberg). When the deportations were in full swing, Einsatzstab Rosenberg handled only art collections and items of "ideological value" (such as Jewish religious and folklore objects and libraries). The confiscation of the contents of expropriated Jewish apartments "for the good of the German people" was left to the Reichsministerium für die Besetzten Ostgebiete (Reich Ministry for the Occupied Eastern Territories), also under Rosenberg, and to the military administration in Belgium. No estimate can be made of the value of the property seized by the Germans when they emptied the Jewish apartments of their contents. According to a figure given in August 1944, the sheer bulk of the furniture confiscated by the military administration was 3,531,450 cubic feet (100,000 cu m). Another stage in the theft of the Jews' possessions took place in the MECHELEN assembly camp, where they were stripped of any valuables still in their possession, such as watches and jewelry, just before boarding the deportation trains.

Forced Labor. The removal of the Jews from economic life was followed, beginning in June 1942, by their exploitation as a cheap source of manpower. There was no direct connection between the drafting of Jews for forced labor and the deportations (they involved different authorities), but because the drafting of Jews for forced labor and the deportation of Jews happened to coincide, they were seen as parts of the same operation. Actually, the forced-labor draft of Jews in Belgium was part of a drive that the Germans were carrying out in all the occupied countries of Europe. The Belgian Jews put on forced labor were employed primarily in the construction of fortifications along the coast of northern France, of which ORGANISATION TODT was in charge. A total of 2,252 Jews from Belgium were put to work there, setting out from Brussels, Charleroi, and Liège from June through August 1942, in seven groups. Other sources of employment for Jews on forced labor were German army construction projects and clothing factories in Belgium. Several groups of Jews also worked for short periods in the Fabrique Nationale d'Armes de

Guerre (F.N. Arms Factory) at Herstal, in stone quarries, and on soil amelioration. Forced-labor workers were given wages that were deposited in their name in a Brussels bank. This pay, however, was left in the bank up to the end of the war, either because the Jews in the forced-labor camps were deported to extermination camps (by way of the Mechelen or DRANCY camps) or because the Jews were afraid to claim it.

Relations between the Jews and the General Population. Relations between the Jews and the various components of the Belgian population were complicated, even before the German occupation of the country. There were a number of negative factors in this relationship: most of the population were Catholic; there was a language war between the Flemings and the Walloons; and most of the Jews were recent immigrants whose mentality was quite different from that of the native population. These factors, however, were balanced by the democratic character of the regime and by the rapid integration of the Jews in the economic life of the country and in some of its political movements. During the occupation, an important positive factor was the stand of the government-in-exile, which on January 10, 1941, issued a statement that declared all the decrees of the German military administration null and void and committed itself to restoring the stolen property to its rightful owners and to punishing Belgians collaborating with the Germans.

On October 10, 1940, the Germans asked the directors general of the Belgian governmental departments to take appropriate action to remove the Jews from the economic life of the country, but these officials refused to comply, citing legal grounds. The Germans did not press further, and published the anti-Jewish decrees on their own, with the Belgian administrative staff cooperating in the implementation of the decrees. Generally speaking, the reaction of the Belgian public to the anti-Jewish legislation in the first two years of the occupation was one of apathy. But there were exceptions: the anti-Jewish decrees of October 28, 1940, especially the one that ordered the elimination of Jews from public administration, aroused a negative reaction among the population; some of-

ficial protests were even lodged. Prominent among these were the protests made by three senior Brussels jurists and by the Free University of Brussels, which had the largest number of Jewish lecturers. The Germans responded by reprimanding the university, but they took no further action; neither, of course, did the protests have any effect on German policy. Several radical right-wing Belgian organizations cooperated with the Germans—for ideological or economic reasons, or because they felt that there was no choice and that Nazi hegemony had to be recognized. These organizations included the Vlaams Nationaal Verbond (National Flemish Movement; VNV), headed by Staf de Clerq, and the Rexist movement, made up mostly of Walloons, and headed by Léon Degrelle. They also provided 400 volunteers for the SS, organized into two legions. These volunteers spread antisemitic propaganda and helped the authorities to implement their policies. In addition, Radio Bruxelles broadcast anti-Jewish propaganda quite often. The total effect of these organizations and institutions was not large, but it appears to have been enough to deter people, in a number of cases, from protesting the anti-Jewish policy. In 1941, a VNV member, Gerard Romsee, was appointed director general of the Ministry of the Interior, a post in which he helped apply the anti-Jewish legislation. On April 14, 1941, during Passover, a small group of Flemish antisemitic nationalists staged what came to be known as the "Antwerp pogrom" (apparently at the instigation of one of the local German agencies), in the course of which two synagogues and the house of Rabbi Marcus Rottenberg were damaged.

The introduction of the yellow badge, in a decree issued on May 27, 1942, led to a number of protests. The Greater Brussels city council refused to distribute the badge, and the AJB too declared that it was unable to undertake this task, but the councils of other cities with a Jewish population (such as Antwerp) did not react in the same manner. Most of the underground newspapers sharply denounced the decree and called upon the population to express its solidarity with the Jews. There was indeed much sympathy for the Jews among the population, and a number of people expressed their solidarity by wearing badges similar to the Jewish yellow badge. This reaction had no immediate effect on the situation, but some have seen it as a turning point, as a result of which the Belgian population was more inclined to help the Jews when the deportations were launched.

The stand taken by the Belgian population when the deportations began, in the summer of 1942, was of great importance. The Belgian resistance movement was not united and consisted of several groups, but there was wide support for resistance as such, and it was this general mood that made it possible, for example, for as many as 80,000 persons (non-Jews) to go into hiding and thereby avoid the forced-labor draft. An illegal press existed with a wide circulation. Some 70,000 people are estimated to have been organized in the resistance, out of a total population of 8 million. The Communist party played a central role in the resistance operations, despite its small size, and it was an important factor in the establishment, in March 1941, of the Front d'Indépendance, which became the largest resistance organization. The various resistance groups also had many Jews among their members. With the help of large sectors of the population, especially leftist party activists and church institutions (as well as individual Belgians not affiliated with any group), some 25,000 Jews were concealed from the Germans. Belgian Jews and Jews from the Netherlands passing through Belgium were helped to escape to France and Switzerland.

Concerning the participation of the Catholic church in providing hiding places for Jews, special mention must be made of Father Joseph André of Namur, of the regional seminary in Bastogne, and Bishop Louis-Joseph Kerkhofs of Liège; the bishop of Mechelen also provided refuge to many Jews. Cardinal Joseph-Ernst van Roey, the highest ecclesiastical authority in Belgium, took action on behalf of the Jews in several instances, although he was very careful about it. In the early phase of the deportations, van Roey intervened on behalf of Jewish converts and the Jewish partners of mixed marriages, as well as on behalf of Jews who were Belgian nationals, and obtained their release. A few weeks later van Roey acted similarly on

behalf of Rabbi Salomon Ullmann and the AJB leaders who had been arrested and imprisoned in the BREENDONCK camp. On the other hand, van Roey's critics claim that by abstaining from a general protest and confining intervention to certain groups of Jews, the cardinal actually facilitated the deportation of the rest of the Jews. The queen mother, Elizabeth, also intervened on behalf of the Jews of Belgian nationality. On August 1, 1942, she met with three of the AJB leaders, and following that meeting she appealed to Hitler himself, through General von Falkenhausen.

The postponement of the deportation of Jews who were Belgian nationals, therefore, was achieved by a combination of intervention on their behalf by Belgian elements, a pragmatic approach on the part of the German military administration, and the consent, for the time being and for its own convenience, of the RSHA. Restricting protection to Belgian nationals, however, implied that the rest of the Jews (meaning most of the Jewish population of Belgium) could be abandoned. The Belgian Red Cross assisted many Jews by providing them with food parcels; in 1943, half the quantity of parcels earmarked for this purpose was distributed among the Jews who were in hiding. Side by side with many manifestations of aid to the Jews in the deportation period, however, there were also instances when Belgians informed to the authorities on Jews in hiding, and some radical right-wing organizations took up an active search for such Jews.

The Jewish Community. During the fighting in May 1940, many Jews tried to escape to France and to Britain. Some made their way to southern France or even to Spain; many others returned to their homes in Belgium after weeks of wandering. In the early months of the occupation, when no anti-Jewish action was taken, the Jews tried to rehabilitate their communal life; the first step in this direction was the formation of aid committees in Brussels and Antwerp.

This was followed by the renewal of activities in the communities and in some organizations, political parties, and youth movements. The flight of veteran leaders and of persons prominent in economic affairs had affected in particular the work of the Consistoire Central, several welfare organizations, and the Orthodox communities of Brussels and Antwerp. It was the leader of the General Zionists, Itzko Kubowitzki—the dominant figure among the remaining leaders—who sought to reorganize Jewish life and in the course of this effort helped integrate many Zionists into the representative bodies of Belgian Jewry. The Chief Rabbi (Grand Rabbin) of Belgium, Joseph Wiener, had fled during the fighting; in September 1940 he was replaced by Rabbi Salomon Ullmann, who in 1937 had become the chief Jewish military chaplain. (His father was the founder of one of the Orthodox congregations of Antwerp.) In addition to the existing organizations of Belgian and eastern European Jews, a committee was formed of German Jews who had settled in Belgium before its occupation and who now constituted 20 percent of the Jewish population. All these organizations underwent a decisive change in their operations when the AJB was formed, in late 1941. Some of the old organizations were integrated into the AJB, and others kept up their independent existence, officially or unofficially; but all of them were affected by the predominant role that was now being played by the AJB.

For a while, the elimination of Jews from jobs in the public administration was of no great consequence, since only a few Jews had held such positions. The same applied, temporarily, to the initial anti-Jewish economic decrees. When the general economic situation deteriorated, however, and Aryanization was launched in the summer of 1941, the effect on the situation of the Jews was marked, and the Jewish organizations were hard pressed to meet the community needs, especially for welfare. Nevertheless, up until the time of the deportations, the Jews were able to maintain a tolerable standard of living. At that point, a wide gulf opened between the Jews who had Belgian nationality and were protected and all the other Jews. Some contacts were maintained with the American Jewish JOINT DISTRIBUTION COMMITTEE, which transmitted financial aid to the AJB, and, later, to the Jewish Defense Committee (see below).

As a rule, the Germans did not interfere with Jewish religious life. The first anti-Jewish decree to be issued, however, outlawing *sheḥitah* (ritual slaughter) without first stunning the animal, discriminated against Jews observing their dietary laws; efforts were made to solve the problem by using electric stunning devices that the Dutch rabbis had sanctioned for this purpose. Orthodox Jewish families, more than the others, felt the impact of the worsening food situation, as of 1942. Jewish religious literary activity was kept up, and one interesting project was the translation of the Talmud into Yiddish, so as to facilitate its study by young students (the project was not completed, but a part of the translation was published after the Holocaust).

Education, in the initial phase, remained unchanged. Most young Jews did not attend Jewish schools and remained in the public school system until April 1942, when the decree expelling Jews from the general school system, issued in late 1941, was applied. The community lost no time in meeting the new need and established several schools and kindergartens, using for this purpose the premises of the Brussels Central Synagogue, among other places. In the 1942–1943 school year, which opened after the deportations had started, the AJB-maintained school network shrank considerably in size. During the 1943–1944 school year, classes were held only in the AJB orphanages, which had the official sanction of the German authorities. Religious schools *par excellence*, such as the yeshiva (rabbinical academy) at Heide, near Antwerp, remained open until the beginning of the deportations.

Zionist youth movements in Brussels and Antwerp (Ha-Shomer ha-Tsa'ir, Bnei Akiva, Maccabi ha-Tsa'ir, Gordonia and Betar) resumed their activities, albeit on a more modest scale, concentrating on educational training, cultural work, and mutual help, in cooperation with the official political parties and organizations. In their work they sorely missed the contact they had previously enjoyed with Palestine. The various youth movements cooperated with one another, the Antwerp religious Bnei Akiva and the Marxist Ha-Shomer ha-Tsa'ir joining in obtaining food in the city's hinterland and distributing it, and in running an agricultural training farm in Bomal, south of Liège.

Rescue Operations and the Underground. The Jews of Belgium were actively engaged in underground operations and efforts for their own rescue, often coming up with original ideas. It is a moot point among historians whether all actions in which Jews were involved can be classified as "Jewish," since many of these actions were initiated and carried out by organizations belonging to the Belgian Left. By 1940 and 1941 the Germans were arresting Jews active in Communist organizations of German emigrés. Numerous Communists were seized by the Germans in June 1941, following the German attack on the Soviet Union, and of these, a considerable number were Jews. Also arrested, in 1941 and 1942, were Jews who had worked in the general underground press. Jews played a dominant role in the RED ORCHESTRA, the spy ring operating for the Soviet Union, and they were among the members of the *Front d'Indépendance* (a Belgian organization, representing various groups, that called for armed resistance).

Specific Jewish acts of resistance first took place in late 1941. Shortly after the AJB was formed, several Yiddish-language underground newspapers made their appearance, published by the Bund and Po'alei Zion, and as late as 1944 a Communist-sponsored Yiddish newspaper was still being published. Two other Jewish papers—one in Dutch and one in French—also appeared. In late 1941 and early 1942 the Jewish underground press expressed opposition to the AJB and its operations.

In July 1942, in view of the deteriorating situation of the Jews, a joint underground Jewish defense organization was initiated called the Comité de Défense des Juifs (Jewish Defense Committee; CDJ). It began its activities in September 1942. The initiative for its creation was taken by Ghert Jospa (who established contact between representatives of the Jewish Communists and the Front d'Indépendance) and various Zionist activists— Abusz Werber, the leader of Po'alei Zion– Left; Edouard Rotkel and Benjamin Nykerk of the General Zionists; and Chaim Perelman, who had a Revisionist party background. Eugene Hellendael, a member of the Brussels local AJB, also joined the founding members of the CDJ. The CDJ had important ties with the general resistance organizations as well as with the AJB, and it played a central role in the rescue and resistance operations during the period from 1942 to 1944. It also had contacts with the Catholic church and various other bodies, and engaged in fundraising. The organization's main purpose was to find hiding places for Jews; its children's section, in cooperation with the Oeuvre Nationale de l'Enfance (National Children's Committee), headed by Yvonne NÈVEJEAN, succeeded in hiding four thousand children. Large numbers of Jewish adults also had the CDJ's help in finding a place to hide.

Jewish armed resistance operations (some of which had no connection with the CDJ) had some impressive successes. On two occasions, in the summer of 1942, the target was the AJB. In one instance, the purpose was to seize the card index that the AJB maintained in its office, and in the other the attack was directed at Robert Holcinger, the official in charge of sending out the call-ups for deportation. The single most significant resistance operation carried out by the Jewish underground was the attack on a deportation train, on the night of April 19–20, 1943, containing a transport of Jews from the Mechelen camp (Transport No. 20) headed for Auschwitz. A recent exhaustive study has shed much new light upon this operation, the only recorded instance of an armed attack in Europe on a train taking Jews to their death.

Individual escapes from the deportation trains originating in the Mechelen camp were quite frequent. Such an escape first occurred in Transport No. 16 on October 31, 1942. Of the 26,500 Jews who were deported from Mechelen, the total number of escapees was 571; of these, 539 escaped from transports 16 to 20. In the attack on Transport No. 20 itself, 231 Jews escaped, of whom 23 were shot to death by the train guards. Most of the escapees, some of whom were members of resistance groups, jumped from the train as soon as they could (a number had tried to escape from an earlier transport). One group of 17 Jews was saved by the outside help of three persons—none of them affiliated with any organization—headed by a Jew. This action was launched near the Mechelen camp, on the stretch between Mechelen and Louvain. The three tricked the train into coming to a halt and managed to open the door of one carriage; some of the Jews in the carriage jumped off, amid a hail of bullets from the train guards. This was not a large operation and it had only limited success, but it was linked to the other escapes and became a legend and a source of pride for the resistance movements. After the Holocaust, credit for this action was claimed by various elements.

In addition to offering resistance and going into hiding, hundreds of Jews attempted to flee to Switzerland and southern France, and from there to Spain. Many dozens of members of the Zionist youth movements succeeded in such attempts. In 1943, a few dozen Jews were saved from imprisonment and deportation because they were on the list of candidates for the exchange of Jews and Germans (*see* EXCHANGE: JEWS AND GERMANS). All in all, initiative on the part of Jews played a central role in the operations that enabled a relatively large proportion of the Jews of Belgium to be saved.

After Liberation. The rehabilitation of Belgian Jewry was a difficult and painful process. At first, the Belgian authorities did not want the Jews who had not been Belgian nationals before the war to remain in the country. The restitution of Jewish property also ran into difficulties. Another problem was the guardianship of the war orphans and the kind of upbringing they were to have; this issue caused friction among the various Jewish organizations, and also between the Jews and the Belgian authorities. The first attempt at reorganizing the Jewish community was made by Jews who came out of hiding after liberation; one body formed at this early stage was the Comité Central Israélite pour la Reconstruction de la Vie Religieuse en Belgique (Central Jewish Committee for the Reconstruction of Religious Life in Belgium). An important role was played in the first few months after liberation by the Jewish chaplains in the Allied forces and by the JEWISH BRIGADE GROUP, which was posted to Belgium in early August 1945, with bases at Tournai and Ghent. Soldiers of the brigade were involved in the renewal of Zionist activity and in the search for Jewish orphans and their return to the Jewish fold.

In the first postwar years the Zionist parties and youth movements were reestablished, amid a good deal of squabbling. The leftist Zionist parties gradually lost ground, and radical non-Zionist leftist parties did not make a comeback. Hundreds of war orphans

and members of the Zionist youth movements left for Palestine, while others emigrated to other destinations. In Antwerp and Brussels, Jewish community life was restored, although on a much smaller scale than in the past; in other places, such as Liège, restoration occurred on a negligible scale.

On April 19, 1970, a memorial for the murdered Jews of Belgium was unveiled at Anderlecht, and on October 16, 1987, a memorial was dedicated in the Valley of the Destroyed Jewish Communities at YAD VASHEM in Jerusalem. Every year, survivors of the Holocaust and former resistance fighters hold a memorial march to the Dossin camp at Mechelen, the point of departure for the deportation of Belgian Jews to the extermination camps. Dozens of non-Jewish Belgians have been awarded the medal of "RIGHTEOUS AMONG THE NATIONS" by Yad Vashem for saving Jews during the war years.

In early 1981 a court in Kiel, Germany, tried Ernst Ehlers, the man who had been chief of the Sicherheitspolizei (Security Police) and the SD (Sicherheitsdienst; Security Service) in Belgium and northern France in the period from 1941 to 1944. Also tried were his successor in that post, Konstantin Canaris, and the head of the Jewish section in the Sicherheitspolizei and SD, Kurt Asche. Ehlers committed suicide before the trial opened, and Canaris was set free because of his poor health. Asche was found guilty as an accessory to murder and was sentenced, on July 8, 1981, to seven years for his part in the deportation of the Jews of Belgium.

BIBLIOGRAPHY

Gutman, Y., and C. J. Haft, eds. *Patterns of Jewish Leadership in Nazi Europe, 1933–1945.* Jerusalem, 1979. See pages 353–376.

Klarsfeld, S., and M. Steinberg. *Die Endlösung der Judenfrage in Belgien: Dokumente.* New York, 1980.

Ministère de la Justice, Commission des Crimes de Guerre. *Les crimes de guerre commis sous l'occupation de la Belgique, 1940–1945.* Liège, 1947–1948.

Steinberg, L. *Le Comité de défense des Juifs en Belgique, 1942–1944.* Brussels, 1973.

Steinberg, M. *Le dossier Bruxelles-Auschwitz: La police et l'extermination des Juifs de Belgique.* Brussels, 1981.

Steinberg, M. *L'étoile et le fusil.* 3 vols. Brussels, 1983–1986.

DAN MICHMAN

BELGRADE, capital of SERBIA in the nineteenth century and of YUGOSLAVIA from 1918. On the eve of World War II, Belgrade had three hundred thousand inhabitants. Jews are known to have lived in the city since the Middle Ages. On the eve of the German occupation of Yugoslavia, there were about eleven thousand Jews, mostly Sephardic (80 percent to 90 percent), in Belgrade, which was also the seat of the Federation of Jewish Communities in Yugoslavia.

On April 6, 1941, Germany, together with its allies Italy, Hungary, and Bulgaria, invaded Yugoslavia. Belgrade suffered heavy bombardment and about three thousand inhabitants were killed, including Jews. On April 13 the Germans occupied the city. A short while later, the authorities were instructed to carry out a census, and about nine thousand Jews were counted. Most of the Jewish men and some of the young women were organized into labor groups and employed mainly in clearing the ruins.

In the first months of the occupation, the military government issued many decrees aimed at harming the situation and livelihood of the Jews and restricting their contacts with the non-Jewish population. After the outbreak of the Serbian revolt against the Germans in July 1941, mass arrests of the Jewish males in Belgrade commenced, and until late August most were interned in the Topovske Šupe concentration camp on the outskirts of the city. From September to November of that year, the prisoners were put to death by firing squads of the German army, on the pretext (as recorded in German sources) that the Jews had participated in the opposition movement. In December 1941 all the Jewish women and children in Belgrade were arrested and taken to the SAJMIŠTE concentration camp near the city. In early March 1942 a gas van was sent from Berlin to Belgrade, and by early May all the women and children in Sajmište had been gassed to death. In August 1942 Dr. Harold Turner, head of the German civilian administration

in Serbia, sent a report to his superiors in which he claimed: "Serbia is the only country in Europe in which the Jewish problem has been solved."

It is estimated that the Germans murdered about 90 percent of the Jews of Belgrade. After the war, about twenty-two hundred Jews returned to the city.

BIBLIOGRAPHY

Browning, C. *Fateful Months: Essays on the Emergence of the Final Solution.* New York, 1985. See chapters 2–4.
Ivanović, L. "Teror nad jevrejima u okupiranom Beogradu." *Godisniak grada Beograda* 13 (1966): 289–316.

MENACHEM SHELAH

BELORUSSIA (White Russia), Soviet republic in the western USSR. Until the thirteenth century the principalities of Belorussia were part of Kievan Russia; following the Mongol invasion of 1240, they became a separate entity. In the fourteenth century Belorussia was part of the principality of Lithuania, whose population, for the most part, was Belorussian and whose official language was also Belorussian. With the unification of Lithuania and Poland in 1569, Belorussia became part of the Polish kingdom.

In the seventeenth century Moscow seized substantial parts of Belorussia and, following the three partitions of Poland (in 1772, 1793, and 1795), it annexed the entire area of Belorussia. This was one of the most backward regions of European Russia: its population had no clear national identity of its own, it faced diverse and vexing social problems, 75 percent of its inhabitants worked on the land, and 71 percent were illiterate. During World War I Belorussia was a battle zone, and after the war it was the scene of fighting between the Soviets and the Poles. Under the Treaty of Riga (March 18, 1921) Belorussia was split up, the western part going to Poland and the eastern part becoming one of the Soviet Union's socialist republics. On September 17, 1939, the Red Army entered western Belorussia and incorporated it with all of its component districts into the Belorussian SSR. These districts were those of Vilna (Vilnius;

except for the city of Vilna and its environs, which were handed over to Lithuania), Novogrudok, BIAŁYSTOK, and Polesye.

Jewish communities were founded in Belorussia as early as the fourteenth century, in BREST-LITOVSK and GRODNO. After the unification of Lithuania and Poland, the authorities encouraged the settlement of Poles and Jews in Belorussia. When Belorussia was incorporated into tsarist Russia, it was included in the Pale of Settlement, the area where Jews were permitted to reside. Belorussian Jews suffered from all the tsarist anti-Jewish decrees and from persecution and pogroms. In the wake of the 1881 pogroms and the subsequent anti-Jewish measures, they emigrated to the West in large numbers.

Belorussia was a center of Jewish religious studies, as was Lithuania. The two Jewish communities were very similar in their way of life and creativity. Renowned rabbinical academies (yeshivas) were established, in VOLOZHIN, MIR, and many other centers. Belorussia was a center of the Hasidic pietistic movement and of the opponents of the Hasidim, known as the Misnagdim. A high proportion of Belorussia's Jews were manual workers, and a broad network of educational and mutual-aid institutions existed.

Western Belorussia. During the period following World War I the Jews of the western part of Belorussia, then under Polish rule, were hard hit by the anti-Jewish policies pursued in that border region by the Polish government. The effects of these policies hastened the pauperization process of the entire Jewish community.

The entry of Soviet forces into western Belorussia, on September 17, 1939, was a relief for the Jews, in view of the Nazi threat they had been facing, but it also aroused mixed feelings among large parts of the Jewish population. As it turned out, during the twenty-one months of Soviet rule the situation of the Jews in many respects underwent a rapid process of deterioration that eroded the very basis of Jewish existence. Many Jews lost their livelihood, Jewish public institutions were dissolved, and the anti-Jewish animosity of the population grew to unprecedented dimensions. The Soviet regime withheld from the Jews information on the basic elements of Nazi policy toward them.

On the eve of the German invasion of the USSR (June 22, 1941), the Jewish population of western Belorussia, including the Jews from western Poland who had taken refuge there, numbered 670,000. The German army advanced at lightning speed, occupying western Belorussia and reaching the old Polish-Soviet border within a week. A wave of pogroms, staged by the local population, swept over large parts of the region, much to the Germans' satisfaction. The Germans themselves, from the very beginning, launched one *Aktion* after another, in which 40 percent of the Jews of the Vilna, Novogrudok, and Polesye districts were murdered. In some places, the majority of the Jews were killed. Except for a part of the Jewish population of the Białystok district, the Jews of Belorussia were murdered in pits near the places where they had lived, and were buried on the spot. The first wave of *Aktionen* lasted until December 1941, and, as in other parts of the Soviet Union occupied by the Germans, they marked the beginning of the "FINAL SOLUTION." The *Aktionen* in this first wave were carried out by Einsatzgruppe B units: Sonderkommandos 7a and 7b, Einsatzkommandos 8 and 9, and units of Vorkommando Moskau, an advance detachment commanded by Franz Walter Six. At a subsequent stage, units of Einsatzgruppe A also participated in the slaughter. The mass murder came to a standstill in the winter of 1941–1942, because the Germans needed the manpower to help cope with the difficulties they were encountering in preparing for a long war, contrary to their earlier expectations. The economic situation in Belorussia and the harsh winter weather also obstructed the extermination program.

The second wave of mass murder began in the spring of 1942, and ended only with the total annihilation of the Jews of western Belorussia. The rise in partisan operations during that period prompted the Germans to accelerate the pace of extermination. According to German data, by the end of 1942 only thirty thousand Jews were left in Belorussia (excluding the Białystok district). In the course of that year most of the ghettos in western Belorussia were liquidated (*see* Table 1); the last to suffer this fate were the ghettos of Glubokoye (August 20, 1943) and Lida

TABLE 1. *Liquidation of Seventy-Four Ghettos in Western Belorussia*

PERIOD OF LIQUIDATION	VILNA DISTRICT	POLESYE DISTRICT	NOVOGRUDOK DISTRICT	TOTAL	PERCENTAGE
To end of 1941	3	1	2	6	8.0
From early to mid-1942	10		8	18	24.0
From mid-1942 to end 1942	5	17	14	36	49.0
From early to mid-1943	7	1	3	11	15.0
Second half of 1943	2		1	3	4.0
Total	27	19	28	74	100.0

(September 18, 1943). From the KOLDICHEVO camp, the last Jews fled on March 7, 1944.

The Jewish underground. The struggle of the Jews of Belorussia had various aspects: exerting a daily effort to stay alive in the ghettos, going into hiding, escaping from the ghetto, and joining armed undergrounds. Thousands of Jews went into hiding in bunkers and various other places of concealment; in the 16 ghettos for which data exist, twelve thousand six hundred persons hid in such places. Underground organizations were set up, following the first wave of *Aktionen*, in the Vilna, Novogroduk, and Polesye districts. In some instances these organizations were the continuation of the Zionist pioneering underground that had operated under the Soviet regime, from 1939 to 1941. In 94 out of 111 ghettos or other places with Jews in western Belorussia (not including the Białystok district and the city of Vilna), there were underground organizations and acts of resistance; 64 had an organized underground and in 30 other places there are recorded cases of resistance, although no organized underground is known to have existed in them. Members of the underground came from the Zionist youth movements Ha-Shomer ha-Tsa'ir, He-Haluts, He-Haluts ha-Tsa'ir, Betar, Ha-No'ar ha-Tsiyyoni, and Gordonia; from the Hebrew Tarbut (Zionist-oriented) schools and the Yiddish schools; and from adult groups. Forty-two of these underground groups had in their possession 500 rifles, 150 pistols, 35 machine guns, and 20 submachine guns. The number of Jews from the Vilna, Novogrudok, and Polesye districts who fled to the forests is estimated as at least twenty-five thousand.

The Jews of the Białystok district. The Białystok district was incorporated into East Prussia on July 17, 1941, thus becoming part of the Reich. Białystok itself had a Jewish population of sixty thousand to seventy thousand. When the Germans took the city in June of that year they launched an *Aktion* in which they murdered two thousand Jews, and several thousand more were killed in July. This was followed by a period of relative quiet in Białystok. In the provincial towns of the Białystok district, large-scale *Aktionen* took place; those who managed to escape from them took refuge in the city of Białystok. The extermination of the surviving Jewish population of the Białystok district was undertaken on November 2, 1942. At that point the number of Jews was still quite substantial. They were rounded up and put into transit camps, and in November and December were taken to the TREBLINKA extermination camp.

In early February 1943 a week-long *Aktion* was conducted in Białystok, in the course of which 12,000 Jews were murdered (2,000 were killed on the spot). Efraim BARASZ, the JUDENRAT (Jewish Council) chairman, continued to believe that the ghetto would not be liquidated, because the Germans needed the manpower it provided. On August 16, 1943, the Germans surrounded the ghetto. The uprising in the ghetto, commanded by Mordechai TENENBAUM, with the participation of the Dror, Ha-Shomer ha-Tsa'ir, Communist, and Betar movements, went on for several days, until the last of the fighters fell. Over 25,000 Białystok Jews were transported to Treblinka, and 1,200 children from Białystok were sent to AUSCHWITZ. Another 2,000 Jews, who had been in the "Small Ghetto," were sent to MAJDANEK. A few Jews from Białystok managed to escape and join the partisans; of these, 60 survived.

LATVIA

LITHUANIA

USSR

NEMAN

• Dvinsk

• Kovno

Glubokoye •

Ilov
Tserkoshchina • • Vitebsk

• Vilna

Lepel •

BELORUSSIA

Smolensk •

Eišiškės •

Pleshchenitsy •

Orsha •

Radun •

• Volozhin

Lida •

Smolevichi •
• Minsk

Mogilev •
Polkovichi •
Pashkovichi •

DNIEPER

• Grodno

Maly Trostinets •

Glinishche
Cherven •

Novogrudok •

• Koldichevo

Gorodishche
Forest

• Mir

Białystok •

POLAND

• Nesvizh

Slonim •

• Baranovichi

Slutsk •

• Bobruisk
• Kiselevich

Polesye •

USSR

Brest-
Litovsk •

• Motol

PRIPET

Gomel •

Pinsk •   Lachva •

in.
0   64 miles   1   0   120 km.   3

cm.

Eastern Belorussia. Large Jewish communities existed in the cities of eastern Belorussia. In the 1897 census, Jews had formed the majority of the population in these cities: in MINSK, 56.4 percent of the total; in MOGILEV, 54.3 percent; in VITEBSK, 56.3 percent; in GOMEL (Homel), 55.9 percent; in Orsha, 62.3 percent, and in Bobruisk, 63.1 percent. Because of emigration, however, and because Jews moved to other cities (including Moscow and Leningrad), the proportion of Jews in these cities went down, and in the 1926 census they no longer constituted the majority of these urban populations.

The October Revolution of 1917 posed new and basic problems for the Jews. As members of the middle class they found themselves deprived of their sources of livelihood, their employment and social status, and their traditional way of life. Jewish culture and education came under sharp attack. The autonomous Jewish community framework was dissolved, and the only official Jewish body permitted was the Communist party's "Jewish Section" (Yevsektsiya), which conducted an aggressive propaganda drive against traditional Jewish religious life. Jewish schools, academies, and synagogues were closed down. Many Jews however, continued to observe traditional customs in the privacy of their homes, and the Zionist youth movements Ha-Shomer ha-Tsa'ir and He-Haluts maintained their operations, clandestinely, until the late 1920s.

Minsk was the center of Yiddish culture and literature, and in the 1932–1933 school year, 36,650 Jewish children attended Yiddish schools. During the following years, however, a sharp turn was made as the Soviet purges were launched. In the mid-1930s the number of Jewish schools declined rapidly. The hundreds of clandestine Jewish schools that had been in existence were liquidated, and Jewish intellectuals were imprisoned, exiled, or executed.

In the 1926 census, 407,000 Jews were counted in eastern Belorussia (8.2 percent of the population). Minsk had a Jewish population of 53,686 (40.8 percent of the total); Gomel, 37,453 (43.7 percent); Vitebsk, 37,013 (37.5 percent); and Bobruisk, 21,558 Jews (42 percent of the total). In the 1939 census the number of Jews was down to 375,000, and on the eve of the German invasion in June 1941 it was 405,000, including Jewish refugees from western Belorussia and other parts of Poland.

With the outbreak of the war, the Germans speedily conquered eastern Belorussia. Minsk was taken on June 28, 1941, Vitebsk on July 11, and by July 16 German forces had reached SMOLENSK. Many Jews fled eastward to save their lives, but German forces dropped by parachutes barred the roads, and most of the refugees who had gone in the direction of Orsha and Moscow were intercepted and had to turn back. However, those who fled to the Gomel area made good their escape, since Gomel was taken by the Germans only on August 19. An estimated 120,000 Jews living in eastern Belorussia succeeded in escaping to the Soviet interior.

The Germans immediately began a program of mass murder, seeing the Jews of the Soviet Union as the personification of "Judeo-Bolshevism." The indifference of the majority of the population to the fate of the Jews encouraged the Germans to accelerate the massacres, and the difficulties they came to encounter on the front had the effect of increasing the rate at which the extermination proceeded. Jews living in small towns and villages were moved into larger ghettos. In some places, such as Bobruisk and Slutsk, the ghettos were set up in the open country. In Lepel the Jews had to vacate their homes and move into the ghetto at two hours' notice. They were left without water or food in houses without windowpanes, thirty to forty persons to each house, without fuel or warm clothing, and in a temperature of minus 77 degrees Fahrenheit (minus 25 degrees centigrade). Similar conditions prevailed in other ghettos in the area.

Reports submitted by the Einsatzgruppen accused the Jews of "maintaining contact with the partisans"; in some instances the reports cite reasons for killing the Jews: for "acts of sabotage," "refusal to obey orders," "offering resistance," and so on. Some of the reports contain figures for the number of partisans killed, in place of the figures for the Jews, and in others, "Jews and partisans" are lumped together.

By the end of 1941 the Jews of thirty-five ghettos had been murdered, among them those in the major cities, which contained the largest concentration of Jews—Gomel, Mogilev, Vitebsk, and Bobruisk. Together, they accounted for a third of the entire Jewish population of eastern Belorussia. In most of the ghettos the Jews had been killed by the end of October 1941. Only the Minsk ghetto, which with 100,000 Jews had the largest single concentration of Jews, remained in existence until October 1943.

The mass murder of Jews was carried out in huge pits that were prepared close to the ghettos. The Jews of Mogilev were murdered in Pashkovo, Pulkovichi, Smolevichi, and the Gorodishche Forest; the Jews of Cherven in Glinishche; those of Bobruisk in Kiselevich; those of Vitebsk in Ilov and Tserkoshchina; and the Jews of Minsk in MALY TROSTINETS. In Minsk, Pleshchenitsy, Gomel, Vitebsk, and Mogilev the Germans used GAS VANS (*dushkovki*). In the Minsk ghetto some ninety thousand Jews were murdered in consecutive *Aktionen*, five of them on a large scale, and several "interim" and "night" *Aktionen*. The killings were carried out by Einsatzgruppe B units, Sonderkommandos 7a and 7b, Vorkommando Moskau, Einsatzkommandos 8 and 9, Police Battalions 316 and 322, Lithuanian units, Belorussian police, and Ukrainian auxiliary units.

The Minsk ghetto had an underground organization that operated up to the very end. Approximately 10,000 Jews escaped from Minsk into the forest. In the period from November 1941 to October 1942, 35,442 Jews from the Reich and the Protectorate of BOHEMIA AND MORAVIA were also brought to Minsk to be killed. A transit camp was set up 5 miles (8 km) from Bobruisk, to which Jews from the west were brought. The first consignment, consisting of 960 Jews from Warsaw, arrived at the camp on May 29, 1942, followed on July 28, 1942, by another 500 Jews, and at a later date by more Jews from Warsaw. A total of 2,000 Jews were assembled in the camp; those who still survived in September 1943 were murdered that month. Mogilev was the site of a transit camp (*Dulag*, from *Durchgangslager*) for Jews and Communist party activists; 196 persons were murdered in that camp.

Belorussian Jews offered resistance in the various ghettos, and a small proportion escaped to the forests. Of the Jews surviving among the partisans in the forests, only a very few returned to their homes at the end of the war. Some five thousand Jews went back to Minsk, most of them from the forest. They were later joined by Jews who in the first few days of the war had fled to the Soviet interior, and Jews from other parts of the country. Throughout the war the majority of the local population evinced an unfriendly or even hostile attitude to the Jews; some, including Communist party activists, were extremely hostile. A very small minority showed a humane attitude, and some of these saved a few Jews.

The 1959 census reported 150,000 Jews in Belorussia, representing 1.9 percent of the total population; the 1970 census showed 148,000 Jews—1.64 percent of the total. Almost a third of all the Jews of Belorussia live in Minsk, the capital of the republic. In the Gomel and Mogilev districts the Jews represent 2 percent of the total population, in the Vitebsk district their proportion is 1 percent, and in the three remaining districts—Minsk, Brest-Litovsk, and Grodno—less than 0.5 percent.

BIBLIOGRAPHY

Cholawski, S. *The Jews in Belorussia (White Russia) during World War II*. Tel Aviv, 1982. (In Hebrew.)

Ehrenburg, I., and V. Grossman, eds. *The Black Book of Soviet Jewry*. New York, 1980.

Kalush, V. *In the Service of the People for a Free Byelorussia: Biographical Notes on Professor Radoslav Ostrovski*. London, 1964.

Krausnick, H., and H.-H. Wilhelm. *Die Truppe des Weltanschauungskrieges: Die Einsatzgruppen der Sicherheitspolizei und des SD*. Stuttgart, 1981.

Orbach, W. "The Destruction of the Jews in the Nazi-occupied Territories of the USSR." *Soviet Jewish Affairs* 6/2 (October 1976):14–51.

SHALOM CHOLAWSKI

BEŁŻEC, extermination camp in Poland. Bełżec was a small town in the southeastern part of the Lublin district, on the Lublin-Lvov railway line. In early 1940 the Germans set up a camp there for Jewish forced labor, which they used to build fortifications and dig anti-tank ditches along the demarcation line between German- and Soviet-occupied Poland. The camp was closed down at the end of the year. On November 1, 1941, as part of AKTION REINHARD, the Germans began construction of an extermination camp at Bełżec. The site they chose was near the Bełżec railway station, about 1,620 feet (500 m) away on a railway siding. It contained some of the anti-tank ditches that had been dug the previous year, and these were now destined to become mass graves for the Jews who were to be murdered in the camp.

Initially, the construction work was carried out by Poles from Bełżec, but these were later replaced by Jews from ghettos in the neighboring towns. Of the SS men who were in charge of the camp construction and operation, most had taken part in the EUTHANASIA PROGRAM, including the camp's first commandant, Polizeihauptmann and SS-Hauptsturmführer Christian WIRTH. When the camp was operating, its staff included twenty to thirty German SS men, who held the command and administration positions and oversaw the extermination program. There were also between ninety and one hundred twenty Ukrainian men from the TRAWNIKI camp—all of

BEŁŻEC

them Soviet prisoners of war who had volunteered to serve the Germans—whose job it was to stand guard over the camp and the extermination process, quash any resistance from Jews being taken off the incoming rail transports, and prevent any attempts at escape. Among the Ukrainian group there were also Soviet VOLKSDEUTSCHE (ethnic Germans) who held junior command positions. The German staff had their quarters outside the camp, while the Ukrainians were housed inside. In addition to the German and Ukrainian staff, the camp used Jewish prisoners for various local jobs and services.

First Stage. In its first stage the Bełżec camp had three gas chambers, located in a 26-by-40-foot (8 × 12 m) barrack. The structure had double walls, with sand in between for insulation, and was divided into three rooms, each 13 by 26 feet (4 × 8 m). The floor of the gas chambers and the walls, up to a height of over 3 feet (1 m), were covered with tin sheets. A corridor led to the three doors of the gas chambers. Each door was 5 to 6 feet (1.8 m) high and 3.5 feet (1.1 m) wide, with rubber strips fastened to its sides so that when it was closed it sealed hermetically. The doors were made of hard wood, to resist pressure from inside the chambers, and could be opened only from the outside. Each gas chamber had an additional opening, for the removal of the corpses. There were pipes in the chambers through which the gas was pumped in.

By the end of February 1942, the gas chambers were ready for a test of their effective functioning. Several groups of Jews were brought in from Lubycze Królewska for this purpose and put into the chambers. The gas that was used (carbon monoxide) came in metal containers and was piped into the gas chambers. In addition to the Jews brought in from the outside, the Jewish prisoners who had been working on the construction of the camp were also gassed in this trial run. In the course of the initial testing, a 250-horsepower diesel engine was installed outside the gas chambers to generate the carbon monoxide gas and pump it into the pipes. This became the method that was to be used throughout the period of the camp's operation.

The Bełżec camp was relatively small, square in shape, with each side measuring 886 feet (270 m), and enclosed by a barbed-wire fence. To camouflage the inside of the camp,

tree branches were affixed to the fence and trees were planted along the perimeter. There was a watchtower in each corner and one in the center of the camp, near the gas chambers. On the north side of the square was the gate through which the trains entered the camp area.

The camp was divided into two sections: the larger one in the northwestern part and the smaller in the eastern part. The former was named Camp I and contained the administration buildings, the staff quarters, the railway platform, and the track leading to it (which was long enough to hold twenty freight cars). The Jews who were taken off the cars were first concentrated in an adjacent lot in which there were two barracks; in one of them the prisoners had to take off their clothes, while the other served as a storeroom. The eastern part, named Camp II, contained the gas chambers and the antitank ditches. This extermination area was separated from the rest of the camp by a fence. Between the barrack in Camp I where the Jews took off their clothes and the gas chambers in Camp II was a path known as the "tube" (Schlauch), 6.5 feet (2 m) wide and several dozen yards long, fenced in on both sides. It was along this path that the Jews, now naked, were led to their death.

By March 17, 1942, the main installations had been constructed and tried out, and the mass extermination program was launched.

Mechanics of Extermination. From among the young males who arrived in the camp, some who were fit were selected and put to work. In the early stage, this "respite" delayed their death only by a day or two, or a few days at the most, until they too were sent to the gas chambers, and their places as workers taken by new arrivals. Later on, for the sake of greater efficiency, groups of men numbering from seven hundred to one thousand were kept alive for a longer period and forced to work in the extermination area. They were split up into work teams of various sizes, ranging from a few dozen to several hundred.

One of the teams was employed on the railway platform, where their job was to clean the freight cars from which the Jews had been forced, to take down those Jews who were unable to get off on their own, and to remove the corpses of the Jews who had not survived the train ride. Another team was assigned to the area where the victims had to undress and

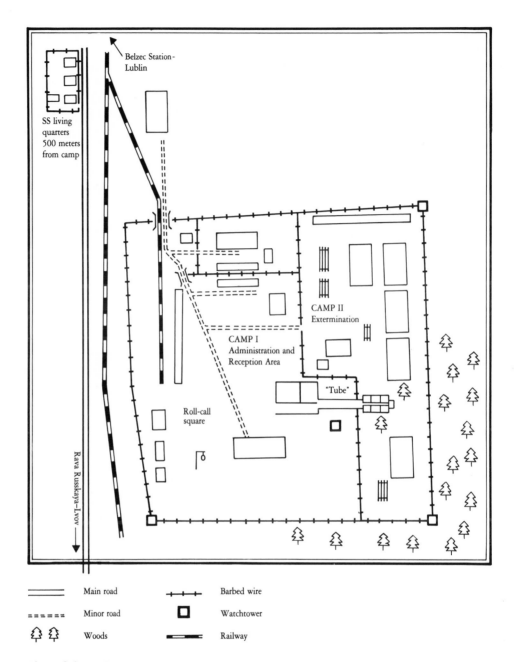

Belzec Station-Lublin

SS living
quarters
500 meters
from camp

CAMP II
Extermination

CAMP I
Administration and
Reception Area

"Tube"

Roll-call
square

Rava Russkaya–Lvov

	Main road		Barbed wire
	Minor road		Watchtower
	Woods		Railway

Plan of the Bełżec concentration camp.

leave their clothes and other belongings behind. This team was divided into several
subgroups for specific tasks, such as collecting
the discarded items, sorting them out, removing the yellow badges from the clothes, and
making a search for money or valuables that
the victims might have hidden in their clothes
or other belongings. Another job for this team
was to prepare all the clothes and other items
for shipment to an outside destination. After a
few months had passed, a new practice was
introduced in the procedure leading to extermination: the women were shorn of their hair
(which was to be used in the manufacture of
felt footwear). This task too was allotted to
one of the teams. The prisoners who made up
the work teams were housed in several barracks in Camp I, together with a group of
artisans—tailors, cobblers, carpenters, and so
on—who worked for the camp staff.

Several hundred Jewish prisoners were allotted to Camp II, their assignment being to remove the corpses from the gas chambers and inter them in the burial pits. A special group, nicknamed "the dentists," had the job of extracting gold teeth from the mouths of the dead Jews.

At all times, the prisoners working in the camp were subject to maltreatment and cruelty, by both the Germans and the Ukrainians, and to *Selektionen*, which meant the immediate execution of those selected. Only a handful of prisoners held out for more than a few months. The murdered prisoners were replaced by other Jews chosen from the new arrivals.

In the first four weeks of operation, from March 17 to mid-April 1942, a total of about 80,000 Jews were murdered in the Bełżec camp: 30,000 from the Lublin ghetto, 15,000 from Lvov, and the rest from other ghettos in the Lublin district and Eastern Galicia.

The *modus operandi* of the Bełżec extermination machine, as devised by Wirth, was as follows. A train consisting of forty to sixty freight cars would arrive at the Bełżec railway station, after a trip lasting several hours—sometimes several days—under horrible conditions, with no water or toilet facilities, and with 100 to 130 Jews packed into each car. Many did not survive the trip and died en route. When the train came to a halt, twenty of the freight cars, with a total of 2,000 to 2,500 Jews aboard, were detached from the train and attached to a locomotive that pulled them into the camp. Once inside, the Jews were ordered out of the cars, and one of the German officers announced that they had arrived at a transit camp, for onward distribution to various labor camps. They were also told that they would now be disinfected and washed, for their own hygiene's sake, and that they had to hand over any money or valuables in their possession. The men were separated

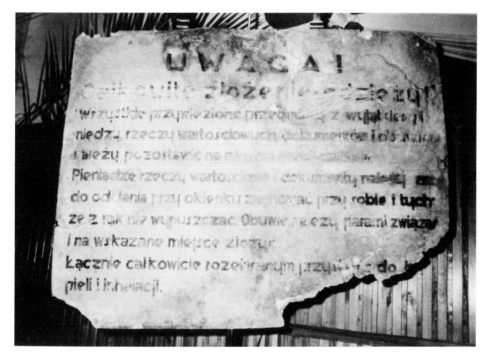

A sign from the Bełżec extermination camp. The Polish text reads: "ATTENTION. All belongings must be handed in at the counter except for money, documents, and other valuables, which you must keep with you. Shoes should be tied together in pairs and placed in the area marked for shoes. Afterward one must go completely naked to the showers."

from the women and children, and both groups were ordered to strip. With the Germans and Ukrainians shouting, threatening, and beating them, the Jews were rushed into the "showers"—that is, the gas chambers. As soon as they were locked in, the engine was started and the carbon monoxide began to flow into the gas chambers, killing all those inside within twenty or thirty minutes.

At first, the whole process, from the arrival of the cars in the camp to the removal of the corpses from the gas chambers, took three to four hours; as time went on, more efficient methods were introduced in the process and it took only sixty to ninety minutes. During the time that the twenty freight cars that had entered the camp were being cleaned and pulled out of the camp, twenty other cars took their place inside. The system was based on subterfuge and deception, to ensure that from the time the prisoners boarded the train to the moment the gas chamber doors closed behind them, they would believe that they were on their way to a labor camp.

Second Stage. In mid-April 1942, the camp ceased operating (the transports had temporarily halted) and was inactive for a month. The murder operation was resumed in May, and the transports that came in now also included Jews from the Kraków ghetto and the Kraków district. The German officers in charge had learned from experience that three gas chambers would not be enough to kill all the victims scheduled to be brought to Bełżec; a decision was therefore made to build larger gas chambers, and in order for this construction work to be carried out, as of mid-June the transports were discontinued for a month.

The existing gas chambers were demolished, and in their place a new building, made of brick and concrete and containing six 13-by-16-foot (4 × 5 m) cells, was erected. In the center of the building was a corridor with three doors on each side for entering the gas chambers. Each chamber had another opening on the outside wall, through which the corpses of the victims were later removed. The new gas chambers had a total capacity of 1,000 to 1,200 victims at a time, about half the number contained in twenty freight cars. Over the entrance to the building was a sign reading "Showers and Disinfection Rooms."

The transports were renewed in the second week of July and kept arriving on a regular schedule until the beginning of December. From July to October, about 130,000 Jews were brought to the camp from the Kraków district, and about 225,000 from the Lvov area in Eastern Galicia; there were also transports from the southern subdistricts of the Lublin and Radom districts. Some of the transports to Bełżec brought German, Austrian, and Czechoslovak Jews who had earlier been deported from their native countries to ghettos in Poland. The Germans were also planning to bring 200,000 Romanian Jews to Bełżec, but this plan was not carried out since the Romanian government refused to surrender Jews to the Germans.

The total number of murder victims in Bełżec was 600,000, virtually all Jews, with a few hundred (or at most a few thousand) Gypsies. This figure was confirmed by the Główna Komisja Badania Zbrodni Hitlerowskich w Polsce (MAIN COMMISSION FOR INVESTIGATION OF NAZI CRIMES IN POLAND) and was accepted by the judicial authorities of the Federal Republic of Germany.

Obliteration of the Camp. In December 1942, the transports to Bełżec and the extermination operation there came to an end. By this time most of the Jews of the GENERALGOUVERNEMENT had been killed, and the SS authorities in charge of Aktion Reinhard shut down the camp. SOBIBÓR and TREBLINKA, two extermination camps that had been constructed after Bełżec, continued to function, as did the AUSCHWITZ-Birkenau extermination camp.

Between December 1942 and spring 1943, the mass graves in Bełżec were opened and the bodies of the murder victims were exhumed and cremated. A special installation was put up to serve as a crematorium, made out of iron rails used for railways. Bones that resisted the flames were crushed, and these remains, together with the ashes, were buried in the ditches from which the corpses had been removed.

When the cremation of the bodies was completed, the camp was dismantled and all visible traces of the mass murder of which it had been the scene were removed. The Jewish prisoners, some six hundred in number, who had been kept behind in the camp were sent to Sobibór to be put to death there. In the final period, from the beginning of August 1942, the camp commander was SS-Hauptsturmführer Gottlieb Hering, who had replaced Christian Wirth. (Wirth had been appointed inspector of all the extermination camps set up under Aktion Reinhard.) After the camp was dismantled, the farmers in the area swarmed over the site, looking for money and gold that the Jews were rumored to have hidden there in the ground. To put an end to this, the Germans posted a Ukrainian guard, converted the grounds into a farm, and gave it to the guard. The area was plowed under and sown, and trees were planted on it. In the summer of 1944 the Bełżec area was liberated by the Red Army and the Polish army. It is now a national shrine.

Only a few individuals succeeded in escaping from Bełżec, and only one survived to tell the gruesome tale—Rudolf Reder, who spent four months in the camp and escaped in November 1942. After the war, Reder gave written testimony, which appeared in the form of a booklet, on what he had witnessed there. Apart from this one source, information on Bełżec has been difficult to come by, compared with evidence on the other extermination camps.

BIBLIOGRAPHY

Arad, Y. *Operation Reinhard Death Camps: Belzec, Sobibor, and Treblinka.* Bloomington, 1987.

Donat, A., ed. *The Death Camp Treblinka.* New York, 1979.

Reder, R. *Bełżec.* Kraków, 1946.

Ruckerl, A., ed. *Nationalsozialistische Vernichtungslager im Spiegel deutscher Strafprozesse: Belzec, Sobibor, Treblinka, Chelmno.* Munich, 1977.

Tregenza, M. "Belzec Deathcamp." *Wiener Library Bulletin* 30 (1977): 8–25.

YITZHAK ARAD

BENEŠ, EDVARD (1884–1948), Czech statesman. In prewar Czechoslovakia, Beneš was closely associated with his mentor, Tomáš G. Masaryk, founder of the Czechoslovak republic. Beneš headed his country's delegation to the Paris Peace Conference in 1919 and served as foreign minister of independent Czechoslovakia. His policy aimed at establishing a balance of power in eastern Europe; he negotiated treaties with Romania and Yugoslavia (the Little Entente) and counted on French hegemony as a spearhead against the German-Hungarian alliance. After the signing of a mutual pact with the Soviet Union in 1935, he also came to rely on that country as a safeguard against foes.

After President Masaryk's resignation in 1935, Beneš was elected as his successor. During the Sudeten crisis in September 1938, Beneš—abandoned by the Western allies—capitulated before Hitler's ultimatum and ceded the Sudetenland to Germany. He resigned on October 5 of that year and went into exile. After the outbreak of World War II, he established in France a Czechoslovak national committee, which moved to London in 1940, and he was recognized on July 21, 1941, as the president of the CZECHOSLOVAK GOVERNMENT-IN-EXILE.

Dr. Edvard Beneš, president of Czechoslovakia. [National Archives]

The Czech army intelligence and its network of agents in Europe had the reputation of being well informed. Consequently, Beneš was requested by the London office of the World Jewish Congress to verify the information about the Nazi extermination plan that reached Geneva in August 1942 (*see* RIEGNER CABLE). In his belated reply, Beneš claimed: "There seems to be no clear indication that the Germans are preparing for a wholesale extermination of all the Jews . . . although innumerable Jews are being severely persecuted and suffer from starvation." But shortly thereafter, the Jewish Agency announced that atrocity reports had been verified, and on December 15, 1942, the Beneš government strongly condemned the murder of Jews. Throughout the war years, Beneš maintained a close and friendly relationship with Jewish leaders and staunchly supported Jewish national aspirations in Palestine and the struggle for a Jewish state. He also took steps to minimize antisemitism in the Czechoslovak armed forces.

As head of the only eastern European government-in-exile allowed to return after the war, Beneš reestablished his government in Czechoslovakia in April 1945. After 1945 Czechoslovakia became a reunited country, and the Jews lost their status as a recognized minority group, having to declare themselves Czechs or Slovaks. In February 1948 Beneš succumbed to Communist demands by accepting a Communist-dominated cabinet, but he refused to sign the new constitution. Increasingly ill (he suffered two strokes in 1947), he resigned on June 7, 1948, and died a broken man in September of that year. His memoirs of the period of turmoil were published in 1954.

BIBLIOGRAPHY

Dagan, A. "The Czechoslovak Government-in-Exile and the Jews." In vol. 3 of *The Jews of Czechoslovakia*, edited by A. Dagan, pp. 449–498. New York, 1984.

Rothkirchen, L. "The Czechoslovak Government-in-Exile: Jewish and Palestinian Aspects in Light of the Documents." *Yad Vashem Studies* 9 (1973): 157–200.

LIVIA ROTHKIRCHEN

BEN-GURION, DAVID (1886–1973), prominent Zionist leader; first prime minister of Israel. Born in Płońsk, Poland, Ben-Gurion was a Zionist from his early youth and settled in Palestine in 1906. He was one of the founders of the socialist movement Po'alei Zion and subsequently of the Ahdut ha-Avoda and Mapai socialist political parties. In World War I he volunteered for the Jewish Legion, the volunteer formation in World War I that fought in the British army for the liberation of Palestine from Turkish rule. He was one of the founders of the Histadrut (the General Federation of Labor) and was its secretary-general from 1921 to 1935; in the latter year he became chairman of the Zionist Executive and of the Jewish Agency, holding both posts up to 1948. Ben-Gurion played a central role in the struggle for the establishment of a Jewish state, which he proclaimed on May 14, 1948. In the subsequent war he led both the political and the military struggles as prime minister and minister of defense, posts he retained until 1963.

Ben-Gurion's attitude toward European Jewry during the Holocaust period and the actions that he took for their rescue have been the subject of controversy. It has even been claimed that he consciously detached himself from the Holocaust events and concentrated on the building up of the YISHUV (the Jewish community in Palestine) and establishment of the state, almost to the exclusion of everything else. The views of scholars are divided: a minority holds that Ben-Gurion did in fact distance himself from the problem of European Jewry during the Holocaust; others maintain that from the early 1930s he was at all times preoccupied with the current and potential threats facing Jewish existence in Europe. Most scholars dealing with the general history of the Yishuv tend to take a more balanced view, and reject a one-sided approach.

The situation was, in any case, extremely complex. On the one hand, the conditions facing the Jews of eastern and central Europe in the 1930s deteriorated rapidly; on the other, there was a crisis in the relations between the Zionist movement and the British government. It reached a climax in May 1939, when the WHITE PAPER—limiting future

David Ben-Gurion (second from left) visiting Jewish survivors at Bergen-Belsen in November 1945. At a meeting in the camp he declared: "We shall not rest until every one of you who so desires joins us in the land of Israel in building a Jewish state."

Jewish development, including immigration, in the country—was issued. The combination of circumstances caused Ben-Gurion to conclude that Zionism had to blaze a new political trail. He spent much of the first two years of the war in the United States, in order to mobilize American Jewry's support for a far-reaching new program. It was ratified by a special Zionist conference held in New York in May 1942 at the Biltmore Hotel, hence its name, the BILTMORE RESOLUTION.

The resolution called for Palestine to be opened for large-scale Jewish immigration and, after the war, to become a Jewish commonwealth, under Jewish authority. In this way, it would provide a solution to the problems of the Jews (even if it could not absorb them all), and the mass immigration would also be the basis for its political and eco-

nomic status. The political solution would be the concern of the Zionist movement, while Jewish organizations in the free world— who had financial means and access to the centers of political power—would have the task of providing immediate aid to the Jews of Europe, and first and foremost to Polish Jewry.

In May 1942, reports of the mass murder of the Jews began to be published, and when in October of that year Ben-Gurion returned to Palestine, he was already in possession of information concerning a German master plan for the systematic annihilation of the Jews. Thus, the millions of Jews for whom the Biltmore program had been conceived were being killed. Ben-Gurion, however, clung to his program, believing that "disaster is the source of strength" that would spur the Jewish people and the Zionist movement to action.

From the end of 1942, Ben-Gurion took part in organizing the Yishuv for rescue operations. He did not permit the establishment of a broad rescue committee under Jewish Agency auspices, since he felt that the Yishuv should have its own official committee; but he did leave political action in the hands of Jewish Agency departments, under the direction and watchful eye of his confidants, among them Shaul Meirov (Avigur), Eliyahu Golomb, and Zvi Yehieli. Ben-Gurion consistently had reservations about mass demonstrations, which were intended to rouse public opinion in the free world and influence Allied governments to help in rescue efforts, because he did not expect them to be effective while the war was in progress. He was against using "national funds" for rescue operations, but was in favor of collecting money for that specific purpose, and himself took part in such fund-raising.

Ben-Gurion's attitude and actions appear to have been based on his conviction that even if the Yishuv were to use its best people and all the resources at its disposal, it would not be able to save many lives, both because of the relentless German annihilation machinery and because the Allied powers, especially Britain, managed to thwart one rescue plan after the other. These included proposals for exchange of Germans for Jews; provision of protective documents to Jews; emigration; cessation of the extermination process in exchange for financial remittances (the EUROPA PLAN, for example); and the dispatch of PARACHUTISTS from Palestine.

Ben-Gurion's doubts about the chances of success for rescue efforts were further reinforced by the BERMUDA CONFERENCE of April 1943 and by various developments in 1944, such as the Allies' refusal to bomb AUSCHWITZ; the failure of the arrangement concerning Hungarian Jewry, proposed by Adolf EICHMANN and his aides, to exchange "blood for goods"; and, above all, Britain's attitude toward a plan on which Ben-Gurion had pinned great hopes — the rescue of thirty thousand Jewish children from German-occupied Europe. These disappointments led Ben-Gurion to concentrate on independent, smaller, and more realistic rescue programs.

This line of reasoning on Ben-Gurion's part and its practical consequences caused tension between him and a significant part of the Jewish population, and within the leadership itself. The approach was criticized not only by the opposition on the right but also by members of Mapai, Ben-Gurion's own party. Moreover, Ben-Gurion did not publicly reveal his analysis of the situation, the intuition that he had, and the way in which he reached his conclusions. The impression created was that he lacked compassion for the suffering of European Jewry and that his course of action was not affected by the Holocaust. In fact, he was deeply moved by the enormity of the tragedy, and his policies were molded by his determination to alleviate the suffering and its root causes by finding long-term solutions.

BIBLIOGRAPHY

Frieling, T. "Ben-Gurion and the Holocaust of European Jewry: A Sterotype Reexamined." *Yad Vashem Studies* 18 (1987): 199–232.

Gal, A. *David Ben-Gurion: Preparing for a Jewish State*. Sede Boker, Israel, 1985. (In Hebrew.)

Porat, D. "Ben Gurion and the Holocaust." *Zionism* 12 (1987): 293–314. (In Hebrew.)

Tevet, S. *David Ben-Gurion: The Burning Ground, 1886–1948*. Boston, 1987.

Tevet, S. *The Zeal of David: The Life of David Ben-Gurion*. Vol. 3. Jerusalem, 1987. (In Hebrew.)

DINA PORAT

BENOÎT, MARIE (b. 1895), French Capuchin monk who rescued Jews during the Holocaust. In the summer of 1942, Benoît was a resident monk in the Capuchin monastery in Marseilles, France. Witnessing the spectacle of Vichy authorities rounding up thousands of non-French Jewish refugees and handing them over to the Germans for deportation, Benoît decided to devote himself to helping Jews escape from France to either Spain or Switzerland, both neutral countries. Under his guidance, the Capuchin monastery was transformed into a nerve center of a widespread rescue network, in collaboration with frontier smugglers (*passeurs*) and in coordination with various Christian and Jewish organizations. A printing machine in the mon-

Father Marie Benoît in 1984.

astery's basement turned out thousands of false baptismal certificates, which the fleeing Jews needed in order to procure other necessary documents.

With the occupation of Vichy France in November 1942, the escape routes to Switzerland and Spain became more difficult to negotiate. The nearby Italian zone of occupation now became the principal escape haven. Journeying to Nice, Benoît coordinated plans with local Jewish organizations. Accompanied by Angelo Donati, an influential local Jewish banker in Nice, he met with Gen. Guido Lospinoso, the Italian commissioner of Jewish affairs (sent to Nice by MUSSOLINI, under German pressure, for the express purpose of instituting anti-Jewish measures), and convinced him that the rescue of the thirty thousand Jews in Nice and its environs was the divine order of the day. Benoît was promised that the Italian occupation authorities would not interfere. Not satisfied with this commitment, and harboring presentiments as to the ultimate fate of the Jews in Nice, Benoît continued on to Rome, and in an audience with Pope PIUS XII on July 16, 1943, he outlined a plan for transferring the majority of the thirty thousand Jews in the Nice region to northern Italy to prevent their falling into German hands. This plan was later expanded to provide for the Jews' transfer to former military camps in North Africa, now in Allied hands. The new Italian government of Marshal Pietro BADOGLIO (Mussolini had been deposed on July 25, 1943) was prepared to provide four ships for this giant undertaking, and ways were found to channel funds from Jewish organizations abroad. However, the premature publication of the Italian armistice on September 8 and the immediate German occupation of northern Italy and the Italian zone of occupation in France foiled this plan.

Benoît's activities now centered on helping Jews in Rome and its vicinity, with the Capuchin College inside the Vatican as his base of operations. To be able to deal effectively with the task of providing food, shelter, and new identities to thousands of Jewish refugees in Rome and elsewhere, he was elected a board member of Delasem (Delegazione Assistenza Emigranti Ebrei), the central Jewish welfare organization of Italy. When its Jewish president, Settimo Sorani, was arrested by the Germans, Benoît was nominated acting president; he chaired the organization's meetings, which were now held inside the Capuchin College. Benoît escaped several attempts by the Gestapo to arrest him, as his fame spread among Jews and non-Jews. He extracted letters of protection and other important documents from the Swiss, Romanian, Hungarian, and Spanish legations. These papers enabled thousands of Jews, under assumed names, to circulate freely in Rome. He also obtained a large batch of ration cards from the Rome police, ostensibly on behalf of non-Jewish homeless refugees stranded in the capital.

After Rome's liberation in June 1944, Benoît was hailed by the Jewish community at an official synagogue ceremony. With the war over and the Jews safe, he returned to his ecclesiastical duties. France awarded him various military decorations; Israel, through YAD VASHEM, conferred on him the title of "RIGHTEOUS AMONG THE NATIONS" in 1966.

BIBLIOGRAPHY

Grossman, K. R. *Die unbesungenen Helden: Menschen in Deutschlands dunkeln Tagen.* Berlin, 1961. See pages 242–284.

Morley, J. F. *Vatican Diplomacy and the Jews during the Holocaust, 1939–1943.* New York, 1980.
Rorty, J. "Father Benoit, Ambassador of the Jews: An Untold Chapter of the Underground." *Commentary* 2/6 (December 1946): 507–513.

MORDECAI PALDIEL

BERDICHEV, town in Zhitomir Oblast (district), Ukrainian SSR, known to have been in existence since the fourteenth century. Jews lived in Berdichev from the sixteenth century. The town became a center of Hasidism, the seat of the renowned rabbi Levi Yitzhak of Berdichev, and, in the nineteenth century, a center of Haskalah (Jewish Enlightenment).

Immediately prior to World War II, Berdichev had a Jewish population of over 30,000, out of a total population of 66,306. When the town was taken by the Germans on July 7, 1941, the Jewish population numbered 20,000. Three days later the military governor imposed a collective fine on the Jews of 100,000 rubles, in cash and valuables. Jews were harassed, some were murdered in groups, and synagogues were set on fire with the congregants inside at prayer.

On August 25, the Jews of Berdichev were ordered to move into a ghetto that had been set up in the poorest part of the town (if they did not live there already), which thus became unbearably congested. On September 4, on orders of the *Höherer SS- und Polizeiführer* (Higher SS and Police Leader) of the Ukraine, 1,500 young Jews were seized and taken out of town to be shot to death. A force of German and Ukrainian police surrounded the ghetto on September 15. Four hundred skilled craftsmen and their families, a total of 2,000 people, were set aside, and the rest, 18,600 persons, were taken out of town to pits that had been prepared in advance, to be shot to death.

Two thousand more Jews were murdered on November 3, leaving only 150 craftsmen alive. The following spring, on April 7, 1942, 70 Jewish women, who were married to non-Jews and lived outside the ghetto, were murdered together with their children. On June 16, the number of craftsmen was reduced to 60; and at the end of October 1943, when Soviet forces were approaching, those Jews who were still left alive were also murdered.

When Berdichev was liberated, on January 15, 1944, 15 Jews were found in the town.

BIBLIOGRAPHY

Ehrenburg, I., and V. Grossman, eds. *The Black Book of Soviet Jewry.* New York, 1981.

SHMUEL SPECTOR

BEREZHANY (Pol., Brzeżany), town in Ternopol Oblast (district), Ukrainian SSR, 31 miles (50 km) west of Ternopol. Between the two wars, Berezhany was part of Poland, and in September 1939 it was incorporated into the Soviet Union, together with the rest of eastern Poland. On the eve of World War II, Berezhany had a Jewish population of over four thousand.

On July 7, 1941, two weeks after the invasion of the Soviet Union, the Germans occupied Berezhany. The Ukrainians lost no time in attacking the Jews; on the morrow of the German entry, they killed three Jews, and a few days later, several dozen more, twelve of them in the Christian cemetery and others in the large municipal park. Various anti-Jewish measures were enacted, such as a dusk-to-dawn curfew, a ban on leaving the city, and the wearing of a Jewish BADGE (a band with a Star of David on the right arm). At the beginning of August 1941 a JUDENRAT (Jewish Council) was set up, consisting of twenty-four members, and its first task was to collect a fine of 300,000 zlotys from the community. The Judenrat also had to supply men for forced labor and to collect and hand over to the Germans valuables, goods, furniture, and household appliances owned by Jews.

On the eve of the Day of Atonement (September 30, 1941), all male Jews aged eighteen to sixty-five were ordered to assemble on the following day in the central town square. A *Selektion* was made that resulted in 700 men being taken to a nearby forest and murdered. On December 18 of that year, 1,200 Jews were moved out of the city, on the pretext that they were being transferred to nearby Podgaitsy. Along the way the German and Ukrainian escorts stopped the convoy and machine-gunned all the Jews to death. Toward the end of 1941, young Jews were seized and sent to labor camps in Zborov,

Kamionka, and Hluboczek Wielki. Most of them met their death there, from hard labor, starvation, and the treatment meted out to them.

On February 17, 1942, several dozen Berezhany Jews were murdered in a place outside the town. In the spring of that year, Jews from neighboring villages were brought into the town. Additional dozens of Jews were murdered in June 1942. In a mass *Aktion* that took place on the Day of Atonement, September 21, fifteen hundred Jews were rounded up and deported to the BEŁŻEC extermination camp. On October 15, the remaining Jews of Berezhany were confined in a ghetto. Another *Aktion* took place on December 4 and 5, after which several hundred Jews were sent to their death in Bełżec. In that period a growing number of attempts were made to go into hiding in the ghetto or take refuge in the nearby forests.

In March 1943, twelve women were shot to death for having left the confines of the ghetto. At the end of that month and the beginning of April, the Germans and their Ukrainian helpers murdered two hundred men in the Jewish cemetery. In May, four hundred men were put into a work camp that was set up in the ghetto area. On June 12, 1943, the last of the Jews in the work camp and in the ghetto were murdered. Only a handful of the community members had remained in hiding and lived to witness the town's liberation in summer 1944.

BIBLIOGRAPHY

Katz, M., ed. *Brzeżany Memorial Book.* Haifa, 1978. (In Hebrew and English.)

AHARON WEISS

BEREZHANY

BERGEN-BELSEN, camp in the concentration camp system of Nazi Germany. Bergen-Belsen was located in Lower Saxony, northern Germany, near the city of Celle. The camp was officially established in April 1943 as an *Aufenthaltslager* (detention camp) for holding persons who were designated for exchange with German nationals in Allied countries whom the Germans wanted to repatriate. A prisoner-of-war camp on the site,

Stalag 311, was partially cleared to make room for the new camp.

From its inception, Bergen-Belsen came under the SS WIRTSCHAFTS-VERWALTUNGSHAUPT-AMT (Economic-Administrative Main Office; WVHA), which was in charge of the administration of concentration camps. Its first commandant was Hauptsturmführer (later promoted to Sturmbannführer) Adolf Haas. Five hundred Jewish prisoners from the BUCHEN-WALD and NATZWEILER camps were taken to Bergen-Belsen to work on the construction of the camp; they were not candidates for exchange and belonged to the Baukommando (construction detachment), whose task was to construct facilities for the intake of the persons who, on the face of it, were candidates for exchange. In the course of the first eigh-

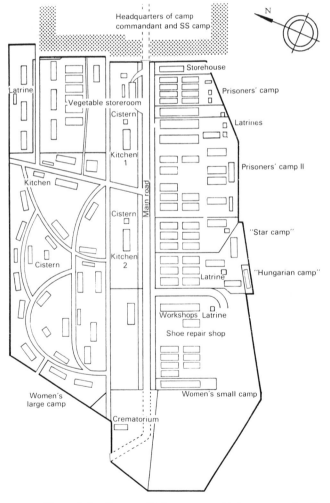

Plan of the Bergen-Belsen camp (February to April 1945). [From *Bergen-Belsen: Geschichte des Aufenthaltslagers 1943–1945;* Hannover, 1962]

teen months of the camp's existence, five satellite camps were set up, unconnected with one another, as follows:

1. A "prisoners' camp" (*Häftlingslager*) for the first 500 prisoners who had been brought in for construction of the camp. This was the first satellite camp to be built at Bergen-Belsen; conditions in the camp were among the worst possible, and the mortality rate was very high. The camp was closed on February 23, 1944, and the few surviving prisoners were transferred to SACHSENHAUSEN.

2. The "special camp" (*Sonderlager*). In mid-June 1943, two transports of Jews from Poland (mainly from Warsaw, Lvov, and Kraków), totaling 2,400 persons, were taken to this camp; these were Jews who had papers (*promesas*) in their possession, issued by various—mostly South American—countries. In late October 1943, 1,700 of these Jews were deported to AUSCHWITZ, where they were all immediately killed. Another 350 suffered the same fate in early 1944. This left 350 detainees in the camp, of whom 266 were in possession of immigration permits to Palestine, 34 were United States citizens, and 50 had South American papers. These prisoners were not assigned to work teams, and no contact was permitted between them and other groups of Bergen-Belsen prisoners.

3. The "neutral camp" (*Neutralenlager*). This camp contained two barracks in which 350 Jewish prisoners were housed from late July 1944 to early March 1945. The prisoners were nationals of neutral countries, among them 155 Spanish, 105 Turkish, 35 Argentine, and 19 Portuguese citizens. Conditions in this camp were better than in any other part of Bergen-Belsen. The prisoners here were not put to work, enjoyed better nourishment and sanitary conditions, and were treated by the SS with less cruelty than were prisoners in the other satellite camps.

4. The "star camp" (*Sternenlager*). This was the largest of the five satellite camps, containing eighteen barracks. It housed Jewish prisoners who ostensibly were designated for exchange (*Austauschjuden*, or exchange Jews). These prisoners did not wear the usual concentration camp uniform and were permitted to wear their own clothes, but they had to wear a yellow BADGE (a Magen David, or Star of David, from which came the name

Bergen-Belsen after the liberation of the camp by the British army on April 15, 1945.

"star camp"). Men and women lived in separate barracks, but members of the same family were able to meet. Most of the prisoners in the "star camp" were Jews from the Netherlands; in the period from January to September 1944, eight transports from the WESTERBORK camp in the Netherlands arrived in Bergen-Belsen, made up of 3,670 persons who were classified as *Austauschjuden*. In the first half of 1944, the "star camp" also took in small transports of Jews from various other countries. These included 200 Jews from Tunisia, Tripoli, and Benghazi who until then had been held in the Fossoli di Carpi camp in Italy; 200 Jewish women from the DRANCY camp in France, whose husbands were French prisoners of war being held by the Germans; and several hundred Jews from Yugoslavia and Albania. According to a count taken on July 31, 1944, the "star camp" contained a total of 4,100 Jewish prisoners classified as *Austauschjuden*.

5. The "Hungarian camp" (*Ungarnlager*), which was set up on July 8, 1944, and held 1,684 Jews from Hungary—the transport organized by Dr. Rezső (Rudolf) KASZTNER. Here, too, the prisoners wore their own clothes but were forced to display the yellow badge.

Only a few of the Jews who were brought to Bergen-Belsen as candidates for exchange were in fact set free in exchange deals (*see* EXCHANGE: JEWS AND GERMANS). On July 10, 1944, 222 Jews with immigration certificates to Palestine landed at the Haifa port. A few weeks later, on August 21, 318 Jews from the "Hungarian camp" reached Switzerland, followed by another 1,365 in December; on January 25, 1945, 136 Jews with South American papers also reached Switzerland.

Beginning in March 1944, Bergen-Belsen gradually became a "regular" concentration camp, the Germans transferring to it prisoners from other concentration camps who

Former SS women guards lowering the bodies of dead inmates into a common grave in Bergen-Belsen (April 1945).

were classified as ill and unfit to work (*Arbeitsunfähige*). The first such group came in late March 1944 and consisted of 1,000 sick prisoners from the DORA camp. They were put into a new section of the camp where the sanitary conditions were extremely poor; they received no blankets, no medical attention, and only minute food rations. Nearly all of them died within a short period; on the day of the camp's liberation, only 57 of the original 1,000 were still alive. More transports of prisoners "unfit for work" kept arriving from various camps, up to the end of 1944, most of them made up of Hungarian Jews. The majority were housed in the former "prisoners' camp", where conditions were at their worst and the mortality rate was the highest. Of the several thousand prisoners brought to this section of the camp in 1944 (the precise figure is unknown), 820 died in the period from April to June alone. Also transferred to this section of the camp were German convicts from the Dora camp, who were appointed "block elders" (*Blockälteste*)

and Kapos (*see* KAPO), and who treated the Jewish prisoners under their authority with great brutality, causing their situation to deteriorate sharply. The prisoners also suffered from the sadistic practices of the camp doctor, Obersturmbannführer Dr. Karl Jäger, who forced them to keep running for long stretches of time. In summer 1944 some 200 prisoners were killed by phenol injections.

In August 1944 a new section was added, to serve as a women's camp, consisting of twelve barracks; 4,000 Jewish women prisoners from Hungary and Poland were brought there, but after a short stay they were sent on forced labor to the Buchenwald and FLOSSENBÜRG satellite camps. Most of the women were sent back to Bergen-Belsen, sick or exhausted by the hard labor that had been forced on them. In September and October of 1944, transports of Jewish prisoners from the PŁASZÓW camp, and 3,000 Jewish women prisoners from Auschwitz, arrived at Bergen-Belsen; they were housed in the "star camp" in new barracks put up for them, with no water, no beds, and no other facilities of any kind. Among these prisoners were Anne FRANK and her sister Margot; in March 1945 both girls succumbed to the typhus epidemic that was then raging in the camp.

On December 2, 1944, the camp commandant, Adolf Haas, was replaced by Hauptsturmführer Josef KRAMER. A census taken that day showed that the camp population was 15,257 persons, of whom some 8,000 were women. Kramer's first step was to convert Bergen-Belsen officially into a concentration camp. The residues of self-administration that still existed in the "star camp" were abolished, and the internal management of the camp was put into the hands of *Blockälteste* and Kapos, as was done in all the other concentration camps. A final and complete deterioration of the conditions under which the prisoners were living in the camp set in when tens of thousands of prisoners poured in—survivors of the DEATH MARCHES of prisoners who had been evacuated from camps in the east. These included 20,000 women prisoners from the Auschwitz and Buchenwald satellite camps, some of whom had passed through the GROSS-ROSEN camp on the death march to Bergen-Belsen.

Rabbi Leslie H. Hardman, British army chaplain, recites Kaddish at a common grave in Bergen-Belsen (April 1945).

In the period from January to March 1945 there were more death marches, which brought thousands of male prisoners from the Sachsenhausen and Buchenwald camps to Bergen-Belsen. The camp administration did not lift a finger to house the prisoners who were streaming in. Most of them had no roof over their heads, and were without water and food. There was now total chaos in the camps, and a typhus epidemic was at its height; in the month of March alone, 18,168 prisoners perished in the camp, and the number of deaths for the period from January to mid-April was 35,000.

On April 15, 1945, Bergen-Belsen was liberated by the British army. There were sixty thousand prisoners in the camp, most of them in a critical condition. Thousands of unburied bodies were strewn all over the camp grounds. The sight put the British sol-

Josef Kramer (seated), the commandant of Bergen-Belsen from December 2, 1944, was apprehended by the British army when it liberated the camp on April 15, 1945.

diers into a state of shock. The British had not anticipated the immediate rescue requirements, and in the first five days following liberation, fourteen thousand persons died; another fourteen thousand succumbed in the following weeks.

After liberation, Bergen-Belsen became the site of a DISPLACED PERSONS' camp, the British army medical corps helping in the physical rehabilitation of the former prisoners. The displaced persons' camp was in existence up to 1951, with the inmates, under the leadership of Josef Rosensaft, managing to organize a lively social, cultural, and political life in the camp.

The trial of forty-eight members of the staff of Bergen-Belsen, among them sixteen women, by a British military court was held in Lüneburg, Germany, from September 17 to November 17, 1945. Eleven of the accused—including the camp commandant, Josef Kramer—were sentenced to death, and on December 12, 1945, they were executed.

[*See also* Trials of War Criminals: Bergen-Belsen Trial; Appendix, Volume 4.]

BIBLIOGRAPHY

Bloch, S. E., ed. *Holocaust and Rebirth: Bergen Belsen, 1945–1965.* New York, 1965.
Hardman, L. H., and C. Goodman. *The Survivors: The Story of the Belsen Remnant.* London, 1958.
Kolb, E. *Bergen Belsen: Vom "Aufenthaltslager" zum Konzentrationslager, 1943–1945.* Göttingen, 1984.
Levy-Haas, H. *Inside Belsen.* Totowa, N.J., 1962.
Napora, P. *Death at Belsen.* San Antonio, Tex., 1967.
Phillips, R., ed. *The Belsen Trial: Trial of Josef Kramer and 44 Others.* London, 1949.

SHMUEL KRAKOWSKI

BERGEN-BELSEN TRIAL. *See* Trials of War Criminals: Bergen-Belsen Trial.

BERGSON GROUP, a group of members of the Zionist Revisionist movement active in the United States between 1940 and 1948. It supported the creation of a Jewish army to fight Nazi Germany, the rescue of Jews from the Holocaust in Europe, and the establishment of a Jewish state.

In the summer of 1940, Vladimir JABOTINSKY and Hillel Kook went to the United States in order to promote the creation of an independent Jewish army that would fight Adolf Hitler. They were joined by members of the Palestine underground group Irgun Tseva'i Le'ummi (Etsel), who had been there for some time, their original purpose being to raise funds for their organization. On Jabotinsky's death in August 1940, Kook took over the leadership of the group, assuming for this purpose the alias of Peter H. Bergson (hence the group's name). Samuel Merlin became Bergson's right-hand man. On December 4, 1941, the Bergson Group formed the Committee for a Jewish Army of Stateless and Palestinian Jews.

In November 1942, when Rabbi Stephen S. WISE made public a report on the systematic murder of several million Jews by the Nazis (*see* RIEGNER CABLE), the Bergson Group decided to concentrate all its efforts on the rescue of Europe's Jews and for the time being to shelve the campaign for a Jewish army. As Palestinian Jews, the members were not responsible to any local Jewish leadership or political group; they also did not have to account for their actions to Etsel headquarters in Palestine, to any community organization, or to the United States government; and they were not beset by any qualms about dual loyalty. This enabled them to use unconventional means in their operation. They disagreed with the American Jewish establishment, Zionists and non-Zionists alike, over the traditional ways of intercession—which they considered obsequious—with the authorities, and they were sharply critical of the paralysis that had taken hold of American Jews, out of the fear of increasing antisemitism.

Perturbed by the administration's reluctance to take action on behalf of Europe's Jews, the Bergson Group decided to make use of the power of public opinion in a democratic society to bring pressure to bear upon Washington to institute special measures in order to save Jews. Using methods of mass communication, such as full-page advertisements and mass demonstrations, the group appealed to the deep-rooted American religious and liberal tradition with outspoken and provocative slogans such as "The Jews don't want just to pray—they want to fight" and "Action, not mercy," which found a growing response among the public.

Launched in February 1943, the propaganda campaign gained in force with the help of a mass demonstration held at Madison Square Garden on March 9, which had at its center a pageant entitled *We Will Never Die*, composed by the author Ben Hecht in memory of the two million Jews known to have been murdered by that time. From New York, the pageant toured other cities throughout the country.

Following the failure of the BERMUDA CONFERENCE, which was to have come up with a solution of the refugee problem, Bergson convened an emergency conference (July 20 to 25, 1943) that called for stepped-up action in behalf of the rescue of Jews, and demanded that pressure be put on the Axis powers to permit the emigration of Jews, or at least to allow the Allies to supply the Jews in their countries with basic needs. The conference also called on the neutral countries to offer temporary asylum to refugees fleeing for their lives. It established the Emergency Committee to Save the Jewish People of Europe, which in turn resolved to devote its efforts to promoting a United States government agency whose sole concern would be to save Jews. The committee launched a two-pronged campaign—a national publicity drive to alert public opinion to the grave situation of European Jews, and the creation of a lobby, based on public support by both Jews and non-Jews, that would seek to convince the president and the Congress of the need to embark upon rescue operations. Emergency Committee members felt that the creation of a refugee council would lead to government recognition of the unique nature of the Jewish problem.

Journalists and intellectuals, such as Ben Hecht and Max Lerner, joined the publicity drive, and the committee's own magazine, *Answer*, also helped in spreading the Bergson Group's proposals. Leading public figures, such as the press magnate William Randolph Hearst, Secretary of the Interior Harold Ickes, New York mayor Fiorello La Guardia, and Will Rogers, Democratic congressman from California, were among the Emergency Committee's supporters and lent their names to its efforts. These included a pilgrimage of rescue to Washington, made by four hundred rabbis who marched on the White House on October 6, 1943, just before the Day of Atonement. President Franklin D. ROOSEVELT, however, arranged to be away from the White House so that he could avoid receiving the rabbinical delegation. On October 10, six thousand churches observed a "day of intercession" on which Christians offered prayers in behalf of "our brethren in Europe." The committee also began the collection of a million signatures on a petition that was to be presented to the president and Congress, calling for a government agency to be set up that would deal specifically with the rescue of Jews.

The attempts to gain the president's support were of no avail, but the lobbying in Congress did lead to some success. On November 9, 1943, two identical draft resolutions were introduced: in the Senate by Guy Gillette (Democrat from Iowa) and in the House by Will Rogers (Democrat from California) and Joseph Baldwin (Republican from New York). The resolutions called on the president to establish a government commission for the rescue of Europe's Jews. The public atmosphere engendered by the discussion of the draft in Congress, coupled with the intervention of Treasury Secretary Henry MORGENTHAU, Jr., may well have caused President Roosevelt to issue an executive order, on January 22, 1944, establishing the WAR REFUGEE BOARD, to deal with refugees of all religions. The campaign for a "free port" where refugees in danger of their lives would be given temporary refuge, which the committee had supported, met with partial success when the Oswego free port came into being (*see* FORT ONTARIO).

Once the War Refugee Board had been established, the Bergson Group turned its attention to issues that would arise when the war was over, and became active in behalf of a "Hebrew" state in Palestine. In May 1944, it set up the Hebrew Committee for National Liberation and a Hebrew Embassy in Washington.

The Bergson Group's independent line of action brought it into conflict with the Zionist leadership and with the American Jewish establishment. The conflict was exacerbated by the group's temporary shelving of the struggle for Palestine, and by the manner in which it once again took up the issue. Bergson himself demanded that the issue of rescuing Jews should be excluded from any controversy that might arise among Jewish political groups or between Zionists and non-Zionists. The omission of the name "Palestine" from the Gillette-Rogers draft resolution, and the Bergson Group's use of the term "Hebrew state" rather than "Jewish state," contradicted Zionist ideology. The Zionist establishment strongly criticized both Bergson's ideology and his strident tactics, and even asked the administration to take action against him and his men.

The Bergson Group took virtually no part in direct rescue or aid operations, but it did play an important role in bringing the Holocaust of European Jewry to the knowledge of the general public. It also prevailed upon public figures to pressure the American administration to take up rescue operations. Scholars are divided in their appraisal of the Bergson Group's contribution to the establishment of the War Refugee Board. Some (such as Lucy Dawidowicz and Jonathan Kaplan) belittle the group's role in this connection, while others (Sharon Lowenstein and Monty Penkower) stress the importance of that role. There seems to be general agreement, however, that the Bergson Group's organizations succeeded in increasing the pressure on key figures in the administration to search for means of rescuing Jews.

The evaluation of the Bergson Group's achievements seems to be linked to the assessment of the overall record of American Jewry during the Holocaust years. Those scholars (including Saul Friedman, Lowenstein, and David Wyman) who fault American Jews for their lack of initiative and their failure to act in behalf of European Jews extol the success scored by a handful of penniless youngsters, by means of unconventional methods, to arouse public opinion—and through it also the administration—to rescue action. Others (such as Yehuda Bauer, Dawidowicz, Henry Feingold, Leonard Dinner-stein, and Penkower) point to American Jewry's weak position at the time, because of which it could not have been expected to bring about a change in the general atmosphere of indifference and even hostility toward Jewish refugees then prevailing in the country. In their opinion, the current tendency to reproach American Jewry for its record in those years is based, in part, on the power that it attained only later.

BIBLIOGRAPHY

Dawidowicz, L. "Indicting American Jews." *Commentary* 75 (June 1983): 36–44.

Friedman, S. S. *No Haven for the Oppressed: U.S. Policy toward Jewish Refugees, 1933–1945.* Detroit, 1973.

Kaplan, J. "Rescue Activities of the Etzel Mission in the United States during the Holocaust." *Yalkut Moreshet* 30 (1980): 115–138; 31 (1981): 75–96. (In Hebrew.)

Lowenstein, S. R. *Token Refuge: The Story of the Jewish Refugee Center at Oswego, 1944–1946.* Bloomington, 1986.

Penkower, M. N. "In Dramatic Dissent: The Bergson Boys." *American Jewish History* 70/3 (March 1981): 281–309.

Wyman, D. S. *The Abandonment of the Jews: America and the Holocaust, 1941–1945.* New York, 1984.

HAIM GENIZI

BERIḤA (Heb.; "flight, escape"), the post–World War II movement of about 250,000 Jewish Holocaust survivors, mainly from eastern Europe, to DISPLACED PERSONS' camps in Germany, Austria, and Italy and to the West; the name applies both to the organization that directed the flow and to the mass movement that often outgrew the organization. The avowed aim was to reach the coasts, from which the wanderers could embark for Palestine.

The organized *beriḥa* began with groups of Jewish partisan survivors in the Vilna, Rovno, and Chernovtsy areas that initially had no contact with one another. They felt that they could not carry on life in their former homes, which had become Jewish graveyards. Many of the survivors had belonged to Zionist youth movements before the war, and their Zionist convictions had been strengthened by disillusionment with the Soviet regime; consequently, their natural path after the liberation was emigration to Palestine. They had heard that it could best be reached by way of Romania, and they therefore tried, each group separately at first, to make their way over the Romanian border. The groups coalesced, but their attempt to reach Romania failed, and they concentrated in Lublin, which had been liberated by the Red Army in July 1944. Here they were joined by a sizable group of their prewar comrades who had spent the war years as refugees in the USSR, mainly in central Asia; in January 1945, when Warsaw was liberated, the remnants of the ghetto rebels from Warsaw joined the group.

An incipient formal structure was created under Abba KOVNER, partisan and poet, and the leadership group made its way to Romania in March. Illegal transit points were established on the Polish border with Czechoslovakia and Romania, and by May about two thousand persons had reached Romania. On April 26, 1945, Kovner established the Organization of Eastern European Survivors, a semipolitical organization that was to unite the Jewish people beyond their party and political allegiances and help create a Jewish state that would be the last refuge for a nation for whom another Holocaust was predicted. The new group was soon to disintegrate, however, after contact with the lively and argumentative democracy of Palestine Jewry. It turned out that no immigration from Romania to Palestine was feasible, and the group turned west to Italy, where the Jewish Palestinian units of the British army (the JEWISH BRIGADE GROUP and others) were stationed. The soldiers had established a central organization for looking after Jewish survivors (Merkaz la-Gola, or Diaspora Center), led by an all-party coalition under Mordechai Surkis, Yehiel Duvdevani, and Aharon Hoter-Yishai.

As a result of the unification of the two elements in July 1945, the Beriḥa in Poland, now led by Moshe Meiri and Mordechai Rosman, directed the flow to Italy, by way of Budapest and Graz. By August 1945, roughly fifteen thousand Jews had reached Italy. However, there were only very limited ("illegal") opportunities for reaching Palestine at that time, and the difficult decision was reached to direct the increasing flow of survivors and returnees from the USSR to Poland, and from there to Germany, where, under United States Army rule, Jews were accepted into displaced persons' camps, housed, and fed. Transit to Italy from Germany and Austria all but ceased, and the soldiers took over some of the central positions, receiving the flow of people directed by the Polish Beriḥa.

In September and October 1945, the first emissaries sent by the Hagana (the Jewish underground in Palestine) arrived in Europe. Isser Ben-Zvi, Zvi Netzer, and Yohanan Cohen, among others, reached Poland and other places and integrated themselves into the loosely organized and illegal Beriḥa structure. The stream moved through various control points by way of the Polish-Slovak mountains, through Upper Silesia into the Náchod area in Bohemia, or by way of Szczecin into Berlin. Those who entered Czechoslovakia went either through Prague and then to Bavaria, or by way of Bratislava to Vienna, then to Salzburg, and on to either Germany or Italy. The Beriḥa activists were not paid, and necessary expenses were covered, often unwittingly but eventually with full knowledge, by the American JOINT DISTRIBUTION COMMITTEE as "transit" expenses for transport, food, and basic lodging. The small amount of property in the refugees' possession was scrupulously guarded, brought over the border by the Beriḥa workers, and delivered to the owners. Beriḥa had no central hierarchy; a coordination office in Bratislava—run by Levi Argov, an emissary from Palestine, more or less at his own initiative—worked out schedules for transports from Poland westward. Parallel points were set up in Hungary and Slovakia, again in coordination with Argov. In Austria another emissary, Arthur (Asher) Ben-Nathan, received the flow from Czechoslovakia and distributed it by way of Salzburg and Innsbruck.

The Soviets, whose control over eastern Europe was tightening, permitted the illegal flow in a halfhearted manner, although sometimes they suddenly pounced on the refugees and organizers and arrested them (some spent years in the Gulag, and a few were killed); but usually they turned a blind eye. The atti-

BERIḤA

© Martin Gilbert 1982

Jewish refugees waiting at the Budapest train station to go to Italy; from there they made their way to Palestine (1945). [Zvi Kadushin; Beth Hatefutsoth]

tude of the British was predictably hostile, while the United States army, after some initial troubles, accepted the *beriḥa* flow because it was wary of a scandal with the administration and the public at home; in any case, it could not order soldiers to shoot at Jewish refugees, which was the only way it could have stopped them from coming.

Between August 1945 and the end of June 1946, Beriḥa figures show 48,106 refugees as having left Poland by means of the organization. If there is added an unknown number who came across without the help of Beriḥa, as well as similar movements of REFUGEES from Hungary and Czechoslovakia, a figure of some 60,000 to 65,000 transients is reached. The flight from Poland was mainly motivated by the murderous antisemitism there, exacerbated by the political struggle between the Communist regime and the strong opposition to it. The anti-Jewish action reached its climax on July 4, 1946, in the pogrom of KIELCE, following a ritual-murder accusation, with forty-two fatalities and a large number of injured. In the wake of the pogrom, 90,000 to 95,000 Jews fled from Poland between July

and September 1946. Some of this flow was so sudden that the Beriḥa organization could not cope with it, and many fled across borders without any organized help. Later in that year the flow abated, and by early 1947 it became a trickle. During the summer and autumn of that year, the cooperation of the Polish and Czechoslovak governments in enabling the refugees to cross the borders was obtained, probably for a mixture of political and genuinely humanitarian reasons.

As the Beriḥa movements decreased in early 1947—a brief revival occurred from March through July, when some nineteen thousand Romanian Jews fled to Vienna by means of the Beriḥa to escape from a combination of hunger and political constriction —Beriḥa became hierarchically organized. Ephraim Dekel of the Hagana in Palestine became the organization's European leader, subject to the ALIYA BET immigration organization, headed by Shaul Avigur in Paris. But the transit points were slowly dismantled as activists moved to the coasts themselves, and in 1948, after the establishment of Israel, immigration became legal. Nevertheless, for countries from which no legal exit was possible, Beriḥa continued to maintain a skeleton framework under Meir Sapir in 1949.

The approximately 250,000 Jews who used the Beriḥa routes made it the largest organized illegal mass movement in modern times. No literature or propaganda of any kind was ever published by Beriḥa. It never needed to call on Jews to leave their homes; on the contrary, it often could not cope with the flow of people who wanted to escape. Thus, it was truly a service organization.

BIBLIOGRAPHY

Bauer, Y. *Bricha: Flight and Rescue.* New York, 1970.

Dekel, E. *B'richa: Flight to the Homeland.* New York, 1972.

YEHUDA BAUER

BERLIN, capital of Prussia and, from 1871 to 1945, of GERMANY. On the eve of World War II, Berlin's population was at its peak—4.34 million—and it was the second largest city in Europe.

Jews had been living in Berlin since the end of the thirteenth century; in 1573 they were expelled, and a hundred years later, in 1671, Jews again came to settle in Berlin. In the seventeenth and eighteenth centuries the Jewish population in Berlin kept growing— despite efforts by the kings of Prussia to limit their number—and by the middle of the nineteenth century it had risen to two thousand. Berlin was the first center of Haskalah, the Jewish cultural enlightenment movement; its most renowned exponent, Moses Mendelssohn, lived there. It was in Berlin, in 1778, that the Jüdische Freischule was established, the first Jewish institution of learning in which the German language was taught and general subjects were included in the curriculum.

In the nineteenth century and the early years of the twentieth century, the Jewish population of Berlin increased greatly—from 3,300 in 1812, to 36,000 in 1871, 94,000 in 1895, and 142,000 in 1910. The rapid rise was the result of a mass influx of Jews from the provincial towns; from the eastern provinces of Imperial Germany, especially from Posen (Pol., Poznań); and from eastern Europe. A high percentage of the Berlin Jewish population was therefore made up of *Ostjuden*— Jews from the east—a situation that had considerable impact on both the Jewish and the non-Jewish population of Berlin.

Jews in Berlin were prominent in various aspects of the city's economic, intellectual, and cultural life. The city was also the seat of the head offices of most of the national Jewish organizations—such as the CENTRAL-VEREIN DEUTSCHER STAATSBÜRGER JÜDISCHEN GLAUBENS (Central Union of German Citizens of Jewish Faith), the Ezra Society, the Zentralwohlfahrtstelle der Deutschen Juden (Central Welfare Organization of German Jews), and the Central Lodge of B'NAI B'RITH in Germany—and of most of the Jewish periodicals published in Germany.

Up to the end of World War I, control of the Jewish community was in the hands of wealthy liberals; after the war, the Jüdische Volkspartei, or Jewish People's Party—an alignment of the Zionists, including Mizraḥi and the Union of Eastern European Jewish Organizations—gained in strength in the Jewish community organization, and in 1928 a representative of that party, Georg Kareski, was elected president of the community. In 1930 the liberals were returned to power and Wilhelm Kleeman became president. The spokesman for the positions taken by liberal Jews was Leo BAECK, Berlin's leading liberal rabbi.

In 1923 the Berlin community took the initiative for the formation of a Preussischer Landesverband Jüdischer Gemeinden (Union of Jewish Communities in Prussia), in order to strengthen its own status among the other communities and to facilitate contacts with the government authorities. In the early 1930s Berlin is estimated to have had 115 Jewish houses of prayer. The community itself maintained 17 synagogues, with a seating capacity of 25,000; on the high holidays, extra halls were rented that doubled the available seating capacity, the services being either liberal or traditional. The community also supported dozens of religious congregations, including Orthodox prayer houses and a Sephardic synagogue. In the 1930s the community school system consisted of fifteen kindergartens, several elementary schools, two junior high schools, and one secondary school (*Gymnasium*). Adas Israel, the separatist Orthodox community, maintained its own elementary and secondary school and a girls' school. By the late 1920s one-seventh of all the Jewish children were attending Jewish schools. There were differences of opinion among the Jews concerning the educational role of the community—whether it should maintain a separate Jewish school system, based on Jewish values, or whether it should prefer a national German framework, with a minimum emphasis on Jewish elements. For the Jewish students attending the public schools, the community provided forty-eight *Religionsschulen* (Hebrew schools).

Jewish youth movements were active in Berlin, supported by the various Jewish politically oriented organizations. The community maintained youth centers, provided summer vacations in the country for thousands of children, arranged foster homes, and made vocational training facilities available. The Jewish youth had their own gyms and playgrounds. Bar Kochba was the leading sports club, and a Maccabi organization was established in 1921.

The Berlin community provided welfare services, with its institutions serving as a model for the entire country. The Jewish welfare office coordinated the operations of the various Jewish welfare organizations. The community maintained twenty four regional welfare and youth offices, an office for aid to the disabled, twelve orphanages, dozens of day nurseries for the infants of working mothers, poorhouses, a network of soup kitchens and school kitchens, and *Winterhilfe* (special aid in the cold season—initially as part of the overall organization and, after Hitler's rise to power, independently). The community also ran its own medical facilities, such as a 350-bed hospital (which operated throughout the war), a hospital for the disabled, two medical clinics, institutions for the blind, the deaf, and the mentally ill, and a training school for the staff of these establishments. The community also had loan institutions, a vocational training and counseling office, a section providing assistance to academically qualified persons, an employment office, and an emigration advisory of-

fice. The Jewish community was the largest Jewish employer, its annual budget for 1928 amounted to some 10 million marks, of which 30 percent was used for religious activities, 12 percent for education and vocational training, 30 percent for welfare and aid, and the remainder for maintenance and miscellaneous purposes. Revenue from taxes covered 60 percent of the expenditures. The separatist community, Adas Israel, in addition to its schools, provided welfare services and maintained its own cemetery.

In 1925, 50 percent of the breadwinners were salaried employees, of whom 80 percent were office workers, 18 percent manual workers, and 2 percent house servants. The economic depression of the early 1930s, coupled with the growing antisemitism, caused many Jews to apply to the Jewish employment office, with 50 percent of such applicants coming from the commercial sector, 25 percent from among the skilled workers, 15 percent from the ranks of unskilled workers, and 10 percent from the professional class.

In that same period a large number of Jews opted out of the organized Jewish community, either in order to convert (mainly to enter into a mixed marriage) or in order to avoid paying the community tax by turning *konfessionslos* (not belonging to any recognized religious denomination).

Under the Weimar Republic, Berlin was Germany's center of culture. Many Jews gained fame as theater directors, actors, playwrights, film producers, musicians, artists, and journalists. Despite the difficulties caused by the economic situation, Jews achieved success in the professions, many earning distinguished reputations in medicine, and held posts in the city's universities and academies. Jews were also prominent as entrepreneurs.

At the same time, however, Jews became the targets of antisemitic attacks. In the wake of the murder of two leaders of the leftist Spartacus League, Karl Liebknecht and Rosa Luxemburg (the latter a Jew, born in Poland), in January 1919, a wave of riots against *Ostjuden* was launched. Similar riots also occurred during the short-lived revolutionary attempt, the Kapp Putsch, in March 1920. In November 1923, an area in the eastern part of Berlin that was inhabited by Jews

Rosa Luxemburg, leader of the left-wing revolutionary Spartaksbund. She was killed by German army officers in January 1919 while being taken to the Moabit prison in Berlin. [Internationaal Instituut voor Sociale Geschiedenis; Beth Hatefutsoth]

from eastern Europe was the scene of a pogrom.

In 1926 Joseph GOEBBELS was appointed *Gauleiter* of Berlin and founded *Der Angriff* (The Attack), a Nazi party organ, which he used to spread Nazi antisemitism and incite the population against Berlin's "Jewish press." Goebbels exploited the February 1930 killing of Horst Wessel, an SA (Sturmabteilung; Storm Troopers) man in Berlin, to launch a campaign against the city's Jews. On the Jewish New Year of 1931, Jews on their way home from the synagogues were attacked on the Kurfürstendamm in western Berlin. The next year, 1932, saw a spate of attacks on Jewish university students and lecturers in the city. The election campaign that year served to intensify the antisemitic

atmosphere. This was followed by a decrease in the number of Jews opting out of Berlin's Jewish community, and a rise in the community's tax revenue and in separate Jewish cultural activities.

In the September 1930 elections the Nazi party received 14.6 percent of the vote, four times as much as in the 1928 elections. The collapse of German democracy was accompanied by a crisis in the functioning of the Berlin city council. In the July 1932 elections the Nazis obtained 28.6 percent of the vote (as against 37.4 percent on the national level); in the November elections that same year, the Nazis lost some of their support and gained only 25.9 percent of the vote (33 percent in the whole of Germany).

On the night of January 30, 1933, the SA celebrated Hitler's appointment as Reich chancellor by staging a torchlight parade in the streets of Berlin. Jews who had been active in anti-Nazi political parties and organizations fled the city. It was at this point that the first wave of suicides hit the Jewish community, a phenomenon that was to repeat itself time and again for as long as the community continued to exist. On the night of the Reichstag fire (February 27, 1933), SA troops attacked the offices of the Centralverein.

The "Aryanization" of Jewish-owned enterprises began in 1933. As early as April 11 of that year, the newspaper announced that the businesses owned by its publisher, Rudolf Mosse, had been Aryanized. On August 1, the Berlin-Lichtenberg municipality revoked trading licenses that had been granted to Jews. On July 20, 1935, Berlin police closed down the Jewish-owned stores on the Kurfürstendamm. Until the KRISTALLNACHT pogrom, however, it was mainly the salaried employees who bore the brunt of Nazi policy in Berlin, as in all of Germany, whereas Jewish businesses continued to operate on the local as well as the international scene.

The Jewish leadership of Berlin made efforts to work out new principles that would assure the city's Jews a continued existence as a religious minority, within the framework of Nazi policies. The community bylaws were adapted to Nazi demands. A wall-to-wall coalition was formed, in which Alfred Klee, of the Jüdische Volkspartei, played a major role; Heinrich Stahl, of the Liberal (Reform Jewish) Association, was president of the community. At the end of 1933 an agreement was reached for the establishment of the REICHSVERTRETUNG DER DEUTSCHEN JUDEN (Reich Representation of German Jews), with its head office in Berlin.

There was an upsurge of Zionist activities in the Nazi period, in which the Zionist organ *Jüdische Rundschau*, edited by Robert WELTSCH, played a major part. He-Haluts and other Zionist youth movements gained substantial strength, and *hakhsharot* (agricultural training centers) were set up for their members, including those of the religiously observant youth organizations. Recha Freier founded YOUTH ALIYA, which aimed to take young Jews to Palestine. Zionist activists, aided by emissaries from abroad, helped organize "illegal" immigration to Palestine. Welfare agencies and educational institutions also greatly increased the scope of their operations; Jewish students from the public schools transferred to the community-maintained schools, and the Hochschule (from 1934, Lehranstalt) für die Wissenschaft des Judentums (College of Jewish Studies) expanded the range of its work. In response to the book burning staged by the Nazis in front of the Berlin Opera on May 10, 1933, the KULTURBUND DEUTSCHER JUDEN (Cultural Society of German Jews) was established, launching its activities in the fall of that year. The Jewish press improved the quality of its contents and raised its circulation. The Jews of Berlin turned inward, beginning a new life that saw the flourishing of Jewish culture.

Like the rest of German Jewry, the Jews of Berlin suffered from the Nazi restrictions and persecution campaign. The relaxation of anti-Jewish measures on the eve of the Olympic games in Berlin, in summer 1936, was of short duration, coming to an end as soon as the games were over. On May 30, 1937, a *Razzia* (raid) against Jews took place in the streets of Berlin, for all passersby to see.

The year 1933 also marked the beginning of a steady rise of Jewish migration, from all over Germany, including Berlin. Detailed figures on the movement of Jews to and from Berlin in the period 1933 to 1937 have not been preserved; of the 22,636 Jews who emigrated from Germany in 1937, 5,558 are known to have had their homes in Berlin. By the end of 1937 the Jewish population decreased to 140,000, and by September 1939 to 82,788—which was about 50 percent of the population figure in 1933. In Germany as a whole, the number of Jews in that period was reduced to approximately one-third of the number in 1933. This disparity between the rate of emigration from Berlin and that from the rest of the country may have meant that the Jews of Berlin felt more secure than other German Jews. In January 1939 the ZENTRALSTELLE FÜR JÜDISCHE AUSWANDERUNG (Central Office for Jewish Emigration) was set up in Berlin, on the model of an office that the Nazis had first established in Vienna.

On March 5, 1938, the Berlin Jewish community, like the other Jewish communities in Germany, was deprived of its status as a recognized public corporate body. In August 1939 it was reestablished as a "society" under the aegis of the Reichsvereinigung der Juden in Deutschland (the successor of the Reichsvertretung); in the interim period, between March 1938 and August 1939, the community was administered by an emergency committee of three (Heinrich STAHL, Moritz Henschel, and Herbert Selinger). From August 1939 on, the community was classified, in legal terms, as a "Jewish religious society," administered by a five-man committee and supervised by the Gestapo. Up to March 1940 Stahl was the chairman of the committee; he was followed by Henschel, who remained in office until February 1943, when the society was dissolved on Gestapo orders.

On *Kristallnacht* (November 9–10, 1938), most of the synagogues of Berlin were burnt down, and Jewish schools, the offices of Jewish public institutions, and Jewish medical clinics came under attack. Jewish department stores were stormed and ransacked, and the shattering of the shopwindows of the Jewish clothing stores on Leipzigerstrasse gave the pogrom its name. Dozens of Jews were murdered, and several thousand were arrested and taken to concentration camps (mainly to the ORANIENBURG camp). In the

A Jewish snowman in Berlin (1939). [Bildarchiv Preussischer Kulturbesitz]

Staatsarchiv), and in the Berlin city council archives. Religious services were permitted in four synagogues only (that number being increased to nine in early 1939). Only one Jewish newspaper, *Das Jüdische Nachrichtenblatt*, was allowed to be published in Berlin after November 1938.

As of December 3 of that year, Jews were no longer free to move about as they liked. Under the *Judenbann* (ban on Jews), they were prohibited from entering government office compounds. The Berlin police also prohibited Jews from using bathhouses and public swimming pools. During the war, the only place where the Jews were allowed to take walks was the Weissensee Jewish cemetery, but in May 1942 even that was put out of bounds.

Also in December 1938, the evacuation of Jews from residences in the prestigious parts of the city was launched, the official pretext being Albert SPEER's plans for the rebuilding of Berlin. At that point the Jewish community's housing advisory office—which was subject to city police orders—was given wide powers regarding the housing of Berlin Jews. In the final stage, when the community was being liquidated, the data accumulated by that office was a major source for drawing up the lists of Jews to be deported to their death.

In the post-*Kristallnacht* period, the Jewish community leaders saw their major task as facilitating the emigration from the Reich of the greater part of German Jewry, and, in the meantime, as creating temporary frameworks that would enable the Jews to hold out until their chance for emigration came.

At the outbreak of the war, an estimated 75,500 Jews were living in Berlin. The community employment office sought to find them productive job opportunities. In March 1941 Berlin Jews were also subjected to a labor draft; they were paid a wage from which various deductions were made, including a head tax that went to the community.

In early 1941 some 74,500 Jews were still living in Berlin; by October 1941 another 1,350 had emigrated, the last group of emigrants leaving the city on October 18 of that year. On October 23 further emigration of Jews from Germany was prohibited. It is known, however, that another 62 Jews managed to get out by December of 1941, and

wake of *Kristallnacht*, twelve hundred Jewish commercial enterprises in Berlin were put up for Aryanization; buyers were found for seven hundred, while the remaining five hundred were declared unsalable.

Other developments that followed *Kristallnacht* were the closing down, looting, and burning of dozens of Jewish institutions and the confiscation of their property, among them the Lehranstalt für die Wissenschaft des Judentums, the rabbinical seminary, the Jewish community library and museum, the archives of the community and of the Centralverein, and the library of the Adas Israel community. Also confiscated were the Jewish manuscripts, documents, and books in the libraries of Berlin universities, in the Bible Research Institute of the University of Berlin, in the Prussian State Archives (Geheimes another 9 Jews left the country legally in the course of 1942. On September 19, 1942, the yellow badge (*see* BADGE, JEWISH) was distributed to the Jews in community offices, for which they had to pay ten pfennig. This well-organized distribution process enabled the community officials to carry out Gestapo orders to update the existing card index of Jewish residents of Berlin.

On the Day of Atonement in 1941, while Rabbi Leo BAECK was preaching, three top officials of the community (the president, Moritz Henschel; his deputy, Philip Kotzover; and the director of the housing office, Martha Mosse) were called out of the synagogue and summoned to Gestapo headquarters. There they were told of an impending operation under which a substantial number of Jews were to be evacuated from Berlin. The community was ordered to submit without delay up-to-date lists of the city's Jews, including their addresses, and to turn the Levetzow Street synagogue into a transit camp for one thousand evacuees. Later, other such assembly points, pending evacuation, were set up in such places as the Jewish home for the aged, the community office building, and the Jewish hospital.

The deportation of Jews, under the cover of evacuation of the apartments they were occupying, now became the established route. A few days prior to the date fixed for their reporting to the assembly place, deportees were advised that in view of their impending departure for emigration (*Abwanderung*), their apartment leases had run out; they were also ordered to submit to the community office a declaration containing a detailed list of all their property. This declaration was used by the community and the chiefs of the housing authority in Berlin in the liquidation of Jewish property in the city. (These lists have survived.) A JÜDISCHER ORDNUNGS-DIENST—a form of Jewish police—was set up to make sure that the deportees would report at the appointed time.

Hundreds of Jews committed suicide rather than face deportation. In order to stem the panic, the publication of obituary notices was restricted, and a special section was formed in the Jewish hospital to handle the suicide cases. Some Jews tried to go underground (a number of them were helped by German organizations), and others tried to escape to neighboring countries. The Gestapo activated a network of Jewish informants that succeeded in locating many Jews who had gone underground.

The first transport left Berlin on October 18, 1941, taking some one thousand Jews to the Łódź ghetto, and from there to their deaths. Up to January 20, 1942, the day of the WANNSEE CONFERENCE, ten thousand Jews from Berlin were deported to their deaths, in nine transports, their destinations being RIGA, MINSK, KOVNO, and Łódź. The first transport for the THERESIENSTADT ghetto left Berlin on June 6, 1942; the first to go straight to AUSCHWITZ left Berlin on July 11 of that year.

In May 1942 the Jewish Communist underground exploded a fire bomb at the anti-Soviet exhibition "The Soviet Paradise"; as retaliation, 500 Jews were seized, of whom 250 were shot to death on the spot and the other 250 were deported to the Sachsenhausen camp. The Haluts underground in Berlin ordered its members to go into hiding. In June, the services provided by the Jewish community were curtailed; the schools were closed down, and some of the community staff were deported to the extermination camps. Alois BRUNNER—Adolf EICHMANN's deputy—was not satisfied with the rate at which the deportations were being carried out and took personal charge of the deportations in November and December of 1942. In December, when some of the Jews summoned for deportation had not reported, a corresponding number of Jews were seized in the Jewish community offices and put on the deportation train or shot to death on the spot. It is estimated that in the course of 1942 the number of Jews in Berlin was reduced from fifty-five thousand to thirty-three thousand.

On January 26 and 27, 1943, the senior officers of the Reichsvereinigung—Paul EPPSTEIN, Philip Kotzover, and Rabbi Leo Baeck—were deported to Theresienstadt. Until the beginning of 1943, Jews employed in the German armament industry were considered safe from deportation; however, on February 27 and 28 such Jews were rounded up at their place of work and taken straight to the assembly points. The large number of prisoners seized on this occasion required the use of improvised places of detention, including the Jewish community building and a concert hall. Among the Jews arrested were the spouses of Aryans, and those who had been exempt from wearing the yellow badge; some of these Jews were released, perhaps because of a demonstration that was staged by their wives.

On January 28, 1943, the Gestapo ordered the Berlin Jewish community legally liquidated, and a month later, on February 22, Henschel reported that the order had been carried out. Jews who were not subject to deportation were trained to take over various posts in the Jewish hospital and in the Rest-Reichsvereinigung (the "rump" association).

The great deportations of February and March 1943 had Auschwitz as their destination. The number of Jews left in Berlin in March of that year is estimated at 27,260, which by the following month had gone down to 18,300. Goebbels noted in his diary on April 11, 1943, that "Berlin's liberation from the Jews" was one of the regime's most important political achievements. In early June 1943 only 6,800 Jews were left in the city. On June 10, the offices of the Jewish community, as well as of all other Jewish organizations in Berlin, were closed down and the remaining employees were deported to their death. The capital of the Third Reich was declared *judenrein* ("cleansed of Jews").

The Jewish hospital, directed by Dr. Walter Lustig, was in operation up to the end of the war; it served mainly as an assembly camp for Jews from Berlin and other parts of Germany, pending their deportation to the extermination camps. The Jewish cemetery in Weissensee was also functioning. The last deportations from Berlin took place on January 5, 1945 (to Auschwitz); February 2, 1945 (to SACHSENHAUSEN and RAVENSBRÜCK); and March 27, 1945 (to Theresienstadt). A total of 63 deportation transports, carrying thirty-five thousand Jews, left Berlin for the various extermination camps, and 117 transports, consisting of a total of fifteen thousand Jews, went to the Theresienstadt ghetto.

It is estimated that forty-seven hundred Jews married to Aryans survived in Berlin, plus another fourteen hundred Jews who had gone into hiding; nineteen hundred Jews returned to Berlin from the extermination camps.

BIBLIOGRAPHY

Bàker, L. *Days of Sorrow and Pain: Leo Baeck and the Berlin Jews.* New York, 1978.

Ball-Kaduri, K. J. "Berlin is 'Purged' of Jews: The Jews in Berlin in 1943." *Yad Vashem Studies* 5 (1963): 271–316.

Bendt, V. "Die Synagogen unter dem Nationalsozialismus." In vol. 2 of *Synagogen in Berlin*, edited by R. Bothe and V. Bendt, pp. 49–123. Berlin, 1983.

Offenberg, M., ed. *Adass Jisroel: Die Jüdische Gemeinde in Berlin (1869–1942): Vernichtet und vergessen.* Berlin, 1986.

Sellenthin, H. G. *Geschichte der Juden in Berlin und des Gebäudes Fasanenstrasse 79/80.* Berlin, 1959.

GABRIEL E. ALEXANDER

BERLIN DOCUMENTS CENTER. *See* Documentation Centers: Berlin Documents Center.

BERMAN, ADOLF ABRAHAM (1906–1978), psychologist, Zionist activist in the WARSAW ghetto underground, and one of the leaders of ZEGOTA (the Polish Council for Aid to Jews) in the Polish part of Warsaw. Berman obtained his D.Phil. degree at Warsaw University and was director of the Jewish center of psychological counseling clinics in Warsaw. He also taught in high schools and published articles dealing with social and educational psychology. From his early years, he was active in the Left Po'alei Zion. Under the German occupation, he was director of CENTOS (Federation of Associations for the Care of Orphans in Poland) in the Warsaw ghetto, a league affiliated with the Jewish self-help organization. Berman was active in the political underground and was one of the founders of the Antifascist Bloc, the precursor to the ŻYDOWSKA ORGANIZACJA BOJOWA (Jewish Fighting Organization; ŻOB) in the ghetto.

In September 1942, Berman moved to the "Aryan" side of Warsaw, together with his wife, Batya, who had been active in the ghetto underground as manager of a network of lending libraries. Posing as a Pole, Berman lived among the Poles up to the end of the war, making strenuous efforts to help the Jews, as representative of the Żydowski Komitet Narodowy (Jewish National Committee) and as secretary of Zegota. Owing to his connections and his non-Jewish appearance, he was able to move about freely and promote widespread efforts for the rescue of Jews surviving in Warsaw after the liquidation of the ghetto. He also helped to save the written records that had been hidden on the "Aryan" side, among them the last of the chronicles recorded by Emanuel RINGELBLUM. In January 1944, Berman fell into the hands of Polish blackmailers, but was freed by the help of his Polish friends and the payment of ransom.

When Poland was liberated, Berman became the chairman of the Central Committee of the Jews of Poland and a member of the Polish parliament. In 1950 he settled in Israel, was active in the leftist political camp, was elected to the second Knesset (Israeli parliament), and was involved in the activities of survivors' organizations and former underground fighters living in Israel. His underground and public activities during the Holocaust period are described in his two books, *The Underground Period* (1971) and *In the Place Where Fate Brought Me: With the Jews of Warsaw, 1939–1942* (1978; both in Hebrew).

BIBLIOGRAPHY

Kermish, J. "The Activities of the Council for Aid to Jews ('Zegota') in Occupied Poland." In *Rescue Attempts during the Holocaust*, edited by I. Gutman and E. Zuroff, pp. 367–398. Jerusalem, 1977.

ISRAEL GUTMAN

BERMUDA CONFERENCE, conference convened by the United States and Great Britain on April 19, 1943, ostensibly to find solutions for wartime refugees. In fact, it marked the high point of efforts by officials in both nations to thwart a move for more effective action to rescue European Jewry.

The idea of convening a refugee conference grew out of a need, felt first by British authorities in the final months of 1942, to defuse public protest after revelations were confirmed that the Nazi regime had actually begun a policy of systematic liquidation of Jews.

The British initiative rekindled a familiar diplomatic game between the two Allied governments. Diplomatic dispatches from both sides were prefaced with long recitations of the efforts they had undertaken in the rescue cause. The American dispatches even mentioned the internment of Japanese-Americans as evidence of the heavy burden the country was supporting. Resentful of the initiative's implication, American dispatches spoke of the forthcoming conference as if the idea had originated in Washington, much to the chagrin of the British, who hastened to correct the misimpression.

The site of the meeting also created some conflict, since neither side wanted to be linked directly to the refugee-rescue debacle—the lack of any serious effort to rescue Jews. Thus, Canada discouraged a suggestion that the conference convene in Ottawa, and the State Department (*see* UNITED STATES DEPARTMENT OF STATE) rejected Washington. Finally Assistant Secretary of State Breckinridge Long suggested the island of Bermuda, which, because of its inaccessibility during wartime, would allow both sides control of the press, and the conference itself could be kept free of the representatives of private agencies such as the JOINT DISTRIBUTION COMMITTEE (JDC) and the WORLD JEWISH CONGRESS.

As preparations for the conference developed, it was clear that both sides had set such severe limitations on what might be discussed and who might speak at the plenary sessions that the conference would have virtually nothing to show for its trouble. There was an insistence that the Jewish character of the problem be played down and a more universal approach assumed. The British, in the face of information that the Germans had earmarked the Jews for extinction, insisted that Jews were merely one of many victimized groups. The State Department continued to employ the term "political refugee," a euphemism to conceal the racial character of the refugee problem. In fact, neither side wanted to discuss the matter of the "Final Solution" but preferred to limit debate to the "refugee question." Even at that, the prohibition on circumventing American immigration laws that had been invoked at the EVIAN CONFERENCE remained in force. In the event (claimed as unlikely) that shipping should become available, the American delegation insisted that prisoners of war receive priority over refugees. Actually, there never was a shortage of ships with empty holds returning to American ports. Discussion concerning Palestine, the likeliest haven, was ruled out, as was the possibility of direct negotiations with Berlin. Not even the suggestion of sending food packages to concentration camp inmates was ac-

cepted for discussion, although the British themselves had established a precedent for such a policy by feeding the inhabitants of occupied Greece throughout the war. The conference found itself in the embarrassing situation of having little left to discuss.

The disparity in rank between the two delegations also caused unforeseen problems. Composed of Richard Law, son of a former prime minister and parliamentary undersecretary of state, and Osbert Peake and George Hall of the Home Office, the British delegation far outranked the American. This was especially so after Myron Taylor, President Franklin D. ROOSEVELT's personal emissary to the Vatican, and James G. MCDONALD, former League of Nations high commissioner for refugees from Germany, declined to head the American delegation. The State Department was compelled to settle for Harold Willis Dodds, president of Princeton University; Sen. Scott Lucas, Democrat of Illinois; and Rep. Sol Bloom, Democrat from Manhattan and chairman of the House Committee on Foreign Affairs. The last-mentioned, a Jew, was destined to become the most controversial member of the American delegation because Jewish rescue agencies found him unacceptable. Two of the technical experts supporting the American delegation, G. Robert Borden Reams and Robert C. Alexander, had earned similar reputations among rescue advocates for their adamant opposition to refugees. The only sympathetic member of the delegation was George Backer, whose leading positions in the Organization for Rehabilitation through Training (ORT) and the Jewish Telegraph Agency made him especially knowledgeable about the fate of European Jewry.

The composition of the American delegation; the refusal to include Joseph SCHWARTZ, head of the European branch of the JDC; the rejection of rescue suggestions by Joseph Proskauer, head of the AMERICAN JEWISH COMMITTEE, and by Rabbi Stephen S. WISE, head of the American and World Jewish congresses; and the fact that the State Department limited the number of press correspondents to five, representing the major news agencies, convinced even the most hopeful rescue advocates (mostly, but not exclusively, American Jewish groups) that the Bermuda Conference

MEMORANDUM

February 22, 1944

Memorandum of Myron C. Taylor re Bermuda Conference and the IGC. (Material obtained from file in Visa Division, State Department)

Myron C. Taylor addressed a memorandum on April 30, 1943, to Welles, Long, and Hull. The occasion was a wire from the Department to London requesting a meeting of the Intergovernmental Committee after the Bermuda Conference. A note in the file states that Mr. Taylor initialled the wire only on condition that his memorandum be presented to Mr. Long and the Secretary.

The text of the memorandum follows:

"Before any meeting is called the position of our own Government with respect to the refugee situation must be clearly developed. The Bermuda Conference was wholly ineffective, as I view it, and we knew it would be. What the IGC may be able to do, of course, is open to question, but with respect to anything that it may be able to do, it will require a commitment and large financial obligation if the plight of the refugees generally is to be relieved. The commitment also obligates this Government, if made, to find not only temporary places of refuge, but permanent places of settlement. It is my opinion, as it was before the Bermuda Conference, that the position of our Government and of the British Government must be thoroughly clarified and clearly understood in advance and if nothing constructive can be assured, such a meeting will only be another failure.

Myron C. Taylor"

The following penciled notation appears at the bottom: "Eu concurs with Mr. Taylor's memorandum. T.B.C.", and below this notation were several initials which could not be deciphered. Opposite Mr. Long's name at the top were the words, in ink, "I agree".

Memorandum from Myron C. Taylor, the principal American representative at the Evian Conference, to Cordell Hull, the secretary of state, and Sumner Welles and Breckinridge Long, assistant secretaries of state, regarding the failure of the Bermuda Conference.

would be simply a ploy to deflect an aroused public opinion.

Yet even that objective eluded the conferees, who tried to find a strategy that could create the illusion of action while at the same time making certain that nothing untoward was in fact done. Much time was devoted to the notion of revitalizing the INTERGOVERNMENTAL COMMITTEE ON REFUGEES (IGCR), which was originally created at the Evian Conference in 1938 to enter into negotiations with Berlin on the refugee question. But the disinterring of the virtually defunct agency posed problems. Since negotiating with the Nazi regime had now been ruled out by the delegations, neither side was willing to fund the IGCR, and certainly the Jewish agencies, which had originally underwritten it, were reluctant to enter into an agreement that they felt was designed to thwart rather than to aid rescue. The second objective—to enhance the flow of refugees out of areas such as Spain and Switzerland, where they had found a precarious haven, by establishing a refugee camp in North Africa—offered more hope. But this suggestion, rather than dealing with the millions in the Nazi grip, focused on those whose lives, though uncomfortable, were at least not in danger. Moreover, there was much opposition by the United States War Department and the British Foreign Office to establishing such a camp in a Muslim area. It was not established until over a year after the conference ended, when it was too late to do any good.

An early press release, sounding a hopeful note, stated that all problems were being discussed openly and good progress was being made. In fact, both delegations manifested the fear that Berlin would "dump" refugees with the Allies and use them as a weapon to compromise the Allied drive for final victory. The conference was in danger of rejecting all proposals and thereby defeating its own goal of soothing an aroused public opinion. It was George Backer, speaking to the conference on April 25, who pointed out this danger. He observed that shipping was in fact available, and that by limiting its concern to those who had found haven in neutral nations the conference would have nothing significant to show. It should at least try, Backer urged, to rescue 125,000 Jews in eastern Europe who imminently faced certain death. Backer made a special plea to save the thousands of Jewish children who could assure a Jewish future despite the radical losses. But this plea too was rejected.

A brief optimistic news bulletin that spoke of the possibility of helping "a substantial number of refugees" marked the end of the conference, but a final report of the deliberations and conclusions was not published until December 10, 1943, eight months later. The public embarrassment that Backer had predicted came to pass. The American Jewish press was virtually unanimous in condemning the conference. Some spoke of it as a particularly cruel duplicity in the midst of a mass-murder operation. Public protest, rather than being stilled, reached new heights. Even the small camp established in North Africa in March 1944 housed only 630 refugees, and strict orders were issued by the State Department that there should be "a good mix" in selecting them.

The use of a conference to assuage an aroused public sentiment reveals much about the American aspect of the Holocaust. It illustrates that even when it was possible to arouse an otherwise lethargic public about the fate of European Jewry, government officials experienced few qualms in devising strategies to deflect its concern. Both the British and American governments were willing to go to extraordinary lengths to avoid doing what needed to be done. The episode gives historians a clue to the atmosphere and intentions surrounding the rescue of the Jews.

BIBLIOGRAPHY

Feingold, H. L. *The Politics of Rescue.* New Brunswick, N.J., 1970.
Wasserstein, B. *Britain and the Jews of Europe, 1939–1945.* Oxford, 1979.
Wyman, D. S. *The Abandonment of the Jews: America and the Holocaust, 1941–1945.* New York, 1984.

HENRY L. FEINGOLD

BERNADOTTE, FOLKE (1895–1948), Swedish statesman; count of Wisborg and nephew of King Gustav V. During World War II Bernadotte represented the Swedish RED CROSS in the exchange of prisoners between Germany and the Allies. In 1943 he became its vice president and in 1946 he was appointed its president. Bernadotte negotiated with Heinrich HIMMLER on behalf of the Swedish Red Cross, and in March and April of 1945 succeeded in persuading him to release more than seven thousand Scandinavian nationals who were being held in Nazi concentration camps; these included over four hundred Danish Jews imprisoned in THERESIENSTADT.

Following a meeting between Norbert Masur, the representative of the WORLD JEWISH CONGRESS in Sweden, and Himmler, Bernadotte also succeeded in arranging for the release of ten thousand women from the RAVENSBRÜCK concentration camp; two thousand of the women, who were nationals of various countries, were Jewish. Most of them were transferred to SWEDEN.

On May 20, 1948, the United Nations Security Council appointed Bernadotte as a mediator on its behalf between Israel and the invading Arab countries. He negotiated a four-week truce, beginning on June 11, 1948, but was unable to obtain from the Arab states an agreement for its extension. Bernadotte then worked out a plan for the settlement of the conflict based on Israeli concessions to the Arabs, but on September 17 of that year he was assassinated in Jerusalem by Hazit ha-Moledet (Fatherland Front), a group connected with the LOḤAMEI ḤERUT ISRAEL organization.

The Jewish National Fund planted a forest in the hills of Jerusalem in honor of Folke Bernadotte. His book, *Instead of Arms*, was published in 1949.

BIBLIOGRAPHY

Hewins, R. *Bernadotte: Sein Leben und Werk.* Frankfurt, 1952.
Svenson, S. *Folke Bernadotte: Fredkämpe och folksforsonare.* Stockholm, 1949.

ELISHEVA SHAUL

Folke Bernadotte.

BERNHEIM PETITION, petition against Nazi ANTI-JEWISH LEGISLATION presented to the League of Nations in May 1933. The Nazis came to power in January 1933 and in April of that year introduced anti-Jewish laws. The Jewish public outside Germany sought ways to protect the civil rights of German Jews. In their search, the Jewish activists cited the German-Polish Geneva Convention of 1922, under which both parties were committed to protect the minorities in Upper Silesia by safeguarding their equal rights and abstaining from any form of discrimination against them. That convention provided that in cases of differences in the interpretation of its provisions, the League of Nations Council would be the arbitrator, and that individuals or groups who felt that their rights under the convention were being violated would also have the right to petition the council. The Jewish activists decided to resort to this latter provision, basing themselves on a petition signed by Franz Bernheim, one of ten thousand Jewish residents of Upper Silesia, in which he complained of the anti-Jewish laws being applied in that area.

In May 1933, after the Bernheim petition had been presented to the council, the German representative informed the council that his government acknowledged that an international convention to which it had subscribed had priority over internal German legislation. On ending its deliberations, in June 1933, the council stated that the complaints raised in the Bernheim petition were valid and that Germany should abolish all discrimination against Jews in Upper Silesia.

The German government, which had reason to be interested in the full observance of the Geneva Convention, was forced to issue specific instructions to the authorities of Upper Silesia that invalidated the application of anti-Jewish legislation in that region. In addition, the German government ordered the country's central authorities to refrain from all anti-Jewish measures in Upper Silesia, and the Nazi party issued similar instructions. Finally, in September 1933, the German government submitted an explicit declaration to the League of Nations Council, in which it stated that all anti-Jewish legislation was null and void in Upper Silesia. The ongoing activities of the Comité des Délégations Juives (the international body set up after World War I to protect Jewish rights), and the measures that the Upper Silesian Jews took to organize themselves to protect their civil rights, also played a role in ensuring that these rights remained inviolate, up to May 1937, the terminal date of the German-Polish Convention. Until then, even the NUREMBERG LAWS were not applied.

Following the termination of the convention, the German and Polish governments signed a joint declaration concerning the protection of minority rights in their respective countries. This was a strictly bilateral statement that did not recognize any role for the League of Nations; in practice, the declaration meant that the Jews of Upper Silesia were being deprived of their rights.

From then on, the Nazi regime embarked upon a systematic policy designed to equate the status of Upper Silesian Jews with that of the Jews in the rest of Germany. The process was completed on March 31, 1938.

BIBLIOGRAPHY

Brugel, J. W. "The Bernheim Petition: A Challenge to Nazi Germany in 1933." *Patterns of Prejudice* 17/2 (1983): 17–25.

Feinberg, N. "Jewish Political Activities against the Nazi Regime in the Years 1933–1939." In *Jewish Resistance during the Holocaust.* Proceedings of the Conference on Manifestations of Jewish Resistance, pp. 74–93. Jerusalem, 1971.

DAVID HADAR

BESSARABIA, region situated between the Prut and Dniester rivers; the larger part is today in the Moldavian SSR and the smaller part in the Ukrainian SSR. Bessarabia was part of the principality of Moldavia until its annexation by tsarist Russia in 1812. In 1918 it was incorporated into ROMANIA, and on June 29, 1940, it was annexed to the Soviet Union, after the NAZI-SOVIET PACT and a Soviet ultimatum. In late June 1941, a few days after the German invasion of the Soviet Union, it again came under Romanian rule.

The Bessarabian Jews numbered about 205,000 in 1939. In June 1940, when the Romanian army retreated from Bessarabia, the Jews were accused of greeting the entering Soviet army as a liberator and of humiliating and striking the retreating Romanian soldiers. They were also accused of being hostile toward Romania, the Romanians, and the local inhabitants, and of collaborating with the Communist regime. In June 1941, shortly before the outbreak of the war between Germany and the USSR, the Soviet authorities deported between five thousand and ten thousand Bessarabian Jews, considered "enemies of the people," to Siberia and other remote regions. The number of Jews who succeeded in fleeing into the interior of the USSR in the first days of the German invasion was relatively small: the Soviet authorities prevented passage to the Ukraine and maintained guard units on the old border along the Dniester, and the German units swept rapidly from north to south on a wide front; within several weeks Bessarabia was in the rear. Some thirty thousand to forty thousand Jews fled, of whom twenty-five thousand were caught by the Soviet army and driven back to Bessarabia. Many escaped to ODESSA and were trapped in the siege there.

On the eve of the invasion of the Soviet Union, the Romanian dictator, Ion ANTONESCU, issued a secret edict, *Curatirea Terenului* (Cleansing of the Ground). It contained three sections, ordering on-the-spot physical extermination of all the Jews living in the villages; arrest of the Jews living in the cities and their concentration in ghettos; and detention of all the Communists and those who had served the Soviets during the year of Soviet rule in Bessarabia, with execution of those proved guilty of such collaboration. Units of gendarmes, who received the order prior to the outbreak of the war, participated in the massacre of Jews in the cities neighboring on the new border: Roman, Fălticeni, and Galaţi. The secret order for the army, code named *Ordine Speciale* (Special Orders), was transmitted to Gen. Ilie Seteflea by Ion Antonescu, and its execution was entrusted to the army administration known as Pretoria, headed by Gen. Ion Topor. The army units were ordered to help the soldiers actually engaged in the killings.

A special killing unit was hastily created from the Security Services, commanded by the deputy prime minister, Mihai ANTONESCU, and called the Esalon Special (Special Echelon). The unit, comprising about 160 soldiers, took part in the massacre of Jews and cooperated with the parallel German units. Together with the German army and Einsatzgruppe D, they massacred about 150,000 to 160,000 Jews during July and August 1941. The Romanians were responsible for most of these massacres, in which nearly all the village Jews were exterminated.

The second stage began in August 1941 with the creation of the camps and the ghettos in which the remaining Jews were concentrated. Most of the camps were established in Jewish villages such as VERTUJENI; in Jewish towns where most of the inhabitants had been killed by the Romanian army, such as MARCULEŞTI; and in Jewish quarters and ruined parts of cities and towns such as Bălţi, Soroca, and Khotin. In KISHINEV a ghetto was established in the poor and partially destroyed Jewish area, and 11,000 of the 50,000 Jews who had lived there before

the war were forced into it. On September 4, 64,176 Jews still remained in all of Bessarabia, and on September 25, there were 43,397.

The third stage began on September 15, 1941, when Ion Antonescu ordered the deportation of all the Jews of Bessarabia to TRANSNISTRIA, the area of the Ukraine occupied by Romania. It took place chiefly on foot, by way of four crossing points: Atachi, Cosauti, Rezina, and Tiraspol. Most of the Jews were deported via Atachi, a Romanian village on the banks of the Dniester. According to an official estimate, about twenty-five thousand Jews were killed during the deportation, and tens of thousands were cast into an improvised communal grave in the Cosauti Forest in central Bessarabia, which was traversed by the convoys on their way to the crossing point. Tens of thousands were drowned in the Dniester River. For about a month convoys of Jews were transferred from place to place without planning or need, the principal aim apparently being to reduce the number of Jews. Anyone falling behind was shot by the Romanian escorts.

All the property of the Bessarabian Jews was plundered in several waves of "spontaneous," organized pillage. The inspectors of the Romanian National Bank "legally" confiscated valuables, jewels, and cash, and civilians and soldiers robbed the contents of

BESSARABIA, June 1940

the deportees' homes and the belongings they had prepared to take with them. Because of massive corruption at all levels of government, only a small part of the "legally" confiscated property reached the coffers of the state treasury. Many acts of violence were committed by the general population, and far more by the Romanian soldiers. The homes, apartments, and business concerns of the Jews became state property (*averea statului*) and were handed over to the National Center of Romanization. The latter gave or sold them to Romanians, principally to ex-servicemen, widows, and Romanians from other regions.

In the census of "those of Jewish blood" conducted in May 1942, only 227 Jews were counted in the whole of Bessarabia, and most of these were Jewish only by virtue of the race laws. After the war, about 7,000 to 10,000 Jews who had fled into the Soviet Union or had been deported by the Soviet government before the war returned to Bessarabia. Some of the approximately 50,000 Jews liberated in Transnistria in the spring of 1944 had been among those deported from Bessarabia.

BIBLIOGRAPHY

Ancel, J. "The Romanian Way of Solving the 'Jewish Problem' in Bessarabia and Bukovina, June–July 1941." *Yad Vashem Studies* 19 (1988): 187–232.

JEAN ANCEL

BEST, WERNER (b. 1903), Nazi official; a senior member of the SS and Sicherheitspolizei (Security Police), and German plenipotentiary in occupied Denmark from 1942 to 1945. Born in Darmstadt to a family of officials, Best studied law and in 1929 was appointed *Gerichtsassessor* (judge) in the Hessian Department of Justice. He entered the Nazi party in 1930 and the SS in 1931. In 1933, very soon after the Nazi seizure of power, he was appointed state commissioner for the Hessian police force and police president for the province.

He progressed rapidly in subsequent years, becoming legal adviser to the Gestapo and deputy to Reinhard HEYDRICH and Heinrich HIMMLER. From 1935 to 1940 he was bureau chief in the head office of the SD (Sicherheitsdienst; Security Service) in Berlin. From September 1939 to June 1940 Best headed Section II of the REICHSSICHERHEITSHAUPTAMT (Reich Security Main Office; RSHA); it was for service in this capacity that he was later accused of complicity in the murder of Jews and members of the Polish intelligentsia in occupied Poland. He then served for two years (June 1940 to August 1942) as *Ministerialdirektor* of the military administration attached to the High Command in occupied France. His tasks included the suppression of the French Résistance and the "de-Judaizing" of France. From November 1942 until 1945, Best served as German plenipotentiary in occupied DENMARK. There is evidence that he tried to avert the impact of the "Final Solution" on the Danish Jews, almost all of whom escaped to Sweden.

In 1949 Best was sentenced to death by a Danish court, but this was commuted to twelve years' imprisonment. He was in fact released in 1951, whereupon he returned to Germany and became legal adviser to the Stinnes group of firms. A Berlin denazification court fined him 70,000 marks in 1958 as punishment for his role in the leadership of the SS. In 1969 he was arrested on charges of mass murder in Poland, but he was released on grounds of health in 1972. The charges were not formally withdrawn.

BIBLIOGRAPHY

Petrow, R. *The Bitter Years: The Invasion and Occupation of Denmark and Norway, April 1940–1945.* New York, 1974.
Yahil, L. *The Rescue of Danish Jewry: Test of a Democracy.* Philadelphia, 1969.

LIONEL KOCHAN

BETAR. *See* Youth Movements: General Survey.

BET LOḤAMEI HA-GETTA'OT. *See* Museums and Memorial Institutes: Bet Loḥamei ha-Getta'ot.

BIAŁYSTOK, city in northeastern POLAND, seat of the district of that name. Records of Białystok's existence date back to the fourteenth century. In 1807 it was handed over to the Russians; during the interwar period, it was part of independent Poland. The presence of Jews there is first mentioned in the mid-seventeenth century. The development of Białystok and of its Jewish community into a great center was the result of the growth of the textile industry in the nineteenth century. From a population of 400 at the beginning of that century, the city had grown to 61,500 by 1913; its Jewish population meanwhile ranged from 66 percent to 75 percent of the total (48,000 in 1913). In the interwar period the Jewish population went down to between 50 percent and 60 percent.

The first Jewish factory was established in 1850; by 1912, almost 90 percent of the textile factories in the city were Jewish-owned. In World War I most of the factories were destroyed; of the new factories and stores opened between 1921 and 1939, 75 percent belonged to Jews. The Jewish community had an intensive educational and cultural network.

Białystok was occupied by the Germans on September 15, 1939, but a week later, on September 22, it was handed over to the Soviet Union, which held it for the next twenty-one months. On June 27, 1941, the Germans took Białystok for the second time, and the same day, two thousand Jews were burned alive, shot, or tortured to death. That day, which the Jews came to call "Red Friday," marked the beginning of the end for the Jews of Białystok. In the first two weeks of the occupation the Jews were attacked repeatedly, and another four thousand were murdered in an open field near Pietraszek—members of the intelligentsia, Communists, and other political figures.

Two days after the occupation, the military commander of the city summoned Białystok's chief rabbi, Dr. Gedaliah Rosenmann, and the chairman of the Jewish Community Council, Efraim BARASZ, to his office and ordered them to form a JUDENRAT (Jewish Council). Within a day or two the Judenrat had come into existence, comprising twelve members, all of them veteran public figures. A month later a new Judenrat, twice the size of its predecessor, was established with Barasz as

acting chairman. A ghetto was set up and, on August 1, 1941, fifty thousand Białystok Jews were confined there (including some from the Białystok district, outside the city itself). They were packed into a small area, a newly developed non-Jewish neighborhood which was split into two parts: east and west, divided by the Biała River. The ghetto's main gate was at 3 Upiecka Street; another gate was set up at 4 Jurowiecka, and there was eventually a third gate. The Judenrat had its offices at 32 Kupiecka, and most of its departmental offices, dealing with the ghetto's day-to-day affairs, were housed there as well.

The history of the Białystok ghetto can be divided into three periods: (1) from its occupation on June 27, 1941, until August 15, 1941, during which time the city was under military rule; (2) from August 15, 1941, to November 1942, when it was under a civilian district administration; (3) from November 1942 to the final liquidation of the ghetto in August 1943, when the Gestapo and the SS were in control.

The ghetto rapidly became a center of industry, a supply base for essential items required by the economic arm of the occupation authorities—and a constant target of German plunder and pillage. Most of the Białystok Jews worked in ghetto industries; a relatively small number were employed in German establishments outside the ghetto. The ghetto had about ten factories and a large number of newly established workshops, manufacturing numerous and diverse items. The Germans made up the orders for the items to be manufactured—the army's requirements figured prominently in these—and passed them on to the Judenrat for implementation. In addition to the "legal" manufacturing operations, which dealt exclusively with the needs of the occupation authorities, the ghetto also ran a variegated, clandestine "illegal" industry, which turned out products for the use of the ghetto inhabitants themselves. There was an open trade in clothes, leather goods, and textile products, as well as other items, which were exchanged for food. Other kinds of transactions also took place, based for the most part on smuggling. The Judenrat derived a handsome income from the tax that every shopkeeper had to pay it for wares sold. By mid-1942, however, the Gestapo ordered the Judenrat to put

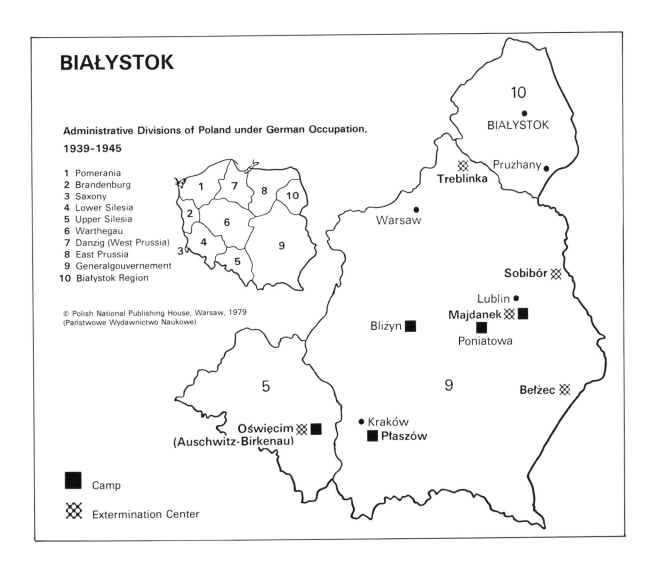

BIAŁYSTOK

Administrative Divisions of Poland under German Occupation,

1939-1945

1 Pomerania
2 Brandenburg
3 Saxony
4 Lower Silesia
5 Upper Silesia
6 Warthegau
7 Danzig (West Prussia)
8 East Prussia
9 Generalgouvernement
10 Białystok Region

© Polish National Publishing House, Warsaw, 1979
(Państwowe Wydawnictwo Naukowe)

■ Camp

✕✕ Extermination Center

an end to the commercial activities in the ghetto.

The German civil administration supplied the ghetto population with its meager rations through the Judenrat. The flow of supplies, however, was irregular, except for bread, which did appear on a more or less regular basis. In order to increase the quantity of food available in the ghetto, the Judenrat encouraged inhabitants to grow vegetables and fruit on plots of land it owned (the former sites of buildings that had been destroyed and cleared of their ruins). These plots were dubbed "Judenrat gardens."

Between September 18 and October 21, 1941, on orders given by the German authorities, the Judenrat transferred 4,500 inhabitants of the ghetto to the town of PRUZHANY, some 62 miles (100 km) south of Białystok. These were the sick, the unskilled, and the unemployed—the poorest among the ghetto population. Some of them made their way back to Białystok, but most were killed when the Pruzhany ghetto was liquidated during the last four days of January 1943.

From the beginning, the various departments of the Judenrat had to deal with difficult and complex tasks. In the ghetto there were several soup kitchens, two hospitals, an outpatient clinic, a gynecological clinic, three pharmacies, a first-aid organization, two schools, a law court, and other institutions. A JÜDISCHER ORDNUNGSDIENST (Jewish police force) was also set up by the Judenrat, with a complement of 200 men.

Under the German occupation the Jewish youth movements, whose activities had come to an almost complete stop under the Soviets, resumed their operations. By early 1942, active cells of the various movements existed in the ghetto: the Communists, the BUND, and the Zionist youth movements He-Haluts–Dror, Ha-Shomer ha-Tsa'ir, Betar, and Ha-No'ar ha-Tsiyyoni. Also at that time, a group of Ha-Shomer ha-Tsa'ir activists came to Białystok from Vilna, with the assignment, *inter alia*, of creating a united front of all the youth movements in the ghetto. There was generally agreement that the goal of such a body was to wage armed struggle against the Germans, but several questions came up, apart from the existing rivalry and mutual distrust among the various movements (especially between the Communists and all the other groups). Would such a united front leave the ghetto for the forests to join the partisans in their fight? Or should its purpose be to prepare for fighting within the ghetto, and, if so, at what point and under what circumstances should an armed struggle be launched?

It was not until August 1942, following prolonged efforts made by two Ha-Shomer ha-Tsa'ir activists, Haika GROSMAN and Adek Boraks, that a headquarters was established for the first united underground in the Białystok ghetto. Named Bloc No. 1 or Front A, the headquarters represented the Communists,

Deportation of Jews from Białystok.

Ha-Shomer ha-Tsa'ir, and a part of the Bund. In November 1942, Mordechai TENENBAUM arrived in Białystok, on behalf of the Dror movement, and Bloc No. 2 then came into being, uniting all the other movements, with the Ha-Shomer ha-Tsa'ir members participating in both blocs. Efforts to join the two blocs in a single organization continued until shortly before the liquidation of the ghetto, but only in July 1943 did a united underground come into being, with Tenenbaum as its commander and Daniel Moszkowicz, a Communist, as deputy commander.

On Tenenbaum's initiative a secret archive was established, under the direction of Zvi Mersik, on the model of the Warsaw ghetto's ONEG SHABBAT. The archive was in operation until April 1943, collecting testimonies and descriptions of events, as well as announcements issued by the Judenrat and reports of its meetings (which were channeled to the archive by Efraim Barasz). The documents, hidden on the Polish side of Białystok, were saved, and constitute an invaluable source of information. Barasz also made considerable sums of money available to Tenenbaum, but the latter's efforts to obtain arms from the Polish underground ARMIA KRAJOWA (Home Army) were all turned down.

From February 5 to 12, 1943, an *Aktion* was conducted in the ghetto, in the course of which two thousand Jews were shot on the spot and ten thousand were deported to TREBLINKA. Defense Bloc No. 1, with its meager resources, was activated and suffered many losses; other fighters, among them the Bloc commander Adek Boraks, were sent to Treblinka.

Barasz still believed that the thousands of Jews who had been deported from the ghetto would serve as scapegoats and that their sacrifice would save the remaining Jews, with the ghetto continuing to exist. In the course of the next six months, until the final liquidation of the ghetto—the threat of which was in the air throughout this period—Barasz made desperate efforts to ensure that the status quo in the ghetto was maintained, seeking to exploit the varied attitudes among the German authorities with this end in mind. The new orders that were coming in from the Wehrmacht reinforced his belief that the Białystok ghetto, which was now an important labor camp for the Germans, would not be liquidated. But this was not to be. Berlin issued the final order for the end of the ghetto, and in August 1943, Odilo GLOBOCNIK was assigned the task of its liquidation.

On the night of August 15–16, the Białystok ghetto was surrounded by three rings of German soldiers and SS men, armed with light and heavy arms, including artillery, and assisted by Ukrainian auxiliaries. One SS unit entered the ghetto and put the factories under guard. The previous night, Barasz had been summoned by the Gestapo. He was told that the ghetto inhabitants were going to be moved to LUBLIN and warned that the move had to proceed in an orderly fashion and that no resistance would be tolerated. Barasz tried in vain to have the order rescinded. The next morning, August 16, 1943, the ghetto population awoke to find the Judenrat's announcement posted on the walls, ordering it to report for immediate evacuation. The size of the ghetto population on the eve of liquidation was some thirty thousand.

At this moment—when tens of thousands of stupefied and exhausted Jews, with as many of their pitiful belongings as they could carry, were making their way to the assembly point on Jurowiecka Street—the underground rose in revolt. The precise moment was 10:00 a.m. According to a predetermined plan, the various cells of the underground took up their assigned positions, where they were to be issued arms and launch the attack. The plan was for the main force to attack the Germans along the Smolna Street fence, in order to breach the German lines and create a gap through which the fighters would make their escape to the forest. Diversionary attacks were to be made at four points, on Fabryczna, Nowogrodzka, Chmielna, and Ciepła streets, along the route where the Jews were making their way to the assembly point. The fighting was planned for the eastern side of the ghetto, where the command post of the revolt, as well as the arms cache and the fighters' bunker (at 7 Chmielna), were situated. Leaflets were passed out urging the population to disregard the evacuation order and not to proceed to the assembly point.

The fighting in the ghetto went on for five days, from August 16 to 20. The main battle in the first two days was fought over the Smolna Street fence. The fighters had only a few arms at their disposal, and over three hundred a day fell in battle. When the fighting was at its height, a large German force entered the ghetto, supported by armored cars and tanks. Realizing that the struggle inside the ghetto was lost, a group of fighters retreated into the Chmielna Street bunker, planning to make their way to the forest and continue the battle from there. On August 19, however, the Germans came upon the bunker and surrounded it, and all the seventy-two fighters in it (with one exception) were shot to death. The next day, which was the fifth day of fighting, the last defense positions—on Ciepła and Fabryczna streets—fell to the Germans. Mordechai Tenenbaum and Daniel Moszkowicz, who had led the uprising, were forced to retreat from the fighters' last stronghold, on Fabryzcna Street. There is no firm information on how they met their death, but it appears that they committed suicide.

The deportations from the ghetto began on August 18 and went on for three days, in the course of which the greater part of Białystok's Jews were deported. Some were sent to Treblinka, where they were murdered, and others to MAJDANEK, where they went through a *Selektion*. Those who were found fit were taken to the PONIATOWA camp the Bliżyn camp, or to AUSCHWITZ. A train with 1,200 Białystok children aboard was sent to THERESIENSTADT; a month later, these children too ended up in Auschwitz. In Białystok itself a "small ghetto" was left, containing 2,000 Jews, but three weeks later it too was liquidated and its occupants sent to Majdanek, among them Efraim Barasz, Gedaliah Rosenmann, and the commander of the Jewish police, Markus. They, too, were murdered in Majdanek, as were the remnants of Białystok's Jews, in the mass killing that took place in that camp on November 3, 1943 (*see* "ERNTEFEST").

In December 1942, small groups of armed men had escaped from the ghetto. By the summer of 1943, after the uprising, 150 fighters from the Białystok ghetto had joined the partisans. Several partisan units, especially the Forois (Yi., "go out") unit, which had merged with the "Jewish Group," engaged the Germans in a long series of raids. A number of young Jewish women, who had remained in Białystok posing as Aryans and had acted as couriers, maintained contact with these units. In some instances, partisan units made up of Białystok Jews received aid from the Polish and Belorussian population. In the spring of 1944, Forois linked up with Soviet partisans, at which time 60 of its Jewish partisans were still alive.

Some two hundred Jews from Białystok survived in the German camps, and several dozen were saved by hiding on the "Aryan" side of the city. Also saved were sixty fighters who had escaped to the forests and joined up with the partisans. Białystok was liberated by the Soviet army in August 1944.

BIBLIOGRAPHY

Blumenthal, N. *Conduct and Actions of a Judenrat: Documents from the Bialystok Ghetto.* Jerusalem, 1962.

Datner, S. *The Fight and Annihilation of the Białystok Ghetto.* Łódź, 1946.

Grossman, H. *The Underground Army: Fighters of the Bialystock Ghetto.* New York, 1987.

Klibanski, B. "The Underground Archives in the Bialystok Ghetto founded by Zevi Mersik and Mordecai Tenenbaum." *Yad Vashem Studies* 2 (1958): 295–330.

Schmulewitz, I., et al., eds. *The Bialystoker Memorial Book.* New York, 1982.

Sohn, D., Ed. *Bialystok: Photo Album of a Renowned City and Its Jews the World Over.* New York, 1951.

SARAH BENDER
and TERESA PREKEROWA

BIBELFORSCHER. *See* Jehovah's Witnesses.

BIBERSTEIN, MAREK (d. 1944), chairman of the JUDENRAT (Jewish Council) in KRAKÓW. Before the war, Biberstein was a prominent figure in the life of the city's Jewish community. When Kraków was occupied by the Germans, he was appointed chairman of the provisional community administration, which before long became a Judenrat, with Biberstein remaining at its head. In this capacity, he did a great deal to alleviate the lot of the community by organizing aid to those in need and by frequently intervening for the release of Jews who for one reason or another had been seized by the Germans. In June 1941, Biberstein was arrested on the charge of having violated foreign-currency regulations, but the real reason seems to have been the Germans' dissatisfaction with his conduct and their desire to remove him from his post. He was kept in prison in Tarnów until the end of July 1942, when he returned to the Kraków ghetto, a sick and broken man. A few weeks later Biberstein and his family were taken to the PŁASZÓW camp, where he perished on May 14, 1944.

BIBLIOGRAPHY

Bauminger, A., M. Bosak, and N. M. Gelber. *The Kraków Book: A Jewish Mother City.* Jerusalem, 1959. (In Hebrew.)

AHARON WEISS

BIEBOW, HANS (1902–1947), head of the ŁÓDŹ ghetto administration. Born in Bremen, Biebow was a businessman who had joined the Nazi party. When the ŁÓDŹ ghetto was established in the spring of 1940, Biebow was put in charge of its food and economic office (Ernährungs- und Wirtschaftsstelle für das Ghetto), which in October was redesignated the "ghetto administration" (Ghettoverwaltung). The office had a staff of 250 German officials. Thanks to his personal ties with Reinhard HEYDRICH, chief of the SD (Sicherheitsdienst; Security Service), and with Arthur GREISER, governor of the WARTHEGAU, Biebow enjoyed wide powers in administering the ŁÓDŹ ghetto. By exploiting the manpower in the ghetto factories that he established and by robbing the Jews of their property, Biebow was able to extract great profits. He personally made sure that the ghetto was hermetically closed and that the inhabitants would starve. He set up special warehouses in the town of Pabianice, where the personal possessions and clothing of the victims of the CHEŁMNO extermination camp were stored, sorted, and sent to Germany for use by the German population.

Biebow was among the officials who organized the transports to Chełmno from Łódź and from the ghettos in the provincial towns of the Warthegau. These transports began in

Hans Biebow (left), Nazi head of the Łódź ghetto administration.

December 1941 and continued throughout 1942. Biebow, however, did not want the ghetto administration to pass into the hands of the SS, and in order to maintain the flow of profits from the ghetto factories he ensured the ghetto's continued existence even after the 1942 deportations, up until the summer of 1944. Nevertheless, once it was decided that the ghetto would be liquidated, Biebow became very active in organizing transports to the Chełmno and AUSCHWITZ extermination camps, from June to August 1944, and in the ghetto's final liquidation. He excelled in deception tactics, convincing the Jews that the transports from the ghetto would take them to work camps attached to German factories. When the ghetto was liquidated in August 1944, Biebow remained in Łódź, and until January 1945 he supervised the removal to Germany of possessions left behind by the ghetto inhabitants. After the war, Biebow was tried by a Polish court in Łódź, sentenced to death, and executed.

BIBLIOGRAPHY

Trunk, I. *Judenrat.* New York, 1972.

SHMUEL KRAKOWSKI

BIELSKI, TUVIA (1906–1987), Jewish partisan commander. Bielski's family were farmers in Stankiewicze, near NOVOGRUDOK. At the age of seventeen he joined the Zionist pioneering movement, and in 1928 he was mobilized into the Polish army, where he rose to the rank of corporal. He married in 1930 and settled in the village of Subotnik, where he opened a textile store. In September 1939 the area was annexed to the Soviet Union.

With the German invasion of the Soviet Union on June 22, 1941, Bielski was mobilized. When the Germans invaded the region he fled to the forest, and from there to his village of birth. After their parents and other members of their family were slaughtered in the Novogrudok ghetto, Bielski and his brothers Zusya, Asael, and Aharon, escaped to the forests. Securing arms, they created a seventeen-member partisan core there, consisting mostly of members of Bielski's family. Elected as commander, Tuvia Bielski sent emissaries to the ghettos in the vicinity, inviting the inmates to join his group. Hundreds of the surviving Jews in the ghettos of the Novogrudok region—men, women, and children—streamed into Bielski's camp, and his partisan band grew daily.

Bielski learned to wage partisan combat, and he considered the saving of Jewish lives a supreme objective. His band inspired terror in the Novogrudok region as it took vengeance on the Belorussian police and on the farmers who massacred Jews. The German authorities offered a reward of 100,000 marks for assistance in capturing him.

With the creation of the band of Jewish partisans in the Naliboki Forest, Bielski won the trust of the Soviet partisan unit in the vicinity, and particularly of its commander, General Platon (Vasily Yehimovich Chernyshev). Bielski opposed the unit's intention of taking away his 150 fighters, leaving him with a civilian camp of refugees, and in order to frustrate this aim he made his camp a maintenance base for the Soviet fighters. His group was not a partisan band in the regular sense but a Jewish community in the forest, with a synagogue, a law court, workshops, a school, and a dispensary (*see* FAMILY CAMPS IN THE FORESTS).

In the summer of 1943, the Germans initiated a massive hunt through the Naliboki Forest in order to destroy the partisan forces, and in particular Bielski's band. The partisans retreated to the densest part of the forest, and the commander of Bielski's area or-

Asael Bielski (left) and Tuvia Bielski.

dered Bielski to pare down his unit to include only single people with arms; married men, women, and children were ordered to abandon the area where the unit had been staying and not follow the fighters to the center of the forest. Knowing that this instruction was a death sentence for the civilians in his group, Bielski disobeyed, retreating to the thickest part of the forest with his entire band. The fighters protected the civilians until they were able to emerge safely from the forest, evading the Germans who surrounded it. In the summer of 1944, with the liberation of the area, Bielski and his 1,230-strong partisan band, known as "Kalinin," marched into the town of Novogrudok. Asael Bielski was killed in battle as a soldier in the Soviet army at Königsberg in 1944.

After the war Bielski returned to Poland. That same year, in 1945, he immigrated to Palestine, and in 1954 he settled in the United States with his two surviving brothers.

BIBLIOGRAPHY

Ainsztein, R. *Jewish Resistance in Nazi-occupied Eastern Europe.* London, 1974. See pages 315–325.

YITZCHAK ALPEROWITZ

BILTMORE RESOLUTION, declaration adopted at a conference of American Zionists in 1942, explicitly advocating the establishment of a Jewish state in Palestine. In the spring of 1942, Zionist fortunes had reached their lowest ebb. Despite the dire straits of European Jewry, the cooperation of the YISHUV in the British war effort, and the collaboration of the Arabs with the Nazis, the British government adamantly refused to modify its WHITE PAPER OF 1939, which limited Jewish immigration into Palestine and contemplated a Palestinian state with an Arab majority. Furthermore, American Zionists had failed to mobilize the crucial support of either American Jewry or the administration of President Franklin D. ROOSEVELT. To counteract this situation, an extraordinary Zionist conference was called for May 10 and 11, 1942. Held in New York's Biltmore Hotel, it was attended by leading Zionist personalities, including Chaim WEIZMANN, Abba Hillel SILVER, Stephen S. WISE, David BEN-GURION, and Nahum GOLDMANN.

Despite the fact that no verified data existed at the time regarding the "FINAL SOLUTION," it was clear to those at the conference that European Jewry was in the throes of a great catastrophe. Article 2 of the resolution offered "a message of hope and encouragement to [our] fellow Jews in the ghettos and concentration camps of Hitler-dominated Europe, and our prayers that their hour of liberation may not be far distant." The resolution further offered warm greetings to Jewish fighting men and women, and sent a proposal of peace and goodwill to the Arabs. However, the conclusion of the resolution was unambiguous: "The conference declares that the new world order that will follow victory cannot be established on foundations of peace, justice, and equality unless the problem of Jewish homelessness is finally solved" (Article 8). Consequently, the resolution urged "that Palestine be established as a Jewish commonwealth integrated into the structure of the new democratic world."

Events in Europe were not yet sufficiently clear for American, or Palestinian, Zionists to fully comprehend. The RIEGNER CABLE was received in August 1942 and verified only late that November. Thus, the conference was responding to partial information and spoke of the need to relocate two million Jewish refugees at a time when nearly that number of Russian, Polish, and Romanian Jews had already been massacred. Even so, the resolution marked the first time that a majority of Zionists called openly for the establishment of Jewish sovereignty as the ultimate goal of Zionism. The resolution became central to the activities of Silver and Wise, as co-chairmen of the AMERICAN ZIONIST EMERGENCY COUNCIL. Indeed, although many non-Zionists in the United States (including those of the AMERICAN JEWISH COMMITTEE) did not support its statist demands, the resolution became the primary statement of Zionist goals until the United Nations opted for the partition of Palestine into separate Jewish and Arab states on November 29, 1947.

BIBLIOGRAPHY

Bauer, Y. *From Diplomacy to Resistance.* New York, 1973.

Shpiro, D. "The Political Background of the 1942 Biltmore Resolution." *Herzl Year Book* 8 (1978): 166–177.

Urofsky, M. *American Zionism from Herzl to the Holocaust.* New York, 1976.

ABRAHAM J. EDELHEIT

BINKIENE, SOFIJA (1902–1984), rescuer of Jews in KOVNO, Lithuania. The widow of a well-known Lithuanian author, Binkiene lived near the Kovno ghetto. Although she had had no previous contacts with Jewish circles and was tending a sick husband, she helped Jews by offering them temporary shelter in her home. Many Jews, fleeing from the Kovno ghetto, found initial refuge in her home. At times, especially during the final liquidation of the ghetto in 1944, Binkiene roved the streets near the ghetto in the hope of bringing straggling Jews into the safety of her home. Many scores of Jews were thus helped and saved.

In 1967, Sofija Binkiene edited a book on Lithuanians who rescued Jews, *Ir be ginklo kariai* (Vilna, 1962). She was awarded the title of "RIGHTEOUS AMONG THE NATIONS" by YAD VASHEM in 1967.

MORDECAI PALDIEL

Sofija Binkiene.

BIRKENAU. *See* Auschwitz.

BLACK BOOK OF SOVIET JEWRY, THE, a book of testimonies and documents (descriptions, letters, and excerpts from diaries) concerning Nazi crimes in the SOVIET UNION, the principal source of which were Jewish survivors and non-Jewish eyewitnesses. As stated in the subtitle, the book covers "the ruthless murder of Jews by fascist German invaders throughout the temporarily occupied regions of the Soviet Union and in the extermination camps of Poland during the war of 1941 to 1945." The *Black Book* was the work of the noted Soviet Jewish writers Ilya EHRENBURG and Vasily Grossman, with Soviet writers and poets, both Jewish and non-Jewish, among the contributors.

The idea of issuing such a book was conceived by Ehrenburg as early as 1943, and by the end of 1944 a first version was ready. At that point, Ehrenburg published excerpts in two volumes under the title *Merder fun Felker* (Murder of Peoples). At the beginning of 1945 the manuscript was given to the JEWISH ANTIFASCIST COMMITTEE in the Soviet Union on the instructions of committee member Shlomo Lozovski; there it was revised and emended. Copies of the manuscript were sent to the United States, Romania, and Israel in 1946. Excerpts from the manuscript were published in the United States in the English-language *Black Book*, which had as its subject the annihilation of the Jews in Europe as a whole. In Romania, the first part of the manuscript was published in 1946, under the title *Cartea neagra*. According to Ehrenburg, the book was printed in the Soviet Union by the publisher Der Emes, but the entire edition, as well as the manuscript, was destroyed in 1948, when the Jewish Antifascist Committee was liquidated.

The manuscript copy that had gone to Israel—in which the chapter on Lithuania is missing—was handed over to YAD VASHEM in 1965 by Shlomo Tsirulnikov, an activist in the V League (a wartime Soviet-YISHUV friendship league). Adapted and edited by Haya Lifshitz and Marek Kipnis, the book was published in Russian (Jerusalem, 1980), English (New York, 1981), and Yiddish (Jerusalem, 1984; this edition included a reconstructed version of the chapter on Lithuania). Among the material in the Ehrenburg archive that was opened to the public at Yad Vashem at the end of 1987 was an almost complete handwritten manuscript of the *Black Book*.

BIBLIOGRAPHY

Ehrenburg, I. *Men, Years, Life.* 6 vols. London, 1962–1968.

Sutzkever, A. "Ilya Ehrenburg: A Chapter of Memoirs from the Years 1944–1946." *Di Goldene Keyt* 61 (1967): 21–37. (In Yiddish.)

HAYA LIFSHITZ

BLECHHAMMER (Pol., Blachownia Śląska), concentration camp established in April 1942 near Koźle, a town 18.5 miles (30 km) west of Gleiwitz (present-day Gliwice). In its initial stage, Blechhammer was a forced-labor camp for Jews (a *Judenlager*). The first group of prisoners, numbering 350, were employed on the construction of the Oberschlesische Hydriewerke (Upper Silesia Hydrogenation Works), a chemical-products plant. After a short time a typhus epidemic broke out, and 120 prisoners who contracted the disease were sent to AUSCHWITZ, where they were killed. That June the remaining prisoners were transferred to a new and larger camp that had been built nearby. Most of the prisoners brought to Blechhammer were Jews from Upper Silesia, but there were other Jews as well, from fifteen different countries. The number of prisoners reached 5,500. They were housed in wooden barracks under appalling conditions, with no toilet or washing facilities. Some 200 female Jewish prisoners were put into a separate section of the camp. Hunger and disease were rife, especially diarrhea and tuberculosis. A crematorium was built, in which were cremated the bodies of 1,500 prisoners who had died from "natural" causes or had been killed.

On April 1, 1944, as part of a reorganization, the camp was put under the authority of the Auschwitz camp administration, and it became the satellite camp Auschwitz IV. Hauptsturmführer Otto Brossmann was the camp commandant until November 1944, when he was replaced by Untersturmführer Kurt Klipp. Throughout the camp's existence, Karl Demerer, a Viennese Jew, was the "camp elder" (*Lagerältester*). He had the courage to stand up to the camp authorities and in many instances was able to help the prisoners.

On January 21, 1945, 4,000 prisoners, including 150 women, were taken out of the camp and put on a death march lasting thirteen days. Some 800 prisoners were killed en route. On February 2, the survivors reached the GROSS-ROSEN camp, where they remained for five days before being moved to BUCHEN-WALD. Several dozen prisoners who tried to hide in Blechhammer during the evacuation were discovered and killed on the spot.

BIBLIOGRAPHY

Brown, J. *In Durance Vile*. London, 1981.
Piper, F. "Das Nebenlager Blechhammer." *Hefte von Auschwitz* 10 (1967): 19–40.

SHMUEL KRAKOWSKI

BLITZKRIEG (lit., "lightning war"), theory of the conduct of war, developed by the German armed forces in World War II, aimed at winning complete victory in as short a time as possible, measured in days and weeks rather than months and years. The term was first used in connection with the German attack on Poland in 1939. In the blitzkrieg, tanks and armored and other motorized vehicles for transporting troops were concentrated, and massive attacks by dive-bombers and self-propelled artillery were directed at selected enemy front-line positions. Dive-bombers also attacked vital enemy localities in the rear. These actions were calculated to create psychological shock and resultant disorganization in the enemy forces and to prevent any concerted reaction by the enemy high command.

The tactics of blitzkrieg were evolved by the German general Heinz Guderian (who drew most of his ideas from the writings of the British military theorists Basil Henry Liddell Hart and John Frederick Charles Fuller). They consisted of a splitting thrust by armored columns on a narrow front and complete disruption of the main enemy position at the point of attack, followed by wide-sweeping encirclement movements of fast-moving armored spearheads, thus creating large caldrons of entrapped and immobilized enemy forces.

The blitzkrieg method was successfully applied by the German Wehrmacht in the campaigns against Poland, France, Denmark, Norway, Yugoslavia, and Greece. However, after initial successes in the attack on the Soviet

The Blechhammer concentration camp.

Union (Operation "Barbarossa"), its failure there in late 1941 was the turning point of World War II and heralded the doom of the Third Reich. The British also used the term "blitz" for the German terror air attacks on British cities from September 1940 to May 1941.

BIBLIOGRAPHY

Guderian, H. *Achtung Panzer*. Stuttgart, 1937.
Liddell Hart, B. H. Strategy: *The Indirect Approach*. New York, 1967.
Miksche, F. O. *Blitzkrieg*. London, 1941.

JEHUDA L. WALLACH

BLOBEL KOMMANDO. *See* Aktion 1005.

BLOBEL, PAUL (1894–1951), SS officer. Born into a Protestant family, Blobel attended a vocational school, where he learned construction and carpentry. In World War I he volunteered for the army and served in the engineering corps. After the war he resumed his studies, became an architect, and settled in Solingen. In the depression he lost his job and could not find any other employment. He

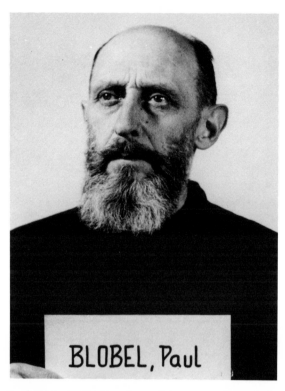

Paul Blobel, SS-*Standartenführer;* member of the SD; commanding officer of Einsatzgruppe C's Sonderkommando 4a. [National Archives]

joined the Nazi party in October 1931, and in January 1932 enlisted in the SS. In March 1933 he entered service with the Staatspolizei (Stapo) in Düsseldorf, and on June 1, 1934, he transferred to the SD (Sicherheitsdienst; Security Service) with the rank of *Untersturmführer* and was appointed SD officer for the Düsseldorf area. He advanced rapidly in the SS hierarchy and became a *Standartenführer* on January 30, 1941.

At the beginning of June 1942, Blobel was summoned to Pretzsch, a town on the Elbe northeast of Leipzig, where candidates for service in the EINSATZGRUPPEN were being assembled to be deployed in German-occupied territory in the Soviet Union. Blobel was appointed commanding officer of Sonderkommando 4a of Einsatzgruppe C, which was assigned to the Ukraine. At the head of this unit Blobel went from Sokal to Kiev by way of Volhynia, engaging in *Aktionen* along the route, in LUTSK, Dubno, ZHITOMIR, BERDICHEV, and other places. When Kiev fell, he entered the city and with his unit organized and carried out the murder of Kiev's Jews at BABI YAR, on September 29 and 30, 1941. His last

Aktion in that area took place in KHARKOV, where his unit murdered 21,685 Jews in Drobitski Yar at the end of December 1941.

On January 13, 1942, Blobel was released from his post for reasons of health—he suffered from a liver ailment that was aggravated by his excessive drinking. When he recovered he was called to the REICHSSICHERHEITSHAUPTAMT (Reich Security Main Office; RSHA) and put in charge of AKTION 1005, an operation whose goal was to obliterate the traces of the mass murders committed by the Germans. Blobel established his headquarters in Łódź; his direct superior was the Gestapo chief, Heinrich MÜLLER, in Berlin.

Until the fall of 1943, the method Blobel used was to cremate the bodies on huge pyres. The first experiments to employ this method were carried out in CHEŁMNO. The permanent camps, such as AUSCHWITZ, were later equipped with crematoria. In the fall of 1943 Blobel set up special units, the Sonderkommandos 1005, for the specific task of disinterring and cremating the bodies from the mass graves in the German-occupied parts of the Soviet Union. These units were manned by Jewish and other prisoners who were killed when their work in a given place was done. Some of these prisoners, especially the Jews among them, succeeded in escaping, notably in Babi Yar, JANÓWSKA, the NINTH FORT in Kovno, PONARY, and Grabowka, near Białystok. At the end of October 1944, when their tasks were completed, the German personnel who had served in the Sonderkommandos 1005—men of the SD, Sicherheitspolizei (Security Police), and ORDNUNGSPOLIZEI (German regular police)—all joined Einsatzgruppe "Iltis," a new unit commanded by Blobel. It was posted to Carinthia, on the Austro-Yugoslav border, to take part in fighting against the Yugoslav PARTISANS.

Blobel was arrested after the war and was one of the principal defendants in The *Einsatzgruppen* Case (Trial 9) at the SUBSEQUENT NUREMBERG PROCEEDINGS. He was sentenced to death in 1948 and hanged at the Landsberg prison in Bavaria on June 8, 1951.

BIBLIOGRAPHY

Tenenbaum, J. "The Einsatzgruppen." *Jewish Social Studies* 17/1 (1955): 43–64.

SHMUEL SPECTOR

BLOMBERG, WERNER VON (1878–1946), German field marshal; minister of war from 1933 to 1938. Born into a military family, Blomberg joined the German general staff in World War I. During the period of the Weimar Republic he took part in the program of clandestine rearmament, especially in the training of officers and the formation of a covert general staff. As adjutant general, his duties took him to Russia and America. In 1932 he served as military adviser to the German delegation at the Geneva disarmament conference. He combined these duties with command of the army corps at Königsberg, and it was in this capacity that he first met Hitler, in 1931.

In 1933, upon the formation of the Hitler–von Papen government, Blomberg was appointed minister of war and enthusiastically supported Nazi rearmament. He strongly opposed Ernst RÖHM's plans to incorporate the SA (Sturmabteilung; Storm Troopers) into the German army, and in the ensuing putsch against Röhm played a central role in consolidating Hitler's power. On the death of President Paul von HINDENBERG in August 1934, Blomberg took a personal oath of loyalty to Hitler as Hindenburg's successor, thereby ensuring Hitler's control over the army. In 1935, Blomberg was appointed commander in chief of the new Wehrmacht. He cooperated in plans for the reoccupation of the Rhineland and was promoted to field marshal in 1936. Blomberg was reluctant to support Nazi war policy, and in 1938 was engineered out of office by Hermann GÖRING and Heinrich HIMMLER. His fall and that of Werner von Fritsch, the army commander in chief, shortly afterward, ensured that party control of the armed forces remained unhampered. Blomberg died in American detention at Nuremberg.

BIBLIOGRAPHY

Brett-Smith, R. *Hitler's Generals*. San Rafael, Calif., 1977.
Humble, R. *Hitler's Generals*. New York, 1974.

LIONEL KOCHAN

BLUM, ABRAHAM ("Abrasha"; 1905–1943), BUND leader and member of the ŻYDOWSKA ORGANIZACJA BOJOWA (Jewish Fighting Organization; ŻOB) in WARSAW. Blum was born in Vilna into a middle-class family, attended a Yiddish secondary school, and graduated with a degree in construction engineering from a Belgian institute. As a young man he became active in the Bund's youth movement. In 1929 he moved to Warsaw and became a full-time party activist. In the 1930s he was a member of the national board of the Bund youth movement, Zukunft (Future), and was active in the Bund-sponsored school network.

In the early days of World War II, Blum was one of the few Bund leaders who did not leave Warsaw. He played a central role in the Bund's clandestine operations as soon as they were launched, and helped run the party's soup kitchens, underground press, welfare services, and political indoctrination efforts.

In the underground's debate concerning the formation of a united fighting organization, Blum, as of the spring of 1942, supported the stand that called for the Bund to join with the Zionist groups in such an organization. Marek EDELMAN, in the report on the Bund's underground operations, *Getto Walczy* (The Ghetto Fights), published in 1945, described Blum as "the spiritual father of our resistance . . . the only person [in the Bund] able to control the situation [during the mass deportation from Warsaw]," and stated: "We owe it to him that we survived that terrible period." In October 1942 the Bund joined the ŻOB, and Blum was appointed the party's representative on the coordinating committee of the Bund and the Jewish National Committee (Żydowski Komitet Narodowy), the two bodies that formed the political leadership of the ŻOB. He rejected an offer to cross over to the "Aryan" side, despite the fact that his wife and children had gone into hiding there.

During the WARSAW GHETTO UPRISING in April 1943, Blum fought with a group of young people in the "Brushmakers" area. He was among the group that succeeded in escaping from the ghetto and reaching the Polish side by way of the city sewage system. For several days he was in hiding in the Kampinos Forest, and from there he returned to Warsaw. When his hiding place there was discovered, he tried to escape through a fourth-floor window by tying bed sheets together and climbing down, but the sheets tore; Blum fell and was injured. He was seized by the Germans and taken to the Gestapo, and all further trace of him was lost.

BIBLIOGRAPHY

Gutman, Y. *The Jews of Warsaw, 1939–1943.* Bloomington, 1980.

ISRAEL GUTMAN

BLUM, LÉON (1872–1950), premier of FRANCE on three occasions. Blum began his political career at the age of twenty-two as a member of the French Social Democratic party, to which he remained attached until the end of his life. From the close of World War I he supported Zionist aspirations in Palestine. Blum first came to power in 1936 at a most unpropitious moment for France, with respect to both domestic and foreign policy: it was faced with Germany's remilitarization of the Rhineland and with a deep internal economic crisis, and Blum had difficulty confronting these issues. With France rocked by mass waves of workers' strikes, Blum opted for far-reaching social and economic reforms, which further upset the internal equilibrium. During his term of office antisemitism grew, with Blum—France's first Jewish premier—at its center. He was forced out of office in early 1937 when he failed to receive the necessary support in the Chamber of Deputies. A short-lived return in 1938 exacerbated his relations with many elements of French society, which saw him as a symbol of all the negative attributes they associated with the Third Republic.

Before World War II, Blum strongly opposed Hitler and National Socialism. His standpoint, however, was more reflective of a Social Democrat who opposed fascism than of a Jew who opposed racism. When attacking National Socialism, Blum did not address the treatment of the Jews in prewar Nazi Germany, but rather Nazi actions against Social Democrats and Social Democratic values. Nevertheless, in 1938, in the wake of the disappointing EVIAN CONFERENCE on refugees and the violent KRISTALLNACHT pogrom, Blum decried the idea of closing France to Jewish refugees from Nazism, and sharply criticized French Jews for supporting this position.

Arrested by the Vichy authorities on September 14, 1940, Blum, together with other French leaders of the Third Republic, was tried in the spring of 1942 at a show trial in Riom, which was never brought to a conclusion. On March 31, 1943, at the age of seventy-one, the former French premier was sent to BUCHENWALD. In early April 1945 he was removed from the camp, and after being shunted from one place to another was imprisoned in DACHAU. On April 28 he was transferred to the hands of the Wehrmacht. Blum was liberated on May 4, and within ten days arrived in Paris. In 1946 he returned to political activity and formed a socialist coalition government, which lasted only a month.

Léon Blum. [Beth Hatefutsoth]

BIBLIOGRAPHY

Birnbaum, P. *Un mythe politique—La "République juive": De Léon Blum à Pierre Mendès-France.* Paris, 1988.
Colton, J. *Léon Blum: Humanist in Politics.* Durham, N.C., 1987.
Lacouture, J. *Léon Blum.* New York, 1982.
Léon Blum before His Judges. Foreword by C. R. Attlee. London, 1943.

RICHARD COHEN and
ISRAEL ELDAR

B'NAI B'RITH, international Jewish organization. Founded in New York in 1843, B'nai B'rith is the oldest secular Jewish organization in the United States, where most of its strength is concentrated. The B'nai B'rith Order was founded by Jewish immigrants from Germany as a "fraternal order," its structure and aims influenced by the FREEMASONS; it set itself the goal of blending humanistic Judaism with general human ideals. The order also assisted Jews in parts of the world where they were being persecuted. B'nai B'rith lodges and chapters sprang up in other countries, including Germany, where a B'nai B'rith order was established in 1882, in reaction to growing ANTISEMITISM in that country.

Reacting to manifestations of antisemitism in Europe, B'nai B'rith in the United States decided in 1913 to establish the Anti-Defamation League (ADL), a body that exists to this day. The ADL concentrated on gaining the support of public opinion. In the 1920s and 1930s it grew beyond the confines of B'nai B'rith and developed into a broadly based community organization, fighting Henry Ford's antisemitic campaign and the Ku Klux Klan. In the late 1930s the ADL worked against Nazi and fascist groups in the United States and became a prime source of information on their activities, to the extent that even the Federal Bureau of Investigation utilized the ADL files on these groups for its work.

B'nai B'rith was not always in accord with the activist line pursued by its offspring. In 1931, when Nazi thugs attacked Jews in the streets of Berlin, Rabbi Leo BAECK asked the president of B'nai B'rith, Alfred Cohen, to refrain from arousing public opinion in America against these acts in Germany. Even after Adolf Hitler's rise to power in Germany, Cohen continued to base his policy on Germany on Baeck's advice. (Baeck was concerned about possible Nazi reaction to a boycott movement of German goods among the Jews of America.) Opposing the stand taken by the Anti-Defamation League, Cohen refused to join the boycott of German goods, on the ground that such action would cause harm to the Jews of Germany, and particularly to B'nai B'rith in that country, which the Nazis permitted to function until 1937. An appeal by B'nai B'rith asking the United States gov-ernment to protest to Germany against the persecution of the Jews was rejected by President Franklin D. ROOSEVELT, who at that point was not prepared to interfere in Nazi Germany's "internal affairs."

On April 9, 1937, the Gestapo seized all the B'nai B'rith chapters in Germany, arresting the officers and conducting searches of their residences, handcuffing the national B'nai B'rith officers, confiscating the order's assets, and liquidating all of its welfare institutions. A shocked Alfred Cohen appealed to Secretary of State Cordell HULL to protest to the German government on humanitarian grounds, but his appeal was turned down. Even at that time Cohen remained opposed to public protest and boycott, and still believed that "quiet diplomacy" could help the Jews of Germany.

In May 1938 Henry Monsky was elected president of B'nai B'rith, the first time that a Jew of eastern European origin had assumed this post. Monsky was a Zionist and his views were close to those held by the leaders of the American Jewish Congress; he supported the boycott of Germany and made it his policy to transform B'nai B'rith into a large-scale organization. A few months later, the KRISTALL-NACHT pogrom took place in Germany (November 1938), followed by the total elimination of the Jews from the German economy and the liquidation of Jewish institutions. Even before that, the Jews of Germany had no place to go; but B'nai B'rith, fearful of arousing antisemitism in the United States—like most American Jews at the time—did not challenge the quota system of the 1924 Immigration Act and did not try to arouse public opinion against the administration's policy of not fully utilizing even the quotas provided by that act. In the wake of *Kristallnacht*, Monsky, together with other Jewish leaders, conveyed to the White House the concern of American Jewry over the existing state of affairs.

When reliable information was received concerning the "Final Solution," Monsky and the other Jewish leaders conferred with Roosevelt on ways of rescuing the Jews. Monsky sought to create unity in Jewish ranks and, with the support of the Zionists, established the AMERICAN JEWISH CONFERENCE, which set the rescue of European Jews as one of its goals. At the founding session of the conference, held in Pittsburgh in February 1943, Monsky formed an emergency committee for the affairs of European Jewry. The committee in turn drafted recommendations to be submitted to the BERMUDA CONFERENCE, and organized mass meetings. At the September 1943 meeting of the conference, the destruction of European Jewry was discussed; no one argued against Monsky's thesis that Jewish unity was a prerequisite for the rescue of Europe's Jews, but the meeting did not come up with a practical contribution to this end.

After the war, B'nai B'rith played an active role in addressing the problem of the Holocaust survivors. In 1946 Monsky testified before the Anglo-American Committee on Palestine, supporting the Zionist solution of the problem.

BIBLIOGRAPHY

Bisgyer, M. *Challenge and Encounter: Behind the Scenes in the Struggle for Jewish Survival.* New York, 1967.

Grusd, E. E. *B'nai B'rith: The Story of a Covenant.* New York, 1966.

Klutznick, P. *No Easy Answers.* New York, 1971.

Moore, D. D. *B'nai B'rith as a Challenge of Ethnic Leadership.* Albany, N.Y., 1981.

MENAHEM KAUFMAN

BOARD OF DEPUTIES OF BRITISH JEWS, the representative body of British Jewry, originating in 1760. Following the Nazi rise to power in Germany and the calamity that it represented for Germany's Jews, the Board of Deputies, then under the presidency of Neville Laski, was confronted by extremely serious issues on which it had to take a stand: the persecution of the Jews in Germany and, later, in the countries occupied by the Germans; the question of Jewish emigration from Germany to Britain; and the absorption and rehabilitation of these refugees. In those years—and even more so during the war—the board faced the problems of maneuvering between British loyalty and Jewish loyalty, and of deciding how to act when British interests did not coincide with, or even contradicted, the interests of the Jews.

The board appealed to the British government, and in particular to the Foreign Office, asking that it intervene with the Nazis to stop the persecution of the Jews, and raise the refugee problem at the League of Nations and other international forums. The British government, however, refused to take any step that could be interpreted as interference in the "internal affairs of Germany." This policy eventually became one of appeasement toward the Third Reich. The board confined itself to legal arguments and confidential, moderate steps, and did not put any public pressure on the government by alerting the Jewish community. It opposed and obstructed attempts by activist groups in the community to resort to more vigorous means. The board also resisted the boycott of Germany and the formation of a protest movement against the persecution of German Jewry.

In the summer of 1932, when Stephen S. WISE called for a preparatory meeting for the formation of the WORLD JEWISH CONGRESS, the board refused to take part and also stayed away from the preparatory meetings that followed; neither did the board join the World Jewish Congress when it was finally established. It did, however, participate with other leading Jewish organizations in the United States and Europe in sponsoring an international Jewish conference in London in October 1933 to deal with the situation of the German Jews and coordinate efforts to help them. The conference was a complete failure, mainly because of the isolationist tendencies of the United States organizations.

The board's position on combating the antisemitic campaign conducted by the British fascist movement under Sir Oswald MOSLEY (mainly in 1936) also displayed caution. It opposed any open clash with the fascists and rejected cooperation with anti-fascist movements. On this issue, as in the case of the boycott, ad hoc bodies sprang up that took energetic steps against the fascist threat. The Jews of London's East End, who had been personally affected by the fascists, were particularly active in these bodies and were angered by the board's failure to act. It was only in response to strong pressure that the board decided to establish a coordinating committee (later named the Defense Committee) whose task it was to counteract the fascist campaign against the Jewish community.

In 1939 a democratic changeover took place when Selig BRODETSKY, of eastern European origin, was elected to the presidency of the board, a position previously the preserve of members of old, established families in the community. With the election of Brodetsky, the strength of the Zionists on the board increased, and in 1943 they became the dominant force. As a result, the influence of the board with the British government lessened. During the war, the board submitted a series of requests and demands to the British government: to intervene in behalf of the Jews in the Nazi-occupied countries; to give wide publicity to Nazi anti-Jewish brutality, deportations, and murder; to issue declarations on the situation of the Jews; to provide assistance for the integration of the refugees in neutral countries or in GREAT BRITAIN; and to bomb AUSCHWITZ from the air. These requests and demands did not, however, meet with any response. As was the case with other Jewish organizations in Britain, the Board of Deputies of British Jews was unable to bring any meaningful influence to bear upon British policy concerning the Jews under Nazi persecution. Nor was the board able, despite all its efforts, to affect policy on such critical issues as the opening of the gates of Palestine to Jewish refugees, or the admission of Jewish refugees from Europe to Britain or other parts of the empire.

BIBLIOGRAPHY

Alderman, G. *The Jewish Community in British Politics.* Oxford, 1983.

Gould, J., and S. Esh, eds. *Jewish Life in Modern Britain.* London, 1964.

Sompolinsky, M. "Anglo-Jewish Leadership and the British Government: Attempts at Rescue, 1944–1945." *Yad Vashem Studies* 13 (1979): 211–247.

Wasserstein, B. *Britain and the Jews of Europe, 1939–1945.* Oxford, 1979.

Wasserstein, B. "Patterns of Jewish Leadership in Great Britain during the Nazi Era." In *Jewish Leadership during the Nazi Era: Patterns of Behavior in the Free World*, edited by R. L. Braham, pp. 29–43. New York, 1985.

NANA SAGI

BOGAARD, JOHANNES ("Uncle Hannes"; 1891–1974), farmer in Nieuw Vennep (Haarlemmermeer), southwest of Amsterdam, who was responsible for the rescue of some three hundred Jews. Bogaard hid fugitive Jews on

Johannes Bogaard (center), planting a tree in the Garden of the Righteous at Yad Vashem, Jerusalem (1964).

his farm, as well as on the farms of relatives and friendly neighbors, for long periods of time. Born into a strict Calvinist family of limited means, he was taught by his father to respect the Jews as the people of the Bible. After the deportation of Jews from the NETHERLANDS began in July 1942, the entire Bogaard family of farmers devoted themselves to helping Jews escape the Nazi dragnet. When Jews were referred to Bogaard as being in need of help, Uncle Hannes ("Oom Hannes"), as he was affectionately known, traveled to Amsterdam once or twice a week to fetch the persons threatened with deportation and persuade them to follow him and place themselves under his care. Most were hidden in the vicinity of his farm, although at times there were up to one hundred Jews on his family's farm alone. He also collected money, ration cards, and identification papers from friends and acquaintances.

In November 1942 the Dutch Nazi police raided the Bogaard farm, capturing three Jews. Two more raids followed in the succeeding months, in which several dozen Jews were apprehended and a policeman was killed. Johannes's father, one of his brothers, and his own son Teunis were taken to a German concentration camp, where they perished.

By the end of 1943, Johannes Bogaard, until then operating largely on his own initiative, was able to link up with underground organizations, but most of his help still came from his own family. Alerted to the increased danger of detection by the authorities, most of the Jews in his charge were moved to other locations in the countryside for safe refuge. Bogaard probably saved more Jews, almost single-handedly, than any other person in the Netherlands. He was recognized by YAD VASHEM as a "RIGHTEOUS AMONG THE NATIONS" in 1963.

MORDECAI PALDIEL

BOGDANOVKA (Rom., Bogdanovca), extermination camp established in October 1941 by Romanian occupation authorities in the village of that name on the Bug River, in the Golta district of TRANSNISTRIA, on orders of Col. Modest Isopescu, the district commissioner. Most of the people deported to Bogdanovka—some forty-eight thousand—came from ODESSA, and about seven thousand from BESSARABIA. The last transport arrived at Bogdanovka on December 1, 1941; by then over fifty-four thousand Jews were being held there.

Several cases of typhus broke out in the camp in mid-December. In consultation with Fleischer, the German adviser to the Romanian administration of the district, Isopescu decided to kill the entire camp population and issued an order to this effect to Vasile Manescu, the military government official in charge of the district. Taking part in the operation were Romanian troops and gendarmerie, Ukrainian police, and civilians from the town of Golta brought in for this purpose, as well as local ethnic Germans (VOLKSDEUTSCHE). The chief of the Ukrainian regular police, Kazachievici, was in overall command.

The mass slaughter began on December 21, 1941. The sick and disabled prisoners, some 5,000 in all, were locked into two stables; layers of kerosene-drenched straw were spread over the roofs and set alight, and all the prisoners packed inside were burned to death. The rest of the prisoners, lined up in columns of 300 to 400 each, were marched to a nearby forest and driven to the banks of a watercourse (*garla mare*, "the great valley," as the Romanian camp commandants called it). They were ordered to remove their clothes, get on their knees, and lean over the valley, and were then shot in the back of

BOGDANOVKA

© Martin Gilbert 1982

their necks with dumdum bullets or killed with hand grenades. The massacre went on for four days, in the course of which 30,000 Jews were murdered. The rest were left freezing in the cold, waiting on the banks of the river for their turn to die. With their bare hands they dug holes in the ground, packing them with frozen corpses and trying in this way to shelter themselves from the cold. Nevertheless, thousands of them froze to death. On Christmas Eve the killing came to a temporary halt, only to be renewed four days later, on December 28. By the end of the day on December 31, the remaining 11,000 Jews were also dead. Isopescu ordered all traces of the slaughter to be obliterated and the corpses to be burned. For two months, in January and February of 1942, 200 Jews who had been selected for this gruesome task were kept busy burning the corpses, piling them up in pyres with layers of straw and timber, and using gasoline to set the fire to the pyres. Of these 200 Jews, 150 died of cold and hunger or were shot to death by their Ukrainian guards.

In early 1945 Isopescu, Manescu, and the camp commandants were put on trial, in the first such proceedings against Romanian war criminals. The men responsible for the mass murder were sentenced to death (although the sentences were commuted to life imprisonment), and the other defendants were given long prison terms.

BIBLIOGRAPHY

Carp, M. *Transnistria.* Vol. 3 of *Cartea Neagră.* Bucharest, 1947.

Lavi, T., ed. *Rumania*, vol. 1. In *Pinkas Hakehillot; Encyclopaedia of Jewish Communities.* Jerusalem, 1969. (In Hebrew.)

JEAN ANCEL

BOHEMIA AND MORAVIA, PROTECTORATE OF, German protectorate proclaimed by Adolf Hitler on March 16, 1939, following the occupation of those territories by the Wehrmacht on the day before. The First Czechoslovak Republic had been established after World War I, on October 28, 1918, after the disintegration of the Austro-Hungarian monarchy. The Second Czechoslovak Republic, the rump state created in the wake of the MUNICH CONFERENCE (September 28–29, 1938) and the German annexation of the Sudetenland, came to an abrupt end. After the German invasion, Bohemia and Moravia, the heartland of the historic Czech lands, became part of the territory of the Reich.

Konstantin von NEURATH was appointed the Reich protector, Karl Hermann FRANK —leader of the Sudeten German party— became state secretary, and all other key positions were filled by Reich officials, who through the Landräte (local German councils) acquired control over the Czech provincial authorities. Nominally there remained the Czech president, Emil Hácha, and an "autonomous" Czech government, whose acts were nonetheless to be completely subordinate to the political, economic, and military interests of the Third Reich. Henceforward, the fate of the Jews differed in each of the former provinces of Czechoslovakia (*see* SLOVAKIA; TRANSCARPATHIAN UKRAINE).

On the eve of the German occupation, a total of 136 Jewish religious congregations existed in Bohemia, Moravia, and Silesia. The Jewish population numbered 118,310 persons, according to the criteria of the NUREMBERG LAWS.

Immediately after the occupation, a wave of arrests, coded Aktion Gitter (Operation Bars), was launched, mostly of emigrés from Germany, Czech public figures, and Jews. Jew-baiting became vociferous, the lead being taken by the most extreme of the fascist organizations, Vlajka (The Flag), which was especially active in Moravia. Anti-Jewish excesses began during the first days of the occupation: the synagogues of Vsetín and Jihlava (Iglau) were burned down. In other localities (Plzeň and Brno), Jews were rounded up in cafés and attacked on the streets under various pretexts.

In June 1939, Adolf EICHMANN arrived in PRAGUE and set up the ZENTRALSTELLE FÜR JÜDISCHE AUSWANDERUNG (Central Office for Jewish Emigration) to encourage large-scale emigration. It is estimated that before October 1941, when emigration was banned, 26,629 Jews managed to leave the country legally or illegally. Among these were 2,500 person who—under the HAAVARA AGREEMENT,

BOHEMIA AND MORAVIA Annexed March 15, 1939

signed on January 13, 1939, between the Czechoslovak Ministry of Finance and the Jewish Agency—reached Palestine in three groups (March 1939, October 1939, and January 1940). Others emigrated to Great Britain, the United States, or South America, or escaped to neighboring Poland. Hundreds of children and young people were transferred by the He-Haluts and YOUTH ALIYA movements to Great Britain, Denmark, and the Netherlands for agricultural training. After the establishment of the Czech National Council in London (later, the CZECHOSLOVAK GOVERNMENT-IN-EXILE, under the leadership of Edvard Beneš, the second and last president of the republic), army reservists in Allied and neutral countries were called upon to enlist in the Allied armies. About 2,000 Czechoslovak Jews who reached Palestine joined the Czechoslovak army units, fighting at Dunkerque, and later as part of the Allied Middle East forces. In 1941 a Czechoslovak division, about 70 percent Jewish, was established in the Soviet Union.

Under a decree of June 21, 1939, Jews in the protectorate were ordered to register and subsequently to sell their gold, platinum, silver articles, and precious jewelry to the Hadega public purchasing agency and to deposit all their stocks, bonds, and securities in a foreign-currency bank. Fraudulent methods, threats, blackmail, and force were used to acquire Jewish enterprises through ARISIERUNG ("Aryanization"). The total value of Jewish assets expropriated by the Germans in the Protectorate of Bohemia and Moravia has been estimated as at least a half-billion dollars.

With the outbreak of war in September 1939, a reign of terror was unleashed. Ordinances were issued curtailing the freedom of movement of Jews. There were dismissals from employment, and certain rations (sugar, tobacco, and items of clothing) were denied to Jews. Hostages arrested, including numerous prominent Jews, were sent to concentration camps.

As early as October 1939, the first expulsion took place. Around three thousand men from Moravská Ostrava and Frýdek-Místek were dispatched to "retraining centers" in the Nisko settlement in the Lublin area (see NISKO AND LUBLIN PLAN). As of November 24, the bilingual weekly *Jüdisches Nachrichtenblatt*—

Židovske Listy made its appearance, censored by the Gestapo, as the organ of the Jewish Religious Organizations, and later of the Ältestenrat der Juden in Prag (Council of Jewish Elders in Prague). The expulsion of Jewish children from schools, and other restrictions, as on the use of telephones and public transportation, posed severe problems for the Jewish population; the burden fell upon the Jews to take care of education, social work, relief for the sick and aged, and, first and foremost, training in languages and new vocations to enable people to emigrate overseas.

The Jewish Religious Congregation (JRC) of Prague, subject to the authority of the Zentralstelle, was led by two members of the assimilationist Czech-Jewish movement: Dr. Emil Kafka, the chairman, and Dr. František Weidmann, the secretary, who, after Kafka's departure to London, was appointed chairman by the Zentralstelle. Jacob EDELSTEIN,

the director of the Palestine Office in Prague, was appointed deputy chairman. Other leading members were Otto Zucker, Hanus Bonn, Marie Schmolka, Hanna Steiner, Dr. František Friedmann, Dr. Franz Kahn, Dr. Adolf Beneš, and Dr. Leo Janowitz.

The various departments of the JRC were gradually turned into unwilling tools of the German authorities, and their functions were redefined; tasks such as the liquidation of Jewish assets, consignment of Jews to forced labor, and assistance to deportees were imposed on their agenda. Any obstruction was regarded as sabotage punishable by death.

Early in September 1941, the JRC was ordered to take a census of the Jewish population. The 88,105 persons, identified in this census were ordered to wear the yellow Jewish BADGE and to live in complete isolation from the rest of the population. Shortly after Reinhard HEYDRICH was appointed acting

Deportation of Jews from Plzeň (Pilsen), 52 miles (83.6 km) southwest of Prague.

Reich protector, he called a meeting at Hrad-cany Palace to discuss the "solution of the Jewish problem." It was decided to concentrate the Jews of the protectorate in THERESIENSTADT and, after "their numbers have been considerably depleted by death," to send them to "the east."

First, five transports were sent from Prague to ŁÓDŹ, and one from Brno to MINSK and RIGA. These deportees were to share the fate of hundreds of thousands of Polish and Russian Jews: the greater part were annihilated in the camps of BEŁŻEC, CHEŁMNO, TREBLINKA, and Lublin (MAJDANEK). Some were massacred in the NINTH FORT in Kovno.

Between November 24, 1941, and March 16, 1945, 122 trains with 73,608 persons aboard were dispatched from the protectorate to Theresienstadt. A great majority of these people (60,399) were deported in the years 1942 to 1944 to AUSCHWITZ and other extermination camps; only 3,227 of them survived the war. As part of the retaliation campaign for Heydrich's assassination in Prague (May 27, 1942), a special transport of 1,000 Czech Jews was dispatched on June 10 to Poland; at Ujazd, they were ordered to dig their own graves before they were executed. The abandoned possessions of Jews, such as textiles, furs, furniture, and glassware, were stored by the Treuhandstelle (Trustee Office) set up by the Nazis in fifty-four warehouses. Eleven synagogues in the capital were utilized for this purpose.

On February 8, 1943, the JRC in Prague was reorganized as the Ältestenrat der Juden in Prag, headed first by Salo Krämer and his deputy, Herbert Langer. The last *Judenälteste* (head of the Jewish Council), from July 1943, was Dr. František Friedmann, and his deputy in charge of administration was Erich Kraus.

The final mass transport of "full Jews" (*Volljuden*) left Prague in the summer of 1943. After this transport, aside from the members of the Jewish Council and their families, only Jewish partners in mixed marriages were left in the protectorate. By December 31, 1944, their number amounted to 6,795. In late January and early February 1945, 4,243 persons were sent to Theresienstadt. On May 5, 1945 (the day of the liberation of Czechoslovakia), the total number of officially registered Jews in the Protectorate of Bohemia and Moravia was 2,803. It is estimated that of the 92,199 Jews living in Bohemia and Moravia before the start of the deportations, 78,154 perished and 14,045 survived the Holocaust.

Before their deportation to the extermination camps, the Jewish community leadership and cultural elite of Prague managed to save from destruction articles of the religious and cultural heritage of the Jews of Bohemia and Moravia. The Nazis intended to display this accumulation of items at a Central Museum of the Extinguished Jewish Race; instead it became the rich collection of Judaica exhibited in the Jewish Museum of Prague, a precious legacy of the 77,297 Jewish victims, whose names are inscribed on the walls of the Pinkas Synagogue.

[*See also* Youth Movements: Bohemia and Moravia.]

BIBLIOGRAPHY

Baum, K. "Nazi Anti-Jewish Legislation in the Czech Protectorate: A Documentary Note." *Soviet Jewish Affairs* 2/1 (May 1972): 116–128.

Dagan, A., et al., eds. *The Jews of Czechoslovakia: Historical Studies and Surveys.* Vol. 3. Philadelphia, 1984.

Duff, S. G. *German Protectorate: The Czechs under Nazi Rule.* London, 1970.

Mastny, V. *The Czechs under Nazi Rule: The Failure of National Resistance, 1939–1942.* New York, 1971.

Mastny, V., and R. Luza. *A History of the Czechoslovak Republic, 1918–1948.* Princeton, 1973.

LIVIA ROTHKIRCHEN

BOMBING OF AUSCHWITZ. *See* Auschwitz, Bombing of.

BONHOEFFER, DIETRICH (1906–1945), German Protestant theologian. Bonhoeffer's execution by the Nazis in the FLOSSENBÜRG concentration camp on April 9, 1945, in the closing stages of World War II, cut short his career as one of Germany's most significant twentieth-century theologians. After completing his studies at the University of Berlin (D.Phil., 1927) as a student of Adolf von Harnack, Germany's famous liberal theologian, Bonhoeffer became attracted to the more critical dialectical theology of Karl BARTH.

Early in his career he realized the dangers of the extremism and racist bias of Nazi ideology, and in 1933 he became an outspoken opponent of the German Christian (Deutsche Christen) faction of the German Evangelical Church (Evangelische Kirche), which lauded Adolf Hitler and gave its support to the rise of the Nazi party. Because of this opposition, Bonhoeffer was sent to be chaplain of the German church in south London from 1933 to 1935, but he was later recalled to lead an illegal training institute for ordination candidates of the anti-Nazi Confessing Church (Bekennende Kirche), until it was suppressed by the Gestapo in 1938. During the war, he was recruited by Adm. Wilhelm CANARIS, head of the ABWEHR (the Wehrmacht intelligence service), for secret contacts with foreign churches, but was arrested in April 1943 and imprisoned in Berlin and Flossenbürg until his execution.

Bonhoeffer came from a Christian tradition that saw the Jews as accursed, as stated in his April 1933 essay "The Church and the Jewish Question." However, he was the first theologian to recognize the implications for Christian theology of the Nazi persecution of the Jews, and in 1933 he warned his fellow churchmen of the perversion of the Gospels that these racist attacks implied. He subsequently became involved in efforts to assist Jews to escape from Germany, including a successful scheme in 1942 to smuggle a party of fifteen Jews to Switzerland, which led to his arrest. Bonhoeffer's sense of moral outrage against the Nazi treatment of Jews was a major factor in his support of the German resistance movement, in which various members of his immediate family were involved and for which they were later executed.

In his theology, Bonhoeffer addressed the deeper causes of the alienation between Judaism and Christianity, showing that all attempts to curtail the theological significance of the Jewish heritage must be regarded as heretical. In his unfinished work *Ethics*, he began to define the basis for a new understanding of the theological solidarity between Christians and Jews, which went be-yond sympathy based on humanitarian feelings. He was continually disappointed by the timidity of the Confessing Church in facing its obligations to the Jewish people. But his involvement in conspiratorial activities after 1939 prevented him from publishing any more outspoken attacks on the regime. There are, however, hints of new approaches in the series of his letters that were smuggled out of prison between 1943 and 1945. A collection of them was first published in 1951, under the title *Widerstand und Ergebung* (Resistance and Surrender). It appeared in English translation in 1953 as *Letters and Papers from Prison* and was published in many subsequent editions.

Bonhoeffer's courageous opposition to the Nazi regime and his subsequent murder greatly enhanced his reputation in the postwar period, and his theological influence has been significantly instrumental in the post-Holocaust rethinking of Christian relationships with the Jewish people. His other major works include *Nachfolge* (1937; published in English as *The Cost of Discipleship*, 1948) and *Sanctorium Communio* (1929; *The Community of Saints*, 1963).

BIBLIOGRAPHY

Bethge, E. *Dietrich Bonhoeffer.* New York, 1977.

Bethge, E., ed. *Ethics.* New York, 1967.

Robertson, E. *The Shame and the Sacrifice: The Life and Martyrdom of Dietrich Bonhoeffer.* New York, 1988.

Willis, R. E. "Bonhoeffer and Barth on Jewish Suffering." *Journal of Ecumenical Studies* 24/4 (1987): 598–615.

Zerner, R. "Dietrich Bonhoeffer and the Jews: Thoughts and Action, 1933–1945." *Jewish Social Studies* 37/3–4 (Summer–Fall 1975): 235–250.

JOHN S. CONWAY

BOR-KOMOROWSKI, TADEUSZ (1895–1966), commander of the ARMIA KRAJOWA (Home Army) in WARSAW and of the WARSAW POLISH UPRISING in 1944. Bor-Komorowski was born in Lvov. His actual name was Komorowski, "Bor" being his later code name in the underground. In World War I he was an officer in the Austro-Hungarian army, and

Tadeusz Bor-Komorowski.

after the war served as an officer in the Polish army, in which he became a colonel. In 1939 he took part in the battle against the German invaders.

At the beginning of the German occupation, Bor-Komorowski was one of the organizers of the Polish underground in the Kraków area. In July 1941 he became deputy commander of the Armia Krajowa and two years later was appointed its commander, the POLISH GOVERNMENT-IN-EXILE promoting him to brigadier general. In his political views he was close to the National Democratic party (the "Endeks"). It was he who gave the order for the Polish uprising in Warsaw, which he led from August to October 1944. When the rebellion was put down, Bor-Komorowski became a prisoner of war. He was liberated at the end of the war and spent the rest of his life in London, where he was active among Polish emigrés. He wrote the story of his experiences in *The Secret Army* (1951), in which he told about the aid offered and the actions taken by the Armia Krajowa in the face of mass deportations and the killing of the Jews. His contentions, however, have no basis in fact.

BIBLIOGRAPHY

Korbonski, S. *The Polish Underground State: A Guide to the Underground, 1939–1945.* New York, 1969.

Zawodny, J. K. *Nothing but Honor: The Story of the Warsaw Uprising, 1944.* Stanford, 1978.

SHMUEL KRAKOWSKI

BORKOWSKA, ANNA (d. 1988), mother superior of a small cloister of Dominican sisters in Kolonia Wilenska, near Vilna, Lithuania. During the PONARY massacres of Jews in the summer months of 1941, Anna Borkowska agreed to conceal in her convent for brief periods seventeen members of Jewish Zionist pioneering groups, including Ha-Shomer ha-Tsa'ir. Later, she helped by smuggling weapons into the Vilna ghetto. Abraham SUTZKEVER, the Yiddish poet, related that the first four grenades received there were the gift of the mother superior, who instructed Abba KOVNER in their proper use. She later supplied other weapons.

As Nazi suspicions of her mounted, the Ger-

Abba Kovner, second from right, presenting Anna Borkowska with the Yad Vashem Righteous among the Nations medal and certificate in Warsaw (August 3, 1984). [Ma'ariv]

mans had Anna Borkowska arrested in September 1943, the convent closed, and the sisters dispersed. One nun was dispatched to a labor camp. In 1984, Anna Borkowska was recognized by YAD VASHEM as a "RIGHTEOUS AMONG THE NATIONS."

BIBLIOGRAPHY

Bartoszewski, W., and Z. Lewin, eds. *Righteous among Nations: How Poles Helped the Jews, 1939–1945.* London, 1969.

MORDECAI PALDIEL

BORMANN, MARTIN (1900–1945?), Nazi leader and close aide of Adolf HITLER. Bormann was born in Halberstadt into the family of a postal worker. Toward the end of World War I he interrupted his high school studies to enlist in the artillery, but the war ended before he reached the front. At the end of the war Bormann joined the Deutsche Freikorps, which carried out acts of violence along the Latvian border after Latvia declared itself independent. Subsequently, Bormann was active in the underground, paramilitary nationalist Frontbann organization, created by Ernst RÖHM, and participated in one of its political assassinations (*Fememorde*). In 1923 he was arrested for this, and sentenced to a year's imprisonment. In prison he became acquainted with Rudolf HÖSS, future commandant of the AUSCHWITZ extermination camp. After Bormann's release in 1925, he joined the Nazi party and the SA (Sturmabteilung; Storm Troopers) in Thuringia, and in 1926 was appointed head of Nazi press affairs and deputy SA commander of the region. In 1928 he rose to the rank of *Gauleiter* of Thuringia. Known in the Nazi party as an active fund-raiser, he was appointed treasurer at the party center in Munich.

With the Nazi rise to power in 1933, Bormann was elected to the Reichstag and became head of the office of Rudolf HESS, Hitler's deputy in the party. From this time Bormann remained at the center of Nazi power around Hitler and was responsible for all financial and administrative affairs. He was always in the shadow of the Führer, ex-

celling as a planner and a behind-the-scenes man, but not as a public speaker.

After Hess's strange flight to Scotland in 1941, Bormann's power increased. In 1942 he was appointed head of the party secretariat and of the party staff, with the rank of *Reichsminister*, and in 1943 he became Hitler's secretary. In this capacity, Bormann also controlled Hitler's appointments calendar, sometimes preventing important figures such as Hermann GÖRING, Joseph GOEBBELS, Heinrich HIMMLER, and Albert SPEER from approaching the leader. He took notes on Hitler's speeches and monologues at luncheons with his favorites, the material known as Hitler's "table talks."

As the war continued and became Hitler's principal occupation, Bormann's status grew, since he was charged in Hitler's name not only with party affairs but with the domestic affairs of Germany. In particular, Bormann was active in fields such as the EUTHANASIA PROGRAM, the war against the church, the pil-

Martin Bormann, Nazi party secretary. [National Archives]

lage of art objects in the occupied countries of eastern Europe, and the expansion of forced-labor programs throughout Europe. Above all, Bormann, who was completely amoral, was the zealous executor of the racist plan of National Socialism and in particular of the persecution and extermination of the Jews. He signed the series of anti-Jewish edicts ordering the deportation of the Jews to the east, the concentration of power in Jewish affairs in the hands of the SS, and the concealment of the massacre as the "transfer of the Jews to labor in the east."

Bormann was appointed commander of the People's Army (Volkssturm), created toward the end of the war, in October 1944. His desire for greater personal power did not cease even after Hitler entered his bunker in Berlin. In the last stage of Nazi rule, Bormann tried to have Göring executed, was a witness to Hitler's marriage to Eva Braun a day before their suicide, and observed the suicide of Goebbels and his family. Before the surrender, it was Bormann who informed Adm. Karl Dönitz that Dönitz had been appointed the Führer's successor.

After Hitler's death, Bormann allegedly tried to conduct negotiations with the Soviets, but after becoming convinced that these were hopeless he gave the order to escape from the bunker. With that his trace vanished. On October 29, 1945, Bormann was indicted *in absentia* with the other Nazi leaders by the International Military Tribunal at Nuremberg, and on October 1, 1946, he was sentenced to death *in absentia*.

Bormann's fate is uncertain. According to unreliable testimony, he was killed by a Soviet shell or committed suicide, and according to rumors that spread in the 1960s he escaped to South America, perhaps to Paraguay. In early 1973 a West German forensic expert determined that one of two skeletons discovered in West Berlin during excavations in 1972 was almost certainly that of Bormann. On the basis of this determination, Bormann was officially declared dead.

BIBLIOGRAPHY

Lang, J. von, and C. Sibyll. *Bormann: The Man Who Manipulated Hitler*. New York, 1979.

McGovern, J. *Martin Bormann*. New York, 1968.
Wulf, J. *Martin Bormann: Hitlers Schatten*. Gütersloh, 1962.

TSVI RAANAN

BOSNIA. *See* Yugoslavia.

BOTHMANN, HANS (1911–1946), commandant of the CHEŁMNO extermination camp in central Poland. Bothmann joined the HITLER-JUGEND (the Nazi youth movement) in November 1932 and the SS in June 1933. In September 1939, following the invasion of Poland, he was assigned to the Sicherheitspolizei (Security Police) in Poznań. He was appointed commandant at Chełmno in the spring of 1942, replacing Hauptsturmführer Herbert Lange, and he directed the mass killing operations in the camp until March 1943, when the transports of Jews to Chełmno were discontinued. The next month Bothmann, together with eighty-five members of the camp staff, was transferred to Yugoslavia, where he formed Sonderkommando Bothmann, which reinforced a company of gendarmerie attached to the "Prinz Eugen" Division of the SS. With these forces, Bothmann engaged in operations against the Yugoslav PARTISANS.

In the late spring of 1944, Bothmann and his unit were ordered back to Chełmno to renew the gassing operations, which continued through June and July. In August, Sonderkommando Bothmann took part in the liquidation of the ŁÓDŹ ghetto. It was then assigned to AKTION 1005, in which the corpses of the victims at Chełmno were burned to obliterate evidence of the killings that had taken place there.

In January 1945 Bothmann escaped to western Germany, where he was captured by the British; on April 4, 1946, he hanged himself in prison.

SHMUEL KRAKOWSKI

BOYCOTT, ANTI-JEWISH. The boycott of April 1, 1933, was the first national action against the German Jews after the Nazi seizure of power on January 30 of that year. The boycott was declared by the Nazi party on March 28, apparently after consultations with the top ranks of power at Hitler's residence in Berchtesgaden on the initiative of Propaganda Minister Joseph GOEBBELS. The declaration was described as an action of both reprisal and warning against world Jewry to cease what the Nazis called *Greuelpropaganda* (horror propaganda) and an economic boycott abroad against the "New Germany." The acts of terror committed by the SA (Sturmabteilung; Storm Troopers) against political rivals and Jews in the first months after the Nazi rise to power had indeed received extensive publicity and aroused public protests throughout the world, though Jewish institutions and organizations generally took a cautious line, fearing to harm German Jewry.

The boycott was organized initially as a Nazi party operation. Julius STREICHER was placed at the head of the organizing committee. Despite the apparently short period of preparation, everything was planned down to the last detail. At 10:00 a.m. on Saturday, April 1, the boycott was to begin simultaneously in every city and town, down to the smallest village. In fact, actions commenced in several places on the previous day or evening—a direct continuation of the harassment and confiscation that had been pursued continuously in the weeks preceding the "official" boycott. The pattern was the same, in accordance with the detailed instructions: guards of uniformed, sometimes armed, Nazis were placed in front of every store or other business owned by Jews, and their clients were prevented from entering. Trucks patrolled the streets with uniformed Nazis and members of the Stahlhelm organization, bearing signs and slogans proclaiming: "Ger-

Boycott of April 1, 1933, in Berlin. The sign in both windows reads: "Germans! Beware! Don't buy from Jews!"

mans! Defend yourselves! Don't buy from Jews!" In the main streets of the large cities an effort was made to avoid open violence, but in more remote places there were many incidents of shattered store windows, pillaging of stores, and physical assault of Jewish business owners. Despite the order not to harm the businesses of Jewish foreign nationals, many attacks did occur, especially on Jews of eastern European origin who lived together in poor sections of towns. An indication of such attacks is the complaints they engendered from diplomatic representations, particularly, in several cities, the representatives of Poland.

Besides retail stores, the liberal professions were a specific target for expropriation activities. Guards were placed at the doors of the offices of Jewish lawyers and doctors. In several cities, uniformed gangs of Nazis broke into law courts and forcibly expelled Jewish judges and prosecutors, both government employees and private lawyers. On the day before the boycott, the ministers of justice in Prussia and Bavaria had already sent the Jewish jurists "on vacation" and had forbidden them to enter the law courts "in order to guarantee their safety and to maintain public order."

The boycott declaration aroused a wave of protests and a series of interventions by government circles and both Jewish and non-Jewish businessmen abroad in an attempt to bring about its annulment. Jewish organizations in Germany and abroad published announcements rejecting the Nazi accusations of *Greuelpropaganda* and proclaiming an economic boycott against German exports. In Germany too the declaration of boycott aroused concern in economic circles over possible harmful consequences, in light of the unemployment and depression. On the afternoon of Friday, March 31, in a government consultation in Hitler's office in Berlin, the possibility had been discussed of annulling the boycott of the following day, on condition that the governments of Great Britain and the United States publish official announcements condemning the *Greuelpropaganda*. It was possibly because of these pressures that the boycott—initially declared for an unlimited period—ceased, by government an-

nouncement, after one day, while the hope was expressed that those spreading *Greuelpropaganda* abroad had learned their lesson. There was no conflict between the intentions of the party, which declared the boycott, and those of the government, which announced its cessation. Goebbels himself, the moving spirit in the organization of the boycott, declared at a party mass meeting on the evening of March 31 that the boycott would be stopped after one day and would be renewed on April 4 if the *Greuelpropaganda* abroad did not cease.

It is the opinion of several scholars that the Nazi leadership organized the boycott day as a "safety valve" for pressures from rank-and-file party members, in particular SA members, who demanded radical steps against the activity of the Jews in the economy, as promised in the Nazi party platform. According to this interpretation, the aim of the boycott was to allow postponement of these steps (1) until the stabilization of the Nazi regime and (2) because of Germany's uncertain financial situation and international position. Yet in fact the boycott was a clear and explicit starting signal for a process of harassment and oppression, designed to undermine the basis of the economic existence of Germany Jewry. Acts of terror, expropriation, and discrimination, which previously could have been interpreted as "individual" or "isolated" acts (*Einzelaktionen*) of violence on a local initiative, were legitimized through the boycott by the highest party and government institutions. In the boycott instructions, the initial and immediate targets of economic oppression were also clearly indicated: Jewish professionals and Jewish retail businesses. From this point of view, the April 1 boycott was the official opening for preparing the legislation passed on April 7 against Jewish professionals and government employees, and the administrative and propaganda campaign of repression against all economic activity among German Jewry.

BIBLIOGRAPHY

Adam, U. D. *Judenpolitik im Dritten Reich*. Düsseldorf, 1972.
Ball-Kaduri, J. *Das Leben der Juden in Deutschland im Jahre 1933*: *Ein Zeitbericht*. Frankfurt, 1963.

Barkai, A. *Vom Boykott zur "Entjudung": Der wirtschaftliche Existenzkampf der Juden im Dritten Reich, 1933–1943.* Frankfurt, 1988.

Schleunes, K. *The Twisted Road to Auschwitz: Nazi Policy toward German Jews, 1933–1939.* Urbana, Ill., 1970.

AVRAHAM BARKAI

BOYCOTTS, ANTI-NAZI, pre–World War II actions to boycott German goods in reaction to the Nazi persecution of the Jews. Following the Nazi rise to power in 1933, there were Jewish protests throughout the world against the policies of the new regime in Germany. These protests developed into boycott movements in many countries, most importantly in the United States.

On March 19, 1933, the Jewish War Veterans organization announced a boycott in the United States. Following the Nazi boycott of Jewish businesses (*see* BOYCOTT, ANTI-JEWISH) in Germany on April 1, 1933, additional boycott groups were formed in the United States and elsewhere. In May 1933, the Yiddish journalist Abraham Coralnik founded the American League for the Defense of Jewish Rights. He was succeeded six months later by Samuel Untermyer, who became a leading figure in the boycott movement until the United States entered World War II. Untermyer changed the organization's name to the Non-Sectarian Anti-Nazi League to Champion Human Rights, in order to emphasize the universality of the cause. In 1933, Untermyer and Coralnik organized the World Jewish Economic Conference in Amsterdam in an unsuccessful effort to coordinate an international Jewish boycott movement.

The American Jewish Congress (*see* WORLD JEWISH CONGRESS) issued its own boycott declaration in August 1933, and its JOINT BOYCOTT COUNCIL, formed in 1935 together with the JEWISH LABOR COMMITTEE's boycott movement, became one of the two leading boycott organizations in the United States. However, efforts to unify the boycott activities of Untermyer's League and the Joint Boycott Council were unsuccessful.

Support for the anti-Nazi boycott was widespread in the United States and elsewhere, but the movement never received the wholehearted backing of many important organizations and leaders, both among the American public in general and in the Jewish community. In the United States, the AMERICAN JEWISH COMMITTEE and B'NAI B'RITH were among the organizations opposing the boycott, while the BOARD OF DEPUTIES OF BRITISH JEWS in England and the Alliance Israélite Universelle in France opposed the movements in their respective countries.

In Britain, the Board of Deputies turned down a proposal to foster an economic boycott of Germany at a meeting held on July 23, 1933. Dissenting members of the board, including Lord Melchett (Henry Mond), formed the Jewish Representation Council. Together with an ad hoc committee, the Organization for Ending Hostilities to German Jews, this council strove to organize a boycott in Great Britain. Lord Melchett also played a role in convening the World Jewish Economic Conference in 1933. After 1934, however, the British boycott movement became splintered and lost most of its effectiveness.

Whereas several British and American organizations opposed international Jewish political activity in principle, the Jewish Agency found itself working against the boycott through the HAAVARA AGREEMENT (Transfer Agreement) reached with Germany. The agency's understanding of the practical necessities of aiding German Jews to leave Germany and emigrate to Palestine with part of their capital led to this conflict.

In January 1936, Simon Marks, Sir Herbert Samuel, and Lord Bearsted went to the United States from England to negotiate with American Jewish leaders on the creation of the COUNCIL FOR GERMAN JEWRY. However, they had to yield to American Zionist insistence that no scheme to transfer German goods out of Germany be considered.

The boycott met with limited success; the fur trade between Britain and Germany virtually ceased, and several American department stores, such as R. H. Macy and Gimbel Brothers, agreed to stop buying German goods. There is also some evidence that leading figures within the Nazi regime were at times concerned about the possible effects of the boycott movement on the German economy. However, the movement failed in its overriding goal of forcing Nazi Germany to change its Jewish policy.

BIBLIOGRAPHY

Gottlieb, M. R. *American Anti-Nazi Resistance, 1933–1941: An Historical Analysis.* New York, 1982.
Tenenbaum, J. "The Anti-Nazi Boycott Movement in the United States." *Yad Vashem Studies* 3 (1959): 141–159.

DAVID SILBERKLANG

BRACK, VIKTOR (1904–1948), senior SS officer (*Oberführer*) and one of the chief functionaries in the EUTHANASIA PROGRAM and the mass gassing of Jews in the EXTERMINATION CAMPS during World War II. The son of a physician, Brack studied economics in Munich. He was friendly with Heinrich HIMMLER and was his chauffeur before becoming liaison officer between the SS and the Führer's Chancellery (Kanzlei des Führers) in 1936. He rose to become deputy to Philip Bouhler, head of the chancellery, and Brack's office in the chancellery, known as T4, was responsible for the killing of more than fifty thousand Germans and Jews under the Euthanasia Program from 1939 to 1941. Brack himself personally interviewed the medical personnel employed in the program.

In the summer of 1941, when the "FINAL SOLUTION" was inaugurated, Brack made his experience available in the efforts to sterilize Jews in X-ray clinics and to exterminate them in the gas chambers of the camps in occupied Poland. As one of the accused in The Medical Case, tried at the SUBSEQUENT NUREMBERG PROCEEDINGS, Brack was sentenced to death by an American military tribunal in 1947 and executed in 1948.

BIBLIOGRAPHY

Lifton, R. J. *The Nazi Doctors: Medical Killing and the Psychology of Genocide.* New York, 1986.
Mitscherlich, A., and F. Mielke. *Doctors of Infamy: The Story of Nazi Medical Crimes.* New York, 1949.

Sereny, G. *Into That Darkness: From Mercy Killing to Mass Murder.* New York, 1974.

LIONEL KOCHAN

BRAND, JOEL (1907–1964), member of the RELIEF AND RESCUE COMMITTEE OF BUDAPEST (known as the Va'ada) during World War II. Born in Năsăud, Transylvania, then under Hungarian rule, Brand embraced Zionism after a stint in the radical leftist movement in Weimar Germany. He returned to Transylvania after Hitler's seizure of power but eventually settled in Budapest, where together with his wife, Hansi Hartmann Brand, he operated a medium-sized glove-manufacturing plant. After the Anschluss and especially after the outbreak of World War II, the Brands became interested in refugee affairs, organizing a variety of rescue and relief activities.

When the Va'ada was established in January 1943 to aid refugees who had escaped from or were seeking to escape from Slovakia

Joel Brand.

and Poland, Brand was chosen to head its Tiyyul (Trip) section, a border-crossing operation whose function was to smuggle Jews out of these countries.

After the German occupation of Hungary on March 19, 1944, the Va'ada's primary concern was the rescuing of Jews within Hungary. Brand was also engaged in the Re-Tiyyul (Return Trip) program, which enabled a number of Polish and Slovak refugees to return to Slovakia, where the situation of the remaining Jews was better, at least temporarily. While the first contact and rescue negotiations with the SS were established through Fülöp FREUDIGER, the Orthodox representative of the Jewish Council (Zsidó Tanács), and continued later by Rezső (Rudolf) KASZTNER, it was Brand whom Adolf EICHMANN summoned, on April 25, 1944, to offer his "Blood for Goods" arrangement. Under the arrangement, which was approved by the higher SS authorities, apparently including Heinrich HIMMLER, Eichmann expressed his readiness to exchange one million Jews for certain goods to be obtained from outside Hungary. These included 10,000 trucks that would be used for civilian purposes or only along the eastern front. Jews could not remain in Hungary, for he had promised to make the country *judenrein* ("cleansed of Jews"). But those covered by the bargain would be permitted to go into any Allied-controlled part of the world except Palestine, for the Nazis had promised the mufti of Jerusalem, Hajj Amin al-HUSSEINI, not to permit this. To effectuate the deal, Eichmann was ready to allow Brand to go abroad to establish contact with the representatives of world Jewry and the western Allies.

The true reason why Brand was chosen remains a mystery, but it appears that he had been recommended by Andor ("Bandi") Grosz, a doubtful character and minor intelligence agent who was in the service of anyone who paid him, including the Germans and the Va'ada. Grosz was reportedly employed by SS-Hauptsturmführer Otto Klages, the head of the SD (Sicherheitsdienst; Security Service) in Hungary; he was assigned to go together with Brand to establish contact with American and British intelligence officers in Istanbul and to discuss with them the possibility of a separate peace between Germany and the western Allies. Brand's mission, according to this scenario, was to camouflage Grosz's more important assignment.

Brand was informed about the completion of his travel arrangements on May 15, 1944, the day that mass deportations from Hungary began. Supplied with a German passport bearing the name Eugen Band, he left Budapest for Vienna in the company of Obersturmbannführer Hermann KRUMEY, a leading member of the Eichmann Sonderkommando, and Grosz left two days later. On May 19 Brand and Grosz arrived in Istanbul, where they were met by local representatives of the JOINT RESCUE COMMITTEE of the Jewish Agency. Since Brand had no Turkish visa, the details of his mission were revealed to Laurence Steinhardt, the American ambassador in Ankara, and to the leaders of the Jewish Agency in Jerusalem by the Agency's representatives in Turkey.

By the end of the month, the leaders of the American and British governments were fully informed about Brand's mission. Grosz was arrested by the British on June 1, shortly after crossing the Syrian border. Thus, he was unable to meet with authorized Jewish and non-Jewish representatives and to complete his assignment. Equipped with a British visa, Brand left—ostensibly for Palestine—on June 5, but was arrested by the British at Aleppo two days later. On June 10 he was given an opportunity (while under arrest) to reveal the plight of Hungarian Jewry and the details of his mission to Moshe Shertok (Sharett), head of the Jewish Agency's Political Department. Shertok was very favorably impressed with Brand, as was Ira A. HIRSCHMANN, the representative of the WAR REFUGEE BOARD, who interrogated him later in the month in Cairo. Before the month was over, Shertok and Hirschmann revealed the details of their interrogations to the YISHUV leaders and to top figures of the American and British governments.

In spite of pleas by the Yishuv leaders, the British decided against having any dealings "with the Gestapo" and even permitting Brand's return to Hungary. Their decision was based on many factors, among them the continuation of the "Final Solution" program in Hungary; the vehement opposition of the

Soviets (who were officially informed about the offer in mid-June) to any discussion on this matter with the Germans; and the concern of the British over acquiring responsibility for one million Jews in case the Nazis kept their side of the bargain. The Americans were more flexible, advocating that the negotiations be continued in the hope of saving lives. Whatever hopes the Jewish leaders of the free world had for Brand's mission dissipated on July 19, when the BBC brought it to public attention. The following day, the British press emphasized that the "monstrous offer" of the Germans to barter Jews was a loathsome attempt to blackmail the Allies.

Immediately after his June 10 meeting with Shertok, Brand was taken to Cairo, where he was intensively debriefed and treated as a "privileged prisoner" until October, when he was allowed to go to Palestine. A frustrated and dejected man, Brand felt for a long time that because of the failure and shortcomings of the Jewish leaders and the passivity and insensitivity of the Allies, the chance to save a million Jews had been missed. However, shortly before his death in Tel Aviv in 1964, Brand came to believe that he had made a "terrible mistake" in passing to the British the Eichmann offer, and that Heinrich Himmler had merely sought to sow suspicion among the Allies as a preparation for his much-desired Nazi-western coalition against Moscow.

BIBLIOGRAPHY

Bauer, Y. *The Holocaust in Historical Perspective.* Seattle, 1978. See pages 94–155.
Brand, J., and A. Weissberg. *Desperate Mission: Joel Brand's Story.* New York, 1958.

RANDOLPH L. BRAHAM

BRATISLAVA (Ger., Pressburg; Hung., Pozsony), city in Czechoslovakia; capital of SLOVAKIA. Bratislava dates back to the tenth century. From 1541 to 1784 it was the capital of Habsburg-ruled Hungary, and until 1848 it was the seat of the Hungarian parliament. In 1918 it became the capital of the Czechoslovak province of Slovakia, and from 1939 to 1945 it was the capital of the Slovak state.

The presence of Jews in Bratislava is mentioned as early as the tenth century, but it was only in the seventeenth century that the Jewish community began to flourish. Rabbi Moshe Sofer (known as the Ḥatam Sofer; 1762–1839) established a large yeshiva (rabbinical academy), and the city became a great center of Orthodox Judaism. The Orthodox influence declined in the second half of the nineteenth century, when modern institutions of both a religious and a secular character were established. The city had an antisemitic tradition, which was expressed in anti-Jewish riots (in 1831, 1848, 1918, and 1937), during the Holocaust, and in the post–World War II period. In December 1940, Bratislava had a Jewish population of some fifteen thousand—about one-sixth of Slovak Jewry.

As a capital city, Bratislava was the seat of central Jewish organizations such as the ÚSTREDŇA ŽIDOV and the Union of Jewish Communities. It was also the home of nationalist bodies, such as the HLINKA GUARD, Hlinková Mladež (Hlinka Youth), the Freiwillige Schutzstaffel (Volunteer Battalions), and the German HITLERJUGEND. These organizations, together with urban mobs, frequently rioted against the Jews. Such riots began in October 1938, immediately after Slovakia was granted autonomy, and subsequently they were launched time and again. Bratislava's Jews—some of whom still lived in the Židovna, the old ghetto—were exposed to organized raids by rioters and to sporadic harassment. Following the attacks that took place in March 1939 to "celebrate" Slovakia's independence, a Jewish self-defense organization was formed in the Jewish quarter, its membership consisting of artisans, members of sports clubs, yeshiva students, and members of youth movements. The Jews defended themselves against sporadic attacks, and in a few instances the attackers had to pay with their lives.

The Bratislava Jews were quick to come to the aid of their brethren in an hour of need. The first to appeal for such help were the Jews of Austria, especially those who lived in the "Seven Communities" of Burgenland and were being persecuted by the SS, and Jewish residents of Slovakia whom the authorities had expelled to Hungary, claiming that they were Hungarian nationals. (The Hungarians had turned them back into the no-man's-land between the two countries.) For the latter, the Jewish organizations rented the premises of a factory that was no longer in operation—known as the "Patronka"—and put it in shape for lengthy occupation; this later became a place that the Jews mortally feared, since it was used as an assembly center prior to their deportation to the east.

Bratislava's port was the departure point for several "illegal" immigration boats that sailed for the Black Sea and the shores of Palestine. The passengers on these boats were refugees from neighboring countries as well as residents of Czechoslovakia; only some of them succeeded in reaching their goal.

The deportation of the Jews of Bratislava was preceded by their eviction from certain parts of the city—specific squares, streets, and quarters—and their removal to the provinces. This operation, known as the *dislokacia*, lasted from the fall of 1941 to the spring of 1942, and in its course 6,700 persons were moved out, that is, half the Jewish population of the city. Their property was confiscated by the authorities, and their apartments were handed over to other inhabitants. The official reason given for the *dislokacia* was the shortage of apartments for the city's growing population, but in fact the operation was a planned prelude to the deportations; the Jews were being gathered into a few places, to facilitate their eventual deportation to extermination camps.

When the deportations were launched, some of the victims were loaded into railway cars at Patronka, and sent straight to the east; others were first taken to assembly points selected for this purpose. In Bratislava the Jews continued to maintain their activities—legally, in the Ústredńa Židov, or illegally, in the PRACOVŃÁ SKUPINA (Working Group). Following the SLOVAK NATIONAL UPRISING in 1944, the city came under German occupation. Many Jews who had not fled in time hid in city bunkers, a refuge for which, in most instances, they had to pay heavily: they were seized by raiding teams and sent to a camp in SERED, and from there to the extermination camps. When the number of Jews seized in this fashion declined, the Germans resorted to surprise checks in the street, often

helped by tip-offs from informants and collaborators, Jewish and non-Jewish. At the beginning of the German occupation, several members of the Pracovná Skupina deluded themselves that they would be able to help the local Jewish population, but later they themselves were caught and taken to Sered. A Jewish underground, headed by Juraj Revesz, was also organized in the city, in order to give financial aid to the Jews in hiding; this group obtained money from the International RED CROSS delegate, Georges Dunand, and distributed it among those in need. Members of the underground who fell into German hands were used by the Gestapo as bait for other Jews roaming the streets; the latter knew these activists and turned to them for help. The result was that many of the Jews in hiding were discovered, along with their families. When the Soviets liberated Bratislava, in April 1945, only a few Jews were left.

Liberation did not put an end to pogroms. Particularly severe were the pogroms of the summer of 1946, when the Jewish hospital was among the places ransacked, and those of the summer of 1948. The latter were the last of the postwar attacks on the Jews of Bratislava, and in their course a self-defense group was formed that was able to capture the rioters. Most of the remaining Jews of Bratislava left in the great emigration wave of 1948 and 1949. Organized Jewish life, of modest dimensions, continues to function in the city.

BIBLIOGRAPHY

Dagan, A., ed. *The Jews of Czechoslovakia*. 3 vols. New York, 1968.

Dunand, G. *Ne perdez pas leur trace*. Neuchâtel, 1950.

Frieder, E. *To Deliver Their Souls: The Struggle of a Young Rabbi during the Holocaust*. Jerusalem, 1986. (In Hebrew.)

Grünhut, A. *Katastrophenzeit des slowakischen Judentums: Aufstieg und Niedergang der Juden von Pressburg*. Tel Aviv, 1972.

YESHAYAHU JELINEK

BREENDONCK, internment camp in Belgium, near the village of that name, south of the city of Antwerp. At the beginning of the century, a fortress was erected near the village, at the junction of the Antwerp-Brussels and MECHELEN-Dendermonde roads, as part of a chain of fortifications; this fortress, surrounded by a moat, consists of a building measuring 656 by 984 feet (200 × 300 m) and is still in existence.

At the end of August 1940 the Germans turned the fortress into a *Polizeihaftlager* (internment camp), and three weeks later, on September 20, the first group of detainees,

numbering twenty persons, mostly "politicals" and Jews of foreign nationality, were brought to the camp. The camp was under the control of the Sicherheitspolizei (Security Police) and was run by ss men, with Wehrmacht personnel serving as guards. At the end of 1941 they were joined by Belgian SS men. The first commandant of the camp was Sturmbannführer Philip Schmitt, who was followed, in 1943, by an Austrian, Karl Schönwetter. The officer in charge of forced labor was Untersturmführer Artur Prauss,

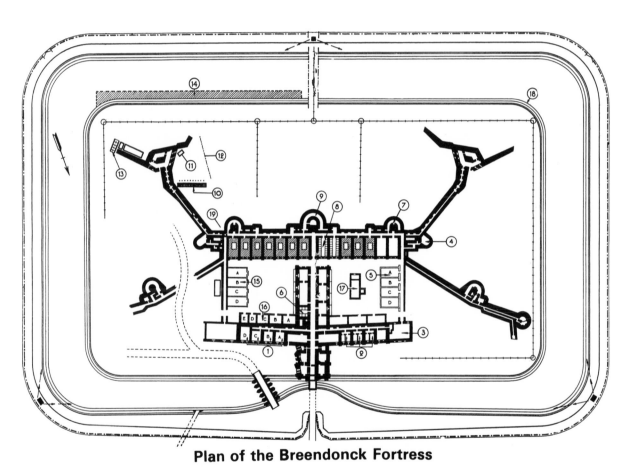

Plan of the Breendonck Fortress

1. SS offices
2. Gestapo preliminary interrogation office
3. Prisoner's latrines
4. Torture chamber
5. Wooden huts
6. Dark cells
7. Morgue (purported to be gas chambers)
8. Cells
9. Dome of the fortress
10. Execution site
11. Gallows
12. Wall for concealing torture area
13. Rabbit hutch where starved prisoners would try to steal the rabbit food.
14. Site where exhausted prisoners were thrown and they then drowned
15. Barracks
16. Storerooms
17. Printing shop
18. Site where prisoners were buried alive

Les Crimes de Guerre — Le Camp de Tortures de Breendonck, Liege 1948.

Plan of Breendonck.

who had the reputation of being the most cruel person in the camp staff. The camp commandant came directly under the authority of the Security Police chief for Belgium and northern France, Konstantin Canaris, and then of his successor, Ernst Ehlers.

In the early stage, conditions in the camp were quite tolerable, and the Jewish prisoners were not separated from the non-Jews. But at the end of 1940, the situation took a sharp turn for the worse; the "Aryan" prisoners were put into separate living quarters, although both groups continued to work side by side.

At first the Jews were in the majority, but during 1942, when the deportations from Belgium began, their numbers decreased. Almost all the Jews of Belgium were then put into the Jewish transit camp at Mechelen, and from there sent to extermination camps. The non-Jewish group consisted mostly of members of the underground (especially the leftist underground), hostages, and black-market operators. The total number of prisoners held in the camp is estimated as having ranged from 3,000 to 3,600 (of whom 7 percent were Jews), but no precise figures are available. Various sources have provided average occupancy figures (apparently for the end of each year):

	1940	1941	1942	1943	1944
Jews	40	200	180	50	45
Non-Jews	35	200	450	650	600

Some 300 persons perished in the camp from torture, harassment, and the harsh conditions; 450 were executed by shooting and 14 were hanged; 54 Jews were deported to AUSCHWITZ; and of the 165 others, 65 died in the camp.

Conditions were among the worst in the camps of western Europe: overcrowded and dilapidated housing, bad food, and harsh punishment; but worst of all was the violence. Prauss set the tone for the cruelty and brutality. One form of punishment used was to drown the prisoners, another to bury them up to the neck and then beat and kick them to death. Political prisoners were executed in groups from the end of 1942 onward, and especially on the eve of liberation in the summer of 1944.

The camp was made into a museum in 1948, and in 1954 a memorial, the work of the sculptor Idel Janchelevici, was erected at the site.

BIBLIOGRAPHY

Halkin, L. E. *Breendonck*. Brussels, 1946.
Ministère de la Justice, Commission des Crimes de Guerre. *Camp de tortures de Breendonck*. Liège, 1948.
Solonevitch, B. *Breendonck: Camp de tortures et de mort*. Brussels, 1944.
Wolf, J. *Le procès de Breendonck*. Brussels, 1973.

DAN MICHMAN

BRESLAU (Pol., Wrocław), city on the Oder River in Lower Silesia; it was part of GERMANY until 1945 and was annexed to Poland after World War II. Breslau was founded in the tenth century; Jews first settled there in the late twelfth century, and they lived there continuously after 1630. On the eve of World War II the city had a population of 630,000.

Breslau had one of the largest and most prominent Jewish communities in Germany. Several of the leading figures of the Wissenschaft des Judentums (the movement for the scholarly study of Judaism and Jewish history) were active there, among them Abraham Geiger, a leader of the Reform movement; Zacharias Frankel, leader of the Conservative trend; and the historian Heinrich Graetz. The Jewish Theological Seminary (Jüdisches Theologisches Seminar), the first modern institution of its kind in Germany, was founded in Breslau in 1854. Breslau was also an important center of Zionism in Germany; in 1912 the Blau-Weiss (Blue-White) Zionist youth movement was founded there.

After World War I a large number of Jews settled in Breslau from the districts of Poznań and southern Upper Silesia, which had been annexed to Poland. In 1925 the Jewish population of the city was 23,240 (4.2 percent of the total), making it the third largest Jewish community in Germany; in 1933 it declined to 20,202.

The period between the world wars saw a rise in antisemitism, which included the desecration of tombstones and the accusation that Jews had murdered a Christian child. In

Jews rounded up in Breslau, awaiting deportation.

1932 the appointment of a Jewish lecturer at the University of Breslau led to riots, causing the university to cancel the appointment.

The Nazi rise to power led to more riots and to the murder of young Jews who were active in the Social Democratic party. Even before the anti-Jewish BOYCOTT of April 1, 1933, SA (Sturmabteilung; Storm Troopers) men stormed into the district courts and evicted the Jewish judges and lawyers. The discriminatory laws against Jews enacted by the central government were applied most severely in Breslau, and Jewish businessmen, under the impact of the official and unofficial boycott, were forced to liquidate their enterprises, or were deprived of them by the official policy of ARISIERUNG ("Aryanization"). In 1936 some four thousand Breslau Jews were in need of the aid offered by the nationwide Jewish relief campaign, the Jüdische Winterhilfe (Jewish Winter Relief). The Breslau Jewish community board did its best to solve the problems caused by the ongoing changes. It supported the actors and musicians who, having been dismissed from their jobs, joined the Breslau branch of the KULTURBUND DEUTSCHER JUDEN (Cultural Society of German Jews); it helped the sports clubs to set up a gym and a swimming pool for the Jewish population; and it expanded the existing *hakhsharot* (agricultural training centers) and vocational training centers in order to promote emigration and Aliya (immigration to Palestine).

During the KRISTALLNACHT pogrom all the synagogues in Breslau were destroyed except for the Orthodox Storch Synagogue, which was not set afire lest the fire spread to the adjoining buildings; however, the interior and the contents were severely damaged. As a result of the many arrests, the personal harassment, and the destruction of property, more and more Jews emigrated, so that by 1939 the Jewish population had dwindled to 10,309.

On March 31, 1941, the Jews in Breslau numbered 9,184. In September of that year Jewish apartments were confiscated and most of the Jews were relocated to special *Judenhäuser* (Jewish houses). In November, the first groups of Jews were sent to transit camps in Silesia (Riebnig, Grüssau, and Tomersdorf). Within a few days of their arrival at these camps, the deportations to the east began. Between November 25, 1941, and April 1944 the Jews of Breslau were deported in fifteen transports, primarily to THERESIENSTADT and AUSCHWITZ. The only Jews spared were 150 persons who were married to "Aryan" spouses.

Following the seizure of Breslau by the Soviet army and the annexation of the city to Poland, more than ten thousand Jews made their way to Breslau, most of them refugees from eastern Europe, and for a while the Jewish community institutions resumed operations. The Jewish community archive, one of the largest in Germany, was taken to Warsaw in 1945. At the end of the 1980s Breslau's Jewish population stood at less than seventy, not enough to maintain the community facilities and the cemeteries.

BIBLIOGRAPHY

Anders, G. *Besuch im Hades: Auschwitz und Breslau 1966.* Munich, 1979.

Polonski, F. "Holocaust we Wrocławiu/na Dolnym Slaku (1941–1944) w świetle dokumentów administracji skarbowej." *Dzieje Najnowsze* 18/3–4 (1986): 235–248.

Schwerin, K. "Die Juden in Schlesien: Aus ihrer Geschichte und ihrem Beitrag zur Wirtschaft und Kultur." *Bulletin des Leo Baeck Instituts* 19/56–57 (1980): 1–84.

Tausk, W. *Breslauer Tagebuch 1933–1940.* Berlin, 1975.

Walk, J., ed. *Als Jude in Breslau: Aus den Tagebüchern von Studienrat a. D. Dr. Willy Israel Cohn.* Gerlingen, West Germany, 1984.

JOSEPH WALK

The Germans handed Brest-Litovsk over to the Soviets on September 22, 1939. In the photo, Generaloberst Heinz Guderian is in the center. [Bildarchiv Preussischer Kulturbesitz]

BREST-LITOVSK (Brisk, in Jewish usage), administrative center of Brest Oblast (district) in southwestern BELORUSSIA. Brest-Litovsk has been known to exist since the eleventh century. It was there that the March 1918 peace treaty was signed between Soviet Russia and Germany. In the interwar period, Brest-Litovsk belonged to Poland.

Jews lived in Brest-Litovsk from the fourteenth century. Until the seventeenth century the city was the center of Lithuanian Jewry's spiritual life and religious scholarship. In 1897 Brest-Litovsk had over 30,000 Jews, constituting more than 75 percent of the total population. During World War I, however, many of the Jews were driven out and in 1931 its Jewish population was 21,440 — 44 percent of the total. The Jewish community maintained many public institutions, among them a Hebrew high school.

Soon after the beginning of World War II the Germans occupied Brest-Litovsk, on September 15, 1939, but they handed it over to the Soviets on September 22. In that one week the Germans arrested several prominent Jews and maltreated them. On June 23, 1941, a day after they had launched their invasion of the Soviet Union, the Germans occupied Brest-Litovsk for the second time; the town fortress, however, held out for another half year, until all of its defenders had fallen in battle. On June 28 and 29, Sonderkom-

4

Radun •

Lida •

• Grodno

Białystok •

P O L A N D

Slonim •

BREST-
LITOVSK

Motol •

P R I P E T

1 | 2 | 3
4 | 5 | 6
B E L O R U S S I A

BREST-LITOVSK

0　　42 miles　　1

in.

cm.

0　　80 km.　　3

mando 7b of Einsatzgruppe B went into action, rounding up five thousand men on the pretext that they were being drafted for work, taking them to the outskirts, and killing them all. In August of that year a twenty-member JUDENRAT (Jewish Council) was appointed, a Jewish police force set up, and a collective ransom payment of 5 million rubles imposed on the Jews. In November, orders were issued for the creation of two ghettos, known as the "small" and the "large" ghetto. A month later the ghettos were sealed off; the gates were guarded strictly and no food was allowed in. Jews in the ghettos were starving despite the efforts made by the Judenrat to help the needy through its welfare agencies. Workshops were set up in order to create employment for the ghetto population.

Early in 1942 a fighting underground with eighty members was established under the leadership of Aryeh Scheinmann. Those members of the underground who worked in the fortress or in the bombed-out airfield stole weapons and ammunition and smuggled them into the ghetto. Plans were made for a

ghetto uprising. In late June, nine hundred skilled artisans were rounded up and sent on forced labor to the east. A few weeks later twelve of them came back; all the others had been murdered.

On October 15, 1942, the ghetto was cordoned off and its liquidation was launched. The Jews were rounded up and put on trains for the Brona Gora station, just north of Kobrin on the Brest-Litovsk–Baranovichi railway line. On arrival they were killed. Some of the Jews hid and others fled, but many days later they were apprehended and executed.

Prior to the liquidation of the ghetto the underground established contact with a group of alleged Russian partisans, and several armed groups left the ghetto to join these partisans in the forests. These so-called partisans, however, turned out to be gangs of robbers and murderers who killed the Jewish fighters and seized their possessions and weapons. On the day the ghetto was liquidated, two armed groups escaped from the ghetto, one consisting of thirteen fighters and the other of ten. While wandering in the forest, the smaller group encounted a "partisan" gang, which disarmed the Jewish fighters and murdered two of them; the others dispersed but some of them, too, were eventually killed. In the spring of 1943 Jewish fighters from Brest-Litovsk joined Soviet partisan units belonging to the Pinsk and Brest-Litovsk partisan formations.

Brest-Litovsk was liberated on July 28, 1944, and about ten Jews, who had been hiding, were found there. After a time some two hundred Jewish survivors of the Holocaust gathered in the city, including some from neighboring towns.

BIBLIOGRAPHY

Steinman, E., ed. *Brest-Litovsk.* Vol. 2 of *Encyclopedia of the Jewish Diaspora.* Jerusalem, 1958. (In Hebrew.)

SHMUEL SPECTOR

BRIZGYS, VINCENTAS (b. 1903), Lithuanian Catholic priest. Brizgys studied in Kovno and Rome. In the 1930s he was one of the leaders of the Center for Catholic Action (Kataliku

Veikimo Centras), a Lithuanian organization, and was appointed bishop of Kovno. During World War II he was auxiliary archbishop of that city.

At the end of June 1941, when LITHUANIA had fallen into German hands, Brizgys appended his signature to several statements thanking Nazi Germany for liberating Lithuania from the Soviet annexation and pledging loyalty to the new occupying power. Nevertheless, in the course of the Nazi occupation, Brizgys met several times with representatives of Kovno Jewry and expressed his sympathy with them. As the war went on, he displayed a benevolent attitude toward the rescue of the children in the Kovno ghetto. He did not, however, agree to intervene on their behalf with the Nazi authorities, claiming that by doing so he would jeopardize the position of the Catholic church in Lithuania. An internal German report, dated January 16, 1942, mentioned that Brizgys specifically prohibited the Catholic clergy from interceding on behalf of the Jews in any manner whatever. When the Germans retreated from Lithuania, in 1944, Brizgys left for Germany. After the war he moved to the United States, where he was active among Lithuanian emigrés.

BIBLIOGRAPHY

Garfunkel, L. *The Destruction of Kovno's Jewry.* Jerusalem, 1959. (In Hebrew.)

DOV LEVIN

BRODETSKY, SELIG (1888–1954), mathematician and Zionist leader. Born in the Ukraine, Brodetsky, while still a child, emigrated to Britain with his family. He studied at Cambridge and Leipzig, and on his return from Germany was appointed a lecturer in applied mathematics at Bristol University. From 1924 to 1949 he was a professor at Leeds University.

Brodetsky became a Zionist as a youth, and from 1928 until the establishment of the state of Israel in 1948, he was a member of the Jewish Agency executive committee and head of its political department in London. From 1939 to 1949, he was president of the BOARD OF DEPUTIES OF BRITISH JEWS, the first person

Selig Brodetsky. [Central Zionist Archives, Jerusalem]

to hold that post who was of eastern European origin and did not belong to the established Anglo-Jewish aristocratic families. His election was made possible by the growing strength of the Zionist element on the board, which succeeded in changing the board's composition and orientation. During Brodetsky's term of office, the board had to deal with fateful issues: aid to the Jews of occupied Europe during the war, postwar aid to the surviving refugees from the Nazi-occupied countries, and the struggle for Palestine. As a leader of British Jewry, Brodetsky bitterly attacked the policy of the British Mandatory government in Palestine, while at the same time emphasizing British Jewry's loyalty to the Crown. In January 1946 Brodetsky testified before the Anglo-American Commission, which was investigating the Palestine problem, denounced the WHITE PAPER policy, and demanded the immediate opening of the gates of Palestine for the entry of displaced persons.

From 1949 to 1951, Brodetsky was president of the Hebrew University in Jerusalem. His autobiography, *Memoirs: From Ghetto to Israel*, was published in 1960.

BIBLIOGRAPHY

Sompolinski, M. "Anglo-Jewish Leadership and the British Government: Attempts at Rescue, 1944–1945." *Yad Vashem Studies* 13 (1979): 211–247.

Wasserstein, B. *Britain and the Jews of Europe, 1939–1945*. London, 1979.

NANA SAGI

BRODY, town in Lvov Oblast (district), Ukrainian SSR. Founded in the sixteenth century, Brody was under Polish rule in the period from 1918 to 1939, and was annexed to the Soviet Union in September of that year. It was one of the important Jewish communities in Galicia, and for many years Jews constituted a majority of the population; in 1939, 9,000 Jews lived there. On July 1, 1941, the Germans occupied the town and lost no time in issuing anti-Jewish decrees: the Jews were ordered to wear an armband with the Star of David (*see* BADGE, JEWISH) and to make punitive payments; they were subject to forced labor; and were restricted in their movements. On July 15, 1941, a group of 250 intellectuals were summoned to the local Gestapo, where they were subjected to two days of torture and then murdered in ditches adjoining the Jewish cemetery. The JUDENRAT (Jewish Council) was ordered to supply hundreds of Jews daily for work on bridge repairs, on road building, and

in military camps. By August, Jewish property was being plundered on a large scale by both Germans and Ukrainians. In December, the Germans began stopping Jewish youths in the street and transporting them to labor camps that had been set up in the area. In the first half of 1942, about 1,500 Jews were imprisoned in these camps. Their number dwindled sharply in the second half of 1942 and the beginning of the following year, owing to the high death rate caused by mistreatment, hard labor, starvation, and disease. In the summer of 1942 the Judenrat, on its own initiative, launched an effort to find jobs in areas that were considered vital to the German economy, in the hope that this would give protection, at least to some degree, from deportation to the labor camps.

On September 19, 1942, German and Ukrainian police arrested Jews on the streets or dragged them out of their houses and hiding places. When this *Aktion* was over, 2,000 Jews were taken to the BEŁŻEC death camp, while 300 were killed on the spot. In another *Aktion,* on November 2, another 2,500 people were sent to Bełżec. During the fall and winter of 1942, the German authorities brought into Brody remnants of other Jewish communities in the area, such as those of Sokolovka, Lopatin, Olesko, and Radechov.

In December 1942 the Germans announced the establishment of a ghetto in Brody, and by January 1, 1943, some six thousand persons had been gathered there, most of them from the vicinity. Many of the inmates died of starvation and typhus epidemics, and many others were shot by the Ukrainian police who guarded the ghetto perimeter. In March and April 1943 there were numerous *Aktionen,* as a result of which thousands of people were rounded up and put to death in the neighboring woods. Some of the young Jews who managed to escape from the ghetto into the forest formed groups and obtained arms with which they tried to resist their German and Ukrainian pursuers. The ghetto was liquidated on May 21, 1943. Over three thousand of its inmates were dispatched to MAJDANEK, and hundreds were murdered while still in the ghetto. In an effort to discover Jews still hidden there, the Germans and their Ukrainian helpers set the houses on fire, and many of those who had sought refuge found their death in the flames. The hunt for more Jews in hiding went on for many weeks; all those who were caught were murdered.

BIBLIOGRAPHY

Gilbert, M. *The Holocaust.* New York, 1985.

AHARON WEISS

BRUNACCI, ALDO. *See* Nicolini, Giuseppe.

BRUNNER, ALOIS (b. 1912), SS officer, one of Adolf EICHMANN's assistants. A native of Austria, Brunner joined the Nazi party in 1931 and the SS in November 1938. Following the German annexation of Austria, Brunner became a staff member of the Sicherheitspolizei and the SD (Sicherheitsdienst; Security Service) in Vienna. In August 1938 he became director of the Vienna ZENTRALSTELLE FÜR JÜDISCHE AUSWANDERUNG (Central Office for Jewish Emigration), which Eichmann had set up. In October and November of 1939, Brunner was in charge of the deportation of Jews from Vienna and Moravia to Nisko, in the Lublin district of Poland (*see* NISKO AND LUBLIN PLAN). In February and March of 1941 he

organized the deportation of Viennese Jews to the Kielce area, and in October of that year he deported more Viennese Jews to the east. Later, in March 1943, Brunner was posted to Greece, to deal with the deportation of the Jews of SALONIKA and of Bulgarian-occupied THRACE and MACEDONIA; in July of that year he went to the region of southern France that until then had been under Italian occupation, to supervise the deportation of the Jews of Nice and other places in the area to AUSCHWITZ, by way of DRANCY. At the end of September 1944, he arrived in BRATISLAVA to complete the deportation of the Jews of SLOVAKIA.

After the war, all trace of Brunner was lost. He was tried *in absentia* in Paris, and sentenced to death in 1954. Eventually he was given asylum in Syria, and has been living in that country under an assumed name.

BIBLIOGRAPHY

Felstiner, M. "Alois Brunner: Eichmann's Best Tool." *Simon Wiesenthal Center Annual* 3 (1986): 1–46.
Felstiner, M. "Commandant of Drancy: Alois Brunner and the Jews of France." *Holocaust and Genocide Studies* 2/1 (1987): 21–47.

SHMUEL SPECTOR

Alois Brunner.

BRUSSELS. First mentioned in the tenth century, Brussels became the capital of Brabant in 1383, of the Low Countries in 1482, and later of the Spanish and Austrian Low Countries. Since 1830 it has been the capital of independent BELGIUM.

When the Germans occupied Belgium on May 17, 1940, thirty-three thousand Jews lived in Brussels, more than half the total Jewish population of the country. Most of them had immigrated to Belgium from eastern Europe and Germany after 1918, but Brussels also had the largest concentration of "veteran" Belgian Jews. They were well integrated into the city's social and economic life, and some held positions of prominence. Ninety-two percent of the Brussels Jews lived in the seven western quarters of the city, mostly in the area containing the main railway station and in the Anderlecht quarter.

Brussels was the location of the national

Jewish organizations: the Consistoire Central (Central Consistory), to which all Jews who held Belgian nationality belonged; the Chief Rabbinate; the Oeuvre Centrale Israélite de Secours (Central Jewish Relief Society; OCIS); and the HICEM office (which in Belgium bore the name BELHICEM), headed by Max Gottschalk, who was of great help to the refugees from Nazi Germany.

Brussels Jewry had its own philanthropic and communal organizations and professional unions, and it took an active part in political life. Among the Jewish umbrella organizations in Brussels were the Foyer Israélite de Bruxelles (Brussels Jewish Welfare Agency); the Conseil d'Associations Juives de Bruxelles (Brussels Council of Jewish Organizations), made up of thirty-three organizations of the lower middle-class Jews and headed by Leon Kubowitzki; and the Oeuvre de la Communauté du Travail des Juifs d'Allemagne (Association of German Jewish Laborers), comprising the Jewish refugees from Germany.

The immediate effect of the German occupation on the Jewish community was total chaos and the disruption of the community services and the work of the Jewish organizations. Many of the organizations' leaders fled while the fighting was going on; of the twelve board members of the official Jewish Community Organization, only one, Marcel Blum, stayed. Of the Orthodox Community Board, only the vice president, David Lazare (a Jew of Polish nationality), remained; and of the rabbis, only Abraham Joseph Feinburg, a Belgian national, stayed.

In the summer of 1940 several persons, on their own initiative, began to revive organized Jewish life in the city, with the emphasis on aid and relief. The OCIS resumed its work on a much larger scale than previously, since thousands of people were now in need. In the first five months of 1941, OCIS spent 220,000 Belgian francs on aid to the needy, and in 1941 as a whole, approximately 1 million francs. About 60 percent of this sum was contributed by the Brussels community, the rest coming from individual donors and the American Jewish JOINT DISTRIBUTION COMMITTEE. A special aid effort was made for the refugees from Germany, with Itzko Kubowitzki (Leon's brother) taking the lead, on behalf

of groups of Brussels residents who were immigrants from eastern Europe. In September 1940 Rabbi Salomon Ullmann accepted the post of Chief Rabbi of Belgium, with his office in Brussels. On November 10 the Brussels Community Board resumed operations, its immediate task being to organize the Jewish population. Marcel Blum was elected president and Itzko Kubowitzki vice president; Edouard Rotkel, a Hungarian Jew who had come to Brussels in 1938, was elected secretary. Salomon van den Bergh, a wealthy furniture merchant, was also on the board. Anti-Jewish decrees issued on October 28, 1940, were met with criticism among some parts of the general population. Three senior jurists and the Université Libre de Bruxelles (Brussels Free University)—which had a larger number of Jewish lecturers on its faculty than any other Belgian university—issued protests against the anti-Jewish measures.

In early 1941 the Comité de Coordination (Coordinating Committee) was set up at the insistence of the Sicherheitspolizei (Security Police), but it did not become an important body. At the end of 1941 the ASSOCIATION DES JUIFS EN BELGIQUE (Association of Jews in Belgium; AJB) was established, with its head office in Brussels. The AJB took up the relief work that had previously been in the hands of OCIS; heading the AJB's social services, until the spring of 1943, was Professor Chaim Perelman.

In 1941 the economic situation of Belgium deteriorated, and the Jews were especially hard hit. As a result, the Jewish political organizations expanded their welfare operations. The relief organizations of the Zionist Po'alei Zion Left and those of the Communists—most of which had been in existence since before the occupation—enlarged the scope of their operations. Jews had been active in leftist organizations before the war, but under the Germans such activities were outlawed; many of the Jewish leftist activists were arrested between 1940 and 1942. From the end of 1941, in reaction to the creation of the AJB, specifically Jewish underground activity was launched. This activity also expressed itself in the publication of underground newspapers, such as Po'alei Zion's *Unzer Wort* (Our Word) and, later on, *Unzer*

Kampf (Our Struggle), the journal of the Brussels branch of the Communist party.

In April 1941 a decree on the expulsion of Jews from the general school system was put into effect, affecting three thousand Jewish children. This posed a particularly serious problem for Brussels Jewry because of the nearly total lack of teachers and school buildings for such a large number of children. University lecturers and students working for the AJB did, however, manage to set up an alternative Jewish school system, which functioned until the deportation of the Jews of Belgian nationality, in September 1943.

During the spring and early summer of 1942 economic pressure on the Jews grew stronger, as the liquidation and "Aryanization" (*see* ARISIERUNG) of Jewish enterprises were speeded up, especially in the textile and leather industries. The wealthy Jews tried to escape to southern France or Switzerland. This was also the time when the Jews were being drafted for FORCED LABOR. On June 26, 1942, a transport of Brussels Jews was sent to the labor camps of the ORGANISATION TODT in northern France. Thousands of other Jews worked for the Germans in various enterprises in Belgium itself.

A German order of May 27, 1942, obliged all Jews to wear the yellow badge (*see* BADGE, JEWISH), the distribution of which was imposed on the municipalities of greater Brussels; the order met with a hostile reaction on the part of the mayors. On June 5, J. Coelst, the acting chairman of the Conférence des Bourgmestres (Conference of Mayors), informed the German authorities of the mayors' refusal to cooperate in the distribution of the yellow badges. Since the AJB also refused to undertake this task, the German headquarters in Brussels had to use its own personnel for the job. Many of the city's residents expressed their solidarity with the Jews by wearing yellow badges similar to the ones that the Jews had been forced to put on.

In late July 1942 a roundup of the Jews was launched, pending their deportation. The Jews were issued summonses to report to the MECHELEN camp, but when an insufficient number turned up at the camp, the Germans began to look for Jews. From August 13 to 18, Jews were arrested in the streets of Brussels in large numbers, and on September 3, Jews were hunted down in the area of the main Brussels railway station. Many of the Jews who were arrested were taken to a school building in the Saint Gilles quarter and from there were transferred to Mechelen. More arrests were made in the months that followed, especially during the winter. The final roundup took place on the night of September 3–4, 1943, as part of Operation "Iltis"—the seizure by the Germans of all Jews of Belgian nationality, who a year earlier had been assured that they would not be deported. Out of the 975 "Belgian" Jews seized in this operation, 750 were from Brussels.

The arrest of Jews for forced labor, and the beginning of the deportation to eastern Europe, were met with increasing resistance on the part of the Jews of Brussels. On September 15, 1942, the Comité de Défense des Juifs (Jewish Defense Committee) was formed, with Jewish Communists and members of various Zionist organizations cooperating with one another. The committee made efforts to find hiding places for Jews, especially Jewish children, and also engaged in relief work; in February 1944 it was giving support to thirty-six hundred persons. The committee was also in touch with resistance fighters. Groups of Jews were active in Belgian resistance operations; most of them—about one hundred—belonged to the leftist partisan organizations, such as the Corps Mobile and the Corps de Bruxelles, which later united into one body. Many of the small resistance cells were made up exclusively of Jews. In the summer of 1942 two significant resistance operations took place in Brussels: in one, the AJB card index of Jews was destroyed by fire; and in the other, Robert Holcinger, the AJB official responsible for ensuring that Jews reported for deportation, was assassinated. Jews were also members of other underground groups, such as the Belgian resistance group Banco. Members of that group provided hiding places for several Jewish refugees from Germany. The refugees in their turn contributed by translating German informational material into French and Dutch, and French and Dutch material into German.

As many as twelve thousand Jews are estimated to have gone into hiding in various places in Brussels. One of them was the painter Felix Nussbaum, a refugee from Germany who eventually fell into German hands and was deported to AUSCHWITZ, where he perished. He left behind paintings in which he depicted his experiences; the largest collection of his work is to be found in the Museum of Cultural History of Osnabrück, his native city.

After the liberation, Brussels served as the center for the reorganization and rehabilitation of Belgian Jewry. The Consistoire and the Zionist Federation of Belgium were reconstituted. Together with the Aide aux Israélites Victimes de la Guerre (Aid Society for Jewish War Victims) and the Comité Central de Reconstruction Religieuse (Central Committee for the Restoration of Religious Life), they dealt with the special problems that arose at the time. These included the status of Jews who had been residents of Belgium before the war but did not hold Belgian nationality, the DISPLACED PERSONS who had reached Belgium, the restoration of Jewish property, and the care of Jewish war orphans.

In the late 1940s, the Jewish population of Brussels was estimated at twenty-seven thousand. Brussels served as the headquarters of the Union des Anciens Résistants Juifs de Belgique (Union of Veteran Jewish Resistance Fighters of Belgium) and the Union des Déportés Juifs et Ayant Droits en Belgique (Union of Jewish Deportees and Their Legatees Eligible for Pension Rights in Belgium). In 1970 a memorial for the victims of the Holocaust was erected in the Anderlecht quarter of Brussels.

BIBLIOGRAPHY

Communauté Israélite de Bruxelles. *La grande synagogue de Bruxelles: Contribution à l'histoire des Juifs de Bruxelles.* Brussels, 1978.
Ministère de la Justice. Commission des Crimes de Guerre. *La persécution antisémitique en Belgique.* Liège, 1947.
Steinberg, M. *L'étoile et le fusil.* 3 vols. Brussels, 1983–1986.

DAN MICHMAN

BRZEŻANY. *See* Berezhany.

BUCHAREST, capital of ROMANIA and before that of the principality of Walachia. Jews lived in Bucharest from the sixteenth century. It was the largest center of Romanian Jewry; during the twentieth century the number of Jews increased rapidly, reaching 76,480 by 1930 (twice as many as at the beginning of the century) and 102,018 by 1941. Several quarters in Bucharest, such as the Văcăresti-Dudest neighborhood and the "Blue Quarter," were considered Jewish areas. Throughout World War II Jewish refugees streamed into Bucharest from provincial towns, believing themselves safer in the capital and among many Jews. The central organizations of Romanian Jewry were in Bucharest, as well as Jewish schools, hospitals, and other institutions. However, Bucharest was also a center of the antisemitic IRON GUARD movement, and this had an effect on the situation of the Jewish community in the city.

As early as 1937, persecutions of Jews in professional, financial, and cultural fields commenced. Government offices and private institutions such as banks, factories, and publishing houses refused to employ them. In 1938, under the government of Octavian GOGA and Alexandra CUZA, Jewish businessmen were removed from the chamber of commerce. Most of the trade unions dismissed Jews from their ranks; the example was set by the Advocates' Association, which elected an antisemitic leadership on December 6, 1938. Many streets were dangerous for Jews.

With the establishment of the ANTONESCU government on September 6, 1940, members of the Iron Guard, known as Legionnaires, began to sow terror among the Jews of Bucharest. Jews were attacked in the streets, parks, and other public places; cars belonging to Jews were expropriated; many Jews were imprisoned and released only on payment of a ransom. The Legionnaires used the offices of the police, who were subordinate to them.

Antonescu failed in his attempt to deter the Legionnaires, to impose order in the capital, and to prevent the destruction of economic and productive life. On January 21, 1941, the Legionnaires rebelled, and attempted to remove Antonescu and seize power. During the revolt there were riots against the Jews of

Bodies of Jews killed in the Bucharest pogrom of January 1941.

Bucharest. Jews were seized in synagogues, on the streets, and in their homes, some according to lists drawn up in advance. About one hundred were placed on trucks and shot to death at various places in the vicinity of the city.

During the killings carried out by the Legionnaires, bands of ruffians attacked the Jewish quarters, plundering, raping, and destroying houses and shops. They were joined by mobs from the suburbs and Gypsies who took advantage of this opportunity to plunder. The riots lasted three days, and 127 Jews were murdered.

With the outbreak of war against the Soviet Union on June 22, 1941, the leaders of the Jewish organizations were declared hostages who would be put to death if the city's Jews worked against the authorities. On September 3 of that year the Jews were obliged to wear a "Jewish sign" (a black star on a white background), but after two days the president of the Federation of the Communities, Wilhelm FILDERMAN, managed to have the edict annulled. Various taxes were imposed on the Jews of Bucharest for the benefit of the army and the civil authorities; these included monetary "donations" and a onetime tax of several hundred million lei (April 1943).

In September 1942, a group of 395 Jews who in 1940 had asked to return to BESSARABIA after its annexation to the Soviet Union, as well as about 200 Jews considered to be Communists, were deported to TRANSNISTRIA. The deportees in the first group were killed by members of the SS in Transnistria. On Antonescu's order, all of the Jews who had settled in Bucharest after January 1, 1940, were deported from the city.

The policy of dispossession, expropriation, nationalization, and dismissals, together with the various levies and taxes, soon impoverished the Jewish population. By late 1941, a total of 8,234 Jewish wage earners had been dismissed. Recruitment of Jews for forced labor completed the process of pauperization. From the fall of 1941, Jews were employed in cleaning the streets and clearing them of snow. Forced-labor gangs were established

BUCHAREST

Annexations from June to September 1940: (1) Bessarabia and (2) N. Bukovina to USSR; (3) N. Transylvania to Hungary; (4) S. Dobruja to Bulgaria.

on August 1, 1941, and in 1942, 28,177 Jewish males were engaged in forced labor. Jews who did not present themselves for recruitment, or who fled from the labor gangs, were arrested and deported to Transnistria with their families. All Jewish youths between the ages of fifteen and eighteen were taken for forced labor in May 1943. In April 1944, when bombing of the city intensified, the local forced-labor gangs were brought to clear the ruins, take away the bodies of the dead, and remove unexploded bombs.

In addition to the national Jewish organizations, the institutions of the CENTRALA EVREILOR (Jewish Center) were also concentrated in Bucharest from February 1942. These included welfare institutions, in particular the Autonomous Aid Committee; the Palestine Office; the directors of the Zionist movement in Romania; the Jewish theater; two higher-education institutions created after the removal of Jewish students from the general system of higher education; and an orchestra made up of musicians who had been dismissed from Romanian orchestras. Until 1942 the journal of the Zionist movement, *Renasterea Noastra*, appeared in Bucharest, and after its closure by order of the authorities, the Jewish Center journal, *Gazeta Evreeasca*, appeared.

The Jews of Bucharest were saved from extermination on August 23, 1944, after the dictator, Ion Antonescu, was arrested by the king. The German forces close to the city did not succeed in entering it. Adolf EICHMANN, who was then in Budapest and was supposed to go to Bucharest to begin preparations for deporting the Jews, postponed his journey when he learned that the Romanians had broken off their alliance with Germany. The immediate opposition of the Romanian army, and the entry of the Soviet army into the city on August 30, 1944, prevented the Nazis from carrying out their scheme.

BIBLIOGRAPHY

Carp, M. *Pogromul dela Iaşi*. Vol. 2A of *Cartea Neagră*. Bucharest, 1948.
Lavi, T., ed. *Rumania*, vol. 1. In *Pinkas Hakehillot; Encyclopaedia of Jewish Communities*. Jerusalem, 1969. See pages 59–75. (In Hebrew.)
Pe Marginea Prapastiei, 21–31 Ianuarie 1941. Vol. 2. Bucharest, 1942.
Safran, A. *Resisting the Storm—Romania, 1940–1947: Memoirs*. Jerusalem, 1987.

JEAN ANCEL

BUCHENWALD, concentration camp, one of the largest on German soil, with 130 satellite camps and extension units. Buchenwald was situated on the northern slope of Ettersberg, a mountain 5 miles (8 km) north of Weimar, in Thüringen (now part of the German Democratic Republic). The camp was established on July 16, 1937, when the first group of prisoners, consisting of 149 persons, mostly political detainees and criminals, was brought to the site. The name "Buchenwald" was given to it by Heinrich HIMMLER on July 28, 1937.

Buchenwald was divided into three parts: the "large camp," which housed prisoners with some seniority; the "small camp," where prisoners were kept in quarantine; and the "tent camp," set up for Polish prisoners sent there after the German invasion of Poland in 1939. Besides these three parts were the administration compound, the SS barracks, and the camp factories. The commandants were SS-Standartenführer Karl KOCH (1937–1941) and SS-Oberführer Hermann Pister (1942–1945).

Large groups of prisoners began to arrive in the camp shortly after its foundation and by the end of 1937 their number reached 2,561, most of them "politicals." In the spring of 1938 the number of prisoners rose rapidly as a result of the operation against "asocial elements," the victims of which were taken to Buchenwald; by July 1938 there were 7,723 prisoners in the camp. Another 2,200 from Austria were added on September 23, 1938, all of them Jews. A further 10,000 Jews were imprisoned after KRISTALLNACHT (November 9–10, 1938), and at the end of November the camp prison population exceeded 18,000. By the end of the year, most of the Jewish prisoners were released, and the camp population had dropped to 11,000.

The outbreak of war was accompanied by a wave of arrests throughout the Reich, which brought thousands of political prisoners to Buchenwald. This was followed by the influx of thousands of Poles, who were housed in the tent camp. As of 1943, following the completion of armament factories in the vicinity of the camp, the number of prisoners grew steadily: to 63,048 by the end of 1944 and to 86,232 in February 1945. In the eight years of its existence, from July 1937 to March 1945, a total of 238,980 prisoners from thirty countries passed through Buchenwald and its satellite camps; of these, 43,045 were killed or perished in some other fashion there (the figure includes Soviet prisoners of war).

The first transports of German Jews arrived in the spring of 1938, followed by Austrian Jews and the *Kristallnacht* prisoners. The Jews were subject to extraordinarily cruel treatment, working fourteen to fifteen hours a day (generally in the infamous Buchenwald quarry) and enduring abominable living conditions. The Nazis' object at this point was to exert pressure on the Jews and their families to emigrate from Germany within the shortest possible time. Thus, in the winter of 1938–1939, 9,370 Jews were released after their families, as well as Jewish and international organizations, had made arrangements for their emigration. Of the *Kristallnacht* detainees, in the short while that these prisoners were held at Buchenwald, 600 were killed, committed suicide, or died from other causes. The number of Jewish prisoners rose again after the outbreak of the war, when Jews from Germany and the Protectorate of BOHEMIA AND MORAVIA were brought to the camp; in September 1939, the Jewish prisoners numbered some 2,700.

In accordance with an order issued on October 17, 1942, which provided for all Jewish prisoners held in the Reich to be transferred to AUSCHWITZ, the Jews in Buchenwald, except for 204 essential workers, were sent to that concentration and extermination camp. In 1944, transports of Hungarian Jews began coming to Buchenwald from Auschwitz; after a short stay in the main camp most of them were distributed among the satellite camps, where they were put to work in the armament factories. Beginning on January 18, 1945, when Auschwitz and other camps in the east were being evacuated, thousands of Jewish prisoners arrived in Buchenwald. The Auschwitz evacuees included several hundred children and youths, and a special barrack, which came to be known as "Children's Block 66," was put up for them in the tent

Under United States military escort, German civilians were forced to view the evidence of atrocities at the Buchenwald camp. Here, they look at a truckload of dead Allied and political prisoners. [United States Army Signal Corps]

camp. This block housed more than six hundred children and youths, most of whom survived. The Jewish prisoners were deprived of the privileges and exemptions granted to the other inmates, and Jewish prisoners were used for MEDICAL EXPERIMENTS.

Resistance cells were formed in Buchenwald from the first years of its existence. In 1938 such a cell was established by members of the German Communist party in the camp, who included some of that party's most prominent figures. At first, the aim of the resistance cells was to plant their members in the central posts available to inmates, to support one another, and to have a say in developments in the camp. Up to the end of 1938 the internal administration of Buchenwald was, for the most part, in the hands of the criminal prisoners. When it was discovered that the criminals and some of the SS personnel were involved in corruption and stealing (from the *Kristallnacht* prisoners), the camp administration removed the criminal prisoners from most of their posts, and their influence gradually passed into the hands of the political prisoners. Some resistance cells, mainly those belonging to the Left, managed to plant some of their members in key positions held by prisoners in the internal camp administration, thereby facilitating their clandestine activities. Later, following the outbreak of the war and the influx into Buchenwald of political prisoners from the occupied countries, more resistance groups were formed, on the basis of nationality. In 1943 a general underground movement that included Jews came into being, called the International Underground Committee. The resistance movement in Buchenwald scored some impressive successes, primarily the acts of sabotage it carried out in the armaments works that employed Buchenwald prisoners. Underground members also smuggled arms and ammunition into the camp.

On April 6, 1945, the Germans began evacuating the Jewish prisoners. The following day, thousands of prisoners of various nationalities were evacuated from the main camps and the satellite camps. Of the 28,250 prisoners evacuated from the main camp, 7,000 to 8,000 either were killed or died by some other means in the course of the evacuation. The total number of prisoners from the satellite camps and the main camp who fell victim during the evacuation of Buchenwald is estimated at 25,500. In the final days of the camp's existence, resistance members who held key posts in the internal administration sabotaged SS orders for evacuation by slowing down its pace, and as a result the Nazis failed to complete the evacuation.

By April 11, most of the SS men had fled from the camp. The underground did not wait for the approaching American forces to take control but did so themselves, together with armed teams of prisoners, in the process trapping several dozen SS men left in the camp. On that day, April 11, some twenty-one thousand prisoners were liberated in Buchenwald, with four thousand Jews among them, including about one thousand children and youths.

In 1947, thirty-one members of the Buchenwald camp staff were tried for their crimes by an American court. Two of the accused were sentenced to death, and four to life imprisonment.

BIBLIOGRAPHY

Bartel, W., et al., eds. *Buchenwald—Mahnung und Verpflichtung: Dokumente und Berichte.* Berlin, 1983.

Briquet, G. *The Buchenwald Case.* Dachau, 1947.
Burney, C. *The Dungeon Democracy.* London, 1945.
D'Harcourt, P. *The Real Enemy.* New York, 1967.
Gutman, Y., and S. Avital, eds. *The Nazi Concentration Camps.* Jerusalem, 1984.

YEHOSHUA R. BÜCHLER

BUDAPEST, capital of HUNGARY. Budapest is situated on both banks of the Danube and consists of the united cities of Buda, Óbuda, and Pest; its population in 1941 was about one million, and in 1976 over two million. The first settlement on the site was the Roman colony of Aquincum. In 1872 the united city of Budapest was formed, and it became the capital of independent Hungary in November 1918.

A grave from the Roman period attests to a Jewish presence in Aquincum. From the twelfth century there was a constant Jewish presence in Buda, except for some short periods in the thirteenth century. Between the world wars, some 200,000 of Trianon Hungary's 450,000 Jews resided in Budapest, making it one of the most important urban Jewish population centers in Europe. It was the center of Hungarian Jewish life, and the Jewish presence in the culture, thought, politics, professions, and economy of the city was of great significance. During the years of restrictive anti-Jewish legislation (from 1938), the predominantly middle-class Jewish community suffered greatly, especially from unemployment. By 1940 the community supported 17,000 of its members with $100,000 in aid. Nonetheless, as the situation of the rest of European Jewry deteriorated during the course of World War II, Budapest Jewry lived in relative comfort and security until the German occupation in March 1944.

Some five thousand refugees from Germany, Austria, and later Poland began to arrive in Budapest in the late 1930s. The Hungarian Jewish relief organizations Magyar Izraeliták Pártfogo Irodaja (Welfare Bureau of Hungarian Jews) and Országos Zsidó Segito Akcio (National Hungarian Jewish Assistance Campaign), the RELIEF AND RESCUE COMMITTEE OF BUDAPEST (known as the Va'ada), and an Orthodox committee headed by Fülöp FREUDIGER, together with the Ameri-

Crowds of Jews in front of the Swiss embassy on Vadasz Street in Budapest, waiting to receive *Schutzpässe*.

can Jewish JOINT DISTRIBUTION COMMITTEE, assisted these refugees. The Joint provided $47,000 in aid during the first six months of the war. With the advent of deportations from SLOVAKIA in March 1942, significant numbers of Slovak Jews began escaping to Hungary. Most of the six thousand to eight thousand Slovak refugees eventually came to Budapest.

With the German occupation (March 19, 1944), the situation of Budapest Jewry deteriorated drastically. A central Jewish council, the Zsidó Tanács, was established under the Neolog leader Samu STERN. It was made responsible for governing Budapest Jewry and forwarding decrees to the provincial Jewish councils. Life was severely restricted in Budapest, as it was throughout Hungary, with orders such as the one calling for the closing of Jewish shops (March 22), which

affected eighteen thousand Jewish stores in the capital. Hundreds of Jews were rounded up and interned in the KISTARCSA camp. Following Allied air raids in early April, the deputy interior minister, László ENDRE, ordered on April 12 that within twenty-four hours the Jewish community turn over 500 apartments to non-Jews who had been left homeless by the bombing. Before the day was over, Adolf EICHMANN, who was responsible for implementing the "Final Solution" in Hungary, had raised the quota to 1,500.

The provincial Jews were systematically concentrated and deported between mid-April and July, but the Jews of Budapest were not put into a ghetto during this, the first, wave of deportations from Hungary. The Hungarian authorities scattered the Jews about the city in 2,639 buildings, which were marked with a Star of David. The move to

Street scene in Budapest (1944).

these buildings, with their 33,294 apartments and 70,197 rooms, was made between June 17 and 24, 1944. Shortly thereafter, 17,500 Jews were dispatched from the outskirts of Budapest to AUSCHWITZ. On July 7 the Hungarian regent, Miklós HORTHY, ordered the stoppage of further deportations, saving the remaining Budapest Jews for the time being.

During the lull in the deportations, the Jews of Budapest continued as best they could, struggling to keep alive. Many looked for ways to protect themselves from renewed deportations. Most commonly, they tried to acquire baptismal certificates or applied for official government exemptions from all anti-Jewish statutes. Some groups, like the Relief and Rescue Committee and the Zionist youth movements, continued the rescue activities they had begun during the deporta-

tions. When Horthy announced that his government was withdrawing from the Axis with Germany on October 15, Budapest Jewry was exultant. But with the immediate fall of Horthy's regime and the establishment of a Nazi-backed government under Ferenc SZÁLASI, they began to face their gravest peril.

During the first days of the new ARROW CROSS PARTY's rule, some six hundred Jews were murdered in Budapest. Soon afterward, Jews were drafted to build fortifications. On November 8, deportations were resumed. Over seventy thousand Jews were taken to the Óbuda brickyards, and from there were marched out of the city on foot toward the Austrian border. The *Fussmarsch* (foot march), as this deportation was known, continued until December 24. In the meantime, on November 13, the Arrow Cross ordered the establishment of a ghetto, and by December 2 most of Budapest's unprotected Jews had been placed within its confines. The ghetto had four main entrances, on Wesselenyi, Nagyatadi Szabo, Nagydiofa, and Kisdiofa streets. It was divided into ten districts, each with a district commander. A ghetto police force was also established, but unlike other such forces under Nazi occupation, it never became enmeshed in the process of deportation. Public kitchens and a hospital also served the ghetto residents. During December 1944 and January 1945, random acts of Arrow Cross violence increased, and between ten thousand and twenty thousand Jews were shot along the banks of the Danube, their corpses making the river run red.

During the Szálasi period, the neutral diplomats—among them Friedrich Born (international RED CROSS), Raoul WALLENBERG (Sweden), Per Anger (Sweden), Carl LUTZ (Switzerland), Angelo Rotta (the papal nuncio), Valdemar Langlet (Swedish Red Cross), and Asta Nilsson (Swedish Red Cross)—exerted great efforts to rescue Budapest Jewry. In most aspects of their work they were joined by members of the Va'ada (especially Ottó KOMOLY); members of the Zionist youth movement; the Zsidó Tanács; and other non-affiliated Jews. Christian organizations, notably the Jo Pasztor (Good Shepherd Society) under Gabor SZTEHLO, and a number of convents and monasteries, also aided Jews. The focus of the rescue was to ensure that the

Jews stayed out of the hands of the Nazis and Arrow Cross, and that they had sufficient food, shelter, and fuel to remain alive until the arrival of the Red Army.

The diplomats often protested to the government about the treatment of the Jews. With the help of the various Jewish rescuers, food, medicines, and fuel were obtained and distributed. Efforts were made to safeguard Jews from deportation by providing them with *Schutzpässe* (protective documents) in the name of the neutral governments and agencies. The Swiss issued 7,800, the Swedes 4,500, the Vatican 2,500, the Portuguese 700, and the Spanish 100; some 100,000 (mostly Swiss) were forged and distributed by the Zionist youth. The bearers of protective documents were placed under diplomatic protection, often taking up residence in the embassies and consulates and their annexes. The largest of these protected buildings was the "Glass House" on Vadasz Street and the annex next door, which were under the protection of the Swiss and housed over three thousand Jews. Special houses also were set up, in which between five thousand and six thousand children were protected from their planned transfer to the ghetto and from Arrow Cross rampages. In addition, the *Schutzpässe* were used to bring deportees back to Budapest before they reached the border. Frequently, bearers of false papers were assisted as well. In early November of 1944 a special "international ghetto" was set up for the bearers of the documents and their families. The extraterritorial status of the houses was not always honored, and many fell victim to Arrow Cross violence.

By December 26, 1944, the Soviets had completely encircled Budapest. On January 18, 1945, Pest was taken, and on February 13 Buda fell to the Red Army. Exact figures on the number of Jews in Budapest at the time of the Soviet entry are not available, but about 70,000 were in the ghetto, about 25,000 were under diplomatic protection, and another 25,000 were hidden, often with false "Aryan" papers—all told, some 120,000.

In the post–World War II period, Budapest remained the center of the diminished Hungarian Jewish community. As of the end of the 1980s, about sixty thousand of Hungary's eighty thousand Jews resided in the capital.

Moving into a Budapest apartment designated for Jews and marked with a Star of David (1944).

BIBLIOGRAPHY

Braham, R. L. *The Politics of Genocide: The Holocaust in Hungary.* New York, 1981.

Cohen, A. *The Halutz Resistance in Hungary, 1942–1944.* New York, 1986.

Lavi, T., ed. *Hungary.* In *Pinkas Hakehillot; Encyclopaedia of Jewish Communities.* Jerusalem, 1976. (In Hebrew.)

ASHER COHEN and
ROBERT ROZETT

BUDZYŃ, forced-labor and concentration camp in Poland. Budzyń was a village and estate in the Lublin district, 3 miles (5 km)

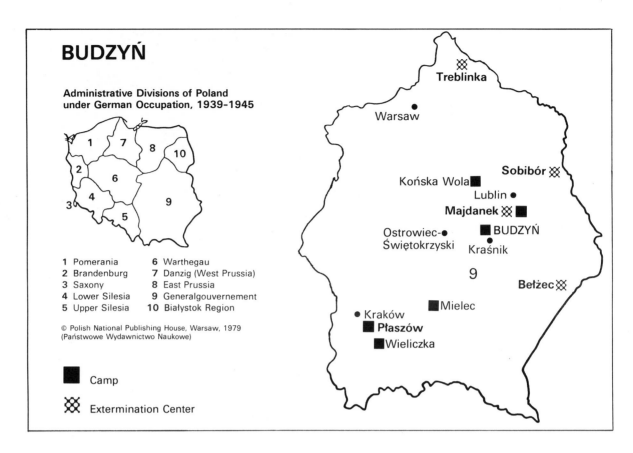

BUDZYŃ

Administrative Divisions of Poland under German Occupation, 1939-1945

1 Pomerania
2 Brandenburg
3 Saxony
4 Lower Silesia
5 Upper Silesia
6 Warthegau
7 Danzig (West Prussia)
8 East Prussia
9 Generalgouvernement
10 Białystok Region

© Polish National Publishing House, Warsaw, 1979
(Państwowe Wydawnictwo Naukowe)

■ Camp

⊠ Extermination Center

northwest of the town of Kraśnik. In the mid-1930s the Poles established a military-industrial combine on this site, including an aircraft industry. Following the German occupation of Poland, the military industries were taken over by the Hermann Göring Works, while the aircraft factory was operated by the Heinkel Company.

During the summer of 1942 a forced-labor camp was set up in Budzyń, and 500 Jews were brought in from the neighboring towns. In the fall, 400 prisoners of war were added from the Końska Wola camp and from the camp on Lipowa Street in LUBLIN. In May 1943, after the WARSAW GHETTO UPRISING had been suppressed, 800 Jews from Warsaw were brought in. By mid-1943 the camp had a prison population of 3,000, including 300 women and children. The prisoners were employed in the military factories, in construction, and in general services. The camp commandant, an SS officer named Feiks, mistreated the prisoners and from time to time killed some of them. In the fall of 1942 some 100 prisoners—sick or old persons, and children—had been taken to the BEŁŻEC extermination camp and murdered there. In August 1943 another 200 prisoners, classified as sick and unfit for work, were sent away, this time to MAJDANEK, to be killed. On October 22, Budzyń became a concentration camp and was attached to Majdanek. Late that winter, on February 8, 1944, dozens of prisoners were killed when the Ukrainian guards opened fire on them.

Owing to the influence exercised by the camp elder, Noah Stockman, a prisoner of war hailing from Brest-Litovsk, conditions in the camp were relatively bearable. In one instance, several groups of youngsters who came from the surrounding towns acquired weapons by stealing them from the military factories and escaped to the forests, where they joined the partisans. Stockman managed to persuade the camp administration to refrain from harsh retaliatory measures. For Passover 1944, again owing to Stockman's influence, unleavened bread was baked in the camp and a Seder ceremony was held. At the beginning of May of that year the evacuation of the camp began, and prisoners were sent in groups to Mielec, Ostrowiec, and Wieliczka, among other places.

BIBLIOGRAPHY

Freiburg, D. *Darkness Covered the Earth.* Tel Aviv, 1970. (In Hebrew.)

SHMUEL SPECTOR

BUKOVINA, historical name of the region covering the northeastern Carpathians and the plain at the foot of the mountains, bordering on the Dniester in the north. Up to 1774 the territory was part of the principality of Moldavia, then under Ottoman suzerainty. From 1774 to 1918 it was ruled by Austria, and during that period was called Bukovina. Many Germans and even more Ukrainians settled there, creating a difficult conflict of nationalities. By the end of the Austrian period the Ukrainians had become the largest nationality in northern Bukovina, although they were not a majority in all of Bukovina. Bukovina was incorporated into ROMANIA in 1918. In June of 1940, northern Bukovina —which had a Ukrainian majority—was annexed by the Soviet Union, following a Soviet ultimatum to Romania (an act that violated the NAZI-SOVIET PACT). A year later, in late June and early July 1941, in the wake of the German attack on the Soviet Union, Romania recaptured northern Bukovina.

Jews had settled in Bukovina in the thirteenth century. During the seventeenth century, Jews from Poland and the Ukraine entered the area in large numbers, and the influx increased sharply during the Austrian period. In 1890 Bukovina had a Jewish population of some ninety thousand. The Jews played an important role in the development of commerce and industry; the wealthy among them acquired landed estates, and some were even raised to the nobility. Under Romanian rule, between the two world wars, the situation of the Jews deteriorated: there was antisemitic rioting, Jews were driven out of various occupations, and their legal status was impaired. A law for the "reexamination of citizenship," passed by the government of

BUKOVINA, June 1940

Octavian GOGA and Alexandru CUZA in early 1938, deprived many Jews of their Romanian nationality.

During the Soviet annexation of northern Bukovina in June 1940 and the withdrawal of Romanian troops from that area, the Romanians vented their spite on the local population, especially the Jews, accusing them of being Communists and Soviet sympathizers and of armed acts of provocation against Romanian soldiers. At this early stage of the Holocaust, and without any connection to the Nazis, Romanian army units murdered hundreds of Jews and committed other grave crimes against them. Infantry Battalion 16, commanded by the antisemitic Maj. Valeriu Carp, killed dozens of Jews with indescribable tortures on its withdrawal from northern Bukovina in the direction of Fălticeni. The murders did not cease even when the withdrawal of the Romanian troops from Soviet-annexed northern Bukovina was completed, with the participation of a number of infantry battalions, in addition to the sixteenth. Jewish soldiers serving in the Romanian army were also the victims of humiliation and torture by Romanian troops, and a number of Jewish soldiers were murdered. Many Jews on their way to join their army units were thrown off the speeding trains.

The Soviet regime in northern Bukovina put an end to traditional Jewish cultural life and education and to the de facto autonomy enjoyed by the Jews under the Romanians. All non-Communist Jewish organizations were disbanded, and a campaign of harassment and arrests was launched against Zionist leaders and activists. On June 13, 1941, a drive was begun to deport to Siberia masses of Zionist leaders and activists, and anyone else who was regarded as an "enemy of the people." The expulsions into exile continued into the first few days of the war. From CHERNOVTSY (Rom., Cernăuţi; Ger., Czernowitz) at least four thousand Jews were exiled, as were hundreds of families from the provincial towns. This was accompanied by a campaign against persons of property and wealth, or against those whom the Soviets regarded as such; many Jews belonging to the middle class were affected, including professionals, whom the Soviets classified as "bourgeois."

Following the invasion of the Soviet Union by the Germans and their allies (which included Romania), on June 22, 1941, thousands of Jews were called up for service in the Red Army, but most of them remained where they were, since no special travel arrangements had been made for them. Only a few Jews were evacuated from Bukovina or managed to escape on their own into the Soviet interior, since many of the people trying to make their way eastward were intercepted by the German and Romanian armies. In many villages, pogroms against the Jews were launched as soon as the Soviet troops had withdrawn and before any Romanian army units had arrived. Organized gangs of peasants, mostly Ukrainians, robbed, tortured, raped, and murdered Jews by the hundreds and thousands. This was the case in Banila pe Ceremus, Sadagura, Rohosna, and other places. The Romanian army encouraged its troops to take "revenge" on the Jews, alleging that the Jews had aided the Soviet regime. In Ciudei, the first village in northern Bukovina that he captured, Major Carp ordered 450 Jews to be murdered. Between July 4 and 31, thousands of Jews were killed by Romanian troops in the villages they occupied.

Chernovtsy was occupied on July 5 and 6, by Romanian and German units. Together with them, Einsatzkommando 10a of Einsatzgruppe D entered the city. The Germans were not satisfied with the performance of their Romanian allies, who were also paying special attention to the removal of Ukrainians from northern Bukovina. Einsatzkommando 10a set an example to the Romanians when it carried out its first massacre in the city, murdering hundreds of Jews, mainly from the intelligentsia and the professional class. At the same time, German and Romanian units staged pogroms throughout the Chernovtsy district. In the Jewish-populated towns along the Dniester, hundreds of Jews were killed by Ukrainians from Galicia, and other Jews were killed on the northern bank of the river, having been forced across by Romanian and German troops. Approximately fifteen thousand Jews were killed in this wave of murder. On June 21, 1941, on orders of Ion ANTONESCU, the Jews living in the towns and villages of southern Bukovina were driven out. Local authorities interpreted the orders as they wished, and included the Jews of Siret in the expulsion. The old people and the women and children were for the most part sent to camps in southwest Romania. The small Jewish communities in the Olteni region were ordered to look after the Jews in the camps, a task they were incapable of carrying out.

In September and October 1941 the Jews in the camps of southwestern Romania were first freed, then "legally" fleeced, and then expelled to TRANSNISTRIA. In northern Bukovina, the Jews who had survived the pogroms and massacres were assembled into several camps and from there were transferred to ghettos, in Storojineti, Cotmani, Vizhnitsa (Vaşcăuti), and Lujeni. Many of them escaped or were transferred to Chernovtsy. On July 11 the Romanian civil administration took over in Bukovina, and Alexandru Rioşanu was appointed governor. The "Romanization" section of the civil administration was devoted to the confiscation of Jewish property. On July 30 a special decree was issued by the governor, ordering the Jews to wear the yellow badge (*see* BADGE, JEWISH). The military section attached to the governor's office, headed by Maj. Stere Marinescu, was responsible for the implementation of all anti-Jewish orders and regulations; it did so with great severity, adding further regulations of its own.

All the existing anti-Jewish laws and regulations in force in Old Romania (the Regat) were also applied in Bukovina. The Jews in Bukovina, however, were not allowed to maintain contact with their brethren in the rest of the country, the prohibition also applying to food shipments. On August 4 the first attempt was made to deport Jews from Bukovina to Transnistria, in a group consisting of Jews from Storojineti and its vicinity. Romanian gendarmes murdered 200 of these deportees by drowning them in the Dniester. On October 10, 1941, a secret order was received from Bucharest to expel all the Jews of Bukovina to the other bank of the Dniester. By then, all the Jews of northern Bukovina had been put into ghettos and camps. On October 11 a ghetto was established in Chernovtsy, and on the next day the deportation was launched. Some of the Jews were transported to Transnistria through the Atachi border crossing, but most of them were driven to hastily improvised camps in northern Bessarabia—SECURENI, EDINETI, and MARCULEŞTI—where many of them died. The survivors were deported to Transnistria between October 3 and 11, 1941. By November 15, when the deportation came to a stop, 57,000 Jews had been deported from Bukovina (including the southern part). The process was carried out in a most brutal manner, and many of the Jews were murdered en route to their destination. Jewish property left behind was pillaged at once by the local population, even though it was classified as property to be confiscated for the government. In Chernovtsy, only 20,000 Jews were left; 4,000 more were deported from there in June 1942.

As a result of efforts made by Jewish leaders in Bucharest, especially Dr. Wilhelm FILDERMAN and Chief Rabbi Alexander SAFRAN, the deportation was halted, the Jews having obtained an assurance from the deputy prime minister, Mihai ANTONESCU, that the Chernovtsy Jews required for the economy would be permitted to stay there. Ion Antonescu, the Romanian dictator, agreed to allow 10,000 Jews to stay, but in fact the number of Jews who remained in Chernovtsy for the rest of the war was 16,000, with several hundred refugees from Poland included in that figure. In October 1943 the wearing of the yellow badge was abolished, and Jews were again permitted to move about on the city streets. When the Red Army was drawing near, the Jews were afraid that the retreating Germans would take revenge on them. The Jews were not, however, permitted to move into the interior.

In February 1944 the Romanian army withdrew from Chernovtsy and the city was left in German hands; it was only the advance of the Soviet army and its swift occupation of the city that saved the Jews from extermination. In April 1945, when the Soviets permitted travel to Romania, most of the local Jews—the remnants of northern Bukovina's Jews—left Chernovtsy. Several thousand Jews, mainly individual survivors of the families that had been deported, returned to Chernovtsy in late 1944 and early 1945, from Transnistria. Most of them took up residence in the towns of southern Bukovina from which they had been driven out in 1941. A few years later the majority of them left Romania and settled in Israel.

BIBLIOGRAPHY

Ancel, J., and T. Lavi, eds. *Rumania*, vol. 2. In *Pinkas Hakehillot; Encyclopaedia of Jewish Communities*. Jerusalem, 1980. (In Hebrew.)

Levin, D. "The Jews and the Inception of Soviet Rule in Bukovina." *Soviet Jewish Affairs* 6/2 (October 1976): 52–70.

JEAN ANCEL

BULGARIA. Located in the Balkan Peninsula, Bulgaria has common borders with Romania, Yugoslavia, Greece, and Turkey. The Bulgarian people was formed by the integration of the Ugaritic Bulgars from the Volga region, who had conquered the area in the seventh century, with its original Slavic, Illyrian, Thracian, and Macedonian inhabit-

BULGARIA, March 1943

ants. The Bulgarian language belongs to the South Slavic group of languages, and most Bulgarians are Orthodox Christians.

From 1396 to 1878 Bulgaria was under Ottoman rule, and after gaining independence it continued to acknowledge Ottoman suzerainty, until 1908. In World War I Bulgaria fought on the side of the Central Powers; after the war it had to give up territory and make large reparations payments. Its regime was a constitutional monarchy, and it had a parliament (Narodno Sobranie, or National Assembly) in which leftist, centrist liberal-democratic, and right-wing nationalist parties were represented. In practice, however, it was the king who held power in the country.

In 1940 Bulgaria's population was 6.2 million, with 407,000 in the capital, Sofia. Up to the end of World War II, peasants constituted 80 percent of the population, and the econ-

omy was based primarily on agricultural production, its industry tiny even by eastern European standards. Eighty-five percent of the population were ethnic Bulgars, and the great majority, 87.5 percent, were Orthodox Christians. Muslim Turks accounted for 10 percent, and an additional 1.5 percent were Muslim Bulgars (Pomaks). There were also small groups of Catholics and Protestants. In 1943 there were 63,403 Jews in Bulgaria, about 1 percent of the population.

The earliest reports on the presence of Jews in the areas of what is now Bulgaria date back to the first century. During the Middle Ages the Jews had special privileges, and their situation in Bulgaria was better than in the other European kingdoms. Under Ottoman rule they were in the good graces of both the Bulgarian and the Ottoman authorities, who regarded them as a mediatory entity. When Bulgaria became independent in 1878, its Jews were granted full and equal rights.

Approximately 90 percent of Bulgarian Jewry descended from Jews who had been expelled from Spain in 1492 and had come to Bulgaria between the sixteenth and the nineteenth century, mostly by way of the SARAJEVO and SALONIKA Jewish communities; 10 percent of the Jews were Ashkenazic, of Austro-Hungarian and Romanian origin. In the interwar period some Ashkenazic Jews from Russia also took up residence in Bulgaria. Sephardic and Ashkenazic Jews lived in complete harmony, and at times the office of chief rabbi was held by an Ashkenazi. In the early twentieth century most of the Jews spoke Judeo-Spanish (Ladino), but over the course of time, with the growth of the Jewish intelligentsia, Bulgarian became the dominant language. Educated Jews were also fluent in German and French. Dozens of Jewish periodicals were published, in both Judeo-Spanish and Bulgarian. Zionism rapidly gained a predominant foothold in Jewish community life, and in 1918 it extended this foothold to the Consistory, the Bulgarian Jewish communities' central council.

The Jewish communities were autonomous financially and administratively. Jews lived only in the cities, and their main occupations were in the retail trade and the professions. They played no prominent role in the country's economy and had little influence on social and cultural life. The rural population scarcely knew the Jews, and it was only in Sofia, where half the retail trade was in Jewish hands, that their presence had an impact. As a result, Bulgaria was free of one of the usual factors contributing to the rise of antisemitism—Jewish competition in the economic sphere. Antisemitism never struck roots in Bulgaria; the Bulgarian people, itself of mixed origin, could not lay claim to "racial purity." During World War II some Bulgarians called for ethnic solidarity with the Japanese, because of the joint "Mongol" origin of the two peoples. After the war, certain ideologists denied that the Bulgarians had any link to the Mongol race, and claimed that they were pure Slavs, "brothers of the Russian people."

Karl Hoffmann, the representative of the REICHSSICHERHEITSHAUPTAMT (Reich Security Main Office; RSHA) in Bulgaria, in a letter to his superiors in Berlin dated April 5, 1943, stated: "Anybody who is familiar with conditions in Bulgaria must realize that as the time draws near for the 'transports' of the Jews, there will be problems. . . . The Jewish Question does not exist in Bulgaria in the sense that it does in Germany. The ideological and racial prerequisites for convincing the Bulgarian people of the urgent need for a solution of the Jewish Question as in the Reich are not to be found here."

This is not to say that there were never manifestations of antisemitism in Bulgaria. Occasional antisemitic incidents took place in the provincial towns and, more frequently, in Sofia. Three cases of blood libel (the accusation that Jews kill gentiles to obtain their blood for Jewish rituals) occurred in the late nineteenth century, and in the early twentieth century there were anti-Jewish riots in the Jewish quarters of several cities. In 1933 the Nazi-oriented nationalist Saiuz na Bulgarskite Natsionalni Legioni (Union of Bulgarian National Legions), known as the Legionnaires' Association, was formed. This was followed by the creation of a youth organization, Branik, modeled on the HITLERJUGEND, and a fascist organization, Ratnitsi Napreduka na Bulgarshtinata (Guardians of the Advancement of the Bulgarian National Spirit), known as the Ratnitsi, led by Petur Gabrovski.

In the 1930s Bulgaria again had close ties with Germany, its World War I ally. Its motivations were to regain the territories it had lost in 1918, to rid itself of the heavy reparations payments, and to free itself of the restrictions that had been imposed on the strength of its armed forces. In addition, Bulgaria's economy was becoming increasingly dependent on Germany, the volume of its trade with Germany rising from 29 percent of its total foreign trade in 1929 to 68 percent in 1939.

On February 15, 1940, King Boris III appointed the pro-German Professor Bogdan Filov (1883–1945) as prime minister. (Filov was sentenced to death after the war and executed.) On March 1, 1941, under an arbitration award made by Adolf Hitler, Bulgaria received back the southern Dobruja

(Dobrudzha) region from Romania. That day, Bulgaria joined the Axis; the following day, German forces entered Bulgaria, and in April Bulgaria took part in the Axis attack on Yugoslavia and Greece. In return it regained THRACE and MACEDONIA, as well as parts of eastern Serbia, thereby realizing its nationalists' dream of a "Greater Bulgaria." Bulgaria declared war on Great Britain and the United States, but not on the Soviet Union, and it did not send any of its forces to the eastern front—the only European member of the Axis to refrain from doing so. This was because King Boris felt he had to take into account the Slavophile sentiments of his subjects, who had not forgotten the role that Russia had played, in 1878, in helping Bulgaria gain independence.

Anti-Jewish Legislation. The rapprochement with Germany also had its effect on the Jewish issue. The German demands that Bulgaria enact anti-Jewish laws accorded fully with the antisemitic sentiments prevailing in Filov's cabinet. As early as July 1940, a government spokesman announced that Bulgaria was planning to "take steps that would restrict the activities of the Jews," and on October 7, 1940, the government approved the Law for the Protection of the Nation, which curbed the rights of the Jews. The chairman of the Jewish Consistory in Sofia, Josef Geron, together with other members of its executive board and Jewish activists, launched an information drive designed to make the government and the population aware of the grave damage that the anti-Jewish law would cause the Bulgarian people. The Consistory representatives also asked for the opportunity to present their case to the king, but he refused to receive them.

The struggle launched by the Jewish leaders had a positive impact on public opinion. In October 1940 a group of twenty-one leading writers sent a protest letter to the prime minister, the final passage of which read: "On behalf of civilization and on behalf of Bulgaria's good name, we beseech you not to accept the law, the repercussions of which would put a dark stain on our legislation and leave an intolerable mark upon our national memory."

The Bulgarian Medical Association lost no time in joining the writers' protest, using even stronger language, and the Bar Association followed suit, in yet more forceful terms. Political leaders from both left and right also appealed to the prime minister. Of special importance was the protest lodged by the Holy Synod (the supreme body of the Orthodox church) and the personal intervention of metropolitans Stefan of Sofia, Cyril of Plovdiv, Neofit of Vidin, and Sofroni of Vratsa.

The arousal of public sympathy for the Jews sparked off a reaction in the opposing camp. Fascist organizations such as the Federation of Reserve Officers (Saiuz na Zapasnite Ofitseri) and the Federation of Reserve Sergeants and Soldiers (Saiuz na Zapasnite Podofitseri i Voinitsi) distributed leaflets in support of the law. These bodies, known for their nationalist and revanchist attitudes, were joined by the Pharmacists' Association (Aptekarski Saiuz) and the Students' Union (Studenskata Organizatsia). Support for the anti-Jewish law was expressed by the Merchants' Association (Targovskoto Sdruzhenie), which had four thousand Jews among its membership. Despite these manifestations of support for the law, the majority of public opinion was opposed. The government, however, decided to adhere to its *Realpolitik* and persisted in its stand, motivated by opportunist political pragmatism rather than by racist antisemitic ideology: the anti-Jewish law was designed to pave the way for a further rapprochement with Germany. The protests against the law are of no avail, and on January 21, 1941, it passed parliament and was ratified by the king's signature that same day. The law provided the government with a legal basis for its anti-Jewish measures. The definition of "Jews" in the law was, basically, copied from the NUREMBERG LAWS, with some slight "improvement" on the Nuremberg text. In its introduction, the law stated that "the Jews are an evil and a foreign element among the Bulgarian People that acts against the State."

The law had three sections, as follows:

1. No branches of international organizations were permitted to exist in Bulgaria. This affected first the B'NAI B'RITH lodge

Members of the Jewish Consistory in Sofia, Bulgaria (1941).

and, a year later, the various component parts of the Zionist movement.

2. Jews could not be elected to public office and could not take part in a vote for such office; Jewish civil servants had to resign immediately; the *numerus clausus* (quota of Jews) was to be applied in the universities; mixed marriages between Jews and Bulgarians were prohibited; Jews were restricted to their current places of residence; and Jewish economic activities were severely restricted.

3. What was considered "anti-national" behavior by Jews and other foreign nationals was defined.

The authors of the law made attempts to conceal its antisemitic intent by applying it to all "foreigners." In February 1941, the Regulations for the Law for the Protection of the Nation were issued, which expanded the restrictions and applied only to Jews. These regulations, in effect, disenfranchised the Jews.

Commissariat for Jewish Questions. In August 1942 another regulation was issued, establishing the Commissariat for Jewish Questions (Komisarstvo za Evreiskite Vuprosi; KEV) in the Ministry of Internal Affairs. Its task was to apply the Law for the Protection of the Nation and the relevant regulations. Under those regulations, the Jewish community boards were stripped of their power and placed under the authority of the KEV. On September 30 of that year, Aleksander Belev (1900–1944) was appointed Commissioner for Jewish Questions. A pro-Nazi lawyer, Belev was one of the few Bulgarians who believed in antisemitism as an ideology. In September 1944, when the Soviet army entered Bulgaria, Belev tried to escape with the retreating Germans, but was caught by partisans and executed.

The August 1942 regulation also contained provisions for the financing of the KEV's wide range of operations. These expenses were to be covered by the blocked bank accounts of the Jews—a certain percentage of which would be set aside for this purpose—and by special fees that "persons of Jewish extraction" would have to pay for official documents issued to them. In other words, the Jews themselves would have to pay the enormous costs of their persecution: of the restrictions imposed on them in the initial stage, and of their eventual expulsion from Bulgaria. The various measures introduced by the KEV on the basis of the anti-Jewish law and regulations were intended as a prelude to the deportation of the Jews to the east. This was stated by Belev in no uncertain terms in a letter he addressed to the minister of internal affairs, Petur Gabrovski, on August 29, 1942: "The radical solution of our Jewish Question will be their emigration, which will have to proceed hand in hand

with the confiscation of their property. . . .
For the present, the possibility for such emigration does not exist, unless Germany were to agree to settle the Jews in Galicia or in another part of Russia. For the present, until such time as conditions arise that would enable the emigration of Jews to proceed, it is imperative to toughen the measures against them."

The "measures against the Jews" were taken during 1942. In the spring of 1943, the plan for the "solution of the Jewish Question" entered its final stage, that of their deportation from the country. First to be deported were the Jews of Thrace, Macedonia, and eastern Serbia, the territories that the Germans had handed over to Bulgaria. This was to be followed by preparatory steps for the deportation of all the Jews from Bulgaria.

Deportation. In November 1941 the Bulgarian foreign minister, Ivan Vladimir Popov, had a meeting with Joachim von RIBBENTROP at which the German foreign minister told him that, according to Hitler's decision, all the Jews would be expelled from Europe when the war ended. As a preliminary stage for the total removal of the Jews, their deportation to Poland was being planned. German Foreign Ministry officials kept a close watch on the development of the anti-Jewish policy in Bulgaria, and believed that they would have no problem in taking the Jews out of that country. On February 22, 1943, an agreement was signed in Sofia between Belev and Adolf EICHMANN's representative in Bulgaria, SS-Hauptsturmführer Theodor DANNECKER. The agreement provided that "as a first step, twenty thousand Jews will be deported to German territories in the east." The text that had been prepared for signature contained the words "from Thrace and Macedonia," but these words were struck out by Belev and Dannecker when they signed the document. A week later, on March 2, the Bulgarian government approved the agreement as it stood. Because of concern about possible adverse public reaction, a note was added to the official approval of the agreement stating that "the approval of this agreement does not require its publication in the official Gazette." (From most of the countries occupied by Germany, and even countries allied with it, such as Italy, Hungary, and Romania, the Jews were deported without any agreement being signed between the Reich and the local government.)

Two days later, on March 4, some 12,000 Jews from the Bulgarian-occupied territories of Thrace, Macedonia, and eastern Serbia were evicted from their homes. Allowed only some personal effects, they were put into concentration camps. They remained there for about a week in the custody of Bulgarian soldiers and police, who stole the Jews' belongings on the pretext of carrying out body searches. It was only when the Jews boarded trains that they were handed over to units of the German Wehrmacht. By the end of March the Bulgarian transports began moving north, with the Danube River port of Lom as their first destination. From there they proceeded on cargo boats to Vienna, where once again they were put on trains, which took them to their final destination, TREBLINKA. On March 20 and 21, 4,226 Jews from Thrace and the city of Pirot were deported, followed, from March 22 to 29, by 7,158 Jews from Macedonia (mostly from Skopje). The total number of Jews deported from the occupied territories was 11,384. Of these, 21 were reported by their escorts to have died en route, leaving 11,363 to be handed over to the Treblinka camp administration.

Reports on what had happened to the Jews of the occupied territories began to circulate among the Jewish communities in Bulgaria. The Bulgarian occupied territories were now emptied of their Jews, but Belev was still short of the 20,000 Jews stipulated in the agreement with Dannecker. Wanting to fulfill the agreement, he was forced to use Bulgarian Jews for this purpose. He chose to deport the Jews of Kyustendil, a town near the old border with Serbia. On March 5, 1943, the KEV representative in Kyustendil issued orders for the confiscation of water containers and other household utensils. The Jews of the town suspected that these items were to be used for a long train journey, and their fears were confirmed by a town official who leaked the information that a deportation order for Jews had been received.

The events that followed, however, were quite different from what might have been expected. Kyustendil became the occasion for an inspiring manifestation of the Bulgarians' solidarity with their Jewish fellow citizens and their determination to protect them. Bulgarian and right-wing Macedonian nationalist functionaries from the town sent a delegation to Sofia that arrived on March 8 and was joined by Dimitur Peshev, deputy speaker of parliament. The next day, the delegation held two meetings. At the first, held with the leaders of the Jewish Consistory, the delegation declared that they would do all in their power to prevent the implementation of the deportation order. The second was held with Minister of the Interior Petur Gabrovski. At this meeting, the Macedonian members of the delegation threatened the minister with "personal sanctions" (that is, assassination) if he did not call off the deportation. The deadline for the deportation was midnight, March 9–10, but Gabrovski agreed to its postponement. The delegation's prompt and determined intervention had achieved its purpose, and for the moment the Jews of Bulgaria were saved from deportation.

Peshev spent the following week, March 10 to 17, in talks with members of parliament, seeking to gain their support for a manifesto protesting the deportation of the Jews. On March 17 he submitted the manifesto to the speaker; it bore the signatures of forty-three parliamentarians. Its text included the following passage: "Such an act must not be permitted, not only because the persons affected have not been stripped of their citizenship and cannot legally be expelled from Bulgaria; an act of this sort would also have grave political consequences for the country as a whole." The government reacted angrily. On March 23, a majority in parliament reprimanded Peshev, who by now was isolated, and removed him from his post as deputy speaker. (After the war, Peshev was sentenced to fifteen years' hard labor as a war criminal, saved from a death sentence by his assistance to the Jews. His sentence was commuted and he lived the rest of his life in poverty.)

Following the postponement of the March 9 deportation, Belev resigned from his post. During April and May, the Jews of Bulgaria again had the threat of deportation hanging over them. The Germans maintained their pressure; on April 5, the German minister in Sofia, Adolf Beckerle, wrote to Berlin that it would not be long before the Jews would be deported from Bulgaria proper. At this point, however, the Bulgarian government was beginning to have its doubts, under the impact of the tumult in parliament and the mood of the people. A new plan was devised whereby 25,000 Sofia Jews would be exiled to the provinces, pending their deportation from the country. On May 22, 1943, a decree containing the new plan was published. The following day (the eve of a national holiday commemorating Saints Cyril and Methodius), the Jews of Sofia held a demonstration in the courtyard of the synagogue, and on May 24 there was a demonstration by Bulgarians, on the initiative of underground Communist groups. Militant Jews as well marched through the city. The police intervened, using brute force to break up both gatherings. The decree on the expulsion of the Jews from Sofia was put into effect, and within twelve days, 19,153 Jews were driven out of the capital and forced to live in some twenty provincial towns. Although this expulsion was the climax of Jewish persecutions, it also removed the threat of deportation to the extermination camps.

In the late summer of 1943, the political climate underwent a change. On August 28, King Boris III died under mysterious circumstances, following his return from a meeting with Hitler. In September, Italy surrendered, and the Allies kept up their advance. The Bulgarian government decided to adopt a more flexible policy. Petur Gabrovski was not reappointed to the cabinet; the United States sought to impress upon Bulgaria that it should change its policy, including its attitude toward the Jews; and in the fall of that year, the Germans stopped pressuring Bulgaria regarding the Jewish issue.

Further provisions of the Law for the Protection of the Nation stipulated that from 1941 all Jewish males between the ages of twenty and forty were to be drafted into special labor battalions. At first the Jews in these battalions worked side by side with Bulgarians, performing the same work and wearing the same uniforms. When the German Labor Service, the Reichsarbeitsdienst, protested against this equal treatment, the Jews were formed into separate units and assigned "very hard work" in the mountains and forests, under the same conditions as convicts sentenced to hard labor. In effect, the Jewish labor battalion camps became concentration camps. The upper age limit for the forced-labor draft was raised in 1943 to forty-six, and the workday was extended to twelve hours. Some twelve thousand Jews were drafted into the forced-labor battalions and put on extremely hard work, constructing new trails in the mountains, building new roads, and cutting trees in the forests.

The Law for the Protection of the Nation involved the same sort of restrictions and humiliations to which the Jews were exposed in other countries of occupied Europe: all Jews aged ten and above had to wear a yellow badge (*see* BADGE, JEWISH) on their clothing; every Jewish house or business had to display a sign identifying it as Jewish; Jews were dismissed from all posts in the schools and universities. The situation of the Jews in the provincial towns was exceptionally bad. The Jews exiled from Sofia were restricted to living only in Jewish houses, and were not allowed to take up employment; they lived in drastically overcrowded conditions, with as many as eight to ten persons to a room; they had only one hour a day in which to make their purchases in the public markets; and in some towns a permanent curfew was in force for Jews, except for one or two hours a day. Jews were prohibited from using the main streets, from entering certain kinds of business establishments, and from attending places of entertainment such as cinemas and cafés. Their radios, automobiles, and bicycles were confiscated, as were valuables such as jewelry and rugs.

The Bulgarian population was divided in its attitude toward the Jews. Some tried to enrich themselves at the expense of the latter, whereas others tried to help them by providing food supplies, by aiding the Jewish communities to maintain contact with one another, and by employing Jews illegally. It would be difficult to assess the precise proportion of the two groups in the population, but the Jews were under the impression that most Bulgarians remained faithful to their humane principles, were not infected by antisemitism, and had compassion for the Jews in their hour of need.

Rescue Efforts and Acts of Resistance. Prior to Bulgaria's alliance with Germany in April 1941, several attempts were made to save Jews without Bulgarian nationality, as well as groups of children and Zionist youth. "Illegal" immigration (ALIYA BET) ships left Bulgaria for Palestine. The first such ship, the *Salvador*, left Varna on December 4, 1940, only to sink twelve days later off the coast of Turkey because it was unseaworthy. Of the 335 refugees on board, 213 drowned, while 122 were saved and made their way to Palestine. Another 170 Jews from Bulgaria joined other Palestine-bound Jewish refugees on a Romanian ship, the *Dorian*, in late February 1941, and a month later a group of 65 children left for Palestine. From April 1941 until late 1943, the borders of Bulgaria were hermetically sealed for Jewish emigration.

In late 1943, Chaim WEIZMANN and Rabbi Stephen WISE, in London and Washington respectively, worked on plans for rescuing Bulgarian Jewry by transporting them to Palestine via Turkey. In Sofia, secret contacts concerning these plans were handled by the Swiss legation, and in Istanbul they were in the hands of Ira HIRSCHMANN, representative of the WAR REFUGEE BOARD. The fact that the Allied powers were taking interest in the fate of the Jews of Bulgaria induced the Sofia government to moderate its Jewish policy. Finally, in August 1944, it repealed the anti-Jewish legislation. On September 9, when the Soviet army entered Bulgaria, the new anti-fascist government that had by then been established declared war on Nazi Germany.

A few dozen Jewish youths joined the partisan units, and some of them fell in battles with the Bulgarian gendarmerie. Among those killed in action who had gained renown for their heroism were Emil Shekerdzhiiski, Violeta Iakova, Mati Rubenov, Menachem Papo, and Yosif Talvi.

The special situation in Bulgaria in those years has not been fully researched, and the question of who was responsible for saving the Jews has yet to be resolved. The Jewish community of DENMARK was the other community under the Nazis that was saved, but this was because they were moved to Sweden by a concerted effort of the Danish people. In Bulgaria the Jews survived in a country that was in the pro-German camp. Thus far, the answers given to this question have been colored by ideological bias and for the most part have not been based on reliable and conclusive evidence.

The official Communist version seeks to credit the Communists with saving Bulgarian Jewry. The Bulgarian Communist resistance did indeed demonstrate its concern for the Jews: its radio station in Moscow made several broadcasts condemning their persecution, and the Communist underground organization in Sofia took part in the May 24, 1943, demonstrations. These efforts, however, did not deter the Bulgarian government from expelling the Jews from the capital. The Communist version is unwarranted; as Nissan Oren has noted (1968), Communist propaganda during the war had no effect on the Bulgarian government.

Benjamin Arditi, one of the leaders of Bulgarian Jewry, has claimed that the Jews of Bulgaria were saved by King Boris's decisions, in March and May 1943, not to permit their deportation from the country. This version, too, does not present the complete story, and no original document exists to prove that the king made such a decision. On the other hand, Minister of the Interior Gabrovski would not have taken the risk of postponing the deportation decreed for March 9, 1943, without the king's authority. King Boris, moreover, was able to resist German pressure on an issue of immense importance: the demand by the Germans that Bulgarian forces join in the fighting against the Soviet army. No evidence has come to light to confirm the legend surrounding King Boris's mysterious death, according to which he was poisoned because he refused Hitler's demand for the surrender of Bulgarian Jewry. To date, the Bulgarian government has not granted scholars from the West access to the Royal Archives for that period. King Boris's acts and decisions on this issue are still shrouded in secrecy, and more research would be required to substantiate the claim that it was he who saved Bulgaria's Jews.

The question of how Bulgarian Jews were saved has two aspects: (1) Who gave the orders to postpone the deportations in March and May 1943, and to refrain from deporting the Jews in the fall of 1943? (2) What were the motives for these decisions?

Until his death on August 28, 1943, King Boris was the supreme authority in the country. The prime minister and all other members of the cabinet were absolutely loyal to the king and abided by his decisions. Not a single instance is known of the cabinet's disobeying the king or acting in defiance of his position. While the Reich representatives in Sofia had direct access to the cabinet, neither Filov nor Gabrovski would have dared to make a decision on such an important issue without the king's consent. It would appear, therefore, that it was the king who gave the orders. It must be borne in mind, however, that the ultimate decision for a moderate Jewish policy was made in September 1943; by then Boris was dead, his son, Simeon II, was a small child, and Filov was still the prime minister.

We may assume that the king had several motives for his decisions. First, the Soviet victory at Stalingrad in February 1943, the subsequent Soviet military advances, and the Allied victories in North Africa made it clear that the German chances of winning the war were growing slimmer. Second, Boris realized that because of the Allies' interest in the fate of the Bulgarian Jews it was worthwhile keeping them alive, as security to be redeemed after the war to expiate for Bulgaria's declaration of war on the United States and Britain in 1941. Fearing that the German forces stationed in Bulgaria might take action against him, Boris decided on a compromise solution for the Jewish problem. He deported the Jews from the newly occupied territories, promulgated anti-Jewish legislation, and expelled the Jews of Sofia to provincial towns, but he did not deport Bulgarian Jews from the country.

Once the drive for deportation lost its momentum, the post–May 1943 delaying tactics had the support of a variety of additional forces: the Holy Synod and the personal involvement of the metropolitans Cyril and Stefan; appeals by leaders of the entire political spectrum, from the Communists to the nationalist bourgeoisie, by various political organizations, and by the leadership of the country's Macedonian minority; the persistent and far-reaching campaign waged by the Consistory and by Jewish and Zionist leaders in the United States, who had the support of influential elements in the United States administration; and the tolerant and humane character of the majority of Bulgarians. A rare combination of international circumstances and internal pressures influenced the king's behavior. However, it would be difficult to assess the specific weight of each of these factors, which together saved the lives of fifty thousand Bulgarian Jews.

From 1948 to 1949, some forty-five thousand Jews—90 percent of the Jewish population—left Bulgaria to settle in Israel. Only a few thousand Jews remained. This phenomenon, of nearly the entire Jewish community's moving to the Jewish state, was based on the strong sense of Jewish national identity that Bulgarian Jewry had long fostered, on their unwillingness to live under a Communist regime, and on their memories of the Holocaust period.

BIBLIOGRAPHY

Chary, F. B. *The Bulgarian Jews and the Final Solution.* Pittsburgh, 1972.
Miller, M. L. *Bulgaria during the Second World War.* Stanford, 1975.
Oren, N. "The Bulgarian Exception: A Reassessment of the Salvation of the Jewish Community." *Yad Vashem Studies* 7 (1968): 83–106.

AVRAHAM BEN-YAKOV

BUNA-MONOWITZ. *See* Auschwitz.

BUND (Yidisher Arbeter-Bund in Russland, Lite un Poiln; League of Jewish Workers in Russia, Lithuania, and Poland), Jewish So-

A Bund May Day parade in Warsaw, May 1, 1936. The banner on the right reads: "Down with Militarism and Wars! Long live International Workers' Solidarity!" The banner on the left reads: "The Strike Is Our Weapon!"

cialist party. The Bund was founded in Vilna in September and October 1897. In its initial stage, the party's aim was to organize Jewish workers and strengthen their revolutionary ardor so that they would join the Russian Socialist movement in its struggle against the tsarist regime. The Bund was totally opposed to Zionism and to Hebrew culture and language, regarding Yiddish as the national language of the Jews of eastern Europe. It aspired to equal rights for Jews within the framework of a Socialist and democratic state in which the Jewish population would enjoy cultural autonomy, like all the other people in the state. After the Bolshevik Revolution in 1917, the Bund gradually ceased to exist in the Soviet Union; most of its members joined the Communist party, and those who did not were persecuted by the new regime.

In the interwar period, independent Poland became the major scene of the Bund's activities; small branches also existed in Romania, Lithuania, Belgium, and France, as well as in the United States. In Poland the party established a broad base of operations, including children's and youth organizations (SKIF and Zukunft, respectively), a sports movement, and a women's organization. The Bund was the moving spirit in the establishment of CYShO (Central Yiddish Schools Organization), the Yiddish school network, and was the leading political body among the Jewish workers' organizations. Two of its outstanding leaders, Henryk Erlich and Wiktor Alter, succeeded in consolidating the party and turning it into an important force among the Jewish population of Poland. After joining the Socialist International, the Bund established close relations with the Socialist parties in the West and with the Polish Socialist party. Between 1936 and 1939, the Bund led a determined drive against antisemitic elements in Poland, and did not hesitate from time to time to activate its party militia, which was formed in the 1920s to react to street attacks on Jews and assaults on Bund members by political rivals. During that period the organization gained substantial representation on city councils, especially in WARSAW, ŁÓDŹ, VILNA, PIOTRKÓW TRYBUNALSKI, and LUBLIN. In parts of Galicia and

Upper Silesia, however, support for the Bund was conspicuously absent, especially in such important centers as LVOV and KRAKÓW. Moreover, despite continued efforts, the Bund never succeeded in having a candidate elected to the Sejm (the Polish parliament) or the senate.

When World War II broke out, most of the Bund's senior leaders left Poland. Most of the members of the party's Central Committee—Shlomo Mendelsohn, Emanuel Sherer, Vladimir Kossowski, Jekuthiel Portnoy (Noah), and Emanuel Nowogrodski—went to the United States, where they established an important center of support for party activities. The two top leaders of the party, Erlich and Alter, were arrested in the Soviet-occupied parts of Poland in September and October of 1939. The Bund made enormous and desperate efforts to have the two men released from Soviet imprisonment, for this purpose soliciting the help of leading personalities in the POLISH GOVERNMENT-IN-EXILE in London and the American labor movement. Their efforts were in vain, and in December 1941 both Bund leaders were murdered in the Soviet Union. In the eastern parts of Poland, which the Soviets had occupied—in Vilna, Białystok, Grodno, and other cities—most of the Bund members were arrested and exiled. In Warsaw, Bund members carried on underground operations. Until the beginning of the deportations to extermination camps, the Warsaw underground organization of the party issued publications that had a relatively wide circulation and were distributed in the provincial towns and cities of Poland. In June 1941 a Polish courier was caught with underground newspapers in her possession, as well as a list of Bund activists in various Polish cities. This led to the arrest and murder of a great number of party members in Piotrków Trybunalski, Kraków, Radom, and Tomaszów Mazowiecki.

The party leadership in Warsaw adamantly refused any political cooperation with Zionist parties or movements. In March 1942, when efforts were undertaken to form a united Jewish fighting organization, the Bund leader in Warsaw, Maurice Oisach, rejected the idea, saying that the Bund maintained ties with underground elements outside the ghetto. The party tried to set up a joint underground organization with the clandestine Polish socialist party, but the attempt failed. The Bund did not join the Antifascist Bloc that was created in the spring of 1942. One of the leaders of the Bund, the head of its youth faction, Abrasha Blum, did not agree with his elders and supported the establishment of a general Jewish organization. However, it was only in October and November of 1942—following the major *Aktion* in Warsaw—that the young Bund members, led by Blum, Berek Schneidemil, and Marek EDELMAN, joined the ŻYDOWSKA ORGANIZACJA BOJOWA (Jewish Fighting Organization; ŻOB), and even then, they refused to take part in the Żydowski Komitet Narodowy (Jewish National Committee) that had been set up. Therefore, a "Coordinating Committee" had to be established, in which both the Bund and the National Committee took part, as equals.

A similar situation existed in Vilna, where the Bund leaders, including Grisha Jaszunski, Berl Waydman, and Joel Fischmann, did not want to join the FAREYNEGTE PARTIZANER ORGANIZATSYE (United Partisan Organization), which was formed at the beginning of 1942. Here too, the young leaders, Abraham Chwojnik and Shmuel Kaplinski, were in favor of joining the Jewish fighting organization, and they did so, in the face of opposition by their elders. In both Vilna and Piotrków Trybunalski, the Bund was very influential in the Judenräte. Bund members Zalman Tennenberg and Yitzhak Samsonowitz headed the Judenrat in Piotrków Trybunalski—the only place where Bund members held these positions. In Vilna, Bund activists Jaszunski and Fischmann were on the Judenrat and wielded considerable influence there, but this came to an end when Jacob GENS became the head of the ghetto. The Bund was an important force in the struggle that the Łódź ghetto employees waged against Mordechai Chaim RUMKOWSKI for better living conditions.

In April 1942, Samuel ZYGELBOJM, a prominent Bund activist who had gone to the United States, was appointed to the Polish National Committee that had been set up in London. As a member of that committee, Zygelbojm was vehemently opposed to the Zionist bodies and their influence in London, and he refused to undertake joint action with the other Jewish member of the council, Ignacy Isaac SCHWARZBART. Two reports reached Zygelbojm—one sent in May 1942 and received the same month, and the other sent in August of that year and received in November—from a Bund activist in Warsaw, Leon FEINER, with detailed information on the annihilation of Polish Jewry. Zygelbojm thereupon sought to enlist the help of Polish authorities in London, the leaders of the major powers, and world opinion for the rescue of the Jews of Poland. Bitterly disappointed by the failure of his efforts, Zygelbojm, in despair, committed suicide in May 1943, as an act of protest against the indifference of the free world in the face of the murder of the Jews. His place on the Polish National Committee was taken by Emanuel Sherer, a Bund activist who went to London from the United States to take up his appointment.

The Bund took part in the WARSAW GHETTO UPRISING of April 1943, with four squads of its members joining in the fighting. In March 1944 the Polish government-in-exile in London awarded a medal of valor posthumously to Michael Kleppfisch, a Bund activist who had fallen in the uprising. Another Bund member, Marek Edelman, was one of the commanders of the ŻOB in Warsaw.

BIBLIOGRAPHY

In the Years of the Jewish Catastrophe: *The Voice of the Underground Bund*. New York, 1948. (In Yiddish.)

Johnpoll, B. K. *The Politics of Futility*: *The General Jewish Workers Bund of Poland, 1917–1943*. Ithaca, N.Y., 1967.

Kruk, H. "Diary of the Vilna Ghetto." *YIVO Annual* 13 (1965): 9–78.

Zygelbojm Book. New York, 1947. (In Yiddish.)

DANIEL BLATMAN

BUND DEUTSCHER MÄDEL. See Hitlerjugend.

C

CAMPS. [*The Nazis established a wide-ranging system of concentration, slave-labor, and extermination camps. Comprised of nearly three thousand camps, it crisscrossed Europe in a vast spiderweb of terror and mass intimidation. For an overview of this system of incarceration, see* Concentration Camps. *Prisoners detained while awaiting transfer to the "east" were held in assembly camps (Sammellager) and transit camps (Aufenthaltslager; Durchgangslager); see* Bergen-Belsen; Edineti; Gunskirchen; Kistarcza; Mechelen; Mogilev-Podolski; Secureni; Theresienstadt; Vaivara; Vertujeni; Vught; Westerbork. *In forced-labor camps (Arbeitslager or Zwangsarbeitslager), prisoners were worked to death; see* Blechhammer; Ebensee; Janówska; Klooga; Płaszów; Poniatowa; Trawniki; *see also* Forced Labor *and* Libya: Forced-Labor and Internment Camps. *Five camps were operated primarily as death factories, chiefly for Jews; see* Extermination Camps. *The Nazi camp system was rounded out by various prisoner-of-war camps and by the internment and detention camps run by some of Germany's client states (Croatia, Hungary, Italy, Romania, Slovakia, and Vichy France); see* Drancy; Ferramonti di Tarsa; Gurs; Les Milles; Vapniarka; Vittel. *After World War II, the British used detention camps on the island of Cyprus to keep Jewish "illegal" immigrants from reaching Palestine; see* Cyprus Detention Camps.]

CANADA. Just one week after the German invasion of Poland in September 1939, Canada joined the war effort against Nazi Germany. Second only to the Soviet Union in geographic area, Canada was economically and militarily unprepared for war. Nevertheless, this sparsely populated country eventually proved one of the leading military and economic mainstays of the Allied cause and a major contributor to the final defeat of Nazi Germany.

But if Canada was a stalwart of the Allied cause, it proved less than sympathetic to the mounting crisis of European Jewry. Most Canadians regarded the tragic plight of European Jews and their desperate need of a safe haven as an immigration problem best avoided. From Hitler's consolidation of power in 1933 to Nazi Germany's final surrender in the spring of 1945, Canada's doors remained closed to Jews. As a result, Canada had arguably the worst record among all the Western states in granting sanctuary to Jewish refugees from Nazi persecution.

Controls on Jewish admissions to Canada predate Hitler's rise. Prior to 1923, Jews entered Canada on equal terms with tens of thousands of other European immigrants. While preference was given to immigrants from Britain and the United States, the need for agricultural settlers to farm the vast Canadian prairies was so great that Canadian authorities actively recruited immigrants in eastern Europe. The Canadian public remained uneasy at the arrival of so many people of different ethnic and cultural origins. Nevertheless, the economic benefits of immigration were reassuring, as was the assumption that the immigrants would remain in

275

rural Canada, where they and their children could gradually be assimilated.

Most Jews who came to Canada, however, seemed to defy the government's policy of agricultural immigration. Rather than go to rural areas or take up farm-based employment, they congregated in Canadian urban centers and competed with Anglo-Canadian artisans and professionals.

As the agricultural lands of western Canada filled with European settlers and anti-immigration sentiment grew stronger, the government restricted immigration. Barriers were raised against all eastern Europeans. However, especially harsh regulations restricted the entry to Canada of Jewish would-be immigrants, irrespective of country of origin (except those from Britain or the United States). After 1923 only those few Jews who had close family members in Canada or who could muster the political influence necessary to obtain a rarely issued entry permit were allowed into Canada.

When the depression of the 1930s deepened and rising European antisemitism sent many Jews in search of refuge, Canada's immigration regulations were further tightened and Canadian authorities turned a deaf ear to every plea on behalf of Jewish refugees. In this, Canadian officials reflected the prevailing national sentiment, which was steadfastly opposed to Jewish immigration. While this opposition was strong all across Canada, nowhere was it stronger than in rural, French-speaking, and Catholic Quebec, on which the government counted heavily for reelection. The government knew only too well that any concession on the Jewish refugee issue would cost it dearly at the polls.

In spite of this opposition, the small immigrant working-class Jewish community of Canada, constituting less than 1.5 percent of the national population and largely concentrated in Montreal and Toronto, lobbied in support of Jewish immigration. As the Nazi threat to European Jewry increased, the Canadian Jewish community, through its national umbrella organization, the Canadian Jewish Congress, also organized a national boycott of German-made goods. If the boycott had limited success, the prewar effort to open Canada's doors to Jewish refugees was a complete failure. Although Canada partici-

pated in the 1938 EVIAN CONFERENCE, it did so reluctantly and only to ensure that Canada did not become the focus of any Jewish refugee resettlement scheme which might be proposed.

With the outbreak of hostilities in 1939, Jewish community support for the national war effort was unreserved. But attempts to convince public servants and political leaders to admit those Jews of Europe who might still be rescued from the Nazis remained a Jewish priority. In spite of the determination of immigration authorities to hold the line against Jewish admissions, the Canadian Jewish Congress did wring several small and hard-won concessions out of the Canadian cabinet. In late 1941 the government approved the admission of 1,000 Jewish children from Vichy France whose parents had been transported to Poland. Unfortunately, this came too late. Before any of the children selected for Canada could be removed, the Nazis seized control of Vichy France. The children followed their parents to the death camps. Later in the war, the Canadian government, under renewed domestic Jewish and international pressure, permitted the entry of several hundred Jewish refugees who had found temporary sanctuary in Spain and Portugal.

Another group of Jewish refugees came to Canada, more by accident than design. After the fall of France in 1940, British fears of imminent invasion grew. So too did fears that German and Austrian refugees in Britain, including Jews, posed a fifth-column threat. Refugees were rounded up and interned pending determination of their loyalty. Individuals declared a national threat were to be imprisoned in Australia or Canada. By error, several thousand innocent young Jewish refugees were shipped to Canada, where they were initially held in prisoner-of-war camps. Long after the error was discovered and long after almost all the internees in Britain were released, Canada still refused to release those it held, for fear they they would want to stay. Canada wanted no Jewish refugees, and certainly not any who had entered through a back door. It took more than two years of pressure by the British government and prodding by the Canadian Jewish community before the young men were finally released to attend Canadian schools or undertake war-related work.

Canadian reluctance to permit the entry of Jewish refugees did not end with the Allied victory in 1945 or with revelations of the Holocaust. Canada, its prewar immigration regulations still intact, rejected any suggestion that it offer new homes to DISPLACED PERSONS, least of all to Jews. When acute labor shortages eventually forced Canada to admit displaced persons, the government devised schemes to permit the immigration of thousands of new settlers to waiting jobs, while keeping Jewish entries to a minimum.

Only in late 1947 did government policy begin to change. After much negotiation, the government reaffirmed its wartime pledge, allowing into Canada 1,000 Jewish children, now orphaned survivors of the Holocaust. At the behest of the largely Jewish-owned Canadian clothing industry, which claimed a shortage of skilled labor, the government also allowed limited recruitment of clothing and fur workers among Holocaust survivors. In addition, the government gradually enlarged the circle of those eligible for reunification with family members in Canada. But a more fundamental shift in policy was in the offing. As the total flow of immigrants grew so large that a gradually increasing number of Jewish displaced persons could hardly be noticed and the newly independent state of Israel promised to absorb the bulk of the remaining Jewish displaced persons, Canadian policy changed. In 1948 a new Immigration Act removed all discriminatory regulations against Jewish immigration.

BIBLIOGRAPHY

Abella, I., and H. Troper. *None Is Too Many: Canada and the Jews of Europe, 1933–1948.* Toronto, 1982.

Dirks, G. E. *Canada's Refugee Policy: Indifference or Opportunism?* Montreal, 1977.

Draper, P. J. "The Accidental Immigrants: Canada and the Interned Refugees." *Canadian Jewish Historical Society Journal* 2 (1978): 1–38, 80–112.

Troper, H., and M. Weinfeld. *Jews, Ukrainians and the Hunt for Nazi War Criminals in Canada.* Toronto, 1988.

HAROLD TROPER

CANARIS, WILHELM (1887–1945), German admiral; between 1935 and 1944 chief of the ABWEHR, the intelligence department of the Armed Forces High Command. Canaris was born at Aplerbeck, Westphalia, the son of a local industrialist. He entered the German navy in 1905 and during World War I served both in an intelligence capacity in Spain and as commander of a U-boat in the Mediterranean.

After the November 1918 revolution in Germany, Canaris participated in the Freikorps activity of the Marine Brigade and in 1919 was for a time adjutant of the Reichswehr (Armed Forces) minister, Gustav Noske. He continued to advance in his naval career, and by 1934 was commandant of the fortress at Swinemünde, northeast of Stettin, on the Baltic Sea. His earlier success in intelligence work secured Canaris the position of head of military intelligence (*Chef der Abwehrabteilung des Kriegsministeriums*) in 1935.

Canaris was a Nazi sympathizer, but he also developed contacts with the military opposition to Hitler, led by Generalmajor Ludwig Beck, chief of the General Staff from 1935 to 1938, and Generalleutnant Franz Halder, chief of the General Staff from 1938 to 1942. Canaris feared the outbreak of war, and sought to deter the regime through his intelligence reports. His protests against the brutalities perpetrated by the SS against the Polish intelligentsia, nobility, and clergy brought him into conflict with Reinhard HEYDRICH, who had been his subordinate as a trainee naval officer. Canaris also opposed Hitler's plans to bring Spain, then under Franco's rule, into the war.

Canaris's opposition to Hitler, combined with his fear of military defeat and Russian invasion, paralyzed to some extent his role in the resistance. After the assassination of Heydrich in 1942, friction increased between Canaris and both the SS and the new head of the REICHSSICHERHEITSHAUPTAMT (Reich Security Main Office; RSHA), Ernst KALTENBRUNNER. In January 1944 the arrest of Count Helmuth von Moltke, one of Canaris's co-conspirators, and the flight of two of Canaris's agents to the British in Turkey led to his dismissal the following month. Shortly after the July 1944 bomb plot against Hitler, Canaris was arrested. In February 1945 he

Adm. Wilhelm Canaris (right), chief of the intelligence service (Abwehr) of the Armed Forces High Command from 1935 to 1944. [National Archives]

was taken to the FLOSSENBÜRG concentration camp together with his longtime collaborator, Gen. Hans Oster, and was executed at Hitler's order on April 9, on charges of treason.

BIBLIOGRAPHY

Amort, C., and M. Jedlicka. *The Canaris File.* London, 1970.
Graml, H., et al. *The German Resistance to Hitler.* London, 1970.
Höhne, H. *Canaris: A Biography.* Garden City, N.Y., 1979.

LIONEL KOCHAN

CARPATHIAN RUTHENIA. *See* Transcarpathian Ukraine.

CATHOLIC CHURCH. *See* Christian Churches; Pius XII.

CDJC. *See* Documentation Centers: Centre de Documentation Juive Contemporaine.

CENTER OF CONTEMPORARY JEWISH DOCUMENTATION. *See* Documentation Centers: Centre de Documentation Juive Contemporaine.

CENTRALA EVREILOR (Jewish Center), Jewish institution in ROMANIA, similar to the JUDENRAT (Jewish Council), which the government of Ion ANTONESCU set up in February 1942, responding to pressure by the German legation in BUCHAREST. The Centrala took the place of the long-established Federatia Uniunilor de Comunitati Evreesti (Union of Jewish Communities), which had been disbanded in December 1941. The Centrala had the task of implementing all orders and decisions on Jewish affairs issued by the government and its various agencies, as well as acting as the representative Jewish body in all contacts with the authorities. Officially, the Centrala was not permitted to be in touch with any branch of the government except the office of Radu LECCA, the commissioner general for Jewish questions, who in turn took orders from Gustav RICHTER, the counselor on Jewish affairs at the German legation.

Heading the Centrala were persons who had previously not been active Jewish leaders. Its first chairman was Stefan Streitman, a convert from Judaism and a journalist by profession, but the real authority was in the hands of Nandor Ghingold, also a convert from Judaism, a physician with professional ties to some of the staff members of the German legation, who had recommended his appointment. One of the department heads was Adolf Willman, who was known to be a German agent, but there were also legitimate representatives of the Jewish population among the officers of the Centrala. Some of them had been kept on in the posts they had held in the federation, while the other officers included members of the Zionist movement who had joined in order to keep an eye on the Centrala and to take charge of the school system. At a later stage, members of the clandestine Communist party also joined the Centrala.

The two tasks assigned to the Centrala were, on the face of it, irreconcilable. On the one hand, it was to participate in preparations for the planned deportation of the Jews to the extermination camps in Poland, as demanded of the Romanian government by the Nazi representatives (headed by Richter). On the other hand, the Centrala was expected to cater to the Romanian authorities who sought to use it as an instrument for extorting money and property from the Jews, and as an agency that would supply forced-labor battalions. As long as the Romanian government agreed with the deportation plans, the Centrala did as the Nazis asked, making a census of the Jews (based on racial criteria) and a list of their addresses. It did not take Ghingold long to discover, as had Jewish leaders before him, that the corrupt regime could be softened by bribes. Ghingold promptly adopted this method, the bribes taking the form of contributions to Antonescu's wife, in her capacity as head of the Con-

siliul de Patronaj (Welfare Council), an umbrella organization of welfare institutions serving the soldiers and the surviving dependents of those killed in action. The total amount of these contributions to the Consiliul by the Centrala under Ghingold's administration exceeded the amount it spent on assisting the Jews who had been forced into the labor battalions or had been deported to TRANSNISTRIA.

The Centrala took no part in the struggle waged by the clandestine Consiliul Evreesc (Jewish Council), founded by Wilhelm FILDERMAN, against the implementation of the plans for the deportation of Romanian Jews to Poland, an issue that was coming to a head in the summer of 1942. The Romanian authorities, for their part, no longer considered Ghingold and his assistants to be genuine representatives of the Jews, and by June 1942, the minister of the interior, as well as other members of the cabinet, resumed the practice of consulting Filderman on all issues affecting the fate of the Jews.

When the threat of extermination by the Germans receded, Ghingold gradually came to change his attitude and was less and less inclined to assist the Zionist movement and the Jews in general. He had never thought of himself as representing the Jews, but rather as dealing with Jewish affairs on behalf of the Romanian government.

With the shift in Romanian policy on the Jews, the Centrala, in 1943 and 1944, increasingly assumed the traditional functions of the Union of Jewish Communities in organizing welfare operations and meeting the spiritual and material needs of the Jews, under the intolerable conditions created by the Romanian authorities. Under the law, the veteran Jewish leaders and institutions had to go through the Centrala; without it they could not send aid to the deportees in Transnistria or help the forty thousand Jews on forced labor and their families. When it became clear that a German defeat in the war was gradually becoming inevitable, more and more funds were made available for welfare operations, drawn from the various regular and special taxes and levies imposed on the Jews. In the Centrala, too, a growing number of officials were willing to be of help to the deportees and to divert funds for that purpose. Ghingold had an understanding of the situation and in general did not interfere with these efforts. On the other hand, he provided the impetus for Filderman's deportation to Transnistria, by transmitting to Lecca and Antonescu a memorandum that Filderman had addressed to him personally, protesting against the special levy of 4 billion lei ($35 million) that Antonescu had imposed on the Jews in May 1943—and against which Ghingold did not protest.

Under Ghingold's lead the Centrala retained power and influence among a part of the Jewish population, especially those Jews who were in need of the coveted certificate of exemption from forced labor. This was a way of extorting special payments from wealthy Jews and members of the professions, in exchange for enabling them to keep on earning a living and staying in their jobs. Using the Centrala staff, Lecca turned the exemption certificate into a lucrative source of income for himself and for the political figures and officials that he favored. Mihai ANTONESCU, the deputy prime minister, also ordered Lecca to provide funds for various purposes from this source. Other recipients of bribes from Lecca, from the same source—the Centrala—were staff members of the German legation. Ghingold himself never took a bribe, but he remained convinced that more money could be obtained from the wealthy Jews and that, willingly or unwillingly, they should contribute more, both for the welfare work of the Centrala and for the large payments that had to be made to the state treasury, or diverted to the pockets of government officials.

When it became obvious that the Centrala's days were numbered, Ghingold and his associates, like the rest of the Romanian establishment under Antonescu, collected recommendations for themselves certifying their "good conduct" and asserting that they had acted in behalf of the repatriation of the orphans and deportees. The Centrala executive officers were well aware of the bad reputation they had among the Jews, owing to the heavy payments they had extracted and their readiness to cooperate with the Romanian authorities.

In December 1944, after the liberation, the Centrala was disbanded and the Union of Jewish Communities was reinstated. The Centrala chiefs were put on trial and sentenced to long prison terms. Ghingold was released after ten years; he was rehabilitated, and until his death in 1988 practiced medicine on the staff of a leading Bucharest hospital.

BIBLIOGRAPHY

Ancel, J. *Romania.* Jerusalem, 1989.
Ancel, J., ed. *Documents concerning the Fate of Romanian Jewry during the Holocaust.* Vol. 7. Jerusalem, 1986.

JEAN ANCEL

CENTRAL COMMITTEE OF GERMAN JEWS FOR RELIEF AND RECONSTRUCTION. *See* Zentralausschuss der Deutschen Juden für Hilfe und Aufbau.

CENTRAL CONSISTORY OF FRENCH JEWS. *See* Consistoire Central des Israélites de France.

CENTRAL OFFICE FOR JEWISH EMIGRATION. *See* Zentralstelle für Jüdische Auswanderung.

CENTRAL OFFICE OF THE JUDICIAL ADMINISTRATIONS OF THE LÄNDER FOR INVESTIGATION OF NAZI CRIMES, LUDWIGSBURG. *See* Ludwigsburger Zentralstelle.

CENTRAL RESETTLEMENT OFFICE. *See* Umwandererzentralstelle.

CENTRAL UNION OF GERMAN CITIZENS OF JEWISH FAITH. *See* Centralverein Deutscher Staatsbürger Jüdischen Glaubens.

CENTRALVEREIN DER JUDEN IN DEUTSCHLAND. *See* Centralverein Deutscher Staatsbürger Jüdischen Glaubens.

CENTRALVEREIN DEUTSCHER STAATS-BÜRGER JÜDISCHEN GLAUBENS (Central Union of German Citizens of Jewish Faith; CV), an organization, active between 1893 and 1938, that aimed to safeguard the civil and social equality of the Jews of GERMANY while fostering their German identity.

With the rise of the antisemitic movement in Germany in the last quarter of the nineteenth century, a central Jewish organization was founded to defend Jewish civil and social equality. At the time of its founding in 1893, the organization was accepted with reservations in the Jewish community; its ideas, however, were quickly absorbed. The number of members rose from 2,000 in 1894 to 72,500 in 1924. Many others belonged through the collective adherence of associated groups. At the peak of its activity the CV was the largest organization of German Jews, and regarded itself as their representative. Its first heads were Maximilian Horowitz (1893–1917) and Eugen Fuchs (1917–1919).

Until World War I the organization worked principally through legal channels and conducted information activity (called *Abwehrkampf*, "defense struggle"), mainly in an apologetic manner. In face of rising antisemitism after World War I, precedence was given to working through political channels. Contacts were made with parties and organizations supporting the republic and taking a stand against extreme German nationalism, especially Nazi nationalism. During the electoral campaigns, propaganda material was distributed in millions of copies. In 1929 a special archive was founded to collect the most complete information in Germany on Nazi activities and intentions. A special service placed material from that data bank at the disposal of newspapers and parties. Prior to the elections of September 1930, in which the Nazis made a decisive political breakthrough, the CV and the Zionists worked together, but the partnership was soon broken owing to doctrinal and practical disagreements.

Alongside this political activity, the CV's information activity expanded. Its monthly journal, *Im Deutschen Reich*, which had appeared since 1894, merged in 1922 with the long-standing Jewish journal *Allgemeine Zeitung des Judentums* and subsequently became a weekly called *Zeitung-CV*, which was also distributed to non-Jewish subscribers. An ideological and literary biweekly, *Der Morgen*, served the intelligentsia. The prominent leaders of the CV between the two world wars were Julius Brodnitz, Ludwig Holländer, and Alfred Wiener.

The CV placed stress on fostering German awareness and saw Jewry as a religious and spiritual group only; consequently, it adopted a negative attitude toward Zionism. At the same time some of its leaders, particularly the younger ones, demanded that the CV view the settlement enterprises in Palestine positively, if only because of the obligation of Jewish solidarity. Eventually most of the CV representatives at the head of the central institutions of German Jewry came from this pro-Palestine circle.

With the Nazi rise to power, the "defense" activity became insufficient, and the CV had to adapt to the new conditions. The *Zeitung-CV* attempted to continue its defense policy through declarations, such as "We shall be on our guard and firmly defend ourselves, in accordance with the constitution, against any effort to encroach on our rights." It continually reminded President Paul von HINDENBURG and the German conservatives participating in Hitler's government of their duty to defend the rights of all citizens without religious differentiation. At the same time, a legal office was established under CV direction, since the organization clearly recognized that only through legal channels could the rights of the Jews still be defended.

The CV launched a comprehensive information campaign, both within its own organization and on the invitation of Jewish communities. Tens of thousands of German Jews, avid for encouragement and guidance, came to hear the heads of the CV, most of whom tried to soothe the community and encourage its attachment to the German homeland. But when Nazi attacks persisted, and particularly after the blow of the anti-Jewish BOYCOTT of April 1, 1933, a new policy was adopted that encouraged independent Jewish organization and activity. CV members also helped sponsor the REICHSVERTRETUNG DER DEUTSCHEN JUDEN (Reich Representation of German Jews), created in September 1933, relying on cooperation between the various Jewish organizations. The CV organized independent educational and religious activities, and for a short time even hoped that this could constitute the basis for an arrangement with the government, a second "emancipation" (the first being the civil and political emancipation, culminating in 1871, of Germany's Jews) that would establish recognition of the Jews of Germany as a separate group in the country. These hopes were shattered by the new government's unrelenting hostility. The CV's change of attitude toward independent Jewish activity could be seen in the *Zeitung-CV*, which expanded, added sections, and began to publicize German Jewish activities in all fields.

In the fall of 1935, after the promulgation of the NUREMBERG LAWS, the CV was obliged to change its name to Centralverein der Juden in Deutschland (Central Union of Jews in Germany). After 1935 the organization increasingly recognized emigration and vocational training as its chief priorities. At the same time, the ideological and organizational struggles with other viewpoints (principally Zionism) continued, both in the CV publications and in the local and national institutions. With the passage of time, however, those disputes were restricted more and more to the theoretical sphere. In 1936 the CV changed its name to the Jüdischer Centralverein. The organization's last chairman, Ernst Herzfeld, stated in 1937 that the only difference of opinion between its members and the Zionists was whether emigration to countries other than Palestine should be welcomed or merely accepted as a necessary evil.

The CV ceased to exist as an independent group after the KRISTALLNACHT disturbances of November 1938. Like other Jewish bodies, it was incorporated into the compulsory new central organization, the Reichsvereinigung der Juden in Deutschland (Reich Association of Jews in Germany), established on July 4, 1939 (*see* Appendix, Volume 4). Its representatives continued to occupy central positions in the leadership of German Jewry.

BIBLIOGRAPHY

Hirschberg, A. "Der Centralverein Deutscher Staatsbürger Jüdischen Glaubens." In *Festschrift für Leo Baeck*. Berlin, 1970.
Paucker, A. *Der Abwehrkampf gegen Antisemitismus und Nationalsozialismus in den letzten Jahren der Weimarer Republik*. Hamburg, 1969.
Paucker, A. "Jewish Self-Defence." In *The Jews in Nazi Germany, 1933–1943*, edited by A. Paucker. Tübingen, 1986.
Reinharz, J. *Fatherland and Promised Land: The Dilemma of the German Jew, 1893–1914*. Ann Arbor, 1975.
Schorsch, I. *The Jewish Reaction to German Antisemitism, 1870–1914*. New York, 1972.

YEHOYAKIM COCHAVI

CENTRAL WELFARE COUNCIL. *See* Rada Główna Opiekuncza.

CENTRE DE DOCUMENTATION JUIVE CONTEMPORAINE. *See* Documentation Centers: Centre de Documentation Juive Contemporaine.

CENTRO DI DOCUMENTAZIONE EBRAICA CONTEMPORANEA. *See* Documentation Centers: Centro di Documentazione Ebraica Contemporanea.

CERNĂUȚI. *See* Chernovtsy.

CFGJ. *See* Council for German Jewry.

CGQJ. *See* Commissariat Général aux Questions Juives.

CHAMBERLAIN, HOUSTON STEWART (1855–1927), racial ideologist and major figure in modern ANTISEMITISM. An Englishman who opted for German nationality, Chamberlain is important for his role as an ideological link between older racist theories and Nazism (*see* RACISM). His book *Die Grundlagen des 19. Jahrhunderts* (The Foundations of the Nineteenth Century; 1899) combined racial theory with a vitalist philosophy and cultural criticism, creating a universal world view with markedly conservative traits.

Holding physical and moral inequality to be the basis of human existence, Chamberlain saw all of Western history in terms of a race struggle. He maintained that Jesus' "Aryan doctrine" had been racially poisoned by Judaism. This deformation of an "Aryan religion" by the Jew Paul in the racial chaos of the Roman empire had determined all of Euopean history and constituted what Chamberlain called "the foundation of the nineteenth century." Since then a constant war had been waged that, he wrote, had still not reached its end. The Germans, the legitimate rulers of the world as the last branch of the Aryan tree, had not attained their goal: the radical suppression of Judaism and redemption of the world from racial chaos. Only the Aryans were capable of a "creative culture," and therefore their intermingling with "inferior races" would lead to decline and degeneration.

Chamberlain's writings are a mixture of Richard Wagner's race mysticism, the racial theories of Joseph-Arthur de Gobineau and Paul de Lagarde, the biblical and philological studies of Julius Wellhausen, popular Darwinism, the vulgar empiricism of Ernst Haeckel, and other contemporary trends. He appealed to the Nazis because of his optimistic historical perspective on Germany's mission to liberate mankind from the Jewish race. Chamberlain rejected Gobineau's racial pessimism and the scientific natural monism of Social Darwinists, whose theories, he thought, led to a passive attitude of resignation toward the inevitable and deterministic process of decay. His racial theories exerted a deep influence on his contemporaries, including Emperor Wilhelm II, who was one of Chamberlain's devoted readers, corresponding with him and awarding him the Iron Cross for his publications; Alfred ROSENBERG's *The Myth of the Twentieth Century* was based largely on his ideas. Chamberlain saw in Adolf HITLER the man who would implement his theories.

BIBLIOGRAPHY

Field, G. G. *Evangelist of Race: The German Vision of Houston Chamberlain.* New York, 1981.

Mosse, G. *Towards the Final Solution: A History of European Racism.* New York, 1980.

Stackelberg, R. J. "Houston S. Chamberlain: From Monarchism to National Socialism." *Wiener Library Bulletin* 31/2 (1978): 118–125.

DAVID BANKIER

CHAMBON-SUR-LIGNON. *See* Le Chambon-sur-Lignon.

CHEŁMNO (Ger., Kulmhof), the first Nazi camp in which mass executions were carried out by means of gas, and the first site for mass killings within the framework of the "FINAL SOLUTION" outside the area of Nazi occupation in the USSR. The camp was destined to serve as a center for the extermination of the Jews in the ŁÓDŹ ghetto and the entire WARTHEGAU region, which had been annexed to the Third Reich. It was located in the Polish village of Chełmno, 47 miles (70 km) west of Łódź, in the Koło district. A total of 320,000 people were put to death there.

The camp was set up on two sites, 2.5 miles (4 km) apart: (1) the camp in the Schloss, an old palace inside the village, which served as a reception and extermination center for the victims and as a residence for the camp staff; and (2) the Waldlager, a camp in the adjacent Rzuwowski Forest, in which mass graves and cremation ovens were later found.

To administer and operate the camp, a special unit was set up, called Sonderkommando Kulmhof, also known as Sonderkommando Lange and, later, Sonderkommando Bothmann, after its first commandant, Hauptsturmführer Herbert Lange and, from March 1942, Hauptsturmführer Hans BOTHMANN.

Sonderkommando Kulmhof consisted of members of the Sicherheitspolizei (Security Police; Sipo) and the Schutzpolizei (regular uniformed police). Twenty members of Sipo held central posts in the camp. Some one hundred and twenty Schutzpolizei were divided into secondary units: the Transportkommando, the Schlosskommando, and the Waldkommando.

The Transportkommando operated mainly at the nearby Powiercie railway station, to which most of the victims were brought. Its function was to reinforce the German guard that had accompanied the deportees and to transport the latter in trucks to the Schloss camp.

The Schlosskommando guarded the palace camp and participated in the killing process. The Waldkommando, which operated in the forest camp, formed two cordons whose purpose was to ensure that no one approached the camp or saw what was happening inside. This unit also supervised the unloading of the victims' corpses, their burial, and, later, their cremation.

Sonderkommando Kulmhof was directly subject to the REICHSSICHERHEITSHAUPTAMT (Reich Security Main Office; RSHA) in Berlin. However, the governor of the Warthegau region, Arthur GREISER; the SS commander in the Warthegau, Wilhelm KOPPE; and the head of the Łódź ghetto administration, Hans BIEBOW, all concerned themselves with the affairs of the camp as well. Members of the camp staff received for their services a special increment of twelve to fifteen reichsmarks in their wages.

The deportees were generally brought in freight trains, to the Koło junction. From there they were transferred to another train, running on a narrow-gauge track, which pro-

Jews of Sompolno, a town 90 miles (145 km) west of Warsaw, waiting to be transported to the Chełmno extermination camp (beginning of February 1942).

ceeded to the Powiercie station. Sometimes the victims were taken in trucks straight from their dwelling places to Chełmno. Throughout the journey, the transports were always heavily guarded by German police. For example, transports from the Łódź ghetto went in a twelve-car train accompanied by a special unit consisting of 155 German police.

The victims were first concentrated in the courtyard of the Schloss, where they were reassured that they were being sent to a work camp and were to wash while their clothes were being disinfected. They were then taken in groups of fifty—men, women, and children together—to the ground floor of the Schloss, where they were told to strip. Here their valuables were collected in baskets that would supposedly be marked with their names.

The victims were then taken to the cellar, past signs reading "To the Washroom" hung on the passage door and stairway. From there they were brought to an enclosed ramp made of boards and slanted downward. At the end of the ramp stood a gas van with its doors open. The moment the victims entered the ramp, the Germans forced them, with blows, to run toward the bottom and into the van. They had no alternative other than to enter it.

Beginning in December 1941, three gas vans were operated in the Chełmno camp. They were Renault trucks, two of medium size and one larger, hermetically sealed inside and with double back doors. On the outside they looked like furniture delivery vans. The enclosed space within the van was from 13 to 15 feet (4 to 5 m) long, 6.75 feet (2.2 m) wide, and 6.5 feet (2 m) high; fifty to seventy people were crammed into each van, which was lined inside with galvanized tin. On the tin floor a wooden lattice was laid, under which a hole had been drilled and a metal pipe soldered into the hole. On the outside of the truck, the other end of this pipe was connected to a flexible exhaust pipe, through which carbon monoxide was pumped into the enclosure within the van.

After the van had been filled with people, the driver closed and locked the doors, entered the truck's cab, and switched on the motor. For ten minutes the victims within suffocated from the gas. Once they were dead, the pipe was detached from its connection

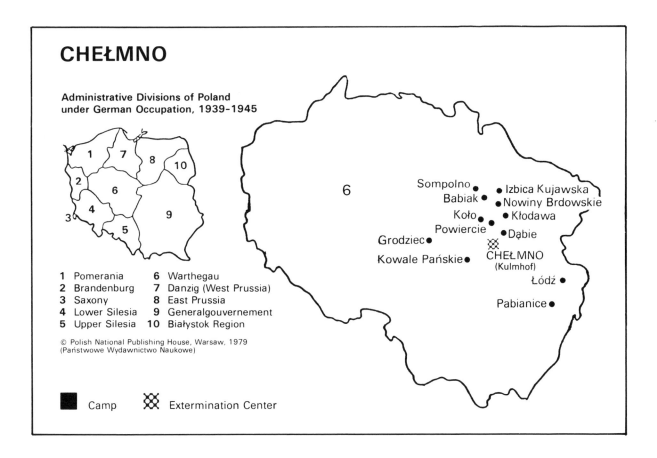

CHEŁMNO

Administrative Divisions of Poland
under German Occupation, 1939–1945

1 Pomerania   6 Warthegau
2 Brandenburg   7 Danzig (West Prussia)
3 Saxony   8 East Prussia
4 Lower Silesia   9 Generalgouvernement
5 Upper Silesia   10 Białystok Region

© Polish National Publishing House, Warsaw, 1979
(Państwowe Wydawnictwo Naukowe)

■ Camp   ⬚ Extermination Center

with the vehicle, which proceeded to the Waldlager. Here there were three clearings, separated by avenues of trees, in which four mass graves were located. Here, as of the summer of 1942, there were also two crematoria, 32.5 feet (10 m) long and 16 to 19 feet (5 to 6 m) wide.

From among the batches of deportees who reached Chełmno, a few men were selected to replenish a group totaling thirty to forty who were compelled to work as gravediggers; the weakest among them were regularly shot. This group had to take the fresh corpses out of the gas vans and bury them in the mass graves in the clearing (and, later, burn them in the cremation ovens). At nighttime the gravediggers were taken back to the Schlosslager and held in a locked room under heavy guard. These prisoners made many attempts to escape, and two of them succeeded, Moroka Podchlebnik and Jacob GROJANOWSKI (this may have been a pseudonym). Grojanowski, who arrived at Chełmno on January 6, 1942, escaped on January 19. At the end of that month he managed to reach the WARSAW ghetto, where he gave very detailed information on what was happening in the camp to ONEG SHABBAT, the underground archive headed by Emanuel RINGELBLUM. Grojanowski's report was passed on to the Polish underground, which sent it to the POLISH GOVERNMENT-IN-EXILE. In this manner, all the details about the Chełmno camp were known in London by June 1942.

The first transports to Chełmno began on December 7, 1941, and the camp began to operate on the following day. The first victims were Jews from the communities in the area: Koło, Dąbie, Sompolno, Kłodawa, Babiak, Dęby Szlacheckie, Kowale Pańskie, Izbica Kujawska, Nowiny Brdowskie, and Grodziec. The early victims also included five thousand GYPSIES who had been imprisoned in a separate section of the Łódź ghetto.

In mid-January 1942, the deportations from the Łódź ghetto began. Between January 16 and 29, 10,003 Jews were taken from the ghetto and killed at Chełmno; from February 22 to April 2, 34,073; from May 4 to 15, 11,680; and from September 5 to 12, 15,859. These numbers included Jews from Germany, Austria, Czechoslovakia, and Luxembourg who had first been expelled to the Łódź ghetto. In addition, 15,000 Jews sent from the Łódź ghetto to forced-labor camps in the Warthegau region were put to death.

In the course of 1942, Jews from all the other thirty-six places of Jewish settlement in the Warthegau region were transported to Chełmno for extermination. A few hundred Poles were also sent there, as well as Soviet prisoners of war and eighty-eight Czechoslovak children from the village of LIDICE.

The possessions and clothes brought by the victims to Chełmno were shipped to warehouses established in the town of Pabianice by the Nazi administration of the Łódź ghetto, headed by Hans Biebow. These articles were then distributed or sold to the German population of the Warthegau.

In March 1943 the transports to Chełmno came to an end, since the entire Jewish population of the Warthegau, except in the Łódź ghetto, had been exterminated. The Nazi authorities dismantled the camp, and the Schloss was demolished. The camp staff was transferred to Yugoslavia and incorporated into the "Prinz Eugen" Division of the Waffen-SS, which fought the Yugoslav partisans.

In April 1944, in connection with the planned liquidation of the Łódź ghetto, the Nazis decided to renew their extermination activities at Chełmno. Hans Bothmann and other members of Sonderkommando Kulmhof were brought back from Yugoslavia for this purpose and were joined by new camp staff, including Walter Piller, who was appointed deputy commandant. The camp was reconstituted in the former Waldlager. Here, two huts, each 66 feet (20 m) long and 33 feet (10 m) wide, were built to receive the victims, in addition to two new crematoria.

On June 23, 1944, transports to Chełmno from the Łódź ghetto began anew, and by July 14, 7,176 persons had been killed. The system was similar to that previously used: the victims, brought by truck, were told that they were going to work in Germany and that they must wash themselves while their clothes were being disinfected. Assembled in groups of seventy to ninety, they stripped, then went through a door with the sign "To the Washroom" on it, to a passageway 78 feet (25 m)

long, fenced off on both sides. The passageway led to a slope, at the end of which stood a gas van.

In mid-July, to accelerate the pace of liquidating the Łódź ghetto, the Nazis halted the transports to Chełmno and began to send the ghetto's surviving residents to AUSCHWITZ, where the pace of extermination by ZYKLON B gas was ten times faster. Sonderkommando Kulmhof was transferred to Łódź and, together with other German units, was occupied until the end of August 1944 with the final liquidation of the ghetto and the deportations of its inhabitants to Auschwitz. At the beginning of September 1944, Sonderkommando Kulmhof returned to Chełmno. Together with Sonderkommando 1005, it oversaw the exhumation and cremation of the corpses, since a decision had been made to obliterate all signs of the mass murders. The work was done by a group of fifty Jewish prisoners.

On the night of January 17, 1945, when the Red Army was approaching, the Nazis abandoned Chełmno. As they were executing the forty-eight Jewish prisoners remaining in the camp, the latter resisted, and three managed to escape. The others were killed.

After the war, a detailed description of the camp, what happened there, and the daily life of the Nazi staff was given to the American authorities in West Germany by Heinrich May, a former Nazi who was *Forstmeister* (forest inspector) in Precinct 77 of the Warthegau during Chełmno's existence.

From 1947 to 1950, trials were held in Poland of two staff members of the camp, Walter Piller and Hermann Gielow. Both were sentenced to death. Later, from 1962 to 1965, a trial of twelve of the camp's staff was held in West Germany. Three of them were sentenced to thirteen years' imprisonment, and one to seven years'; the others received only light punishment.

BIBLIOGRAPHY

Bednarz, W. *Obóz stracen w Chełmnie nad Nerem.* Warsaw, 1946.

Gutman, Y., and A. Saf, eds. *The Nazi Concentration Camps: Structure and Aims; The Image of the Prisoner; The Jews in the Camps.* Proceedings of the Fourth Yad Vashem Historical Conference. Jerusalem, 1984.

Krakowski, S. "In Kulmhof stationierte Gaswagen." In *Nationalsozialistische Massentötungen durch Giftgas,* edited by E. Kogon, H. Langbein, and A. Rückerl, pp. 110–145. Frankfurt, 1983.

SHMUEL KRAKOWSKI

CHERNOVTSY (Rom., Cernăuţi; Ger., Czernowitz), district center of Chernovtsy Oblast and former capital of BUKOVINA. Up to 1918, Chernovtsy was under Austrian rule; from 1918 to 1940 it was part of Romania. Its Jewish population in 1930 was 46,000, 40 percent of the total. In June 1940, Chernovtsy was incorporated into the Soviet Union. At first many Jews welcomed the Soviets, in the hope that they would put an end to antisemitic persecution, which had become much worse in the final phase of the Romanian regime's control of the province. The Soviets, however, brought Jewish national life to an end, and their policy of confiscating property and other assets severely affected the Jews. On June 13, 1941, some ten thousand Jews were arrested, most of them from Chernovtsy, and exiled to Siberia—among them community and Zionist leaders, persons who had owned property, and others who were seized at random. Many of these deportees were to perish in the camps from cold, starvation, and disease.

On June 30, 1941, eight days after the German invasion of the Soviet Union, the Soviets evacuated Chernovtsy after setting fire to several public buildings, thereby causing fires in the city center. Earlier, many Jews had been drafted into the Soviet army and moved from the city. Romanian and German troops who entered Chernovtsy, as well as local Romanian and Ukrainian inhabitants, systematically ransacked Jewish houses, murdered Jews, raped Jewish women, and abused the Jews in various ways. A large number of Jews were arrested, and some six hundred were killed by Einsatzkommando 10b and its Romanian helpers.

Einsatzgruppe D moved its headquarters into Chernovtsy on July 10, and on the insistence of its commander, Otto OHLENDORF, even more stringent measures were adopted against the Jews. Approximately 1,500 Jews were seized by Einsatzkommando 10b, most of them young people and intelligentsia, and murdered with the help of the Romanian police. The chief rabbi, Dr. Abraham Mark, was among the victims; the Great Synagogue was also set on fire on this occasion. In early August, Einsatzkommando 10b murdered another 682 Jews. The Romanian authorities, who had been given full control of the city, introduced various discriminatory measures: Jews had to wear the yellow badge (*see* BADGE, JEWISH), Jewish houses had to bear the sign *Jude* on them, Jews were prohibited from moving about at certain hours and in certain districts, and they had their food rations reduced, were put on unpaid FORCED LABOR, and were used as hostages.

On October 11, 1941, all the Jews in the city, over fifty thousand in all, were concentrated in a small area consisting of a few side streets; their property and assets were confiscated in favor of the Romanian National Bank. This action was taken on the order of the Romanian governor, Corneliu Calotescu, despite the opposition of the mayor, Traian Popovici. Most of the Romanian government officials were antisemites, supporters of the movements led by Alexandru CUZA and the IRON GUARD. On October 10 the local authorities were told of the order given by Ion ANTONESCU, the Romanian dictator, to deport the city's Jews to TRANSNISTRIA. The order was transmitted verbally, by two high-ranking officers of the Romanian general staff, to ensure that no written evidence of it would remain.

During the Festival of Tabernacles (October 12, 1941), the deportation to Transnistria began. The first transport consisted of 6,000 Jews, who were taken away in cattle cars. Heading the column of deportees were Rabbi Mordechai Fridmann of Boian and Rabbi Eliezer Hager; they carried Torah scrolls in their arms and were surrounded by Hasidim. The second transport left on October 17. The transports continued until November 15, when Antonescu ordered a halt. A total of 28,391 Jews were deported in October and November 1941 to Transnistria, by way of the MARCULEŞTI camp in Bessarabia. The 20,000 Jews left in Chernovtsy had been issued special permits certifying that they were "useful" for the economy. In the hope that this would save them from deportation,

CHERNOVTSY

GREATER GERMANY

USSR

TRANSNISTRIA

CHERNOVTSY
2
Atachi

HUNGARY
•Satu-Mare
Marculeşti

3
•Oradea
Cluj
Tîrgu-Mureş
Kishinev

1

•Timişoara

ROMANIA
Galaţi

Bucharest •

Black Sea

YUGOSLAVIA

4

BULGARIA

0   160 miles   1 in.

0   300 km.   3 cm.

Annexations from June to September 1940: (1) Bessarabia and (2) N. Bukovina to USSR; (3) N. Transylvania to Hungary; (4) S. Dobruja to Bulgaria.

1,500 Jews converted to Christianity, but the authorities strongly disapproved, and many Jews were put on trial and sentenced to prison for having gone through a mock conversion. On June 4, 1942, the transports were resumed: 2,000 Jews were deported to Transnistria by way of the Atachi border post. Some were handed over to the SS and taken across the Bug River, where most of them were murdered. A second transport left on June 13 with 200 Jews aboard, some of them mentally ill; a third transport left on June 28. Altogether, 5,000 Jews were deported to Transnistria in the three transports, and by November 1943, 4,500 were dead. The mortality rate among the children deported to Transnistria was 100 percent, and among adults it reached 70 percent.

While the transports were leaving Chernovtsy, and for some time thereafter, Romanians from all over the country—businessmen and others—flocked into the city and seized control of the industrial plants and commercial enterprises that the Jews had left behind or that had been confiscated from them; some of the plants were dismantled and moved to the interior of the country. The sixteen thousand Jews left in Chernovtsy were in dire straits, most of them having taken on any work that could save them from deportation. In October 1943 the yellow

badge and the restrictions on movement in the city were abolished. When the Red Army was approaching, the authorities barred the Jews from leaving the city as the Romanian residents were doing. Early in February of 1944, Chernovtsy was under the control of the German army, and it was only the city's swift liberation by the Soviet forces that made it impossible for the Germans to liquidate the remnants of the Jewish community. In April 1945 all but two thousand of the surviving native Chernovtsy Jews left the city and, by way of Romania, made their way to Palestine.

BIBLIOGRAPHY

Ancel, J., and T. Lavi, eds. *Rumania*, vol. 2. In *Pinkas Hakehillot; Encyclopaedia of Jewish Communities.* Jerusalem, 1980. See pages 487–511. (In Hebrew.)

Carp, M. *Transnistria.* Vol. 3 of *Cartea Neagră.* Bucharest, 1947.

Mircu, M. *Pogromurile din Bucovina si Dorohoi.* Bucharest, 1945. See pages 66–96.

Yavetz, Z. "Youth Movements in Czernowitz." *Jewish Heritage* 14 (Spring 1972): 9–18.

JEAN ANCEL

CHETNIKS (Serb., Četniki, from *četa*, "platoon"), Serbian guerrilla units that fought against the Turks and, in World War I, against Austro-Hungarian and German forces. In World War II, the Chetniks were armed bands of Serbs active in YUGOSLAVIA during its occupation (1941–1945). They had in common their loyalty to the Yugoslav royal house, aiming to restore it to the throne after the war, and their commitment to a relentless struggle against the partisan forces led by TITO.

The first Chetnik units came into being shortly after the Yugoslav army's surrender to the Germans in April 1941, on the initiative of Col. Draža Mihajlović, an officer of the Yugoslav general staff. Mihajlović gathered around himself Yugoslav soldiers fleeing the Germans and began to organize them in the Fruska Gora Mountains of central Serbia.

Mihajlović's men in Serbia took part in the uprising against the Germans in July and August of 1941, even cooperating with the partisans under Tito. The uprising was suppressed by the Germans with unspeakable cruelty, causing many deaths and widespread destruction. This brought the Chetniks to three conclusions: (1) there was no point in waging a hopeless armed struggle against the Germans, a struggle that would threaten the very existence of the Serbian people; (2) the proper course was to organize and gain strength, so as to be ready for an Allied invasion of the Balkans; (3) the pro-Communist partisans were the most dangerous enemy of all, and it was the struggle with them that would decide Yugoslavia's fate after Germany was defeated.

These conclusions exacerbated the differences between the partisans and the Chetniks, which before long turned into a civil war. The Chetniks' struggle with the invaders came to a complete stop at the end of 1941, and gradually evolved into cooperation with the Italians and the Germans against Tito.

At first, the western Allies had viewed the Chetniks as the core of the resistance movements in Yugoslavia against the invaders. But reports from British parachutists who had joined the fighting forces in Yugoslavia began to reach the West, indicating that the Chetniks' policy was to fight the partisans under Tito, rather than the Germans and their allies. Consequently, the attitude of the western Allies underwent a change in the second half of 1942, and they switched their aid to the partisans who were fighting the Germany enemy. By the end of 1943, the break between the West and the Chetniks was complete. The Chetniks had become collaborators and had joined the forces fighting the partisans. After the occupation of Serbia by the partisans and the Red Army, the Chetniks were hunted down. Shortly after the end of the war, Mihajlović and his men were captured and brought before a Yugoslav national tribunal; most were hanged.

At the initial stage, there were some Jews among the Chetniks, but when it turned out that the Chetniks were not fighting the invaders and their collaborators, and in fact were inclined to cooperate with them, the Jews switched to the ranks of the partisans. As the Chetniks increased their cooperation with the Germans, their attitude toward the Jews in the areas under their control deteriorated, and they identified the Jews with the hated Communists. There were many instances of Chetniks' murdering Jews or handing them over to the Germans.

BIBLIOGRAPHY

Millazzo, M. *The Chetnik Movement and the Yugoslav Resistance.* Baltimore, 1975.
Tomasevich, J. *The Chetniks: War and Revolution in Yugoslavia, 1941–1945.* Stanford, 1975.

MENACHEM SHELAH

CHILDREN. *See* André, Joseph; Beccari, Arrigo; Frank, Anne; Korczak, Janusz; Nèvejean, Yvonne; N.V. Group; Oeuvre de Secours aux Enfants; Rescue of Children, United States; "Tehran Children"; Union des Juifs pour la Résistance et l'Entr'aide; Van der Voort, Hanna.

CHILDREN'S AID SOCIETY. *See* Oeuvre de Secours aux Enfants.

CHIŞINĂU. *See* Kishinev.

CHOMS, WŁADYSŁAWA (1891–1966), Polish rescuer of Jews during the Holocaust. Choms headed the Lvov branch of ZEGOTA (the Polish Council for Aid to Jews), a Polish underground organization based in Warsaw. Before the war, in Drogobych, Eastern Galicia, where she headed the municipal welfare department, and in Lvov, where she was active in combating antisemitism, she showed a particular concern for the welfare of the Jewish people. With the German occupation of Lvov in June 1941, she became wholeheartedly involved in charitable work on behalf of destitute Jews. Collecting jewelry and money from wealthy Jews, she created a fund for extending aid to Jews, and rallied around her a group of devoted persons.

Aid came in various forms: the forging of false documents for Jews living outside the restricted ghetto perimeter; provision of money, food, and medical care for Jews inside and outside the ghetto; and the removal of Jewish children and adults from the ghetto

Władysława Choms in the Hall of Remembrance at Yad Vashem, Jerusalem, on May 22, 1963, when she received her award as a "Righteous among the Nations." She is in the front row, fourth from the left. To the right is the Eternal Flame.

to secure shelters in convents and with private families. Some sixty Jewish children were under her personal supervision.

Sought by the Germans (her officer-husband and son had fled to England and were known to have enlisted in the struggle against Nazi Germany), Choms was constantly on the move, ever changing names and addresses. In November 1942, while supervising a well-established rescue network in Lvov, she was elected by the Warsaw-based Zegota to establish and head a local branch in Lvov. Nicknamed the "Angel of Lvov" by her Jewish beneficiaries, she continued her charitable activities until November 1943, when, with the increasing threat to her personal safety, she was dispatched to Warsaw by her underground superiors.

After the war, Choms learned that her son, a pilot in the Royal Air Force, had been shot down and killed in 1941. She was recognized as a "RIGHTEOUS AMONG THE NATIONS," and planted a tree at YAD VASHEM in Jerusalem in 1963.

BIBLIOGRAPHY

Bartoszewski, W., and Z. Lewin, eds. *Righteous among Nations: How Poles Helped the Jews, 1939–1945*. London, 1969.

MORDECAI PALDIEL

CHORTKOV (Pol., Czortków), city in Ternopol Oblast (district), Ukrainian SSR. Until 1918, Chortkov belonged to Austrian-held Eastern Galicia, and in the interwar period to independent Poland. In September 1939, together with the rest of eastern Poland, Chortkov was occupied by the Red Army and annexed to the Ukrainian SSR.

Jews had been living in Chortkov since the sixteenth century. In the nineteenth century it was a center of Hasidism and the residence of a Hasidic rabbi. On the eve of World War II its Jewish population numbered six thousand.

The Germans took the city on July 6, 1941. On July 10 the Ukrainians, with German help, staged a pogrom, seizing Jews in the streets and murdering 300 of them in the city jail. On July 28 German police killed 150 Jews in the adjacent Czarny Las (Black Forest). Various decrees were enacted against the Jews, restricting their economic activities and freedom of movement and drafting them for forced labor. At the end of July a JUDENRAT (Jewish Council) was appointed, and on August 20 a 25,000-ruble collective fine was imposed on the Jews. Some members of the Judenrat, including the chairman, were arrested on October 12 and were murdered a few days later. On October 15 the Germans seized 200 Jews, mostly professionals, and murdered them in the Czarny Las.

Over a period of two months, beginning in the middle of November, groups of Jews were sent for forced labor to the Kamionka, Hluboczek, Borki Wielkie, and Stupki camps, and even as far as the JANÓWSKA camp in Lvov. In April 1942 a ghetto was established in Chortkov. Many of its inhabitants fell victim to the overcrowding, the lack of sanitation, and the epidemics that broke out. On August 27 an *Aktion* was carried out in which some six hundred Jews were murdered in the streets. It was followed by a *Selektion* that resulted in the deportation to the BEŁŻEC extermination camp of 2,000 Jews, most of whom were not in possession of work passes. In September the ghetto area was further reduced and conditions deteriorated even more. A second *Aktion* took place on October 5 that led to the sending of five hundred Jews to Bełżec.

On December 15 the Germans set up a work camp in Chortkov, populating it with over five hundred artisans and putting them to work,

BIBLIOGRAPHY

Austri-Dunn, Y. ed. *Memorial Book of Czortków.* Haifa, 1967. (In Hebrew and English).

AHARON WEISS

On March 23, 1944, Chortkov was liberated by the Soviets, but the Germans launched a counterattack and the Soviet forces withdrew, together with about one hundred Jewish survivors from the city. It was only in the summer of 1944, when the Soviets returned to Chortkov, that the Germans were driven out from the entire sector.

CHRISTIAN CHURCHES. [*The two articles in this entry survey the major developments taking place in Jewish-Christian relations during the Holocaust and afterward. For discussion of these relations in specific national settings, see the entries for those countries; see also under* Rescue.]

General Survey

Christian anti-Judaism derives from the earliest years of the Christian community, when the majority of Jews refused to accept the supernatural claims made for the person of Jesus of Nazareth. Its character changed in the fourth century, by which point most Christians were gentiles and Christianity became the state religion of the Roman empire. The theologians of the fourth and fifth centuries codified and extended anti-Judaic hostility by claiming that all Jews, as a community, shared the blame for the crucifixion of Jesus, that the destruction of Jerusalem in the year 70 was a divine punishment, that the Jewish people were to be treated with severity because of their obstinate blindness in refusing the promises made in their own traditional scriptures, and that the church had now superseded Judaism as the vehicle for salvation. These themes became the basis of traditional Christian teachings for many centuries, providing theological justification for repeated acts of persecution and violence. Despite the fact that successive popes issued edicts that Jews were to be considered witnesses of the original truth of divine relation to man—and, as such, regarded as potential

mainly for the German army. During the rest of 1942 and the early part of 1943, the Germans murdered many dozens of Jews from the work camp. Most of the camp's remaining inmates were killed on June 23, 1943, in a forest on the road to Jagielnica; the rest were transferred to the Hluboczek labor camp and to a farm at Swidowa. In September of that year the liquidation of the ghetto was complete.

During the ghetto's existence, attempts were made to organize an underground. A group of young people, led by Reuven Rosenberg, managed to obtain several handguns, and in the spring of 1943 they escaped to a forest in the area. Before long the Germans and their Ukrainian helpers discovered the group. In the ensuing clash most of the group's members were killed, while the rest continued to roam in the forest and fight the Germans. Another underground group in the ghetto was led by Meir Wassermann. Acquiring weapons, they escaped from the ghetto and operated against the Germans in the forests between Tluste and Jagielnica. Most members of this group fell in battle against the Germans and their Ukrainian collaborators.

converts—the triumphalist and monopolistic views of orthodox Christianity led to the imposing of social and physical segregation on the Jewish communities in ghettos or as minorities throughout Christian Europe; to widespread expulsions of Jews from Christian countries such as Spain and England; and to the repressive and often murderous policies of the Catholic Inquisition.

The influence of Martin Luther, especially in his rabid diatribes against the Jews at the end of his career, carried over the same theological antipathies into Protestantism, and contributed to the frequent persecution and the expulsions of Jews from German territories and city-states during the Reformation. Some of the followers of John Calvin, however, demonstrated a warmer sympathy for the Jews as the originators of Hebraic morality and of the sacred scriptures.

The rise of secularist thought in the eighteenth century, and of romanticism in the nineteenth, led to increasing skepticism in western Europe about traditional Christian dogmatic teachings, including Christian attitudes toward Judaism. The ingrained religious prejudices, however, remained entrenched in popular culture, especially in eastern Europe. Other forms of antisemitism, based on social, economic, or national ideas, increasingly came to overlap and supersede theological antipathies, adapting the stereotypes of earlier centuries and infusing the religious vocabulary with political and racist connotations. This incremental process was notable in the antisemitic propaganda of the early twentieth century, and in the formation of explicitly antisemitic political parties in Germany, France, and Austria. Only isolated Christian protests were voiced against the extremism of these racist views—notably the writings of the Protestant theologian Karl BARTH and Pope Pius XI's 1938 statement, "Antisemitism is inadmissible. We are all spiritually Semites." But the prevalence of dogmatic Christian attitudes, coupled with xenophobia and heightened ethnocentricity, prevented the growth of any more positive stance toward Judaism and the Jews. Christian theology provided no adequate defense against the escalating violence and mass murders of the Holocaust.

Roman Catholicism. Catholic attitudes toward the Nazi persecution of the Jews were ambivalent throughout the period of the Third Reich. The new Nazi regime's signature of a Reich Concordat with the Vatican in July 1933, and German Catholic support for its authoritarian and nationalist stances, gave rise to widespread illusions about the nature of Hitler's rule, illusions that were to be much criticized in the aftermath. This early collaboration preempted the possibility of mobilizing German Catholic opposition to the regime, even when the Nazis' pursuit of their totalitarian goals led to the increasing abrogation of the Concordat and persecution of the church. Despite the condemnation of Nazi ideology and RACISM in general in the papal encyclical *Mit brennender Sorge* (With Burning Concern) of March 1937, German Catholic sympathy for the Jews was evident only in individual cases, notably for Catholics of Jewish origin. Opposition was expressed more toward the methods employed by the Nazis than toward their repressive policies. The attitudes of such leading Catholics as the presiding bishop, Cardinal Adolf Bertram of Breslau, were characterized by deep-rooted hostility to the Jews, strong expressions of national loyalty, and the desire to protect their own church institutions. They led to silent acquiescence in face of the NUREMBERG LAWS of 1935 and the KRISTALLNACHT pogrom of 1938.

The episcopate's continued attempts to reach a workable compromise with the Nazi regime inhibited any forcible protests against the "FINAL SOLUTION." During the war, the German Catholic bishops took no clear stance in support of the Jews, in striking contrast to their strong protests against the Nazi EUTHANASIA PROGRAM. Reports of atrocities in eastern Europe and of the mass murders of Jews were disbelieved or were regarded with indifference. Limited support was given to the St. Raphael's Society (St. Raphaelsverein), which promoted emigration, principally for Catholic converts, and protests were made against the Nazi plans to annul marriages between Christians and Jews; these protests did secure protection for a few of those living in so-called mixed marriages.

The Vatican's policy under Pope PIUS XII (1939–1958) was dominated throughout the war years by the pursuit of a peaceful settlement by diplomatic means. Early illusions about the tractability of the Nazi leadership were shed only reluctantly, when the ineffectiveness of all protests to Berlin against Nazi persecution measures became clear. The reluctance of the German bishops to challenge the Nazi government, and the weakness of the papal nuncio in Berlin, contributed to the Vatican's passivity in face of the Nazi crimes. Stronger interventions on behalf of the victims of the war were, however, made to other governments more amenable to papal pressures, as in Slovakia, Hungary, and Romania. The Vatican condemned the antisemitic legislation passed in these countries, protested the deportations of Jews, whether converts to Catholicism or not, and demanded that the rights of all Catholics, including those of converts from Judaism, be respected. These efforts contributed to saving a minority of the Jewish populations in these states. Direct assistance by the Vatican in securing entry visas to Catholic countries (in Latin America, for example) was only modestly successful, and no efforts were made to cooperate with other relief agencies, either Protestant or Jewish. In Italy, a Vatican protest against German deportations of Italian Jews was lodged only after the initial roundup of Jews in Rome in October 1943. Similar interventions in Yugoslavia were limited in their success.

Pope Pius's pronouncements about the sufferings of the war victims were general in tone, and omitted any direct condemnation of the perpetrators, in the continuing but contentious belief that diplomatic representations would be more effective than open protest. The exaggerated belief in the efficacy of Vatican diplomacy led to the maintenance of a prudent reserve, which in hindsight has been vigorously criticized. The subsequent frustration of the Vatican's humanitarian moves by all the combatant powers induced a sense of pessimism and caution, and revealed the restricted influence of the Catholic church on national wartime policies. In the claustrophobic atmosphere of the Vatican, the unwillingness to admit the Church's impotence was accompanied by a failure to grasp the extent of Nazi atrocities against the Jews, as evidenced by the lack of sympathy for Zionist plans to secure a haven for Nazi victims in Palestine.

Throughout Nazi-occupied Europe, Catholic reactions were highly varied. In Italy itself, the Vatican and Catholic clergy played a significant role in helping and hiding Italian Jews. In France, traditional anti-Judaic antipathies combined with xenophobic resentment against the influx of foreign Jews to produce indifference to their plight; on the other hand, many younger clergy regarded assistance to the Jews as part of their resistance to the German invader. The French Catholic hierarchy was notably divided. More sympathetic attitudes were displayed after the first deportations of the Jews in the summer of 1942 and the occupation of Vichy-controlled southern France in November of that year. Significant support was given in the diocese of Lyons by Cardinal Pierre Gerlier, with the clandestine publication of the journal *Témoignage Chrétien* and the founding of the organization L'Amitié Chrétienne. A strong protest was issued in 1942 by Archbishop Jules-Gérard SALIÈGE of Toulouse. Numerous individual efforts were made to hide Jews, especially children, or to organize escape routes to Spain or Switzerland.

In Poland, the Nazi campaign of terrorization and persecution included measures designed to exploit the widespread Catholic antipathy to the Jews. The initial territorial separation and later annihilation of the Jews, on the one hand, and the decimation of the Catholic clergy and suppression of Catholic organizations, on the other, precluded any public protest. Nevertheless, a number of rescue attempts were made, particularly efforts by religious orders to save children. In Slovakia—whose president, Jozef TISO, was a priest, and whose parliament included numerous members of the clergy—harsh antisemitic measures, including deportations, were approved by the government in 1941 and 1942. Not until later in 1942, under pressure from the Vatican, did Slovak Catholic attitudes demonstrate more sympathy for the plight of the Jews. In Hungary, widespread indifference marked the stance of the Catholic population, and no public protests from the Catholic hierarchy were issued, although individual exemptions, were obtained, mainly for Jewish converts to Catholicism. In the Netherlands, a resolute protest by the Catholic bishops in 1942 led to an intensification of measures against Dutch Catholic Jews, which intimidated further public steps but also resulted in numerous rescue efforts on an individual basis. In Belgium, too, the Catholic clergy took many steps to help Jews.

The long centuries of being taught contempt for the Jews had inured Catholics to regarding the Jewish people as outside their circle of obligation. In the circumstances of Nazi persecution and annihilation, assistance to Jews was prompted more by the dictates of Christian charity than of solidarity. The events of the Holocaust did not lead at the time to any revision of Catholic theological doctrines, but the impact of the Holocaust was to produce major changes in Catholic attitudes toward the Jews from the Second Vatican Council Declaration on the Jews (1965) onward.

Protestantism. The main branch of Protestantism to give support to the Nazi ideological campaign against the Jewish people was the so-called German Christian movement, which formed the radical wing of German Lutheranism. This movement's enthusiastic support for Hitler personally, and its appeal to the latent antisemitism of Lutheran churchmen, resulted in its victory in the church elections of July 1933. The movement's attempts to reconcile Christian doctrine with its nationalist and political sympathies for Nazism—such as their claim that Jesus must have been of "Aryan blood"—led to the demand for the removal of all Jewish elements from Christian liturgy and practice, including the Testament and the teachings of the "rabbi" Paul. These excesses were quickly condemned as theological heresies by the conservatively orthodox members of the rival Confessing Church (Bekennende Kirche), which repudiated all Nazi efforts to control its teachings or to expel converted Jews from church office or membership. The German Christians movement was soon discredited, and it cannot be seen as influential in the implementation of the Nazis' plans to eradicate Jews.

But despite the Confessing Church's refusal to accept the tenets of Nazi ideology or to abandon the Jewish scriptures as a source of revelation, leading figures, such as Martin NIEMÖLLER and Otto DIBELIUS, still maintained the traditional Lutheran antipathy to the Jews on theological and social grounds. The majority of German Protestants did not challenge the right of the state to enact discriminating legislation against the Jews, and raised no objections to the initial Nazi measures taken against non-Christian Jews, though many shared the widespread public feelings of outrage against the excesses of the *Kristallnacht* pogrom. Their illusions about the nature of the Nazi regime, as well as their national and political loyalties, meant that protests were made solely in defense of the church's autonomy, or on behalf of Jewish converts. During the war, these feelings were only heightened. The young theologian Dietrich BONHOEFFER was virtually alone in recognizing the centrality of the Jewish persecution as an issue for Christians (although he too never abandoned theological anti-Judaism), and he was active in organizing efforts to enable a limited number of Jews to escape into exile.

The Confessing Church also sponsored the work of Pastor Heinrich Grüber in establishing a relief organization, principally to promote emigration of Jewish Protestants, that was tolerated if not approved by the Nazis. Grüber was, however, sent to a concentration camp in 1940, and further limited rescue efforts had to be undertaken clandestinely, notably in Württemberg, where a group of Confessing Church pastors offered sanctuary. In 1943 the bishop of Württemberg, Theophil WURM, though still denying any philosemitic tendencies, made a strong if belated series of protests against the mass murders without trial of Jews and members of other nations. In particular, he urged the abandonment of plans to deport and annihilate those Jews who still remained in Germany as partners or children of Christian Germans. The sense of moral outrage against these annihilations was a factor in the cre-ation of the ill-fated German resistance movement, led mainly by Protestants, although the traditional antisemitism of these conservative circles was reflected in their fragmentary plans for postwar reconstruction. Above all, the absence of any widespead public protest against the "Final Solution" indicated the success of the Nazi attempt to invalidate the Jews as an object of concern for the German churches.

The Reformed, or Calvinist, churches of France, Switzerland, the Netherlands, and

Hungary were more sympathetic to Judaism on theological grounds. In addition, their own history of resisting tyrannical persecutions led to a sense of identification with the Jewish victims of Nazism. In France, leading Protestants protested against the anti-Jewish measures of the Vichy regime. Relief efforts in concentration camps, such as GURS, and escape routes to Spain and Switzerland, were organized by CIMADE (Commission Inter-Mouvements auprès des Evacués), a French Protestant youth movement. Thousands of Jewish refugees were hidden in remote Protestant villages such as LE CHAMBON-SUR-LIGNON.

In Switzerland, the Geneva headquarters of the nascent World Council of Churches became a center for courier activities and relief efforts to aid Jews escaping from other parts of western Europe. The council also cooperated closely with Jewish organizations in informing Protestant communities worldwide about the extent of the Nazi atrocities. The Dutch and Danish Protestant churches actively assisted in rescue efforts. In Britain, strong leadership was given by the archbishop of Canterbury, William Temple, and by Bishop George Bell of Chichester. Both aroused public concern for the Jews' fate and urged the government to make more generous provision for the admission of refugees, whether Christian or not, and for their friendly reception in Britain. Wartime restrictions and the refusal of the British government to alter its policy on immigration into Palestine revealed the limitations of these representations.

The Protestant churches were slow to find an adequate response to the Nazi persecution of the Jews. The failure of the German Protestants to take a stronger stand, and the absence of a well-organized international Protestant agency, hampered relief efforts. Only after 1938 were effective international measures taken, and these were curtailed by the outbreak of war. The recognition that Protestant indifference was due largely to the survival of prejudicial stereotypes and the absence of a sense of theological affinity became the chief incentive in the postwar Protestant reassessment of Christian relations with the Jewish people.

BIBLIOGRAPHY

Busch, E. *Juden und Christen im Schatten des Dritten Reiches.* Munich, 1979.

Conway, J. S. *The Nazi Persecution of the Churches, 1933–1945.* London, 1968.

Friedlander, S. *Pius XII and the Third Reich: A Documentation.* London, 1966.

Gutteridge, R. *Open Thy Mouth for the Dumb: The German Evangelical Church and the Jews, 1879–1950.* Oxford, 1976.

Hay, M. *The Roots of Christian Anti-Semitism.* New York, 1981.

Kulka, O. D., and P. R. Mendes-Flohr, eds. *Judaism and Christianity under the Impact of National Socialism.* Jerusalem, 1987.

Lewy, G. *The Catholic Church and Nazi Germany.* New York, 1964.

Morley, J. F. *Vatican Diplomacy and the Jews during the Holocaust, 1939–1943.* New York, 1980.

Rengstorf, K., and S. von Kortzfleisch, eds. *Kirche und Synagoge: Handbuch zur Geschichte von Christen und Juden.* 2 vols. Stuttgart, 1968, 1970.

Scholder, K. *The Churches and the Third Reich: Preliminary History of the Time of Illusions, 1918–1934.* Vol. 1. London, 1987.

Snoek, J. M. *The Grey Book: A Collection of Protests against Anti-Semitism and the Persecution of the Jews, Issued by Non–Roman Catholic Churches and Church Leaders during Hitler's Rule.* Assen, Netherlands, 1969.

JOHN S. CONWAY

After the Holocaust

Since the collapse of Adolf Hitler's Third Reich there has been increased sensitivity in the Christian churches to the problem of ANTISEMITISM. Modern antisemitism, that is, antisemitism used as a political and ideological tool, has been widely condemned by church assemblies and courts of justice. There is also an emerging realization that the river of modern antisemitism has been fed by ancient streams of theological and cultural Jew-hatred.

The river reached flood proportions in the German Third Reich, when streams of ethnic (*völkisch*) racism and pseudoscientific racial anthropology combined with motives of blatant economic pillage and political expediency. The river of anti-Jewish violence then overflowed the familiar channels of nonviolent discrimination and occasional mob violence that had long carried the ill will of Christendom toward Jews. The force of the flood was not accidental, however: its power was purposefully harnessed to rational engines of destruction intended to wipe Jewry from the face of the earth.

Since the end of World War II, Nazism and political antisemitism have been readily condemned in most Western churches, along with other forms of racial prejudice (there has been no parallel development in the Eastern churches). Although the number of books and articles on the subject has greatly increased since the 1960s, still comparatively rare is evidence that the churches' officials and courts have come to terms with Christianity's own contribution to the attempted destruction of the Jews. The greatest progress has been made in local centers.

Even resolutions against "antisemitism" and "racism" are usually cast in such form as to make it clear that the unpleasant acts were something that was done by other people. Still protected from radical surgery, still unthreatened by any deep and insightful repentance, both theological and cultural antisemitism are alive in most of the Christian world—including circles that readily condemn what they call "racial prejudice," "anti-Judaism," or "anti-Semitism" (that is, political antisemitism).

Nevertheless, in contemporary theological writing the focus is on the frontier between the Christian churches and the Jewish people. The acid tests as to whether hierarchies and churches have made the pilgrimage of faith in the shadow of Auschwitz are three: (1) the attitude toward teaching the Holocaust and the lessons of the Holocaust; (2) the attitude toward a restored Israel; and (3) the attitude toward organized missions to the Jews (*Judenmissionen*). The red thread that ties these three issues together is the response to the question, "How do you stand on the question of the survival of the Jewish people?"

The major centers of theological change have been in West Germany, the Netherlands, and the United States.

Germany. German leaders in such change have been well aware that the Barmen Declaration (May 1934) of the Confessing Church (Bekennende Kirche), the cornerstone of Christian resistance to Nazism, condemned the idolatry of the dictatorship (*Führerstaat*) but did not deal with antisemitism. Dietrich BONHOEFFER—later to be martyred by the Nazis for complicity in the July 20, 1944, attempt on Hitler's life—tried to induce the Christian resistance to give attention to the importance of the *Judenfrage* ("Jewish question"), but he was unsuccessful. As church leaders such as the theologian Karl BARTH and Martin NIEMÖLLER later confessed with regret, they did not at the time see the significance for Christians of the assault on the Jewish people.

Neither did the Stuttgart Declaration of Guilt (October 1945)—adopted in the presence of foreign church delegates by leading German churchmen who had been opponents of Nazism and who earnestly repented of the churches' weakness in the face of the Third Reich's violation of human rights—mention what had happened to the Jews. The first postwar conferences and synods of the churches in Germany, as well as Christian consultations elsewhere in the world, regretted whatever injustices may have occurred and reaffirmed the traditional approach to the evangelization of the Jews. The issue of Jewish survival had not yet penetrated the thinking of ecclesiastical circles.

The mystery of Jewish survival was working, nonetheless, in the spiritual undertow of Christian thought. At a Protestant rally (*Kirchentag*) of 275,000 people in Berlin in 1961, some 28,000 participants flooded discussion sessions on "The Christian Obligation to the Jews." Out of this came Working Group (*Arbeitsgemeinschaft*) VI, which has since sponsored dozens of conferences and the publication of many collectively and individually written volumes. A chief center has been the Arnoldshain Adult Education Academy, near Frankfurt.

The first German Conference on the Holocaust and the Church Struggle was held in Hamburg in June 1975, under the joint sponsorship of the Gesellschaften für Christlich-Jüdische Zusammenarbeit (Societies for Christian-Jewish Cooperation), the National Council of Christians and Jews (United States), and the International Council of Christians and Jews.

The cooperative work with colleagues in

other churches, especially in America, has been important for German developments. A large German delegation participated in the International Theological Symposium on the Holocaust held in Philadelphia in 1978, returning home to press more vigorously for a reform and reconstruction of official teaching. In January 1980 the Synod of the Church of the Rhineland issued a powerful statement calling for basic changes. Co-responsibility for the Holocaust was accepted, theological antisemitism was condemned, the state of Israel was affirmed, and targeting Jews for conversion was repudiated. Although some units—conspicuously the Theology Faculty at the University of Bonn—reacted conventionally, the Rhineland Declaration gained widespread attention and approbation in Germany and in the ecumenical world.

The Netherlands. In 1961 an important initiative was undertaken in Israel by a committee of Dutch Protestants. Believing that remorse was not enough and that action was called for, under the leadership of Johan Pillon they founded Nes Ammim, a Christian *moshav* (cooperative settlement) in western Galilee. Nes Ammim has outlived the suspicion of missionary intention and has contributed worthily to the fraternal goal of helping to build up the land.

Postwar Dutch theology has been deeply influenced by the Leerhuis (House of Study) movement, centered in lay Bible study, which owes much to the Jewish thinkers Franz Rosenzweig and Martin Buber. Also important have been the *Vormingscentren* (theological training centers), fraternally related to the German *Evangelische Akademien* (evangelical academies). The first center, Kerk en Wereld (Church and World), was founded by Hendrik Kraemer, a close associate of Karl Barth and other leaders of theological renewal and resistance to Nazism. Kraemer—like Bonhoeffer, Barth, Reinhold NIEBUHR, and others close to Wilhelm Adolf Visser 't Hooft and the World Council of Churches in Process of Formation (from 1938 until the founding Assembly in Amsterdam in 1948)—combined the theme of biblical theological renewal with opposition to Nazi idolatry and antisemitism.

By 1970 both of the major Dutch Protestant churches, the Reformed and the Christian Reformed, had adopted official statements condemning antisemitism, affirming the importance of Israel—people, land, and state —and withdrawing from the traditional line on missions to the Jews.

The United States. During World War II the only American Christian theologian of rank to point to the theological significance of the Nazi assault on the Jews, and one of the very few to assay the meaning of the church struggle against idolatry, was Reinhold Niebuhr. His students have in their generation constituted the major Protestant phalanx leading the reform and reconstruction of preaching and teaching in the shadow of the Holocaust.

On the Roman Catholic side, the primary impulse to change has come from the conciliar reforms initiated by Pope John XXIII. On October 28, 1965, Vatican II issued *Nostra aetate* (Declaration on the Relation of the Church to Non-Christian Religions), in spite of desperate diplomatic efforts by Arab governments to prevent any change in the church's traditional teaching of contempt of the Jews. Followed a decade later by "Guidelines for Catholic-Jewish Relations" and twenty years later by "Notes on Jews and Judaism in Preaching and Catechesis," the directives of the Vatican have moved steadily toward greater recognition of the continuing indebtedness of Christians to their Jewish heritage, the sinfulness of antisemitism, and the Jewish right to self-definition. Nowhere has Vatican II had greater response than among American Catholics.

Landmarks in opening a deeper level of self-examination on the part of the churches in America were two self-study projects reported in Bernhard Olson's *Faith and Prejudice* (1963): a study of four publishers of Protestant church school lessons, and John T. Pawlikowski's book *Catechetics and Prejudice* (1973), an examination of the Roman Catholic church's teachings about Jews, Protestants, and racial minorities based in part on unpublished research conducted during the 1960s. Both books were distinguished by the way they revealed the layers of Christian theological antisemitism.

The year 1967 was a turning point in the preaching, teaching, and public alignment of American Jews, Protestants, and Roman

Catholics. American Jews responded to the perceived threat of a "second Holocaust" in the Six-Day War with greatly increased financial and political support of Israel. Against the background of a thunderous silence on the part of church bureaucrats, a number of Protestant conservatives, Protestant liberals, and concerned Roman Catholics launched three agencies that since that time have had increasing influence in the seminaries and congregations. The three were founded within a few weeks of each other.

One was Christians Concerned for Israel, which in 1978 expanded into a federation of many groups called The National Christian Leadership Conference for Israel. Its literature, newsletters, and advertisements have helped to educate the churches in articulate support of Israel and to make clear to political leaders of both parties that millions of church people of many denominations are united in a commitment to Jewish survival. The federation's predecessor organization was important in causing Christian congregations to observe Holocaust Memorial Day annually from 1972.

The second agency was the Israel Study Group, consisting of ten Roman Catholic and ten Protestant theologians, meeting in seminar three times a year to read and discuss theological papers on a restored Israel and related issues, such as the Holocaust, antisemitism, the Christian meaning of Jewish survival, and basic Christian dogmas in the shadow of Auschwitz. Now called the Christian Study Group on Israel and the Jewish People, the seminar has resulted in several major books and many articles, and has influenced denominational statements (Episcopal, Presbyterian, and United Church of Christ) reworking official stands on Christian-Jewish relations.

This study group has provided an important testing ground for the work of such Roman Catholic leaders as Father Edward Flannery (*The Anguish of the Jews*, 2nd ed., 1985) and Dr. Eugene Fisher (*Faith without Prejudice*, 1977) of the United States Catholic Conference, and of such Protestants as Roy Eckardt and Alice Eckardt (*A Long Night's Journey into Day*, 2nd ed., 1988) and Paul van Buren (*A Theology of the Jewish-Christian Reality*, 4 vols., 1980–).

The third new foundation was an interfaith, international, and interdisciplinary conference of college, seminary, and university people that became the Annual Scholars' Conference on the Holocaust and the Church Struggle. Meeting the first weekend in March of every year, the Scholars' Conference has brought together hundreds of professors, graduate students, and public educators and has led to the publication of a host of articles and several dozen books.

In July 1988 an international conference, Remembering for the Future, was held in Oxford and London, with 650 educators from twenty-four nations present. The first of two themes was "Christian-Jewish Relations during and after the Holocaust." The chairperson of the conference was Dr. Elisabeth Maxwell. Two of the six members of the executive committee were leaders in all three of the agencies mentioned above, and over half of the registrants at Oxford were alumni of the Annual Scholars' Conference (USA).

The prominence of Americans in these efforts, which are often carried on in close cooperation with colleagues in Israel, reflects the degree to which religious liberty and pluralism are accepted facts of life in the United States. The Jewish, Roman Catholic, and Protestant communities are all of great strength and their members are equally entitled to citizens' rights before the law.

This parity of strength and legal status has practical consequences in terms of sharing mutual concerns. One of the two oldest centers of Holocaust education in the United States, the Anne Frank Institute of Philadelphia (formerly the National Institute on the Holocaust), is independent of any single denominational or faith alignment and is strictly interfaith in its programs. The largest department of religion in the country, that of Temple University in Philadelphia, is oriented toward interfaith dialogue rather than seminary or divinity school apologetics. Its *Journal of Ecumenical Studies* is the preeminent quarterly journal in the field.

When Holocaust Memorial Day became a public calendar event in America, all chaplains of the army, air force, and navy were sent the book *Liturgies on the Holocaust*, by M. S. Littell (1986), and regardless of their own denominational affiliation were expected to lead services of participation in remembering the Holocaust and its lessons for all persons of conscience. Just as those reforming and reconstructing the churches' preaching and teaching about the Jewish people have looked to Jewish teachers for counsel and encouragement, so Jewish leaders, remembering the heavy losses of their people in an age of genocide, have been able more and more to look to the churches for participation in services of mourning and healing.

During the German church struggle those who opposed Nazism found support at the parish level, not in the hierarchies. In the reform of church preaching and teaching about the Jewish people carried out in Germany, the Netherlands, and the United States, with few exceptions the strongest impulses have continued to come from the parish and congregational levels rather than from the front offices.

FRANKLIN H. LITTELL

Poland. In Poland, the Catholic church had historically played a significant part in the spread of antisemitism. During World War II Polish priests helped to save Jews, and the Catholic church in Poland itself suffered a great deal from Nazi persecutions. Hundreds of Jewish children were given refuge in convents and church-sponsored children's asylums, although the church itself did not engage in an organized massive effort of saving Jews.

In the initial postwar phase, especially after the KIELCE pogrom of July 4, 1946, the hesitant and ambiguous attitude of Polish church leaders came in for a good deal of censure, but as time went on a change took place in the attitudes of many of the leaders, as well as of the entire Catholic public. An important contribution to this development was made by *Tygodnik Powszechny*, a leading Catholic weekly published in Kraków, which took a consistent position against antisemitism and gave the subject prominent space in its columns. The public appearances of Pope John Paul II also had an effect on the ongoing process of change in the influential sector of the Catholic population. Among the Catholic intelligentsia there is a growing interest in the history of the Jews and the relations between Jews and Poles, and from the mid-1980s there has been some soul-searching

and an effort to analyze the complicated pattern of that relationship. This process has been furthered by numerous meetings of Jewish and Polish scholars at Oxford and in Poland, and by the studies in this field that have been published. In 1987 *Tygodnik Powszechny* published an article by a noted literary scholar, Jan Blonski, that raised the painful issue of the relations between Poles and Jews in a courageous and candid form. This article aroused much interest in Poland. In addition, the Polish Catholic periodicals *Znak* and *Wieża* have published special issues on Judaism in general and on the question of the Jews in Poland.

ISRAEL GUTMAN

BIBLIOGRAPHY

Cargas, H. J. *A Christian Response to the Holocaust.* Denver, 1981.
Fasching, D. J. *The Jewish People in Christian Preaching.* New York, 1984.
Fisher, E. "The Holocaust and the State of Israel: A Catholic Perspective." *Judaism* 75: 16–24.
Gerlach, W. *Als die Zeugen schwiegen: Die Bekennende Kirche und die Juden.* Berlin, 1987.
Littell, F. H. *The Crucifixion of the Jews.* Macon, Ga., 1987.
Littell, F. H., and H. G. Locke. *The German Church Struggle and the Holocaust, 1933–1945.* Detroit, 1974.
Littell, M. S., ed. *Liturgies on the Holocaust.* New York, 1986.
Osten-Sacken, P. von der. *Christian-Jewish Dialogue: Theological Foundations.* Philadelphia, 1986.
World Council of Churches. *The Theology of the Churches and the Jewish People.* Geneva, 1988.

CHRONICLES OF THE ŁÓDŹ GHETTO. *See* Łódź Ghetto, Chronicles of the.

CHURCHILL, WINSTON LEONARD SPENCER (1874–1965), British statesman and wartime leader. Churchill's political career, which extended from 1900 to the mid-1950s, spanned a period of tumultuous developments within the Jewish world: the growth of the Jewish national home in Palestine, the Holocaust, and the creation of the state of Israel. His political responsibilities during this period, as well as his personal pro-

Zionist sympathies and his imperial perspective, ensured him a central role in twentieth-century Jewish history.

During 1921 and 1922, as secretary of state for the British colonies, Churchill was closely involved with the formative years of the British Mandate in Palestine and with the early development of post–World War I Jewish settlement there. Firmly committed to the concept of a British Empire as vital to the interests of the United Kingdom, Churchill looked to the growing Jewish national home as a pro-British bastion. He was a leading opponent of Prime Minister Neville Chamberlain's foreign policy of APPEASEMENT (1937–1939), and called constantly for an active rearmament program against Adolf Hitler's Germany. He was also the leading parliamentary opponent of the 1939 WHITE PAPER, which limited Jewish immigration to Palestine and the purchase by Jews of land there; he supported continued Jewish immigration to Palestine.

When Britain declared war against Germany in September 1939, Churchill joined Chamberlain's government as First Lord of the Admiralty. From within the War Cabinet, Churchill tried to induce the government to abandon the White Paper. In January 1940, he convinced the cabinet to accept a *modus vivendi* whereby the White Paper would remain in force but nothing would be done that would prejudice a reconsideration of Palestine policy after the war. In effect, this meant that the constitutional provisions of the 1939 policy would be frozen.

This compromise agreement remained in force, even after Churchill succeeded Chamberlain as British prime minister in May 1940. Although Churchill attempted a number of times during the war years to propose alternative policies that would permit the creation of a Jewish state, his pro-Zionist stand was firmly opposed by the other members of the cabinet and by the British senior civil service. On each occasion, Churchill informed his colleagues of his intention to support the creation of an independent state with "three or four million Jews" after the war against Germany had been won. Only in 1943, following the final elimination of the Axis threat to the British position in the Middle East, did Churchill decide to confront the supporters of the White Paper and advocate new discussions on the political future of the Palestine Mandate. A Cabinet Committee on Palestine was formed which ultimately recommended that Palestine be partitioned between Jews and Arabs. This decision was accepted by the British cabinet in January 1944, and active planning for the partition began. However, the November 1944 assassination in Cairo of Lord Walter Moyne by members of the LOHAMEI HERUT ISRAEL underground led Churchill to suspend any further deliberations until after the end of the war. The defeat of Churchill's Conservative party in the elections of 1945 meant that the wartime partition proposal was not revived.

Churchill's views regarding the future of the Jews in Palestine, together with the absolute primacy he gave to winning the war, deflected any concern for the immediate circumstances of European Jewry under the Nazis. Although he was sympathetic to Jewish matters, he was only rarely consulted regarding the fate of Jewish communities in occupied Europe. He consistently supported efforts to liberalize British restrictions on Jewish immigration into Palestine (one of the main avenues of escape from Europe), but he did nothing to foster active British support for programs of rescue. Despite his outspokenly pro-Jewish stance, there was no British equivalent of the American WAR REFUGEE BOARD. In a letter of February 1943 (drafted by the Foreign Office but signed by Churchill), the prime minister set out the reasons why Britain would not take an active role in rescue: transport was a major problem; the lines of escape passed through areas of vital military importance and would disrupt the war effort; and it would not be possible to rescue Jewish refugees while abandoning the far greater number of Allied citizens in German-occupied areas.

In July 1944, Churchill and Anthony EDEN both endorsed the appeals by the Jewish Agency that Auschwitz be bombed (*see* AUSCHWITZ, BOMBING OF). Nevertheless, neither intervened with sufficient force to overcome the obstacles created by British bureaucracy, and no bombing mission ever took place.

The Jewish issue remained a marginal one for British leaders. Although he was sympa-

Prime Minister Winston Churchill and Madame Chiang Kai-shek (Soong Mei-ling, sister-in-law of Sun Yat-sen), wife of Generalissimo Chiang Kai-shek, at the First Cairo Conference, November 25, 1943.

thetic to Jewish concerns and actively supported Zionist aspirations, Churchill shared the official British consensus that the rescue of European Jewry could only be achieved by the total defeat of Nazi Germany.

[*See also* Great Britain.]

BIBLIOGRAPHY

Cohen, M. J. *Churchill and the Jews*. London, 1985.
Gilbert, M. *Winston Churchill*. Vols. 6, 7. London, 1983, 1985.
Zweig, R. W. *Britain and Palestine during the Second World War*. Woodbridge, England, 1986.

RONALD W. ZWEIG

CLAIMS CONFERENCE. *See* Reparations and Restitution from Germany.

CLAUBERG, CARL (1898–1957), SS physician infamous for his experiments in sterilizing Jewish women at the AUSCHWITZ extermination camp during World War II. Clauberg was born at Wupperhof and served in the infantry during World War I. He later studied medicine at the universities of Kiel, Hamburg, and Graz, qualifying as a doctor in 1925. He had a successful medical career and in 1937 was appointed professor of gynecology and obstetrics at the University of Königsberg. At the same time he was chief doctor at a women's clinic in Upper Silesia and published numerous papers in his specialty. Clauberg was an enthusiastic Nazi, joining the party in 1933 and rising to the rank of *Brigadeführer* in the SS.

The sterilization program was initiated in 1941, and in 1942 Heinrich HIMMLER entrusted Clauberg with its experimental implementation at Auschwitz. He had the cooperation of internee doctors there (including the Polish camp doctor, Władysław Dering, whose experiments were later the subject of a famous libel case in England in 1964). The experiments at Auschwitz lasted until 1944; they involved sterilization by means of injections into the womb, which caused unimaginable suffering to the victims, Jewish and Gypsy women. Clauberg conducted similar experiments in the women's concentration camp of RAVENSBRÜCK in 1945.

Arrested by the Russians at the end of the war, Clauberg was tried in 1948 for his role in the "mass extermination of Soviet citizens." He was sentenced to twenty-five years' imprisonment, but was released in 1955 under the German-Soviet prisoner repatriation agreement. Clauberg showed no regrets for his experiments, and even boasted of his "scientific achievements." At the initiative of the Central Council of Jews in Germany, an action to prosecute Clauberg was undertaken in the West German courts. The council accused Clauberg of "having caused severe bodily harm" to Jewish women. The Kiel police put him under arrest, but he died in a hospital shortly before the date of the trial.

[*See also* Medical Experiments; Physicians, Nazi.]

BIBLIOGRAPHY

Lifton, R. *The Nazi Doctors: Medical Killing and the Psychology of Genocide.* New York, 1986.

LIONEL KOCHAN

CLERGY IN NAZI GERMANY. *See* Bonhoeffer, Dietrich; Christian Churches; Dibelius, Otto; Galen, Clemens August Graf von; Lichtenberg, Bernhard; Niemöller, Martin; Wurm, Theophil.

CLUJ (Cluj-Napoca; Hung., Kolozsvár; Ger., Klausenburg), capital of Cluj county and of Hungarian-ruled northern TRANSYLVANIA (1940–1944). In 1941, Cluj had a population of 110,956, of whom 16,763 were Jewish. The Jewish community was one of the largest in the province, with a well-developed network of educational, cultural, and charitable institutions. It boasted many politically active Zionist leaders, including Hillel Danzig and Rezső (Rudolph) KASZTNER. The last head of the Orthodox community was Zsigmond Léb; that of the large Neolog (Conservative) community was Dr. József Fischer, Kasztner's father-in-law, who during the pre-1940 era also served in the Romanian parliament as a representative of the Jewish party.

The ghettoization of the Cluj Jews began on May 3, 1944, and was completed within a week. The Jews were concentrated in the Iris brickyard in the northern part of the city. Consisting mostly of shacks used for drying bricks and tiles, the ghetto had practically no facilities for the approximately eighteen thousand Jews who were assembled there from Cluj county. The concentration of the Jews was carried out by the local administrative and police authorities with the cooperation of SS advisers, including SS-Hauptsturmführer Dieter WISLICENY. The ghetto was under the command of László Urbán, the city's police chief. Its internal administration was entrusted to a JUDENRAT (Jewish Council), whose members included Fischer (as head), Rabbi Akiba Glasner, Rabbi Mózes Weinberger, and Ernö Marton. As in all the other ghettos in Hungary, the local brickyard also had a "mint," a special building where the gendarmes and police tortured Jews into confessing where they had hidden their valuables.

Kasztner, who had been in the midst of controversial negotiations with the Eichmann Sonderkommando on a rescue arrangement, visited the city on May 4 and 5. Shortly thereafter, 388 Jews, including many of Kasztner's relatives and closest friends,

CLUJ

Annexations from June to September 1940: (1) Bessarabia and (2) N. Bukovina to USSR; (3) N. Transylvania to Hungary; (4) S. Dobruja to Bulgaria.

were taken out of the ghetto and transferred to Budapest. From there, together with some 1,300 other Jews, they were eventually taken to Switzerland via BERGEN-BELSEN—a rescue mission that engendered great controversy (*see* RELIEF AND RESCUE COMMITTEE OF BUDAPEST).

The Cluj ghetto was liquidated through the deportation of the Jews to AUSCHWITZ in six transports between May 25 and June 9, 1944. After the war, the city reverted to Romania. In 1947, it had a Jewish population of close to sixty-five hundred, including not only survivors but also some who moved there from other parts of Romania.

BIBLIOGRAPHY

Braham, R. L. *Genocide and Retribution.* Boston, 1983. See pages 24–27, 123–141.
Carmilly-Weinberger, M., ed. *Memorial Volume for the Jews of Cluj-Kolozsvár.* New York, 1970. (In English, Hebrew, and Hungarian.)

RANDOLPH L. BRAHAM

COHEN, DAVID (1882–1967), Dutch Zionist leader and public figure. Born in Deventer, Cohen was an expert in papyrology and became a professor of ancient history, first in Leyden and then in Amsterdam. He was active in Jewish affairs from an early age, joined the Zionist movement in 1904, and held key posts in it. He was one of the sponsors and organizers of the Zionist Students' Union and the Jewish Youth Federation. In World War I Cohen was active in providing assistance to Jewish refugees, mainly from Germany, and became the secretary of the Committee for Refugees. He was a member of the Jewish Council in The Hague and then in Amsterdam, and in 1934 was elected to the Standing Committee of the Union of Ashkenazic Communities. In 1933, when the Nazis rose to power in Germany, it was on Cohen's initiative that the Comité voor Bijzondere Joodse Belangen (Committee for Special Jewish Affairs) was established, and he became the executive chairman of its subcommittee on refugees.

Following the German occupation of the NETHERLANDS in May 1940, Cohen was among the sponsors of the Jewish Coordinating Committee set up in December of that year. On February 12, 1941, Cohen, together with Abraham ASSCHER, formed the JOODSE RAAD (Jewish Council) at the "suggestion" of the Germans. He was one of the council's two chairmen (the other being Asscher), taking part in its daily operations and determining its policy toward the Germans. During the war years the Joodse Raad came under severe attack from Lodewijk Ernst VISSER and from the Dutch government-in-exile for its policy of cooperation with the Germans. This was the background for Cohen's conflict with Visser, who was opposed to such cooperation. In the Joodse Raad itself there was also opposition to Cohen's policy, but he was always successful in overcoming this resistance and obtaining majority support for his position in the Coordinating Committee.

On September 23, 1943, Cohen was arrested, together with the other members of the Joodse Raad who were still in Amsterdam, and taken first to WESTERBORK and from there to THERESIENSTADT. When he came back to the Netherlands after the war, the Dutch government instituted judicial proceedings against him, charging him with collaborating with the enemy. Cohen was arrested, but after an investigation the file was closed. In 1947 Cohen was also charged before a Jewish community tribunal, where he put up a passionate defense of his policy during the war; but he was found guilty and was barred from holding office in any Jewish institution. In 1950 the sentence was annulled; Cohen returned to his university post, but did not again become active in Jewish public life. In 1955 he published his reminiscences, *Zwervend en Dolend* (Fugitive and Vagabond).

BIBLIOGRAPHY

Michman, J. "The Controversial Stand of the Joodse Raad in the Netherlands." *Yad Vashem Studies* 10 (1974): 9–68.
Michman, J. "The Controversy Surrounding the Jewish Council of Amsterdam." In *Patterns of Jewish Leadership in Nazi Europe, 1933–1945.* Proceedings of the Third Yad Vashem International Historical Conference, edited by Y. Gutman and C. J. Haft, pp. 235–258. Jerusalem, 1979.
Michman, J., H. Beem, and D. Michman. *The Neth-*

erlands. In *Pinkas Hakehillot; Encyclopaedia of Jewish Communities.* Jerusalem, 1985. (In Hebrew.)

Presser, J. *The Destruction of the Dutch Jews,* New York, 1969.

JOZEPH MICHMAN

COHN, MARIANNE (1924–1944), French Jewish underground activist. Born in Mannheim, Germany, Cohn was a member of the ECLAIREURS ISRAÉLITES DE FRANCE (French Jewish Scouts) and in 1942 joined the Mouvement de la Jeunesse Sioniste (Zionist Youth Movement). She belonged to the underground sponsored by both organizations, which smuggled into Switzerland Jewish children whose parents had been expelled from France. On June 1, 1944, Cohn was seized by a German patrol, together with a group of twenty-eight children, and all were imprisoned in the town of Annemasse. The underground succeeded in establishing contact with Cohn and devised a plan to get her out of jail, but she was not prepared to escape, fearing that the children would suffer if she were to do

Marianne Cohn.

so. On July 8, two members of the Nazi-sponsored French militia broke into the prison, took Cohn out, and killed her with an ax. The children were all saved.

BIBLIOGRAPHY

L'activité des organisations juives en France sous l'occupation. Paris, 1947.

Hammel, F. C. *Souviens-toi d'Amalek: Témoignage sur la lutte des Juifs en France (1938–1944).* Paris, 1982.

Latour, A. *The Jewish Resistance in France, 1940– 1944.* New York, 1981.

LUCIEN LAZARE

COLLABORATORS. *See* Hilfswillige; Nachtigall Battalion; Ostbataillone; Policiniai Batalionai; Quisling, Vidkun; Ukrainische Hilfspolizei; Vlasov, Andrei; *see also under* Police in Occupied Countries.

COLUMBIA HAUS, concentration camp in Berlin, used mainly for detaining the victims of Nazi persecution who were under interrogation by the GESTAPO at its headquarters on Prinz-Albrecht Street. In the late summer of 1933, the basement of the Gestapo headquarters building was equipped with cells, but these could hold only about fifty prisoners at most. Many of the prisoners in "protective custody" were also held in the police jail on Alexanderplatz for their questioning by the Gestapo. Beginning in early 1934 (no exact date is available), the Gestapo also utilized Columbia Haus—a concentration camp set up by the SS—to hold prisoners who were under direct Gestapo investigation. Columbia Haus, located near the Tempelhof airfield, had originally served as a military prison. Like the Gestapo headquarters itself, it was loathed for the torture methods employed there. Owing to its close connection with the SA (Sturmabteilung; Storm Troopers) and, later, with the SS and Gestapo headquarters, Columbia Haus, instead of being disbanded when the initial 1934 persecution phase came to an end, was taken over by the Inspectorate of Concentration Camps. A Gestapo headquarters circular dated January 8, 1935, stated that henceforth "Columbia Haus

Prison" was to be designated "KL [*Konzentrationslager*] Columbia Haus"; at that time, it appears, Columbia Haus came administratively under the direct control of the Gestapo.

In late 1935, the Gestapo decided to increase its headquarters' prison capacity, and by fall 1936 the planned additional cells were ready for occupation. At that time the SS was in the process of liquidating all the camps it had been using in the first few years following the Nazi seizure of power—with the exception of DACHAU—and constructing new and larger concentration camp complexes. Columbia Haus was no longer needed. On November 5, 1935, the camp was closed.

BIBLIOGRAPHY

Krausnick, H., et al. *Anatomy of the SS State.* London, 1968.

FALK PINGEL

COMISIA AUTONOMA DE AJUTORARE (Refugee Aid Committee), organization established in BUCHAREST to render assistance to Jews in ROMANIA who underwent suffering under the Ion ANTONESCU regime. The committee was formed at the end of January 1941, following the suppression of the IRON GUARD revolt and the pogroms in Bucharest (January 21 to 23, 1941). It was founded on the initiative of leading figures in the Federatia Uniunilor de Comunitati Evreesti, or Union of Jewish Communities (Wilhelm FILDERMAN, Fred Saraga, and Emil Costiner); representatives of the Zionist movement (Misu Benvenisti and Dr. Cornel Iancu); businessmen; and a group of women who had already achieved a reputation for extending aid to Jews victimized by the regime. The committee, headed by Arnold Schwefelberg, a lawyer, collected funds and supplies needed by the victims of the Bucharest pogroms. Subsequently, it concentrated its efforts on alleviating conditions for the forty thousand Jews who had been expelled from their homes in towns and villages and were being detained in camps in various parts of the country. Sometimes the aid provided consisted of no more than a meal or a piece of clothing—just enough to keep the refugees

alive. After the German (and Romanian) invasion of the Soviet Union, on June 22, 1941, and the mass deportation of Jews to TRANSNISTRIA, the committee—a voluntary body—could no longer cope with the growing needs, and schoolchildren and additional volunteers from all sectors of the Jewish population joined in helping its operations.

These activities, and the initiatives undertaken by the committee's leaders, reflected the disasters that befell Romanian Jewry: the IAŞI pogrom and the deportations that cost the lives of twelve thousand Jews from Iaşi in the period from June 29 to July 8, 1941; the camps, especially at Calaras-Ialomita, to which the survivors were taken; the removal of the Jews from the city of Constanţa to the Osmancea camp; and the transfer of Jews from small villages to large population centers. All these developments created an urgent need for financial and material aid to ensure at least the bare existence of the victims.

In the spring of 1941, before the outbreak of the war against the Soviet Union, the committee launched a major campaign for contributions. This was necessitated by the rapid impoverishment of new sectors of the Jewish population as a result of anti-Jewish measures undertaken by the Antonescu regime—the confiscation of houses and other properties, the imposition of special levies, the expulsion of Jews from villages, and, particularly, the dismissal of Jews from their posts and their exclusion from various professions. Sufficient money was collected in this drive to cover the needs. The committee also provided tools, money, food, kitchen utensils, and drugs to the Jews drafted into forced-labor battalions, and it tried to help the families of these draftees as best it could.

Filderman made efforts to channel aid to the Jews of BESSARABIA and BUKOVINA in the first few days of the murder campaign conducted by Romanian and German forces in July and August of 1941, but they were all rejected by the Romanian authorities. On December 17, 1941, the Union of Jewish Communities was disbanded, and on the same day permission was granted to provide aid to the Jews who had been deported to Transnistria. In place of the union the authorities installed the CENTRALA EVREILOR (Jewish Center), which was also supposed to take over the functions of the Refugee Aid Committee. The center, however, was not permitted to aid the Jews deported to Transnistria; its operations were restricted to the Jews in Romania proper. The committee kept up its work, but it added the term "autonomous" (*autonoma*) to its title, to distinguish it from the Jewish Center's aid committee, under whose auspices it formally operated.

In the fall of 1942 the committee was called upon to extend aid to new categories of deportees to Transnistria: Jewish political prisoners suspected of Communist activity; Jews who in the summer of 1940, following the annexation of Bessarabia and northern Bukovina by the Soviet Union, had applied—in vain—to return to the Soviet Union; and Jews who had violated the laws and regulations concerning forced labor. From 1942 to 1944 the committee was able to aid the deportees in Transnistria in various ways, in most instances helping to save their lives. In 1942 the committee also sent work tools to Transnistria to aid the cooperative societies that had been set up in the ghettos and camps of the region. In early 1943, after long and persistent efforts, the committee was permitted to send a delegation (headed by Fred Saraga) to visit several ghettos in Transnistria. This visit, coupled with those of representatives of the International RED CROSS and of the papal nuncio in Bucharest, Archbishop Andrea Cassulo, expedited the provision of relief to the deportees and the establishment of orphanages in Transnistria.

At the end of 1943 permission was granted for the repatriation of the Jews from Transnistria. The committee organized the return of six thousand Jews from the DOROHOI district and of four thousand orphaned children, providing food and clothing and arranging for rail transportation. The repatriation operation was halted in April 1944, following the liberation of northern Romania and northern Transnistria by the Soviet army and the seizure of the Dniester crossings by German forces. Many of the Jews who had not yet been repatriated were killed by the Nazis. The committee provided temporary housing and upkeep for the returnees. As of late 1943, the committee was receiving funds from the JOINT DISTRIBUTION COMMITTEE, transmitted to it by the International Red Cross.

The committee's operations grew in size after the fall of the Antonescu regime, and it began extending aid to thousands of Jews who had been released from forced-labor battalions, detention camps, and prisons, in addition to the returnees from Transnistria. At the end of 1944 and the beginning of 1945, Jewish Communists seized control of the committee, incorporating it into the Comitetul Democrat Evreesc (Jewish Democratic Committee). Although the Refugee Aid Committee's operations did not come to an end overnight, they were soon phased out, and what remained of the committee ceased to exist. A substantial part of its assets was diverted by the Jewish Communists for aid to Romanian gentiles.

BIBLIOGRAPHY

Ancel, J., ed. *Documents concerning the Fate of Romanian Jewry during the Holocaust.* Vols. 5, 8. New York, 1987.

JEAN ANCEL

COMMISSARIAT GÉNÉRAL AUX QUESTIONS JUIVES (Office for Jewish Affairs; CGQJ), agency established by the Vichy government in March 1941 to coordinate French anti-Jewish policy and to prepare and administer legislation in this field.

During his first contacts with the French authorities on the "Jewish question," in early 1941, Adolf EICHMANN's Paris representative, Theodor DANNECKER, advised Adm. François DARLAN, the head of the Vichy government, of the Nazis' intent to sponsor a Zentraljudenamt (Central Jewish Office) for the occupied zone. Consistent with their opposition to the division of their country, the French proposed instead a French-directed agency whose jurisdiction would extend to both zones. Technically, therefore, French sovereignty would be preserved. Delighted with the French willingness to cooperate, Dannecker agreed. Darlan established the new agency on March 29, 1941, and named the French war veterans' leader, Xavier VALLAT, a rabid antisemite but also an anti-German, to be its head.

Under Vallat, the CGQJ attempted to codify an anti-Jewish policy in the French national interest. The idea was to unify anti-Jewish actions throughout both zones, and to do so energetically and efficiently. Implicit in Vallat's approach was the hope that the Germans would gradually withdraw from this field, leaving the task to the French alone. Dissatisfied with the existing STATUT DES JUIFS (Jewish Law), Vallat put forward a new law on June 2, 1941, that aimed to define the Jews and to intensify Vichy's anti-Jewish program. All loopholes were to be closed. Basing itself on this second *Statut des Juifs*, the CGQJ soon prompted a flurry of decrees drastically limiting the number of Jews in commerce and the professions. On June 2, another law announced a forthcoming detailed census of Jews in the unoccupied zone—a grave step that profoundly shocked Jewish opinion and that was to have fatal consequences later, when Jews in France were rounded up and deported. Finally, by a law of July 22, 1941, the CGQJ launched a vast process of "Aryanization" (*see* ARISIERUNG)—the confiscation of Jewish property—in the unoccupied zone.

"Aryanization" became one of the major tasks of the CGQJ. Eager to ensure that Jewish property did not find its way to the Reich, the French government designated the CGQJ as the agency to take charge of confiscating Jewish property throughout France. Vallat entered into complex negotiations with the Germans, consulted with ministries, industrialists, and businessmen, and administered a complicated bureaucracy of inspectors and trustees. The goal was to liquidate or sell all Jewish holdings for the benefit of France. The vast scale of this project, which eventually involved more than forty-two thousand Jewish enterprises, drained the legislative and administrative energies of the CGQJ. Corruption and inefficiency followed, despite Vallat's efforts to combat both.

Because of his relatively moderate approach, the German authorities finally replaced Vallat, in May 1942, with Louis DARQUIER DE PELLEPOIX. An outsider at Vichy and far more at home in the pro-German milieus of Paris, Darquier did not have the legalistic or technical scruples of his predecessor. He and his staff increasingly went their own way, clashing with various ministries and indulging their taste for brutality and personal enrichment. Propaganda and repression assumed far more importance than under Vallat. The CGQJ spawned a parapolice organi-

zation, the Sections d'Enquête et de Contrôle. Darquier and his lieutenants were not averse to working with the Nazis, notably when roundups and deportations were conducted throughout France in the summer of 1942. When possible, the Vichy leaders kept the CGQJ at arm's length; Marshal Philippe PÉTAIN himself allegedly referred to Darquier as *Monsieur le tortionnaire* ("Mr. Torturer"). But the anti-Jewish machinery continued to function, and even to accelerate the rate of persecution.

In late 1943 the Germans pressured Vichy to drop Darquier, recognizing that he was unable to bring the Vichy government fully into line with Nazi policy. Darquier was succeeded in February 1944 by Charles Mercier du Paty de Clam, an undistinguished civil servant descended from the famous officer who arrested Alfred Dreyfus in 1894. Du Paty de Clam seems to have made efforts to reverse the Commissariat's anti-Semitic orientation, with some minor success. With the end of the war in sight, du Paty de Clam took leave from his office in May. Pierre LAVAL, who sought until the end to maintain control and government continuity in this sphere as in others, named Joseph Antignac, one of Vichy's top officials and most virulent antisemites, to head the Commissariat. Remarkably, "business as usual" remained the policy of the CGQJ even after the Allies went ashore in Normandy. When France was liberated, the agency, along with the rest of the Vichy administration, ceased to exist.

BIBLIOGRAPHY

Billig, J. *Le Commissariat Général aux Questions Juives (1941–1944)*. 3 vols. Paris, 1955–1960.
Knobel, M. "C.-M.-V. du Paty de Clam, commissaire général aux questions juives." *Le Monde Juif* 117 (1985):18–24.
Marrus, M. R., and R. O. Paxton. *Vichy France and the Jews*. New York, 1981.

MICHAEL R. MARRUS

COMMISSAR ORDER. *See* Kommissarbefehl.

COMMITTEE FOR THE JEWS OF OCCUPIED EUROPE. *See* Joint Rescue Committee.

CONCENTRATION CAMPS (Ger., *Konzentrationslager*; KZ), camps in which persons are imprisoned without regard to the accepted norms of arrest and detention. Although the term "concentration camp" is sometimes used as a generic term for Nazi camps, not all the camps eventually established by the Nazis were designated as concentration camps proper. Their extensive camp system also included labor camps (*Arbeitslager*), transit camps (*Durchgangslager*), prisoner-of-war (POW) camps (*Kriegsgefangenlager*), and ex-termination camps (*Vernichtungslager*). This entry focuses on the network of concentration camps.

Concentration camps were an essential part of the Nazi regime of oppression. The regime imprisoned in such camps political adversaries and persons considered socially or racially undesirable. Forced labor performed by the prisoners became a central element of the imprisonment. During World War II the concentration camps also played a part in the Nazi fight against the resistance

CONCENTRATION CAMPS

Corporal punishment by whipping at the Buchenwald concentration camp.

movements, and some camps (such as AUSCHWITZ and MAJDANEK) were centers for the systematic extermination of Jews, GYPSIES, Soviet PRISONERS OF WAR (POWs) and other groups in the Reich and the occupied territories.

The history of the concentration camps can be divided into three periods: (1) 1933 to 1936; (2) 1936 to 1942; and (3) 1942 to 1944–1945.

From 1933 to 1936. In the earliest period, the concentration camps were used primarily for incarcerating internal political adversaries from the left and liberal circles, as well as members of the proscribed German labor movement organizations. Special places of detention for political prisoners came into being in the wake of the *Razzien* (raids) that were carried out after the Reichstag fire of February 28, 1933 (*see* LAW AND JUDICIARY IN NAZI GERMANY). The main categories taken into "preventive protective custody" (*vorbeugende Schutzhaft*) were Communist party members, as well as members of the trade unions and the Social Democratic party after these were outlawed on May 2 and June 21, 1933, respectively. At the end of July, when the first wave of arrests came to an end, a total of twenty-seven thousand persons were being held in "protective custody." To cope with this large number of political detainees, Germany's police and juridical authorities, as well as the SA (Sturmabteilung; Storm Troopers) and SS, established special detention centers (their precise number cannot be determined). In Prussia alone there were twenty separate detention camps for *Schutzhaft* prisoners. In the spring of 1934 these camps were put under the authority of Heinrich HIMMLER, who was also in charge of the political police in the various states of the Reich. This meant that the regular police, the juridical authorities, and the SA no longer exercised any control over the concentration camp prisoners, who passed to the control of the SS.

On July 4, 1934, Himmler appointed Theodor EICKE, the commandant of the DACHAU concentration camp, as *Inspekteur der Konzentrationslager und SS-Wachverbände* (Inspector of Concentration Camps and SS Guard Units). These guard units became known as SS TOTENKOPFVERBÄNDE (Death's-Head Units), after the death's-head symbol they wore on the collar of their uniforms. Eicke fixed the prisoners' daily routine, the methods of punishment, and the duties of the SS guards. He stressed what he considered to be the proper relationship between the guards and the prisoners, calling the latter "the enemy of the people." Eicke's system was accepted, with variations, in all the concentration camps, and in the course of time many of his subordinates occupied key positions in the camps. From the organizational aspect, the inspectorate of concentration camps came under the SS Main Office (SS-Hauptamt), headed by SS-Gruppenführer August Heissmeyer, but for the most part it acted on its own. Most of the small "protective custody" camps established in 1933 were now abolished. In September 1935 the official concentration camps were Dachau, Lichtenburg (on the Elbe, in the Prussian province of Saxony), Sachsenburg (in the state of Saxony), Esterwegen (in eastern Friesland, Prussia), and ORANIENBURG and COLUMBIA HAUS (near Berlin). A total of about six thousand prisoners were held in these camps.

Beginning in the autumn of 1933, persons other than "political" prisoners were also put into concentration camps. They included tramps and beggars, who in the Nazi jargon were dubbed "asocial elements," as well as persons with several previous criminal convictions, the *Berufsverbrecher* (habitual criminals). This reduced the percentage of political prisoners to about 75 percent by 1936. At a certain stage, a discussion was held in the Nazi hierarchy on whether the camp system should be continued, in light of the consolidation of the regime. Hitler decided the argument by supporting those who favored the continuation of the camps. The number of detainees fell in 1935 and 1936, but later grew again as new categories of prisoners, such as the asocials, were imprisoned.

From 1936 to 1942. The war preparations and the war itself led to an expansion of the concentration camp system. Except for Dachau, the camps established in the initial period were dissolved or put to other uses, and new and larger concentration camps were set up in their place: SACHSENHAUSEN (1936), BUCHENWALD (1937), MAUTHAUSEN and Flossenbürg (1938), RAVENSBRÜCK, the concentration camp for women (1939), Auschwitz (1940), and NATZWEILER (1941). In June 1940 NEUENGAMME, which until then had

been a Sachsenhausen satellite camp, became an independent camp, and in May of 1941 GROSS-ROSEN as well became independent. In February 1942, STUTTHOF, which had been under the authority of the police and SS chief in Danzig, became a regular concentration camp. At the beginning of the second period, the Dachau camp's capacity was enlarged to accommodate six thousand prisoners.

In addition to these detention installations, which were officially designated as concentration camps, there were also hard-labor and "reeducation" camps, run by the Sicherheitspolizei (Security Police; Sipo), the Ministry of Justice, and even private enterprises. Late in 1941 CHEŁMNO began operating as an extermination camp, and in the spring of 1942 the extermination camps TREBLINKA, SOBIBÓR, and BEŁŻEC were established as part of AKTION REINHARD. Auschwitz-Birkenau (Auschwitz II) and Majdanek, which were existing concentration camps, had extermination centers established within them as well. These sites became the main places in which the Jews of Europe were killed. Chełmno and the three Aktion Reinhard camps were not part of the concentration camp system, whereas Auschwitz and Majdanek were both concentration camps and extermination centers. All the prisoners who were not killed immediately upon arrival in these two camps were considered concentration camp inmates.

In June 1936 Himmler assumed the newly created position of *Reichsführer-SS und Chef der Deutschen Polizei* (Reich Leader of the SS and Chief of the German Police). Three years later, in October 1939, the criminal police (KRIMINALPOLIZEI; Kripo) and the political police (the GESTAPO, which was responsible— among other things— for making arrests and transferring concentration camp prisoners) were both incorporated into the REICHSSICHERHEITSHAUPTAMT (Reich Security Main Office; RSHA). In his capacity as chief of the German police, Himmler was able to increase the number of nonpolitical prisoners incarcerated in concentration camps, especially habitual criminals, tramps, beggars, and Gypsies, and also HOMOSEXUALS and convicted prostitutes.

In taking charge of nonpolitical prisoners in such large numbers (which reached their

The remains of the Majdanek concentration camp have been preserved as a Polish national memorial. In the photo are prisoners' three-tier wooden bunks.

height in 1937 and 1938), the SS chiefs also had economic considerations in mind. The implementation of the FOUR-YEAR PLAN, whose objective was to prepare the army and the economy for war, led to a labor shortage especially in the area of construction. For this reason the SS sought to exploit the concentration camp prisoners for military and civil construction projects, and thereby to reinforce its own standing. Camps that were established from 1937 on had a quarry or brickyard near them, where the prisoners were put to work. The SS also set up its own factories for this purpose. Beginning in the summer of 1938, and reaching a peak in the wake of the KRISTALLNACHT pogrom, Jews were interned in the camps solely because they were Jews.

The rise in the number of nonpolitical prisoners, together with the general intensification of persecution during the period of war preparations, led to a constant increase in the number of concentration camp prisoners during the second period. When the war broke out there were about 25,000 prisoners in the camps; thereafter, there was a steep rise in their number, far exceeding the camps' capacity, as a result of which congestion in them took on catastrophic proportions. At the end of 1941 the concentration camps contained some 60,000 prisoners.

In the wake of the ANSCHLUSS in March 1938, prisoners from Austria, and later from the annexed areas of Czechoslovakia, were sent to the concentration camps. Prisoners from all the occupied countries followed, although the great majority were from Poland. These were primarily political and Jewish prisoners. However, the raids against actual or presumed resistance fighters (especially in Poland) were so sweeping that all segments of the population were affected, regardless of political convictions or involvement with concrete political actions.

With the expansion of the war into the Soviet Union, the concentration camp population was swelled by Russian POWs. Most of them were soon killed in the KOMMISSARBEFEHL extermination operations, for which special installations were put up where the prisoners were shot to death. By the spring of 1942, in Buchenwald and Sachsenhausen alone, about 21,500 Soviet POWs were shot to death. In the meantime a small gas chamber had been built in Auschwitz I (the main Auschwitz camp), and experiments with ZY-KLON B gas were carried out in it. Some 600 Soviet POWs and 250 other prisoners were killed during the course of these experiments. All told, by May 1942 approximately 15,000 additional Soviet POWs had died in Auschwitz and in the SS POW camp at Lublin, having either been shot to death or perished from the intolerable conditions prevailing there.

From 1942 to 1944–1945. In the third period, concentration camp prisoners were systematically drafted for work in the armaments industry. The great losses suffered by the Germans in the fighting, especially on the eastern front, forced the Nazi leadership to draft growing numbers of Germans from the labor force into the army. Their places were mostly taken by forced labor from the occupied territories and, to a lesser degree, by concentration camp prisoners. Previously, forced labor in the concentration camps had been a method of punishment and persecution intended to humiliate the prisoners and lead to their deaths through overwork. Now, through an arrangement made by the SS with Minister of Armaments Albert SPEER, concentration camp prisoners were to be put at the disposal of state-owned and private companies that were in need of manpower for arms production. The newly created SS WIRTSCHAFTS-VERWALTUNGSHAUPT-AMT (Economic-Administrative Main Office; WVHA), especially in 1943 and 1944, established, in the vicinity of industrial plants, a large number of satellite camps, which were put under the control of the existing main camps.

Speer's reorganization of the armaments industry also led to a corresponding change in the SS structure. Its two central departments, Haushalt und Bauten (Budget and Construction) and Verwaltung und Wirtschaft (Administration and Economy) were merged into the WVHA, with Oswald POHL in charge. The concentration camp inspectorate was also taken over by this office as its Section D, headed by Richard GLÜCKS. Section D was largely independent of the WVHA and had its offices at a considerable distance from it (at Oranienburg, near Sachsenhausen).

In the third period the SS did not establish any additional central concentration camps, but a number of existing camps that hitherto had not been under the control of the concentration camp inspectorate were taken over and run as such. These included the small Niederhagen camp, whose inmates were drafted to enlarge the Wewelsburg assembly site for the SS elite; the VUGHT and PŁASZÓW camps; the KAISERWALD camp; Majdanek, which had previously been the SS POW camp in Lublin; and the BERGEN-BELSEN camp for Jewish internees. In October 1944 Dora, which had been a Buchenwald satellite camp, became an independent camp, DORA-MITTELBAU (Nordhausen). The prisoners in Dora were employed in the production of V-2 rockets.

In the meantime, the Auschwitz and Majdanek camps were integrated, in 1942, into the systematic extermination of Jews. The SS oversaw the installation of gas chambers there, and most of the Jews deported to these camps were killed on arrival, especially children, women, the old, and the weak. Entire communities of Jews were brought to Auschwitz: from the Netherlands in 1942 and 1943, from Slovakia between 1942 and 1944, from Greece in 1943, and from Hungary and various parts of Poland, Germany, France, Belgium, and other countries in 1944. In Auschwitz the Jews were sent to the new section, Birkenau, which originally had been planned to house Soviet POWs; a large area there was used for female prisoners. Only a few of the other concentration camps had gas chambers installed in them. These were used for a limited time only and on a much smaller scale than in Auschwitz and Majdanek. By far, most of the prisoners in the third period were Jews, Poles, and Soviets. A large proportion of the Soviets had first been drafted as forced foreign laborers (*see* FORCED LABOR: FREMDARBEITER). Their presence in the concentration camps was a punishment for violating the exceptionally harsh rules that were applied to the *Ostarbeiter* (workers from the east). Next, by number, were the French, the Italians (after Italy's surrender), and the Yugoslavs. In the fall of 1944, as the war fronts were drawing near, the camps were gradually closed and the prisoners sent on long DEATH MARCHES to other camps still in existence.

Conditions. Living conditions in the concentration camps varied greatly among the camps and from one period to another. In the first period, prisoners were rarely incarcerated longer than a year, and the housing, food, and working conditions were tolerable, compared to the later years. The deaths that occurred were usually the result of deliberate maltreatment, or of SS and SA men shooting to death prisoners against whom they had a personal grudge.

In the second period the mortality rate rose as a result of maltreatment, the kinds of work the prisoners were assigned, the more primitive working conditions that prevailed, and the physical exertion called for in the quarries, as well as undernourishment and overcrowding in the barracks. Most of the victims were Poles, Russians, and Jews, but the so-called Spanish fighters—men who had fought on the republican side in the Spanish Civil War—also had only a very slight chance of surviving between 1940 and 1942, especially in Mauthausen. Up to the outbreak of the war in September 1939 the best conditions (relatively) were to be found in Dachau; the worst in Mauthausen. Between October 27, 1939, and February 18, 1940, Dachau was cleared of prisoners and served as a training camp for the Waffen-SS. After that it took in chiefly prisoners from other camps who were in poor physical condition, and as a result the mortality rate rose rapidly there too.

In 1943 living conditions for most concentration camp prisoners improved slightly, notwithstanding the large new intake, and the differences among the camps were less pronounced. The demands of the armaments industry and the wish to exploit the labor potential of the prisoners more rationally forced the SS, and the companies involved, to improve their treatment of the prisoners and provide them with adequate nourishment. Such improvement, however, applied only to places where the prisoners' work required technical knowledge and skill; in the construction projects—of which there were many—the general decrease in the mortality rate was not felt. In Auschwitz and Majdanek, the decrease did not apply to every sector: at Auschwitz-Birkenau, which contained the Jewish prisoners, the mortality rate remained at an extremely high level, whereas in the Auschwitz camp as a whole it decreased from 15 percent in March 1943 to 3 percent in August. In the liquidation phase of the camps, however, the rate rose again, to unbelievable heights.

The total number of people who perished in the concentration camps, not including those sent directly to extermination centers, can only be guessed at. Existing documentation accounts for more than 450,000, but the real number may be assumed to have been from 700,000 to 800,000. Eugen Kogon's estimate in *The Theory and Practice of Hell* of 1.2 million seems too high. On the other hand, his figure for the total number of concentration camp prisoners, 1.6 million, appears reliable. As far as is known, the highest total number of prisoners held at any given time was 714,211, the figure registered by the SS in January 1945.

Camp Routine. The prisoners had little choice in their daily actions. The SS dictated the day's course of events, down to the smallest detail. Violations of orders in the camp were severely punished—by flogging, solitary confinement, withholding food rations, and so forth. Some prisoners were assigned positions supervising their fellow inmates and working in the camp administration, as room, block, and camp "elders" and as KAPOs, who were in charge of work crews. Prisoners also worked in the camp kitchen, in the hospital, and in the office. The way these prisoners carried out their jobs was of great importance for the prison population as a whole. Some were just as brutal as the SS and exploited their positions for their own benefit only. Others made efforts to mitigate the SS terror regime and to protect prisoners who were in danger. The role played by functionaries among the prisoners is evaluated in widely divergent ways in Holocaust memoirs, and depends to a considerable degree on the personal experiences of the author.

The prisoners were categorized by the SS according to their national origin and the grounds for which they had been put into the concentration camps. Each category had its own conditions of imprisonment, which in turn affected the chances of survival. The different categories were identified by the color of the badges worn by the prisoners on their clothes. The prisoners—especially the "politicals" (the "reds") and the criminals (the "greens")—competed with one another for the assignments that carried influence. As a

Survivors of the Flossenbürg concentration camp after their liberation by the American army on April 23, 1945.

rule, German prisoners held the top posts; in Auschwitz, the Polish prisoners also played an important role. Soviet prisoners and Jews (irrespective of their nationality) had very little chance of obtaining any appointment. The criteria applied by the SS to the different categories were determined by its racist ideology.

Composition of Prisoners. In the first period the composition of the prison population was relatively homogeneous; most were anti-Nazis. It was therefore much easier for prisoners at that time to establish solidarity among themselves than in the following years. In the second period, the struggle for survival encouraged the emergence of cliques, who cheated and fought one another in efforts to obtain a share of the little food and inadequate accommodation available. On the other hand, there were also illegal groups of prisoners who organized mutual help; the first to do so were the German Communists in the camps. The influence exercised by these illegal groups increased in the third period, during which living conditions

in the camps underwent temporary improvement. They managed to smuggle their members into important assignments and into the camp administration. Other groups, especially those made up of Soviet POWs, engaged in sabotage in the arms factories. In some camps, underground "international" prisoners' committees were set up, which made it their task to prepare for their self-liberation when the front line came closer.

The fate of the prisoners depended to a large extent on their practical skills, ideological views, and past social ties. Most of the newly arrived prisoners had to fend for themselves. From the SS they could expect harsh punishment and maltreatment if they committed an error. Only in rare instances was it possible for the other prisoners to help the new arrivals, or at least to sympathize with them. There was also a certain understandable tension between newcomers and old-timers familiar with the conditions, who had undergone a long period of adaptation and survival to attain a certain status in the camp.

For the new prisoner the first shock was usually his (or her) total humiliation as a human being: he had to relinquish all personal possessions, his hair was shorn, and he was tattooed with an identification number. This, added to the strenuous physical labor, the terrible living conditions, and the brutality of those in charge, made the danger to his life greatest in the first few months, when many perished. If, on the other hand, the prisoner had skills that could be put to practical use and was therefore attached to a work gang with a relatively easy assignment, or if he belonged to a social or ideological group that kept together in the camp (such as the Communists, JEHOVAH'S WITNESSES, or the conservative national resistance groups among the Polish prisoners), he had a chance of finding protection, escaping harassment, and becoming acquainted with appropriate conduct in the camp.

Some camps, such as Auschwitz-Birkenau and Stutthof, contained separate sections for women, and Ravensbrück was entirely a women's camp. The humiliation, loss of personal identity, absence of the most elementary sanitary conditions and of any privacy, and the cutting off of their hair had an especially damaging effect on the women prisoners, and led to a high rate of collapse and death among them. Sometimes there were children and youth in the camps. Their distress was especially intense, but often the hardest and most veteran prisoners took pity on them and tried to protect them.

Jews in the Camps. There were also tensions between the different ethnic groups, with Jews at the bottom of the ladder. During the first period the Jews were a relatively small group in the camps. In Dachau, for example, only 10 percent of the prisoners were Jews. Most of them belonged to the outlawed organizations of the labor movement or had been taken into "protective custody" because of their political activities. This situation changed in the second period, and as a result of the *Razzien* against "asocial" elements ordered by Himmler in 1936, as many as one-third of the persons taken to the camps were Jews. This was one of a series of intensified anti-Jewish measures introduced that year, resulting in a rapid deterioration of the situation of the Jews in Germany. Be-

ginning with Dachau, the number of Jews in the concentration camps rose to between 15 percent and 20 percent of the camp population. A new height was reached in the wake of the November 9, 1938, *Kristallnacht* pogrom, when within a few days thirty-six thousand Jews were detained in the Reich (including Austria). Of these, eleven thousand were taken to Dachau, between ten thousand and twelve thousand to Buchenwald, and about six thousand to Sachsenhausen, creating catastrophic congestion in these camps. No single group underwent such sufferings in the period before the war as did the Jews on that occasion.

From the very beginning, the treatment meted out to Jews was worse than that given other prisoners. As early as 1933, the Jewish share in the prisoners' mortality rate at Dachau was disproportionately large. In the second period, conditions in the camps for Jewish prisoners deteriorated drastically. Following the mass influx of Jews in November 1938, the overall mortality in all the concentration camps multiplied rapidly, and most of the victims were Jews. The SS exploited the terrible conditions in the camps to force the Jews to emigrate from Germany. As a rule, at that time any Jewish prisoner who could produce an emigration visa was set free, and by the spring of 1939 most of the Jews who had been brought to the camps in November 1938 had been released.

Once the war broke out, Jews taken to concentration camps had little chance of survival. The groups of Polish Jews imprisoned in Buchenwald and in Mauthausen were nearly all annihilated within a few months. In the fall of 1941, when a medical commission carried out a selection of certain categories of prisoners in the camps, weeding out the feeble, the sick, and the "politicals" (whom the SS particularly disliked) to send them to gas chambers under the EUTHANASIA PROGRAM, the percentage of Jewish prisoners among those selected was extremely high. In the conditions prevailing during the second period, Jewish prisoners were rarely able to form groups of their own. Many, especially the German Jews, had the word *Jude* stamped on their clothes by the SS. For the individual Jewish prisoner this mark of identification had a variety of social and ideological meanings: some of the Jews among the prisoners were Social Democrats or Communists who were divorced from Jewish religious practice and faith; others had been close to traditional right-wing parties and were rooted in national bourgeois ideology; still others were strictly Orthodox Jews.

Even before the arrival of the Polish Jews, the German Jewish prisoners had a varied social background. This was now reinforced by the "national" differences between the two communities, the Polish and the German. At first the strongest bond between them was the persecution from which they all suffered. The perilous conditions of life and the careful watch kept by the SS over the Jewish prisoners during the second period as a rule precluded the emergence among the Jews of the kind of group cooperation and core associations that the "politicals" and the "criminals" had managed to create. Nevertheless, in some of the concentration camps, and also in Auschwitz, illegal Jewish groups engaged in mutual assistance and in activities of a political nature. Even among the SONDERKOMMANDO prisoners in Birkenau, who were part of the concentration camp but worked in the extermination center, an underground group was organized, and in October 1944 a revolt broke out in the camp.

In the third period, the deportation of the Jews from the Reich to ghettos and camps in the east also had its consequences for the Jews in the concentration camps in Germany. An order issued by the WVHA on October 5, 1942, called for all the concentration camps on the soil of the Reich to be made *judenfrei* ("free of Jews"). The Jewish prisoners were deported mostly to Auschwitz and Lublin (Majdanek), where they suffered the same fate as the other Jews sent to those camps. It was not until 1944 that some of Hungary's deported Jews, instead of being sent to extermination camps, were put on a march to the Reich for forced labor there. The majority of them were caught up in the chaos of the evacuation marches.

Once liberated, many former prisoners were unable to free themselves from the anguish of their experience in the concentration camps. Months, and often years later, they still felt the detrimental effects on their mental and physical health, which in some cases was irreparably damaged. Among the symptoms were a frequent inability to establish close contact with others, to hold a regular job, or to sustain a marital and family relationship, in addition to sleep disorders, anxiety attacks, body tremors, and gastritis. Some of the more typical of these symptoms have been described in the medical literature as the "concentration camp syndrome," although its precise manifestations and frequency of occurrence remain in dispute.

Effects of the Camps. Research on the effects of imprisonment in concentration camps—some of it based on personal experience—has, for the most part, taken the form of psychoanalytical studies. These seek to analyze the behavior of concentration camp inmates and to explain such phenomena as the formation of groups and the rivalry among them, emotional insensitivity, and the adoption of patterns of behavior that might aid in survival. Best known is *The Informed Heart*, by Bruno Bettelheim, who maintains that the prisoners adopted the standards of the SS, or at least had to build up a kind of schizophrenic conscience in themselves. From the beginning, however, there were also studies based on the sociological method (Kogon), which were later expanded by behavioral studies. While the rules laid down by the SS in the camps had to be observed by the prisoners to ensure their survival, there always existed groups of prisoners who adhered to their own set of standards and behaved accordingly. They often had to restrict such behavior to underground and "illegal" activities, with the result that not all their fellow prisoners were aware that such standards of behavior did indeed exist in the camps.

[See also Italy: Concentration Camps; Muselmann; Survivors, Psychology of; see in addition under Camps.]

BIBLIOGRAPHY

Bettelheim, B. *The Informed Heart: The Human Condition in Modern Mass Society.* London, 1961.

Des Pres, T. *The Survivor: An Anatomy of Life in the Death Camps.* New York, 1976.

Gutman, Y., and A. Saf, eds. *The Nazi Concentration Camps: Structure and Aims; The Image of the Prisoner; The Jews in the Camps.* Proceedings of the Fourth Yad Vashem International Historical Conference. Jerusalem, 1984.

International Tracing Service. Records Branch. *Catalogue of Camps and Prisons in Germany and German-occupied Territories, September 1939–May 1945.* 2 vols. Arolsen, West Germany, 1949–1950. Supplement, 1951.

Kogon, E. *The Theory and Practice of Hell: The German Concentration Camps and the System behind Them.* New York, 1950.

Pawelczynska, A. *Values and Violence in Auschwitz: A Sociological Analysis.* Berkeley, 1979.

Pingel, F. "The Concentration Camps as Part of the National-Socialist System of Domination." In *The Nazi Concentration Camps: Structure and Aims; The Image of the Prisoner; The Jews in the Camps.* Proceedings of the Fourth Yad Vashem International Historical Conference, edited by Y. Gutman and A. Saf, pp. 3–18. Jerusalem, 1984.

Rousset, D. *The Other Kingdom.* New York, 1947.

Segev, T. *Soldiers of Evil: The Commandants of the Nazi Concentration Camps.* New York, 1987.

FALK PINGEL

CONFERENCES. *See* Bermuda Conference; Evian Conference; Munich Conference; Wannsee Conference.

CONFISCATION. *See under* Expropriation.

CONSEIL REPRÉSENTATIF DES JUIFS DE FRANCE (Representative Council of French Jews; CRIF), umbrella organization of French Jewish societies, founded in January 1944. CRIF's foundation ended the long-standing divisions in FRANCE between French-born and immigrant Jewish associations, which were motivated by two factors: the fate of the remaining Jews, and postwar considerations. Joseph Fisher (later Ariel), president of the Zionist Federation, was instrumental in its establishment. From mid-1943 Fisher pursued a policy of unification, and by August 1943 he had succeeded in uniting the immigrant organizations into the Comité Général de Défense (CGD). Fisher pursued, however, a much broader objective: the unification of the immigrant organizations and the CONSIS-

TOIRE CENTRAL DES ISRAÉLITES DE FRANCE (CC), the representatives of French Judaism. The divisions by then were more superficial than real; previous political obstacles, the evaluation of Vichy's policy, and the CC's perception of its role, which had hindered French Jewry's unity, had been overcome.

The CC and the CGD entered into negotiations in December 1943, and by early 1944 the broad principles of the CRIF were accepted. Shortly thereafter, debates developed concerning its charter. They ranged over three issues: the closure of the UNION GÉNÉRALE DES ISRAÉLITES DE FRANCE (General Council of French Jews; UGIF); resistance; and postwar policy on the establishment of a Jewish national home in Palestine. Questions of resistance and the UGIF were partly resolved. Divergences developed over the issue of Palestine: Communists and Bundists demanded a binational home, and the CC was concerned about the implications of too firm a commitment. A general consensus, however, overrode the differences. The CRIF was formed, with Léon MEISS as president. At liberation, it represented all the political tendencies and organizations, and it was able to act on behalf of a united community and to present the Jewish case to the provisional government.

BIBLIOGRAPHY

Adler, J. *The Jews of Paris and the Final Solution: Communal Response and International Conflicts, 1940–1944.* Oxford, 1987.

Conseil Représentatif des Juifs de France. *C.R.I.F.: Vingt-cinq années d'activités, 1944–1969.* Paris, 1970.

JACQUES ADLER

CONSISTOIRE CENTRAL DES ISRAÉLITES DE FRANCE (Central Consistory of French Jews), the hierarchical religious organization of French Jewry, established in 1808. During the 1930s, in the face of rising antisemitism, the Consistoire cautioned against overt public demonstrations and tried to curb the political activism of immigrant Jews. With the fall of FRANCE, the Consistoire's leadership relocated from Paris to Lyons, in the unoccupied zone.

Slow in responding to the catastrophe befalling French Jewry, the Consistoire began to function under the new circumstances in the spring of 1941 under the presidency of Jacques HELBRONNER, a sixty-eight-year old member of the Conseil d'Etat (Council of State). Following closely the Consistoire's traditional course of diplomacy, Helbronner advised the Jewish community to observe the anti-Jewish restrictions and thus to maintain the honor of French Jewry. On the community's behalf, the Consistoire filed numerous solemn protests against the Vichy racial legislation, and Helbronner intervened with Marshal Philippe PÉTAIN on many occasions. In this vein, the Consistoire led the campaign against the creation of the UNION GÉNÉRALE DES ISRAÉLITES DE FRANCE (UGIF) and tried to uphold its own unique position in French Jewry. Not disbanded by the Vichy law establishing the UGIF, the Consistoire remained responsible for Jewish religious life, maintaining open synagogues until the end of the war and involving itself in welfare projects through the work of the Aumônerie Générale Israélite (Jewish Chaplaincy) and the Chief Rabbi's Fund. As the historical representative of French Jewry, the Consistoire continued to advocate moderation even after the deportations of the summer of 1942, although it registered a most vehement protest to Vichy.

After the German occupation of the south in November 1942 and the mass deportations from Marseilles in January 1943, the Consistoire withdrew its opposition to the UGIF, and on several occasions they jointly determined Jewish responses. However, a major change in the Consistoire's orientation ensued only after Helbronner was deported in October 1943, during the all-out effort of the SS to round up French Jews. Under the leadership of Helbronner's successor, Léon MEISS, the Consistoire undertook discussions with all elements of the community, including the Communist factions, in an effort to establish a united Jewish position against the renewed German drive. Resistance groups and official representatives of established Judaism eventually set up the CONSEIL REPRÉSENTATIF DES JUIFS DE FRANCE, an all-encompassing Jewish organization that was to direct French Jewry from early 1944 until the liberation of France. At the head of this unique body was the president of the Consistoire, Léon Meiss.

BIBLIOGRAPHY

Adler, J. *The Jews of Paris and the Final Solution.* New York, 1987.

Cohen, R. I. *The Burden of Conscience: French Jewish Leadership during the Holocaust.* Bloomington, 1987.

Cohen, R. I. "French Jewry's Dilemma on the Orientation of Its Leadership (From Polemics to Conciliation: 1942–1944)." *Yad Vashem Studies* 14 (1981): 167–204.

Szajkowski, Z. "The French Central Jewish Consistory during the Second World War." *Yad Vashem Studies* 3 (1959): 187–202.

RICHARD COHEN

CORFU, northernmost Greek island in the Ionian Sea. Massive emigration from Corfu beginning after 1891 had reduced its Jewish population from five thousand to two thousand. Many of the older inhabitants spoke Italian, attesting to the long cultural and occasional political influence of Italy. The Italians occupied the island in April 1941, but after the Italian surrender to the Allies on September 8, 1943, the Germans conquered the island from its Italian garrison. The Jewish quarter was heavily bombed in mid-September and several Jews were killed.

Corfu's Jews had been convinced that the Germans would not cross from occupied Epiros to their island. They knew of German antisemitism, but, ignorant of the Holocaust, they did not feel threatened, and ignored warnings to flee given by the Italians, whose occupation had been relatively mild. The Germans quickly closed the Jewish school and instituted measures to keep the Jewish population under their control.

The commander of Corfu, Karl JÄGER, reported to his headquarters in Ioannina that the deportation of the Jews was not feasible under the circumstances, citing logistic problems, the presence of the Red Cross, and the potential intervention of the local population. On June 9, 1944, 1,795 Jews were arrested by German military police units from Ioannina and by local Greek police, assisted by the Jews Ino Recanati and Joseph Recanati of Athens, and were interned in the old fortress. At least 30 Jews escaped and were hidden by their Christian neighbors or reached Epirus, where they joined the partisans or were protected by them. After a tortuous seven-day journey to Athens, during which several young men escaped, later to fight with the resistance, the Jews were transported to AUSCHWITZ, where two-thirds were killed on arrival (June 30, 1944); only some 200 returned to Corfu. During the deportations, much of the Greek population showed considerable sympathy, especially in Lefkas; others, however, engaged in looting after Jewish shops and homes were systematically stripped by the Germans.

BIBLIOGRAPHY

Gilbert, M. *The Holocaust.* New York, 1985. See pages 698–699.

STEVEN B. BOWMAN

COUNCIL FOR AID TO JEWS. *See* Zegota.

COUNCIL FOR GERMAN JEWRY (CFGJ), British Jewish organization established in 1936 with the goal of aiding German Jews to leave GERMANY in coordinated emigration. Organizationally, the CFGJ succeeded and absorbed the Central British Fund for German Jewry (CBF), established in May 1933, and occupied the same premises in Woburn House, in London. Many of the CBF's officers became officers of the council as well, and the CBF became the council's financial arm.

In reaction to the NUREMBERG LAWS of September 1935, British Jewish leaders held a number of meetings at the Rothschild home at New Court, London. Through long discussions and consultations with German Jewish leaders, a consensus was reached between Zionists and non-Zionists in December 1935 in the form of an outline for an emigration plan. A delegation consisting of Sir Herbert Samuel, Lord Bearsted, and Simon Marks traveled to the United States in January 1936 with the aim of establishing a partnership with American Jewry in order to raise $15 million to assist in the emigration of 100,000 German Jews aged seventeen to thirty-five. Half of the emigrants would settle in Palestine, and the other half in other countries around the world. It was hoped that the young emigrants would quickly succeed in finding employment and would then bring their families out of Germany. In addition, it was hoped that another 100,000 German Jews would emigrate without assistance, thereby ensuring the emigration of a large part of German Jewry in a brief time.

Personal and organizational differences nearly prevented the formation of a joint council. American Zionist and non-Zionist leaders distrusted each other, and each organization was reluctant to yield any of its independence to the proposed umbrella group. The American Jewish organizations did not wish to submit their allocations of funds to British scrutiny.

The council's executive board held its first meeting in London on March 15, 1936, but the two major American groups, the JOINT DISTRIBUTION COMMITTEE and the United Palestine Appeal, joined formally only in August. The council never achieved the stature its British founders sought, since it lacked the power to make independent decisions. The coordination achieved succeeded in funding numerous vocational-training programs in Germany and elsewhere, as well as in assisting approximately 100,000 Jews to emigrate by the outbreak of World War II. More than $15 million was raised in this period, but events quickly overtook the council's plans and work, leaving the self-help aspect of the plan largely unrealized. British immigration policies in Palestine, emigration obstacles in Germany, and the growing impoverishment of German Jewry combined to limit severely the council's success.

The ANSCHLUSS of Austria, creating more potential refugees, and the heightened persecution of German Jewry in 1938 (*see* KRISTALLNACHT), threw the council's emigration plan into a shambles. Organized and planned emigration now became subsidized flight. With the outbreak of World War II, the council was forced to limit its activities to refugees in Britain, and its name was changed accordingly, to the Central Council for Jewish Refugees. Following the war, the needs of DISPLACED PERSONS and REFUGEES brought another reorganization and name change, to the Central British Fund for Relief and Rehabilitation. This organization still exists at Woburn House.

[See also Great Britain.]

BIBLIOGRAPHY

Bauer, Y. My Brother's Keeper: A History of the American Joint Distribution Committee, 1929–1939. Philadelphia, 1974. See pages 151–160.
Bentwich, N. They Sought Refuge: An Account of British Jewry's Work for Victims of Nazi Oppression. London, 1956.
Stiebel, J. "The Central British Fund for World Jewish Relief." Transactions of the Jewish Society of England 27 (1978/80): 60–61.

DAVID SILBERKLANG

CRACOW. See Kraków.

CRIF. See Conseil Représentatif des Juifs de France.

CRIMES AGAINST HUMANITY. Article 6 of the charter of the International Military Tribunal (IMT), which was to conduct the NUREMBERG TRIAL, empowered the IMT to try the major war criminals of the European Axis countries for three categories of crimes: crimes against peace, war crimes, and crimes against humanity.

Among the crimes defined as war crimes were violations of the laws or customs of war, such as murder, ill-treatment, deportation, forced labor, or wanton destruction not justified by military necessity. The IMT found that such acts, including also ill-treatment of civilian populations and prisoners of war, had been committed by the Führer and his cohorts in total disregard of the fundamental principles of international law, and had been based instead on cold-blooded, criminal considerations. The IMT therefore decided to deal with the entire category of war crimes in great detail and to determine the individual defendants' guilt for such crimes. Included in the tribunal's deliberations were acts of murder and ill-treatment of prisoners of war and civilian populations, especially the persecution of Jews.

Such acts of persecution were also defined as crimes against humanity, even if they were committed before the war but were connected to preparations for the war. Article 6(c) of the IMT charter defines crimes against humanity as "murder, extermination, enslavement, deportation, and other inhumane acts committed against any civilian population, before or during the war; or persecution on political, racial, or religious grounds in execution of or in connection with any crime within the jurisdiction of the tribunal, whether or not in violation of the domestic law of the country where perpetrated." It follows from this that the IMT was empowered to try crimes against humanity only if they were perpetrated in the execution of or in connection with war crimes or crimes against peace. Some of the acts defined as war crimes—such as murder, ill-treatment, and deportation—were also defined as crimes against humanity. These acts, however, were deemed war crimes only when they were a violation of the laws and customs of war, affecting the rights of fighting forces and the civilian population in occupied territory or in the course of warlike actions. Crimes against humanity, on the other hand, were defined as applying to acts against any civilian population—including the population of the country that commits the acts, and commits them on its own soil—at any time, in times of peace as well as in times of war. The latter feature—application to acts committed both in times of peace and times of war—also appears in the definition of crimes against peace, a category that includes not only the initiation and conduct of war, but also acts committed in times of peace, such as planning and preparation of aggression.

A corollary of this is that it is neither the time in which the act is committed nor the act itself that constitutes the exclusive characteristic of a crime against humanity and sets it apart from the other crimes defined in the IMT charter. What distinguishes crimes against humanity from other crimes are the extraordinary brutality and diversity of means that the Nazis employed to commit these crimes, the unprecedented policy of persecution and extermination on which they were based, and the fact that while initially they were related to a policy of aggression, they exceeded by far the definition of war crimes in the traditional sense. Among the victims of the Nazi crimes against humanity were populations for which the laws and customs of war provide no protection—such as nationals of neutral countries, stateless persons, nationals of countries that were partners in the Axis, and, of course, nationals of Germany itself. Above all, most of the victims of the Nazi crimes against humanity were Jews, who, prior to the Nuremberg Trial, were not deemed to have protection based on international law.

There is some substance to the view that the introduction of the category of crimes against humanity was designed to serve as a support to the categories of war crimes and crimes against peace, or to cover a side effect related to these two categories. Crimes against humanity related to acts committed in times of peace as well, in the framework of planning and preparation for war, and on the territory of the aggressor or any other territory (not necessarily Nazi-occupied areas), against the aggressors' own nationals, the nationals of countries that were not at war with Germany, or stateless persons. Since these acts were related to preparations for war, the persons responsible for them could not be convicted under the laws and customs of war, which deal with situations involving actual warfare. The separate category of crimes against humanity also seeks to take into account another element: while the crimes to which it refers affect various populations —groups that were persecuted on national, racial, and religious grounds—the crimes all have in common the element of "inhumanity": the cruel methods that were employed, and the unprecedented purpose of mass extermination of victims simply for belonging to a certain group (or being classified, by the criminals, as belonging to that group), without the victims' having committed any offense whatsoever.

Every crime is an offense not only against the victim, but also against the established

order of the country in which it takes place—the country as a social organization that includes all its citizens, irrespective of color, political views, and origin. Similarly, every international crime, especially when it is a crime against humanity, is an attack on the international community as a whole, threatening the safeguards of its peace, and indeed its very existence. Nevertheless, what distinguishes crimes against humanity from the other categories of crimes is their "inhumanity," rather than the injury they inflict upon "humanity" as a worldwide community; this was why they were designated as crimes against "humanity" in the abstract sense of the term. However, acts defined as crimes against peace or war crimes can also be regarded as crimes against humanity, since the planning and carrying out of aggression prepares the conditions for inhumane offenses against human rights.

The element of humanity and the condemnation of and punishment for inhumane acts are not recent innovations in international law, the dictates of human conscience having long been regarded as one of international law's sources. Thus, the Petersburg Declaration of 1868 stated that the dictates of humanity must take precedence over the needs of war; and the fourth Hague Convention (1907) specified that in situations not specifically provided for in the convention, the civilian population and the fighting forces would also be protected by the principles of humanity and the dictates of society's conscience. This principle has since been reconfirmed time and again in various international treaties and conventions, such as the 1949 Geneva Convention and the 1977 Supplementary Protocols.

The IMT extended this principle to apply also to criminal acts that are not war crimes, in order to provide protection to every civilian population and to every individual, irrespective of his nationality and his country's policy and laws. Evidently, the principle is valid under all circumstances and takes precedence over every national law and every bilateral or multilateral international agreement; it is a universal and cogent principle, which is not subject to challenge and cannot be deviated from by unilateral decision; it can be changed or replaced only by a humanitarian principle that is of an even higher order (as stated in the 1969 Vienna Convention on Treaties). This means that, in formal terms, the definition of inhumane acts as being criminal in nature does not depend on the legal system or established policy of the country in which such acts occur. In this respect, too, crimes against humanity are *sui generis*, different from other criminal acts.

The criminal nature of crimes against humanity is far worse and of a totally different order than that of any other criminal act defined as such by the criminal codes of all civilized nations. This criminal practice was demonstrated in its most radical form by the Nazi policy and acts of brutal mass murder and extermination of entire peoples and population groups (*see* GENOCIDE). The unique character of a crime against humanity can also be recognized in other acts that in the European continental system of law have long been classified as inherently criminal (*malum per se*), and that in Soviet legal terminology constitute a threat to society and public order.

These aspects of crimes against humanity and crimes against peace are disregarded by those who have challenged the justice and the very nature of the Nuremberg Trial because it included these categories in the stated principles upon which it based the indictment. Such acts, so their argument goes, were political acts, for which those who committed them cannot be held accountable, as heads of sovereign entities who were not subject to any other entity or to any law other than a law declared as valid by their own state. It is true that in a certain respect the crimes defined by the IMT charter are of a political character, since their planning, preparation, and execution were possible only in the framework of operations, guidelines, initiatives, and decrees emanating from and authorized by the political administration of a state. This, however, is no reason to treat the persons responsible for these crimes as political criminals in the accepted sense of that term, since their acts were linked to the theory of RACISM and to other inhumane concepts that have no precedent in the annals of mankind. Thus it was declared, in legal theory and practice, that such criminals may be tried by any country that does not want to, or has no reason to, extradite them for trial in other countries or by international tribunals.

Furthermore, their status is like that of other categories of criminals to whom the principle of universal jurisdiction and punishment applies. Nor may these criminals seek to justify their acts by claiming that they were performing their official duties or acting on orders from their superiors. One restriction that the IMT charter did impose was that in order for crimes against humanity to be tried, they had to be related to war crimes or crimes against peace, either as side effects of such crimes or in support of them.

Many legal experts and human-rights activists seek to abolish this restrictive condition in the codification of international criminal law. They point out that while this condition applied to those tried at the Nuremberg Trial and the Tokyo trial of major Japanese war criminals, it should not be applicable to other criminals charged with crimes against humanity, and consequently their prosecution should not be linked to war crimes or crimes against peace. Indeed, such a link is conspicuous by its absence in Allied Control Council Law No. 10, of December 20, 1945, and in the laws of other countries, among them Israel's Nazis and Nazi Collaborators (Punishment) Law 5710-1950.

It is true that in most of the trials the Allies held in their zones of occupation in Germany, the judges preferred to follow the IMT precedent and held defendants responsible for crimes against humanity only when the acts were committed in the preparation of aggression or in violation of the laws and customs of war. This was so in the SUBSEQUENT NUREMBERG PROCEEDINGS, held by the Americans, in which the Nuremberg Military Tribunals tried Nazi judges, industrialists, and Einsatzgruppen personnel, among others. Those who call for the complete separation of the concept of crimes against humanity from war crimes and crimes against peace do so in order to endow this concept with the status of a human-rights principle that would protect all human beings at all times and under all conditions, completely independent of warlike events.

[*See also* Trials of War Criminals.]

BIBLIOGRAPHY

Falk, R. A., B. Kolko, and R. J. Lifton. *Crimes of War: A Legal, Political, Documentary, and Psychological Inquiry into the Responsibility of Leaders, Citizens, and Soldiers for Criminal Acts of War.* New York, 1971.

Goldstein, A. "Crimes against Humanity: Some Jewish Aspects." *Jewish Yearbook of International Law* 1 (1948): 206–225.

Schwelb, E. "Crimes against Humanity." *British Yearbook of International Law* 23 (1946): 178–228.

MARIAN MUSHKAT

CROATIA (Nezavisna Država Hrvatska, or Independent State of Croatia; NDH), puppet state in YUGOSLAVIA, established during World War II, that was in existence from April 1941 to May 1945. Its area—which underwent many changes owing to annexations—consisted of what are today the Federative Republic of Croatia and the Federative Republic of Bosnia and Herzegovina, a total of approximately 38,600 square miles (100,000 sq km). Its capital was Zagreb; it had a population of 6.3 million, of whom 3.3 million were Catholic Croats, 1.9 million Orthodox Serbs, 700,000 Muslim Croats, 170,000 Germans, 75,000 Hungarians, 40,000 Jews, 30,000 Gypsies, and 100,000 members of other minorities.

Serbian Minority. Croatia was set up by the Germans and the Italians on April 10, 1941, as part of their plan for the dismemberment of Yugoslavia. Ante PAVELIĆ, leader of the secessionist USTAŠA movement, was made head of state. Shortly after taking control, the Ustaša, with the support of many Croatians, embarked upon what it called "the purge of Croatia from foreign elements," which had as its main purpose the elimination of the Serbian minority. In a brutal terror campaign, more than half a million Serbs were killed, a quarter-million expelled, and two hundred thousand forced to convert to Catholicism. The Ustaša regime in Croatia, and particularly this drive in the summer of 1941 to exterminate and dispossess the Serbs, was one of the most horrendous episodes of World War II. The murder methods applied by the Ustaša were extraordinarily primitive and sadistic: thousands were hurled from mountaintops, others were beaten to death or had their throats cut, entire villages were burned down, women raped, people sent on death marches in the middle of winter, and still others starved to death.

Jews. The Jews of Croatia lived mainly in the larger cities: Zagreb (11,000), Sarajevo (10,000), Osijek (3,000), and Bjelovar (3,000). Sixty percent are estimated to have been Ashkenazim and the rest Sephardim. Most of the Jews belonged to the middle class; they were civil servants, merchants, and professionals such as doctors and lawyers. Zionists controlled the communities. Croatian Jewry carried on a wide range of activities; it had its own school network, weekly newspaper, welfare institutions, and youth movements. The NDH regime categorized the Jews as one of the "foreign elements" that had to be purged, and the Ustaša's German patrons encouraged it in its drive against the Jews. In pursuing this course, the Ustaša was motivated by desires to please the Germans and to acquire the Jews' property, rather than by ideological antisemitism. Three government departments were involved in Jewish affairs. The Ministry of the Interior, with Andrija Artuković as minister, dealt with anti-Jewish legislation; the security police (Ustaška Nadzorna Služba), under Eugen Dido Kvaternik, arrested, imprisoned, and murdered Jews, and ran the concentration camps; and the Ministry of Finance, under Vladimir Kosak, was charged with the depredation of Jewish property.

Anti-Jewish legislation. A few days after taking control, the Ustaša enacted anti-Jewish legislation, most of it based on the precedents set in the Third Reich, the GENERALGOUVERNEMENT, and SLOVAKIA. It included racial statutes on the model of the NUREMBERG LAWS, which defined who was a Jew and stripped the Jews of their civil rights. But there was an innovation in these laws—a paragraph empowering the head of state to bestow the title of "Honorary Aryan"—which provided an opportunity for corrupt practices. Most of the legislation dealt with economic affairs: Aryan trustees

CROATIA, 1941 to 1945

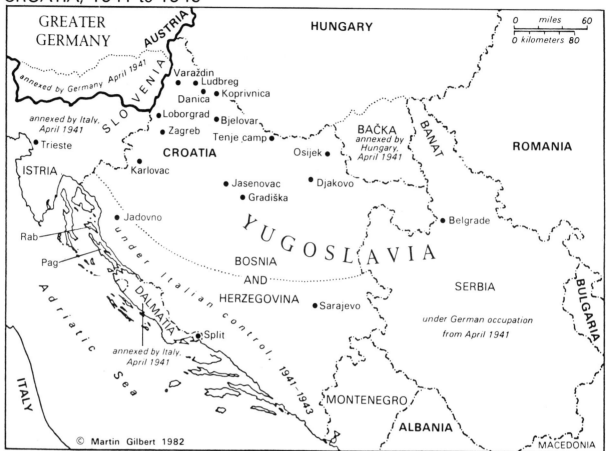

were appointed to take over Jewish businesses; Jewish factories, enterprises, and real property were "nationalized"; Jewish civil servants were dismissed; and Jewish professionals (lawyers, doctors, veterinarians, and so on) were prohibited from dealing with non-Jewish clients. Collective fines, which had to be paid in gold or its equivalent, were imposed on the Jewish communities. Overnight, a pseudolegal expropriation drive was launched, which before long turned into an unbridled countrywide campaign of plunder and pillage in which everyone who stood to profit took part—trade unions, youth organizations, sports clubs, the armed forces, and government officials of all ranks. Ordinary citizens also took part in this campaign wherever they could; indeed, the share of "private" elements in the plunder was enormous—at least half of the property of which the Jews were robbed apparently never reached the state treasury but remained in the hands of individual Croatians.

According to an estimate by the Ministry of Finance published in 1944, the value of the Jewish property it acquired was 25 billion dinars ($50 million, according to the prewar rate of exchange). Presenting the state budget for the 1942–1943 fiscal year, the minister of finance, Vladimir Kosak, said that the deficit would be covered by proceeds from the sale of Jewish property.

In the first few months of Ustaša rule, various other decrees were passed, mostly by local authorities, designed to restrict the Jews' freedom of movement and the places where they could live, and thereby to isolate them from the rest of the population. In May 1941 an order was announced under which the Jews had to wear the yellow Jewish BADGE with the letter Ž (from Židov, "Jew") prominently displayed on it.

Roundup, incarceration, and murder. The first arrests made among the Jews were part of a general preventive measure to forestall the rise of any anti-government organiza-

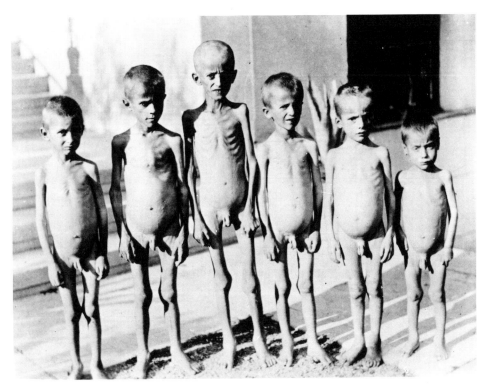

Children liberated from a Croatian concentration camp.

tions. It affected the active members of left-wing parties, Serbian parties, democrats, and left-wing intellectuals. Included in that wave of arrests were some one hundred Jewish youngsters who had been active in Zionist youth movements in Zagreb, as well as the Jewish lawyers in that city; both groups were taken to concentration camps that had been established in the country, where most of them were killed. Following the German invasion of the Soviet Union in June 1941, the incidence of sabotage acts in Croatia rose sharply and the situation of the Jews deteriorated further, as acts of sabotage led to retaliatory measures in which many Jews were executed (with the authorities stressing their Jewishness). The mass arrest of Jews was set in motion with a decree issued by Ante Pavelić on June 26, 1941, that accused the Jews of spreading lies in order to incite the population and of interfering with the orderly supply of essential commodities, "well-known black-marketeers that they are. . . . I declare that the Jews are collectively guilty and order them to be imprisoned . . . in concentration camps."

The onslaught on the Jews of Zagreb had begun a few days earlier, on June 22. By the end of the month several hundred Jewish families had been seized and, for the most part, put into the Pag and Jadovno concentration camps. In July it was the turn of the smaller communities, such as Varaždin, Koprivnica, Ludbreg, Karlovac, and Bjelovar. The prisoners were first assembled in the former trade-fair grounds in the heart of Zagreb and from there dispatched to various camps.

This was followed, at the beginning of August, by a drive against the Jews of Bosnia and Herzegovina. In the first stage, those living in small towns were arrested; at the end of the month, it was the turn of Sarajevo, where the roundup of the Jews took longer than expected and was completed only in November 1941. The concentration camp of JA-SENOVAC was constructed in August 1941, and after its completion most arrested Jews were sent there. Some Jewish women of Sarajevo were imprisoned in a special women's camp that had been set up in the town of Djakovo for lack of space in the other camps.

By the end of 1941, two-thirds of Croatian Jewry had been taken to Croatian concentration camps; most were killed on arrival or soon after. The Jews who had not yet been imprisoned were regarded as indispensable to the state's economy, were married to non-Jews, or had personal ties to members of the ruling clique. Some Jews also managed to flee to the Italian zone of occupation. In an interview with a German newspaper at the end of the summer of 1941, Pavelić declared: "The Jews will be liquidated within a very short time."

Jews were imprisoned in the following concentration camps:

1. Danica, near Zagreb. This camp was established in April 1941 and was disbanded at the end of the year. Most of the inmates were political prisoners; the Jewish lawyers of Zagreb were also incarcerated here.

2. Jadovno, in the Velebit Mountains. Established in May 1941 and disbanded in August of that year, when the area was about to be handed over to the Italians. It was here that the Jewish youngsters from Zagreb were imprisoned and murdered.

3. Pag, on Pag Island in the Adriatic. Established in June 1941 and dismantled by the end of August of that year. In the few weeks of its existence, hundreds of people were murdered in this camp. An inquiry commission set up by the Italian army when it took control of the area in August 1941 reported that shocking acts had been committed there. Among the murder victims were many of the people who had been seized in the first wave of arrests.

4. Kruscica, in Bosnia. Established at the beginning of August 1941 and disbanded by the end of the following month. This was mainly a transit camp for the Jewish women arrested in Bosnia and Herzegovina.

5. Loborgrad, in northern Croatia. Set up in September 1941 and dismantled in October 1942. It served as a camp for women and children and was run by VOLKSDEUTSCHE (ethnic Germans). In May 1942 the women and children prisoners were deported to AUSCHWITZ.

6. Djakovo, in southeast Croatia. Established in December 1941; in existence until June 1942. This was another camp where women and children were imprisoned. Sev-

eral hundred prisoners died in a typhus epidemic that broke out there; the rest were transferred, in the summer of 1942, to Jasenovac, where they were killed on arrival.

7. Tenje, near Osijek. Set up in March 1942 and disbanded in August of that year, when all its prisoners were deported to Auschwitz to be gassed.

8. Jasenovac, 62 miles (100 km) from Zagreb. Established in August 1941; in existence until April 1945. This was the largest and best-known concentration camp in Croatia, the place where most of its Jews went to their death. It was also in Jasenovac that hundreds of thousands of people belonging to other nationalities were killed—Serbs, GYPSIES, and various non-Jewish opposition elements.

German role in deportation and extermination. Croatian Jews, for the most part, were murdered by fellow Croatians, but there is no doubt about the role played by the Germans. From the beginning of Ustaša rule, it was the Germans who supervised the "solution of the Jewish question." An SS officer named Müller was posted to Zagreb in May 1941 and took charge of the "solution." In Sarajevo, it was SS-Sturmbannführer Dr. Alfred Heinrich who handled the Jews. A major role was also played by the German ambassador in Zagreb, SA-Gruppenführer Siegfried Kasche, a veteran member of the diplomatic corps and a zealous antisemite. It was Kasche who pressured and exhorted the Croatian leaders to lose no time in killing all the Jews in the country, and who urged his colleagues in Berlin to make sure that the Jews in the Italian-occupied zone were seized and subjected to the same fate as their brethren in the other parts of Croatia. Kasche's right-hand man on Jewish affairs was SS-Sturmbannführer Hans Helm, who served as the embassy police attaché and belonged to the staff of the REICHSSICHERHEITSHAUPTAMT (Reich Security Main Office; RSHA).

As long as the Croatians continued to kill Jews, the Germans did not interfere, but German involvement grew at the beginning of 1942, when it appeared that the Croatians might call a halt to the killing. At the WANNSEE CONFERENCE of January 20, 1942, it was decided that the Germans would propose to the Croatians that they transfer the Jews

The Jewish Rab battalion, formed after the prisoners of the Rab internment camp were liberated in September 1943.

of Croatia to eastern Europe. In the negotiations that followed, Hans Helm, who was an expert on Yugoslav affairs, represented the German side, while Dido Kvaternik, chief of security services, was the Croatian representative. The Germans may have decided to take over the murder of Croatian Jews because the Croatians had lost some of their enthusiasm following the successes of the Red Army in the winter of 1941–1942. In the spring of 1942 the two sides agreed on the deportation of Croatian Jews to the east; the Croatian government undertook to arrest the Jews, take them to the railheads, and pay the Germans 30 reichsmarks per person for the cost of transporting the prisoners to the extermination camps. In return, the Germans agreed that the property of the Jewish

victims would go to the Croatian government.

SS-Hauptsturmführer Franz Abromeit, an "expert" on the staff of Adolf EICHMANN's section, was sent to Zagreb to take charge of the deportation. Between August 13 and 20, 1942, five trains left Croatia for Auschwitz with 5,500 Jews aboard, half from the Tenje concentration camp and the rest from the Loborgrad camp and from Zagreb and Sarajevo. In May 1943, while Heinrich HIMMLER was on a visit to Zagreb, another series of deportations to Auschwitz was conducted, with the Germans joining the Croatians in drawing up the list of deportees. In two trains on May 5 and 10, a group of 1,150 Jews was deported, including the leaders of the Zagreb and Osijek Jewish communities. Of the thousands of Croatian Jews who were deported to Auschwitz, only a few dozen survived. In Croatia itself, a mere few hundred Jews remained alive, most of them because they were protégés of Croatian political leaders or were married to non-Jews.

Italian protection. Most of the Croatian Jews who survived owed their lives to the Italians. In their zone of occupation (the Dalmatian coast, Albania, and Montenegro), the Italians resolutely protected the Jews; some five thousand Jews were saved by the Italians in Yugoslavia.

In the summer of 1943 all the Jewish refugees in Dalmatia were put into a camp in RAB. Following the Italian surrender in September 1943, the area was liberated by the partisans, and most of the Jews were moved to liberated areas in the center of the country. Those who were fit to bear arms or perform other military service joined the partisan army, while the others were given the protection of the fighting forces.

Catholic Church. In the interwar period the Catholic church in Croatia had been a staunch supporter of Croatian nationalism, and it welcomed the establishment of the Croatian state. The Vatican had always supported the stand of the Croatian church and had encouraged Croatian separatism. The Ustaša extermination drive against Serbs, Jews, and Gypsies presented the church with a dilemma.

Many Catholic priests, mainly of the lower rank, took an active part in the murder operations. Generally speaking, the reaction of the Catholic church was a function of military and political developments affecting Croatia; when the standing of the NDH regime was weakening and the war was drawing to an end, protests by the church against Ustaša crimes became more and more outspoken. This was not the case in the earlier stages. A bishops' conference that met in Zagreb in November 1941 was not even prepared to denounce the forced conversion of Serbs that had taken place in the summer of 1941, let alone condemn the persecution and murder of Serbs and Jews. It was not until the middle of 1943 that Aloysius Stepinac, the archbishop of Zagreb, publicly came out against the murder of Croatian Jews (most of whom had been killed by that time), the

Serbs, and other nationalities. The Vatican followed a similar line. In the early stage, the Croatian massacres were explained in Rome as "teething troubles of a new regime" (the expression of Monsignor Domenico Tardini of the Vatican state secretariat). When the course of the war was changing, the leaders of the Catholic church began to criticize the Ustaša, but in mild terms; it was only at the end, when Allied victory was assured, that Vatican spokesmen came out with clear denunciations. In some instances, Croatian clerics did help Jews. Their main effort was to save the lives of the Jewish partners in mixed marriages, and most of these did in fact survive. The church also extended help to the Zagreb Jewish community in providing food, medicines, and clothing for Jews in the concentration camps.

Communities. Jewish communities in Croatia were severely restricted in their activities during the Holocaust, mainly because most of them were liquidated at an early stage. Of the three major communities, that of Sarajevo ceased functioning at the beginning of 1942 and the Osijek community by the middle of that year. Only the Zagreb community remained in existence throughout the war.

The Zagreb community was the center of all Jewish activities. It stayed in touch with the Jewish institutions in Hungary (the RELIEF AND RESCUE COMMITTEE OF BUDAPEST), Switzerland, and Turkey; it received financial aid from abroad; and its representatives negotiated with Croatian government officials and others. Until the last deportation to Auschwitz, in May 1943, the community was headed by the Chief Rabbi of Zagreb, Dr. Shalom Freiberger, and the secretary, Aleksa Klein. Thereafter, the few Jews left in the city dealt mainly with the dispatch of food parcels to Jewish prisoners in concentration camps and with extending aid to the needy.

It is estimated that thirty thousand Jews were murdered in Croatia—80 percent of its Jewish population.

BIBLIOGRAPHY

Hory, L., and M. Broszat. *Der kroatische Ustacha Staat, 1941–1945.* Stuttgart, 1964.
Jelić-Butić, F. *Ustaše i N.D.H.* Zagreb, 1977.

Lederer, Z., ed. *The Crimes of the Germans and Their Collaborators against the Jews of Jugoslavia.* Belgrade, 1953.

Morley, J. F. *Vatican Diplomacy and the Jews during the Holocaust, 1939–1943.* New York, 1980. See pages 147–165.

MENACHEM SHELAH

CRYSTAL NIGHT. *See* Kristallnacht.

CULTURAL SOCIETY OF GERMAN JEWS. *See* Kulturbund Deutscher Juden.

CUZA, ALEXANDRU (1857–1946), founder of modern antisemitism in ROMANIA. A professor of economics at the University of Iaşi, Cuza propagated racist views of Jew-hatred and general xenophobia, accusing the Jews of having taken over Romania's cities and deprived them of their Romanian character, and of aiming to seize control of the entire country. In 1895 Cuza, together with Nicolae Jorga (a historian, writer, and political figure) and the Frenchman J. de Biez, established an international antisemitic organization, the Alliance Antisémitique Universelle. In 1910 Cuza and Jorga formed the National Democratic party, a protofascist political party based on Christian national ideas, whose main platform was the removal of the Jews from the professions and the army and a ban on their settlement in villages. Under Cuza's leadership the city of Iaşi, and especially its university, became the country's center of antisemitic activities. In 1923 he set up a fascist organization, the Liga Apararei Nationale Crestine (League of National Christian Defense), with Corneliu Codreanu as its secretary. Codreanu left the league in 1927 and established the IRON GUARD, in its initial form.

Cuza called for the imposition of a *numerus clausus* on Jews, that is, their restriction to a specific quota at the universities and in all other spheres—in effect, their removal from any position of influence in the cultural, intellectual, and literary life of the country. His fascist and antisemitic ideas preceded Nazi influence in Romania by many years, and he was able to boast that he had sounded the alarm of the Jewish "peril" much earlier than Hitler.

In 1935 Cuza and Octavian GOGA joined in forming the National Christian party by merging Cuza's league with the National Agrarian party headed by Goga. Goga came to power in 1937, with Cuza's help, and formed an outspokenly antisemitic government, the second of its kind in Europe. It remained in power for only forty-four days, but in that short time it succeeded in stripping a quarter-million Jews of their Romanian citizenship, and in ideological terms it paved the way for Ion ANTONESCU's dictatorship. The Communist authorities who assumed power after the liberation of Romania in 1944 did not take any action against Cuza and did not put him on trial "because of his advanced age."

BIBLIOGRAPHY

Ancel, J., ed. *Documents concerning the Fate of Romanian Jewry during the Holocaust.* Vols. 1, 5. Jerusalem, 1986.

Fischer-Galati, S. "Fascism, Communism, and the Jewish Question in Romania." In *Jews and Non-Jews in Eastern Europe, 1918–1945,* edited by B. Vago and G. L. Mosse, pp. 157–175. New York, 1974.

Weber, E. "Romania." In *The European Right: A Historical Profile,* edited by H. Rogger and E. Weber, pp. 501–574. Berkeley, 1966.

JEAN ANCEL

CYPRUS DETENTION CAMPS, transshipment and detention camps on the Mediterranean island of Cyprus in which the British authorities held Jewish "illegal" immigrants, most of them European survivors of the Holocaust trying to enter Palestine. On August 7, 1946, the British government made a decision to detain these Jews in Cyprus, hoping that this deterrent would put an end to Jewish immigration. The decision was geared to the British policy of breaking the power of the "Hebrew resistance movement" in Palestine. But before long the British came to realize that detention was not achieving the desired aim; the would-be immigrants continued their attempts to reach Palestine despite vio-

The former Canadian corvette (escort ship) *Josiah Wedgwood*, sailing under Panamanian flag from Italy with 1,259 Jewish refugees. It was intercepted by British warships on June 27, 1946, off the coast of Haifa in Palestine. The refugees were taken into custody by the British and then deported to the Cyprus detention camps.

lent clashes with British troops and transshipment to Cyprus. By December 1946 the British government, under pressure from the Jewish Agency and in view of the rapid rise in the number of people interned in the Cyprus camps, was allotting half the legal immigration quota (that is, 750 visas, or certificates, a month) to the Cyprus detainees.

The use of the Cyprus detention camps began on August 13, 1946, and ended on February 10, 1949, when the last group of detainees left for what had become the state of Israel. During this period, fifty-two thousand Jews passed through the Cyprus camps, having been taken off thirty-nine boats in their attempts to get to Palestine. To this number must be added twenty-two hundred children who were born in the camps. Some of the detainees spent only a few months in Cyprus, but many were held there for a year and

longer. Responsibility for setting up the camps and for their administration and security was that of the British army in Cyprus, which handled the camps as though it were dealing with prisoners of war and according to the rules applicable to prisoner-of-war camps.

There were two kinds of camps. The "summer camps," of which there were five, were located at Kraolos, near Famagusta, and the detainees in them were housed in tents. The seven "winter camps" were located at Dekalia, north of Larnaca; here the housing consisted of tin huts and some tents. Conditions in the camps were quite harsh, especially for mothers of children and babies. The tents and barracks were overcrowded. there was no privacy, and families had to share accommodations with single persons. There were no partitions, no lighting fixtures, and no furni-

"Illegal immigrants" detained by the British in one of the "winter camps" in Cyprus (1947). [Bet Loḥamei ha-Getta'ot]

ture except beds. The food supplied by the British army was of poor quality; because of the inadequate facilities in the field kitchens, some of it was wasted and people went hungry. The detainees also suffered from a lack of shoes and clothing, which the British supplied only in limited quantities, from army surplus. The insufficient supply of water, particularly in the hot summer months, caused sanitary conditions to deteriorate and led to skin diseases and infections. Most of the British officers and troops in charge of the camps carried out their duties indifferently or unwillingly. Some, for humanitarian reasons, wanted to ease the refugees' lot, but they had little authority or resources. The British administration in Palestine, which was charged with establishing and maintaining the camps, had to bear the costs out of its budget, which in any case showed a deficit, and it sought to put the responsibility for the welfare of the detainees on the Jewish Agency and the JOINT DISTRIBUTION COMMITTEE (also known as the Joint).

This put the Jewish Agency in a dilemma. It

did not recognize the legality of the detention, nor did it want to relieve the British authorities of their responsibility for the maintenance of the camps and the detainees' state of health. The Agency therefore asked the Joint Distribution Committee to take on responsibility for the welfare of the camp population, which the Joint readily did. As early as September 1946, a few weeks after the camps were set up, the Joint was already engaged in welfare operations there, which they maintained throughout the camps' existence.

The Joint greatly reduced the hardships from which the refugees suffered. It recruited medical and welfare teams in Palestine to run nurseries and clinics in the camps, it improved the quality of food rations for those in special need and supplemented the basic food supplies of the general camp population, it catered to religious requirements, and it set up a bureau for the search of missing relatives. The provision of educational facilities for the children and teenagers (of whom there were large numbers in the camps, most having been orphaned in the Holocaust) was yet another task taken on by the Joint, in partnership with YOUTH ALIYA. The majority of the youngsters were put into one camp, Camp 65, which became a kind of youth village. There, Youth Aliya educational teams established a school system based on the few teachers found among the refugees. The welfare teams recruited in Palestine included Jewish Agency–appointed emissaries of various political movements. Morris Laub, the Joint's director in Cyprus, became the spokesman and representative of the detainees vis-à-vis the British authorities on the island.

The detainees in the Cyprus camps were relatively young, with 80 percent of them between the ages of thirteen and thirty-five. Thus, they were among the more spirited and lively survivors of the Holocaust. They came to the camps as members of YOUTH MOVEMENTS, immigration groups, and political parties imbued with a strong Zionist ideology. Their ideology and self-discipline enabled

them to adapt to the conditions in the camps.

In addition to being deprived of their liberty and exposed to harsh physical conditions, the detainees also suffered greatly from the enforced idleness of the camps. Efforts to keep them busy with cultural activities met with difficulties, owing to lack of means and scarcity of qualified personnel. An important contribution was made by emissaries from Palestine who lived with the refugees in the camps. Some of these were "legal": representatives of the various Zionist movements, welfare workers under Joint auspices, and teachers dispatched to Cyprus by the Rutenberg Teachers' Seminary. Others were "illegal"; they had been sent to Cyprus by the Palmah, the underground strike force of the Hagana (the Yishuv's underground military organization), to provide the young people in the camps with military training and prepare them for service with the Hagana when they arrived in Palestine. Living among the detainees and sharing their lot, these emissaries had great influence; they represented the Jewish national institutions and were the link between the refugees and the Jewish population in Palestine.

A few of the refugees who had second thoughts applied to the British authorities to return to the country from which they had set out. But generally, despite all their suffering, the Cyprus detainees displayed impressive moral strength and staying power during their internment. Though there were no written laws and no real sanctions that could have been applied, not a single criminal act was recorded among the detainees.

BIBLIOGRAPHY

Laub, M. *Last Barrier to Freedom.* Berkeley, 1985.
Oren, M. *You May View the Land from a Distance: Education of Youth in Cyprus.* Tel Aviv, 1987. (In Hebrew.)
Schaary, D. *The Cyprus Detention Camps for Jewish "Illegal" Immigrants to Palestine, 1946–1949.* Jerusalem, 1981. (In Hebrew.)

NAHUM BOGNER

Refugee children learning Hebrew in one of the Cyprus detention camps (1947). [H. Fin]

CZECHOSLOVAK GOVERNMENT-IN-EXILE. After the MUNICH CONFERENCE (September 29–30, 1938), the president of Czechoslovakia, Edvard BENEŠ, resigned and went into exile. Following the outbreak of World War II, he established in France a Czechoslovak National Committee, which, after moving to London in 1940, functioned as a government-in-exile, one of several such London-based governments-in-exile of European countries that had been overrun by Hitler.

The government-in-exile was recognized by the Soviet Union and by the British government (July 21, 1941). From its establishment, President Beneš's main objective was to gain international recognition for the legal continuity of the Czechoslovak republic and its pre-Munich boundaries. One of its first moves was the setting up of a State Council (Statni Rada), a quasi-provisional parliament to act as a unifying body for resistance activities in exile. The Czechoslovak government-in-exile conducted extensive negotiations with the POLISH GOVERNMENT-IN-EXILE under Władysław SIKORSKI in order to obtain a far-reaching agreement, but the mutual efforts were unsuccessful. Jewish refugees from Czechoslovakia who reached Poland, the Soviet Union, Palestine, France, and Great Britain constituted a high percentage (estimated at 50 percent) of the Czechoslovak army units formed in exile. Members of the intelligentsia who managed to escape to Britain before the outbreak of the war, and who had a working knowledge of English, made themselves available to the government-in-exile for various services, particularly the information service and the Foreign Ministry.

Ernst Frischer, former head of the Jewish party in Czechoslovakia (1935–1939), was appointed the representative of the Jewish national group on the State Council. He developed a network for rescue activities and assistance and—together with the government's representatives in Geneva, Stockholm, and Lisbon—organized the sending of food parcels, medicine, and funds to the concentration camps, especially the ghetto of THERESIENSTADT. The official line of the government-in-exile on resistance inside Czechoslovakia was that no hazardous ventures should be undertaken that might entail the sacrifice of hundreds or thousands of lives. Yet a spectacular anti-Nazi action, conceived in London and eventually costing some five thousand lives, was the assassination, on May 27, 1942, of Reinhard HEYDRICH, the acting Reich Protector of BOHEMIA AND MORAVIA. It led to German retaliation in the form of mass murder, with the destruction of two villages in Bohemia (LIDICE and Lezaky) and the killing of their entire male population.

The flow of information between Prague and London, and the informants employed in the Protectorate by the Czech army intelligence in London, enabled the Czech government to furnish important information to the Allies. When asked by the WORLD JEWISH CONGRESS in August 1942 to confirm information regarding the German extermination plan (resulting from the RIEGNER CABLE), Beneš's belated response of November 1942 omitted mention of the wholesale deportations of Jews taking place in the Protectorate. However, the president and the government cooperated closely with the Jewish leadership in the free world and in Palestine. They made several diplomatic moves, including intervention with the Vatican and the Allied governments on behalf of persecuted Jews, and they openly condemned antisemitism. Foreign Minister Jan Masaryk was especially active on the Jewish issue, and his addresses over radio and at rallies were most sympathetic to the Jewish plight. It was the representative of the government at Geneva, Dr. Jaromir Kopecky, who in mid-June 1944 transmitted to the free world the so-called AUSCHWITZ PROTOCOLS, which reached him from Bratislava through underground channels and contained information on the annihilation process at AUSCHWITZ-Birkenau.

The Czechoslovak government-in-exile, the only one of its kind in eastern Europe to be allowed to return after the war to its native country, implemented some radical changes in its minority policy, with the objective of making the republic as nationally homogeneous as possible. The German minority and part of the Hungarian minority were transferred to their homelands (the TRANSCARPATHIAN UKRAINE was annexed to the Soviet Union according to the Czechoslovak-Soviet Treaty of June 29, 1945). The Jewish remnants in Czechoslovakia were given the option of declaring themselves either of Czech or of Slovak nationality.

BIBLIOGRAPHY

Dagan, A. "The Czechoslovak Government-in-Exile and the Jews." In vol. 3 of *The Jews of Czechoslovakia*, edited by A. Dagan, pp. 449–498. Philadelphia, 1984.

Rothkirchen, L. "The Czechoslovak Government-in-Exile: Jewish and Palestinian Aspects in the Light of Documents." *Yad Vashem Studies* 9 (1973): 157–199.

LIVIA ROTHKIRCHEN

CZECHOSLOVAKIA. *See* Bohemia and Moravia, Protectorate of; Slovakia; *see also* Czechoslovak Government-in-Exile.

CZERNIAKÓW, ADAM (1880–1942), head of the Warsaw JUDENRAT (Jewish Council). Czerniaków was born in WARSAW to a middle-class assimilationist family. He completed his chemical engineering studies in 1908. Later, he taught at the Jewish community's vocational school in Warsaw and served in various posts in independent Poland.

For many years Czerniaków represented Jewish artisans in several Polish organizations. From 1927 to 1934 he was a member of the Warsaw Muncipal Council, and in 1931 he was elected to the Polish Senate. Before World War II, he was a member of the executive council of the Jewish community. But in his public career between the wars Czerniaków was not regarded as a leader by the Jews, since he was not a member of any political party and had trouble expressing himself in Yiddish.

During the first week of the war, Maurycy Mayzel, chairman of the Jewish community's council, was one of the many who fled Warsaw. On September 23, in the midst of the siege of the city, Czerniaków noted in his diary that Stefan Starzynski, the mayor and commissar for civil defense, had appointed him "head of the Jewish religious community in Warsaw." On October 4, a few days after the city's surrender and the beginning of the German occupation, Czerniaków wrote: "I was taken to Szucha Avenue, where I was ordered to add twenty-four people to the community council and to serve as its head."

The official titles used by Czerniaków until the middle of 1941 were Head of the Judenrat and President of the Jewish Religious Community of Warsaw. From the middle of May 1941, his functions and authority were defined in the ghetto as corresponding to those of the mayor in the Polish part of the city.

The first Judenrat, established in October 1939, consisted of twenty-four members, including persons of recognized stature within Jewish society and outstanding figures in political organizations. Among them were the Zionist leader Maximilian Hartglas; Samuel ZYGELBOJM, a leader of the BUND; Isaac Meir Levin, the outstanding figure in Agudat Israel; and Abraham Weiss, a leading member of Mizrahi. Most of the party activists included in the first Judenrat left Warsaw and traveled abroad during the first month of the occupation, when it was still possible to leave. Czerniaków too had this opportunity, but he refused to leave and sharply criticized the leaders who fled the city claiming that they would secure aid in the free world for the masses suffering under the heel of the Nazi conqueror.

However, even after a number of the Judenrat members had left, there still remained in it persons with wide experience in public work, among them Abraham GEPNER; Joseph Jaszunski, the director of ORT in Poland; and Stanisław Szereszewski, the chairman of TOPOROL, an association that promoted agriculture.

The Jewish community in Warsaw during the interwar period had provided for religious and educational needs and for relief work. After the ghetto was established, in October 1940, the scope of the Judenrat's activities widened considerably, and it had to deal with matters of food, work, health, housing, and sanitation—functions normally carried out by the municipality and the state authorities. The structure and bureaucracy of the Judenrat also broadened considerably. At one point during the ghetto period it had twenty-five different departments and 6,000 workers, as compared to 530 in the prewar Jewish community.

The Judenrat clerks, particularly in the higher administration and the police force, included agents planted by the German authorities and opportunists prepared to collaborate at any price. Czerniaków despised these people, but he realized that they were a necessary evil. Groups arose in the ghetto that for various reasons tried to oust Czerniaków, and some of them, like the one led by Abraham Gancwajch, had the support of members of the German police and the SD (Sicherheitsdienst; Security Service). All these attempts failed since Czerniaków was supported by the civil authorities in the GENERALGOUVERNEMENT. The Jewish underground severely criticized Czerniaków and the Judenrat's policy. At a certain stage in the ghetto's existence, public control committees were set up to strengthen supervision of the Judenrat and to improve the functioning of its personnel, but they brought no real results.

In studies of the Warsaw ghetto, much attention has been devoted to evaluating Czerniaków's activities. An analysis of this material shows that Czerniaków endeavored to prevent the direct intervention of the German authorities, and sought to organize the internal affairs of the Jews with a minimum of outside involvement. This approach made possible clandestine economic activity, the illegal smuggling of food, and so on. At the same time, there is no proof that Czerniaków maintained contact with the Jewish underground or sided with secret political activities. On the other hand, he persistently promoted education for the ghetto's children, and strove to save Jews in danger of being put to death.

During the years of Czerniaków's tenure as Judenrat head, he came into daily contact with the German police and the civil authorities, who changed five times until the mass deportation of the summer of 1942. In particular, from May 1941 onward, Czerniaków maintained constant contact with Max Bischoff, the German official in charge of moving merchandise in and out of the ghetto.

Until the ghetto was set up, Czerniaków was permitted to maintain contact with the Poles in the Warsaw municipality, chiefly the Polish mayor, Julian Kulski. In his contacts with the Germans, Czerniaków sought ways to influence them and arouse some sort of sensitivity to and consideration for the ghetto situation. These attempts were of no avail. He was twice beaten up by the Germans and

Adam Czerniaków.

suffered many insults. Czerniaków gained a certain measure of understanding through his ties with the ghetto commissar, Heinz AUERSWALD, but Auerswald too misled Czerniaków in the end by hiding from him the real facts of the mass deportation.

Chroniclers and diarists of the Warsaw ghetto are divided as to Czerniaków's personality and characteristics. Some, such as Emanuel RINGELBLUM and Itzhak KATZENELSON, both with a public background and close to the underground, were severely critical, seeing in Czerniaków an assimilator who mixed with assimilators, a man lacking close contact with the Jewish masses, who tended toward self-esteem and absurd public ceremonies in the midst of the grim reality of the ghetto. However, people who worked with Czerniaków praised the man and his qualities. He did indeed place assimilators in key positions, as when he made Joseph Szerynski (a police officer who had converted to Christianity) commander of the ghetto police, a choice considered miserable by all. But the accusation of a tendency toward self-aggrandizement and hollow ceremony is unfounded. It is generally accepted that Czerniaków had great personal decency and good intentions. A member of the underground and a leader of the ghetto fighters, Mordechai TENENBAUM (Tamaroff), noted in his diary that there were only three truly honest persons among the heads of the Judenrat, one of them being Czerniaków. Unlike the Judenrat leaders Mordechai Chaim RUMKOWSKI and Jacob GENS, Czerniaków was not at all guided by personal ambition, and was willing to cooperate with the Nazis only up to a point.

Refusing to help in the roundup of Jews destined for deportation, Czerniaków committed suicide at 4:00 p.m. on July 23, 1942. According to one version, a note was found on his desk addressed to his wife, saying: "They are demanding that I kill the children of my people with my own hands. There is nothing for me to do but to die." His death was interpreted as the protest of a man who was not prepared to cross the line between conducting ghetto activities and handing over Jews.

In the mid-1960s, YAD VASHEM received Czerniaków's wartime diary, which he kept regularly from September 6, 1939, until the day of his death. It consists of eight notebooks with 1,009 small pages in chronological order. The fifth notebook, covering the period between December 14, 1940, and April 22, 1941, has been lost. Czerniaków's diary, published in Hebrew, English, German, and Polish, is one of the most important surviving documents from the period of the Holocaust. It casts light on the man who stood at the head of the Warsaw Judenrat, provides a wealth of information about people and events, and reveals many details concerning the nature of the German rule over the Jews.

BIBLIOGRAPHY

Gutman, Y. "Adam Czerniaków: The Man and his Diary." In *The Catastrophe of European Jewry*, edited by Y. Gutman and L. Rothkirchen, pp. 451–489. Jerusalem, 1976.

Hilberg, R., S. Staron, and J. Kermisz, eds. *The Warsaw Diary of Adam Czerniakow: Prelude to Doom.* New York, 1979.

Tartakower, A., and K. R. Grossmann. "Adam Czerniakow the Man and His Supreme Sacrifice." *Yad Vashem Studies* 6 (1967): 55–67.

ISRAEL GUTMAN

CZERNOWITZ. *See* Chernovtsy.

CZĘSTOCHOWA, Polish city located about 124 miles (200 km) southwest of Warsaw, famed for Jasna Góra (Bright Mountain), the church containing a shrine with the icon of the Black Madonna of Częstochowa, revered all over Poland.

The Jewish community in Częstochowa was founded in 1765, when it numbered 75. It grew to 500 by 1808, and fifty years later there were 3,000 Jews, forming a third of the total population. When World War II broke out, 28,500 Jews lived in the city. In the Częstochowa area, on the banks of the Warta River, there are rich deposits of ores, forming the basis for steelworks. Częstochowa became a wealthy industrial center in the nineteenth century with the construction of roads and railways in the area. Jews took an active part in all the industries, as well as in banking, domestic and international trade, and crafts. A Jewish agricultural training farm and a trade school operated in Częstochowa during the interwar years, in addition to networks of religious and secular Jewish schools, as in most large Jewish communities in Poland.

The Germans entered Częstochowa on Sunday, September 3, 1939, the third day of the war, and persecution of its Jews began at once. More than 300 Jews were killed on the following day, which became known as "Bloody Monday." On September 16 a JUDENRAT (Jewish Council) was formed, headed by Leon Kopinski. Confiscation of Jewish property and household effects, beatings, mockery, and degradation went on incessantly. In August 1940, 1,000 young Jews were rounded up and sent to the Ciechanów forced-labor camps; very few survived.

A ghetto was established on April 9, 1941, by order of the *Stadthauptmann* (city commissioner), SS-Brigadeführer Dr. Richard Wendler, in the eastern, old part of the city. The ghetto was sealed off on August 23. Some

CZĘSTOCHOWA

■ Camp

✖ Extermination Center

Administrative Divisions of Poland under German Occupation, 1939–1945

1 Pomerania
2 Brandenburg
3 Saxony
4 Lower Silesia
5 Upper Silesia
6 Warthegau
7 Danzig (West Prussia)
8 East Prussia
9 Generalgouvernement
10 Białystok Region

© Polish National Publishing House (Państwowe Wydawnictwo Naukowe) Warsaw, 1979

twenty thousand Jews from other cities (Łódź, Płock, Kraków) and villages were sent to the Częstochowa ghetto, which eventually held more than forty-eight thousand persons. The main places of work outside the ghetto were the German Metallurgie military factories on Krótka Street.

In preparation for the forthcoming liquidation of the ghetto, in May 1942 the Germans seized and killed the Jewish social, cultural, and political activists. Large-scale *Aktionen* began on September 22 and lasted until October 8. In each deportation, some eight thousand Jews were packed into sixty freight cars. A total of thirty-nine thousand Jews were sent in this way to the TREBLINKA extermination camp. Elderly people in the home for the aged and the children in the orphanage were killed on the spot. About two thousand Jews managed to escape or to hide in the city.

After the deportations, the northeastern part of the ghetto, called the "small ghetto," held some five thousand able-bodied Jews with skills or professions. On September 2, a privately owned German munitions factory

(*Apparatenbau*) belonging to the HASAG network was established in the suburb of Stradom. This forced-labor camp existed for two years, and a total of three thousand Jews from Poland, Germany, and Austria passed through it. When a typhoid epidemic broke out the camp was closed (January 16, 1945), and the surviving inmates were deported to an unknown destination.

In June 1943, the HASAG Rakow steel mill was opened, in which five hundred to one thousand Jews from Slovakia and Poland were exploited. It was closed on January 16, 1945, and the workers sent to the BUCHENWALD and RAVENSBRÜCK camps. The largest camp in the Częstochowa area was HASAG Pelzery, which functioned from June 1943 until January 16, 1945. This was a munitions factory employing, at any given time, about five thousand Jews, from Poland, Germany, Austria, and Bohemia. Finally, there were an average of three thousand Jews working in the munitions factories of Warta and Częstochowianka.

In December 1942 the ŻYDOWSKA ORGANIZACJA BOJOWA (Jewish Fighting Organization;

Jewish slave laborers from Częstochowa (c. 1940 or 1941).

ŻOB) created a resistance unit in Częstochowa, with some 300 participants. They maintained contact with the Warsaw center. In January 1943 this group, under the leadership of Mendel Fiszlewicz, offered armed resistance to a German *Aktion*. During the clash 251 Jews were killed; the rest were deported to Radomsko and from there to Treblinka. The reprisals that followed included the murder of 127 of the Jewish intelligentsia, and 250 children and elderly people. In other resistance groups there were two relatively large units of partisans, who were killed by Polish rightist partisans, and several small units that joined the leftist Polish partisans. On June 25, 1943, another ŻOB group tried to resist the liquidation of the small ghetto. When the Soviet army liberated Częstochowa, there were still some 5,000 Jews in the area. In June 1946, 2,167 Jews were living in Częstochowa. After the KIELCE pogrom on July 4, many of them joined the BERIḤA for Palestine.

BIBLIOGRAPHY

Glicksman, W. M. "Daily Record Sheet of the Jewish Police (District I) in the Czestochowa Ghetto (1941–1942)." *Yad Vashem Studies* 6 (1967): 331–358.
Glicksman, W. M. *A Kehillah in Poland during the Inter-War Years.* Philadelphia, 1969.
Schutzmann, M. *The Czestochowa Book.* 2 vols. Jerusalem, 1967, 1968. (In Hebrew.)
Tenenbaum, J. *Underground.* New York, 1952.

SINAI LEICHTER

CZORTKÓW. *See* Chortkov.

D

DACHAU, one of the first Nazi CONCENTRATION CAMPS, located in the small town of Dachau, about 10 miles (15 km) northwest of Munich. Dachau was chosen because it was the site of an empty munitions factory from World War I, which provided the needed space. The opening of the camp, with a capacity for 5,000 prisoners, was announced by Heinrich HIMMLER at a press conference held on March 20, 1933.

The first group of so-called protective-custody prisoners, consisting mainly of Communists and Social Democrats, was brought to Dachau on March 22, 1933. They were guarded by Bavarian state police until the camp was taken over by the SS on April 11.

On becoming commandant of the camp in June 1933, Theodor EICKE set up a scheme of organization with detailed regulations for camp life. Later, when Eicke was appointed inspector general for all concentration camps, these regulations were used, with local variations, elsewhere. With Dachau as his model, he developed an institution that was intended, by its very existence, to spread fear among the populace, an effective tool to silence every opponent of the regime. Dachau became a useful training ground for the SS. There, its members first learned to see those with different convictions as inferior and to deal with them accordingly, not hesitating to kill when the occasion arose. In later years, the members of the SS TOTENKOPFVERBÄNDE (Death's-Head Units) were able, without a thought, to annihilate many hundreds of thousands of people in GAS VANS and GAS CHAMBERS. The transformation of the terror system of Na-

tional Socialism into bloody reality began in the Dachau concentration camp. Besides the guards and SS camp personnel, large numbers of SS military units were trained and instructed there.

When the camp opened, only known political opponents of the Nazis were interned. Communists, Social Democrats, and a few monarchists, who had passionately opposed one another (as well as the Nazis) before 1933, now found themselves together behind barbed wire. From about 1935, it was usual for all persons who had been condemned in a court of law to be taken automatically to a concentration camp after they had served their prison sentences. The first Jewish prisoners came as known political opponents of the Nazis. At Dachau, as elsewhere, they received even worse treatment than the other prisoners. Gradually, more and more groups were interned: JEHOVAH'S WITNESSES, who resisted the draft; GYPSIES, who, like the Jews, were classified as racially inferior; clergymen who resisted the Nazi coercion of the churches; HOMOSEXUALS; and many who had been denounced for making critical remarks of various kinds.

The number of Jewish prisoners increased with the systematizing of the persecution of the Jews. After KRISTALLNACHT (November 9–10, 1938), more than ten thousand Jewish citizens from all over Germany were interned in Dachau. Those who could prove their intention to leave Germany were released, and indeed most of them were released within a few months of detention. When systematic extermination of the Jews began in 1942, the

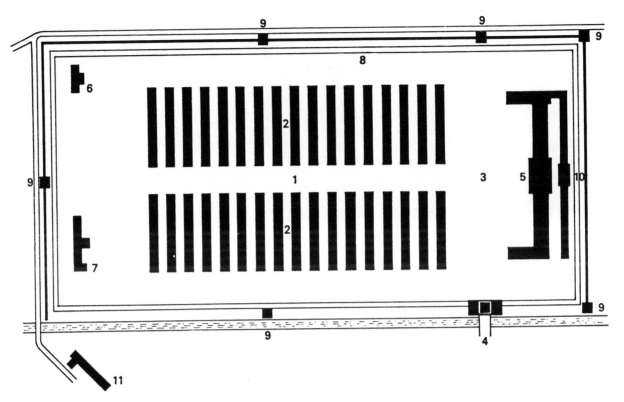

1. *Lagerstrasse* (main road)
2. Barracks
3. Parade ground for roll call
4. *Jourhaus* (entrance to the camp and guard room)
5. *Wirtschaftsgebäude* (kitchen, laundry, showers, etc.)
6. Disinfection hut
7. Vegetable garden
8. Ditch with live barbed-wire fence and camp wall
9. Watchtowers
10. *Bunker* (prison block)
11. Crematorium

Plan of the Dachau concentration camp.

Jewish prisoners were transported from Dachau and the other camps within the German Reich to the mass extermination camps in occupied Poland. When, during the summer and fall of 1944, additional subsidiary camps were installed near armament factories to increase production there, thousands of Jewish prisoners, mostly from Hungary but also from Poland, Czechoslovakia, Romania, and the USSR, were brought to the Dachau subsidiary camps. At the liberation of Dachau and its subsidiary camps in April 1945, about 30 percent of the total number of inmates were Jewish.

During its twelve-year existence, Dachau was always a "political camp": the political prisoners, who had been there first and knew the conditions best, held most of the key positions in the so-called prisoners' internal government, which had been instituted by the SS. Since this body organized the daily life in the camp, it could prevent criminal prisoners from reaching positions that would give them power over the others—power that criminal prisoners in other camps often misused for their own advantage. In 1937 and 1938, a new camp was built by the prisoners alongside the old buildings of the munitions factory: thirty-two barracks; the camp entrance building, containing the offices of the SS administration; the *Wirtschaftsgebäude* ("farm buildings," containing the kitchen, workshops, showers, and so on); and a camp prison. The camp was enclosed by a water-filled ditch, fortified by an electrified barbed-wire fence, and surrounded by a wall with seven guard towers.

During the summer of 1938, several thousand Austrian prisoners were brought to Dachau. Their arrival marked the beginning of the deportations that would reflect the course of the war: transports were sent to Dachau from each country as it was invaded by the German army. Prisoners included resistance fighters, Jews, clergymen, and others who refused to collaborate with the occupation. At the liberation, inmates from more than thirty countries were found in Dachau, with Germans forming only a minority.

All prisoners underwent the same fate when they entered the camp. They left all legal status behind, their remaining possessions were confiscated, their hair was shaved off, and they were dressed in striped fatigues. They were allocated a number as well as a colored triangle indicating the category of prisoner to which they belonged. The daily routine was filled with work, hunger, exhaustion, and fear of the brutality of the sadistic SS guards. The value of the cheap labor that the prisoners provided (the only cost involved was that of their miserable food rations) was quickly recognized and ruthlessly exploited.

At first, besides being employed in camp management and maintenance, the Dachau inmates worked in handicraft industries set up within the camp itself, as well as in so-called branch detachments outside the camp. They built roads, worked in gravel pits, and drained marshes, rehabilitating them as arable land. Initially, production in the camps was directly under the control of the individual camp commandant. But as the camps continued to grow, the range of production expanded, and the SS industries that were served by the camp labor were centralized under their main office in Berlin. In the first winter of the war, 1939–1940, the Dachau camp was used to set up the SS Totenkopf-Division. During this time the prisoners were sent to the camps at BUCHENWALD, FLOSSEN-BÜRG, and MAUTHAUSEN, where they had to work in quarries under the harshest conditions without any safety precautions whatever.

In the course of the war, the work force of the concentration camps became increasingly important for the German armaments industry. The network of camps, which gradually extended over the whole of central Europe, took on gigantic proportions. Dachau alone had, besides numerous smaller camps, thirty-six large subsidiary camps in which up to

thirty-seven thousand prisoners worked almost exclusively on armaments. Private firms had the opportunity to hire slave laborers from the camps. For the prisoners, who worked under SS guard, they paid a daily rate to the SS WIRTSCHAFTS-VERWALTUNGSHAUPT-AMT (Economic-Administrative Main Office; WVHA). The prisoners, however, received nothing. Those who fell ill were sent back to the main camp; this usually meant death. The firms received new, healthier laborers until these too could no longer meet the demands of their employers.

In Dachau there was no mass extermination program with poison gas. But out of the total number of 206,206 prisoners registered there were 31,591 registered deaths, most of them during the war. However, the total number of deaths in Dachau, including the victims of individual and mass executions and the final death marches, will never be known.

In Dachau, as in other Nazi camps, MEDICAL EXPERIMENTS were performed on helpless inmates. Himmler provided the opportunity for

Prisoners of the Dachau concentration camp (June 28, 1938).

SS physicians to use prisoners as guinea pigs. Dr. Sigmund Rascher played a key role in the "decompression" or "high-altitude" experiments. The alleged purpose was to examine the effect of a sudden loss of pressure or lack of oxygen, such as that experienced by army pilots whose planes were destroyed and who had to make parachute jumps at great heights. From mid-March to mid-May 1942, about 200 inmates were used for these experiments; according to the eyewitness testimony of the prisoners' nurse, Walter Neff, out of this number at least 70 or 80 died. Rascher was also responsible for the series of "freezing experiments," which were carried out from the middle of August to October 1942. Their ostensible object was to determine how pilots shot down at sea who suffered from freezing could be quickly and effectively helped. The air force expressed its readiness to conduct these experiments under the direction of Dr. Ernst Holzlöhner, who worked with a Dr. Finke and Dr. Rascher in Dachau. Holzlöhner and Finke broke off their work after October 1942, and Rascher continued alone until March 1943. According to the testimony of witnesses, from a total of 360 to 400 prisoners used in these experiments, 80 to 90 died.

Professor Dr. Claus Schilling, a well-known researcher in tropical medicine, opened a malaria experimental station in the Dachau camp. He hoped to discover possible methods of immunization against malaria, and for this purpose had about 1,100 inmates infected with the disease. The exact number of fatalities from these experiments cannot be determined, since the survivors returned to their previous work in the camp after the disease had subsided and many, physically weakened, then fell victim to other illnesses.

Besides these, a variety of other medical experiments were performed on Dachau prisoners. There was a tuberculosis experimental station; sepsis and phlegmon (purulent inflammation) were artificially induced in a group of prisoners to test and compare the effects of biochemical and allopathic remedies. In addition, there were attempts to make seawater drinkable and experiments with medications to stop bleeding.

The systematic killing within the concentration camp of people who were sick and incapable of work began after the official termination of the EUTHANASIA PROGRAM on September 1, 1941. In the summer of 1941, the camp physician at Dachau was commanded to register those prisoners who were sick or unable to work. Some weeks later, a medical commission from Berlin arrived to pass judgment, and during the winter of 1941–1942 "invalid transports" departed from Dachau in quick succession to the Hartheim castle, near Linz, which had served as an asylum for the insane before the war. There, 3,166 inmates from Dachau were gassed. In 1942 a gas chamber was built in Dachau, but it was not put into use. It was located within the camp's second crematorium, erected when the first crematorium, with only one incinerator, proved inadequate.

From 1934, when the leaders of the SA (Sturmabteilung; Storm Troopers) and opponents of National Socialism were murdered, Dachau was also used as an execution site. In addition, mass shootings of Soviet PRISONERS OF WAR took place there from October 1941 to April 1942, on an SS shooting range located outside the camp grounds. The exact number of these victims cannot be determined, since they were not listed in camp files. Later, Soviet prisoners of war were incorporated instead into the powerful forced-labor system and set to work for the armaments industry. Executions thereafter were carried out individually until the end of the war.

During the last months before the liberation, the prisoners at Dachau had to live under extremely inhuman conditions, which even they would not have been able to imagine. The gigantic transports continually arriving from other Nazi camps evacuated in the face of the advancing Allies brought human beings who were, for the most part, reduced to skeletons and exhausted to the point of death. During this period up to 1,600 prisoners were crowded into barracks intended for 200. In early 1945, over 100 inmates daily, and for a time over 200, fell victim to the typhus epidemic that had been raging in many of the camps since December 1944. An underground camp committee was organized to try to ensure the survival of the prisoners and, if necessary, to organize resistance to SS plans of action.

A memorial, *Dachau*, by the Yugoslav sculptor Nandor Glid, erected at Yad Vashem, Jerusalem, on April 24, 1979. The Yad Vashem memorial is a copy of the one erected on the site of the roll-call area at Dachau in 1967. Bronze, 21 × 52 feet (6.3 × 16 m).

On April 26, 1945, there were 67,665 registered prisoners in Dachau, among them 22,100 Jews; on this day more than 7,000 of them were forced, under SS guard, to march south. During the march anyone who could continue no longer was shot, and many others died from hunger, cold, or exhaustion. At the beginning of May, American troops overtook the remnants of those columns on the march; the SS guards had disappeared shortly before. After the war, it was revealed that plans had existed to kill all the inmates by bombs and poison.

On April 29, 1945, the camp was liberated by the Seventh Army of the United States armed forces. Forty former members of the camp's SS staff were tried by an American court at Dachau between November 15 and December 14, 1945. Of the forty accused, thirty-six were sentenced to death.

BIBLIOGRAPHY

Benz, W., ed. *Dachau Review*. Vol. 1. New York, 1987.

Berben, P. *Dachau, 1933–1945: The Official History*. London, 1975.
Konnilyn, F. *Hitler's Death Camps*. New York, 1981.
Wallner, P. *By Order of the Gestapo*. London, 1941.

BARBARA DISTEL

DALUEGE, KURT (1897–1946), Nazi official. In 1916, Daluege volunteered for army service and became a lieutenant. He was a member of the notorious Rossbach Freikorps, which conducted partisan activity against France. He studied engineering at the Berlin Technical College, and from 1924 worked for the Berlin garbage-disposal department as a construction and civil engineer. Daluege joined the SA (Sturmabteilung; Storm Troopers) in Berlin in 1926 and transferred to the SS in 1928, having been appointed commander of SS Group East. On January 12, 1933, he became a member of the Reichstag; that May he was named chief of the police department of the Prussian Ministry of the

Kurt Daluege (far left), general of the German police. [National Archives]

Interior, with the rank of *Ministerialrat* (senior counselor).

Daluege was short on intellectual ability (his nickname was "Dumm-Dummi") but possessed organizational talent. With no interest or personal involvement in ideology, he served as a willing instrument for the automatic execution of orders; he had little interest in racial issues and left "Jewish affairs" in the hands of Reinhard HEYDRICH.

Under Daluege's direction, the Prussian police was infiltrated with SS men. Following the RÖHM putsch (the action against the SA on June 30, 1934), Daluege was promoted to SS-*Obergruppenführer*, and when Heinrich HIMMLER became chief of the German police, Daluege was appointed head of the Hauptamt Ordnungspolizei (the main office of the regular uniformed police). After Heydrich was assassinated in June 1942, Daluege became acting *Reichsprotektor* of the Protectorate of BOHEMIA AND MORAVIA, a post he held for a year, during which time the LIDICE massacre was perpetrated. For this and other crimes, Daluege was executed in 1946 in Czechoslovakia.

BIBLIOGRAPHY

Wistrich, R. *Who's Who in Nazi Germany.* New York, 1982.

UWE ADAM

DANNECKER, THEODOR (1913–1945), SS officer who specialized in organizing the deportation of Jews from Nazi-occupied Europe. Born in Tübingen, Dannecker was a lawyer by training but in 1937 became a member of Adolf EICHMANN's staff and later an essential collaborator in carrying out the "FINAL SOLUTION." He was sent to Paris in 1940 by Eichmann's bureau (IV B 4) as head of its French branch. In this capacity, Dannecker worked directly under Eichmann and supervised the preparation of lists of French Jews whose arrest followed in May and August of 1941. The following year, Dannecker prepared a set of rules governing the deportation of French Jews and "stateless" Jews in France not effectively protected by a foreign power. He constantly urged the Vichy government to accelerate the deportations to the east, surprising even Vichy officials by the vehemence of his hatred for Jews.

Eichmann recalled Dannecker to Berlin at the end of 1942 for abuse of office, and in January 1943 he was transferred to Bulgaria, where he organized the deportation of eleven thousand Jews from Macedonia and Thrace. In October 1944 Eichmann appointed him Jewish Commissioner in Italy, where he remained until the end of the war. He committed suicide in an American prison camp at Bad Tölz in December 1945.

BIBLIOGRAPHY

Hilberg, R. *The Destruction of the European Jews.* 3 vols. New York, 1985.

LIONEL KOCHAN

DANZIG (Pol., Gdańsk), city on the shores of the Baltic Sea, held alternately over the centuries by Germany and Poland, with both claiming sovereignty over it. This rivalry became dangerous after World War I, when Danzig was made a "free city" under the auspices of the League of Nations, thus providing Poland with access to the Baltic Sea via a corridor that cut off East Prussia from the Reich. Ninety-six percent of the city's population were Germans wanting to be reunited with their fatherland. Their militant nationalism contained elements of antisemitism.

DANZIG, SEPTEMBER 1939

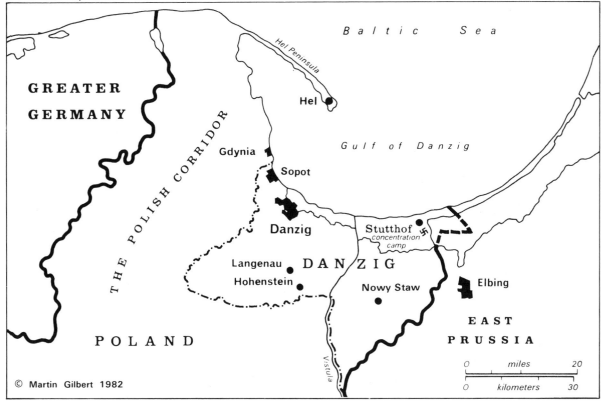

GREATER GERMANY

THE POLISH CORRIDOR

Baltic Sea

Hel Peninsula

Hel

Gulf of Danzig

Gdynia

Sopot

Danzig

Stutthof
concentration
camp

Langenau

Hohenstein

DANZIG

Nowy Staw

Elbing

POLAND

Vistula

EAST PRUSSIA

0   miles   20

0   kilometers   30

© Martin Gilbert 1982

Since entrance to the free city was not restricted, tens of thousands of Jews fleeing from war, revolution, and pogroms passed through it on their way to countries abroad, and thousands of these refugees settled in Danzig, increasing the local Jewish population from twenty-five hundred to twelve thousand. Entrepreneurs among them contributed considerably to the city's industrial development and its transit trade. This economic impact, combined with Poland's protection of its citizens, strengthened the Jews' position, and their struggle for equal rights was also supported by the League of Nations as the guarantor of Danzig's democratic constitution. The League's presence was manifested by a high commissioner who acted on its behalf.

In the 1920s the governing body, the senate, was dominated by a coalition of parties from the Center and the Right, but in the elections of May 1933 the National Socialists became the leading power, winning more than 50 percent of the votes. The Christian conservative Hermann RAUSCHNING became

head of the senate. For practical as well as ideological reasons he was opposed to racial antisemitism, one of the subjects he covered in his book *Gespräche mit Hitler* (1939; published in English as *Hitler Speaks*, 1939).

In November 1934, however, Rauschning was dismissed by the head of the Nazi party, Gauleiter Albert FORSTER, who named the veteran Nazi Arthur GREISER head of the senate. Greiser, like his predecessor, felt himself compelled to honor Danzig's international obligations and to refrain from complete identification with the politics of Nazi Germany. Even though the senate had already, in the 1920s, curtailed the Jews' civic rights —hampering their economic activities; preventing their naturalization; expelling foreign Jews; and discriminating against German Jews, who were not allowed to become officials—Greiser promised to safeguard the Jews' civic equality and to restrain the boycott propaganda. These promises were not kept.

The Jewish community, fighting for its rights, appealed in 1935 to the League of

"Danzig Salutes Its Führer!" Hitler (standing in front car) in a triumphant procession passing through Danzig on September 19, 1939. Albert Forster, the local *Gauleiter,* had declared the union of Danzig with Germany on September 1.

Nations through the offices of its high commissioner in Danzig, the Irishman Sean Lester, but since the impact of the League was already weakened, this proved of little avail. However, although the NUREMBERG LAWS had been promulgated in Germany in 1935, the Jews' situation in Danzig did not significantly change; in 1937 they still numbered twelve thousand, maintaining their key positions in the transit trade. The high commissioner from 1937 to 1939, Carl Jacob Burckhardt of Switzerland, tried to postpone actions against the Jews in order to avoid international complications, telling the Nazi government that he was acting for its benefit. In September 1937, he even obtained Hitler's consent to postpone the promulgation of the Nuremberg Laws in Danzig for reasons of foreign policy. Nevertheless, from October 20 to 23, 1937, a pogrom broke out, affecting mainly the Jewish traders and shopkeepers. In the following weeks the terror increased,

and the government started to intensify the process of ousting the Jews from the economy and confiscating their property. On November 21, 1938, following KRISTALLNACHT, the Nuremberg Laws were promulgated, with certain local modifications.

In the meantime the Jewish community had shrunk to about four thousand, mainly through emigration, and the threats on the lives of those who remained increased. Under the circumstances, the board of the Jewish community proposed to evacuate the remaining Jews through emigration, or, if there was no other alternative, by organizing illegal immigration to Palestine. In the arrangement concluded with the senate, the latter agreed to stop the terror and facilitate the issuing of passports and the obtaining of visas in return for a public announcement by all the Jews that they were willing to leave the city. This announcement was made at a meeting of the entire community on December 17, 1938. Because of the difficulties in implementing the plan, however, sixteen hundred Jews, many of them elderly people, still remained in Danzig when war broke out in September 1939. The board continued its efforts to organize illegal immigration, and the last group of Jews sailed on the *Patria*, which was blown up in the Haifa harbor. At the end of February 1941, the government started to deport the remainder of the Jewish population, six hundred in number, to Poland and THERESIENSTADT.

Even though a number of the city's Jews were eventually murdered, the community's agreement with the senate saved thousands of Danzig's Jews from expulsion and death.

BIBLIOGRAPHY

Levine, H. S. *Hitler's Free City: A History of the Nazi Party in Danzig, 1925–1939.* Chicago, 1973.
Lichtenstein, E. *Die Juden der Freien Stadt Danzig unter der Herrschaft des Nationalsozialismus.* Tübingen, 1973.
Stern, E. *The Jews of Danzig, 1840–1943: Integration, Struggle, Rescue.* Tel Aviv, 1983. (In Hebrew.)

ELIYAHU STERN

DARLAN, FRANÇOIS

DARLAN, FRANÇOIS (1881–1942), French admiral and statesman. In 1939 Darlan was appointed commander of the French fleet. When the Vichy government was established under Marshal Philippe PÉTAIN, Darlan joined it and held several portfolios in the cabinet. In 1940, after Pierre LAVAL's ouster, Pétain appointed Darlan prime minister. Darlan, pressured by the Germans as well as for internal reasons, in March 1941 created the COMMISSARIAT GÉNÉRAL AUX QUESTIONS JUIVES (General Office for Jewish Affairs). He introduced legislation under which all existing Jewish organizations were closed down and dissolved, to be replaced, late in that year, by the UNION GÉNÉRALE DES ISRAÉLITES DE FRANCE (General Council of French Jews; UGIF). Darlan, however, rejected the German demand that the Jews of France be forced to wear the yellow badge (*see* BADGE, JEWISH).

On April 14, 1942, Laval was reappointed prime minister, in response to German pres-

Adm. François Darlan of France visiting Hitler at Berchtesgaden. [National Archives]

sure. Darlan became the French government representative in North Africa a few days before its invasion by the Allies (November 8, 1942), and he persuaded the French army commanders on the spot to offer no resistance to the invading forces. President Franklin D. ROOSEVELT recognized Darlan as chief of state in French North Africa. Darlan retained the Vichy legislation, including the laws against the Jews. However, he was opposed both by the supporters of Pétain, who regarded him as a traitor, and by de GAULLE's Free French, who did not acknowledge the authority of the Vichy regime. On December 24, 1942, Darlan was killed by an anti-Vichy assassin.

BIBLIOGRAPHY

Lacouture, J. *Le rebelle.* Vol. 1 of *Charles de Gaulle.* Paris, 1984.
Marrus, M. R., and R. O. Paxton. *Vichy France and the Jews.* New York, 1981.

LUCIEN LAZARE

DARQUIER DE PELLEPOIX, LOUIS

DARQUIER DE PELLEPOIX, LOUIS (pseud. of Louis Darquier, 1897–1980), French coordinator of Vichy's anti-Jewish program from 1942 to 1944. A notorious antisemitic rabble-rouser, Darquier was chosen to head the Vichy government's COMMISSARIAT GÉNÉRAL AUX QUESTIONS JUIVES (Office for Jewish Affairs) in

May 1942, succeeding Xavier VALLAT, whom the SS in France found too moderate. At this point, the Nazis were about to begin the massive deportation of Jews from France to AUSCHWITZ. Darquier helped coordinate these deportations, and worked closely with the German authorities in PARIS. Quite apart from its brutality and its persecution based upon biological racism, which had hitherto been de-emphasized, Darquier's administration was characterized by corruption and incompetence. The Germans requested his removal, and he left office in February 1944. Darquier fled to Spain, where he lived until his death.

BIBLIOGRAPHY

Laloum, J. *La France antisémite de Darquier de Pellepoix.* Paris, 1979.
Marrus, M. R., and R. O. Paxton. *Vichy France and the Jews.* New York, 1981.

MICHAEL R. MARRUS

DARRÉ, RICHARD WALTHER (1895–1953), German *Reichsbauernführer* (Reich Farmers' Leader) as of April 1933, and *Reichsminister für Ernährung und Landwirtschaft* (Reich Minister of Food and Agriculture) from June 1933 to May 1942. Darré was born of German parents in Argentina. He studied at a high school in England and volunteered for army service in World War I, after which he pursued his studies in agriculture. He was regarded as one of the Nazi ideologists. Darré, a longtime friend of Heinrich HIMMLER—also a farmer—joined the Nazi party and the SS in 1930. In 1931, with Himmler's cooperation, he established the SS RASSE- UND SIEDLUNGSHAUPT-AMT (Race and Resettlement Main Office). He was the author of *Das Bauerntum als Lebensquell der nordischen Rasse* (The Peasantry as the Life Source of the Nordic Race; 1928) and *Neuadel aus Blut und Boden* (The New Aristocracy of Blood and Soil; 1930), in which he opposed further urbanization and industrialization and developed a *Lebensraumprogramm* (Program for Living Space). The peasant was at the center of Darré's ideology, and he believed in a mythical connection between the blood of the German race and the soil (*Blut und Boden*, or "blood and soil"; Blubo). His abstract approach and his inability to cope with problems of war supplies led to a rift with Himmler and, before long, also with Hitler, and Darré was removed from his posts. At the SUBSEQUENT NUREMBERG PROCEEDINGS, the Nuremberg Military Tribunals (the Ministry Case, November 15, 1947, to April 14, 1949) sentenced him to five years' imprisonment, but he was released in 1950.

BIBLIOGRAPHY

Farquharson, J. E. *The Plough and the Swastika: The NSDAP and Agriculture in Germany, 1928–1945.* London, 1976.

UWE ADAM

Richard Walther Darré testifying at his trial before the Nuremberg Military Tribunals.

DAUGAVPILS. *See* Dvinsk.

DAW. *See* Deutsche Ausrüstungswerke.

DEATH CAMPS. *See* Extermination Camps.

DEATH MARCHES (Ger., *Todesmärsche*), forced marches of long columns of prisoners under heavy guard, over long distances, and

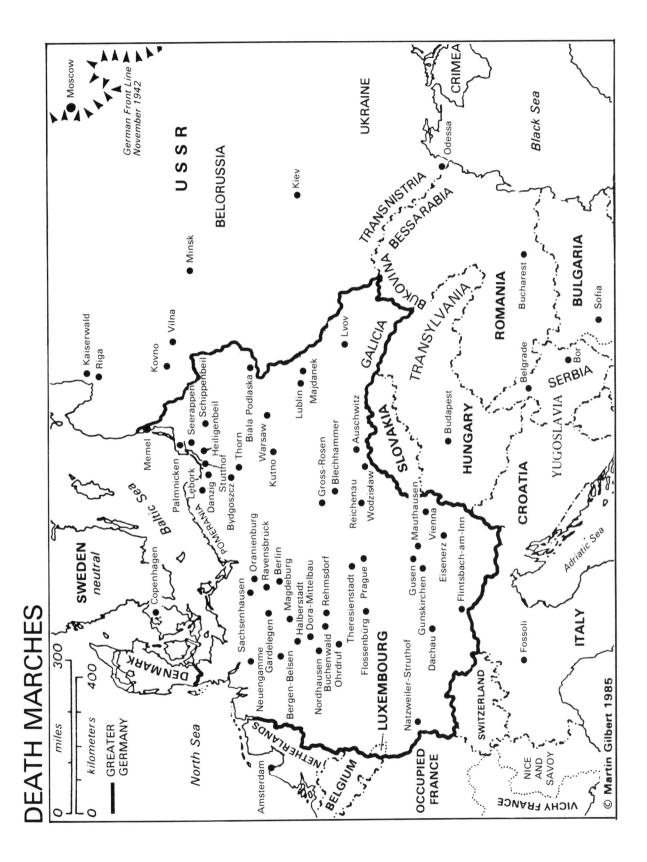

DEATH MARCHES

Hungarian Jews in Austria, victims of the notorious death march from Budapest in November 1944.

under intolerable conditions, in the course of which the prisoners were brutally mistreated and many killed by their escorts. The term was coined by prisoners in the Nazi CONCENTRATION CAMPS and was later used by historiographers of the Nazi regime.

Death marches are known to have taken place especially in the final stage of the war, when concentration camps were being evacuated, but they were a fairly frequent phenomenon throughout the war period. The first death march organized by the SS took place in Poland, in mid-January 1940. On January 14 of that year, eight hundred Jewish prisoners of war from the Polish army were removed from their camp on Lipowa Street in Lublin, and a few days later, escorted by a troop of mounted SS men, they were marched in bitter cold to Biała Podlaska, a distance of approximately 62 miles (100 km). All along the route the Nazis killed prisoners, individually and in groups, and only a few dozen survived to reach their destination.

Following the German invasion of the Soviet Union in the summer of 1941, hundreds of thousands of Soviet PRISONERS OF WAR were moved along the highways of the occupied Ukraine and Belorussia while being transferred from one camp to another, and murdered in their masses en route or at prearranged slaughter sites. In July and August 1941, tens of thousands of Jews from BESSARABIA and BUKOVINA were marched to TRANSNISTRIA, with thousands shot to death along the way by their German and Romanian military and gendarmerie escorts.

Tens of thousands of Jews were also forced on marches when the ghettos of eastern Europe were being liquidated in 1942 and 1943. Many of them were the inhabitants of small ghettos who were moved to larger ghettos or other collection points many miles away— for the most part, their last steps before they were deported to the EXTERMINATION CAMPS. On the way, many of the Jews were murdered by their German escorts or by auxiliary police (Ukrainians, Lithuanians, and others).

The liquidation of the concentration camps began in the summer of 1944, during the great Red Army offensive in the east and the Allied landings in the west. The first camps to be evacuated were those in the Baltic states and in eastern and central Poland; in the west, the NATZWEILER camp was emptied at this time. Most of the moves were made by rail and, in the case of the KAISERWALD camp, also by boat, but some of the prisoners were forced on foot marches.

The first major death march began on July 28, 1944, when the camp on Gesia Street in WARSAW was evacuated. This camp had been established on the ruins of the Warsaw ghetto as an extension of the MAJDANEK camp network. At the time it was evacuated the camp held some 4,400 Jews from various countries, most from Greece and Hungary. About 3,600 prisoners were forced to march to Kutno, a distance of 81 miles (130 km). During the march, anyone too weak to keep up the pace was shot by the Nazis. No food was supplied to the marchers, nor were they allowed to stop for a drink of water. About 1,000 prisoners were murdered on the march to Kutno. When the remainder reached their destination they were put on a freight train, 90 persons to a car; several hundred died on the train, and the rest—who now numbered

fewer than 2,000—arrived at DACHAU on August 9.

Even harsher and longer was the march from the Bor camp in Yugoslavia. About four thousand Jewish prisoners were taken out of that camp, put on the road to Belgrade, and marched for eight days, during which they received hardly any food. From Belgrade they proceeded to Hungary, also on foot. Most of the prisoners were killed on the way and no more than a few hundred survivors were left when the column reached Hungary, where they were dispatched to the ORANIEN-BURG camp by train. One of the prisoners murdered on this death march was the Hungarian Jewish poet Miklós Radnoti, who composed his last poems on the march.

The death march from Budapest began on November 8, 1944, and lasted an entire month. In that march seventy-six thousand Jews—men, women, and children—were made to walk to the Austrian border, es-

The American military authorities ordered the German civilians of the town of Schwarzenfeld, 25 miles (40 km) north of Regensburg, to dig a huge grave for the bodies of concentration camp prisoners who were shot by SS troops on a death march (April 25, 1945). [United States Army]

corted by Hungarians. Thousands were shot to death en route, and thousands more starved to death or succumbed to cold and disease. Several hundred were saved by neutral diplomats such as Raoul WALLENBERG, who pulled Jews out of the columns, put them under their protection, and escorted them back to Budapest. On the Austrian border the Germans took over, leading the columns to various concentration camps, primarily Dachau and MAUTHAUSEN.

The Jewish concentration camp inmates lived with the constant fear that the German exploitation of their labor was a temporary measure which would terminate at the end of the war, when they would all be murdered. In November 1944 Himmler ordered the cessation of murder by gas at AUSCHWITZ, a turning point in the Nazi policy toward the Jews, attributed to Germany's imminent defeat in the war. The Jews were, therefore, included among the other camp inmates in the continuous evacuation operation.

In the wake of the renewed Soviet offensive in mid-January of 1945, the Nazis undertook the evacuation of the remaining concentration camps in Poland. In that month large death marches were launched, primarily from Auschwitz in the south and STUTTHOF in the north. The Germans began evacuating Auschwitz and its satellite camps on January 18, 1945; sixty-six thousand prisoners, mostly Jews, were marched to Wodzisław (Ger., Loslau). There they were put on freight trains and transported to various concentration camps, principally GROSS-ROSEN, BUCHENWALD, Dachau, and Mauthausen. At least fifteen thousand perished in that march.

On January 21, 1945, four thousand prisoners, most of them Jews, left the BLECHHAMMER camp on foot. On February 2 they reached Gross-Rosen, and after staying there five days, left for Buchenwald by train. During the foot march, at least eight hundred prisoners were murdered; the commander of the escort, an SS-*Untersturmführer* named Klipp, excelled in his cruelty.

The evacuation of the Stutthof camp complex was exceptionally brutal and tragic. On the eve of the evacuation, in the middle of January 1945, these camps had a prisoner population of 47,000, over 35,000 of them Jews, of whom most were women. On January 20, the Seerappen camp in East Prussia, a satellite of Stutthof, was evacuated; 1,400 Jewish women and 100 Jewish men were put on the road. The next day they were joined by convoys from other satellite camps in the area (Jessau, Heiligenbeil, and Schippenbeil), making a total of 7,000 Jews—6,000 women and 1,000 men. The march took ten days, and during its course 700 Jews were murdered. On January 31 the convoy arrived at Palmnicken, on the shores of the Baltic. The same day, the Nazis drove all the prisoners into the sea and machine-gunned them. Only 13 persons are known to have survived this massacre.

The first evacuation of the main Stutthof camp was launched on January 25, 1945. That facility contained twenty-five thousand prisoners, half of whom were Jewish women. Another twenty thousand were in various Stutthof satellite camps in Pomerania; most of these were included in the death marches. The main route led from Stutthof to the town of Lebork (Lauenberg), where the convoy halted because the area was encircled by Red Army troops. The surviving prisoners were sent back to the main camp. The large satellite camps in Pomerania were Thorn (Pol., Torun) and Bromberg (Bydgoszcz), containing six thousand Jewish women prisoners; of these, 90 percent were murdered on the death marches following the evacuations.

The evacuation of the main camp of Gross-Rosen and its satellites began in early February 1945. A total of forty thousand prisoners were moved out; thousands were murdered en route, and the remainder were put into the Mittelbau, FLOSSENBÜRG, Buchenwald, Mauthausen, Dachau, BERGEN-BELSEN, and SACHSENHAUSEN camps. Of the twenty thousand Jewish prisoners employed as forced laborers in the Eulengebirge camps, nearly all were killed, most of them either just before the evacuation or during the death march in February 1945.

In the course of March and April 1945, when the American and British armies were advancing in the west and the Red Army in the east, the Germans evacuated one concentration camp after the other, moving the prisoners into the territory still under their control. In mid-March, Nazi Germany still held seven hundred thousand prisoners in concentration camps, among them two hundred thousand women. Approximately forty thousand SS men were still employed in running the concentration camps, guarding the prisoners, and escorting the death marches. In those last two months of the Third Reich's existence, at least a quarter-million prisoners, men and women, were sent on death marches, some of which lasted for weeks. The graves of the murder victims and the others who perished on the highways were spread over central Germany and western Austria. In that final phase, the evacuation of the camps was generally a combined operation: the prisoners made their way partly on foot and partly by train. The train trip was no less harsh or cruel than the foot march; the prisoners suffered from intolerably foul air in the cars, which held an average of seventy persons each, and from lack of food and water.

Some of the death marches in the final months of the war were particularly brutal. In late March and early April 1945, masses of prisoners were moved out of the main Buchenwald camp and its satellites and were sent on long-distance marches in which they incurred heavy losses. Thus, on April 3 and 4 a convoy of prisoners from the Nordhausen camp was forced to march to Flintsbach-am-Inn, a distance of 549 miles (885 km); another convoy originating in Nordhausen marched to Bergen-Belsen, 214 miles (345 km) away; and a group from Ohrdruf was sent to Dachau, a march of 245 miles (395 km). On April 4, a convoy left Halberstadt for Giessen, 316 miles (510 km) away; on April 7, another group from Halberstadt was dispatched to Appendorf, a distance of 327 miles (527 km); and on April 8, a third Halberstadt convoy was sent 162 miles (262 km) to Burstendorf.

In the evacuation of the main Buchenwald camp, the first convoy left on April 6. It consisted of 3,100 Jewish prisoners, of whom 1,400 were murdered on the way. In the next few days, April 7 to 10, some 40,000 prisoners left the camp, of whom 13,500 were murdered during the march. Twenty-one thousand prisoners remained in Buchenwald, among them a few Jews. Rehmsdorf was one of the last of the Buchenwald satellite camps to be evacuated, on April 13; 4,340 Jewish prisoners left the camp, but no more than 500 reached their destination, THERESIEN-STADT, the rest being murdered en route or perishing from other causes.

The evacuation of the DORA-MITTELBAU camp started on April 1, with most of the prisoners marched to Bergen-Belsen, a march lasting about two weeks. In one of the convoys the prisoners were forced into a barn that was then set on fire; the next day, when the American forces reached the site (near the town of Gardelegen), they found hundreds of burned corpses.

On April 25, 1945, there were about forty-five hundred prisoners in Stutthof, among them seventeen hundred Jews, when the final evacuation of the main Stutthof camp began. It was the continuation of the January death marches from the Stutthof satellite camps. Since the area of the camp was surrounded by Red Army forces, the prisoners were removed by sea, on ferryboats; two hundred Jewish women prisoners were first driven to the seashore and shot to death. Prisoners who tried to hide in the barracks were forced out and the barracks were set alight. Of the four thousand prisoners who left on five ferryboats, two thousand drowned or were shot to death by the Germans on the open sea. In the two evacuation operations of the Stutthof camps and the ensuing death marches, twenty-six thousand prisoners perished.

At the end of April, about two weeks before Nazi Germany's final surrender, death marches were launched from Flossenbürg, Sachsenhausen, NEUENGAMME, Magdeburg, Mauthausen, RAVENSBRÜCK, and several of the Dachau satellite camps. The marches of these last two weeks are believed to have cost the lives of tens of thousands of prisoners. On one short stretch alone, between Gunskirchen and Mauthausen, a distance of 37 miles (60 km), thousands of prisoners were buried, most of them Jews from Hungary. In another spot, near the town of Eisenerz, a mass grave was discovered after the war containing the bodies of thirty-five hundred prisoners who were on a death march to Mauthausen.

The evacuations and death marches were kept up literally until the Third Reich's last day. The final camp from which prisoners were sent on a death march was at Reichenau, in the Sudetic Mountains; this took place on May 7, the day on which Germany surrendered to the Allies.

Approximately a quarter of a million prisoners of the Nazi concentration camps were murdered or otherwise died on death marches between the summer of 1944 and the end of the war.

BIBLIOGRAPHY

Bauer, Y. "The Death Marches, January–May 1945." *Modern Judaism* 3/1 (February 1983): 1–21.

Krakowski, S. "The Death Marches in the Period of the Evacuation of the Camps." In *The Nazi Concentration Camps: Structure and Aims; The Image of the Prisoners; The Jews in the Camps.* Proceedings of the Fourth Yad Vashem International Historical Conference, edited by Y. Gutman and A. Saf, pp. 475–491. Jerusalem, 1984.

Strzelecki, A. *Ewakuacja, likwidacja, i wyzwolenie KL Auschwitz.* Oświęcim, 1982.

SHMUEL KRAKOWSKI

DEATH'S-HEAD UNITS. *See* Totenkopfverbände.

DEBRECEN, third largest city in HUNGARY, located in the northeastern part of the country on the Nagy Alfold (Great Plain), near the present-day Romanian border. Debrecen is a major center of Hungarian Calvinism. In 1941, 9,142 Jews lived there, comprising 7.3 percent of the population. An officially recognized Jewish community existed in the city from the mid-nineteenth century.

Like the other Jews of Hungary, the citizens of Debrecen were greatly affected by the first and second Hungarian anti-Jewish laws (1938 and 1939), which severely limited Jewish participation in economic life. Many Debrecen Jews became destitute. One reaction of the community was to turn inward, and as a consequence, Jews gravitated toward Zionism or sought solace in exploring their Jewish heritage more deeply.

Jewish men from Debrecen were drafted into the MUNKASZOLGÁLAT (Labor Service System) shortly after its creation in the summer of 1939. By 1941 the rate of conscription had increased significantly, and most of the area's Jews were sent to the Ukraine, from which few returned. Gen. Károly Beregffy, known to be particularly antisemitic, was the head of the Debrecen area draft board for the labor units and commander of the sixth labor camp, located near the city in the town of Hajdúbőszőrmény. In the fall of 1944, he served as a minister in Ferenc SZÁLASI's ARROW CROSS PARTY regime, for which he was hanged in 1945.

During the period of German occupation, the Jews of Debrecen, like those of SZEGED, were assigned to the fourth anti-Jewish operation zone (for the purpose of deportation, Hungary had been divided into six zones). For the city's Jews, the road from occupation to extermination was short and direct. German soldiers entered Debrecen on March 20, 1944. They promptly ordered the disbanding of the Jewish community and forced it to reorganize as a Zsidó Tanács (Jewish Council), under the leadership of Rabbi Pal (Meir) Weisz. A Jewish police force was set up under a former army captain, Béla Lusztbaum. On the last day of March a decree called for Jews to wear the Jewish BADGE. Early in April, Jewish automobiles were confiscated and Jewish telephones disconnected. On April 8 (during Passover), a handful of Jewish leaders were taken hostage by the authorities and imprisoned at nearby Hajdúszentgyorgy. Eventually, three hundred Jewish notables from the Debrecen area were confined there. On April 21, Jewish stores were forcibly closed. The following week witnessed a public burning of books considered "Jewish" or too liberal for the Hungarian right wing; it was directed by the antisemitic newspaper editor Mihály Kalosvari Borsca.

On April 28, 1944, the order to set up a ghetto was issued by the mayor, Sándor Kolcsey. Ironically, Kolcsey and the city secretary, József Zold, voiced their opposition to erecting a ghetto; this led to their ousting by Lajos Bessenyei, the Debrecen area chief magistrate. Lajos Csoka became the new mayor. On May 9, the boundaries of the ghetto, which was to be established in the western side of the city, were set. It had two parts, known as the "large" and the "small" ghetto, which were divided by Hatvan Street. The Jews of the city were forced to build the wall of the Debrecen ghetto, which stood 8.9 feet (2.7 m) high. On May 15 the ghetto was declared completed. A handful of Jews refused to enter it and hid in bunkers until the Soviet army arrived that fall. Local Hungarian police guarded the ghetto, whereas the Jewish police were charged with keeping order within the walls and were ordered to hand over those Jews whom the authorities wished to interrogate. Each Jew was allocated 43 square feet (4 sq m) of space, which meant that most rooms contained at least one entire family and often more. On June 7, all traffic in and out of the ghetto was ended, including that of Jews leaving the ghetto for work.

Two weeks later, on June 21, 1944, Hungarian gendarmes entered the ghetto and removed the Jews to the nearby Serly brickyards. There they joined the Jews from the neighboring communities of Balmazújvaros, Hajdúbőszőrmény, Hajdúdorog, Hajdúhadház, Hajdúnánás, Hajdúsamson, Hajdúszoboszló, Teglas, and Vamospercs—altogether, 13,084 Jews. At the brickyards, the Jews were stripped of their remaining valuables. A small group was sent to Hajdúszentgyorgy, from where the Jews were deported beginning on June 26. The first two trains, with 6,841 relatively fortunate passengers, were sent to STRASSHOF, in Austria, where the deportees were dispersed and put to work in agricultural and other enterprises for ORGANISATION TODT. Most of the other Jews from Debrecen were deported to AUSCHWITZ, where they arrived on July 3. About half of the Debrecen contingent of the Strasshof group survived the war. Among those killed in the Strasshof group were 233 Debrecen Jews, supposedly on their way to THERESIENSTADT; they were shot by SS men in Bratislava in May 1945.

During the period of ghettoization and deportation, news of the so-called Kasztner train (see KASZTNER, REZSŐ) reached Debrecen via messengers from the Zionist youth movement who posed as gentiles. They told the leader of the Orthodox community, Shlomo Strasser, that anyone from Debrecen could be included in the designated quota for the city. During the deportations, ten families, including those of Rabbi Weisz, Rabbi Strasser, and Zionist leaders, were taken to the Columbus Street camp in Budapest. Soon thereafter they embarked on the Kasztner train, which eventually brought them to freedom in Switzerland. A handful of Zionist

youth activists led by Dr. Adoniyahu Billitzer also escaped from Debrecen. They reached Budapest, where they took part in rescue and defense activities.

Debrecen was taken by the Soviet army on October 20, 1944, and became the administrative center of the antifascist provisional government. Some four thousand Jews from Debrecen survived the war. In 1970, twelve hundred Jews were living there.

BIBLIOGRAPHY

Braham, R. L. *The Politics of Genocide.* New York, 1981.

Gonda, M. E. *A Debreceni Zsidok szasz eve: A martirhalalit halt Debreceni es kornyekbeli Zsidok emlekere.* Tel Aviv, 1970. (In Hebrew and Hungarian.)

Lavi, T., ed. *Hungary.* In *Pinkas Hakehillot; Encyclopaedia of Jewish Communities.* Jerusalem, 1976. (In Hebrew.)

ROBERT ROZETT

DEFFAUGT, JEAN, mayor of Annemasse, a French town on the Swiss border, where many clandestine escape routes for fleeing Jews converged. Deffaugt took it upon himself to visit Jews who were caught by the Germans while trying to cross the border and incarcerated in an annex of the Pax Hotel, where they had to withstand brutal interrogation of the Gestapo. He collected food, medicines, blankets, and other supplies,

Jean Deffaugt and his wife.

which he brought to the Gestapo prison to deliver to the inmates. Deffaugt pleaded with the Gestapo on behalf of the imprisoned Jews. As he later reminisced, "I was afraid, I admit. I never mounted the Gestapo stairways without making the sign of the cross, or murmuring a prayer." On one occasion, the Gestapo agreed to release into Deffaugt's care a group of children under the age of eleven, arrested while on their way to the border, on the basis of the following statement: "I, Jean Deffaugt, mayor of Annemasse, acknowledge receiving from Inspector Mayer, chief of the Security Services, eleven children of Jewish faith, whom I pledge to return at the first order." Deffaugt soon placed them in the hands of a Father Duret, who hid them in Bonne-sur-Menoge until the Allied liberation in the following weeks.

With the liberation of Annemasse by the United States Army, all the children were reunited by Deffaugt and turned over to Jewish hands. Jean Deffaugt was recognized by YAD VASHEM as a "RIGHTEOUS AMONG THE NATIONS" in 1965.

BIBLIOGRAPHY

Lazare, L. *La résistance juive en France.* Paris, 1987.
Minc, R. *L'enfer des innocents—Les enfants juifs dans la tourmente nazie: Recits.* Paris, 1966. See pages 132–137.

MORDECAI PALDIEL

DE GAULLE, CHARLES. *See* Gaulle, Charles de.

DEGESCH. *See* Trials of War Criminals: Zyklon B Trial; Zyklon B.

DEJ (Hung., Dés), former capital of Szolnok-Doboka county, in northern TRANSYLVANIA; part of the territory acquired by Hungary from Romania in September 1940. According to the census of 1941, the city had a population of 16,353, of whom 3,719 (19.3 percent) were Jews. The overwhelming majority of the Jews belonged to the Orthodox community;

many of these were Hasidim. Between 1862 and 1944, the community had many well-established denominational and ecclesiastical institutions, which were under the overall leadership of the Paneth rabbinical dynasty. The last spiritual leader of the community was Rabbi Jacob Elimelech Paneth. Its secular head was Ferenc Ordentlich, who also served as head of the local branch of the Zsidó Tanács (Jewish Council), formed after the ghetto was established on May 3, 1944.

The ghetto was located in the nearby Bungur Forest, where most of its 7,800 Jews, including those brought in from the rural communities in the county, lived under the open sky, without shelter from the elements. Surrounded by barbed wire, the ghetto was guarded by the local police and a gendarme unit brought in from the nearby district of Zilah. The wealthier elements of the Dej community were subjected to particularly cruel treatment by the gendarmes, who were in pursuit of Jewish wealth.

The Jews in the ghetto were deported to AUSCHWITZ in three transports between May 28 and June 8. During the period immediately following the war, Dej, which had reverted to Romania, had a Jewish population of 1,020 (1947). This consisted of the local survivors, as well as those who had moved into the city from neighboring villages and from other parts of Romania.

BIBLIOGRAPHY

Braham, R. L. *Genocide and Retribution.* Boston, 1983.
Singer, Z., ed. *Volt egyszer egy Dés.* . . . Tel Aviv, 1970.

RANDOLPH L. BRAHAM

DE-JUDAIZATION. *See* Entjudung.

DELEGATURA, the POLISH GOVERNMENT-IN-EXILE underground representation in POLAND in the period from 1940 to 1945. Heading the Delegatura were a *delegat* (the government representative, who in 1944 was given the rank of deputy prime minister) and three deputies (who were given the rank of minister). The *delegaty*, in order of succession, were Cyril Ratajski, Jan Piekalkiewicz, Jan Jankowski, Stefan Korbonski, and Jerzy Braun. Assisting the *delegat* was a committee made up of representatives of the four political parties on which the government-in-exile was based. By decision of the four coalition partners, the Polish government-in-exile issued two declarations of principle, as well as several appeals to the Polish people and to the world.

The committee, which was an advisory as well as a decision-making body, had various names at different times: Polityczny Komitet Porozumiewawczy (Coordinating Political Committee; 1940–1943), Krajowa Reprezentacja Polityczna (National Political Representation; 1943), and Rada Jedności Narodowej (National Unity Council; as of January 1944). Its last chairman was Kazimierz Puzak, of the Polish Socialist party. In July 1945, when the Provisional Government of National Unity was established, the Delegatura and the council went out of existence.

The central structure of the Delegatura, which was an executive body, consisted of numerous sections. Their assignments corresponded to the departments of a regular administration. The Delegatura also established provincial, district, and municipal missions, the entire system amounting to an alternate government, rivaling the occupation authorities—an "underground state," with its own systems of education and law and its own armed force, the ARMIA KRAJOWA.

Until 1943, the Delegatura did not concern itself with the problem of Jews in occupied Poland, nor did it establish an organization for this purpose. Early that year a Jewish-affairs bureau was set up, headed by Witold Bienkowski, with Władysław BARTOSZEWSKI as his deputy, within the internal-affairs department. The task of this bureau was to organize the Delegatura's activities with regard to the Jewish population, to keep in daily touch with ZEGOTA (the Polish Council for Aid to Jews), and to process material on the fate of the Jews, for transmission to the Polish government-in-exile in London. The *delegat* himself also dealt with these subjects, as did the Civil Struggle Directorate (Kierownictwo Walki Cywilnej), which had been set up under his auspices. The latter's task was to co-

ordinate popular resistance to the occupying power, and it frequently came out with denunciations of the Nazi crimes against the Jewish population. Thus, in a statement published on September 17, 1942, the Civil Struggle Directorate declared:

> For nearly a year now, in addition to the tragedy of the Polish people, which is being slaughtered by the enemy, our country has been the scene of a terrible, planned massacre of the Jews. This mass murder has no parallel in the annals of mankind; compared to it, the most infamous atrocities known to history pale into insignificance. Unable to act against this situation, we, in the name of the entire Polish people, protest the crime being perpetrated against the Jews; all political and public organizations join in this protest.

BIBLIOGRAPHY

Bartoszewski, W., and Z. Lewin. *Righteous among Nations: How Poles Helped the Jews, 1939–1945.* London, 1969.
Duraczynski, E. *Między Londynem a Warszawa, VII 1943–VII 1944.* Warsaw, 1986.
Engel, D. *In the Shadow of Auschwitz: The Polish Government in Exile and the Jews, 1939–1942.* Chapel Hill, 1987.
Gutman, Y., and S. Krakowski. *Unequal Victims: Poles and Jews during World War Two.* New York, 1986.
Korbonski, S. *The Polish Underground State: A Guide to the Underground, 1939–1945.* New York, 1981.

EUGENIUSZ DURACZYNSKI

DEMJANJUK TRIAL, trial held in the Jerusalem District Court; the second trial in Israel in which the death penalty was imposed under the Nazis and Nazi Collaborators (Punishment) Law 5710-1950 (the first was the EICHMANN TRIAL).

In 1975, information reached the United States Department of Justice that John Iwan Demjanjuk, a resident of Cleveland, Ohio, had collaborated with the Nazis as a member of the SS, and had served as a guard in the SOBIBÓR camp. His photograph, taken from an immigration application form he had filled out in 1951, was sent to Israel and was shown to survivors of the TREBLINKA extermination camp. All those who saw the photograph identified it conclusively as being that of a Ukrainian SS staff member at Treblinka who, because of his fearful cruelty, was called "Ivan the Terrible." A short time later the same survivors were shown a photograph taken in 1942, removed from an identification card used in the TRAWNIKI training camp for SS guards, and it too was identified as the same individual from Treblinka.

At the end of August 1977 the Cleveland state prosecutor submitted a request to the local district court asking for the annulment of Demjanjuk's citizenship, granted on November 14, 1958, on the ground that in his immigration application he had concealed the fact that he had been a member of the SS and a guard in the above extermination camps. On June 23, 1981, after a series of trials, Frank Batisti, senior judge of the Northern District Court of the State of Ohio, ruled that Demjanjuk had lied when filling out the immigration application form in 1951, had concealed his membership in the SS, had been in the Trawniki SS training camp, and had served in the Treblinka and Sobibór extermination camps. The judge ruled that Demjanjuk's American citizenship be annulled, in effect sentencing him to deportation from the United States. In October 1983, after Demjanjuk's appeals against the sentence had failed, the state of Israel submitted an extradition request for him to stand trial under the Nazis and Nazi Collaborators (Punishment) Law 5710-1950. At the end of 1985, after further hearings on the extradition, Israel's request was granted, and on February 28, 1986, Demjanjuk was taken to Israel and imprisoned there.

On February 16, 1987, the trial of Demjanjuk began in the Jerusalem District Court, before Supreme Court Judge Dov Levin and the Jerusalem District Court judges Dalia Dorner and Zvi Tal. The prosecution was represented by the attorney general, Yona Blattman, and the attorneys Michael Shaked, Michael Horowitz, and Dafna Beinwall, supported by a number of expert assistants. The defense consisted of the attorneys Mark O'Connor, John Gill, and Paul Chumak from the United States, and Yoram Sheftel of Israel. The prosecution charged Demjanjuk under the 1950 Punishment Law and under Clause 300 of the 1977 criminal law, on a number of counts: crimes against the Jewish people, crimes against humanity, war crimes, crimes against persecuted individuals, and murder.

Demjanjuk was born in 1920 in the village of Dub Makarenzi, in the Kazatin subdistrict of Kiev Oblast (district). In 1940 he was recruited into the Soviet army and from June 1941 fought against the Germans. He was wounded and hospitalized, returned to service, and during the battle in the Kerch region of the eastern Crimea in May 1942, was taken prisoner by the Germans. At the beginning of July he was brought to the prisoner-of-war camp in Chełmno, near Lublin. Soon afterward, in mid-July, Demjanjuk volunteered for service in the SS auxiliary units and was sent to the SS training camp at Trawniki, where he was trained as a concentration camp guard. At the beginning of October, Demjanjuk was posted to the Treblinka extermination camp, where he supervised the gas chambers and operated the machine that circulated the gas into the chambers. He forced the victims into the gas chambers with the utmost cruelty, flogged them with a whip or an iron pipe, slashed and stabbed them with a sword or dagger, and shot others. He served in Treblinka until September 1943, except for a short period during which he was in Sobibór.

The prosecution called sixty witnesses, among whom were many survivors of Treblinka, as well as criminal-identification experts, police investigators, historians, legal interrogators from Israel and West Germany, and experts from the United States. With the aid of these witnesses the prosecution described AKTION REINHARD (the extermination of Polish Jewry), the annihilation operation in the extermination camps, and the events of the Treblinka camp.

The defense did not deny what had taken place during the Holocaust, and especially the killings in the Treblinka camp, but it repudiated the identification of the defendant, claiming that John Demjanjuk was not "Ivan the Terrible" of Treblinka. The defense attorneys argued that the identification of the accused was erroneous from the outset, because it had been made by survivors many years after the events described by the prosecution, and the accuracy of their memory could not be relied upon. The defense also argued that Demjanjuk's identification card from Trawniki (the "Trawniki document"), which had been received from the Soviet Union, was a forgery made by the Soviet security services, and that Demjanjuk had never been in either Trawniki or the Treblinka and Sobibór extermination camps. It claimed that at the beginning of 1944 Demjanjuk had been sent from the Chełmno prisoner-of-war camp to Graz in Austria, to join the First Ukrainian Division under the command of Gen. Pavlo Shandruk; he was transferred from there, several weeks later, to Heuberg in Bavaria, to the camp of Gen. Andrei VLASOV's army, where he remained until the end of the war.

With the aid of psychological experts, the prosecution refuted the argument that the human memory could not be relied upon after such a long time; by means of the testimony of experts in criminal identification it rejected the argument that the "Trawniki document" was a forgery; and with the aid of historians it refuted Demjanjuk's alibi. On April 18, 1988, the judges found Demjanjuk guilty of all the charges in the indictment and sentenced him to death. The defense lodged an appeal in the Israeli Supreme Court.

[*See also* Trials of War Criminals.]

BIBLIOGRAPHY

Wagenaar, W. A. *Identifying Ivan: A Case Study in Legal Psychology.* Cambridge, Mass., 1988.

SHMUEL SPECTOR

DENAZIFICATION, the process of expurgating Nazism and its influence and punishing its practitioners. At the Yalta Conference, held in February 1945, six months before World War II ended, the three participants —Franklin D. ROOSEVELT, president of the United States; Winston CHURCHILL, prime minister of Britain; and Joseph STALIN, leader of the Soviet Union—in a joint statement announced that they were "determined to wipe out the Nazi party, Nazi laws, organizations, and institutions, remove all Nazi and militarist influences from public office and from the cultural and economic life of the German people, and take such other agreed measures in Germany as may be necessary for the future peace and safety of the world." Whereas the Moscow Declaration by the Allied powers (November 1, 1943) had spoken of the punishment of individuals responsible for Nazi crimes, the Yalta statement signified that the Allies were aiming, above all, at a radical reform of Germany's political institutions by the systematic elimination of all their Nazi and militarist elements.

The Potsdam Agreement, signed on August 2, 1945, by the leaders of the United States, Britain, and the Soviet Union, contained the following declaration:

All members of the Nazi party who have been more than nominal participants in its activities and all other persons hostile to Allied purposes are to be removed from public or semi-public office and from positions of responsibility in important private undertakings. Such persons shall be replaced by persons who by their political and moral qualities are deemed capable of assisting in developing genuine democratic institutions in Germany.

By the time the Potsdam Agreement was signed, a large number of persons who were to be removed from office according to the above declaration were already being held in custody. Long before the occupation of Germany had been accomplished, the Supreme Headquarters of the Allied Expeditionary Forces had drawn up lists of persons who were subject to "mandatory arrest," on the assumption that they had taken part in Nazi crimes. When the war ended, these lists were extended to include persons thought to be particularly dangerous because of their prominent positions in Nazi organizations, the Wehrmacht, the administration, and the economy. A total of 178,000 persons were placed under "mandatory arrest" by the three western Allies and put into internment camps—95,000 in the American zone, over 64,000 in the British zone, and 19,000 in the French zone. In the Soviet-occupied zone, more than 67,000 persons were detained.

In German resistance circles, it had also been agreed as early as 1943 that in principle, when the war was over and the Hitler dictatorship had collapsed, all Nazi elements would have to be eliminated from public life, and that persons who had taken part in the crimes of the Nazi regime would be put on trial. Shortly after the Allied occupation of Germany, German opponents of the Nazi regime began to organize in various places to undertake such "self-purge" operations on their own; these attempts, however, were stifled by the western Allies' military administrations. Only the Soviets, for a short while, permitted feelings of loathing and resentment to be expressed in their zone by spontaneous lynch trials.

Neither the Yalta statement nor the Potsdam declaration contained any guidelines for implementing the announced policy of ridding Germany of Nazism and militarism. The result was that each zone had its own policy in this area, depending on the specific interests and goals of the occupying power.

In the American zone, two influences were at work among the military administration: on the one hand, a desire to reeducate the German people for life in a democratic society; and on the other hand, a belief in collective German guilt and, as a corollary, a general distrust of Germans that did not differentiate between supporters and opponents of the Nazi regime. The requirements of the economy and proper administration were given little weight; American officers, even of higher rank, who employed German experts with a Nazi past in the management of local institutions, were suspended on the spot.

In the British zone, the prevailing inclination was to institute a radical purge of Nazi and militarist influences. This zone, which contained the Ruhr district, had the highest population density, and in the war its housing, transportation, and manufacturing facilities had sustained greater damage than any other part of Germany. In this situation the British were soon ready to pursue a pragmatic policy and seek compromise, out of concern that life would break down completely if Germans familiar with local conditions and problems were to be excluded from employment in responsible posts. Under the Nazi regime all leading officials in the economy and administration, even those on a middle or lower level, had belonged to some sort of a Nazi organization, at least nominally. In these circumstances, the British oc-

cupation authorities felt forced to make use of persons who, by the criteria in force at the time, were to be regarded as politically incriminated. German antifascists protested strongly against this practice, but to no avail.

France—which had not taken part in either the Yalta or the Potsdam conference—also subscribed to the principle that Nazi elements had to be removed, but in the French zone the issue was never accorded the degree of importance that it had in the American or even in the British zone. France's goals were to weaken Germany, its "traditional enemy," by decentralizing Germany's political framework, and also to exploit the resources still to be found in the French zone of Germany for the restoration of the French economy, which had declined sharply as a result of the war. The French not only were ready to retain in their posts persons who were incriminated by activities in Nazi organizations, but often went so far as to engage German experts from other zones who had been dismissed from office for that very reason.

In the Soviet zone, from the start, denazification measures were designed to serve the Soviets' main objective—restructuring society in accordance with Communist principles. Leaders of industry and large landowners were dispossessed without hesitation. In many instances, property of the middle class was also nationalized, if the owner was regarded as having been a Nazi sympathizer. All key positions in the administration, the economy, and cultural life were staffed by Communists loyal to the official line, without consideration for their professional qualifications. Jurists who had served under the Nazi regime as judges or state attorneys were dismissed, with hardly any exceptions. Persons suspected of having taken part in Nazi crimes were taken into custody, and some were exiled to the east; but most of the rank-and-file members of Nazi organizations were not affected by the denazification measures—provided they showed that they were prepared to participate in the creation of a Communist society, as by joining the Communist party.

In order to avoid too great divergences in their respective denazification policies, the four powers, through the Allied Control Council for Germany, issued a regulation

(No. 24, dated January 12, 1946) that provided uniform guidelines to be applied in all the zones of occupation. Attached to the regulation was a list of offices and positions from which former Nazis were barred. Had these guidelines been observed, the denazification measures would have been much harsher than they were in practice. However, it was too late for that; developments had reached the point where the trend toward moderation could no longer be reversed by a Control Council regulation, especially in the French and British zones.

Another Control Council regulation, No. 38 (of October 12, 1946), required that former Nazis be classified in one of five categories:

1. Major offenders
2. Offenders (activists, militarists, profiteers)
3. Lesser offenders
4. Followers
5. Persons exonerated

Persons in categories 1 to 4 were subject to punishment or some form of "reparation": detention in a labor camp, for terms ranging from two to ten years (major offenders); banning from employment; confiscation of property; loss of pension rights; special deductions from current income; restriction of voting rights. Persons in category 4 who were born after January 1, 1919, were exempt from reparation in a "youth amnesty." In the French zone, other amnesties were announced in 1947 and 1948 affecting persons in category 4.

The basis for the classification was a questionnaire that had to be filled in by the person to be denazified, in which he had to give his personal data and divulge his activities during the Nazi regime and his association with Nazi organizations. If the questionnaire showed grounds for incrimination, the case came before a panel of three (one professional jurist, as chairman, and two lay judges) for decision. The Control Council regulation provided for the presumption of guilt, and it was up to the person so affected to prove his innocence; this resulted in many instances of similar cases leading to totally different outcomes.

In view of the difficulties encountered by the denazification procedure, the occupying powers soon sought to transfer its implemen-

tation to the Germans. At the Four-Power Foreign Ministers' Conference, which took place in Moscow in the spring of 1947, it was decided to recommend to the military commanders in the different zones that they transfer the responsibility for implementing Control Council regulations 24 and 38 to the Germans, and that they leave it up to the German authorities to decide on the measures required for such implementation; the occupying power, however, would retain its supreme authority on the subject. In the wake of this recommendation, denazification was handed over to the German authorities in 1947 and 1948.

The change in the international climate and the ensuing deterioration in relations between East and West reduced the interest of the powers in denazification. In March 1948, denazification was brought to an abrupt end in the Soviet zone. On October 15, 1950, the Bundestag (the West German parliament) recommended to the German states that they suspend current classification procedures affecting categories 3, 4, and 5; abstain from introducing any new procedures; and abolish the existing bans on practicing certain professions, on the blocking of bank accounts or other assets, and on the restriction of voting rights. The Bundestag also recommended the granting of pardons to most of the persons who had been sentenced to serve in labor camps. The German states complied with these recommendations by various laws enacted in the period from 1950 to 1954, and they thereby brought denazification to an end.

According to an (incomplete) table made by the West German Ministry of the Interior at the end of 1949, 3,660,648 persons had by then been processed in the three western zones; 1,667 had been classified in category 1 (major offenders); 23,060 in category 2 (offenders); 150,425 in category 3 (lesser offenders); and 1,005,874 in category 4 (followers). A total of 3,410,728 sentences of punishment and reparation were imposed.

Denazification had been launched with great zeal, but it ran out of steam when neither the procedures laid down nor the authorities charged with its implementation proved adequate for the task. Nazi activists who had committed the gravest crimes in the occupied countries did not, needless to say, admit to them in their questionnaires, and more often than not passed unharmed through the denazification process. On the other hand, it was not rare for persons who had been only nominal party members—who had succumbed to pressure from superiors in order to hold on to their jobs and had only held minor "honorary" posts in the party— to have severe sanctions applied to them. Numerous questionnaires were forged, and discrimination, as well as denunciations, occurred quite frequently. Since the motivation in these cases was based on personal and economic rather than political grounds, denazification was put in an even more questionable light. Moreover, depending on which occupation zone was responsible, similar cases were given quite different treatment, a situation that was naturally regarded as unfair and unjust. The less serious cases were dealt with in an early stage of the occupation, when the sentences imposed were relatively severe, whereas the more serious cases were put off. By the time they reached trial, the Allies were no longer as concerned about denazification as previously, with the result that the offenders escaped relatively lightly.

In the end, it was not only those subjected to denazification who opposed it; the process itself came to be rejected, even by opponents of the Nazi regime.

BIBLIOGRAPHY

Bower, T. *The Pledge Betrayed: America and Britain and the Denazification of Postwar Germany.* Garden City, N.Y., 1982.

Friedmann, W. *The Allied Military Government of Germany.* London, 1947.

Fuerstenau, J. *Entnazifizierung: Ein Kapitel deutscher Nachkriegspolitik.* Neuwied, West Germany, 1969.

Griffith, W. E. *The Denazification in the United States Zone of Germany.* Cambridge, Mass., 1966.

Johnson, J. *Dilemmas of Postwar Germany.* New York, 1948.

Lenz, H. *Der Schlusstrich: Gedanken zur Entnazifizierung.* Cologne, 1948.

Niethammer, L. *Entnazifizierung in Bayern: Säuberung und Rehabilitierung unter amerikanischer Besatzung.* Frankfurt, 1972.

ADALBERT RÜCKERL

DENMARK, the southernmost of the Scandinavian countries. Jews settled in Denmark in the late seventeenth century; in 1814 they were granted citizenship, and in 1849, under the constitution adopted that year, they received full rights. Denmark's Jews belonged to the lower and upper middle class; many made a name for themselves in science, literature, the arts, and journalism, or held senior posts in banking and the administration. The rate of mixed marriages was among the highest in the world. In the twentieth century most of Denmark's six thousand Jews lived in the capital, Copenhagen.

During the 1930s the Jewish community of Denmark, like that of every country bordering on Germany, was called upon to assist Jewish refugees. In 1940 a special body, the May Fourth Committee, was established by the community to care for the refugees, which it did in cooperation with several non-Jewish committees that had been formed for the same purpose. One special project was an agricultural-training program set up in coop-

DENMARK

eration with the Zionist pioneering movement He-Haluts, in which the Ministry of Agriculture issued a special permit enabling fifteen hundred youngsters to work on farms and some of them to engage in fishing as well. Shortly before the outbreak of World War II, YOUTH ALIYA groups from Germany, Austria, and Czechoslovakia came to Denmark, thanks to the efforts of Danish women's organizations.

On the whole, however, Danish policy on refugees was reserved; as in other European countries, it differentiated between "political" refugees and other kinds—the "other kinds" being the Jews. Political refugees—most of whom were Social Democrats or Communists—were taken care of by the Danish Social Democrat party's Matteotti Foundation, and were given preference as far as residence and work permits were concerned. On behalf of the government, the relevant ministries, mostly the Ministry of Justice and the Ministry of Social Affairs, handled refugee affairs.

Between 1934 and 1938 the laws and regulations applying to refugees became increasingly restrictive, and non-Scandinavians encountered great difficulties in entering the country and even more so in trying to obtain work permits. Most of the Jewish refugees who did succeed in reaching Denmark—their number is estimated at forty-five hundred—did not remain, and left the country for overseas destinations. When the Germans occupied Denmark in 1940, fifteen hundred Jewish refugees were still in the country, including several hundred *halutsim* (agricultural pioneers) and Youth Aliya children. During the 1930s, the Rigsdag (the Danish parliament) debated government policy on the refugees, with the conservative parties calling for a reduction in their number and a ban on further entries into the country, while the liberal groups expressed disapproval of government policy on the issue. Both the government and the general public expressed their opposition to antisemitism and joined the Jewish community in combating its manifestations.

In the first years following the German occupation (on April 9, 1940), the situation of the Jews remained unchanged—unlike that

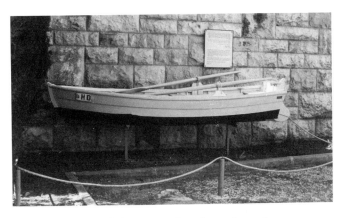

One of the Danish boats used to ferry Jews from the town of Gilleleje to fishing boats at sea, which then brought them to safety in Sweden (October 1943). This boat is on permanent display at Yad Vashem in Jerusalem.

in other countries occupied by the Nazis. The Danes (in contrast to the Norwegians) did not offer any real resistance to the Germans, and reached agreement with the German government on the continued operation of the country's democratic administration. They followed a so-called policy of negotiations, under which the Danish government, and even the Danish army, remained in existence; only the conduct of foreign affairs was no longer in Danish hands. Relations between the two countries were still on a diplomatic basis, with the German minister to Copenhagen, Cecil von Renthe-Fink, staying in his post. The agreement between the Danish government and the occupation authorities contained a provision committing the Germans to refrain from causing harm to the Jews. The protection of Danish Jews by the Danish government remained in force even in times of crisis between the government and the Germans, and the Danish people resolutely resisted occasional German pressure on the Jewish issue, as well as the efforts of the small Danish Nazi party to stir up antisemitism. In the winter of 1941–1942, a public debate was held on the "Jewish question," in which the moderator, Hal Koch, a professor of theology, called on the Danish people to reject out of hand any suggestion that they discriminate against the Danish Jews, not only because justice and honor demanded it, but also because it was a prerequisite for preserving Danish liberty and the rule of law.

The steadfast stand on this issue by the Danish people and the Danish government persuaded the Germans that for the time being it would be preferable not to touch the Danish Jews; at the WANNSEE CONFERENCE, Martin LUTHER, representing the German Foreign Office, proposed that the Scandinavian countries be excluded for the time being from the "FINAL SOLUTION" because of the attitude of the local populations toward the Jews, and the small number of Jews in those countries. The Germans took it for granted that the issue would be resolved after victory had been achieved. This policy remained in force when von Renthe-Fink was replaced, in the fall of 1942, by Dr. Werner BEST.

A change came in the spring of 1943. With the growing strength of the Allied forces on the battlefronts, Danish resistance operations gathered momentum (in the early stage of the occupation such resistance had hardly existed). The strikes and sabotage acts created tension between the Danes and the Germans, and the "Jewish question" was put on the agenda. Throughout this period, and from the beginning of the occupation, the Jewish community had kept a low profile and its quiet life was not seriously disturbed. He-Haluts, however, showed greater sensitivity, became aware of the changing situation, and made plans for escaping from the country. An attempt by some of the young people to reach the coast of southern Europe by hiding under train carriages failed; on the other hand, a group of He-Haluts fishermen on Bornholm Island obtained a boat and used it to flee to Sweden. The Germans learned of the escape and issued a stern warning to the Danish government, which passed it on to the Jewish community. This incident caused friction between the Jewish community—which bore part of the cost of maintaining the Zionist training farms—and the He-Haluts trainees, with the community leaders threatening to take action if such attempts were repeated.

In late August 1943, a crisis erupted between the German authorities and the Danish government when the latter refused to accede to new demands made by the Germans. The Danish government resigned, and the German military commander in Denmark declared a state of emergency. Werner Best regarded this as an opportune moment for proposing to Berlin that the Jews of Denmark be deported; he probably felt that his proposal would bring German police reinforcements to Denmark and that this would have the effect of bolstering his own position, which had suffered as a result of the crisis. Best himself, it turned out, was not sure that his proposal should be carried out, fearing that his own relations with the Danes would be compromised.

On the night of October 1–2, 1943, the German police began arresting Jews. Reports of the planned deportation of the Jews were leaked to various Danish circles by several German sources, the most important of which was the German legation's attaché for shipping affairs, Georg Ferdinand DUCKWITZ. The reaction was spontaneous. The Danes alerted the Jews, helping them move into hiding places and from there make their way to the seashore, and, with the help of Danish fishermen, cross into Sweden. At first this was an unorganized and spontaneous operation, but soon the Danish resistance joined in and helped to organize the massive flight that followed the Swedish government's proclamation that it was ready to take in all the refugees from Denmark. In Denmark, all groups of the population went into action in order to save the Jews. Dozens of protests poured into the offices of the German authorities from Danish economic and social organizations; King Christian X expressed his firm objection to the German plans; the heads of the Danish churches published a strong protest and used their pulpits to urge the Danish people to help the Jews; and the universities closed down for a week, with the students lending a hand in the rescue operation. The operation went on for three weeks, and in its course seventy-two hundred Jews and some seven hundred non-Jewish relatives of theirs were taken to Sweden. The costs of the operation were borne partly by the Jews themselves and to a large extent by contributions made by the Danes. The Danish resistance movement grew in size and strength as a result of the successful rescue effort and was able to keep open a fairly reliable escape route to Sweden.

Rolf Günther—Adolf EICHMANN's deputy, who had come to Copenhagen in order to organize the deportation of the Jews—failed in his mission; the Danish police not only refused to cooperate with Günther but also helped the rescue operation. An order was also issued prohibiting German police from breaking into apartments in order to arrest Jews. Despite all these efforts, some five hundred Jews were arrested, including some *halutsim* and Youth Aliya children, and sent to THERESIENSTADT. The Danish public and the administration (which continued to function after the government had resigned) did not give up their concern for the fate of their Jewish countrymen in Theresienstadt. They sent food parcels to them and had the Danish Foreign Ministry bombard the Germans with warnings. The ministry also put forward a demand that a Danish delegation be permitted to visit the detainees in the Theresienstadt camp. Eichmann exploited this Danish demand by setting up a fake "model ghetto" in Theresienstadt when a Danish delegation, together with International RED CROSS representatives, visited Theresienstadt in the summer of 1944. However, the fact remains that the Danish Jews were not deported to AUSCHWITZ, and in the end were included in a Swedish Red Cross operation, carried out under Count Folke BERNADOTTE, in which Scandinavian nationals were transferred from concentration camps to Sweden, in the spring of 1945, before the war came to an end.

The Danish people's resolute refusal to discriminate against their Jewish fellow citizens and to surrender them, or the refugees among them, to the Germans; the rescue operation launched to transfer the Jews to a safe haven in Sweden; and the unwavering support and protection they gave to the Theresienstadt deportees—all represent an exercise of high moral and political responsibility, outstanding and exceptional for the time in which it took place. It has aroused profound admiration, and its echo reverberates to this day.

BIBLIOGRAPHY

Goldberger, L., ed. *The Rescue of the Danish Jews: Moral Courage under Stress.* New York, 1987.
Petersen, H. U. "Die dänische Flüchtlingspolitik 1933–1941." In *Deutschsprachiges Exil in Dänemark nach 1933: Zu Methoden und Einzelergeb-* *nissen; Vorträge des Kolloquiums am 1. und 2. Oktober 1984*, edited by Ruth Dinesen et al., pp. 73–94. Copenhagen, 1986.
Petrow, R. *The Bitter Years: The Invasion and Occupation of Denmark and Norway, April 1940–May 1945.* New York, 1974.
Valentin, H. "Rescue and Relief Activities in Behalf of Jewish Victims of Nazism in Scandinavia." *YIVO Annual of Jewish Social Science* 8 (1953): 224–251.
Yahil, L. *The Rescue of Danish Jewry: Test of a Democracy.* Philadelphia, 1969.

LENI YAHIL

DENYING THE HOLOCAUST. *See* Holocaust, Denial of the.

DEPARTMENT OF STATE. *See* United States Department of State.

DEPORTATIONS. As early as September 1919, Hitler wrote of the need for systematic measures in Germany to achieve "the removal of the Jews altogether." Thus, from the beginning, the physical removal of the Jews from Germany in one way or another was basic to Hitler's approach to the "Jewish question." But it was not until the mid-1930s that at least one party organization, Reinhard HEYDRICH's SD (Sicherheitsdienst; Security Service), a branch of Heinrich HIMMLER's SS, began to formulate policy based on this axiom by articulating as the final goal of Nazi Jewish policy a Germany "cleansed" or "free" of Jews (*judenrein; judenfrei*). This was to be achieved through intensifying pressures for emigration. It was with the annexation of Austria in March 1938 that the SD was first able to experiment freely in this regard, when Adolf EICHMANN established the ZENTRALSTELLE FÜR JÜDISCHE AUSWANDERUNG (Central Office for Jewish Emigration) in Vienna. However, Eichmann's methods still constituted forced emigration or expulsion rather than deportation.

The first experiment in actual mass deportation of Jews was carried out in the fall of 1938. In March of that year, Poland had decreed that Polish citizens living abroad who did not have their passports renewed with a special stamp by October 31 would be denationalized. The Germans realized that they would soon have on their hands as many as seventy thousand resident Polish Jews, who, without valid passports, would be unable either to return home or to emigrate further. As the deadline approached, Foreign Minister Joachim von RIBBENTROP urged the police to take preventive action. The Gestapo rounded up about seventeen thousand Polish Jews on the night of October 28, 1938, in order to deport them to Poland. The Poles closed their border on October 31, trapping most of the unfortunate deportees in a no-man's-land in the area of ZBĄSZYŃ, and their fate became the subject of prolonged German-Polish negotiations. Deportation without control of the area of reception had proved to be a fiasco.

The conquest of Poland in September 1939, however, offered the shapers of Nazi Jewish policy precisely what they had lacked the previous year. Almost immediately, plans emerged for large-scale deportations of Jews from the ever-expanding Third Reich into German-occupied Poland—to a Lublin Reservation, in particular (*see* NISKO AND LUBLIN PLAN). The first such deportations, in October 1939, were organized by Eichmann and involved five trainloads of Jews from Vienna; Mährisch-Ostrau, in the Protectorate of BOHEMIA AND MORAVIA; and Katowice, in the newly incorporated territory of Eastern Upper Silesia. They were transported to a transit camp at Nisko, on the San River, from which most

Deportations from Würzburg, Germany.

of the deportees were chased over the demarcation line into the Soviet zone.

However, Jewish deportations were only part of a much vaster scheme of demographic engineering approved by Hitler at that time, involving the resettlement of ethnic Germans (VOLKSDEUTSCHE) from the Soviet sphere and the deportation of all Poles from the incorporated territories as well. Eichmann was named the SS expert in charge of "Jewish affairs and evacuations," coordinating the outgoing deportations of Poles and Jews. Amid the chaotic conditions, "wild deportations" (the Nazis' term), and conflicting priorities that characterized German-occupied Poland, systematic deportation of the Jews proved once again unrealizable. Eichmann's Nisko operation was canceled, and the deportation of Jews from the incorporated territories into the GENERALGOUVERNEMENT was repeatedly postponed. Most of those deported by the Germans at this time—over 380,000 into the Generalgouvernement by March 1941, according to SS statistics—were Poles rather than Jews. In addition, several hundred thousand Jews—stripped of their homes, livelihood, and human dignity—fled eastward on their own.

In the summer of 1940, MADAGASCAR replaced the Lublin Reservation as the prospective goal of Jewish deportation, but this plan too proved impracticable. Jewish deportations remained sporadic and tied to other population movements. When more than 70,000 "undesirable" Frenchmen (including, of course, French Jews) were deported from Alsace-Lorraine into Vichy France, the *Gauleiter* (district leaders) of neighboring Baden and Saarpfalz exploited the opportunity to make their own territories *judenfrei* by deporting their 6,500 German Jews there as well, on October 22 and 23, 1940. And when a renewed wave of deportations into the Generalgouvernement was undertaken in early 1941, 5,000 Jews from Vienna and some 4,000 from the incorporated territories were included, until the whole resettlement action was suspended during preparations for the invasion of the Soviet Union. Thus, although total removal of the Jews through deportation was the centerpiece of Nazi expectations in the first eighteen months of the war, in reality such moves comprised only a small fraction of

Nazi deportation programs in this period.

With the invasion of the Soviet Union and the EINSATZGRUPPEN massacres of Soviet Jewry, Nazi Jewish policy shifted from expulsion to mass murder. But the mobile firing-squad methods used in the Soviet Union could not be employed on European Jews. They could not be shot down in the streets of Amsterdam, Paris, or Salonika as they were behind the front in the Soviet Union. Hence the Nazis came to a decision that Jewish deportations would be not an end in themselves, but the means of bringing the Jews to killing centers in the east. However, in late September 1941, before these centers were constructed, Hitler ordered that Germany be cleared of Jews by the end of the year. Between mid-October and mid-December, some fifty thousand German Jews were deported either to ŁÓDŹ or to the occupied areas of the Soviet Union. Many of the latter group were shot on arrival in Riga or Kovno; meanwhile, space was made in the overcrowded Łódź ghetto when deportations of its inhabitants to the first extermination camp, at nearby CHEŁMNO, began in December 1941. But a deportation program on the scale necessary to clear Germany, Poland, and other European countries of their Jews could not begin until the major extermination camps (BEŁŻEC, SOBIBÓR, TREBLINKA, AUSCHWITZ, and, later and on a much smaller scale, MAJDANEK) were ready to go into full operation, between March and July of 1942.

The intended victims (*see* WANNSEE CONFERENCE) were scattered throughout Europe in countries with varying degrees of sovereignty, many of them not under German occupation. The victims in Poland were already ghettoized and under total German control, but deportation of Jews from other parts of Europe would be a far more complex problem. Eichmann had gained considerable experience in both "Jewish affairs" and "evacuations," and his department, Section IV B 4 of the REICHS-SICHERHEITSHAUPTAMT (Reich Security Main Office; RSHA), became the coordinating center of these deportations to the extermination camps. Eichmann had only a small staff directly under him (twelve to thirteen officials plus secretarial help in the Berlin office), but it was nonetheless a far-reaching network. The German embassies in many vassal and

The last Jewish families of Hohenlimburg (near Essen) in Germany being deported to a concentration camp (April 23, 1942).

allied states already had "Jewish advisers" who were in close contact with Eichmann. Himmler had also established his own police networks in areas under German military control, and here Eichmann had direct access to the local Sicherheitspolizei (Security Police; Sipo). The task of Eichmann's small outfit was to get others to perform the functions vital to the deportation program; thus a number of other agencies were of great importance.

Vital logistic support was provided by the Transport Ministry; the German RAILWAYS (Reichsbahn) under its jurisdiction, supervised by State Secretary Albert GANZEN-MÜLLER; and the Reichsbahn's Polish auxiliary, the Ostbahn. Securing "special trains" (*Sonderzüge*) for the Jews despite the immense demands made on German rail capacity throughout the war was crucial. For deportations within Poland, the local Sipo made arrangements directly with the Ostbahn. For all other deportations in Europe, Eichmann's deputy Rolf Günther and Eichmann's transportation expert, Franz NOVAK, worked with Reichsbahn authorities. The Jews were booked as passengers (one-way group fares, children half price, and infants under four free) but were transported for the most part as cargo, that is, in freight cars. In the end the railways carried nearly three million people to six obscure destinations in Poland and the incorporated territories, from which clothing and luggage, but no people, returned.

Another important agency in the deportation program was the Foreign Office. Its Jewish desk had long offered advice concerning the foreign-policy implications of Nazi Jewish programs, especially when foreign Jews were involved. Now it secured the right to be consulted by the SS concerning the "FINAL SOLUTION" in all European territories of the German sphere where foreign-policy considerations still had to be taken into account. The Jewish desk of the Foreign Office worked zealously to facilitate the frictionless implementation of the deportation program in many ways: urging preparatory anti-Jewish legislation, on the German model; negotiating agreements on the fate of Jewish property; exercising diplomatic pressure to assist Eichmann's representatives in attaining final agreement for the deportations, local help in conducting roundups, and in some cases even money to pay for deportation costs; and smoothing out complications arising from the presence of large numbers of Jews with foreign citizenship, who required special consideration if embarrassing incidents were to be avoided.

The actual deportations required the involvement of many other elements. In Poland, special ghetto-clearing units had to be mobilized and assembled for each operation. Even a single deportation from a German city was a major undertaking. The entire police force was mobilized; a large assembly area, usually the cargo depot, was taken over and sealed off for the day. Large numbers of municipal officials were involved: representatives of the Finance Office collected property inventories, liquidated property, and turned the proceeds over to officials of the Tax Office; personnel of the Labor Office collected workbooks; and those from the Housing Office collected keys and disposed of vacant apartments. In foreign countries the process was even more complicated, because allied and satellite governments had to be persuaded to perform not only all these essential functions of the deportation itself but also the preliminary steps of definition, registration, marking, expropriation, and concentration.

By the spring and summer of 1942, the extermination camps were ready and the full-scale deportation program of the "Final Solution" commenced. The onslaught against the Polish ghettos began in southern Poland in March, continued in Warsaw in July, and reached a climax in the fall, when the extermination camps (some of them now equipped with new, larger gas chambers) were virtually flooded with deportees beyond their killing capacity. In the WARTHEGAU, deportations from Łódź were carried out from mid-January until mid-May and again in September, while in the intervening summer months all the other ghettos of the Warthegau were systematically liquidated. By fall, only those Jews capable of physical labor were still alive in the Warthegau.

Added to this stream of victims sent from the ghettos to the extermination camps were the first deportations from other parts of Europe. In mid-February 1942 the Slovak government was approached with a request for 20,000 strong, young Jews for labor in the east, a proposal it eagerly accepted. In March, Eichmann requested the deportation initially of 1,000 and then of an additional 5,000 French Jews; this too encountered no difficulties. Full-scale deportations then quickly followed, as Germany informed Slovakia of its willingness to take all of the remaining Slovak Jews, of whom 58,000 were deported by the end of the summer. In July 1942, mass deportations began from France, Belgium, and the Netherlands, at first composed primarily of foreign Jews in order to facilitate local cooperation and acquiescence. In August, some 5,500 Croatian Jews were added to the deportations, though most of the Jews in Croatia were in fact killed locally by the native fascist USTAŠA. And in November, over 500 Norwegian Jews were rounded up and deported.

A second wave began in early 1943. Deportations continued from France, Belgium, and the Netherlands, along with a trickle from Norway and Croatia, but the center of German attention shifted to the Balkans. Through the efforts first of the Foreign Office and then of Eichmann's traveling representative, Theodor DANNECKER, an agreement was reached with Bulgaria, which rounded up and handed to the Germans over 11,000 "alien" Jews from Macedonia and Thrace. Plans to deport native Bulgarian Jews as well foundered, however, as domestic opposition emerged and Germany's prospects for victory began to dim after the defeat at STALINGRAD in February 1943. Indeed, wherever Germany had to rely on foreign collaborators, its leverage in extracting cooperation in deporting Jews began to weaken in the post-Stalingrad era. While Romania had cooperated with the operations of Einsatzgruppe D along its Russian front and had carried out its own deportation of the "alien" Jews of Bessarabia and Bukovina to Transnistria, where most of them perished, the Romanians now backed out of deporting their "own" Jews. The Jews in the Italian occupation zones of coastal Croatia, southern Greece, and southern France were similarly protected from the German onslaught by the Italian authorities. But the majority of Greek Jews lived in SALONIKA, in northern Greece. This region was occupied by the German military, which provided all the help Eichmann and his local representatives, Dieter WISLICENY and Alois BRUNNER, needed to deport 46,000 Greek Jews between March and May of 1943. The attempt to deport Jews from Denmark in October 1943 failed when the local population first hid the Danish Jews and then smuggled them to nearby Sweden. In the same month, however, following the German occupation of Italy, 1,000 Jews were deported from Rome to Auschwitz.

In 1944, even when the war was clearly lost, deportations continued from western Europe, northern Italy, and the former Italian occupation zone in Greece. Deportations were also resumed in 1944 from Slovakia and from the last remaining ghetto, in Łódź. But all of this was dwarfed by the single largest deportation operation of the "Final Solution"—the attempt to destroy Hungarian Jewry. Following the German occupation of Hungary in March 1944, Eichmann mobilized his entire team of experts and descended on Budapest. Once again willing collaborators were found, who helped to concentrate and deport 437,000 Jews between mid-May and early July of that year, before the head of state, Miklós HORTHY, reasserted himself and brought an end to the deportations, which could proceed only with Hungarian cooperation.

Ultimately, a great part of the victims of the Holocaust fell prey to starvation and disease in the ghettos, to German mobile firing squads, or to brutal murder by local fascists. But for the majority, deportation was the essential step that brought them to their death in the Nazi gas chambers and labor camps.

BIBLIOGRAPHY

Browning, C. R. *The Final Solution and the Foreign Office.* New York, 1978.

Hilberg, R. *The Destruction of the European Jews.* 3 vols. New York, 1985.

Hilberg, R. *Sonderzüge nach Auschwitz.* Mainz, 1981.

Reitlinger, G. *The Final Solution.* New York, 1953.

CHRISTOPHER R. BROWNING

DERECHIN (Pol., Dereczyn), town in the Belorussian SSR. Between the two world wars, Derechin was part of independent Poland. In September 1939, together with all of eastern Poland, it was occupied by the Red Army and annexed to the Soviet Union. On the eve of World War II, four thousand Jews lived in the town. Following the occupation by the

DERECHIN

Germans on June 25, 1941, Jews from the nearby towns of Kholinka and Kolonya were deported to Derechin.

A ghetto was established, and all the "useless" Jews were moved into it. Artisans initially lived outside the ghetto. When rumors of the murder of Jews in SLONIM reached Derechin, the town's Jews began to talk about escaping to the nearby forests. The "useful" Jews opposed this, believing that their usefulness would save their lives and that escape would place them in danger. A youth underground arose; its aims were to escape to the forests and to offer resistance in the ghetto if its members were surrounded there before leaving. The young people smuggled twenty guns and automatic firearms, as well as ammunition, out of the Germans' munitions stores and hid them outside the town.

In the spring of 1942, partisan activity increased, and the police stations in Kholinka and the Puzeviche labor camps were attacked. The Jews of the ghetto began to hope that the partisans would reach Derechin as well. In July of that year, the first Jews left the ghetto and went to the Borelom Forest.

On July 24 an *Aktion* was carried out in the ghetto. Jews who had prepared bunkers went into hiding; some took axes with them to attack anyone breaking into the hiding place. About three hundred Jews fled to the surrounding forests, some to Borelom. Among those who fled to the forest were several who subsequently became well-known partisans, including Eliyahu Lipszowicz, a platoon leader in the unit of Dr. Yeheskel ATLAS. Lipszowicz's brothers Chaim Yehoshua and Gershon; his sister Taiba; the brothers Benjamin and David Dombrowski; Chaim Szelkowicz; and the brothers Moshe Chaim, Miszka, and Shalom Ogolnik were known in the forest as partisan fighters. Some who escaped to the forest were organized into a "family camp," with the aid of the partisan commander Boris Bulat.

On August 10, 1942, 120 partisans, headed by Atlas and Bulat, attacked the German garrison in Derechin. Jewish partisans led the attackers. The Belorussian and Polish police who were caught were shot next to the Jewish communal grave. In that battle three Jewish partisans from the town were killed. Sixty-four Jews who had escaped from Derechin fell in combat in the forest.

Derechin was liberated in mid-July 1944. Over two hundred of its Jews survived.

BIBLIOGRAPHY

Bornsztejn, S. *The Doctor Atlas Brigade: The Story of a Jewish Partisan.* Tel Aviv, 1965. (In Hebrew.)
Raban, Y., ed. *Deretchin: Memorial Book.* Tel Aviv, 1972. (In Hebrew and English.)

SHALOM CHOLAWSKI

DÉS. *See* Dej.

DEUTSCHE AUSRÜSTUNGSWERKE (German Armament Works; DAW), one of the SS's most important economic enterprises, established in May 1939, with headquarters in Berlin; Standartenführer Walter Salpeter was appointed as its head. DAW assumed control of the production plants that the SS had established in order to exploit the labor of inmates of the DACHAU, SACHSENHAUSEN, BUCHENWALD, and, later, AUSCHWITZ concentration camps. As time went on, more such factories were set up, in the LUBLIN, Puławy, STUTTHOF, Fürstenwalde, RAVENSBRÜCK, and NEUENGAMME camps. The number of prisoners employed in these plants rose from 1,220 in 1940 to 15,500 in 1943. The largest factories were in the JANÓWSKA concentration camp in Lvov and the Jewish prisoner-of-war camp in LUBLIN-LIPOWA, which together employed some 8,000 Jews. Most of the prisoners who worked in the DAW factories perished, either through the policy of *Vernichtung durch Arbeit* (extermination through work) or by massslaughter *Aktionen*. The largest *Aktion* was the murder of 2,000 Jewish prisoners of war, who were removed from Lublin-Lipowa on November 3, 1943, and taken to the crematoria at MAJDANEK, where they were shot to death.

[*See also* Forced Labor.]

BIBLIOGRAPHY

Ennos, G. "Die wirtschaftlichen Unternehmungen der SS." *Schriftenreihe der Vierteljahresheft für Zeitgeschichte* 7 (1963).
Hilberg, R. *The Destruction of the European Jews.* 3 vols. New York, 1985.

SHMUEL KRAKOWSKI

DEUTSCHER VORTRUPP, GEFOLG-SCHAFT DEUTSCHER JUDEN (German Vanguard, German Jewish Adherents), organization founded in February 1933 by a group of Jewish university students in GER-MANY led by a student of religion, Hans Joachim Schoeps. It started with about one hundred and fifty members, and its membership declined gradually until it was dissolved by the Gestapo in December 1935.

The organization represented an odd attempt to retain Jewish religious identity while stressing its profound links with German culture. Wishing to participate as a Jewish political movement in the "German national regeneration," it advocated an authoritarian leadership within the Jewish community. As a group of ultrapatriotic Germans, the Deutscher Vortrupp had a highly negative attitude toward eastern European Jews and opposed Zionism, Marxism, and liberalism. Jewish religious observance, however, was part of its program. It opposed Zionism as a form of assimilation because of the Zionist goal of becoming "a nation like all nations"; and it believed that Jews belong to the German *Volk*, having no more than a religious specificity. Schoeps, who was the group's leading figure, was deeply influenced by proponents of a conservative revolution and defined himself as a conservative Prussian Jew. Grounding his world view in the writings of the conservative German Jewish statesman Friedrich Julius Stahl and the philosopher Franz Rosenzweig, he maintained that Prussianism and Jewish religion were based on common values. Schoeps developed a German conservative and nationalist ideology into which Judaism was fused. Failing to comprehend the racist basis of Nazism, he believed that the Third Reich would develop as a corporate state, allowing the Jews to integrate into it. Politically, the Deutscher Vortrupp allied itself with the REICHSBUND JÜDISCHER FRONTSOLDATEN (Reich Union of Jewish Frontline Soldiers) in a common anti-Zionist front. Fearing arrest, Schoeps left Germany for Sweden in 1938. In the war years he maintained a correspondence with German conservative political circles in exile, in which he proposed the establishment of a *numerus clausus* (the quota permitted) policy for the Jews after their return to Germany as the only way to guarantee their proper integration once Germany had been liberated.

BIBLIOGRAPHY

Grossman, K. "Zionists and Non-Zionists under Nazi Rule in the 1930s." *Herzl Year Book* 4 (1961/1962): 329–344.

Rheins, C. J. "Deutscher Vortrupp, Gefolgschaft Deutscher Juden: 1933–1935." *Leo Baeck Institute Year Book* 26 (1981): 207–229.

DAVID BANKIER

DIARIES, HOLOCAUST. The extensive literature about the Holocaust, written in many languages, takes various forms, the most important being diaries, personal memoirs, and fiction. For the purpose of documentation, the diaries are the most valuable: as on-the-spot compositions or notes written at the time of, or shortly following, the events they describe, they can serve the historian as an authentic and reliable source of information. In some cases, memoirs or diaries reconstructed *post factum* by survivors also contain significant information and faithfully depict the reality of the Holocaust and the atmosphere prevailing in it. But a clear distinction must be made between diaries kept while the writers were in direct contact with the horror and the uncertainty, and memoirs written after liberation, which inevitably bear the marks of hindsight.

The Jews have a long and deep-rooted tradition of recording their tribulations. At times of distress and persecution, as during the Crusades and the 1648–1649 Chmielnicki massacres in southern Russia, Jews poured out their hearts in chronicles, descriptions of the events they were witnessing, so that the memory of these events could be kept alive for the future.

However, never has so much been written by Jews who were incarcerated, tortured, and doomed as during the Holocaust. Emanuel RINGELBLUM, in his description of the ONEG SHABBAT Archive in Warsaw, relates that when the first fearful months of the German occupation had passed, the Jews came to realize that "while the Nazi authorities selected entire groups and sectors of the population for harassment, they paid no attention to what the individual Jew was doing in the privacy of his home. And so the Jew began to write; everybody was writing—journalists, writers, teachers, public figures, the teenagers, and even the children. Mostly they kept diaries, in which they described the tragic events unfolding before their eyes as the personal experiences that they indeed were."

It has since become known that the Jews wrote in every place—in the occupied countries, in the camps, and in their hideouts among the non-Jewish population. Whatever their age, the Jews wrote—both those who were writers by profession, and ordinary people for whom this was the only writing they had ever attempted. The urge to write seems to have been prompted by two motives: the need to find an outlet to express, in free and unfettered writing, the helplessness of their condition, their persecution and humiliation; and, for many Jews, wittingly or unwittingly, the sense that what they were recording might well be the only evidence, the only indictment that would be left behind, of their fate, which would perhaps also serve as a deterrent for the future. Many of the diarists were Jews who were hiding among the Christian population or under their protection (as was the case of Anne FRANK), and the isolation and quarantine in which they lived prompted them to give written expression to the stark tragedy they were experiencing.

Many of the diaries and other writings composed during the Holocaust have been lost. It is therefore impossible to estimate how much was written, its quality, and the number of persons writing at a particular time or over a prolonged period. Even so, a tremendous amount of material has been preserved. In the Warsaw Jewish Historical Institute (ŻYDOWSKI INSTYTUT HISTORYCZNY), which has a large collection of diaries, 272 items are listed under "diaries," 65 of them from the Warsaw ghetto, in Polish and Yiddish. Most of these diaries were written during the war and were saved as a result of coincidental circumstances. A relatively large number of important diaries were rescued as part of the Ringelblum Archive. Of the 65 manuscripts from the Warsaw ghetto classified as diaries at the Warsaw Jewish Historical Institute, only 8 were dictated or written

about the time of the liberation; all the others are documents dating from the Holocaust period. So rich is the Warsaw diary collection in both quantity and quality, regarding the life of the Jews in the ghetto, the structure of the ghetto with its various institutions, and a range of details, that a day-by-day history of the Warsaw ghetto can be reconstructed based on this material alone.

The diaries can be classified according to several distinct categories: day-by-day records of events; public diaries; private diaries; and teenagers' and children's diaries.

1. The diaries that contain a daily record of events are devoid of personal observations or interpretations by the person or persons who kept them. The most significant example of this category is the chronicles of the ŁÓDŹ GHETTO, in which the staff of the JUDENRAT (Jewish Council), following instructions of the Judenrat members, recorded current events in the ghetto from January 1940 to July 1944. The Łódź chronicles have the disadvantage of being an officially inspired document, but their continuity, the wealth of events and developments they contain, and the information they provide combine to present a detailed picture of a major aspect of life in the Łódź ghetto.

2. Among the diaries of a public character, two different types can be distinguished. One is similar in its makeup to a chronicle and has as its major purpose the recording of general events as they occur, but it puts the emphasis on details that the author considers important, interpreting and evaluating them and describing their impact on the Jewish population. This pattern is found in the diaries of the historian Emanuel Ringelblum in the Warsaw ghetto and of Herman KRUK in Vilna. Both these diaries reveal their authors' sense of history; indeed, the writers may have planned to use the original material as the basis for an eventual broader historical treatment of the era. Similar to these records in style and relative importance are the diaries of Adam CZERNIAKÓW, head of the Warsaw ghetto Judenrat, and Ludwik Landau, who lived on the Polish side of Warsaw. Czerniaków's diary contains a concise account of his actions from the beginning of the occupation until the great deportation in the summer of 1942, the period in which he headed the largest ghetto in Europe. The account is interspersed with comments that reveal the author's state of mind. Landau, by profession an economist, devotes most of his comprehensive diary to the events on the Polish side and among Polish society, but he also deals extensively with the Jewish aspect. Of a similar nature are the diaries of Raymond-Raoul (Heshel) LAMBERT, a leading figure in the UNION GÉNÉRALE DES ISRAÉLITES DE FRANCE (General Council of French Jews), and Eliezer Yerushalmi of the ŠIAULIAI (Shavli) ghetto in Lithuania. Two other diaries that concentrate on public affairs—and shed light on important episodes in the story of the Jewish underground and armed resistance movement—are those that were kept by two prominent figures in the underground in Poland. One was Mordechai TENENBAUM, a founder of the Vilna underground and of the ŻYDOWSKA ORGANIZACJA BOJOWA (Jewish Fighting Organization; ŻOB) in Warsaw, and head of the Białystok Fighting Organization and uprising. The other was Tova DRAENGER (*Justina's Diary*), a leader of the Akiva movement and the Fighting Haluts movement in Kraków.

Many diaries are a combination of the public and the private. Their authors devote a great deal of attention to public affairs, but also record their personal experiences and make subjective, critical comments on the course of events. Such are the important diaries of two Warsaw teachers, Chaim Aaron KAPLAN and Abraham Lewin; the Yiddish cultural scholar and YIVO (Institute for Jewish Research) leader Selig Kalmanowitz, of Vilna; the engineer Henryk Brisker of Warsaw; Jakub Poznański of the Łódź ghetto; two Jewish police officers in Warsaw, Stanisław Adler and Stefan Ernst; and the Piotrków rabbi, Shimon Huberband (who at one point joined the inner circle of the Oneg Shabbat Archive in Warsaw).

3. Personal or private diaries are those in which the authors concentrate on their own or their relatives' experiences, conduct a kind of dialogue with themselves, and at best give only a patchy description of current events or restrict themselves to those happenings in which they were themselves involved. Examples of this kind are the diaries of Ruth Leimanson-Engelstern and Naomi Schatz-

Weinkranz, two Jewish women who had gone into hiding in Poland among gentiles.

4. The diaries of teenagers and children have a special place among the private diaries. These are very moving writings and impressive human documents, some with literary value. In a number of these diaries the authors lay bare their souls and cry out against mankind and the world, which have ceased to protect them and have abandoned them to the hands of wicked people whose intentions and evil designs they do not understand. The most famous of these diaries is the one by Anne Frank, written in a hideout in Amsterdam where she was living with her own and one other Jewish family. This description of a gifted girl growing into maturity while shut off from the world, suffering from shortages, and with a constant threat hanging over her head, is a gripping literary creation. David Rubinowicz, a village boy living in the Kielce district, was twelve years old when he began recording in a school notebook the sufferings that his family and neighbors were experiencing. David Shrakovik, a diarist in the Łódź ghetto, was a few years older. Sarah Pishkin of Rubevichi in Belorussia, who began her diary when she was fifteen, expresses the pain and tribulations of a girl who has based her hopes on religious faith and is now beset by doubts and despair. David Flinker, a boy living in Brussels, is firm in his religious beliefs, and his mature thoughts are concerned with a search for the meaning of the disaster that has struck the Jewish people. Yitzhak Rudaszewski, a boy from Vilna, describes the general feeling of helplessness that prevails in the ghetto, yet his diary abounds with references to public life and to the interest that he takes in his studies and in the youth movement's program of activities. Eva Heyman, a Hungarian girl, was thirteen in February 1944 and far removed from Jewish life, absorbed by her own and her family's pursuits; her diary records her sudden descent into an atmosphere of catastrophe, from which there is no escape. The diary of Tamara Lazarson, of Kovno, depicts a girl from an assimilated Jewish family who, under the impact of persecution and destruction, discovers her people and comes to believe in its future.

Diaries written in concentration camps

have an enormous value. Some were discovered in the ruins of the AUSCHWITZ-Birkenau crematorium; their authors were men of the Sonderkommandos, who were in daily contact with murder and with the victims who were being led to their deaths. These diaries, and other notes found in Birkenau, were kept by Polish Jews from religious backgrounds—Zalman Gradowski, Zalman Levental, and Leib Langfuss. Full of horror and pain, they also appeal to the world to understand how they had been forced to take part in such awful abominations. These diaries contain revealing details about the preparations for the Sonderkommando uprising in Birkenau and about the uprising itself, an event on which hardly any reports from other primary sources exist.

The diaries and notes kept by Jews who were experiencing the reality of the Holocaust constitute an authentic historical documentation of great importance. They reveal the inner world and thoughts of human beings in extreme distress and under constant tension, and provide an insight into the complexity of the predicaments, the problems, and the decisions faced by the organized Jewish population and its leaders.

[*See also* Literature on the Holocaust.]

BIBLIOGRAPHY

Adler, S. *In the Warsaw Ghetto: Memoirs of Stanislaw Adler.* Jerusalem, 1982.

Czerniakow, A. *The Warsaw Diary of Adam Czerniakow.* New York, 1979.

Dawidsohn-Draengerowa, G. *Pamiętnik Justyny.* Kraków, 1946.

Fishkin, S. "Excerpts from the Diary of Sarah Fishkin." *Yalkut Moreshet* 4 (July 1965): 21–35. (In Hebrew.)

Frank, A. *Diary of a Young Girl.* New York, 1967.

Grynberg, M., ed. *Pamiętniki z getta warszawskiego: Fragmenty i regestry.* Warsaw, 1988.

Heyman, E. *The Diary of Eva Heyman.* Jerusalem, 1974.

Kaplan, C. A. *Scroll of Agony.* New York, 1965.

Lambert, R.-R. *Carnet d'un témoin (1940–1943).* Paris, 1985.

Landau, L. *Kronika lat wojny i okupacji.* 3 vols. Warsaw, 1962.

Lazarson-Rostowski, T. *Tamara's Diary: Kovno, 1942–1946.* Tel Aviv, 1975. (In Hebrew.)

Lewin, A. *A Cup of Tears: A Diary of the Warsaw Ghetto.* Oxford, 1988.

Mark, B. *The Scrolls of Auschwitz.* Tel Aviv, 1985.

Poznanski, J. *Pamiętnik z getta łódzkiego.* Łódź, 1960.

Ringelblum, E. *Notes from the Warsaw Ghetto: The Journal of Emanuel Ringelblum.* New York, 1958.

Rubinowicz, D. *The Diary of David Rubinowicz.* Edmonds, Wash., 1982.

Rudashevski, Y. *The Diary of the Vilna Ghetto, June 1941–April 1943.* Naharia, Israel, 1973.

Wajnkranc, N. S. *Przemineto z ogniem.* Warsaw, 1947.

Yerushalmi, E. *Pinkas Shavli: A Diary from a Lithuanian Ghetto (1941–1944).* Jerusalem, 1958.

ISRAEL GUTMAN

DIATLOVO (Pol., Zdzięciół; Yi., Zhetl), town in Grodno Oblast (district), Belorussian SSR. In the interwar period it belonged to Poland, and in September 1939 it was annexed to the Soviet Union. Diatlovo had a Jewish population beginning in the sixteenth century, and by the end of the nineteenth century a majority of its inhabitants were Jewish. On the eve of World War II, 4,000 Jews lived in the town. From 1939 to 1941, Jews from German-occupied western Poland took refuge there.

The Germans entered Diatlovo on June 30, 1941. On July 15, 6 Jews who had been betrayed as Communists were put to death, and on July 23, 120 Jewish intellectuals were executed. That winter, on December 15, 400 Jews were sent to a work camp in Dvorets. To Diatlovo itself the Germans sent Jews from the towns of Kozlovshchina, Novoyelnia, and Bielitsa. A ghetto was established, in which all the Jews were concentrated, and a JUDENRAT (Jewish Council) was appointed.

At the end of 1941 an underground was formed in Diatlovo on the initiative of Alter DVORETSKI, the Judenrat's deputy chairman and leading personality, that included Moshe Pozdunski, Eliyahu Kowenski, Shalom Gerling, and Joseph Bitenski. Of the sixty members of the underground, ten were induced by Dvoretski to join the ghetto police, whom Dvoretski formed into a self-defense unit.

The underground set itself the goal of organizing the ghetto so as to stage an armed uprising in the event of an *Aktion* and thereby facilitate escape into the forest. It also sought to arouse anti-German feelings among the non-Jewish population. Using the Judenrat's

5

● Volozhin

● Minsk

● Bielitsa
●
Novogrudok   Cherven ●

● **DIATLOVO (ZHETL)**

● Novoyelnia   ● Nesvizh
● Dvorets

Slutsk ●

Pinsk ●   Lachva ● P R I P E T

DIATLOVO (ZHETL)

0   42 miles   1

in.

0   80 km.   3

1 2 3
4 5 6
B E L O R U S S I A

of Jewish partisans, made up of inhabitants of the Diatlovo ghetto and other ghettos nearby, in order to fight the Germans and save the lives of the Jews remaining in the ghettos. The other was to forge an alliance with Soviet partisan units in order to build up a large force that would seize control of the area and fight the Germans. But the partisans in the forests had no such ideas in mind. Returning from a conference with them, Dvoretski and Pozdunski fell into an ambush set by non-Jewish partisans and were killed in the ensuing fight.

In the wake of this incident, the escape of the Diatlovo Jews into the forests came to a halt, and they concentrated on constructing bunkers and hiding places. A second *Aktion* was launched on August 6, 1942, but this time the streets of the ghetto were empty since the Jews had taken refuge in the places prepared earlier. That morning, three Jewish partisans were on their way to the ghetto to lead Jews out to the forest, but they were killed as they tried to break through the cordon that had been placed around the ghetto. A group of 50 Jews, led by Hirsch KAPLINSKI, managed to escape into the forest. Altogether, about 600 Jews broke out of the Diatlovo ghetto and tried to reach the forests in the area. Those who succeeded were among the founders of such partisan groups as the ATLAS and BIELSKI units.

About three hundred and seventy Jews from the Diatlovo ghetto survived the war, 90 percent of them by escaping into the forests. One hundred and sixteen Diatlovo Jews fell while fighting in the forests or in the ranks of the Red Army.

BIBLIOGRAPHY

Kaplinski, B. *Zhetel Record: A Memorial to the Jewish Community of Zhetel.* Tel Aviv, 1957. (In Hebrew.)

SHALOM CHOLAWSKI

funds, Dvoretski acquired arms, and in January 1942 he smuggled two rifles into the ghetto, as well as a submachine gun and ammunition. Opinions in the underground differed on whether to fight in the ghetto or in the forest; the decision would determine where the arms were to be hidden. Dvoretski was in favor of fighting inside the ghetto.

In the spring of 1942, groups of Soviet partisans made their apppearance in the Diatlovo neighborhood. Dvoretski then resolved that the underground should aim at escaping to the forest. On April 20, 1942, following the arrest of Shalom Fyolvn, an underground member who had been caught in the act of trying to purchase arms, Dvoretski escaped from the ghetto together with a group of other members. The Germans put a price of 25,000 reichsmarks on his head.

On April 30, 1,200 Jews were taken from the ghetto and put to death. Dvoretski and his comrades did not attempt to attack the Germans while this *Aktion* was under way because the Soviet partisans refused to take the risk. Dvoretski now sought to accomplish two objectives. The first was to form a large force

DIBELIUS, OTTO (1880–1967), Protestant bishop, theologian, and member of the German church resistance to the Nazis. Born in Berlin, Dibelius studied theology there and at Edinburgh, and was later pastor and, from 1925, general superintendent of the Evangelical (Lutheran) church in the Kurmark diocese in Prussia. Dibelius was always a German nationalist, and when the Nazis came to power his sermon at the inaugural service for the 1933 Reichstag in the garrison church at Potsdam was cautiously benevolent, although he also emphasized the irreconcilability of totalitarianism and the will of God. He was dismissed from his post and turned to the Confessing Church (Bekennende Kirche), founded by his close associate Martin NIEMÖLLER. Together they confronted the theory of the "total state" and the Nazi-organized "German Christian" movement.

During World War II Dibelius fought for freedom of religious expression and opposed Nazi church policy. On a number of occasions he was arrested and forbidden to preach. He was also in touch with some of the participants in the abortive plot against Hitler in 1944, but took no active part in the conspiracy. Though made aware by Kurt GERSTEIN of the mass killing of Jews at Bełżec and other extermination camps in Poland, Dibelius did not openly protest, always remaining within the limits of what was ecclesiastically legitimate. After the war he was appointed bishop of Berlin-Brandenburg. He was the first German to become a president of the World Council of Churches.

BIBLIOGRAPHY

Gutteridge, R. *Open Thy Mouth for the Dumb*. Oxford, 1976.

Littell, F. H., and H. G. Locke, eds. *The German Church Struggle and the Holocaust*. Detroit, 1974.

LIONEL KOCHAN

DIRLEWANGER, OSKAR (1895–1945), senior SS officer and war criminal. Dirlewanger was born in Würzburg, studied political science, and specialized in commerce; he was an officer in World War I and was wounded and awarded the Iron Cross. From 1919 to 1921 he served in various units of the Freikorps, which led to his arrest on two occasions. In 1923 he joined the Nazi party for the first time; in 1926 he joined it once more, and on March 1, 1932, he made it final. He was arrested in July 1934 for indecent behavior and sentenced to two years in prison. From 1937 to 1939 he served as a volunteer in the German "Condor" Legion, which fought on Franco's side in the Spanish Civil War.

In July 1940 Dirlewanger was accepted by the SS with the rank of *Obersturmführer*, and at his own suggestion, he set up and trained a special detachment (Sonderkommando) within the SS TOTENKOPFVERBÄNDE (Death's-Head Units), made up of persons who had been convicted of poaching and other offenses. In early 1941 Dirlewanger and his special SS battalion (SS-Sonderbataillon Dirlewanger) were posted to the Lublin district and attached to Odilo GLOBOCNIK's command. Here Dirlewanger became commandant of a Jewish labor camp in Dzikow, supervised the construction of fortifications on the Bug River in the BEŁŻEC region, and then fought against the Polish partisan movement in the GENERALGOUVERNEMENT. In late February 1942 he and his unit were posted to Belorussia to combat the partisans in that area. In Belorussia, Dirlewanger and his men outdid the other Nazis in the mass murder of the civilian population and the havoc and destruction they wrought upon many places of habitation. Because of these extraordinarily brutal activities, an investigation was launched against Dirlewanger and its findings were submitted to an SS court, but he was not put on trial.

In March 1944 Dirlewanger was promoted to SS-*Standartenführer* in the Waffen-SS, and in August of that year he was posted to Warsaw to help quell the WARSAW POLISH UPRISING, where he again made a name for himself by his great brutality; that same month he was promoted to SS-*Oberführer*. Late in 1944 he was posted to Slovakia with his unit to suppress the SLOVAK NATIONAL UPRISING. In June 1945 Dirlewanger died in Althausen under mysterious circumstances.

BIBLIOGRAPHY

Reitlinger, G. *The SS: Alibi of a Nation*. Englewood Cliffs, N.J., 1981.

SHMUEL SPECTOR

DISPLACED PERSONS, JEWISH. At the end of World War II, the Allied powers found approximately 7 million to 9 million people in Europe who had been uprooted by the war. Before the end of 1945, more than 6 million had been repatriated, leaving 1.5 million to 2 million displaced persons (DPs) who refused to return to their prewar homes, either out of free choice or because they feared retribution, economic deprivation, or annihilation.

On VE Day, May 8, 1945, the DPs included 200,000 Jews—survivors of the forced-labor camps, concentration camps, extermination camps, and DEATH MARCHES. Many Jewish survivors and REFUGEES were not prepared to resume their lives in Holocaust-haunted Europe, especially in antisemitic eastern Europe. Most of these survivors gathered in displaced persons' (DP) camps and organized as a group with its own national consciousness and political objective—to be enabled to emigrate from Europe, primarily to settle in Palestine. The Jews organized under the Hebrew name She'erit ha-Peletah ("surviving remnant"; 1 Chr. 4:43), existing as such from the end of the war in Europe in 1945 until December 1950, when this organization's Central Committee went out of existence.

Many thousands of Jews were at the very end of their strength by the time they were liberated, and died from exhaustion, disease, and also from the shock of liberation and from the effects of eating food that their emaciated bodies were not able to assimilate. Others, by the thousands, made their way to their countries of origin, within the Allies' repatriation program, or left for ports in southern Europe in the hope of being able to continue from there to Palestine. The rest of the Jewish survivors, about 50,000 persons, converged on camps in the Allied zones of occupation in Germany and Austria, mainly in the British zone in the north and the American zone in the south. Before long they were joined by a great number of Jewish refugees fleeing from eastern Europe with the BERIḤA (the organized exodus). These were mostly Jews from Poland, including repatriates from the Soviet Union, and refugees from Czechoslovakia, Hungary, and Romania. At the end of 1946 the number of Jewish DPs was estimated at 250,000, of whom 185,0000 were in Germany, 45,000 in Austria, and 20,000 in Italy.

The DPs were largely Jews from eastern Europe, primarily Poland, whereas most of the survivors from western Europe returned to their countries of origin. The great new influx changed the demographic composition of the DP population. At the time they were liberated, they consisted exclusively of persons who had been in and had survived the Nazi hell, as individuals, with no children or elderly people among them. At the end of 1946 about two-thirds of the DPs were "refugees," that is, they had not themselves had immediate experience of the Holocaust. Many were repatriates from the Soviet Union, and they included a larger number of family units and children, as a result of the Beriha and the marriages that had taken place among the original survivors.

Political Struggle. The existence of the She'erit ha-Peletah organization stemmed from nationalist Jewish motives and from external factors, the latter including the very limited number of emigration opportunities available in overseas countries and the British policy of keeping the gates of Palestine closed, as laid down in the 1939 WHITE PAPER. The struggle for a solution of the DP problem was therefore part and parcel of the Zionist struggle for the immigration of Jews to Palestine and for the establishment of a Jewish state there. The She'erit ha-Peletah played an active and important role in that struggle, together with the greater part of the Jews in the world, led by American Jewry. The following are the stages in the struggle.

1. The mission of Earl G. Harrison, the special envoy whom President Harry S. Truman appointed in the summer of 1945, to inquire into the conditions of the Jews in the DP camps in the American zone in Germany. Harrison was convinced that the only solution to the problem was the emigration of the Jewish DPs to Palestine, and he recommended that the British be asked to issue, without delay, 100,000 entry permits ("certificates"), without waiting for the overall settlement of the Palestine question. The Harrison mission was a decisive turning point, both because of the effect it had on the living conditions of the DPs, and because it resulted in President Truman's involvement in the struggle for the opening of the gates of Palestine.

2. David BEN-GURION's visit to the camps in Germany late in October 1945, in his capacity as chairman of the Jewish Agency. That visit strengthened and consolidated the joint political struggle being waged by the She'erit ha-Peletah, by the Jews of Palestine, and by Jews elsewhere. It persuaded the American occupation authorities to direct the Beriha into the American zone, facilitated the refugees' absorption in the camps, and made the camps a focus of Zionist political pressure.

3. The Anglo-American Commission of Inquiry's visit to the DP camps in February 1946. The commission included the DP problem in its investigation of the Palestinian question, and it too reached the conclusion that the great majority of the Jewish DPs wanted to settle in Palestine. It recommended the immediate settlement in Palestine of 100,000 refugees from Germany and Austria. The commission's recommendations were rejected by Britain, and the political

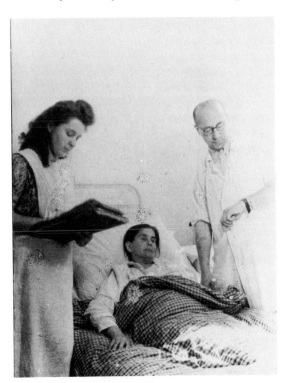

Sanatorium for displaced persons, Bad Wörishofen. [Collection of Toby Knobel Fluek, photograph courtesy A Living Memorial to the Holocaust— Museum of Jewish Heritage, New York]

struggle thereafter used different channels. The She'erit ha-Peletah concentrated on organizational affairs, education, and preparations for immigration to Palestine; the last also included efforts for "illegal" immigration continued in the face of mounting difficulties and the British decision, in August 1946, to deport the "illegal" immigrants to camps in Cyprus (*see* CYPRUS DETENTION CAMPS).

Life in the DP Camps. When the war ended, most of the Jewish DPs were in the British zone in northern Germany and the American zone in the south. They lived behind barbed wire in dozens of severely overcrowded former labor or concentration camps, together with non-Jewish DPs. They were guarded and were exposed to humiliating treatment and, at times, to antisemitic attacks. Nutrition, sanitary conditions, and accommodation in the camps were poor, although they differed from one place to another. Better conditions prevailed, for example, in the Saint Ottilien convent near Munich, where the DPs themselves had set up a hospital soon after VE Day, and in several large camps, containing four thousand to six thousand DPs each, in Feldafing, Landsberg, and Foehrenwald, also in the American zone. Most of the survivors in the British zone were concentrated in the former BERGEN-BELSEN camp. In both zones, however, DPs were also lodged in residential houses in cities that the occupation authorities had requisitioned for this purpose, as well as in public buildings.

Following the Harrison mission and the subsequent implementation of his recommendations, living conditions in the American zone improved considerably, compared to those that continued to prevail in the British zone. In the American zone, the Jewish DPs gained recognition as a special ethnic group that had its own requirements. They were put into separate camps, where they had a wide degree of autonomy; at their request, they were allowed to live outside the camps, and German properties were set aside to be used for their accommodation; and the large Jewish welfare agencies, based in the United States, were able to expand their operations. A special adviser on Jewish affairs was appointed to American military headquarters in Germany, and living conditions in the camps were greatly improved.

Further improvements took place in the wake of Ben-Gurion's visit in October 1945, and the influx of refugees into the American zone was permitted to continue. In the course of 1946, wave after wave of refugees from the east converged upon the American zone, and by the end of the year by far the greatest number of DPs was to be found there. In the British zone, on the other hand, for quite a while the Jews continued to live with the non-Jewish DPs, political activities were restricted, and, in December 1945, the further entry of refugees was prohibited. As a result, only a small proportion of the DPs lived in that zone.

Employment presented a special problem. It was not essential, since the basic necessities of life were provided by the UNITED NATIONS RELIEF AND REHABILITATION ADMINISTRATION (UNRRA) and the welfare agencies, but it was required for other aspects of the rehabilitation of the DPs. Some of the adults were employed in camp services, or in vocational and agricultural training establishments. Only a few DPs were prepared to take up employment in German or Austrian economic enterprises, or were capable of doing so. The refusal of the Jewish DPs to manufacture goods and supply them to the German market, or to integrate in some other way in German economic life, presented a serious obstacle to the effort to engage the DPs in productive occupations. Other factors—such as the psychological effects of their past experience, the uncertainty about their future, the welfare regime under which they lived (which included the supply of items that they could trade in), and the general condition of the postwar German economy—were all good excuses for idleness and black-market activities, which took place despite the efforts of the various organizations to suppress such manifestations.

External Welfare Agencies. The DP camps were under the control of the military authorities, and the care of the DPs was entrusted to UNRRA (which had been set up as far back as 1943) and, as of July 1947, the International Refugee Organization (IRO). UNRRA supplied the basic necessities of life and also acted as the principal coordinating and supervisory agency of the nongovernmental welfare agencies.

A considerable number and variety of Jewish agencies were active among the DPs. First to reach the Jewish survivors were the Jewish military chaplains, and it was they who established the first link between the survivors and the outside world. Of special importance was the work of Abraham Klausner, who introduced a system for locating survivors, publishing lists of their names and where they were to be found, under the title *She'erit ha-Peletah* (the first volume of which appeared in June 1945). Klausner also helped to establish the Central Committee of the She'erit ha-Peletah and to organize the Jews in the DP camps.

In June 1945 a delegation of the JEWISH BRIGADE GROUP, headed by Aharon Hoter-Yishai and Yaakov Lifshitz, arrived in the DP camps—the first group of Palestinian Jews to establish contact with the survivors. They came from Treviso, Italy, where the brigade was stationed. The meeting with Jewish soldiers, serving in a Jewish military formation and wearing Jewish insignia on their uniforms, was a moving experience for the survivors. Men of the brigade assisted in transferring survivors and refugees to ports in southern Europe, and also helped organize schooling and welfare in the camps.

The American Jewish JOINT DISTRIBUTION COMMITTEE (known as the Joint), headed by its European director, Joseph J. SCHWARTZ, sent its first teams to the camps in June 1945. By August 1945 its operations gained official recognition and were expanded. The Joint augmented the DPs' rations, financed the greater part of their welfare and educational activities in the American zone, and took upon itself other assistance programs, such as those for psychological therapy and legal aid. It also contributed financially to the costs of emigration and of immigration to Palestine. It kept in close touch with refugee organizations, the Zionist Organization, the Central Committee of the She'erit ha-Peletah, and the camp committees. The Jewish vocational education organization, ORT, took on the task of establishing an employment and vocational training network for youths and adults.

The appointment of a special adviser on

Ceremonies at Bremerhaven, July 13, 1949, marking the departure of the 50,000th displaced person to the United States. [Collection of Ben Kaplan, photograph courtesy A Living Memorial to the Holocaust—Museum of Jewish Heritage, New York]

Jewish affairs to work with the American military headquarters—one of the results of the Harrison mission—was designed to facilitate ongoing contact with the Jewish DPs and consideration of their problems, as well as to advise the American military authorities and UNRRA on policy regarding them. The office was held by prominent American Jewish personalities, selected by a board representing the five major Jewish organizations: the AMERICAN JEWISH COMMITTEE, the Joint, the AMERICAN JEWISH CONFERENCE, the American Jewish Congress, and the Jewish Agency for Palestine. The office remained in existence until the end of 1949.

In the British zone, a Jewish Relief Unit, sponsored by British Jewry, was engaged in welfare operations. The Jewish Agency's Palestinian delegation, headed by Chaim Hoffman (Yahil), established itself in Germany in December 1945. In its initial stage it consisted of a staff of twenty made up, in effect, of representatives of Jewish political parties in Palestine. The delegation concerned itself with educational and cultural activities among the DPs, the organization of political work, counseling, and representational functions.

Also active in the DP camps were emissaries of Jewish YOUTH MOVEMENTS and agricultural settlement organizations from Palestine; a teachers' delegation (arriving in 1947), also from Palestine; and a variety of other Jewish aid, educational, and migration bodies such as the OEUVRE DE SECOURS AUX EN- FANTS, the United HIAS Service, and the religious women's educational organization, Beis Yaakov.

Internal Organizations, Institutions, and Movements. From the very beginning, the internal organizations of the Holocaust survivors bore a distinctly Zionist character, for a number of reasons. Taking the lead in organizing the survivors were wartime leaders of the Zionist youth movements and fighters of the Jewish underground, who were highly respected and wielded great influence. The survivors, including those who had not been Zionists in the past, found in Zionism the only acceptable answer to their hopes and demands for the future, both as individuals and as victims of the Holocaust. Most of the survivors who were opposed to Zionism (mainly members of the BUND) were among those repatriated to their countries of origin; the ultrareligious anti-Zionists did not arrive in the camps in large numbers until a later stage, and even then they had to cooperate with the Zionist Beriḥa organization in order to get there. Above all, the Zionist solution appeared to be the only one that held out the hope of realizing the goal on which all the Jewish DPs agreed: to abandon blood-drenched Europe and open a new chapter of Jewish life, based on justice and independence rather than charity and subservience. The lack of emigration opportunities, and the anti-Zionist policy and actions of the British government, only served to reinforce the Holocaust survivors' support of Zionist goals and demands. In addition to its other activities, the She'erit ha-Peletah sought to achieve a greater unity among Zionists; to track down relatives among the survivors; to assist in bringing Nazi criminals to trial; and, owing to its strong sense of history, to participate in the efforts to document the Holocaust and commemorate its victims.

The first steps to establish a general survivors' organization were taken as soon as some of the survivors were liberated. In Bergen-Belsen, which was in the British zone, a provisional committee was set up as early as April 1945, chaired by Joseph (Yossele) Rosensaft. In Munich, in the American zone, a festive concert was arranged on May 27, 1945, to celebrate the liberation. It took place in the Saint Ottilien convent, which had been converted into a hospital.

The Central Committee. The survivors' organization in the American zone was initiated by the survivors themselves, with the support of American Jewish army chaplains and soldiers of the Jewish Brigade Group. The goal was to unite all the DPs under a single umbrella organization. On June 20, 1945, in Freimann-Flakkaserne, the First Congress of Zionists in Bavaria was held, at which the bylaws of the Union of Jewish Survivors in the American Zone of Bavaria were adopted. Under the charter, the union's major tasks were to represent the DPs and safeguard their interests. The charter contained a paragraph that called for close cooperation with the Zionist Organization, and henceforth the two bodies in large measure overlapped. A twenty-one-member council was elected, with Samuel Gringauz as chairman and Rabbi Abraham Klausner as honorary chairman; also elected was a small executive committee, with Dr. Zalman Grinberg as its director.

The committee established offices in the German Museum in Munich and set up various departments to deal with DP interests. On July 25, 1945, a conference of Jewish survivors in Germany was held in Saint Ottilien, attended by ninety-four representatives delegated by forty-six groups of survivors in Austria and Germany, including those at Bergen-Belsen. The conference's purpose was to establish a comprehensive organization of all DPs. Present were American army officers, newspapermen, and the head of the Jewish Agency's Immigration Department, Eliyahu Dobkin, who was the first official agency representative to visit the DPs. The overriding tone of the deliberations was one of activist Zionism. Clear-cut demands were formulated for organizing the survivors' life in Germany for as long as they had to stay there, especially with regard to educational facilities and vocational and agricultural training, and a DP Central Committee was formed. It soon transpired that a single survivors' organization for both the American and British zones was not feasible, and the new Central Committee was confined to the Jewish survivors in Bavaria. With the rapid growth of the number of Jews in the American zone, however, the Central Committee gradually became the DPs' principal representative body. In the second half of 1946 the Central Committee was officially recognized by the Americans as the authorized representative of the Jews in the American zone. Officials were elected at each of the three congresses held by the Central Committee: in January 1946, February 1947, and March and April 1948.

In the British zone, the provisional committee elected in Bergen-Belsen was active, and in addition a Central Committee of Jewish Survivors in the British Zone was formed, with Rosensaft serving as chairman of both organizations. Elections of officers were held at two conferences, in September 1945 and in the summer of 1947. The first of these was attended by Professor Selig BRODETSKY, member of the World Zionist Executive; representatives of the Jewish Brigade Group; and many guests. The committee also acted as the representative of the Jews in the British zone of Germany.

Once the Jewish survivors were separated from the others and had their own autonomous camps (in the summer of 1945), each camp elected a camp committee. While they did not have a budget of their own, the committees were supported by the Joint and the Jewish Agency emissaries and assumed responsibility for the camps' internal administration, including hygiene and sanitation, cultural activities, and education and religious life.

As soon as the war ended, the drive to unify the Zionist movement among the groups organized by the surviving partisans and ghetto fighters of eastern Europe gained momentum. One such group was formed in Bucharest, under the leadership of Abba KOVNER; another was the Partisans-Pioneers (it later added "Soldiers" to its title), formed by the Zionist youth movements Dror and Ha-Shomer ha-Tsa'ir.

On December 11, 1945, the United Zionist Organization, with the linked United Pioneer Youth Movement, was formed at a meeting in Landsberg, Germany. The two organizations, however, had only brief life spans as "united" bodies. Party and movement loyalty, nurtured by the movements' eastern European tradition; the party divisions existing

Representatives of the Jewish Committee and the Va'ad he-Haluts in Hannover, Germany. They were arrested on November 11, 1945, because they organized a meeting to protest recent British actions in Palestine.

in Palestine; and the psychological needs of the survivors for a proxy home and family all proved stronger than the drive for unification. The two bodies became identified with Mapai, the socialist party in Palestine.

In addition to the Zionist parties, there were the non-Zionist ultrareligious movements, Agudat Israel and Po'alei Agudat Israel. Their numbers grew when refugees from Hungary and Romania began to flow into the camps, but their political influence was limited, and they were active primarily in education, vocational training, and the publication of newspapers.

Education and Agricultural Training. An elaborate school system was established in the camps, initiated under great difficulties by the survivors. The system, assisted by Jewish Brigade Group soldiers, by emissaries of the Jewish Agency and of the Palestine Jewish community, and by the different welfare agencies, grew rapidly. It consisted of nursery schools; elementary schools; two high schools, one in Munich and one in Bergen-Belsen; educational institutions for the ultrareligious, such as Beis Yaakov girls' schools, teachers' seminars for women, and several Talmudic academies (yeshivas); and a vocational training network run by ORT. The formal educational institutions were complemented by "children's houses" and "kibbutzim," established mainly by the Zionist pioneering youth movements, which often took the place of the family structure. The formal educational system suffered from a shortage of instructors and textbooks, and the complementary institutions were hampered by partisan rivalries. It was only in 1947 that the Central Committee, the Jewish Agency, and the Joint set up an autonomous educational system.

Despite all the difficulties and shortcomings, the dedicated teachers and instructors coped successfully with the extraordinary problems of the mental and emotional rehabilitation of the children of the Holocaust. The educational institutions and kibbutzim were the centers of cultural life in the camps. The kibbutzim, moreover, became the main instrument for preparing the youth for immigration to Palestine, by means of the agricultural training they established on farms that the authorities requisitioned for this purpose.

In the American zone, at the end of 1946, forty-two such farms were in operation, on which 3,500 youngsters were undergoing training. The first such model was "Kibbutz Buchenwald," formed as early as the beginning of June 1945. Its first group of graduates left for Palestine that August.

Newspapers and Documentation. The acute and highly developed political sense of the DPs found its expression in more than seventy newspapers that they published, some in Hebrew but most in Yiddish. Noteworthy were *Ha-Nitsots—Bita'on ha-No'ar ha-Leumi* (The Spark—Organ of the National Youth), which had begun to appear as early as the final days of the war in the Dachau concentration camp, and the mimeographed *Tehiyyat ha-Metim* (Resurrection of the Dead), which came out from early May 1945 in Buchenwald. The organ of the Central Committee in the American zone was *Unzer Veg* (Our Path). Of special importance, because of the role it played in molding public opinion, was the *Landsberger Lager-Zeitung* (Landsberg Camp News), later renamed *Yiddishe Zeitung* (Jewish Newspaper). In the British zone the major periodical was *Unzer Shtimme* (Our Voice). Most of the other newspapers were put out by political parties or *Landsmanshaften* (societies made up of persons from the same town or district). The majority were Zionist, but some were published by Agudat Israel.

Commemoration and documentation projects included the work of the Tsentraler Historisher Komisiye (Central Historical Commission), established in December 1945 by the Central Committee in Munich, to assist in bringing Nazi criminals to trial. A network of regional committees was set up under the commission's auspices whose task it was to take evidence and collect documentary material, including material on the DPs. In August 1946 the commission published the first issue of the monthly *Fun Letzten Hurban* (Concerning the Last Holocaust).

The DP chapter came to an end with the establishment of the state of Israel, when the survivors living in the camps in Europe and in Cyprus began to converge en masse on the Jewish state. About two-thirds of them made their way to Israel after the long struggle; the rest emigrated to the United States, which was now relaxing its immigration regulations. In late 1949 and early 1950 the Adviser on Jewish Affairs, the Jewish Agency mission, and the Central Committee, one by one, wound up their operations; in 1953 the last Jewish DP camp in existence in Germany was disbanded.

HAGIT LAVSKY

Attitude of the United States. At the end of the war, the primary burden of the care of the DPs fell upon the United States military, with Great Britain and France assuming responsibility for smaller numbers. Eighty percent to 90 percent of these refugees were Christians, the rest Jews. The relatively small number of Jews received disproportionate attention because they had been treated more brutally during the war and because their co-religionists in the United States, Great Britain, and Palestine lobbied their respective governments for more humane treatment. They also helped publicize the ways in which the world's two leading democracies—the United States and Great Britain—were failing to help rehabilitate the Holocaust survivors and relocate them to places where they could begin new lives. The problems created by the inability of Great Britain and the United States to agree on a common plan strained the relationship between these nations and exacerbated the difficulties of Europe's surviving Jews.

The problem of DPs had been anticipated. The Allies had established UNRRA in 1943 to help the DPs until they could be sent on their way. In addition, DP centers were established by the American, British, and French armies. (The Soviet government did not admit to having a DP problem in its zone of occupation.)

At first the military assumed that UNRRA would adequately administer and supplement the social services required by these DPs. The Supreme Headquarters of the Allied Expeditionary Forces (SHAEF) and UNRRA then signed a pact outlining their mutual responsibilities, but without any assurance that UNRRA personnel would be utilized. UNRRA functioned as an administrative and subordinate branch of the military. According to these agreements, the army would provide food, shelter, clothing, medical sup-

plies, and security to the assembly centers housing the DPs; UNRRA's responsibilities included administering the camps and providing additional supplies, as well as recreational facilities, health and welfare services, and amenities such as tobacco and toilet articles. Self-help programs and vocational guidance also came under UNRRA. Furthermore, UNRRA claimed that it would provide the necessary professional and technical staff personnel, and give emotional sustenance while the DPs awaited repatriation. Another agreement, concluded in 1946, required UNRRA to operate a records office and tracing bureau, to prepare statistics and research reports, and to supervise educational programs; the army retained ultimate responsibility for DP care, movements of United Nations citizens and DPs, and overall management of the camps.

After the war ended in May 1945, hundreds of thousands more DPs remained in Germany and Austria than had been anticipated. Assembly centers that were established to hold 2,000 to 3,000 people contained more than 10,000. Former New York governor Herbert H. Lehman, the director general of UNRRA, hoped for 5,000 to 6,000 workers to process the DPs that summer, but only 2,646 were on the job in July.

Hurriedly recruited and poorly trained, too many of the original UNRRA workers lacked competence. Confused policies, inadequate supervisors, uncoordinated programs, generally poor administration, and conflicts with the military left a stigma that UNRRA never overcame. A Canadian major representing the organization in SHAEF was virtually ignored by superior officers in the rank-conscious military environment. Individual teams found themselves directionless, broken up and reshuffled, used and then unused. Many of the most efficient UNRRA personnel came from France, England, the Netherlands, Norway, and Poland, where they had experienced the savageries of Nazism and war, and understood the problems of the DPs. The least competent officials did not speak any of the DP languages, knew nothing of the DPs' background, and even profiteered from black-market activities. By December 1945, more than one thousand of the original employees were dismissed for a variety of reasons, including incompetence, inefficiency, lack of adaptability, and misconduct. The quality of operations began to improve thereafter, but the situation remained somewhat chaotic.

Word about the problems at the assembly centers soon reached American and British government officials. Jewish leaders, in particular, complained about the desperate position of their co-religionists in the DP camps. Thousands of Jews in the United States felt themselves morally bound to lead and finance the work of rehabilitating and resettling the Holocaust survivors. The continued maltreatment of their co-religionists grieved them deeply. After several requests, the army finally allowed the Joint to enter the DP centers, in June 1945, to minister to those in need.

Europe had been torn asunder during the war, and the DPs first and foremost needed new homes. However, most countries of the world snubbed European refugees fleeing totalitarianism and communism, and few were willing to harbor foreign immigrants. Everyone knew, of course, that the United States was the only nation that could probably absorb all of the DPs with little difficulty, but rigid immigration restrictions precluded the admission of more than a few thousand. Moreover, Zionist activity in both the United States, where Jews had some political influence, and Great Britain, where they had less, focused on Palestine as the only home for European Jewish survivors who wished to leave the Continent. The British government refused to countenance such an idea. It was keenly aware that the Arabs opposed entry of more Jews, and to keep its options open for Middle Eastern oil, strategic ports, and waterways, it tried to straddle the issue. At the conclusion of the war the British relented somewhat on the number of Jews who might go to Palestine (1,500 a month), but they refused to bend to further pressure from either the United States or the Zionists.

As a result of their stance, the British took other unfortunate and inhumane positions. Despite all that the Jews had suffered during World War II, the British refused to acknowledge in the fall of 1945 that Jews were living under worse conditions than any other victims of Nazi persecution. This situation was made clear in Earl Harrison's report, which

concluded: "We appear to be treating the Jews as the Nazis treated them, except that we do not exterminate them."

Harrison and his entourage had toured more than thirty DP camps during July 1945. His mission had been endorsed by President Truman after the State and Treasury departments, as well as several members of Congress, had heard complaints about the desperate conditions plaguing the war's survivors following their liberation from the concentration camps. Truman thought that accurate information was necessary before proceeding further and for that reason he had appointed Harrison to undertake an inspection.

The findings of Harrison and his associates proved to be a devastating indictment of the Allied military policies in force immediately after the war ended:

1. Jewish DPs lived under guard, behind barbed-wire fences, in centers that included former concentration camps. In some instances, concentration camp victims were housed together with their former guards and tormentors.
2. Housing, medical, and recreational facilities were inadequate, and nothing was being done to improve the quality of life or to rehabilitate the inhabitants.
3. Two months after the war had ended DPs still wore their old concentration camp uniforms because no other clothes had been issued.
4. No efforts were being made to reunite families or to help survivors look for lost relatives. In fact, the army did not allow the survivors to help themselves, since they could neither send nor receive mail.
5. Many army officers and soldiers believed that the survivors must be criminals, since otherwise they would not have been locked up in this fashion. Some army personnel even told Harrison that perhaps Hitler had been right in his treatment of the Jews.

Apart from urging admission to Palestine for those Jews wanting to settle there, Harrison recommended that the United States and other countries should take some of them as immigrants. The Harrison Commission report led to significant changes in the administration of the American DP centers, and it also prompted President Truman to write to British Prime Minister Clement Attlee, urging him to open the gates of Palestine to Jews wanting to go there. (Truman conveniently ignored the suggestion in the report that the United States also take some of the DPs.) Truman's petition was not warmly received in Britain.

Attlee cautiously informed Truman that his cabinet would look into the matter. The decision that the British cabinet reached in October of 1945 was to launch a joint Anglo-American inquiry into the problems and to seek eventual settlement of the displaced persons. Truman agreed, the commission was established, and the investigation began in January 1946.

The committee's ten-point report, which recommended several solutions to the Arab-Jewish conflict in Palestine, was delivered to the president and the prime minister at the end of April 1946. The British and American governments responded differently to the conclusions. Truman pounced on the statement that 100,000 Jews should immediately be admitted to Palestine and ignored the nine other recommendations. Attlee, on the other hand, emphasized the conclusions in the report that called for the nations of the world, and not just Palestine, to admit the DPs, and that appealed for the suppression of violence and terrorism in Palestine. Publicly, Attlee commented that the British would not implement the recommendations unless (1) the United States provided financial and military assistance; and (2) the illegal armies (that is, the Hagana) in Palestine disbanded.

In private, Attlee was even more vitriolic. Neither he nor the members of the cabinet had anticipated a unanimous committee report or a recommendation that 100,000 Jewish displaced persons be admitted to Palestine. The cabinet had hoped to inveigle the United States into joint action, but had never quite made the point directly.

During the summer of 1946 the increased influx from eastern Europe into the DP camps hardened the British against allowing more Jews into Palestine, and forced Truman to reconsider ways of handling the DP situation. The DP centers became more crowded, and the army felt helpless because

it lacked the facilities for dealing with all the additional refugees, yet Truman, because of Jewish pressure at home, refused to allow the camps to be closed to them.

While the exodus of Jews from Poland was taking place in 1946, an American and British delegation was once again trying to work out a plan that would bring 100,000 Jewish DPs into Palestine. The plan formulated by this new group would have divided Palestine into Arab and Jewish sections, with the Arabs receiving three times as much land as the Jews. Although Truman was ready to accept the compromise, pressure from American Jews once again forced him to reject the new plan.

Another event during the summer of 1946 that helped propel Truman into action was a Jewish dissident underground group's bombing of the King David Hotel in Jerusalem, in which ninety-one people lost their lives. This hardened British attitudes toward Jews. Truman finally announced, in August, that he would recommend to Congress that legislation be passed admitting some of the DPs to the United States. He was deliberately vague, and suggested no specific number that he thought should be admitted. This was the first time, however, that any responsible American official had made such a recommendation publicly.

The reaction within the United States to Truman's announcement was mixed, but among the majority of the Jews it was tepid. Most American Jews wanted to see a Jewish homeland established in Palestine; they believed that efforts to bring displaced Jews to the United States would dilute the problem in Europe and weaken the Zionist cause. On the other hand, they did not lack sympathy for the survivors of the Holocaust, and did not want to do anything to harm their chances for resettlement in any place.

The primary role, therefore, in bringing displaced Jews to the United States was assumed by the two leading non-Zionist American Jewish organizations, the American Jewish Committee and the anti-Zionist American Council for Judaism. The former provided the executive and staff leadership, and the president of the latter organization, Lessing Rosenwald, supplied most of the funds.

Most members of the American Jewish

Committee and the American Council for Judaism, as well as other Jews, feared to act openly on behalf of their European coreligionists. Antisemitism and opposition to bringing more Jews to the United States were quite open. Because of the strong prejudices, the leaders of these organizations joined to establish the Citizens' Committee on Displaced Persons, a nonsectarian group chaired by Earl Harrison.

The Citizens' Committee functioned as a lobby to inform the public and Congress of the plight of the DPs, and it urged appropriate legislation. At the outset, its leaders emphasized that 80 percent of the approximately 1 million DPs in Europe were Christian, which was not widely known at the time. The committee tried to awaken an apathetic nation to the facts that most DPs had no place to go and that out of humanitarian concerns the United States should take its fair share of these people.

This publicity helped develop a climate of favorable opinion for concrete legislation. To this end, the Citizens' Committee prepared a bill, based on recommendations made by the American Jewish Committee, providing that the United States would accept 400,000 DPs. Leaders of the Citizens' Committee had decided earlier that to receive the widest possible support, their legislation should be presented by a member of the majority party from the isolationist Midwest. They approached Republican senators Homer Ferguson and Arthur H. Vandenberg of Michigan, and Robert Taft of Ohio, but each refused to sponsor the measure. They then turned to the House of Representatives, where William G. Stratton, congressman-at-large from Illinois, who not only sympathized with their objectives but also saw an opportunity to develop a national reputation, agreed to sponsor it. On April 1, 1947, Stratton introduced a bill that would allow 400,000 DPs, in addition to those who entered under the immigration quotas, to enter the United States during the next four years.

Most congressmen knew little about DPs, could not understand why they had not gone home after the war, and feared a depression or a glut on the labor market if a large number of immigrants began coming to the United States. Hearings on the Stratton mea-

sure were held in the summer of 1947, but no bill was presented on the floor of the House of Representatives. President Truman, first in January 1947 and again in July, called upon Congress to produce suitable legislation to aid DPs but did not endorse the Stratton bill.

The key to the passage of DP legislation lay in the Senate. The House of Representatives was not prepared to pass any bill unless favorable action seemed likely in the upper house. After an initial period of hesitation, during which it appeared that no bill would be passed, propaganda from the Citizens' Committee, letters to representatives and senators, and newspaper editorials urging action began to take effect. Congress received more mail, most of it favorable, on assisting the DPs than on any other subject since Prohibition.

Unfortunately for the DPs, Senator Chapman Revercomb of West Virginia chaired the Immigration Subcommittee of the Senate Judiciary Committee, and his views were anything but favorable toward helping them. He had made a study of the DPs for the Republican Steering Committee in December 1946. His conclusions were negative and showed contempt for those who had suffered most from the war and during its aftermath, whom he characterized as "imbued with a communistic line of thought." When the Senate appeared ready to consider DP legislation in the summer of 1947, Revercomb urged his colleagues to schedule a Senate inspection tour of the camps in Europe before taking action. After lengthy debate the Senate agreed to this proposal, and Revercomb was appointed to head the tour.

In the fall of 1947 both the House of Representatives and the Senate sent committees to investigate the DP camps. The Citizens' Committee sponsored an inspection tour of the camps by Commander Paul Griffith of the American Legion, who thereafter changed his position and endorsed emergency legislation to aid DPs. Both the House and Senate committees also reached the conclusion that something should be done for the people in the camps. The House report noted: "If the Jewish facet of the problem could be cleared up, the solution of the remainder of the problem would be facilitated. The opening up of Palestine to the resettlement of Jewish displaced persons would break the logjam." Around the same time, the governors of several Midwestern states established local commissions to study the possibilities of resettling DPs in their midst. Finally, and perhaps most important for the future passage of legislation, Robert A. Taft, the Republican leader of the Senate, called for "immediate action" to help the DPs. As winter began it seemed likely that Congress would act.

In the second session of the Eightieth Congress, Frank Fellows of Maine, chairman of the Subcommittee on Immigration of the House Judiciary Committee, proposed a measure calling for the admission of 200,000 DPs from among those who had registered by April 21, 1947, with the DP camps. The DPs admitted were to be charged against future immigration quotas for their countries of origin. In the Senate, Revercomb's committee proposed legislation that would admit 100,000 DPs over a two-year period, confine eligibility to those who had been in the DP camps on or before December 22, 1945, and reserve 50 percent of the visas for agricultural workers. It also suggested that 50 percent of those admitted come from the nations of Europe that had been annexed by the Soviet Union after the war.

These restrictions alarmed American Jews. First, most of the Jews who had been in the DP camps in 1945 had meanwhile gone elsewhere—to Palestine, to the United States, and to other countries. Second, the mass exodus of Polish Jews to West Germany took place in 1946, and none of them would be eligible if the December 22, 1945, cutoff date remained. Third, very few Jews came from "annexed territories," by which the senators meant Estonia, Latvia, and Lithuania, which had been absorbed by the Soviet Union. And finally, very few Jews were agricultural workers. Adherents of a generous immigration bill considered the Revercomb bill a disaster.

The Revercomb proposal reached the Senate floor in May 1948. Two significant amendments to the bill passed. One increased the total number of DPs to be admitted to the United States to 100,000 per year for two years, and the other, proposed by Senator William Langer of North Dakota, gave preference to the VOLKSDEUTSCHE (ethnic Germans), those Germans expelled from eastern Europe after the war. Langer, the only member of the Senate Judiciary Committee to oppose the Revercomb plan in a committee vote, believed that the *Volksdeutsche* were worse off than other DPs, especially the Jews, all of whom he assumed had relatives in New York City.

The measure passed the Senate by a vote of 63 to 13. Harrison urged the House to reject the Fellows bill, which discriminated on religious, national, and occupational grounds. He considered the clause on the *Volksdeutsche* "a mockery of American justice" that was tantamount to accepting Nazi racial doctrine. Harrison's statement did not dissuade the House of Representatives from passing the Fellows bill essentially as presented, by a vote of 289 to 91. The two houses of Congress then selected conference committees to reconcile the bills.

The Senate conferees included Revercomb, Ferguson, Harley Kilgore of West Virginia, James Eastland of Mississippi, and Forrest Donnell of Missouri. In the conference, Revercomb, Eastland, and Donnell remained adamant against accepting provisions that might help Jewish DPs. They gave the House members an ultimatum: either the Senate measure or nothing. As a result, the conferees went along with modified aspects of the worst features of both the House and Senate bills. Consequently, DPs had to have arrived in Germany, Austria, and Italy by December 22, 1945, to be considered eligible for admission to the United States, whereas *Volksdeutsche* qualified if they had arrived by July 1, 1948.

The report so displeased some of the conferees that four refused to sign it. Despite the fact that many members of Congress believed that the bill was deliberately intended to exclude Jews, President Truman reluctantly signed it, while denouncing the measure as antisemitic and anti-Catholic. It was the former, but not the latter; Catholics predominated among both the DPs and the *Volksdeutsche*.

Jews and Jewish groups were incensed. Many Jewish groups wanted the act vetoed by the president, but on this point there was no unity. Truman appointed three liberals—Ugo Carusi, Edward M. O'Connor, and

Harry N. Rosenfield—to head the Displaced Persons' Commission in August 1948. Their interpretation of the Displaced Persons' Act was so broad, and their acceptance of questionable documents so frequent, that they undermined the thrust of the bigoted legislation, and more Jews entered the United States than had been anticipated. When Senator Pat McCarran of Nevada, a conservative Democrat, investigated the Displaced Persons' Commission in 1949, he accused it of lax procedures that allowed Communists and other subversives into the United States (the senator did not mention fascists or Nazis, since their admission apparently did not upset him). The frightened commissioners thereupon began adhering to the letter of the law. They also led the campaign to liberalize the Displaced Persons' Act of 1948, which Congress did in June 1950. Thereafter, the DPs ceased being a significant concern of America's Jews or of Congress.

By 1950, those Jews who had wanted to eliminate what they considered to be the specifically antisemitic provisions of the 1948 Displaced Persons' Act had accomplished their purpose. Congress changed the cutoff date to 1949 and did away with the preferences for agricultural workers and persons from annexed territories. Furthermore, by 1950 most of the Jewish DPs had left the assembly centers for Israel, the United States, or other nations.

On the international scene, the formation of the International Refugee Organization (IRO) in 1947, an agency designed to help resettle the DPs still in Europe (numbering over a million), helped to unplug the bottleneck in the DP centers and promoted the exodus to other countries. By 1947, in fact, several of the world's nations, realizing that they needed able-bodied people, sought DPs from the European assembly centers. Most countries wanted young, strong gentiles; none expressed a preference for Jews. Belgium selected twenty thousand Balts and Ukrainians to work in its mines, and the British took about thirty thousand single adults for agriculture, mining, and domestic tasks.

After the establishment of Israel in 1948, most of the Jewish DPs thought that the IRO would facilitate their movement there. However, more than 200 of the IRO's 435 admin-istrative officers were British, and the agency reflected Britain's hostility to Israel. Consequently, it took the position that it could not send people to any place that had not been recognized by all of the United Nations. And, since the Arabs had attacked Israel as soon as the new nation came into being, it could not send DPs to "belligerent" countries in the Middle East. Thus, the European Jews made their way to Israel without the assistance of the IRO, but often with the overt aid of American army officials and the Beriha. For their part, the non-Jews had no difficulty being taken into Canada, Latin America, and the European nations.

Between 1945 and 1952, the United States accepted about 400,000 DPs, of whom perhaps 20 percent were Jewish. (Exact figures are impossible to obtain.) Great Britain admitted about 100,000 people, but figures are not available for the percentage of Jews. Some 136,000 Jewish DPs went to Israel, but here again statistics are only estimates.

The problem of the DPs need not have lasted as long as it did. Great Britain, however, was slow to realize that it would have to relinquish control of Palestine, and the United States was even slower in realizing that unless it made some attempt to receive DPs, the problem simply would not go away. All nations looked to America to take the lead. The fact that so many DPs were Jews also complicated the matter. The world did not want them. With the establishment of Israel in 1948, Jews were at last able to go there.

[See also Survivors, Psychology of; United States Army and Survivors in Germany and Austria.]

LEONARD DINNERSTEIN

BIBLIOGRAPHY

Abzug, R. H. *Inside the Vicious Heart: Americans and the Liberation of Nazi Concentration Camps.* New York, 1985.
Bauer, Y. *Out of the Ashes.* Oxford, 1989.
Dinnerstein, L. *America and the Survivors of the Holocaust.* New York, 1982.
Marrus, M. R. *The Unwanted: European Refugees in the Twentieth Century.* New York, 1985.
Proudfoot, M. J. *European Refugees, 1939–1952: A Study in Forced Population Movement.* Evanston, Ill., 1956.

Wilson, F. M. *Aftermath*. London, 1947.

Ziemke, E. F. *The U.S. Army in the Occupation of Germany*. Washington, D.C., 1975.

DNEPROPETROVSK, district capital in the Ukrainian SSR. On the eve of World War II, Dnepropetrovsk had a Jewish population of some 80,000, out of a total of 500,662. As the German armies approached on August 5, 1941, the evacuation of the city was begun and some 60,000 Jews left. The Germans took the city on August 25. In the first few days of the occupation, the Ukrainian population was extremely hostile to the Jews, plundering their property and informing on many of them to the Germans. The Jews were ordered to wear a Jewish BADGE (a blue Star of David on a white background) and to elect a committee that was referred to as the "community leadership." Its first chairman was a lawyer named Gorenberg. House managers were ordered to provide the command headquarters in the city with a list of their Jewish tenants, and the military administration made preparations to establish a ghetto for Dnepropetrovsk's Jews.

On October 8, 1941, the military governor imposed a collective fine of 30 million rubles on the city's Jews. On October 13, even before the fine was collected, Einsatzkommando 6 (of Einsatzgruppe C) began rounding up the Jews and confining them in a large department store in the city; from there the Jews were taken in groups to a nearby ravine, to be murdered. A total of fifteen thousand Jews were killed in this operation, which was followed at a later stage by the killing of the remaining five thousand Jews.

When Dnepropetrovsk was liberated by the Red Army on October 25, 1943, only fifteen Jews were left alive in the city.

BIBLIOGRAPHY

Ehrenburg, I., and V. Grossman, eds. *The Black Book of Soviet Jewry*. New York, 1981.

SHMUEL SPECTOR

DOCTORS, NAZI. *See* Physicians, Nazi.

DOCUMENTATION CENTERS. [*This entry consists of eight articles that describe major centers for the documentation of the Holocaust:*

  Berlin Documents Center
  Centre de Documentation Juive
    Contemporaine
  Centro di Documentazione Ebraica
    Contemporanea
  Leo Baeck Institute
  Main Commission for Investigation
    of Nazi Crimes in Poland
  Rijksinstituut voor Oorlogsdocumentatie
  Wiener Library
  Żydowski Instytut Historyczny

See also Yad Vashem *and the articles under* Museums and Memorial Institutes.]

Berlin Documents Center

The Berlin Documents Center is an archive consisting of material discovered by the United States Army in a Munich paper fac-

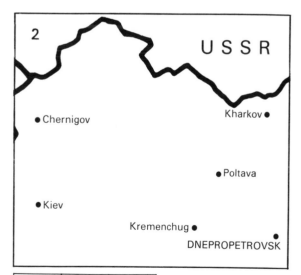

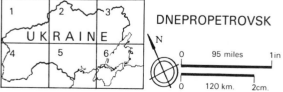

DNEPROPETROVSK

N

0   95 miles   1in

0   120 km.   2cm.

tory (where it was scheduled to be recycled), as well as papers that the Nazis had hidden in the mountains of the Harz and the Tirol. The center, situated in the Dahlendorf district of West Berlin, is to this day under guard by a United States military unit. Access to it is controlled and restricted to authorized representatives of governments and to scholars who show proof that the material they are looking for is essential to their research. Even for such requests, the center prefers to reply in writing, which is the usual practice when requests either are made for documents containing personal data, pension rights, and so on, or emanate from courts of law, official investigation agencies, or DENAZIFICATION proceedings.

The center contains some 30 million files, information sheets, and questionnaires on the persons who set up the Third Reich and ran it —from the lowest echelon up to the very top —and especially on the leaders of the Nazi regime, such as Joseph GOEBBELS, Hermann GÖRING, Julius STREICHER, and Joachim von RIBBENTROP. The center has 10.7 million individual sheets on members of the National Socialist party, over half a million files on SS members, and a similar number of files on SD (Sicherheitsdienst; Security Service) personnel. These files include questionnaires that the subjects themselves had filled in, information on disciplinary proceedings and district court proceedings against them (115,000 of the latter category), and correspondence of Nazi party and government offices ranging from the *Gaue* (the territorial units into which the Reich was divided for Nazi party purposes) all the way up to the Reich chancellery; also included in this category of files are the documents of the People's Court, the party's—and the Reich's—supreme court.

Other categories of papers include those containing data on Nazi doctors (forty thousand) and on teachers and university lecturers (several thousand); documents of the SS RASSE- UND SIEDLUNGSHAUPTAMT (Race and Resettlement Main Office), which dealt with the "Germanization" of occupied territories (2.5 million documents); and papers concerning the Reichskulturkammer (Reich Cultural Affairs Office) and other offices that decided on important appointments in all spheres of life. The material is stored in wooden boxes

and in files that bear the relevant names and numbers.

The following are some of the most interesting documents held by the center, both in political terms and for research purposes:

1. A letter from Adolf HITLER, written in his own hand at 4:00 p.m. on April 29, 1945, in which he declares that he and his wife have decided to choose death rather than suffer the shame of defeat, and asks to be buried in the place where he had spent most of the last twelve years of his life;

2. The cable that the Nazi film director and photographer Leni Riefenstahl sent Hitler when France was conquered, expressing her joy and congratulations on the accomplishment of this task, "one of the most significant in human history";

3. Information that was used to identify a body, found on a South American seashore, that was said to be that of Josef MENGELE; the file describes Mengele as an honest, trustworthy, consistent, steady, and disciplined person, who meticulously carried out the orders he was given and remained loyal to his task even under the most trying circumstances;

4. The file on Adolf EICHMANN, in which he is described as a "perfect Nordic type"—a friendly, trustworthy, and ambitious person, who acts properly under all circumstances, is endowed with a lively intellect and a strong will, and conducts his work in accordance with the principles of National Socialism.

The Berlin Documents Center is one of the most important sources of archival material for the study of the structure of the Nazi regime and the way its staff was selected and behaved. SS men who wanted to marry had to produce documentary evidence, going back two hundred years, on their "pure" racial descent; the women had to produce documents and testimonies on their racial "purity," their moral standards, love of children, state of health (including the most intimate physical details), their suitability to be the mothers of a racially improved generation, and hair and skin color.

The center's material provides information not only on the Nazi ideological indoctrination and the persons in charge, but also on the steps that were taken to ensure that the Nazis possessed the biological and physical properties required for the planning of the right type of future generation. Those who did not possess these qualifications were entered on blacklists of the disqualified. Sometimes persons who had merely played pool or other games with Jews, or had spoken with Jews in their youth, had their names entered on these lists.

In the postwar period, most of the Germans who had served under the Nazi regime as district attorneys, judges, teachers, university lecturers, and government officials kept away, as best they could, from the center, in an effort to forget the past and to ease their reabsorption into German society as it had emerged from the defeat. As the United States high commissioner for the American zone of occupation, John J. McCloy, stated in a 1978 television interview, he at times had to bar access to the center's information to avoid embarrassing former Nazis who had assumed positions in the new German regime.

The Berlin Documents Center is financed by the West German government out of funds allocated for the maintenance of the offices of the Allied occupation authorities.

MARIAN MUSHKAT

Centre de Documentation
Juive Contemporaine

The Centre de Documentation Juive Contemporaine (Center of Contemporary Jewish Documentation; CDJC) is an institution created in France to preserve the evidence of Nazi crimes for future generations. Established clandestinely in Grenoble in 1943 by Isaac Schneersohn and a team representing various Jewish organizations, it embarked upon the task of collecting and protecting documents relating to the fate of the Jews under German occupation.

The liberation of France in August 1944 enabled CDJC to operate openly and, thanks to the hasty departure of the Germans and their Vichy French collaborators, to collect a large quantity of files, with the assistance of the new regime.

Now located at 17, Rue Geoffroy-L'Asnier, the CDJC building was erected in 1956 on a plot of land allotted by the Paris city council, which is also the site of the Memorial for the Unknown Jewish Martyr. CDJC's rich archive contains documents of the German and French authorities relating to the history of the Jews in France during World War II; documents of the SD (Sicherheitsdienst; Security Service) and Sicherheitspolizei (Security Police), including lists of names of all persons deported to the extermination camps of AUSCHWITZ-Birkenau and SOBIBÓR; and the files of Alfred ROSENBERG and of the COMMISSARIAT GÉNÉRAL AUX QUESTIONS JUIVES (General Office for Jewish Affairs). The Rosenberg files are among the most important sources for the study of the organization and activities of the Third Reich and the Nazi party.

The research carried on in CDJC concentrates on four objectives: conducting basic research; disseminating information; bringing Nazi criminals to justice; and seeking indemnification for all categories of Nazi victims. CDJC has provided documents and legal opinions to establish the rights of the victims of the Nazi occupation.

Apart from its collection of documents, CDJC possesses a library of over twenty thousand volumes dealing with the Holocaust period, Nazi and neo-Nazi publications, speeches prepared for Nazi and neo-Nazi spokesmen, and an important collection of periodicals put out by French collaborators with the Nazis (including *Le Cahier Jaune*, *Le Franciste*, and *L'Action Française*).

Since 1946 the center has published *Le Monde Juif* (The Jewish World), a quarterly containing research studies, documents, commentaries, and book reviews.

CDJC has published over fifty books, most of them based on the documentary material contained in its archives. The center also organizes panel discussions, roundtable talks, and lectures dealing with the persecution of the Jews, their sufferings, and resistance activity during the German occupation in France and other countries. CDJC has mounted exhibitions, including "Auschwitz," "Bergen-Belsen," "Life and Revolt in Warsaw and Other Ghettos in Eastern Europe," and "The Jewish Fight against Hitlerism" (the last on permanent display).

BIBLIOGRAPHY

La France de l'Affaire Dreyfus à nos jours: Catalogue no. 1. Paris, 1964.

La France, Le Troisième Reich, Israel: Catalogue no. 2. Paris, 1968.

Le Monde Juive 80 (October–December 1975): entire issue.

Ten Years of Existence of the Jewish Contemporary Documentation Center, 1943–1953. Paris, 1953.

ADAM RUTKOWSKI

Centro di Documentazione Ebraica Contemporanea

The Centro di Documentazione Ebraica Contemporanea (Center for Contemporary Jewish Documentation; CDEC) was established to study the role of Jews in the Italian resistance movement and the history of the persecution of the Jews by the Fascists and the Nazis. It was founded in Venice in 1955, and later moved to Milan.

Over the course of time the center's tasks expanded broadly, and it now deals with three separate, but interconnected, fields, as follows.

1. Historical archives: the collecting of documentation on the Jews in Italy from the end of the nineteenth century until the present day, with special emphasis on the period of persecution from 1938 to 1945. The center conducts independent research on the latter subject.
2. Antisemitism in contemporary Italy: the center collects testimonies and documentation, undertakes research, and supports independent studies on the subject.
3. The collecting of books and periodicals in Italian and other languages on the persecution of the Jews from 1938 to 1945, contemporary antisemitism, the history of the Jews in Italy and the world, and Jewish culture and tradition.

In these three fields the center is the principal scholarly institution in Italy for Italian and foreign scholars. In the years since its founding the center has issued ten publications. It is preparing a memorial book on the Jews deported from Italy in World War II.

MICHELE SARFATTI

Leo Baeck Institute

The Leo Baeck Institute (LBI) is a research institute concerned with the history of the Jews in Germany and of German-speaking Jewish groups in other countries, from the time of the Emancipation of the Jews in the nineteenth century. The LBI collects documentary materials, and it sponsors and advances research in this field.

The LBI was founded in Jerusalem in 1955 by the Council of Jews from Germany. Its founders included major figures from the last generation of German Jewry, including Martin Buber, Siegfried Moses, Ernst Simon, and Gershom Scholem. The institute is named after Rabbi Leo BAECK (1873–1956).

It was not the institute's original intention to include within its scholarly work the history of German Jewry after the Nazi rise to power. Nevertheless, many studies published by the institute deal with Jewish life during the period of the Third Reich, covering among other things the REICHSVERTRETUNG DER DEUTSCHEN JUDEN (Reich Representation of German Jews), educational and cultural activities, the organization of mutual aid, and the policy of emigration, including the HAAVARA AGREEMENT. Studies on the history of the Jews under Nazi rule have also been published in the *Leo Baeck Institute Year Book* and in the institute's *Bulletin*, which since 1957 has appeared three times a year in German. The LBI has also published the memoirs of public figures who were active under the Third Reich, and of people from all sectors of the population between 1780 and 1945, together with historical and sociological surveys of those years. The growing emphasis of the institute on research into the history of German Jewry under the Nazis was reflected in particular in an international symposium, the first of this kind to be sponsored by the LBI. Held in 1985 in Berlin, it was devoted to the topic of "Self-Assertion in Adversity: The Jews in National Socialist Germany, 1933–1939"; among the participants were German historians.

The LBI has branches in the three principal centers of immigration of German Jewry—Israel, the United States, and Great Britain. The archives and library of the New York institute are among the largest and most comprehensive on the subject of German Jewish history. The editorial board of the English-language *Year Book*, which was headed by Robert WELTSCH from its foundation until 1978, is located in London. Since 1978 the

Year Book has been edited by Dr. Arnold Paucker. The Jerusalem institute publishes the German-language *Bulletin* and Hebrew translations of the classical works of Jewish thinkers in Germany. Representatives of the three branches meet at regular intervals under the chairmanship of the president of the institute, in order to coordinate their activity and in particular their research programs. The first president of the LBI was Leo Baeck (until his death in 1956), and the second was Dr. Siegfried Moses. After Dr. Moses's death in 1977, Rabbi Max Gruenewald became president.

BIBLIOGRAPHY

Moses, S. "Leo Baeck Institute of Jews from Germany." *Leo Baeck Institute Year Book* 1 (1956): xi–xviii.

Schorsch, I. "The Leo Baeck Institute: Continuity and Desolation." *Leo Baeck Institute Year Book* 25 (1980): ix–xii.

JOSEPH WALK and
OTTO DOV KULKA

Main Commission for Investigation of Nazi Crimes in Poland

The Main Commission for Investigation of Nazi Crimes in Poland (Główna Komisja Badania Zbrodni Hitlerowskich w Polsce; GKBZHwP) was created by the Polish National Council on March 29, 1945, as part of the Ministry of Justice; it was headed by the minister of justice. The commission's aims are to investigate Nazi crimes committed in Poland or perpetrated on Polish citizens outside Poland's borders; to cooperate with and provide legal aid to tribunals and bodies dealing with pursuit of Nazis in other countries; to conduct research into the occupation period; and to collect documentation and maintain a special archive.

A reform of April 6, 1948, established the Instytut Pamięci Narodowej (Institute of National Remembrance), whose members are chosen from outstanding experts on Nazi crimes and the period of the Nazi occupation. The institute's rich archival collections are available for scholars from Poland and abroad. By 1989, 382 volumes of its bulletins and books had been published.

STEFAN BIERNACKI

Rijksinstituut voor Oorlogsdocumentatie

The Rijksinstituut voor Oorlogsdocumentatie (Netherlands State Institute for War Documentation) is an official research institution, records depot, and library in Amsterdam devoted to the history of World War II, administered by the ministry of education and sciences. The institute was founded on May 8, 1945, after preparations for it had been made in the German-occupied country since 1943 with the moral support (since the spring of 1944) of the Dutch government-in-exile in London. Its directors have been Louis de Jong (1945–1979) and Harry Paape (since 1979), and it has thirty staff members.

By 1987, the Rijksinstituut had published sixty-two volumes: monographs, source publications, and miscellaneous works, as well as over 160 mimeographed reports on a great variety of subjects. Its Holocaust publications include B. A. Sijes's *The Strike of February 25–26, 1941* (1954), J. Presser's *The Destruction of the Dutch Jews* (1969), D. Giltay Veth and A. J. van der Leeuw's *The Weinreb-Report* (1976), and Harry Paape, Gerrold van der Stroom, and David Barnouw's *The Diaries of Anne Frank* (1986). Louis de Jong also paid much attention to several aspects of the Holocaust in his series The Kingdom of the Netherlands in the Second World War, which he was commissioned to write in 1955. The first volume appeared in 1969, and members of the institute's staff have participated in the preparation of this definitive study. The series will consist of fourteen parts (twenty-eight volumes), covering some sixteen thousand pages. It was completed in 1989.

The records depot contains several hundred archives and collections of documents. Those on the Holocaust include the archives of the Comité voor Joodsche Vluchtelingen (Committee for Jewish Refugees), the JOODSE RAAD (Jewish Council), the WESTERBORK transit camp, the VUGHT concentration camp, the IV B 4 section (the section dealing with Jews) of the REICHSSICHERHEITSHAUPTAMT (Reich Security Main Office; RSHA) branch in The Hague, the ZENTRALSTELLE FÜR JÜDISCHE AUSWANDERUNG (Central Office for Jewish Emigration) in Amsterdam, the Omnia Treuhandgesellschaft (Trust Company), whose branch in The Hague dealt with the ARISIERUNG ("Aryanization") of Dutch Jewish enterprises, and many other public and private collections.

The Rijksinstituut's special collections include more than 1,200 private diaries; 120,000 photographs; 200 films; 2,000 drawings; underground newspapers, pamphlets, poems, and doggerels; Allied and German propaganda leaflets; and 5,000 posters. The library of the institute contains about 45,000 titles.

Important tasks in the fields of education and social welfare (especially on behalf of survivors of the Holocaust, resistance fighters, and victims of acts of war), as well as general information, have been entrusted to the institute. It was also responsible for compiling and designing permanent exhibitions in the Netherlands War and Resistance Museum, the State Museum in Auschwitz, and the Westerbork Remembrance Center. The institute publishes annual reports in Dutch and progress reports in English.

HARRY PAAPE

Wiener Library

A research center on Nazism, the Wiener Library was founded by the CENTRALVEREIN DEUTSCHER STAATSBÜRGER JÜDISCHEN GLAUBENS (Central Union of German Citizens of Jewish Faith; CV) and originally operated clandestinely to accumulate material about the Nazi party. The only archive of its kind in the Weimar Republic, it was administered in cooperation with other German organizations and utilized for anti-Nazi propaganda. With Hitler's rise to power, the archive had to be destroyed.

Alfred Wiener (1885–1964), the general secretary of the CV, who had been very active in the fight against antisemitism, emigrated from Germany in 1934 and founded the Jewish Central Information Office in Amsterdam.

This office gathered material on the situation in the Third Reich in order to provide information to all those interested in fighting Nazism. With the help of Dutch and other antifascists, Dr. Wiener collected the available press reports and Nazi literature stemming from Germany. By 1938 the office already had more than eight thousand books and some ten thousand press clippings, with sets of Nazi and anti-Nazi periodicals. The following year, the office was transferred to London and served as the basis of the Wiener Library.

During World War II, the materials were used by various British governmental departments, especially the Ministry of Information. The library became a leading research center on Nazism, fascism, and other totalitarian movements. It came to hold a vast collection of books, eyewitness reports, forty thousand prosecution documents from the International Military Tribunal of the NUREMBERG TRIAL, over a million newspaper clippings, and other archival material, mainly on twentieth-century antisemitism and, especially, Nazism. In 1980, most of the books and the original archival material were transferred to Tel Aviv University; microfilmed copies of the material remain in London.

BIBLIOGRAPHY

Weltsch, R. "About Alfred Wiener." *Leo Baeck Institute Year Book* 9 (1964): 29–30.
Wiener Library. *The Wiener Library: Its History and Activities, 1934–1945.* London, 1946.

DAVID BANKIER

Żydowski Instytut Historyczny

The Żydowski Instytut Historyczny (Jewish Historical Institute) is a research institute in Warsaw focusing on the history of the Jews of Poland, primarily during World War II and the Holocaust period. The institute is an autonomous unit within the Polish Academy of Sciences and is subject to the academy's scholarly supervision (and, according to Polish practice, also the academy's political and ideological supervision). Because of its special character, it has shared the vicissitudes of the Jewish community of Poland and of its cultural and public organizations. The work it has carried out, as well as its methods, have reflected the condition of the surviving Jewish remnants and the Polish regime's attitude toward the country's Jewish population.

The institute has its origins in the Central Jewish Historical Commission, founded in Lublin in 1944 (as soon as the city was liberated from the Germans). The commission moved in 1945 to Łódź, and, at the end of 1947, to Warsaw. It had branches, or at least representatives, in provincial towns and cities with a Jewish population, the largest such branch located in Kraków. The institute's activities involved primarily the collection of historical documentation, mainly on the Jews of Poland during the Holocaust; the collection of Jewish books and art that survived the war; and the taking of testimonies from Holocaust survivors. The commission also embarked upon the publication of collections of documents, diaries, and testimonies, and on research into the history of Polish Jewry in World War II. In 1948 it became the Jewish Historical Institute of Warsaw.

In the several decades of the institute's (and its predecessor's) existence, vast treasures have accumulated in all branches of its activities, and the research conducted by its staff has been an important contribution to Jewish historiography. The largest and most important collection is that of documents and papers from the Holocaust period, including the ONEG SHABBAT Archive (the Ringelblum Archive), which was found in the ruins of the Warsaw ghetto; documents from various ghettos—sometimes only fragments —such as those of Warsaw, Białystok, Łódź, Radom, Będzin, Sosnowiec, and Zamość; col-

The Oneg Shabbat (Ringelblum) Archive, which was hidden in metal containers in Warsaw and discovered in two parts, in September 1946 and December 1950. It is being examined by members of the Jewish Historical Institute.

lections of documents of German institutions from the Holocaust period; a collection of about 250 diaries, most dating back to the Holocaust period; some 7,000 testimonies taken in the period from 1944 to 1970 (the greater part from 1944 to 1947); important collections of notes written by prisoners in concentration and extermination camps; and a card index of Jewish prisoners of war, beginning in 1939.

Also of importance are collections that belonged to Jewish communities during the war period, and to Jewish organizations and institutions that went into operation as soon as Poland was liberated but were liquidated between 1948 and 1951. The institute also has sixty thousand books in various languages, dealing with the different branches of Judaica; some seven thousand pre-1800 printed items; twenty-five hundred periodicals; and a collection of manuscripts, some originating between the eleventh and the eighteenth century.

Research works published by the institute (or by the commission) include more than forty books and collections of documents. The institute staff also publish their research papers in learned journals, including the *Bleter far Yidishe Geshichte* (Pages of Jewish History), which the institute has been producing since 1948 and which by the end of 1986 had reached No. 137–138. The commission, and subsequently the institute, has been headed by the historians Philip Friedman, Nachman Blumenthal, Bernard Mark, Artur Eisenbach, and, most recently, Maurycy Horn. Its research scholars have included Joseph Kermish, Isaiah Trunk, Tatjana Bernstein, Szymon Datner, Franciszek Kupfer, Abraham Wein, and Rata Sakowska, to name only a few.

During the waves of Jewish emigration from Poland, most of the scholars who had been working at the institute left the country, resuming their work in their new places of residence, mainly in Israel.

BIBLIOGRAPHY

Wein, A. "The Jewish Historical Institute in Warsaw." *Yad Vashem Studies* 8 (1970): 203–214.

ABRAHAM WEIN

DOHMEN, NICO. *See* Van der Voort, Hanna.

DOLCHSTOSSLEGENDE ("stab-in-the-back" myth), fabricated version of the German defeat in World War I that gained popularity under the Weimar Republic. It claimed that the German army had not been defeated on the field of battle but rather that the home front had forced the military leaders to lay down their arms, as a result of the defeatist actions taken by the liberals, the Socialists, and the Jews. This fabrication was without any basis in fact, but it provided motivation for the Freikorps, the paramilitary organizations that sprang up. Both in the Weimar Republic and in the Third Reich, it was the version accepted by nationalist circles and by all those who sought revenge for Germany's defeat in the war and for the peace agreement that Germany had been compelled to sign.

Much of the support for this falsehood and its propagation came from Gen. Erich LUDENDORFF, one of the outstanding German commanders in World War I, who in fact had taken the lead in pressing the German government to ask for an immediate cease-fire in the fall of 1918.

BIBLIOGRAPHY

Bauer, Y. *A History of the Holocaust.* New York, 1982. See pages 73–76.

ISRAEL GUTMAN

DOMANEVKA, county seat in the Golta district of TRANSNISTRIA, 77.5 miles (125 km) northeast of Odessa. Domanevka was the site of one of the three mass-murder camps established in October 1941 in the Golta district, on orders of the district governor, Col. Modest Isopescu. In the period from November 1941 to January 1942, twenty thousand Ukrainian Jews and Jews who had fled from BESSARABIA were brought to Domanevka from Odessa, Ochakov, and Berezovka, all of them survivors of the massacre campaign conducted by Einsatzgruppe D.

In December of that year, Isopescu issued

DOMANEVKA

© Martin Gilbert 1982

the order for the murder of these Jews, and they were shot to death in groups of five hundred. Taking part in the massacre were Romanian gendarmes and troops, as well as Sonderkommando R, made up of Germans living in nearby villages. The latter were attached to the VOLKSDEUTSCHE MITTELSTELLE (Ethnic Germans' Welfare Office), which had organized all the VOLKSDEUTSCHE living outside the borders of Germany, and which in 1941 had been attached to the SS. Also participating in the mass murder were Ukrainian militiamen. Some eighteen thousand Jews were murdered, after they had been robbed of their belongings. Their bodies were left lying in the fields, to fall prey to dogs. The murder drive came to an end in February 1942, and the transports coming to Domanevka after that date, consisting of Jews from Odessa and its environs, escaped immediate death. Another sixty Jews from Bessarabia were also seized and taken to Domanevka in this period. There were no more murders, but starvation, diseases, and exposure to the cold took a fearful toll among those who had survived the first wave of massacres.

Some two thousand to three thousand prisoners were now left in the camp. They were crowded into two broken-down stables, pigsties, and several roofless houses. They were not permitted to leave their filthy quarters, and only those who were fit for work were sent on forced labor and were given a small amount of food. The rest were simply left to

starve to death, and every day several dozen died. The prisoners looked so terrible—sick, naked, ravaged by worms and rats—that when the governor of Transnistria, Gheorghe Alexianu, was scheduled to visit the camp in the summer of 1942, the Jews were removed so that he would not see them.

Control of the camp was in the hands of Romanian gendarmes. When the snow melted, a group of sixty Jews was charged with burning the victims of the great massacre, for fear of epidemics. It took two months to burn the bodies, layer upon layer, in fires fed by timber and petroleum. One guard unit of Sonderkommando R asked the Romanian gendarmes for permission to kill Jews, which was granted, and they thereupon murdered hundreds of Jews in the vicinity of the camp.

By the end of 1942 about one thousand Jews were left in Domanevka, the majority of them women. At the end of 1943 most of these were transferred to the Akhmetchetka camp, where they were murdered, as were two hundred and fifty Jews—including fifty children—who had managed to escape the deportation. At the beginning of March an SS unit crossed the Bug and killed several dozen Jews from the Ukraine.

On March 28, 1944, the Soviet army liberated Domanevka; about five hundred Jews were still alive, mostly expellees from Romania. A people's tribunal sentenced Isopescu to death, but the sentence was commuted to life imprisonment.

BIBLIOGRAPHY

Ancel, J., ed. *Documents concerning the Fate of Romanian Jewry during the Holocaust.* Vol. 6. Jerusalem, 1986. See pages 57–113.

JEAN ANCEL

DORA-MITTELBAU (also known as Dora-Nordhausen), concentration camp in the Harz Mountains, 3 miles (5 km) from Nordhausen, Saxony (now in East Germany). The Dora-Mittelbau camp was first mentioned on August 27, 1943, as an external unit of the BUCHENWALD concentration camp. On October 28, 1944, it became a major concentration camp under its own name, with twenty-

One of the underground tunnels where V-2 missiles were manufactured in the Dora-Mittelbau concentration camp.

three branches, most of them in the vicinity, inside a restricted military area.

In the second half of 1943, thousands of prisoners were transferred to Dora-Mittelbau, mostly from Buchenwald, and put to work excavating underground tunnels that were to serve as the site of a huge plant for the manufacture of V-2 missiles and other arms. Until the plant was put into operation (in the late spring of 1944), the ten thousand prisoners working on the site had no living quarters and were housed inside the tunnels under unbearable conditions, deprived of daylight and fresh air for weeks at a time. They had to work at a murderous pace, in twelve-hour shifts. The unspeakable sanitary conditions and lack of security precautions led to a mortality rate much higher than that in any other concentration camp in Germany. Only after production began was a camp of wooden barracks constructed in Dora-Mittelbau, to which the prisoners were transferred in the summer of 1944. That fall, when maximum production was attained in the camp, Dora-Mittelbau had a permanent prison population in the main camp of over

twelve thousand, with another twenty thousand in the satellite camps.

When construction was completed and the plant went into operation, thousands of Jewish prisoners from various countries were brought to Dora-Mittelbau. They were treated with great brutality and were assigned the most physically exacting jobs; their mortality rate was higher than that of any other group of prisoners. Jewish prisoners who were exhausted and could not keep pace with the work were sent to AUSCHWITZ and MAUTHAUSEN in special transports, to be killed there.

The first group of prisoners sent to Dora-Mittelbau from Buchenwald included several individuals who had been active in the underground organization in that camp. Together with other groups of prisoners of various nationalities, they formed an underground while Dora-Mittelbau was still under construction, in order to sabotage the work and slow it down. When production began in 1944, the sabotage operations were intensified, seriously damaging the manufacturing process and upsetting the timetable for the delivery of the weapons so sorely needed by the Nazis in the final months of the war. Large numbers of prisoners were jailed on charges of sabotage; many were killed during their interrogation or were subsequently executed. More than two hundred prisoners suspected of sabotage, including several of the underground leaders, were hanged in public.

On April 1, 1945, the Nazis began the evacuation of the camp. Within several days most of the prisoners had been taken out, with the majority transferred to BERGEN-BELSEN. Thousands were murdered en route; at one point, near the village of Gardelegen, several thousand prisoners—mostly Jews—were crowded into a barn that was set afire, burning them all to death. Others succumbed to disease after they reached Bergen-Belsen, on the very eve of liberation. On March 25, 1945, Dora-Mittelbau and its satellites contained 34,500 prisoners. The camp was liberated on April 9 by United States forces, who found only a few prisoners there.

Between August 7 and December 31, 1947, an American military tribunal, which was independent of the International Military Tribunal at Nuremberg, tried nineteen former staff members of the Dora camp; fifteen were found guilty. The protective-custody camp leader, SS-Obersturmführer Hans Karl Moeser, was sentenced to death by hanging. In his trial statement he said: "The same way, with the same pleasure as you shoot deer, I shoot a human being. When I came to the SS and had to shoot the first three persons, my food didn't taste good for three days, but today it is a pleasure. It is a joy for me." The other defendants received sentences that ranged from five years to life imprisonment.

BIBLIOGRAPHY

Aalmans, W. J., ed. *The 'Dora'-Nordhausen War Crimes Trial*. N.p., 1947.

Bornemann, M., and M. Broszat. "Das KL Dora-Mittelbau." In *Studien zur Geschichte der Konzentrationslager*, pp. 154–198. Stuttgart, 1970.

Caspiva, J., F. Giessner, and K. Pelny. *Geheimwaffen in Konstein: Lager Dora*. Nordhausen, East Germany, 1964.

Diekmann, G., and P. Hochmut. *KZ Dora-Mittelbau*. Nordhausen, East Germany, 1971.

YEHOSHUA R. BÜCHLER and
SHMUEL KRAKOWSKI

DOROHOI, town in ROMANIA, in northern Moldavia, bordering on BUKOVINA. In 1930, Dorohoi had a Jewish population of 5,820. Its Jews suffered more in World War II than others living in the Old Kingdom (Romania in its pre-1918 borders) because the town was near the new border with the Soviet Union, established at the end of June 1940 when the Soviets annexed northern Bukovina, and also because it was a Jewish center in northern Moldavia.

On July 1, 1940, Dorohoi was the scene of the first outbreak of violence against Jews in Romania, when a Romanian army unit that was withdrawing from Bukovina shot to death dozens of Jewish soldiers in its ranks and murdered Jewish inhabitants of the town, including women and children; a total of 200 Jews were killed. This took place before Romania had allied itself with Nazi Germany and before a single German soldier had set foot on Romanian soil. In June 1941, when Romania joined Germany in its invasion of the Soviet Union, a new drive of anti-Jewish persecution was launched. Jews from the nearby towns of Saveni, Darabani, Mihăileni, and Rădăuți were expelled from their homes and forced into Dorohoi; at the same time, 300 Jews from Dorohoi—among them the community leaders—were interned in camps in western Romania (mostly in Tîrgu-Jiu), on suspicion of being Communists. In Dorohoi the Jews were forced to wear the yellow badge (*see* BADGE, JEWISH). At the end of August and the beginning of September 1941, 2,000 Jewish males from other places in the district were brought to Dorohoi; at the same time, the 300 Jews who had been interned in western Romania were permitted to return. All the Jews in the town were forced to subscribe to the war fund.

On November 5, 1941, the authorities informed the community leaders that an order had been issued for the expulsion of the Dorohoi Jews from their hometown. For this purpose, the Dorohoi district was administratively attached to Bukovina, the province from which all the Jews were expelled to TRANSNISTRIA. The expulsion order had in fact originated in Bucharest, and was part of a plan designed to thin out the Jewish population of northern Moldavia. The Jews were forced to "sell" their property to the Central Bank of

DOROHOI

Annexations from June to September 1940: (1) Bessarabia and (2) N. Bukovina to USSR; (3) N. Transylvania to Hungary; (4) S. Dobruja to Bulgaria.

0   160 miles   1 in.

0   300 km.   3 cm.

Romania, and their houses were plundered by their Romanian neighbors.

On November 7 the Jews of Darabani and Rădăuţi were expelled, followed the next day by the Jews of Mihăileni and Saveni. The expulsion of the Dorohoi Jews began on November 12. Some four hundred and fifty Jews had obtained (through bribery) permits to stay in the town, ostensibly as being essential to the economy; even some of these, however, joined in the general expulsion, since they did not want to be separated from those members of their families who were not included in the residence permits. Eight thousand Jews were expelled from Dorohoi and the neighboring area in two transports. Many of them died en route, even before they had crossed the Dniester. In many families only the women and children were sent to Transnistria, with the men kept behind in Romanian forced-labor camps.

The Jews who remained in Dorohoi set up a new community leadership, and its members, together with the leaders of Romanian Jewry, made strenuous efforts to have the Dorohoi district reincorporated in the Old Kingdom and thereby to facilitate the return of the Jews from Transnistria. In the end, their efforts succeeded; the required authorization was given when the Soviet army was making its advance. A delegation of the Jewish Aid Committee was able to go to Transnistria in order to make arrangements for the repatriation of the Jews who had been expelled there. At the end of December 1943, 6,053 Jews from the Dorohoi district, out of the 10,368 who had been expelled from it, returned, together with 2,000 out of the 3,074 expelled from the town of Dorohoi. The local authorities continued to harass the returnees, and only after Dorohoi was liberated by the Red Army in April 1944 did their sufferings at Romanian hands come to an end.

BIBLIOGRAPHY

Carp, M. *Transnistria*. Vol. 3 of *Cartea Neagră*. Bucharest, 1947.
Lavi, T., ed. *Rumania*, vol. 1. In *Pinkas Hakehillot; Encyclopaedia of Jewish Communities*. Jerusalem, 1969. See pages 104–110. (In Hebrew.)

JEAN ANCEL

DOUWES, ARNOLD (b. 1906), Dutch rescuer of Jews during the Holocaust. The son of a pastor in the Dutch Reformed church, Douwes joined the Dutch underground and devoted himself to the rescue of Jewish adults and children. At first, he worked under the guidance of Johannes Post (an important underground figure who aided Jews), who was shot by the Germans. Douwes enlarged the scope of his mentor's rescue operations. Jewish families who had received notification to report for deportation to the WESTERBORK camp were referred to him by the Dutch underground. He concentrated his activities in the vicinity of the town of Nieuwlande, in the northeastern province of Drenthe. There, almost every household sheltered a Jewish person. Douwes looked after all the needs of these Jews, helping to supply them with food and other necessities, false identification papers, and financial support (through the underground). Together with Max Leons (nicknamed "Nico"), a Jew who posed as a Protestant colleague and friend of Douwes, he scoured the countryside and enlisted several hundred Dutch families in their mutual rescue activities.

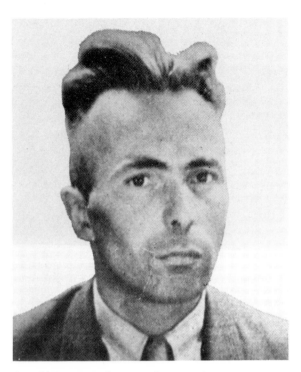

Arnold Douwes, from a photograph on a German "Wanted" poster of May 21, 1942.

Douwes personally met the children in Amsterdam, or at the train station upon their arrival in the Drenthe district. When the Germans staged raids in the vicinity, Douwes went for nocturnal rides on his bicycle, moving Jews—under the very noses of the Germans—to safer locations.

An operation of this magnitude could not go undetected for long, and Douwes was wanted by the authorities. To avoid arrest, he changed his appearance, growing a mustache and wearing a hat and eyeglasses. In spite of these precautions, he was apprehended in January 1945 and imprisoned in Assen, where he awaited his execution. The underground, however, succeeded in freeing him before that could take place. After the war, Douwes lived for a time in South Africa and then moved to Israel in 1956.

Arnold Douwes was responsible for saving the lives of hundreds of Jews, including some one hundred children. In 1965 he was recognized as a "RIGHTEOUS AMONG THE NATIONS" by YAD VASHEM. More than two hundred residents of the Nieuwlande area were later awarded the title as well.

BIBLIOGRAPHY

De Jong, L. *Het Koninkrijk der Nederlanden in de Tweede Wereldoorlog.* Vols. 6, 7. The Hague, 1975–1976.

MORDECAI PALDIEL

DRAENGER, SHIMSHON (1917–1943?), underground leader. Draenger, who was known as Simek, was born in Kraków. At the age of thirteen he joined the Akiva movement, and later became one of its main leaders. Until the outbreak of World War II he edited the movement's journal, *Divrei Akiva*, and the weekly *Tse'irim*, a newspaper for young people. On September 22, 1939, a short time after the German occupation of Kraków, Draenger was arrested because of the articles of Irene Harand, an Austrian anti-Nazi, that he had published in *Divrei Akiva*. Together with his future wife, Gusta Dawidson (*see* DRAENGER, TOVA), who was arrested at the same time,

Shimshon Draenger.

Draenger was held at the prison camp in Troppau, Czechoslovakia. Following his release in December 1939, he reassembled his followers under the guise of educational activity, thereby reconstructing the Akiva cell in Warsaw. At the beginning of the war Draenger tried, unsuccessfully, to save the members of his movement by smuggling them into Slovakia. From December 1941 to August 1942 he managed a training farm at Kopaliny, which was a cover for Akiva and its underground activity.

Draenger was one of the youth movement activists who from the beginning of the war maintained that the Jews had no chance of survival under the Nazi occupation, and this approach dictated his radical position and methods of activity. In August 1942 he helped found HE-HALUTS HA-LOHEM, a combat organization of Jewish pioneer youth, and was a member of its command. He set up the organization's Technical Office, which forged permits for the members giving entry to and exit from the ghetto, and sold these permits to finance arms purchases. He also edited the underground journal *He-Haluts ha-Lohem.*

In January 1943 Draenger was seized and was imprisoned in the MONTELUPICH PRISON, where he organized Bible and other study circles for his friends in jail. On April 29 of that year he escaped and was reunited with his wife, Gusta, who had also escaped from Montelupich. Both became partisans in the Wiśnicz Forest. There Draenger also resumed publication of *He-Haluts ha-Lohem,* exhorting the Jewish youth remaining in the forest to resist the Germans actively, urging the last residents of the ghetto to flee for their lives, and appealing to the Poles not to betray Jews to the authorities. His articles also sketched the history of the pioneer underground.

On November 8, 1943, Draenger was apprehended by the Germans and, presumably, was killed.

BIBLIOGRAPHY

Ainsztein, R. *Jewish Resistance in Nazi-occupied Europe.* London, 1974.

Dawidson, G. *Justina's Diary.* Tel Aviv, 1978. (In Hebrew.)

YAEL PELED (MARGOLIN)

DRAENGER, TOVA (1917–1943?), underground member and chronicler. Draenger's maiden name was Gusta Dawidson. Born in Kraków, by 1938 she was one of the leaders of the Akiva movement there. Together with Shimshon DRAENGER (who became her husband early in 1940), she edited *Tse'irim,* a weekly for young people. During the Nazi occupation she was one of the founders of HE-HALUTS HA-LOHEM, an underground combat movement in Kraków, and played an active role in its operations.

On September 22, 1939, she was arrested, together with Shimshon Draenger, and charged with belonging to the Austrian anti-Nazi Irene Harand group. In December 1939 they were released from the prison camp in Troppau, Czechoslovakia, where they had been interned. They resumed their activities in Kraków and Warsaw and, in 1940, reorganized Akiva in both cities.

In He-Haluts ha-Lohem, Draenger's main task was, with her husband, to produce forged documents for the organization's use. On January 18, 1943, having learned that her husband had been arrested, she surrendered to the Gestapo, as she and her husband had pledged to do if either was seized. She was put in the MONTELUPICH PRISON and, while there, until April 29 of that year, wrote her memoirs in the form of a diary, her purpose being to record the story of the final uprising in Kraków. Years later, these memoirs were published under the title *Justina's Diary.* She wrote on toilet paper, in several copies, helped by fellow members of the underground who shared the cell with her. The diary presents, in Draenger's own words, "the true story of the last and most daring revolt of the young fighters," and deals with the history of Akiva and He-Haluts ha-Lohem between April 1941 and March 1943. Miraculously, fifteen of the diary's twenty chapters were preserved, covering the period from August 23 to November 26, 1942.

Draenger escaped from prison on April 29, 1943, and, together with her husband, resumed underground activities, this time in the Wiśnicz Forest. The two also recommended publication of *He-Haluts ha-Lohem,* the underground movement's journal.

On November 9 of that year, following her

Tova Draenger and pages from her diary.

husband's arrest, Draenger again surrendered to the Nazis. Nothing is known of the subsequent fate of either, and it is assumed that they were both executed.

BIBLIOGRAPHY

Dawidson, G. *Justina's Diary.* Tel Aviv, 1978. (In Hebrew.)

                                        YAEL PELED (MARGOLIN)

DRANCY, assembly camp (*Sammellager*) and detention camp for the Jews of FRANCE, from which they were sent to forced-labor and extermination camps. The camp was established in August 1941 in the northeastern Paris suburb of Drancy. It was situated in an oblong, reinforced concrete four-story building, which before the war had served as a gendarmerie barracks. The camp area cov-

ered 656 by 131 feet (200 × 40 m), with a 10-foot (3-m) lookout tower at each of its four corners. The camp was under twenty-four-hour guard by French gendarmes armed with machine guns. The outer road had a barbed-wire fence on each side. Four satellite camps were added to the camp, as part of the EINSATZSTAB ROSENBERG operation, to serve as depositories for artworks, valuable furniture, household goods, and books that had been confiscated from the homes of Jews who had been arrested, imprisoned, and deported. The camp was able to hold 4,500 prisoners; in the period from August 21, 1941, to August 17, 1944 (liberation day), some 70,000 prisoners passed through it. Its organization and structure were modeled along the lines of Nazi CONCENTRATION CAMPS.

The Drancy camp went through two distinct periods, one lasting from August 21, 1941, to July 1, 1943, when it was administered by the French, and the other from July 2, 1943, to August 17, 1944, during which it was run by the Germans. In the first, "French" period, three high-ranking French police officers named Savart, Laurent, and Gilbert succeeded one another in running the camp, although it was at all times under the control of the German Sicherheitspolizei (Security Police) and SD (Sicherheitsdienst; Security Service) commanders in France.

On July 2, 1943, Alois BRUNNER took over command of the camp, removing from their posts all the Vichy-appointed French commanders and running the camp with the help of four SS officers. The period was marked by a severe deterioration of the inmates' conditions and an intensive effort to deport a larger number of Jews to Auschwitz. Under Brunner's administration, prisoners were assigned functions previously performed by the French police. From August 25, 1942, when they took over from the French gendarmerie, the members of this internal police service (known as Membres du Service d'Ordre) played an important role in the life of the camp.

On June 22, 1942, the first transport, consisting of 1,000 Jews, left Drancy for AUSCHWITZ-Birkenau; the last such transport left Drancy on July 31, 1944. Between these two dates a total of sixty-four transports left Drancy, with 64,759 Jews aboard; of these, sixty-one transports, with 61,000 persons, went to the Auschwitz extermination camp, and three transports, with 3,753 persons, were sent to the SOBIBÓR extermination camp. Of the 65,000 Jews who went to their death from Drancy, more than 20,000 were French (born in France), 15,000 were Polish, and 6,000 were German nationals.

Solidarity and mutual help became the rule among the Drancy prison population, and this conduct was the first manifestation of resistance in the camp. The first escape took place within ten days of the camp's establishment. From August 21, 1941, to August 17, 1943, there were forty-one successful attempts to escape, and an untold number of unsuccessful attempts. In September 1943 the prisoners developed and began working on a plan for digging an escape tunnel, through which all the prisoners would be able to disperse. Running 4.5 feet (1.4 m) below the surface, the tunnel had its starting point underneath the camp commandant's office, and from there it passed under the barbed-wire fence. The planned place of exit was an underground air-raid shelter beyond the camp perimeter. Seventy prisoners worked in three shifts on the tunnel, day and night, beginning on September 15, 1943. On November 8, 1943—when no more than 98 feet (30 m) remained to be excavated (a day's work)—the Germans discovered the tunnel. As punishment, many prisoners were sent to their death, among them the leader of the camp underground, Robert Blum.

At the beginning of August 1944 the Allied forces reached Paris, and on the night of August 15–16 the Germans in Drancy hastily burned all the camp documents. The next day they fled, leaving 1,542 prisoners behind them. On August 17, the consul general of Sweden, Raoul Nordling, took over control of the camp and asked the French Red Cross to care for the inmates; the camp was now liberated.

Until November 15, 1942, food rations in the camp were tiny, and the prisoners were severely undernourished. The shortage of food was a constant feature, with the daily ration ranging from six hundred to eight hundred calories per person; 800 cases of edema and cachexia were recorded. The situation improved after mid-November, with the help of French Jewish organizations and the Red Cross; food parcels were also received in the camp from the families of the prisoners. However, after the advent of Brunner, there was a turn for the worse in this regard as well.

Cultural and religious life persisted in Drancy despite the difficult conditions. Jewish religious customs were observed, and hundreds of prisoners attended prayer services and religious ceremonies. The Jewish New Year (Rosh Hashanah) and the Day of Atonement (Yom Kippur) were celebrated in the synagogue, established in September 1941, and many prisoners also attended regular Sabbath services. On July 20, 1942, the Germans prohibited any further Jewish religious observance, but as late as the fall of 1943 the high holidays were still being celebrated, according to both the Ashkenazic and the Sephardic ritual. Many cultural activities took place in the camp; concerts and literary evenings of a wide variety were held. Books were smuggled into the camp, and a school was set up for the children. The school continued to function, clandestinely, even after January 1943, when it was officially closed down on German orders.

Men, women, and children were among the

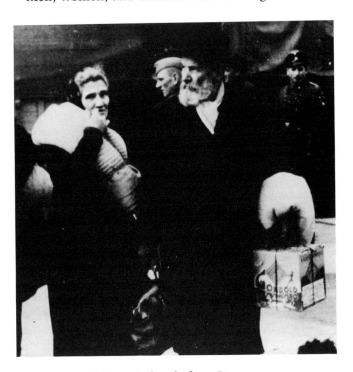

Deportation of the Brin family from Drancy.

prisoners detained in Drancy and deported from there, among them some famous people: the French poet Max Jacob, who died in the camp in 1944; Pierre Masse, a senator who had been a member of Clemenceau's cabinet; the ballet director René Blum, the brother of Léon BLUM; the writer Tristan Bernard; Marcel Dassault, the aircraft constructor; Simone VEIL; Itzhak KATZENELSON; and Jankiel Handelsman (Snopek) and Joseph Dorembus (also known as Jacques Warszawski), later among the organizers of the Sonderkommando mutiny in Auschwitz-Birkenau, on October 7, 1944.

After the war a monument was erected, at the place where the camp's front gates once stood, to commemorate the Jews who were deported to the extermination camps from Drancy.

BIBLIOGRAPHY

Darville, J., and S. Wichens. *Drancy la Juive; ou La 2ᵉ Inquisition.* Paris, 1945.

Felstiner, M. "Commandant of Drancy: Alois Brunner and the Jews of France." *Holocaust and Genocide Studies* 2/1 (1987): 21–47.

Klarsfeld, S. *Le mémorial de la déportation des Juifs de France.* Paris, 1978.

Marrus, M. R., and R. O. Paxton. *Vichy France and the Jews.* New York, 1981.

Rutkowski, A. "Les déportations des Juifs de France vers Auschwitz-Birkenau et Sobibor." *Le Monde Juif* 26/57–58 (1970): 33–75.

Wellers, G. *L'étoile jaune à l'heure de Vichy: De Drancy à Auschwitz.* Paris, 1973.

ADAM RUTKOWSKI

DROGOBYCH (Pol., Drohobycz), city in Lvov Oblast (district), in the Ukrainian SSR. Now an oil-industry center, Drogobych is an old city that from 1772 to 1918 belonged to Austrian-held Galicia, and in the interwar period was part of Poland; between 1939 and 1941 it was in Soviet hands. Jews had lived intermittently in Drogobych since the fifteenth century, and on the eve of World War II the community numbered some fifteen thousand, over 40 percent of the city's population. In September 1939, hundreds of Jews who had escaped from German-occupied parts of Poland found refuge there.

Following the German invasion of Soviet Russia on June 22, 1941, groups of young Jews tried to flee from Drogobych to the east, and many were killed in the attempt, either during German air attacks or at the hands of Ukrainian nationalists who were active in the area. German forces entered the city on June 30 and the next day a pogrom took place. It lasted for three days, and over its course Ukrainians, assisted by Wehrmacht soldiers, murdered over three hundred Jews. In July, various measures against the Jews were introduced. Jews were seized at random and made to perform forced labor; the movement of Jews in the main streets was restricted; many Jews were compelled to vacate their apartments so that German officers could move in; Jews were banned from the city market; and they had to wear on their right-hand sleeve a white band with a blue Star of David.

The JUDENRAT (Jewish Council), which was set up in July, sought to reach an agreement with the German authorities regarding forced labor by Jews; in order to avoid the random seizures, it undertook to supply fixed quotas of laborers. These efforts, however, met with only limited success. The Judenrat also opened soup kitchens that dispensed meals to the needy.

In September and October of 1941, several dozen Jewish intellectuals were arrested and all trace of them was lost; later it became known that they had been tortured and then murdered in a forest near the city. On November 30 over three hundred Jews were murdered in the Bronica Forest outside Drogobych. That winter, many Jews died of starvation and a typhoid epidemic. In the spring of 1942 the Judenrat set up workshops to create employment for the Jewish population in the hope that this would save them from being sent to the work camps that had been set up nearby, where harsh conditions caused the death of many of the inmates. Hundreds of the city's Jews were also employed in local oil refineries and in the processing of oil products.

At the end of March 1942 an *Aktion* took place that resulted in 2,000 Jews being sent to their death in the BEŁŻEC extermination camp. A second large *Aktion*, launched on August 8, lasted until August 17. *Selektionen* were made at the various assembly points and only workers with employment cards from essential jobs in the oil industry were permitted to remain free. Germans and Ukrainian collaborators hunted down Jews in hiding and anyone they found was murdered. More than 600 Jews were killed in the city's courtyards and alleys, and over 2,500 were deported to Bełżec.

At the beginning of October 1942 a ghetto was established in which 10,000 Jews were confined, among them the remnants of Jewish communities in the vicinity. Another *Aktion* took place on October 23 and 24; 2,300 Jews were sent to Bełżec and 300 patients in a Jewish hospital were killed. Still another *Aktion* was launched in November and went on uninterruptedly for an entire month. Ten days after it began, 1,000 Jews were taken to Bełżec by train, and a few days later several hundred more. Hundreds of others were killed in the ghetto. At the end of 1942 and the beginning of 1943, the Jews who worked in the oil industry were put into separate work camps.

On February 15, 1943, 450 Jews were taken out of the ghetto to the Bronica Forest, where they were murdered. The liquidation of the ghetto began on May 21 and was completed by June 10. At the same time the Judenrat ceased to function. Many of the ghetto houses

Deportation of Jews from Drogobych.

were set on fire in order to force out any Jews who had hidden inside. The last Jews found in the ghetto were put on trucks and taken to the Bronica Forest, where they were killed and buried in pits. The destruction of the ghetto was followed by the murder of the Jews in the work camps, with only the most essential workers left alive. Following the Soviet advance of April 1944, these workers were sent west, to the PŁASZÓW camp. When the Soviet army entered Drogobych in August 1944, 400 Jewish survivors emerged from hiding places.

BIBLIOGRAPHY

Gelber, N. M., ed. *Memorial to the Jews of Drohobycz, Boryslaw, and Surroundings.* Tel Aviv, 1959. (In Hebrew.)

Gilbert, M. *The Holocaust.* New York, 1985.

AHARON WEISS

DROR (DEROR). *See* Youth Movements.

Simon Dubnow.

DUBNOW, SIMON (1860–1941), one of the great Jewish historians and thinkers of modern times and one of the founders of Autonomism, the movement that advocated Jewish national autonomy in the Diaspora. Dubnow was born in Mstislavl, Belorussia, received a traditional Jewish education, and acquired a broad general education on his own; he was close to the circle of the Jewish Enlightenment in Russia. Dubnow's first works on Jewish history were published in the 1880s. His greatest achievement was his pioneering approach to the study of the history of the Jews in eastern Europe and their spiritual and religious movements. In his research work, Dubnow stressed the periods of Jewish autonomy in Poland and Lithuania and the history of Hasidism. His major work was the ten-volume *Weltgeschichte des jüdischen Volkes* (World History of the Jewish People), which traced the history of the Jews from their beginnings to modern times; it was first published in its German translation between 1923 and 1929, and then in other languages, including the original Russian.

In his early work as a historian, Dubnow followed the trail of the nineteenth-century German Jewish historian Heinrich Graetz, but he later discarded the view that saw the Jewish people as a unique phenomenon in history with its own spiritual and religious mission. He adopted instead a secular concept, which regarded the Jews as a national entity that, despite the passage of generations and the rise and fall of its "centers of hegemony," has preserved its autonomous spiritual framework. In Dubnow's view, it was the spiritual and cultural elements that represented the highest degree of a people's development. Since the Jews, thanks to their unique history, had retained their specific spiritual essence more than any other people, they were ripe to assume this highest level of a people in progressive human society.

This was the source of Dubnow's political philosophy, which regarded the Emancipation as a turning point in Jewish history and called for the granting of spiritual and cultural autonomy to the Jewish populations of Europe. Dubnow regarded such a grant of autonomy as providing the basis for national Jewish existence and for the realization of Jewish strivings, especially in the countries of eastern Europe. This political concept was the ideological base upon which Dubnow and his associates established the Jewish People's Party (Volkspartei) in 1906.

In 1922 Dubnow succeeded in leaving the Soviet Union and settled in Berlin. When Hitler came to power, Dubnow moved to Riga, the capital of Latvia, and continued his work. When Riga was occupied by the Germans in early July 1941, the eighty-one-year-old scholar was put in the city's ghetto, and his library was confiscated. In his final days he reportedly told the people he met, "Jews, make sure that everything is written down and recorded." According to one account, Dubnow was sick and feverish when he was shot to death while being taken out of the ghetto, in December 1941.

BIBLIOGRAPHY

Pinson, K. S. "Simon Dubnow: Historian and Political Philosopher." In *Nationalism and History: Essays on Old and New Judaism,* by Simon Dubnow, edited by K. S. Pinson. New York, 1970.
Rawidowicz, S., ed. *Simon Dubnow in Memoriam: Essays and Letters.* London, 1954. (In Hebrew.)
Steinberg, A., ed. *Simon Dubnow: The Man and His Work.* Paris, 1963.

ISRAEL GUTMAN

DUCKWITZ, GEORG FERDINAND (1904–1973), German diplomat, one of the "RIGHTEOUS AMONG THE NATIONS." Duckwitz was born in Bremen, the son of a prominent merchant family, and in the early 1930s was a businessman in Copenhagen. He joined the Nazi party in 1932, and from 1933 to 1935 served in Alfred ROSENBERG's foreign-policy office, but left that post of his own accord and took a civilian job in a shipping firm.

At the beginning of World War II, Duckwitz was posted to DENMARK by the ABWEHR, the German intelligence organization. When Denmark was occupied by the Germans, Duckwitz was appointed shipping attaché at the German mission in Copenhagen. He established ties with the leaders of the Danish Social Democrat party and gained their trust. When the Germans were about to deport the Jews of Denmark to Nazi camps in the east at the beginning of October 1943, Duckwitz informed his Danish contacts of the German plans. It was mainly this advance warning that enabled the Danes to organize the operation that saved the Jews by smuggling them out to Sweden. Duckwitz even went so far as to travel to Sweden, where he met with the prime minister, Per Albin Hansson, who promised that the Swedish government would help in the effort to rescue Denmark's Jews.

After the war, Duckwitz remained in the foreign service of the Federal Republic of Germany (West Germany), and from 1955 to 1958 he served as the German ambassador in Denmark. His last post was that of director-general of the Foreign Ministry. For Duckwitz's share in the rescue of the Jews of Denmark, YAD VASHEM awarded him the title of "Righteous among the Nations."

BIBLIOGRAPHY

Kirchhoff, H. *Georg Ferdinand Duckwitz: Skitser til et politisk portraet.* Lyngby, Denmark, 1978.
Yahil, L. *The Rescue of Danish Jewry: Test of a Democracy.* Philadelphia, 1969.

LENI YAHIL

DÜNABURG. *See* Dvinsk.

DUTCH NATIONAL SOCIALIST MOVEMENT. *See* Nationaal Socialistische Beweging.

DVINSK (Latv., Daugavpils; Ger., Dünaburg), city in southeast LATVIA, on the Western Dvina (Daugava) River. In 1935 Dvinsk had a Jewish population of 11,116, out of a total of 45,160. In June 1940, together with the rest of Latvia, it was incorporated into the Soviet Union; and on June 26, 1941, four days after their invasion of the Soviet Union, the Germans occupied the city.

At some point between June 29 and July 2, all the Jewish males aged sixteen to sixty were assembled in the main square and from there were taken to prison. For a week they were subjected to torture, humiliation, and forced labor, and then the Germans began killing them. By July 16, according to official

German accounts, 1,150 Jews had been murdered. The rest underwent the same fate as time went on, with the exception of a few physicians and skilled workers who were released and some young Jews who managed to escape. Those Jews who had not been imprisoned also suffered from maltreatment, had their property confiscated, were thrown out of their homes, and were put on forced labor. Latvian police and volunteer helpers burned down the synagogues—sometimes while Jews were inside or after they had been forced in—and only two synagogues were left intact. In the second half of July, a decree was issued requiring the Jews to wear a yellow badge (*see* BADGE, JEWISH).

During the last week of July, the Jews were put into a ghetto; the site chosen for this purpose was the Latvian cavalry barracks on the banks of the Dvina, north of the city. The place was unfit for human habitation: it had no running water or other sanitary facilities, and was much too small for the number of Jews crowded into it. A few days later, thousands of other Jews were brought into the ghetto from the neighboring towns of Griva, Krāslava, Preiļi, Viski, and Līvanī. By early August, fourteen thousand to sixteen thousand Jews were packed into the ghetto, living there under unspeakable conditions. A JUDENRAT (Jewish Council) was put in charge, and its various subcommittees tried to improve the housing and sanitary conditions. The ghetto had a Jewish police force, a hospital staffed by fifteen doctors and a substantial number of auxiliary personnel, a pharmacy, an orphanage, and a burial society; in the course of time, many workshops were established.

Having set up the ghetto, the Germans embarked upon the systematic murder of its population, with the assistance of the Latvian auxiliary police. In late July or early August 1941, several hundred elderly Jews were murdered; a short while later, thousands of Jews from the neighboring towns were shot to death in pits that had been prepared in the Pogulanka Forest, 5 miles (8 km) from the city (Operation Province). In *Aktionen* that took place on August 8 and 9 and on August 18 and 19, thousands of Dvinsk Jews were murdered in the Pogulanka Forest, including 400 children from the ghetto or-

phanage. According to official German accounts, 9,012 Jews were killed in the period from July 13 to August 21. By the end of August 1941, 7,000 Jews were left in the ghetto, most of them workers employed by the German army or surviving members of the Jewish police force with their families, in addition to a small number of ghetto staff and workshop employees.

On November 7, 1941, a major *Aktion* was launched that lasted until November 9. In its course three thousand to five thousand Jews were murdered at Pogulanka. The first to be killed were the old, the ill, and the orphans, followed by persons who were unemployed or whose work was not essential in German eyes. "Essential" workers had been issued special pink passes (*Scheine*) on the eve of the *Aktion*, but their families were not spared, their turn coming at the end of the *Aktion*. In late November, the ghetto was put under strict quarantine because of a typhus epidemic that had broken out. The quarantine was in force for four months, and while it lasted, the ghetto was cut off from its supply sources and suffered from starvation, as a result of which more people died.

When the quarantine was lifted, in the spring of 1942, 1,000 Jews had survived—the ghetto staff, holders of the pink passes and some members of their families, plus a few who had managed to escape the *Aktion*, among them children hidden by local farmers. Half of these Jews lived in the ghetto and the others in their place of work. On May 1 the ghetto and all its institutions were liquidated, and the several hundred Jews who were in it at the time—among them members of the Jewish Council and the Jewish policemen—were killed. In Dvinsk itself, 450 Jews were left, mostly young men and women with no family ties, and a few unattached children. Many of the young people acquired arms and practiced using them, and some tried to escape in order to join the partisans in Belorussia, but these attempts, for the most part, were unsuccessful. In late October 1943 the Germans moved the surviving Jews of Dvinsk to the KAISERWALD camp; some of the young Jews resisted arrest with the arms they had, but only a few managed to escape. Several dozen Jewish craftsmen were left in the city, working for the security police, and on the eve of the German withdrawal in 1944, they too were taken to the camps. In April of that year, in the course of AKTION 1005, the Germans opened the mass graves in the pits at Pogulanka and other places, and burned the corpses in an effort to obliterate the traces of their crimes.

On July 27, 1944, the Red Army occupied Dvinsk. About twenty Jews were found there, having survived by hiding. By 1946, two thousand Jews had gathered in the city. They established an official Jewish community organization that maintained a cemetery, a synagogue, a Yiddish drama circle, and a Jewish (Yiddish) culture society.

In the course of the following years, the Jewish community in Dvinsk dwindled in size and its cultural activities were discontinued; in 1972 the Jewish cemetery was closed. A memorial for the Nazi victims, which the authorities put up in the city, makes no mention of Jews.

BIBLIOGRAPHY

Levin, D. *With Their Back to the Wall: The Armed Struggle of Latvian Jewry against the Nazis, 1941–1945.* Jerusalem, 1978. (In Hebrew.)

Levin, D., ed. *Latvia and Estonia.* In *Pinkas Hakehillot; Encyclopaedia of Jewish Communities.* Jerusalem, 1988. See pages 98–105. (In Hebrew.)

ESTHER HAGAR

Alter Dvoretski.

DVORETSKI, ALTER (1906–1942), partisan commander. Dvoretski was born in DIATLOVO (Zhetl), studied law at the University of Vilna, and was admitted to the bar in 1938. He was a member of Po'alei Zion, where his main interest was sports activities. Under the Soviet regime (1939–1941) he practiced law in Novogrudok, in the Belorussian SSR.

At the beginning of the German occupation in 1941, Dvoretski settled in Diatlovo and was appointed chairman of its JUDENRAT (Jewish Council). Under the impact of the events he witnessed, he issued a call for rescue and revenge and organized an underground partisan group in the Diatlovo ghetto, with himself at the helm. He devised a plan to arm the Jewish youth in the surrounding towns and take them to the densely wooded Lipiczany Forest, in order to fight the Germans from there; this plan was also to be a means for saving Jews who were physically unfit for fighting.

Dvoretski met with the Germans from time to time, while organizing the acquisition of arms and smuggling them into the ghetto. At all times, he carried a loaded pistol so as to be prepared for any eventuality. He provided weapons to a group of Soviet prisoners of war who had escaped from the camps in which they had been held, and steered them to the Lipiczany Forest. Another group of Jewish youth—refugees with no local family ties or property—also made its way out of the ghetto with Dvoretski's support in the form of advice, arms, and clothing.

Dvoretski worked out a detailed plan for armed resistance in case the Germans tried to carry out a massacre in the ghetto, but the plan was foiled by an act of betrayal. When Dvoretski himself went to the forest, he tried to implement his daring plans of rescuing the Jews of Diatlovo and the neighboring ghettos, and he dreamed of forming Jewish partisan regiments. What he found in the forest, however, were small groups of Soviet partisans—former prisoners of war—who had few arms in their possession and were not prepared to take the initiative in genuine attacks on the Germans. They had no contact with Moscow, lacked a proper command, and were altogether undisciplined; many had antisemitic tendencies. Dvoretski pressured the commander of several partisan groups to agree to launch an attack on the Diatlovo garrison in order to liberate the Jewish youth who were confined in the ghetto.

On the night of April 29, 1942, the partisan group made its way to Diatlovo, coming to a halt at the Christian cemetery on the outskirts of the town. A local peasant was sent to reconnoiter, and he returned with a report that a strong German detachment had come to the town in order to massacre the Jews on the next day, April 30. The Soviet partisans were not ready to risk an attack, and made their way back to their refuge in the forest. The plan for saving the Jews of Diatlovo had been frustrated. The commanders of the various partisan groups treated Dvoretski's proposals with a mixture of fear and envy; in the end, the partisans set an ambush and murdered Dvoretski and one of his comrades.

Dvoretski's activities in the ghetto enabled more than six hundred Jews from Diatlovo to flee during the liquidation of the ghetto on August 6, 1942, and to make their way to the Lipiczany Forest. There they formed a fighting battalion of partisans, commanded by Hirsch KAPLINSKI. This battalion eventually became a Jewish company (the third such) in the Soviet Orlianski-Borba battalion.

BIBLIOGRAPHY

Kahanovich, M. *The Fighting of the Jewish Partisans in Eastern Europe.* Tel Aviv, 1954. (In Hebrew.)

Kaplinski, B., ed. *Zhetel Record: A Memorial to the Jewish Community of Zhetel.* Tel Aviv, 1957. (In Yiddish.)

ELISHEVA SHAUL